STEVEN RAICHLEN'S
PLANET BARBECUE!

An Electrifying Journey Around the World's Barbecue Trail

WORKMAN PUBLISHING • NEW YORK

To my three girls:
Barbara,
Betsy, and
Ella Francesca

Library of Congress Cataloging-in-Publication Data
Raichlen, Steven.
 Planet barbecue! / by Steven Raichlen.
    p. cm.
Includes bibliographical references and index.
ISBN 978-0-7611-4801-2 (alk. paper)
ISBN 978-0-7611-5919-3 (hc)
1. Barbecue cookery. I. Title.
TX840.B3R355145 2010
641.7′6--dc22   2010008444

Cover design by David Matt
Book design by Lisa Hollander with Lidija Tomas
Cover photo credits, see page 616

Workman books are available at special discounts when
purchased in bulk for premiums and sales promotions as
well as for fund-raising or educational use. Special editions or
book excerpts also can be created to specification. For details,
contact the Special Sales Director at the address below or send
an e-mail to specialsales@workman.com.

WORKMAN PUBLISHING COMPANY, INC.
225 Varick Street
New York, NY 10014-4381
www.workman.com

Printed in U.S.A.
First printing March 2010

10 9 8 7 6 5 4 3 2 1

Acknowledgments

"The most enjoyable part of writing any book is thanking the people who helped make it possible." I wrote these words back in 1986 in one of my early books. They ring even truer today. *Planet Barbecue!* represents the enormous creativity and bone-crushing labor of an army of family, friends, colleagues, experts, and grill masters around the world. What follows is an attempt to thank the hundreds of people who have contributed to the effort, with apologies to any I may have inadvertently omitted.

Family and friends: First and foremost, my wife, Barbara, stoker of my fire, nurturer of my dreams, companion on my travels around Planet Barbecue, editor of all my writing, *consigliari* for all the challenges encountered on the barbecue trail, and wind beneath my wings. My byline appears on the cover; hers should be written on every page.

Our kids: Jake, a fine chef in his own right (several of his recipes are in the book), and Betsy—and her husband Gabriel—who, smack in the middle of everything, delivered the most precious baby and future pit-mistress ever, our granddaughter Ella Francesca. Gabriel helped me communicate with Spanish-speaking grill masters around Planet Barbecue.

My assistant, Nancy Loseke, tested every recipe, proofread every page, deftly handled every emergency, and managed to keep me on point (as much as that is possible) through TV shows, book tours, product development, and a thousand other activities. No doubt she got way more than she signed up for; the grace with which she handles it all is a tribute to her, not me. Assisting Nancy with the recipe testing were the amazing Arthur "A. J." Mindermann, Heidi Robb, Stephanie Leonard, and Heidi Toledo. Greer Flax and Bianca Rojas provided additional editorial help.

Workman Publishing: When you look back over your life, there are certain encounters that change the course of your destiny. Meeting my editor, Suzanne Rafer, tops my list. With friendship, enthusiasm, fidelity, and unimaginable conscientiousness, Suzanne has brought ten of my books to life. That an inchoate manuscript of more than 1,200 pages eventually became this book, and that everyone involved with *Planet Barbecue!* survived the arduous editorial process, bear witness to her reputation as the best in the business. Of course, we owe it all to our head honcho and publisher-in-chief, Peter Workman (and his wife, Carolan), who graced this and all of my books with characteristic intelligence, vision, and wit.

Barbara Mateer copyedited the manuscript with fanatic attention to detail; Peggy Gannon and Beth Levy saw to the editorial management; Barbara Peragine got the copy inputted so that Lisa Hollander could create the handsome design and Lidija Tomas, the layout; David Matt designed the bold cover; and Anne Kerman and Aaron Clendening corralled 5,000 photographs into the more than 600 you see here.

A book without a sales effort to back it up is like, well, smoke without fire. A huge thanks to Workman's sales, marketing, editorial, and publicity departments, including Page Edmunds, Andrea Fleck-Nisbet, Erin Klabunde, Selina Meere, Kristin Matthews, Jenny Mandel, Melissa Possick, Melissa Broder, Mell Perling, Kristina Peterson, Sara High, David Schiller, Pat Upton, Jody Weiss, James Wehrle, and Walter Weintz.

Photography: The more than 600 photographs in *Planet Barbecue!* reflect the work of several gifted photographers. Ben Fink shot the beauty and how-to photos, assisted by food stylist Jamie Kimm and prop stylist Sara Abalan. Penny de los Santos shot the Russian sequences and Nuts and Bolts photos; Anastasios Mentis photographed Greece. Philip Hoffhines worked wonders with Photoshop. A special thanks to Mic Garofolo at the Broadmoor. I shot many of the remaining photos, which may remind you why my day job is writer.

History: I was first made aware of the evolutionary consequences of using fire to cook meat by my anthropology professor-cousin, David Raichlen. He in turn introduced me to Dr. Richard Wrangham, whose *Catching Fire: How Cooking Made Us Human* belongs on the bookshelf of anyone interested in cooking and human history. Alain Turq shepherded me through the awe-inspiring Musée Nationale de l'Homme Préhistorique, while Bernard Ginelli and Jacques Collina-Girard showed me how early man would have made fire.

Travel: The researching and writing of *Planet Barbecue!* took me to six continents and fifty-three of the sixty countries included. I could not have done it without the expert advice of Nikolai Baratov, Anya Von Bremzen, Anita Cotter, Marian Goldberg, Mark Miller, Debra Rainey, and Patricia Schultz. Here are some of the people who generously shared their time and expertise in the various countries I visited.

Suzanne with me at Barbecue University

Argentina: Nelida Bernal, Sam Blum, Puppe Mandl

Australia: Vic Cherikoff, Robert Hart, Lee Gilmour, Leilani Mason, Merilyn Newnham

Azerbaijan: Mehman Huseynov, Amina Maharramova

Belgium: Peter de Clercq

Brazil: Arri and Jair Coser, Claudio Nunes, Tiego Ribeiro and Maeve O'Meara, Fuad "Dinho" Zegaib, Paulo Zegaib

Cambodia: Chhive and Ngoy, Siddharth Mehra, Jonathan Phillips

Canada: Sylvie Archambault, Sebastian Arsenault, Pierre Bourdon, Pierre Lesperence

Colombia: Carlos Gómez and Juan Pablo Gómez, Andrés Jaramillo, Andres Reyes and Martha Izquierdo, Ricardo Restrepo

Denmark: Martin Eriksen, Dennis Lange Kristensen, Stig Pedersen

France: Rosa Jackson, Olivia Mathe of L'Hôtel de Toiras

Germany: Manfred Abrahamsberg, Deitmar, Anna, and Andreas Brunk, Gerrit Ervig, Marco Greulich, Victoria Larsen and Julia Pluger of the German National Tourist Office, Claus Marx, Ralph Menn, Jurgen Putz

Greece: Aglaia Kremezi and Costas Moraitis, Anastassios Mentis

Guam: Steven Cruz, Rueben Olivas

Holland: Otto Haan and Chris de Graaf of Karakter Uitgevers

Hungary: Attila Zoltan Garai, Judy Raichlen

India: Tehmu Anklesaria, Robyn Bickford, Stephen Vincent Fernandez of the Imperial Hotel, Salma Husain, Jamie and Russell Kaplan, Narendra Kothiyal, Deepak Kumar, Anurag Masson

Indonesia: Liv Gussing, Morgan Lonergan

Israel: Phyllis Glazer

Italy: Paola Canali, Chiara Centamori, Giorgina Mazero and Giovanni Fracassi of Da Ivo, Fabio Tedesco

Jamaica: Helen Ames and Elisa Fershtadt of Ruder Finn, Paul Bowen, Carey Dennis and Cynthia Perry of the Jamaica Tourist Board

Japan: Noriko Akashi, Etsuko Kawasaki, and Yuu Morakami of the Japan National Tourism Organization, Elizabeth Andoh of a Taste of Culture, Michael Kowamura of Artist House, Tachi Nagasawa and Miko Yamanouchi, Shiori Suzuki

Kenya: Samuel Kariuki and Daniel Kiplagat of the restaurant Carnivore

Malaysia: Azlina Abdul Aziz and Nor Ashikin Samat of Tourism Malaysia, Bong Geok Choo, Haj Samuri Haj Juraimi, Azlinah Kudari, Nor Ashikin Samat

Mexico: José Calan Mut y Mirna Couoh Poot of Antojitos "Calan," Francisco Hernandez Romero, Rubi Sandores Lopez, Roger Sauri, Gustavo Rivas-Solis

Morocco: Rafih and Youssef Benjelloun, Abdel Kader Bou Egudada

Philippines: Alex Paman, Michael Profeta

Russia: Nikolai Baratov, Stalic Khankishiev, Sergei Logvinov, Alexei Sobolev of the restaurant Uzbekistan, Arutyun Yengoyan

Serbia: Milica Bookman, Verica Ignjatovic, Uros Markovic, Milenko Samardzich

Singapore: K. F. Seetoh of Makansutra

South Africa: Paul Appleton of Nando's, Simon Nash and Justine Lawson of Cadac

South Korea: Wendy Chan, Jangbae Yoon and Young-ho Moon of the Korea Agro-Fisheries Trade Corporation

Spain: Victor Arguinzoniz, Rosello Bas, Gerry Dawes, Matías Gorrochategui

Thailand: Karnon "Ton" Chartisathian, Allan Dresner, Cholthicha "Ja-aey" Kamviengchan

Turkey: Engin Akin, Ferhat Boratav, Hamit Ertas, Patrick Hannish, Filiz Hosukoglu, Bilge Hosukoglu

Uruguay: Francis Mallmann, Mikey Roel, Diego Sielbach, Fernando Velázquez, Filipe Velázquez

Vietnam: Michael Montella, Ngo Tung Thanh, Nguyen Dinh Thanh

Finally, a huge thanks to some of the other people behind the scenes who keep the barbecue machine running: Chuck Adams and the whole crew at The Companion Group; Matt Cohen and the whole crew of Resolution Pictures; Steven Schupack and the whole crew at Maryland Public Television; Craig Reed and the whole crew at the Broadmoor, and Tony Herreira and the whole crew at Delta Force; Jim Stephen, Mike Kempster, Sherry Bale, and Jeanine Thompson at the Weber Stephen Products Company.

Contents

Introduction:
Dateline: Planet Barbecue vii

The Discovery of Fire and the
Invention of Barbecue ix

Time Line:
Two Million Years of Barbecue
History (in 2,000 Words) xiv

Grilling with a Conscience xviii

Starters

Starters 1

Your passport to Planet Barbecue. Fire-charred vegetable dips and kebabs. Smoked Egg Pâté. Grilled Quesadillas, Pork Jerky, and Israeli Spiced Foie Gras. Get your barbecue off to a fiery start.

Salads

Salads 59

When it comes to grilled salads, eggplant reigns supreme—with peppers not far behind. As proof— Filipino Grilled Eggplant Salad and Bell Pepper Salad with Capers and Pine Nuts. A chapter's worth of recipes with smoky, snappy, rich flavors that you'll remember long after the flames have died.

Grilled Breads

Grilled Breads 81

Whether simply toasted over the flames, like Crostini and Bruschetta, or baked from scratch on the grill, like Naan Crusted with Pumpkin, Poppy, and Nigella Seeds and Turkish Puff Bread—you can't beat bread that's spent time on the grill.

Beef, Veal, and Game

Beef, Veal, and Game 115

A world of fiery options, including Caveman T-Bones with Hellfire Hot Sauce, Butterflied Sesame-Grilled Beef Short Ribs, and the infamous Buenos Aires "Heart-Stopper," a butterflied New York strip steak with bacon and eggs. Plus Baby Veal Chops with Garlic, Dill, and Russian "Ketchup."

Pork

Pork 191

Go hog wild! The recipes in this chapter give you every opportunity: Puerto Rican Pork Shoulder, Kansas City–Style Spareribs, Pepper-Spiced Spit-Roasted Pork, Russian Onion and Pork Kebabs; even a Whole Hog in the Style of a Greek Island.

Lamb and Goat

Lamb and Goat 265

Lamb is the meat of choice for most of Planet Barbecue and the recipes show the love: Enjoy Australian Lamb on a Shovel, Méchoui of Lamb or Goat with Berber Spices, and Peanut-Crusted Lamb Kebabs in the Style of Burkina Faso. And if you haven't tried goat, start with peppery, tongue-tingling Piri-Piri Goat Kebabs.

page 83

page 119

page 112

page 167

Ground Meat 305

Across cultures and continents, every grill master speaks the language of ground meats. Sample some of the best: "Kobe" Beef Sliders, Really Big Bosnian "Burgers," Ground Lamb Kebabs with Coriander and Cumin, Bratwurst "Hot Tub," and so much more.

Poultry 351

The world's barbecue trail offers up an astonishing array of grilled poultry: Beer-Can Chicken with Asian "Pesto," Francis Mallmann's Salt-Roasted Chicken, Cumin-Grilled Chicken Breasts with Fiery Bolivian Salsa, Israeli Smoked Goose, and Brown Sugar- and Orange-Brined Smoked Turkey. Who needs a stove when you have a grill?

Fish 419

Fish the way it was meant to be cooked—fire roasted. Treat yourself to Planked Salmon with Juniper Rub and Berry Glaze, Tuna Steaks alla Fiorentina, Grilled Hake with Fried Garlic, and Mexican Grilled Fish Tacos. The possibilities are endless.

Shellfish 481

Bring out the briny ocean flavors of fresh shellfish with a blast of smoke and fire. Shrimp on the Barbie (#2), Grilled Oysters with Ginger, Soy, and Jam, Mussels Grilled on Pine Needles, and Hanoi-Style Grilled Squid with Chiles and Lime. These are just a few of the killer recipes included in this chapter.

Vegetables and Vegetarian Dishes 527

Imbued with rich, smoky flavors, these dishes elevate vegetables to crisp, crackling new heights: Coconut-Grilled Corn, Bacon-Grilled Eggplant, Grilled Shishito Peppers with Sesame Oil and Salt, and Paella "Primavera" on the Grill. Meatless grilling just doesn't get better than this.

Desserts 567

Live fire has a way of transforming familiar desserts into jaw-dropping surprises. Grilled Ice Cream? You bet. Smoke-Roasted Apples with Japanese Sweet Bean Paste, Grilled Bananas with Coconut-Caramel Sauce, Fair Trade Chocolate Banana S'mores—don't put out the fire till you finish dessert.

The Nuts and Bolts of Live-Fire Cooking 597

All you need to know to get your grill fired up and at the ready.

Metric Conversion Charts 615

Photography Credits................................616

Index 618

page 205

page 415

page 450

page 578

Dateline: Planet Barbecue

Grilling is the world's most ancient and universal method of cooking. As I write these words at 9 A.M. Eastern Standard Time on a Friday morning, it's:

10 A.M. *in Argentina*
An *asador* (grill master) roasts whole lambs on upright stakes around a bonfire to make a traditional *gaucho asado* (cowboy-style barbecue).

3 P.M. *in South Africa*
A South African *braai* (barbecue) master grills a buttery fish called snook and *rooster brood* (yeast dough rolls) over the embers of driftwood.

4 P.M. *in Greece*
A *taverna* owner roasts an oregano-scented hog on a charcoal-burning rotisserie.

6 P.M. *in India*
A *kababi-wallah* in Old Delhi grills an assortment of meat kebabs on a charcoal-burning grill called a *sigri*.

9 P.M. *in Malaysia*
A grill mistress wraps a spice-slathered stingray in banana leaves to be grilled over coconut shell charcoal, while her counterpart in Indonesia (also female) oxygenates the same fuel with a straw fan to flame-sear the world's smallest kebabs—saté.

11 P.M. *in Melbourne*
Down Under, an Aussie grill buff pulls the final 'roo (kangaroo) kebabs off the barbie, letting her malee root charcoal burn to ash.

Welcome to Planet Barbecue, where grilling over a live fire is practiced 24-7 on all seven continents. (Even in Antarctica, where on September 13, 2008, a band of Russian scientists braved double-digit sub-zero weather to grill Russia's beloved *shashlik,* pork shish kebab.)

For some people (especially if they live in the southern half of the United States), barbecue means the low (typically 250°F), slow (a half day or so) smoke roasting of Texas brisket or North Carolina pork shoulder. For others—the vast majority of citizens of Planet Barbecue—the process involves direct grilling steaks, chops, kebabs, burgers, breads, vegetables, and fruits quickly over a hot fire. Almost everywhere, live-fire cooking results in a communal meal, usually prepared and served outdoors. (Two notable exceptions are Italy and Korea, where much of the grilling takes place indoors in the fall and winter.)

Thus, for practical purposes, the meaning of barbecue in this book embraces the ancient art of cooking with live fire, a specific cooking technique involving wood smoke, a series of iconic dishes, a meal prepared and eaten outdoors, and a communal food experience. When I say "barbecue," as in "Planet Barbecue," I mean all of the above.

Almost two million years ago, our prehistoric ancestors discovered the art of cooking with live fire. (You can read all about this amazing discovery in the chapter coming up.) For the past fifteen years, I have traveled the world's barbecue trail, and for the past five years, I have visited over fifty countries on six continents to research this book.

In it you'll find every imaginable variation on a theme of grilling, barbecuing, and smoking—from the rustic *fogo de chão* (campfire cooking) of Brazil to the high-tech grilling of Spain's culinary avant-garde. I've covered every major food group—from the obvious beef, pork, lamb, and seafood to less expected grilled salads, breads, and desserts. I've included all the icons of barbecue—ribs, brisket, shish kebab, *bistecca alla fiorentina*—as well as many of Planet Barbecue's singular dishes, such as Colombia's *lomo al trapo* (beef tenderloin wrapped up with salt in a cotton cloth and roasted on the embers) and grilled ice cream from Azerbaijan.

I hope reading and cooking from *Planet Barbecue!* gives you as much pleasure as I had researching and writing it.

Steven Raichlen

The Discovery of Fire and the Invention of Barbecue

I'm standing before a life-size (if not terribly lifelike) statue of a Neanderthal woman holding a hunk of red meat on a stick over a campfire. Welcome to Préhisto Parc, a Neanderthal theme park located in Tursac in southwest France. I've come here—to the cradle of prehistoric culture, the Dordogne Valley—to help me answer a question of both personal and professional interest that has intrigued me for two decades. Why do human beings feel such fierce passion about barbecue?

Neanderthal barbecue in southwest France, circa 40,000 B.C. (as recreated at Préhisto Parc).

For impassioned we are, arguing about what constitutes the best barbecue, who are the world's best practitioners, and what's the best way to prepare it at home. We debate the fine points of live-fire cooking—fuels, seasonings, techniques—with the ferocity of medieval theologians arguing the number of angels that can dance on the head of a pin. (The theological metaphor is intentional, for not a few people regard barbecue as a religious experience.) Grilling stirs passions in people in a way you don't get when you boil soup, steam vegetables, or bake bread. It has to be more than a question of taste or technique, and I'm hoping my visit to Préhisto Parc can help me find the answer.

Actually, by the time the Neanderthals came on the scene some 130,000 years ago, the art of live-fire cooking was well advanced. A quick tour around the park—scenes of hunting and trapping, technological competence in tool and fire making, communal dining, living, and even worshipping—shows just how much the act of cooking meat over fire had already influenced human existence. For grilling and roasting turn out to be far more than early cooking techniques—they had a profound effect on how we think, how we relate to others, and even how we look.

The fossilized skull of Homo erectus, the first human ancestor to cook with fire.

So when did it all begin? Not with Lucy—the pint-size *Australopithicene,* whose 3.5 million-year-old skeleton was discovered in Ethiopia's Olduvai Gorge in 1974 by anthropology student Donald Johanson. Lucy may have been the first human ancestor to walk upright (the first major step toward humankind), but her brain (less than a third the capacity of ours) was too small to allow toolmaking (much less fire making) or advanced communication.

Man Discovers Fire

Nor is it likely that barbecue began with a subsequent human ancestor called *Homo habilis* ("Handy Man," literally), who seems to have invented stone toolmaking around 2.3 million years ago. To judge from the numerous cut marks on fossilized animal bones of the period, the *Habilines* developed an important ancillary skill for barbecue—the art of butchering and meat cutting. But the large teeth, massive jaws, and bony-ridged skull characteristic of *Homo habilis* would not have been necessary had Handy Man known how to cook.

No, that honor falls to a more immediate human ancestor, *Homo erectus,* who first appeared on the savannahs of Africa 1.9 million years ago. This "Upright Man" was an extraordinary creature—restless, resourceful, and ambitious. Not the least of his accomplishments was global domination, for by 800,000 B.C., Upright Man had traveled from Africa to Europe, to the Middle and Near East, and clear over to Asia.

Homo erectus had a larger brain than his predecessors (950 to 1,200 cubic centimeters—not that far off from our 1,400), a more efficient digestive system, advanced toolmaking abilities, a complex social organization, and possibly even language. He owed it all to a revolutionary discovery: the use of fire for cooking. In other words, this manlike, if not fully human, ancestor of modern man invented barbecue.

Anthropologists debate the site and date of the first barbecue. Was it Swartkrans, South Africa, where researchers discovered the remains of flame-charred animal bones dating from 1.5 to 1 million B.C.? Or perhaps Gesher Benot Ya'aqov near the Jordan River in Israel, a prehistoric campsite, where hand axes, flints, animal bones, and grapes show burn marks made around 790,000 B.C. Perhaps it was at Dragon Bone Hill near Beijing, China—resting place of the legendary "Peking Man"—where charred bones and flame-darkened stones suggest the use of fire for cooking by *Homo erectus* as early as 750,000 B.C.

Homo erectus *masters the art of fire.*

Were fire making and cooking learned skills, spread from father to son (or mother to daughter), from community to community? Or did they arise in several locations at once—as spontaneous and random as the lightning strikes that very likely provided our prehistoric ancestors with their first source of fire?

For that matter, how did live-fire cooking first begin? Undoubtedly, it was opportunistic—perhaps a forest fire roasted an aurochs (an ancestral steer) or *hippidion* (an early horse) on the hoof, and a hungry *Homo erectus* (and they were likely hungry all the time) tasted it and uttered the first grunt of gastronomic pleasure in history.

However it happened, somewhere between 1.8 million and 800,000 years ago (anthropologists debate the precise moment), *Homo erectus* started eating fire-cooked meat—barbecue—on a regular basis. The act had monumental evolutionary consequences. It was, perhaps, the most important human invention of all time.

In his fascinating book, *Catching Fire: How Cooking Made Us Human,* Richard Wrangham points out how much easier a diet of cooked food is to chew than the raw foods eaten by other primates then and now. According to Wrangham, our modern primate cousins spent up to six hours per day chewing. That's six hours a day not spent hunting, toolmaking, socializing, organizing, and developing language, art, and culture.

Barbecue:
The Original Brain Food

But more important, cooking makes food easier to digest and metabolize. And guess what part of the body demands the most energy in a modern human (up to 20 percent of what we eat)? The brain. Barbecue was the original energy food—both the prerequisite for and the enabler of the development of the part of the body that gives human beings their competitive edge: a large brain. The anatomical changes that took place once *Homo erectus* starting eating cooked food are astonishing: smaller teeth and smaller jaws (which make the mouth and tongue more agile for eventual speech); a larger cranium and forehead to house a larger brain. Within 100,000 years of discovering live-fire cooking (an eye-blink in history), *Homo erectus* evolved from an apelike creature to someone who—from a distance at least—looked human.

The social consequences of the first barbecue are even more revolutionary. Fire meant protection against predators. Fire meant leaving the safety of sleeping in trees for encampments based on the ground. Fire meant the shared communal activities of cooking, eating, sitting, and sleeping around a fire. Fire meant socializing and sharing food with the other members of your community. Fire meant a division of labor, first between man and woman, then between hunters and gatherers, and eventually between people who tended the home fires (literally and figuratively) and people who did their work (as it were) in the world at large. Thought, speech, family, community, the division of labor, and, eventually, civilization—all owe their existence to this amazing invention called live-fire cooking.

Of course, it's a long way from the opportunistic use of fire found in nature to grilling on command. Hundreds of thousands of years passed before our hominid ancestors figured out not only how to use fire, but how to make it. Along the way, there were baby steps—the transfer of fire by carrying a burning log or torch or a tortoise shell full of embers; the conservation of fire for days, weeks, and months in carefully tended fire pits. (For a highly entertaining look at the challenges of procuring fire in prehistoric times, rent the movie, *Quest for Fire.*) So how did we learn to make fire at will? Once again, my trip to Préhisto Parc suggests an answer.

Making Fire— Harder Than It Looks

Bernard Ginelli doesn't look much like a caveman—not in his Nike sneaks and DSX T-shirt. But if ever a time machine were to strand me in Paleolithic times, he's the guy I'd want as my guide. Ginelli grew up in the Dordogne, near the very spot where we're standing, and as a kid on a farm, he unearthed hundreds of Paleolithic stone axes and spearheads. He's the resident toolmaker, spear hurler, and fire starter at the park—a sort of cultural interpreter between the Neanderthal Stone Age and twenty-first century France.

There are two basic ways early man made fire, Ginelli explains: percussion and friction. The first involves striking together two pieces of stone to create sparks to light your fire. Which makes it sound a lot easier than it really is. Strike two pieces of flint together, for example, and you'll get plenty of sparks, but no fire. That's because you need a hot spark, not to mention the right tinder (cottony, shredded, dried fungus), the right crucible (a sort of bird's nest made of dry straw), and the right blowing or fanning motion once the spark hits to nurture it into a fire.

After a dozen tries, Ginelli kindly shows me what I'm doing wrong. The key is the stones: To produce a hot spark, one of the stones must contain metal, like marcasite. A *Homo erectus* could pound two pieces of flint together for a lifetime (and many probably did), making enough sparks to fill an Independence Day sky, but without producing fire. Strike flint on marcasite with the right tinder and ventilation and you can make a fire—as Ginelli did for me—in two minutes. Hominids have been striking stones together to make tools since the days of *Homo habilis* more than two million years ago. Over time, some surely noticed that if one of those stones was marcasite, the spark had the potential to start a fire.

Or maybe not. A few weeks later, I caught up with another prehistorian—this one, Jacques Collina-Girard, a professor at the University of Marseille. Girard argues for friction as the possible

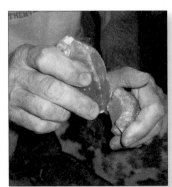

LEFT TO RIGHT: *Bernard Ginelli strikes marcasite with flint to produce a hot spark; the spark ignites tinder in a nest of dry straw; aerating the straw to build the fire.*

first means of making fire—friction as in rubbing two sticks together. If you've ever tried this as a kid—or as the contestant on a reality show—you know how difficult it can be. In fact, without the use of a bow and spindle, the task is darn near impossible.

I met with Professor Girard on the docks in Marseille. (An avid scuba diver, the geologist-prehistorian often pursues his archeological research underwater.) To dispel my skepticism, he produced a bow and a spindle and had a small fire going in about sixty seconds. Of course, it took him years to learn the right kinds of wood, the right kindling, and the right size and shape of the spindle hole to produce fire so quickly and easily. It must have taken *Homo erectus*—or the next human ancestors—*Homo heidelbergus* (a bigger-brained hominid who appeared on the scene about 600,000 years ago) or even early *Homo sapiens* (who appeared about 200,000 years ago)—thousands of years of trial and error to figure out how to make fire by friction.

The Birth of a New Profession—Grill Master

But once we figured it out, the innovations came fast and furious. Which brings me to my final stop—the Musée National de Préhistoire in Les Eyzies-de-Tayac. France's National Prehistory Museum houses one of the largest collections of prehistoric artifacts in the world. On display are many of the immediate consequences of man-made fire—and this revolutionary new art of cooking. Bows and arrowheads, bolos, and lassos for hunting, for example. Fishhooks and spears for fishing. Knives of every imaginable sharpness and shape for butchering the meat.

Also on display is an early hearth, where 24,000 years ago, Cro-Magnons (biologically and intellectually indistinguishable from modern man) perfected the arts of direct grilling, spit roasting, cooking in the embers, and roasting on stakes in front of the fire (a sort of radiant heat cooking still practiced today). A nearby case displays another early barbecue pit—a *four polynesian* ("Polynesian oven")—consisting of two large flat stones sandwiched with beds of embers—last lit around 20,000 B.C. Argentinean grill master Francis Mallmann (you can read about him on page 576) might call the set up an *infiernillo* ("Little Hell")—a sort of grill with fires above and below that anticipates modern indirect grilling.

As to what these first grill masters put on the fire, obviously, the evidence is harder to come by. But flame-blackened animal bones, not to mention the glorious cave paintings at Lascaux and Pech Merle, France, show us some of the early meats our ancestors grilled: aurochs, deer, horse, reindeer, bison, and salmon, to name a few. Other carbonized foods found at stone-age hearth sites

Professor Jacques Collina-Girard demonstrates the friction method of making fire with a bow and spindle.

include acorns, peas, and crab apples. According to *L'Alimentation Préhistorique*—a fascinating study of the prehistoric diet of southwest France—early man fire roasted more than one hundred different documented meats, plants, and seafoods. Salt deposits and fossilized mustard seeds at other prehistoric sites may even suggest how early barbecue tasted.

It's a long way from that first primitive fire used by *Homo erectus* to the stainless steel supergrills we grill on today. And yet, we still share a common bond: our fascination with and dependence on fire. Which brings me one last time to my original question: Why *do* we human beings feel such passion about barbecue? The answer is simple: because the discovery of that primal cooking technique—grilling—set us on the inexorable march to civilization and modern man.

Time Line Two Million Years of

1.8 MILLION B.C.

The emergence of *Homo erectus,* the first human ancestor to use fire to cook food.

750,000 B.C.

Fire-charred bones found in Dragon Bone Hill cave near Beijing—some of the first physical evidence that *Homo erectus* cooked meat with fire.

650,000 TO 250,000 B.C.

Early man gradually learns to make fire at will.

Homo erectus

By striking two stones together (flint and marcasite), he (or she) produces a spark hot enough to ignite tinder and straw.

30,000 B.C.

The first documented use of charcoal—as a black pigment used in European cave paintings. To make charcoal, early man partially burned wood buried in dirt

Fire making in prehistoric times. By percussion (left) and by friction (right).

or sealed in a cave or kiln, extracting the moisture and concentrating the combustibles. Charcoal burns hotter and cleaner than wood and is much easier to transport; it will become the world's most prevalent fuel for grilling.

View of a bison painted at Lascaux approximately 17,000 years ago.

20,000 B.C.

Cro-Magnon invents the process of indirect grilling by sandwiching meats between flat stones with glowing embers on the top and the bottom. One such stone barbecue pit—dubbed a *four polynesian* ("Polynesian oven")—is on display at the Musée National de Préhistoire in Les Eyzies-de-Tayac in the southwest of France.

14,000 B.C.

Prehistoric artists begin painting the walls of the Lascaux Caves in the Vézère valley in southwest France. The nearly 2,000 images catalog many of the meats grilled by prehistoric man, including aurochs (an ancestral steer), horse, deer, and reindeer.

10,000 B.C.

A prehistoric hearth excavated in the Lot region of France and on display at the Pech Merle cave shows the growing repertoire of early grill masters in the form of carbonized crab apples, peas, hazelnuts, wheat, and acorns.

8,500 B.C.

Early wood-burning hearths are found in Sarai Nahar Rai, in the Pratapgarh district in Uttar Pradesh, India.

2,600 B.C.

An early grill master builds an urn-shaped clay barbecue pit in the Ganganagar district in Rajasthan about 400 km from Delhi. Indians still use this device—known today as a tandoor.

850 B.C.

A blind poet named Homer is born in what today is northwest Turkey. His *Iliad* and *Odyssey* become the first two masterpieces of Western literature. The former includes descriptions of grill sessions involving beef wrapped in fat, seasoned with salt, and basted with olive oil and wine.

Homer

800 TO 300 B.C.

The ancient Sanskrit holy book, the *Vedas,* describes *shulyam* (meat roasted on spits) and five kinds of *rotis* (flatbreads), including *kandu pakva* (flatbread roasted in a tandoor) and *angara pakva* (bread cooked over charcoal).

8TH CENTURY B.C.

In his *Theogany,* the Greek poet Hesiod recounts the myth of Prometheus. Son of Titan and brother of Atlas, Prometheus steals fire from Zeus and gives it to man hidden in a giant fennel stalk. In angry retribution, Zeus sends Pandora to punish mankind (a long story) and has Prometheus chained to a mountain in the Caucasus Mountains, where each day a giant eagle eats out his liver.

70 A.D.

Animal sacrifice—long practiced in Biblical times—reaches its apotheosis in Jerusalem, where according to the Roman historian Flavius Josephus, more than 250,000 lambs were grilled as burnt offerings.

Barbecue History {IN 2,000 WORDS}

Oviedo's Natural History of the West Indies. *Contains the first written reference to the word "barbecue."*

1ST CENTURY A.D.

The writer Petronius, gives a fictionalized account of a Roman food orgy— Trimalchio's feast—where the pièce de résistance is a giant spit-roasted sow brought to the dining room on a litter. A slave splits it open with a giant scimitar to reveal a belly full of glistening grilled sausages. You can watch a recreation of the scene in Federico Fellini's film *Satyricon.*

258 A.D.

Saint Lawrence is put to death by the Roman emperor Valerian by being burned alive on a gridiron. According to early accounts of his martyrdom, the saint tells his torturers: "This side is done; turn me over and have a bite" (*Assum est, inquit, versa et manduca*). Lawrence becomes the patron saint of grill masters and cooks.

1095

Pope Urban II calls on the Christians of Western Europe to embark on a military campaign to liberate the Holy Land from the Turks. Over the next two centuries, nine Crusades would take place. Crusaders return to Europe with a taste for cubebs, galangal, mastic, saffron, and other exotic Middle Eastern spices, ushering in an enthusiasm for complex seasoning mixtures that foreshadow today's barbecue rubs.

1248

Les Oyers, the Goose Roasters Guild, is founded in Paris under the reign of Louis IX. In 1509 the guild changes its name to *Les Rôtisseurs*—the first professional organization for grill masters. Its coat of arms features two crossed turnspits and larding needles surrounded by the flames of a hearth. The *Chaîne des Rôtisseurs* (founded in 1950) is one of the oldest international gastronomic societies.

1320

Birth of the most famous chef in medieval Europe: Guillaume Tirel, aka Taillevent. His book, *Le Viandier (The Victualer)* abounds with grilling recipes. (Of course, most medieval cooking was done over a wood fire.) Among Taillevent's more singular recipes: how to grill crane, swan, and peacock, and how to grill whole eggs in the shell. Taillevent is the namesake of the famous Michelin starred restaurant in Paris.

1360

Henry de Vick designs a mechanical clock for Charles V of France. Clocks proliferate throughout Europe to help monks adhere to their daily religious schedule. Chefs adapt the escapement mechanism to power turnspits in the kitchen— the precursor of the modern motorized rotisserie.

1492

Columbus sails west from Spain in a tiny armada of three ships, determined to find a quicker route to the spice producing nations of Asia. On the way, he bumps into the Bahamas and West Indies, accidentally discovering the New World. Among the curiosities he brings back to Europe is the capsicum—a chile pepper. Within a century, grill masters from South Africa to India to Indonesia will spice up their barbecue with chiles.

1516

Spanish adventurer-writer Gonzalo Fernández de Oviedo y Valdés becomes the first European to describe a *barbacoa*, a wooden grill positioned high over a fire used by Taíno Indians of Hispanola to smoke roast fish and wild game. The term *barbacoa* appears in print for the first time in 1526 in Oviedo's *Historia Natural de las Indias (Natural History of the West Indies),* published in Toledo, and gave us the word "barbecue."

A Native American barbacoa, as described by Gonzalo Fernández de Oviedo y Valdés. Note how the food cooks on a wooden grate high over a smoky fire. (Engraving by the Belgian-born artist, Theodore de Bry, circa 1590.)

Time Line Two Million Years of

1575

André Thevet's world atlas, *La Cosmographie Universelle*, gives Europeans a more sinister view of New World barbecue—a cannibalistic feast of human limbs and heads grilled on a wooden gridiron in Brazil. Accounts of cannibalism are used to justify the barbarous treatment of the indigenous peoples by the European colonizers.

1564

The French artist Jacques le Moyne de Morgues accompanies the explorer René de Laudonnière on an expedition to Florida to establish the Huguenot colony of Fort Caroline (near modern day Jacksonville—the French arrived in North America long before the Pilgrims). Le Moyne gives us one of the earliest visual depictions of a New World barbecue—fish, snakes, even alligators roasted on a wooden grate over a smoky fire.

Mixed grill Florida-style, circa 1564 A.D.

1582

The Antonio de Espejo expedition introduces the Mexican chile to what would eventually become the American Southwest. In the years that follow, Spanish farmers and shepherds settle the region, introducing a technique of spit-roasting lamb called *al pastor* ("shepherd style"). Today, *tacos al pastor* (spiced spit-roasted pork and pineapple tacos) are popular in Mexican-American communities across North America.

1650s

One of the first laws promulgated in the English colony of Virginia forbids the discharge of firearms at a "barbicue [sic]." Thus begins America's dual obsession with smoke-roasted meat and guns.

1666

French surgeon Alexandre-Olivier Exquemelin signs on to a Dutch navy ship bound for the West Indies. Captured by pirates off the coast of Haiti, he becomes a pirate himself (as ship's surgeon to Henry Morgan), offering one of the first descriptions of *boucan* (French West Indian barbecue), made by salting and drying meat and smoking it in a smokehouse. A person who ate *boucan* became known as a buccaneer.

Buccaneer

1732

Birth of George Washington—barbecue enthusiast (his diaries abound with references to barbecue—including one that lasted three days)—and the first of a long line of American presidents to use barbecue as a tool for fund raising, consensus building, and diplomacy.

George Washington

1806

Thomas Lincoln marries Nancy Hanks at a barbecue wedding that includes "bear meat, venison, wild turkey . . . a sheep barbecued whole over coals of wood burned in a pit, and covered with green boughs to keep the juices in and a race for the whisky bottle," in the words of Carl Sandburg. Their son, Abraham, will become the 16th president of the United States. By emancipating the slaves, Lincoln helps create a new merchant class of pit masters, who will go on to open some of America's first commercial barbecue businesses.

1882

Canadian-born financier, inventor, and rancher William Soltau Davidson installs the first refrigeration system on a cargo ship called the Dunedin, and uses it to transport beef from Argentina to Europe. The ensuing meat boom makes Buenos Aires the wealthiest city in South America. For a great description of a Buenos Aires *asado* (barbecue) during those boom years, read the novel *2666* by the Chilean author Roberto Bolaño.

1886–1920

The birth of a uniquely American institution, the barbecue joint. The Southside Meat Market—specializing in "hot guts" (smoked beef sausage)—opens in Elgin, Texas, in 1886. The Kreuz Market—specializing in barbecued brisket and beef clod—opens in Lockhart, Texas, in 1900. Former riverboat steward, Henry Perry, opens Kansas City's first barbecue restaurant, the

Barbecue History {IN 2,000 WORDS}

Banks Alley Barbecue Stand, in 1907. In 1915, Adam Scott sells pulled pork in Goldsboro, North Carolina, while in 1918, Charles Foreman opens the Old Hickory Bar-B-Que, specializing in a dish much loved in Owensboro, Kentucky—barbecued mutton.

1921

Industrialist Henry Ford—eager to use scrap wood left over from car manufacturing—licenses Orin F. Stafford's process for turning wood scraps, sawdust, coal dust, borax, limestone, and sodium nitrate into charcoal briquets, and launches the Ford Charcoal Briquet Company. His friend, Thomas Edison, designs the first factory. Lumberman and early Ford dealership owner, E. G. Kingsford, takes charge of the factory, which eventually acquires his name. In 1973, the Kingsford Products Company is acquired by Clorox, which also owns KC Masterpiece (of barbecue sauce fame).

Tandoor oven in Kochi, India. The charcoal in the tandoor glows bright.

1948

India receives its independence from Britain. The subsequent partition of India and Pakistan fills Delhi with thousands of refugees from the disputed province of Kashmir. The new arrivals bring their traditional method of barbecue—roasting breads and meats in a clay barbecue pit called a tandoor. The first tandoori restaurant, Moti Mahal, opens around this time, launching what will become a world-wide Indian barbecue craze.

Weber Kettle Grill

1952

Grilling enthusiast and metalworker George Stephen has the idea to attach legs and vents to half of a spherical nautical buoy. The other half gets vents and a handle. Because at the time he's working at the Weber Metal Works Company in Palatine, Illinois, he calls the device a Weber Kettle Grill. The lid makes it possible for the first time to indirect grill and smoke in your backyard.

1959

Lark Hunter demonstrates the first gas grill, the "Arklamatic," for Arkla Industries (a subsidiary of the Arkansas and Louisiana Power Company) in Baton Rouge, Louisiana. Two years later, the Ohio Fuel Gas Company introduces the first residential natural gas grill: the Charmglow. In 1960, Walter Koziol introduces the "Perfect Host," the first gas grill in a portable cart capable of burning liquid propane. Koziol goes on to invent the first rectangular grill, and the first rust-free solid aluminum grill construction.

The Big Green Egg

1974

An Atlanta, Georgia–based importer named Ed Fischer starts selling a large, ovoid, clay, charcoal-burning Asian grill called a *kamado*—primarily to GIs who discovered it while stationed in China and Japan during World War II. Eventually, Fischer switches to a space-age green ceramic material from Mexico. The Big Green Egg becomes one of the world's most successful cult grills.

1985

Chris Schlesinger and Cary Wheaton open the East Coast Grill in Cambridge, Massachusetts. In an age when serious chefs fussed with painterly plate presentations and baby vegetables, the East Coast Grill becomes the first modern restaurant in America to make a wood-burning grill its focal point. Big portions, bold in-your-face-flavors, and casual service usher in a new sort of American bistro. In 1990, Chris Schlesinger and John Willoughby write *The Thrill of the Grill*, launching a new literary genre: the barbecue cookbook.

1998

Workman Publishing publishes *The Barbecue! Bible*, marking my professional entry in the world of live-fire cooking.

Grilling with a Conscience:
A Word About Ingredients and Shopping

A barbecue book may seem like an odd pulpit from which to preach a gospel of healthy eating. Yet much has changed in America since I wrote my first book on the subject, *The Barbecue! Bible:* There have been chronic outbreaks of *E. coli* in ground beef and salmonella in chicken, not to mention in such seemingly innocent vegetables as spinach and jalapeño peppers. Many fish species have been overfished and the proliferation of fish farms of questionable cleanliness is having an environmental impact. Not to mention the proliferation of genetically modified crops and a global-food supply chain that adds an average of 1,500 miles of travel to the foods we buy in the supermarket.

Each of these changes has an impact on our health, our communities, and the planet. The problems and their solutions are way beyond the scope of this book. Nonetheless, over the past few years I have changed the way I shop and eat, and I have come to believe that if we all make similar changes, we can effect powerful changes in the world around us. Or to paraphrase Michael Pollan, author of *In Defense of Food: An Eater's Manifesto,* each time you shop, you can vote for change with your fork.

So here are ten principles my family and I try to apply to our shopping and cooking. Perhaps some will make sense for you.

SHOP LOCAL: Food grown in your region supports local farmers and requires less fossil fuel to transport. It often costs less and tastes better.

SHOP SEASONAL: Sure, you can buy corn, apples, and scallops (to name three foods featured in this book) year round. But they taste best and cost less when you buy them in the peak season in your area. Plus, it's good to have something to look forward to when they're not.

SHOP FARMERS' MARKETS: Farmers' markets are a great place to buy fresh, local, seasonal food, and by supporting your local growers and farmers, you get great-tasting ingredients, while ensuring that there will be local food for your children and grandchildren.

BUY FREE-RANGE: Animals that feed, graze, and move around in the open air are healthier than chickens crammed into factory coops or steers crowded into feedlots. The process is a lot more humane—and you can taste it in the meat.

BUY ORGANIC: I don't know about you, but I don't like the idea of eating meat from animals fed hormones to accelerate their growth and antibiotics to keep them alive in crowded conditions. The USDA Organic label means your food is drug- and synthetic chemical–free and that it will taste more like, well, food.

CHECK THE TEMPERATURE: Cook *all* chicken and turkey to at least 170°F. Cook all burgers and sausages to at least 160°F. Use an instant-read meat thermometer to check for doneness.

BUY FAIR TRADE: The World Fair Trade Organization makes sure that growers and food producers in developing countries are paid a fair living wage for their labors. Look for the words "Fair Trade" when you buy coffee, sugar, chocolate, bananas, and other staples. The cost may be a few pennies more per pound. The satisfaction of doing good? Priceless.

BUY WILD: When Barbara and I want to grill or smoke salmon, we wait until we can buy wild fish. Yes, it's not always available and it costs more, but the texture and flavor of the fish is superior to farmed—and likely better for you in the long run, too.

BUY UNDERUTILIZED SPECIES: Overfishing has depleted many of the world's fish species, among them cod and sea bass. Other species—especially the dark, oily fish prized by grill masters on much of Planet Barbecue—are plentiful, cheap, and perfect for grilling. The short list of these includes kingfish, bluefish, mackerel, and sardines. The list of endangered species changes from region to region and from year to year—for more information, check a Web site like www.montereybay aquarium.org.

GRILL GREEN: If you're a charcoal griller, use natural lump charcoal, made from pure wood, and light it in a chimney starter. This cuts down on petroleum residue and fumes.

Starters

In the beginning there was fire. And in the beginning there was grilling. The primal urge to gather around the fire led to the equally primal impulse to nibble something grilled while waiting for dinner. Now the world's grill masters are only too happy to oblige, bringing us to the opening chapter of *Planet Barbecue*, grilled appetizers: Here you'll find such fire-charred vegetable dips as *htipiti*, a Greek bell pepper and feta dip and a Kurdish dip made with grilled pumpkin. There are tongue-blistering kebabs, like the Peruvian *anticuchos*. Of course, where there's fire, there's smoke. Israeli smoked eggs make an unexpected pâté, and Mexican grilled quesadillas sandwich smoked chicken and cheese between flour tortillas. You'll also find Kenyan grilled ostrich meatballs and the

Japanese grilled chicken dumplings that are known as *tsukune*, all in the pursuit of bold flavors to get your gastric juices flowing.

Of course, no survey of the world's grilled appetizers would be complete without saté and its cousins from Asia, tiny kebabs with disproportionately big flavors that are dipped in peanut sauce in Malaysia and Thailand or slathered with a 7UP-based barbecue glaze in the Philippines. From "village hammers," Serbian cheese-stuffed, bacon-grilled prunes, to grilled foie gras, a specialty of both Israel and France, the recipes in this chapter are designed to blast all your barbecues off to a fiery start.

Previous page: Fanning the fire keeps the satés grilling in Malaysia.

Bacon-Grilled Enotake Mushrooms

Enotakes are the Modiglianis of mushrooms—long slender beauties with toothpick-thin stems and ivory-colored caps (they look like oversize straight pins). Their flavor is mild and woodsy, and best of all, enotakes come in cork-shaped clusters that are perfect for wrapping and grilling. The Japanese grill them in bacon; the Koreans in thin slices of soy-marinated beef (you'll find the Korean version on page 4). Either way, the contrast of sweet mushrooms and salty meat is a knockout. **SERVES 4**

BACON-GRILLED ENOTAKE MUSHROOMS | facing page
and KOREAN-STYLE ENOTAKES GRILLED WITH BEEF | page 4

JUST THE FACTS:
Despite their exotic name, enotakes can be found at most natural and specialty food stores, and of course, at Japanese markets. Other mushrooms, from chanterelles to creminis, would work well prepared this way. You'd need to cook them shish kebab–style, on bamboo skewers.

4 clusters of enotake mushrooms
   (each about 1 ounce)
4 slices of bacon (about 4 ounces)

YOU'LL ALSO NEED
4 pieces of butcher's string (each 6 inches long)

ADVANCE PREPARATION
None

1 Cut most of the spongy base off each cluster of enotakes, leaving enough intact to hold the mushrooms together. Wrap each cluster crosswise with a slice of bacon, tying it in place with a piece of butcher's string.

2 Set up the grill for direct grilling and preheat it to medium-high. Leave one section of the grill fire-free for a safety zone.

3 When ready to cook, brush and oil the grill grate. Arrange the enotakes on the hot grate and grill them until the bacon and mushrooms are browned on all sides, 2 to 3 minutes per side, 8 to 12 minutes in all, turning with tongs. If the dripping bacon fat causes flare-ups, move the enotakes to another section of the grill.

Barbecue in the Far East: where the grilling is often done at your table and your waitress doubles as grill jockey.

4 Transfer the grilled enotakes to a platter or plates. Snip off and discard the strings. Serve the mushrooms at once.

VARIATION
Korean-Style Enotakes Grilled with Beef: When Koreans grill enotakes they use beef rather than bacon, achieving a sweet, salty flavor by adding sugar and soy sauce. There are several options for the cut of beef: You can use anything from tenderloin to top sirloin—just make sure it's sliced paper-thin across the grain. You only need 4 ounces, so the next time you buy a piece of beef, set this much aside for grilling with the mushrooms.

Make a sesame-soy glaze by combining 3 tablespoons of Asian (dark) sesame oil or unsalted butter, 3 tablespoons soy sauce, 3 tablespoons sugar, and ½ teaspoon freshly ground black pepper in a small saucepan over high heat. Boil it until thick and syrupy, 3 to 5 minutes.

Prepare and grill the enotake mushrooms following the instructions in Steps 1 through 3, on this page and substituting the beef for the bacon. Start basting the mushrooms with some of the sesame-soy glaze after 2 minutes and baste them well. Transfer the grilled enotakes to a platter or plates, snip off and discard the strings, and spoon any remaining glaze over the mushrooms before serving.

Village Hammers: Serbian Bacon-Grilled Prunes
{ SEOSKI CEKIC }

If you've ever had an image of what an eastern European restaurant should look like, no doubt Dacho (pronounced Da-ko) will match it: It's cavernous but cozy, with wreathes of dried red peppers and tables draped with colorful cloths. Every square inch of the walls is covered with Serbian handicrafts, painted crockery, weavings, and wall hangings. It looks, in short, like a rustic farmhouse picked up from the Serbian countryside and plunked down in a gritty working-class suburb of Belgrade. Which in a sense it is. The only way Dacho owner Damir Ashmi could get his mother to follow him to the big city, so the story goes, was to move the family cottage stick by stick and brick by brick to Belgrade. As with any Slavic restaurateur, Damir's first order of business was to install a waist-high fireplace in the kitchen and a brick smokehouse in the courtyard.

Damir built his menu around the sort of country cooking that makes Serbs' mouths water: marinated fire-grilled hot peppers (page 542), for example, and cornmeal- and paprika-crusted pork kebabs (see page 247). What better way to start dinner than with "village hammers," supernaturally sweet prunes stuffed with salty cheese and grilled in bacon. Prunes may lack the cachet in North America that they have in, say, the Balkans or France, but their rich plummy sweetness definitely belongs at a barbecue—especially when the sweet, tart, jam-textured prune in question comes from a Serbian *sljiva* (plum). (That's the same plum used to make the famous Balkan brandy slivovitz, and that's what you should drink with these.) So where does the hammer come in? Well, with a little imagination (and a lot of slivovitz), the bacon-wrapped prune skewered crosswise at the end of a toothpick does look a little like a hammer. **SERVES 4**

THE SCOOP

WHERE: Serbia

WHAT: Prunes stuffed with piquant cheese, wrapped with smoky bacon, and grilled—it's hard to imagine easier, tastier finger food anywhere.

HOW: Direct grilling

JUST THE FACTS: Serbian prunes are decidedly sweeter than those found in North America, so if you can buy imported fruit (for example, prunes from Agen, France), your "hammers" will strike all the more forcefully. Serbian bacon is a lot smokier than ours—use the smokiest country-style bacon you can find; one good brand is Nueske's (www.nueskes.com).

Sitting at the confluence of the Sava and Danube rivers, Belgrade is home to lively nightlife, with some traditional restaurants dating back to the nineteenth century.

4 ounces Gouda cheese

16 pitted prunes

4 lean slices of bacon, or more as needed

YOU'LL ALSO NEED

16 short, thin bamboo skewers or wooden toothpicks, soaked for 1 hour in cold water to cover, and drained; an aluminum foil grill shield (see Note and page 611)

ADVANCE PREPARATION

None needed, although the "hammers" can be assembled several hours ahead.

HOW TO MAKE HAMMERS

1. *Stuff the prunes with cubes of cheese.*

2. *Roll the stuffed prunes in strips of smoky bacon.*

3. *A novel way to keep the toothpicks from burning: wrap them in foil.*

1 Cut the cheese into ¼ x ¼ x 1–inch pieces and stuff them inside the prunes.

2 Cut each slice of bacon crosswise into 4 pieces; each piece should be just large enough to wrap around a prune. Wrap each prune in bacon and secure it through the side with a bamboo skewer or toothpick so that it resembles a hammer. The hammers can be prepared several hours ahead to this stage.

3 Set up the grill for direct grilling and preheat it to high. Leave one section of the grill fire-free for a safety zone.

4 When ready to cook, brush and oil the grill grate. Arrange the wrapped prunes on the hot grate, with an aluminum foil shield under the exposed ends of the skewers or toothpicks to keep them from burning. Grill the hammers, turning with tongs, until the bacon is crisp and the cheese is melted, 1 to 3 minutes per side. In the event you get flare-ups, move the hammers on top of the grill shield or to the safety zone. Transfer the hammers to a platter and serve immediately.

NOTE: For a picturesque variation on the grill shield, wrap the exposed end of each skewer or toothpick with aluminum foil as pictured in photo number 3, this page. The effect will be the same—to keep the bare portion from burning.

"Village hammers": sweet, salty, fruity, and smoky in a single bite.

Poppers

{ STUFFED GRILL-ROASTED JALAPEÑO PEPPERS }

Some people call them poppers. Others call them rattlesnake or arma- dillo eggs. But whatever you call them, these jalapeño peppers, stuffed with cheese, wrapped in bacon, and grilled with wood smoke, embody American barbecue at its most ingenious, irreverent, and diabolical. You may be alarmed by the notion of eating an appetizer that has a jalapeño pepper as its primary ingredient (in Texas it might be considered a vegetable side dish). Rest assured that seeding the peppers removes much of the heat and much of the rest departs in the grilling. This particular rendition plays the smoke of bacon and ham against the piquancy of cheddar cheese, but the permutations on the fillings are limited only by your imagination. **MAKES 24 POPPERS, SERVES 4 TO 6**

24 large jalapeño peppers
    (about 3 inches long and of uniform size)
3 ounces sharp cheddar or Jack cheese,
    cut into 1½ x ¼ x ¼-inch strips
3 ounces smoked or spiced ham,
    cut into 1½ x ¼ x ¼-inch strips
1 bunch fresh cilantro, torn into sprigs
12 thin slices of bacon, cut in half crosswise

YOU'LL ALSO NEED
Wooden toothpicks; a jalapeño roaster (optional);
    2 cups of hickory, oak, or mesquite chips or
    chunks, soaked for 1 hour in water
    to cover, then drained.

ADVANCE PREPARATION
None, but the poppers can be assembled several
    hours ahead.

1 Cut the stem end off each jalapeño pepper and set it aside. Using a coring tool or vegetable peeler, remove the seeds. Place a strip of cheese and ham and a sprig of cilantro in each popper. Wrap the bacon around the outside of the jalapeño like the stripe on a candy cane and secure it with a toothpick. Place the caps on top of the jalapeños and place the poppers in a jalapeño roaster. Alternatively, you can secure the top of the jalapeño in place with a toothpick and grill the jalapeños on their sides.

2 Set up the grill for indirect grill- ing, place a drip pan in the center, and preheat the grill to medium-high. If you are using a gas grill, add the wood chips or chunks to the smoker box or place them in a smoker pouch under the grate (see page 603).

THE SCOOP

WHERE: Texas, U.S.A.

WHAT: Smoke-roasted jalapeño peppers stuffed with bacon and cheese (or any stuffing you desire)

HOW: Indirect grilling or smoking

JUST THE FACTS: Like beer-can chicken, poppers bring out the tinkerer in a lot of grill masters. Consequently, you can buy a number of stainless-steel racks for grilling poppers, including one made by yours truly— not that you need to buy a special piece of gear. Should you want to, go to www.barbecuebible.com /store.

3 When ready to cook, brush and oil the grill grate. If you are using a charcoal grill, toss the wood chips or chunks on the coals. Place the rack with the poppers in the center of the grate over the drip pan and away from the heat. Or arrange the stuffed jalapeños in the center of the grate. Cover the grill and cook the poppers until the bacon is browned and crisp, the cheese is melted, and the peppers are soft, 20 to 30 minutes. Serve at once, removing and discarding the toothpicks.

Cream Cheese and Chutney Open-Face Poppers

Here's a great way to grill poppers when you don't have a jalapeño roaster. You cut the jalapeños in half lengthwise and stuff and wrap them. Then you arrange the stuffed peppers flat on the grill grate. I could suggest a hundred alternative fillings and that wouldn't even scratch the surface. Here are a couple of my favorites. A filling of cream cheese and mango chutney makes these jalapeños sweet, hot, and smoky. **MAKES 24 POPPERS**

12 large jalapeño peppers (about 3 inches long and
    of uniform size)
½ cup mango chutney or apricot jam
½ cup (8 tablespoons) cream cheese
6 to 8 slices of bacon, cut crosswise into 3-inch pieces

1 Cut each jalapeño in half lengthwise and scoop out the seeds. Place 2 teaspoons of mango chutney in each jalapeño half and top it with 2 teaspoons of cream cheese. Wrap each jalapeño crosswise with a piece of bacon, securing it with a toothpick.

2 Set up the grill for indirect grilling, place a drip pan in the center, and preheat the grill to medium-high.

3 When ready to cook, brush and oil the grill grate. Arrange the jalapeños in the center of the grate over the drip pan and away from the heat and cover the grill. Grill the jalapeños until they are soft, the bacon is sizzling and browned, and the filling is bubbling, 15 to 20 minutes. Serve at once.

Goat Cheese and Dried Tomato Poppers

Here are poppers for nonmeat eaters. Stuff the jalapeño peppers with a soft, creamy goat cheese like Montrachet. **MAKES 24 POPPERS**

12 large jalapeño peppers (about 3 inches long and
    of uniform size)
8 ounces (1 cup) soft goat cheese, at room temperature
6 sun-dried tomatoes (not oil packed), soaked in
    warm water for 30 minutes, then drained and
    thinly slivered
6 fresh basil leaves, thinly slivered

1 Cut each jalapeño in half lengthwise and scoop out the seeds. Place 2 teaspoons of goat cheese in each jalapeño half and top it with a couple of tomato and basil slivers.

2 Set up the grill for indirect grilling, place a drip pan in the center, and preheat the grill to medium-high.

3 When ready to cook, brush and oil the grill grate. Arrange the jalapeños in the center of the grate over the drip pan and away from the heat and cover the grill. Grill the jalapeños until they are soft and the filling is bubbling, 15 to 20 minutes. Serve at once.

Grilled Bell Pepper and Feta Cheese Dip
{ HTIPITI }

Mezes are to Greece what tapas are to Spain: a colorful array of dips, salads, meatballs, tiny kebabs, and other snacks served with drinks—in the case of Greece, an anise-flavored spirit called ouzo. Several Greek and Eastern Mediterranean dips and salads owe their smoky flavor to grilling (see the Salad chapter, starting on page 59). In Greece *htipiti* (pronounced chtee-pee-TEH; "ch" like you are clearing your throat) would be made with a fiery red pepper, a sort of Greek jalapeño. To approximate the effect, you can use grilled bell peppers with a spoonful of hot pepper flakes. **SERVES 4 TO 6**

2 large or 4 small red bell peppers

4 ounces feta cheese, drained and crumbled (about 1 cup)

½ to 1 teaspoon hot red pepper flakes

¼ cup extra-virgin olive oil, or more as needed

Coarse salt (kosher or sea) and freshly ground black pepper

Pita bread or Grilled Pita Wedges (recipe follows), for serving

ADVANCE PREPARATION
The peppers can be grilled a day ahead.

1 If you are using a charcoal grill, set it up for grilling in the embers (see page 601). If you are using a gas grill, set it up for direct grilling and preheat it to high.

2 When ready to cook, arrange the bell peppers directly on the coals or on the hot grate of the gas grill. Grill the peppers until charred black on all sides, 3 to 4 minutes per side, 12 to 16 minutes in all. Don't forget to grill the peppers on the tops and bottoms, 1 to 2 minutes each. The idea is to char the skins completely. The peppers can be grilled up to 24 hours ahead and refrigerated, covered.

3 Transfer the grilled bell peppers to a cutting board and let them cool to room temperature. (No, you don't need to place them in a paper bag or bowl covered with plastic wrap. I've found no appreciable difference in ease of peeling.) Using a paring knife, scrape the charred skins off the peppers. There's no need to remove every last bit; a few black spots will add color and flavor. Cut the peppers in half, remove the cores, scrape out the seeds, and cut the flesh into 1-inch pieces.

4 Place the bell pepper pieces, feta, and hot pepper flakes in a food processor fitted with a chopping blade and puree to a smooth paste. Work in the olive oil; start with ¼ cup, adding oil as needed to obtain a diplike consistency. Taste for seasoning, adding salt (you won't need much; the feta is already salty), black pepper, and more hot pepper flakes to taste.

5 Transfer the dip to a serving bowl and serve it with wedges of fresh or grilled pita for dipping.

Grilled Pita Wedges

Traditionally, you'd serve the grilled pepper dip with wedges of fresh pita for dipping, but grilling gives the pita more flavor and a chiplike crispness. **MAKES 24 WEDGES**

4 pita breads
2 to 3 tablespoons extra-virgin olive oil
1 tablespoon white sesame seeds

1 Brush the pitas on both sides with olive oil and sprinkle both sides with sesame seeds.

2 Set up the grill for direct grilling and preheat it to high.

3 When ready to cook, brush and oil the grill grate. Arrange the pitas on the hot grate and grill them until they are toasted and browned on both sides, 1 to 2 minutes per side. Watch the bread; it can burn quickly. Transfer the grilled pitas to a cutting board and cut each into 6 wedges. Serve at once in a cloth-lined basket or bowl.

Kurdish Grilled Pumpkin Dip

THE SCOOP

WHERE: The Kurdish region of Turkey

WHAT: Grilled pumpkin with walnuts, yogurt, and olive oil

HOW: Direct grilling

If Turkish barbecue were sushi, Zübeyir is the place you would want to eat it. You sit at a low table built around a charcoal-burning grill. Overhead is a massive copper hood embossed with scenes from the owners' native Van in eastern Turkey. The grill master—one of the five brothers who own the restaurant—sits across and perhaps three feet away from you, grilling garlic- and paprika-crusted chicken wings or tiny lamb tenderloins spiced with yogurt and Aleppo peppers, or lamb's liver seasoned with garlic and turmeric (which tastes better than it sounds), or eggplants and peppers so astonishingly sweet, you'll feel like you're eating them for the first time. He cooks these items to your desired degree of doneness and serves them sizzling off the coals. So why have I chosen neither grilled meat, nor grilled poultry—the pride of any Turkish restaurant—but a smoky fire-roasted pumpkin dip to represent this remarkable grill parlor? Because while there are thousands of restaurants in Istanbul that serve the other items, I've never seen this traditional Kurdish *meze* (a Near Eastern *tapa*) anywhere else. It's great for nonmeat eaters as part of a *meze* spread or as a prelude to a Near Eastern barbecue. **SERVES 4 TO 6**

1 pound pumpkin, butternut squash, or
    other orange squash, cut in pieces
    and seeded
½ cup walnuts, toasted (optional) and coarsely
    chopped
1 to 2 cloves garlic, minced
⅔ cup thick (Greek-style) plain yogurt
⅓ cup extra-virgin olive oil or vegetable oil
Coarse salt (kosher or sea) and freshly ground
    black pepper
3 tablespoons finely chopped fresh flat-leaf
    parsley
Grilled Pita Wedges (facing page), for serving

ADVANCE PREPARATION
The pumpkin can be grilled a day ahead.

1 Set up the grill for direct grilling
and preheat it to medium.

2 When ready to cook, brush and oil
the grill grate. Arrange the pumpkin
on the hot grate skin side down. Grill
the pumpkin until darkly browned on
the outside and tender, 10 to 15 minutes per side. Use a metal skewer to
test for doneness; it should penetrate
the pumpkin flesh easily. Transfer the
grilled pumpkin pieces to a cutting
board and let them cool, then trim off
the skin and cut the pumpkin flesh into
1-inch pieces. The pumpkin can be
grilled up to a day ahead and refrigerated, covered.

3 Set aside 1 tablespoon of walnuts
for garnish. Place the remaining walnuts and the garlic in a food processor
fitted with a metal blade and very
finely chop them. Add the pumpkin and
puree to a smooth paste. Work in the
yogurt and about ¼ cup olive oil and
process to the consistency of a thick
dip. Season the dip with salt and pepper to taste. Add the parsley and pulse

the machine once or twice to mix. Do
not overprocess or the dip will turn
green.

4 To serve, mound the pumpkin dip
in a serving bowl. Make a depression
in the center of the dip and fill it with
the remaining 1 tablespoon of olive
oil. Sprinkle the reserved 1 tablespoon
of walnuts on top of the pumpkin and
serve the dip with grilled pita.

NOTE: For a really interesting, if not
strictly traditional pumpkin dip, grill
the pumpkin using the indirect method,
adding 2 cups of soaked, drained wood
chips on the coals. Preheat the grill to
medium; the pumpkin will take 40 minutes to 1 hour to grill. Smoked pumpkin
dip is outrageous.

*A typical Turkish-
Kurdish meze
(appetizer) spread,
including grilled
pumpkin dip
(lower left).*

*Kurdish journalists
Heja and Abdullah,
who introduced me
to the restaurant
Zübeyir in Istanbul.*

Red Pepper Dip

Red pepper dips turn up throughout the Middle and Near East (for example, see *htipiti* from Greece on page 9). The Turkish version comes turbocharged with Aleppo pepper, the Near Eastern version of North American hot pepper flakes. Named for a Silk Road city in Syria, Aleppo peppers have a brassy, smoky flavor and moderate heat. Fire charring gives the bell peppers an incredible smoke flavor, while intensifying their innate sweetness. **SERVES 4 TO 6**

3 red bell peppers
1 to 2 cloves garlic, coarsely chopped
1 to 3 teaspoons Aleppo pepper or hot pepper flakes, soaked in 1 tablespoon hot water for 10 minutes
½ cup thick (Greek-style) plain yogurt
3 to 4 tablespoons extra-virgin olive oil
Coarse salt (kosher or sea) and freshly ground black pepper
Grilled Pita Wedges (page 10), for serving

ADVANCE PREPARATION
The peppers can be grilled a day ahead.

1 If you are using a charcoal grill, set it up for grilling in the embers (see page 601). If you are using a gas grill, set it up for direct grilling and preheat it to high.

2 When ready to cook, arrange the bell peppers directly on the coals or on the hot grate of the gas grill. Grill the peppers until charred black on all sides, 3 to 4 minutes per side, 12 to 16 minutes in all.

3 Transfer the grilled bell peppers to a cutting board and let them cool to room temperature. (No, you don't need to place them in a paper bag or bowl covered with plastic wrap. I've found no appreciable difference in ease of peeling.) Using a paring knife, scrape the charred skins off the peppers. There's no need to remove every last bit; a few black spots will add color and flavor. Cut the peppers in half, remove the core, scrape out the seeds, and cut the flesh into 1-inch pieces.

4 Place the bell pepper pieces, garlic, and soaked Aleppo peppers or hot pepper flakes in a food processor and puree to a smooth paste. Add the yogurt and pulse to blend. Work in 2 to 3 tablespoons of olive oil, enough to obtain a thick dip but not so much that the dip becomes runny. Season the dip with salt and black pepper to taste; the dip should be highly seasoned.

5 Transfer the dip to a serving bowl, make a depression in the center of the dip, and fill it with 1 tablespoon of olive oil. Serve the bell pepper dip with the grilled pita.

Smoked Egg Pâté

Eggs loom large in the landscape of Jewish religious symbolism. Eggs are eaten for the break fast, for example, at the end of Yom Kippur, the Jewish Day of Atonement. And a roasted egg—symbol of spring and new beginnings—appears on the Sedar plate (the platter of ritual foods) at the Jewish feast of Passover. So it seemed appropriate that our dinner at the Auberge Shulamit began with a smoked egg pâté. This historic inn, built in the 1930s and used as a lodging house for British officers during the Mandate period, houses a French-Israeli restaurant that doubles as Rosh Pina's barbecue central. Rosh Pina is an artist town overlooking the Sea of Galilee, and it was here, more than a decade ago, that an American friend of the restaurant's founders, Gadi Berkuz and her daughter Lea, introduced the art of American barbecue (smoking low and slow over hickory and cherry wood) to local Israelis, who licked their chops in wonder. You will, too, when you taste what smoking can do to commonplace egg salad. **SERVES 4**

*The Auberge Shulamit,
housed in a 1930s inn in
Rosh Pina, Israel.*

THE SCOOP

WHERE: Israel

WHAT: Egg salad barbecue style (smoked and served with grilled bread)

HOW: Indirect grilling on a charcoal grill or smoking; direct grilling for the toast points

JUST THE FACTS: For a milder smoke flavor, hard cook the eggs, then tap them against the work surface to crack the shell. Do not peel. Smoke the eggs in their cracked shells.

8 large eggs
½ cup mayonnaise,
  preferably Hellmann's
Coarse salt (kosher or sea) and freshly ground
  black pepper
About 1 tablespoon prepared horseradish
  (optional)
Fresh lemon juice (to taste)
4 slices of dense white bread or 4 pita breads,
  cut in half on the diagonal
Finely chopped fresh flat-leaf parsley

YOU'LL ALSO NEED
2 cups hardwood chips or chunks,
  such as cherry or hickory, soaked for
  1 hour in water to cover, then drained

ADVANCE PREPARATION
1 hour for smoking and cooling the eggs

HOW TO SMOKE EGGS

1. *Hard-boiled eggs, peeled and ready for smoking. Soak the wood chips in water to cover so they smolder, not catch fire.*

2. *Place the eggs on the grill over the drip pan and smoke until covered with a thin brown film of smoke.*

Smoked Egg Pâté with grilled pita.

1 Place the eggs in a saucepan and add cold water to cover by 2 inches. Bring to a boil over high heat. Reduce the heat so that the water simmers and cook the eggs exactly 10 minutes. Drain the eggs in a strainer and rinse them under cold running water until they are cool enough to handle. Peel the eggs. The recipe can be prepared up to a day ahead to this stage.

2 To grill: *If you are using a smoker,* set it up following the manufacturer's instructions and preheat it to 250°F. When ready to cook, place the eggs in the smoker and smoke them until they are covered with a light brown film of smoke, 40 minutes to 1 hour.

If you are using a charcoal grill, set up the grill for indirect grilling, place a drip pan in the center, and preheat the grill to medium. When ready to cook, toss the wood chips or chunks on the coals. Place the eggs in the center of the grate over the drip pan and away from the heat. Cover the grill and cook the eggs until they are covered with a light brown film of smoke, 15 to 20 minutes.

3 Transfer the eggs to a plate and let them cool about 20 minutes. Quarter the eggs, place them in a food processor, and coarsely chop them, running the machine in short bursts. Work in the mayonnaise and then season the eggs with salt and pepper to taste. If desired, for a slightly more complex flavor, add a few drops of lemon juice or a spoonful of horseradish. Transfer the egg pâté to a bowl or mound it into a neat cylinder, using a metal ring. The egg pâté can be refrigerated, covered, for several days—not that it will last that long.

4 Just before serving, set up the grill for direct grilling and preheat it to high.

5 When ready to cook, brush and oil the grill grate. Arrange the bread on the hot grate and grill it until toasted, 1 to 2 minutes per side. Watch the bread carefully; it can burn quickly. Sprinkle parsley on top of the egg pâté and serve with the grilled bread.

Smoked Chicken Quesadillas with Cilantro and Pepper Jack Cheese

Quesadillas are often described as Mexican grilled cheese sandwiches, but the truth is that most Mexicans cook quesadillas by deep-frying or pan-frying them. So leave the grilling to us. Like so much in our food culture, we Americans not only embrace the specialties of our neighbors and immigrants, we transform them and make them our own. These quesadillas explode with barbecue flavor—from the smoked chicken, from the pepper Jack cheese, and of course, from charring the quesadillas on the grill. The *pico de gallo* salsa is optional. MAKES 4

4 large (8 to 10 inches across) flour tortillas
1 cup shredded smoked chicken
2 cups shredded cheese (I like a half-and-half mixture of pepper Jack cheese and sharp cheddar)
½ cup coarsely chopped fresh cilantro
2 scallions, both white and green parts, trimmed and finely chopped
2 fresh or pickled jalapeño peppers, thinly sliced crosswise
2 tablespoons (¼ stick) butter (either salted or unsalted is OK), melted
Pico de Gallo (optional, page 130)

ADVANCE PREPARATION
You can assemble the quesadillas up to 30 minutes ahead, but you don't need to. The whole point of a quesadilla is its speed and spontaneity.

1 Place a tortilla on a work surface. Sprinkle one half of the tortilla with a quarter of the chicken, cheese, cilantro, scallions, and jalapeños. Fold the other half on top to make a half-moon–shaped quesadilla. Assemble the remaining quesadillas the same way. Lightly brush both sides of each quesadilla with the butter, turning them carefully. The quesadillas can be prepared to this stage up to 30 minutes ahead.

2 Set up the grill for direct grilling and preheat it to medium-high.

3 When ready to cook, brush and oil the grill grate well. Arrange the quesadillas on the hot grate and grill them until the bottoms are golden brown, 1 to 3 minutes. Using a spatula, turn the quesadillas and grill the second side the same way. Keep an eye on them—quesadillas burn easily. Serve the quesadillas at once, with the *pico de gallo* on the side, if desired.

THE SCOOP

WHERE: U.S.A.

WHAT: A main course quesadilla you truly cook on the grill

HOW: Direct grilling

JUST THE FACTS: For the full flavor effect, you need smoked chicken. Cook the chicken following the instructions in Grilled Chicken Salad with Chiles and Coconut on page 78 or use a good commercial smoked bird. You can also use smoked turkey from the recipe on page 407.

The Satrap of Saté

The year was 1950. He wasn't sure how to make a living but he had a family recipe for Malaysia's best chicken satés.

Planet Barbecue abounds with Horatio Alger-esque success stories. Like child-psychiatrist-turned-barbecue-mogul Dr. Rich Davis, who converted his family sauce recipe into the blockbuster brand, KC Masterpiece. Or Colombian artist and restaurateur Andrés Jaramillo (see page 136), who built a six-seat grill shack into a national landmark that runs the length of a city block. Malaysia has similar grilling success stories, but none can top the saga of Haji Samuri Bin Haji Juraimi.

I'm sitting at one of his restaurants (or more precisely, at one of his seventeen restaurants), a cavernous five hundred–seater named for the house specialty, Saté Kajang. By the entrance there's a curious artifact in a glass showcase—a portable saté kitchen on a bamboo yoke. On one side is a tiny saté grill with the tools of the Malaysian grill master's trade: a straw fan for fanning the charcoal, a basting brush, and a bowl of oil for basting. The other side turns into a tiny table complete with stools, serving plates, condiment bowls, and a kerosene lantern.

Carrying one of these portable kitchens is how Samuri's great-uncle, Haji Tasmin Bin Sakiban, got his start. The year was 1950. The seventeen-year-old Tasmin had just immigrated from Pekalongan, Java, Indonesia. He wasn't sure what he would do for a living, but he did have a family recipe for chicken satés seasoned in a fragrant spice paste. Serving satés to

Walking the walk: Haji Samuri mans the grill at his flagship restaurant, Saté Kajang.

passersby on Club Road, the young Tasmin built a loyal following. Over time, the portable kitchen gave way to a pushcart, then to a proper grill stall.

Tasmin had a young grand-nephew from a nearby village who came to live with him so he could attend high school. To earn his keep, Samuri would help his

great-uncle pound the marinade in a giant mortar with a pestle, cut and skewer the meat, and fan the charcoal to the proper temperature for searing the kebabs. When his great-uncle died in 1985, the grand-nephew opened a second grill shack, then a third. Today, Samuri presides over an empire that stretches across Malaysia with a commissary that turns out tens of thousands of kebabs each day. His flagship restaurant, where I'm dining now, serves four thousand people on a typical weekend.

When you order saté at Saté Kajang, you get a complete meal. It includes a salad (diced cucumbers and onions, eaten off the ends of the bamboo skewers), sticky rice cakes, cooked and served in palm frond packets, and a dish of Malaysia's creamy peanut sauce. So how many satés can you eat for one meal without seeming to make a hog of yourself? "Fifteen satés is a reasonable serving for a man," says Samuri. "Ten satés for a woman."

NAME: Haji Samuri

TERRITORY: Malaysia

CLAIM TO FAME: Owner of the Saté Kajang restaurant chain

SPECIALTIES: *Saté kajang*—saté marinated with lemongrass, ginger, garlic, and other Malaysian spices and grilled over coconut shell charcoal. Available made with chicken, beef, venison, rabbit, and other meats.

SAMURI SAYS:

▶ The most important ingredient in any saté is freshness: fresh lemongrass, shallots, and other ingredients for the marinade—all ground or pounded in a mortar with a pestle daily.

▶ When it comes to marinating saté, don't take shortcuts. You can't get the right flavor in less than twenty-four hours.

▶ The way you control the heat is by oxygenating the fire. In the old days, we fanned the fire with straw paddles. Today, we use electric oscillating fans. The principle remains the same.

Chicken Satés in the Style of Kajang
{ SATE KAJANG }

If you've been to a grill joint or street food center in Malaysia, chances are you've eaten satés. And if you've eaten these tiny kebabs, often made of chicken and served with a creamy peanut sauce, chances are you've had *saté kajang*. Named for a lively city a short drive south of Kuala Lumpur, Kajang is the ground zero of Malaysian satés, the place where an Indonesian immigrant and his family transformed a simple pushcart grill business into a barbecue empire that serves tens of thousands of people each day (you can read about it on the facing page). What you need to know here is that for not much more time than it takes to haul out your food processor, you can make chicken skewers fragrant with Malaysian spices—in short, one of the world's great kebabs. **SERVES 6 TO 8 AS AN APPETIZER, 4 AS A MAIN COURSE**

4 stalks lemongrass
4 cloves garlic, coarsely chopped
2 shallots, coarsely chopped
1 piece (2 inches) fresh ginger, peeled and
    coarsely chopped
2 tablespoons sugar
2 teaspoons coarse salt (kosher or sea)
2 teaspoons ground turmeric
2 teaspoons ground coriander
1 teaspoon ground cumin
1 teaspoon freshly ground black pepper
6 tablespoons vegetable oil
½ cup unsweetened coconut milk or water
1½ pounds skinless, boneless chicken,
    preferably dark meat
1 small cucumber, such as a Kirby,
    cut into ¼-inch dice and placed in
    a serving bowl
1 small red onion, cut into ¼-inch dice and
    placed in a serving bowl
Creamy Asian Peanut Sauce (recipe follows),
    or your favorite Asian peanut sauce

ADVANCE PREPARATION
4 to 12 hours for marinating the satés

YOU'LL ALSO NEED
Butcher's string; 8-inch bamboo skewers; an
    aluminum foil grill shield (see page 611)

1 Trim the green leaves (the top two-thirds) off the lemongrass. Using butcher's string, tie the green ends of the lemongrass together at the cut end and trim the top ends off evenly to make a sort of brush. You'll use this brush for basting the satés. Discard the root and outside layer of the lemongrass bulb and coarsely chop the core.

2 Place the chopped lemongrass and the garlic, shallots, ginger, sugar, salt, turmeric, coriander, cumin, and pepper in a heavy mortar and pound them to a coarse paste with a pestle, then work in 2 tablespoons of the oil and the coconut milk. If you do not have a mortar and pestle, puree the chopped lemongrass and the garlic, shallots, ginger, sugar, salt, turmeric, coriander, cumin, and pepper in a food processor, then work in 2 tablespoons of the oil and the coconut milk. Transfer the marinade to a nonreactive baking dish.

3 Cut the chicken into strips that are 3 inches long, ½ inch wide, and ¼ inch thick. Weave the chicken onto the skewers, leaving the bottom half of each skewer bare for a handle and ¼ inch exposed at the pointed end. Add the chicken to the marinade and stir to coat. Let the chicken marinate in the refrigerator, covered, for 4 to 12 hours; the longer it marinates, the richer the flavor will be.

4 Drain the chicken strips, discarding the marinade. The recipe can be prepared several hours ahead to this stage. Cover and refrigerate the satés until you are ready to grill.

5 Set up the grill for direct grilling and preheat it to high. To be strictly authentic, you'd grill over charcoal (preferably coconut shell charcoal) on a long slender grill just wide enough to expose the meat, but not the skewers, to the fire.

6 When ready to cook, brush and oil the grill grate. Arrange the satés on the hot grate with the aluminum foil shield under the exposed ends of the skewers to keep them from burning. Grill the satés until they are browned on the outside and cooked through, about 2 minutes per side. Baste the satés with the remaining oil as they grill, using the lemongrass leaves as a basting brush.

7 Serve the satés at once. To eat, impale a piece of cucumber and/or onion on the exposed point of the skewer. Dip the saté in the peanut sauce, then eat it.

VARIATIONS
More Kajang Satés: Using the marinade from the *saté kajang,* you can make a wide variety of satés.

Other satés popular in Kajang include chicken livers, beef, lamb, rabbit, venison, and fish.

Creamy Asian Peanut Sauce

Pretty much anywhere you eat satés in Southeast Asia, you'll find some sort of peanut sauce. Malaysia's is lighter and creamier than Indonesia's or Thailand's. Tradition calls for the sauce to be made with deep-fried shelled peanuts. Peanut butter gives you similar results with a lot less labor. **MAKES 2 CUPS**

2 tablespoons vegetable oil
1 small onion, finely chopped
2 cloves garlic, finely chopped
1 tablespoon minced peeled fresh ginger
¾ cup smooth peanut butter
1 cup unsweetened coconut milk
¼ cup chicken stock or water, or more as needed
1 tablespoon sugar, or more to taste
2 tablespoons soy sauce, or more to taste
1 to 2 teaspoons fish sauce (optional)
1 teaspoon Malaysian chile sauce, sambal ulek,
　　or other Asian chile paste
½ teaspoon freshly ground black pepper

Heat the oil in a saucepan over medium heat. Add the onion, garlic, and ginger and cook until lightly browned, about 3 minutes, stirring well. Whisk in the peanut butter, coconut milk, chicken stock or water, sugar, soy sauce, fish sauce, if using, and the chile paste and pepper. Let the sauce simmer until it is thick and richly flavored, about 5 minutes, stirring well. Add more chicken stock or water as needed; the sauce should be thick but pourable. Taste for seasoning, adding more sugar, soy sauce, and/or chile paste as necessary. The peanut sauce can be made up to 24 hours ahead and refrigerated, covered. Serve the sauce at room temperature.

Thai Chicken Satés

What's your "Bingo!" moment? Mine is walking into a grill parlor where the flames leap up from the grill and where there's standing room only, with scarcely a foreigner in sight—like Kuang Heng in Bangkok. Don't be misled by the shop's bare-bones decor, which runs to a wall-mounted Buddhist shrine, a handful of Formica tables, and the ubiquitous photos of Thailand's king and queen. On any given night (the restaurant is open until 5 A.M.), you'll feast on satés here in the company of Thai politicians and movie stars. According to third generation owner Apirak Jirachaithorn, the business began more than a half century ago as a sweet shop. Today, the satés are so popular, Apirak serves five thousand sticks a day (an order comprises ten sticks). What gives his satés their distinctive richness and flavor is the use of evaporated milk in the marinade. **SERVES 6 TO 8 AS AN APPETIZER, 4 AS A MAIN COURSE**

THE SCOOP

WHERE: Just about any street corner in Bangkok, Thailand

WHAT: Thailand's favorite street food—grilled chicken kebabs

HOW: Direct grilling

JUST THE FACTS: Thais would use the dark meat of the chicken, but basting with coconut milk will keep even white meat from drying out on the grill.

FOR THE CHICKEN AND MARINADE

1½ pounds skinless, boneless chicken, preferably dark meat and be sure to include some fat

1 cup evaporated milk

¼ cup soy sauce or ¼ cup Asian fish sauce, or 2 tablespoons of each

1 tablespoon vegetable oil

3 tablespoons sugar

1 tablespoon curry powder

1 teaspoon coarse salt (kosher or sea)

1 teaspoon freshly ground black pepper

FOR THE CUCUMBER SALAD

2 tablespoons rice vinegar

2 tablespoons sugar

½ teaspoon coarse salt (kosher or sea), or more to taste

2 baby or Kirby cucumbers, or 1 large cucumber

1 shallot, thinly sliced

1 to 2 Thai chiles or serrano peppers, thinly sliced

1 cup unsweetened coconut milk, for basting the satés

Creamy Asian Peanut Sauce (facing page), for serving

YOU'LL ALSO NEED

Small bamboo skewers; an aluminum foil grill shield (see page 611)

ADVANCE PREPARATION

1 to 4 hours for marinating the chicken

1 Prepare the chicken and marinade: Cut the chicken into strips about 3 inches long, ¾ inch wide, and ¼ inch thick. Weave the chicken onto the skewers, leaving the bottom half of each skewer bare for a handle and ¼ inch exposed at the pointed end. Arrange the satés in a nonreactive baking dish.

2 Place the evaporated milk, soy sauce, fish sauce, oil, sugar, the curry powder, and salt and pepper in a mixing bowl and whisk to mix. Pour the marinade over the chicken, turning the skewers to coat the chicken well on both sides. Let the chicken marinate in the refrigerator, covered, for 1 to 4 hours; the longer it marinates, the richer the flavor will be.

3 Make the cucumber salad: Combine the rice vinegar, sugar, and salt in a mixing bowl and whisk until the sugar and salt dissolve. Taste for seasoning, adding more salt as necessary. If you are using baby or Kirby cucumbers, thinly slice them. If you are using a full-size cucumber, cut it in half lengthwise, remove and discard the seeds, and thinly slice the cucumber. Add the sliced cucumber, shallot, and chile(s) to the rice vinegar mixture and toss to mix. Place the cucumber salad in small bowls for serving.

4 Set up the grill for direct grilling and preheat it to high.

5 When ready to cook, brush and oil the grill grate. Drain the satés and discard the marinade. Arrange the satés on the hot grate with the aluminum foil shield under the exposed ends of the skewers to keep them from burning. Grill the satés until they are nicely browned, about 2 minutes per side, basting them with the coconut milk. Serve the satés at once with the cucumber salad and peanut sauce.

Piri-Piri Chicken Wings in the Style of Nando's

I don't normally eat at fast food joints—especially not at airports. However, I make an exception whenever I'm in Johannesburg or Cape Town: Nando's. Over three decades, Nando's founders, Fernando ("Nando") Duarte and Robert Brozin, have built traditional African-Portuguese chile-grilled chicken into an empire spanning five continents. The pair uses a two-step process, soaking chicken overnight in their *piri-piri* marinade, then glazing it with a lemon, herb, and chile sauce as it comes off the grill. So how do you make their *piri-piri* marinade and basting sauce? As you can imagine, Duarte and Brozin aren't talking. But they did suggest some broad guidelines. The following gets you in the infield, and it definitely gives Buffalo wings a run for their money. Note: Nando's spells this specialty *peri-peri;* elsewhere on Planet Barbecue it's *piri-piri*. Take your pick. **SERVES 4**

FOR THE WINGS AND MARINADE

½ cup South African peri-peri sauce, Brazilian piri-piri sauce, Tabasco, or other hot sauce *or* ¼ cup hot sauce plus 3 to 4 fresh piri-piri chiles, cayennes, red serranos, or other hot, fresh red chiles, stemmed and cut in half, and seeded (for hotter wings, leave the seeds in)

6 cloves garlic, peeled

1 small onion, peeled and quartered

1 piece (3 inches) fresh ginger, peeled and cut into ¼-inch slices

¼ cup chopped fresh cilantro

¼ cup vegetable oil

¼ cup fresh lemon juice

2 teaspoons coarse salt (kosher or sea)

1 teaspoon freshly ground black pepper

3 pounds whole chicken wings (about 12 wings)

FOR THE GLAZE

4 tablespoons (½ stick) salted butter

3 tablespoons chopped fresh cilantro

2 cloves garlic, minced

3 tablespoons South African or Brazilian piri-piri sauce, Tabasco hot sauce, or other hot sauce

2 tablespoons fresh lemon juice

ADVANCE PREPARATION

6 to 24 hours for marinating the wings

1 Prepare the marinade and wings: Place the ½ cup of hot sauce or ¼ cup sauce and the chiles, the garlic, onion, ginger, cilantro, oil, ¼ cup of lemon juice, and the salt and pepper in a blender and puree until smooth. Or you can puree the *piri-piri* chiles, if using, and the garlic, onion, ginger, cilantro, salt, and pepper in a food processor, then work in the hot sauce, if using, and the oil and lemon juice. Transfer the marinade to a large non-reactive bowl or roasting pan.

2 Rinse the chicken wings under cold running water and blot them dry with paper towels. Cut the chicken wings in half, cutting off and discarding the tips. Add the wings to the marinade and stir to coat. Let the wings marinate in the refrigerator, covered, for at least 6 hours, or as long as overnight, stirring them every few hours. The

PIRI-PIRI CHCKEN WINGS
IN THE STYLE OF NANDO'S

longer the wings marinate, the richer the flavor will be.

3 Make the glaze: Melt the butter in a saucepan over medium-high heat. Add the cilantro and garlic and cook until sizzling and aromatic, about 2 minutes; do not let the garlic brown. Stir in the hot sauce and lemon juice and let the glaze simmer until blended and flavorful, about 2 minutes.

4 To grill: Grilling the chicken wings using the direct method is truer to the way they do it at Nando's but requires a little more care than grilling them using the indirect method. Whichever method you use, drain the wings, discarding the marinade, before grilling.

If you are using the direct method, set up the grill for direct grilling and preheat it to medium. Leave one section of the grill fire-free for a safety zone. When ready to cook, brush and oil the grill grate. Arrange the chicken wings on the hot grate skin side down

and grill them until crisp and golden brown and cooked through, 8 to 12 minutes per side, turning with tongs. Should any flare-ups occur, move the wings to the safety zone.

If you are using the indirect method, set up the grill for indirect grilling, place a drip pan in the center, and preheat the grill to medium. When ready to cook, brush and oil the grill grate. Arrange the chicken wings skin side up in the center of the grate over the drip pan and away from the heat. Cover the grill and grill the wings until they are crisp and golden brown and cooked through, 30 to 40 minutes.

5 To test for doneness, make a small cut in the thickest part of one of the wings; there should be no traces of red or pink at the bone. Transfer the grilled chicken wings to a platter and pour the glaze over them. Toss to mix, then serve at once.

VARIATIONS

Whole Chicken *Piri-Piri:* This is the dish that made Nando's famous. Substitute a 3½- to 4-pound chicken for the wings in the Piri-Piri Chicken Wings, spatchcocking the chicken as described on page 370. If you use the direct method, it will take 15 to 20 minutes per side for the chicken to grill. Using the indirect method will take 40 minutes to 1 hour. Spoon the glaze over the bird and serve at once.

Chicken Kebabs *Piri-Piri:* Another Nando's best-seller is a fiery twist on shish kebab. Start with 1½ pounds of skinless, boneless chicken breast or thighs, cut into 1-inch squares. Marinate the chicken in the *piri-piri* marinade for 3 to 4 hours, then drain it

FOR PIRI-PIRI CHICKEN

1. Puree fiery piri-piri chiles and the other ingredients in a blender to make the marinade.

2. Cut each chicken wing into two sections, discarding the wing tip.

well and skewer it alternating with 1-inch squares of green bell pepper, red bell pepper, and pieces of onion. Grill the kebabs using the direct method until the chicken is browned on the outside and cooked through, 2 to 3 minutes per side, 8 to 12 minutes in all. During the last 3 minutes, start basting the kebabs with the *piri-piri* glaze. Spoon the remaining glaze over the kebabs before serving.

Honey and Soy Spit-Roasted Chicken Wings

Like most Southeast Asians, Malaysians love street food, a fact not immediately apparent if you stay at one of the swanky hotels near Kuala Lumpur's equally swanky Petronas Twin Towers. But hop in a cab to Jalan Alor (Alor Street) and you'll find yourself transported to a rowdy world of hawkers' stalls and streetside kitchens, with leaping flames, sizzling woks, and crowded tables and stools on the sidewalk. Nicknamed "Twenty-Four Hour Food Street," Jalan Alor is where Kuala Lumpurians of all ethnic backgrounds come day or night for some of the best street food in Malaysia. These chicken wings are a specialty of the Chinese cook stalls, where they're roasted on special charcoal-burning rotisseries to the sheen of polished mahogany and the crispness of old-fashioned cellophane. To this add a honey-sweet marinade and you've got world-class wings. Here's how a pit mistress named Wendy Lokechan Thow makes Malaysian-style wings at the popular W•A•W Restaurant. SERVES 4

THE SCOOP

WHERE: Kuala Lumpur, Malaysia

WHAT: Chicken wings marinated with soy sauce and honey and spit roasted until crisp and golden, served with a sweet, hot hoisin-chile dip

HOW: Spit roasting or indirect grilling

3 pounds whole chicken wings (about 12 whole wings)
¼ cup light (regular) soy sauce
¼ cup dark (sweet) soy sauce (see Note)
¼ cup honey
¼ cup Asian (dark) sesame oil
¼ cup Chinese rice wine, sake, or dry sherry
3 tablespoons oyster sauce (optional)
2 slices (¼ inch thick) peeled fresh ginger, crushed with the side of a cleaver
1 teaspoon Chinese five-spice powder or anise seed

1 teaspoon freshly ground black pepper
½ teaspoon ground cinnamon
2 to 3 tablespoons vegetable oil or more Asian (dark) sesame oil, for basting
¼ cup hoisin sauce (optional)
¼ cup chile sauce, such as Thai Sriracha (optional)

ADVANCE PREPARATION

4 to 6 hours for marinating the chicken wings

1 Rinse the chicken wings under cold running water and blot them dry with paper towels. Make one or two deep slashes to the bone in the top (the thickest part) and middle segment of each chicken wing. Place the wings in a large nonreactive mixing bowl.

2 Place the light and dark soy sauces, honey, sesame oil, rice wine, oyster sauce, if using, ginger, five-spice powder, pepper, and cinnamon in a mixing bowl, and mix well. Add the marinade to the wings and stir to coat. Let the chicken wings marinate in the refrigerator, covered, for 4 to 6 hours, turning them several times.

3 To grill: Drain the wings well, discarding the marinade, before grilling.

If you are using a rotisserie, Asians have special dual-spit rotisseries for spit-roasting chicken wings; the wings are pinned between the spits in such a way as to stretch them out and expose as much of them as possible to the fire. The best way to achieve this in North America is to use a rotisserie with a flat basket attachment. Spread the wings out and place them in the basket. Alternatively, you can skewer the wings crosswise on a single spit rotisserie. Set up the grill for spit roasting, following the manufacturer's instructions, and preheat to high. When ready to cook, attach the spit to the grill and turn on the motor. Spit roast the wings until they are crisp skinned, darkly browned, and cooked through, about 30 minutes.

If you are using the indirect method, set up the grill for indirect grilling, place a drip pan in the center, and preheat the grill to medium. Arrange the chicken wings skin side up in the center of the grate over the drip pan and away from the heat, stretching the wings out as far as possible. Cover the grill and grill the wings until they are crisp skinned, darkly browned, and cooked through, 30 to 40 minutes.

4 To test for doneness, make a small cut in the thickest part of one of the wings; there should be no traces of red or pink at the bone. Whichever method you use, start basting the wings with vegetable oil after 15 minutes and baste them several times as they grill.

5 Transfer the wings to a platter or plates. Normally, they're so flavorful, you don't need a sauce, but sometimes they're served with hoisin sauce and chile sauce. Place 1 tablespoon of each, side by side, in each of 4 tiny bowls. Mix the two sauces together with the tip of a chopstick and use the resulting mixture as a dip for the chicken.

NOTE: If dark (sweet) soy sauce is not available, use an additional ¼ cup of regular soy sauce and two more tablespoons of honey.

Iranian Saffron Lemon Chicken Wings

WHERE: Iran and Azerbaijan

WHAT: Persian grilling on the wing—crisp, buttery chicken wings scented with saffron, lemon, and yogurt

HOW: Direct grilling or indirect grilling

JUST THE FACTS: Saffron comes in both threads and in a powder form. The threads are more likely to be pure saffron. Pomegranate molasses, known as *rob-e anar* in Farsi and *narsharab* in Arabic, adds a sweet-sour flavor. I've made it optional, but I like the way it rounds out the chicken—you can find pomegranate molasses at Middle and Near Eastern grocery stores.

So close, but so far away. That's how I felt as I stood on the balcony of my hotel room in Baku, Azerbaijan, looking out over the Caspian Sea. A half day's ferry ride, and I could be in one of the world's great grill cultures, known in Alexander the Great's day as Persia and today as Iran. But this is one case where politics and religion trump barbecue, so I had to settle for dinner at one of the many fine Iranian restaurants in Baku. Which, as it turned out, really wasn't settling at all. Here's how a Buffalo wing would be made on the southern shore of the Caspian Sea: marinated in yogurt and perfumed with saffron and lemon juice. The crisp skin and the succulent meat transcend national borders. SERVES 4

1 teaspoon saffron threads

1 medium-size sweet onion, peeled

1 cup plain Greek-style whole-milk yogurt (see Note)

2 teaspoons coarse salt (kosher or sea), or more to taste

1 teaspoon freshly ground black pepper, or more to taste

¼ cup plus 2 tablespoons fresh lemon juice

¼ cup extra-virgin olive oil

3 pounds whole chicken wings (about 12 wings)

4 tablespoons (½ stick) salted butter

3 tablespoons pomegranate molasses (optional), for serving

3 tablespoons chopped fresh flat-leaf parsley (optional), for serving

2 lemons, cut into wedges, for serving

YOU'LL ALSO NEED

Flat metal skewers (optional)

ADVANCE PREPARATION

6 to 24 hours for marinating the wings

1 Prepare the marinade and wings: Place the saffron threads and 1 tablespoon of hot water in a small bowl and let the saffron soak for about 5 minutes. Transfer half of the saffron and water mixture to a small bowl and set it aside for the glaze.

2 Grate the onion on the coarse holes of a box grater into a large nonreactive mixing bowl. (You can also grate the onion in a food processor.) Add the yogurt, salt, pepper, and remaining soaked saffron and stir to mix. Gradually whisk in the ¼ cup of lemon juice and the olive oil. Taste for seasoning, adding more salt and/or pepper as necessary; the mixture should be highly seasoned.

3 Rinse the chicken wings under cold running water and blot them dry with paper towels. Cut the chicken wings in half, cutting off and discarding the tips. Add the wings to the marinade and stir to coat. Let the wings marinate in the refrigerator, covered, for at least 6 hours, or as long as overnight, stirring them every few hours. The longer the wings marinate, the richer the flavor will be.

4 Make the glaze: Melt the butter in a saucepan over medium-high heat. Add the reserved saffron and water mixture and the remaining 2 table-spoons of lemon juice and let the glaze simmer until blended and flavorful, about 2 minutes.

5 To grill: Drain the wings, discarding the marinade, before grilling.

If you are using the direct method, set up the grill for direct grilling and preheat it to medium. Leave one section of the grill fire-free for a safety zone. When ready to cook, brush and oil the grill grate, if using. Arrange the chicken wings on or over the hot grate, skin side down, and grill them until crisp and golden brown and cooked through, 8 to 12 minutes per side, turning with tongs. Should any flare-ups occur, move the wings to the safety zone. In Iran they would grill the wings on a grate-less grill; you'll find instructions for doing this on page 599. If you are using the grateless method, preheat the grill to medium-high and skewer the wings crosswise on flat metal skewers.

If you are using the indirect method, set up the grill for indirect grilling, place a drip pan in the center, and preheat the grill to medium. When ready to cook, brush and oil the grill grate. Arrange the chicken wings skin side up in the center of the grate over the drip pan and away from the heat. Cover the grill and grill the wings until they are crisp and golden brown and cooked through, 30 to 40 minutes.

6 To test for doneness, make a small cut in the thickest part of one of the wings; there should be no traces of red or pink at the bone. Whichever method you use, once the wings start to brown, start basting them with the saffron glaze (you never want to touch the basting brush to raw meat). Baste the wings several times.

7 Transfer the grilled chicken wings to a plat-ter and pour any remaining saffron glaze over them. Drizzle the pomegranate molasses, if using, over the wings and sprinkle them with parsley, if using. Serve the wings at once, with the lemon wedges.

NOTE: You can substitute 1½ cups regular plain whole-milk yogurt for the Greek-style yogurt. Drain it for 45 minutes in a strainer lined with cheesecloth or a coffee filter.

VARIATIONS

Whole Persian Saffron Lemon Chicken: Substitute a 3½- to 4-pound chicken for the wings in the Iranian Saffron Lemon Chicken Wings, spatchcocking the chicken as described on page 370. If you use the direct method, it will take 15 to 20 minutes per side for the chicken to grill. Using the indirect method will take 40 minutes to 1 hour. Baste the chicken with the saffron glaze and serve the bird as described in Step 7.

Persian Saffron Lemon Chicken Kebabs: A popular Iranian shish kebab can be made by start-ing with 1½ pounds of skinless, boneless chicken breast or thighs, cut into 1-inch squares. Marinate the chicken in the yogurt marinade for 3 to 4 hours, then drain it well and skewer it alternating with 1-inch squares of green bell pepper, red bell pepper, and pieces of onion. Grill the kebabs using the direct method until the chicken is browned on the outside and cooked through, 2 to 3 minutes per side, 8 to 12 minutes in all. During the last 4 min-utes, start basting the kebabs with the saffron glaze. Spoon any remaining glaze over the kebabs before serving and top them with the pomegranate molas-ses and parsley, if using. Serve the kebabs with the lemon wedges.

PLANET BARBECUE

Japan: Grilling Where Less Is More

Grilling in the Land of the Rising Sun

Surrounded by the sea, Japan has always been a fish lover's paradise, but the grilled meats and poultry are first-rate, too.

Neon blazes in the Ginza District in Tokyo.

Not your typical North American barbecue: octopus on the grill.

When it comes to barbecue, the Japanese are at least as grill crazy as we North Americans are. This truth becomes apparent almost the moment you venture out to eat. Barbecue turns up everywhere in the Land of the Rising Sun: at neighborhood yakitori joints and noisy street festivals, in elaborate *kaiseki* (tea ceremony–inspired) meals, and at exclusive grill restaurants where dinner for two costs more than I paid for my first car.

Japan's most popular form of barbecue—and certainly the best known in the United States—is yakitori. But as with so much in Japanese culture, yakitori is a lot different on its home turf than at Japanese restaurants in North America. *Yaki* means "grilled," and *tori,* chicken; but this simple definition doesn't begin to do justice to the wondrous array of grilled fare you find at a yakitori bar. The chicken options alone include grilled thigh meat, wings, skin, liver, heart, gizzards, and embryonic chicken eggs. You'll also find grilled *negi,* a

Seafood robatayaki, salt-crusted fish roasted on vertical stakes in front of a binchotan fire.

leeklike scallion; *shishito* peppers; and *nasu,* grilled eggplant doused with *dashi* (smoky bonito broth) and sprinkled with tuna shavings—all enjoyed in close proximity to your neighboring diners.

If yakitori represents Japanese grilling at its most populist, *robatayaki* is Japanese grilling at its most exclusive. *Ro* refers to the simple charcoal-burning hearth once found in peasant cottages, but the typical *robatayaki* restaurant in Tokyo is anything but pastoral or

cheap. The array of raw ingredients is stunning: giant king crab claws and softshell crabs so small you can eat them in a single bite; all manner of fish, eel, bivalves, octopus, and other cephalopods; Kobe and the less well known, but infinitely tastier Saga beef, so generously marbled it looks like white lace on a red tablecloth; supernaturally sweet Chiba corn; even *mochi* (cinnamon-dusted sticky rice cakes), which the servers pound to order in a waist-high mortar using a pestle.

Presiding over this spectacle on a raised dais is a master griller, who cooks the items you select on a tiny hibachi and delivers them on an eight-foot-long wooden paddle. (The paddle symbolizes the oars off of which seaside grill masters traditionally served grilled seafood.) The meal is served with ostentatious generosity: Wooden sake boxes, for example, are filled to overflowing amid incessant ceremonial shouting. Relaxed? No. Unforgettable? Absolutely.

Pristine seafood awaits the grill at the sprawling Tsukiji Fish Market in Tokyo.

THE GRILLS: Like most grills in Asia, the Japanese restaurant grill is long and slender—two or more feet long and just a couple of inches across, the ideal size for cooking a tiny kebab without burning the exposed end of the bamboo skewer. Lined with refractory brick, Japanese grills achieve extremely high temperatures, in excess of 1,000°F. At home, grilling enthusiasts use small, freestanding, lidless charcoal-burning hibachis.

THE FUEL: Japan is home to the world's most exclusive charcoal, a hard, slow, and extremely hot burning fuel called *binchotan* (or *binchō-tan*). Made from *ubamegashi* oak, it has an almost metallic ring when you strike two pieces together. It burns hot and long, with no discernable aroma of its own (so much for a "charcoal" flavor), the reason it's so highly prized by Japanese grill masters. According to Japanese cultural authority, Elizabeth Andoh, *binchotan* takes its name from a seventeenth century nobleman who lived in what is now the Wakayama prefecture in western Honshu, which is southwest of Osaka—the source of the best *binchotan* today.

THE FLAVORINGS: Yakitori traditionally comes seasoned with sea salt or with *tare*, a dark, thick, sweet-salty barbecue sauce made from soy sauce, mirin (sweet rice wine), sake, and sugar. The chicken kebabs are dipped twice in the *tare*—first when cooked about three quarters of the way through and again right before serving. Each time a chicken kebab is dipped it adds flavor to the sauce (the outside of the chicken is cooked, so there's no danger of contamination). The *tare* ingredients are replenished as needed to keep the pot bubbling and full. Like the master sauce of China, yakitori sauce tastes good after a week, great after a month, and spectacular after a decade.

MUST TRY DISHES: *Yakiniku* is the general term for grilled meat. *Kushiyaki* means foods cooked on skewers. Specific specialties include:

Dengaku: Skewered grilled tofu with miso barbecue sauce; the skewers resemble *dengaku*—stilts.

Negi-ma: Thinly shaved beef rolled around Japanese leeks and grilled with sweet-salty teriyaki sauce; a popular variation features beef rolled around asparagus, then grilled.

Teriyaki: Meats or seafood grilled with a sweet-salty glaze

Tsukune: Grilled chicken dumplings or meatballs

Yaki nasu: Grilled Japanese eggplants sauced with *dashi*, bonito broth, and dusted with shaved dried tuna

Yaki onigiri: Grilled rice balls, often stuffed with miso or sweet bean paste

Yakitori: Every imaginable cut of grilled chicken

Teppanyaki: What you get at a traditional Japanese steak house (an experience typified in North America by restaurants like Benihana). The cooking technique used here is griddling, not grilling.

THE CONDIMENTS: "Japanese food is minus food, not plus food," says Tokyo master chef Akio Saito. In other words, it's more about what you leave out than what you put in. When asked about his favorite condiment for barbecue, he named a single ingredient: salt. You might also get toasted or black sesame seeds, chopped scallions, a paste made from tart salty *umeboshi* (pickled plums), or fiery Japanese mustard.

IF YOU CAN EAT AT ONLY ONE RESTAURANT: Birdland in Tokyo (see page 404)

WHAT TO DRINK: Japanese beer, such as Kirin, Asahi, or Sapporo, or sake

THE MOST SINGULAR DISH IN THE REPERTORY: Lots of candidates for this one: *Ginnan kushiyaki*, grilled ginkgo nut skewers. Grilled *torigai*, flame-toasted dried cockles. *Ayo*, a small river fish grilled and eaten whole, with head, guts, and bones intact.

Tokyo-Style Grilled Chicken Dumplings
{ TSUKUNE }

A meal at a Japanese yakitori parlor would be incomplete without a luscious, crusty, intensely flavorful grilled chicken dumpling or meatball called *tsukune.* In fact, many Japanese grilling aficionados will judge a yakitori bar by its *tsukune,* and if it is not up to snuff, they won't bother sticking around to try anything else. (Traditionally, *tsukune* are grilled on bamboo skewers, but in at least one restaurant—Aburiya Kinnosuke in New York—they cook the dumplings on the backs of wooden spoons, which are stood in front of a blazing charcoal fire.) The most complicated thing about this dish is reading this introduction; the recipe is really just a series of simple steps. **SERVES 6 AS AN APPETIZER, 4 AS A MAIN COURSE**

1¼ pounds skinless, boneless chicken thighs or
    breasts, cut into ½-inch pieces
2 ounces chicken fat or fatty bacon
    (optional; see Note), cut into ½-inch pieces
2 scallions, both white and green parts,
    trimmed and thinly sliced crosswise
1 teaspoon minced peeled fresh ginger
½ teaspoon freshly ground black pepper
1½ teaspoons coarse salt (kosher or sea)
½ teaspoon ground coriander
¼ teaspoon ground sansho pepper, or
    ⅛ teaspoon each additional freshly ground
    black pepper and ground coriander
2 teaspoons cornstarch
1 egg white

YOU'LL ALSO NEED

Small flat bamboo skewers; an aluminum foil
    grill shield (optional, see page 611)

ADVANCE PREPARATION

For the best results, make the dumpling mixture
    1 to 2 hours ahead and refrigerate it until firm.

1 Place the chicken pieces, chicken fat or bacon, if using, scallions, ginger, black pepper, salt, coriander, *sansho* pepper, cornstarch, and egg white in a food processor fitted with a metal blade. Process the mixture to a coarse puree, running the processor in short bursts. Do not overprocess; the mixture should be lumpy—this is essential for the proper texture. Transfer the dumpling mixture to a bowl (or leave it in the processor bowl) and freeze it, covered, until firm, but not frozen, 20 to 30 minutes.

2 Using a large spoon, scoop out a 1½ inch ball of dumpling mixture and mold it onto the end of a skewer to make a flattish oval about 2 inches long, 1 inch wide, and ½ inch thick. Place the skewer on a plate or baking sheet lined with plastic wrap. Repeat until all of the dumpling mixture is used up, wetting or oiling your hands as needed to prevent sticking. You should have 16 to 18 dumplings; refrigerate them, covered, for 1 to 2 hours.

3 Set up the grill for direct grilling and preheat it to high.

4 When ready to cook, brush and generously oil the grill grate. Arrange the dumplings on the hot grate at a diagonal to the bars, placing the aluminum foil shield under the exposed ends of the skewers to keep them from burning. Grill the dumplings until golden brown and cooked through, 3 to 4 minutes per side, 6 to 8 minutes in all. Give each skewer a quarter turn after 1½ minutes to create an attractive crosshatch of grill marks (it also helps the dumplings cook more evenly). Transfer the grilled dumplings to a platter and serve at once.

NOTE: I've made the chicken fat optional, but to get the luscious mouthfeel of a proper *tsukune* you should add it. I save and freeze the lumps of fat from the cavity whenever I roast a chicken; that way I always have some chicken fat on hand. You could substitute diced bacon and you'd get the right texture. Even if the flavor is completely different—and would probably horrify a Japanese person—the result would not be any less amazing.

Grilled Ostrich Meatballs

Think of these meatballs as a warm-up to a full-blown Kenyan barbecue—the sort of cookout that features a half-dozen grilled meats: beef, lamb, pork, goat, plus maybe some impala or kudu. Speaking of game, hunters could substitute ground venison or elk for the ostrich. **SERVES 4**

4 slices white bread (crusts discarded),
    cut into 1-inch squares
1 cup milk
1½ pounds ground ostrich or lean ground beef
1 medium-size onion, finely chopped
3 tablespoons finely chopped fresh flat-leaf
    parsley
½ teaspoon dried thyme
½ teaspoon ground bay leaves
2 large eggs, lightly beaten with a fork
1½ teaspoons coarse salt (kosher or sea)
½ teaspoon freshly ground black pepper
About 2 tablespoons vegetable oil, for basting
Tomato-Pepper Salsa (optional, recipe follows),
    for serving

ADVANCE PREPARATION
Although you can form the meatballs as little as an hour in advance, for the best results, do this 3 to 4 hours ahead and refrigerate until grilling.

1 Place the bread in a mixing bowl, pour the milk over it, and let soak for 10 minutes. Drain off the milk, squeezing the bread to extract the excess.

2 Add the ostrich, onion, parsley, thyme, bay leaves, eggs, salt, and pepper. Beat with a wooden spoon or knead with your fingers to mix.

3 Form the ostrich mixture into flattish meatballs (they should look like miniature burgers), each about 2 inches across and 1 inch thick. Arrange the meatballs on a plate lined with plastic wrap and refrigerate them, covered, for at least 1 hour or as long as 4 hours before grilling (chilling helps firm up the meatballs so they're less likely to stick or fall apart on the grill).

4 Set up the grill for direct grilling and preheat it to high.

5 When ready to cook, brush and oil the grill grate. Arrange the meatballs on the hot grate and grill them until nicely browned on both sides and cooked through, 2 to 3 minutes per side, basting them with oil. Serve the meatballs at once with the Tomato-Pepper Salsa, if desired.

Tomato-Pepper Salsa

Variations on this fiery salsa (think Mexican salsa minus the lime) turn up throughout Africa. For many Kenyans, there is no better accompaniment for grilled meat than *kachumbari,* as the salsa is called in Kenya. **MAKES 1½ TO 2 CUPS**

2 luscious, ripe red tomatoes
1 to 3 hot green peppers, such as serranos or jalapeños, or
    green Scotch bonnet chiles, if you want to make a statement
1 small or ½ medium-size sweet onion
3 tablespoons finely chopped fresh cilantro
½ teaspoon coarse salt (kosher or sea), or more to taste
2 tablespoons vegetable oil, such as corn oil

1 Cut each tomato in half crosswise and squeeze out the seeds. Cut the tomato into ¼-inch dice. Cut the pepper(s) in half lengthwise and remove the seeds (or for a hotter salsa, leave the seeds in). Cut the pepper(s) and onion into ¼-inch dice.

2 Place the diced tomato, pepper, and onion, and the cilantro, salt, and oil in a nonreactive mixing bowl and toss to mix. Taste for seasoning, adding more salt as necessary. You can assemble all the ingredients for the salsa in the bowl several hours ahead, but do not mix them until just before serving.

The Best Beef Satés in Singapore

THE SCOOP

WHERE: Singapore

WHAT: Tiny flame-seared beef kebabs—the cumin, coriander, and turmeric marinade rocks

HOW: Direct grilling

Satés in Singapore play the same role as hot dogs in New York, a popular, affordable, and democratic street snack enjoyed at all hours of the day and night by rich and poor and everyone in between. So to have your saté named the best in Singapore by *The Straits Times* (think *The New York Times* of Southeast Asia) is no small accomplishment, especially if you're an *ang moh,* foreigner—in this case, an American: my stepson, Jake Klein. These satés were first served at the restaurant Wood, which featured Asia's first, and only, exclusively wood-burning kitchen (wood-burning grill, oven, smoker, and rotisserie). But even if you cook on a gas grill, the robust spicing of these satés will blast through loud and clear. For centuries Singapore and the Strait of Malacca were the epicenter of the Asian spice trade; the legacy lives on in these electrifying satés. **SERVES 6 AS AN APPETIZER, 4 AS A LIGHT MAIN COURSE**

1½ pounds rib eye steaks (about ½ inch thick)

3 tablespoons light brown sugar

2 tablespoons ground coriander

1 tablespoon ground turmeric

1½ teaspoons ground cumin

1½ teaspoons freshly ground black pepper

3 tablespoons Asian fish sauce or soy sauce

3 tablespoons vegetable oil

Singapore Cucumber Relish (optional, recipe
    follows), for serving

Fried Garlic Peanut Sauce (optional, recipe
    follows), for serving

YOU'LL ALSO NEED

8-inch bamboo skewers; an aluminum foil grill
    shield (see page 611)

ADVANCE PREPARATION

2 to 12 hours for marinating the beef

1 Cut the steaks, including the fat, into ½-inch cubes and place them in a nonreactive mixing bowl. Stir in the brown sugar, coriander, turmeric, cumin, pepper, fish sauce, and oil. Let the beef marinate in the refrigerator, covered, for at least 2 hours; the longer it marinates, the richer the flavor will be.

2 Drain the cubes of beef, discarding the marinade. Thread the beef onto bamboo skewers, leaving the bottom half of each skewer bare for

a handle and ¼ inch exposed at the pointed end. The satés can be prepared several hours ahead to this stage. Refrigerate the satés, covered, until ready to grill.

3 Set up the grill for direct grilling and preheat it to high.

4 When ready to cook, brush and oil the grill grate. Arrange the satés on the hot grate, with the aluminum foil shield under the exposed ends of the skewers to keep them from burning. Grill the satés until cooked to taste, 1 to 2 minutes per side for medium-rare, a little longer for medium. (In general, Southeast Asians prefer their satés medium to medium-well done.) Use the poke test to check for doneness (see the box on page 612).

5 Serve the satés with Singapore Cucumber Relish and Fried Garlic Peanut Sauce, if desired. The traditional way to eat the satés is to skewer a piece of cucumber on the pointed end of the skewer, then dip the saté in the peanut sauce.

JUST THE FACTS: What makes these satés so extraordinary is the cut of beef, rib eye, the most generously marbled steak you can buy. When assembling the satés, be sure to intersperse cubes of lean beef with fattier cubes of meat or steak fat (that's how they do it in Singapore). Remember: Fat equals flavor. Chicken, pork, lamb, or goat satés can be made the same way.

Jake, my wife, Barbara, and me at the first all-wood-burning restaurant in Singapore.

THE BEST BEEF SATES IN SINGAPORE | page 32

Singapore Cucumber Relish

Variations on this simple relish/salad turn up throughout Southeast Asia. The purpose is to give you a bite of cool, crisp, crunch to counterpoint the spicy hot meat. **MAKES 1 TO 1½ CUPS**

2 Kirby (pickling) cucumbers, or 1 medium-size cucumber,
    cut in half lengthwise and seeded (see Note)
1 shallot, minced (2 to 3 tablespoons), or 1 scallion,
    both white and green parts, trimmed and minced
1 small hot red chile, such as a bird or cayenne pepper,
    stemmed, seeded, and minced
2 tablespoons rice vinegar
1 tablespoon sugar
Coarse salt (kosher or sea) and freshly ground black pepper

Cut the cucumber(s) into ¼-inch dice. Place the cucumber(s), shallot, chile, rice vinegar, and sugar in a mixing bowl and toss gently to mix. Season with salt and pepper to taste. The relish can be made up to 2 hours ahead.

NOTE: It is not necessary to seed Kirby cucumbers.

Fried Garlic Peanut Sauce

To most North Americans barbecue sauce is some variation on a combination of ketchup, brown sugar, and vinegar, but on any given day on Planet Barbecue probably far more people are dipping grilled meats in peanut sauce. The basic formula starts with deep-fried peanuts or peanut butter and the flavorings typically include garlic and ginger for pungency, sugar for sweetness, and fish sauce or soy sauce for saltiness. The peanut-sauce belt begins in Indonesia (its probable birthplace) and extends through Singapore, Thailand, and Malaysia, all the way to Hong Kong. The Singaporean version owes its fragrance to fresh lemongrass and ginger. Dried shrimp are available in Asian and Hispanic markets. Fish sauce isn't a bad substitute, although you can omit it and still wind up with a killer sauce. The addition of fried garlic chips is very characteristic of Southeast Asia. **MAKES ABOUT 2½ CUPS**

2 tablespoons vegetable oil
5 cloves garlic, 3 cloves thinly sliced crosswise and
    2 cloves minced
1 shallot, minced
1 stalk lemongrass, trimmed and minced, or 2 strips
    (each ½ by 2 inches) lemon zest
1 to 3 small hot chiles, such as Thai chiles or serrano or
    jalapeño peppers, stemmed, seeded, and minced
    (for a hotter peanut sauce, leave the seeds in)
1 tablespoon dried shrimp, minced, or 1 teaspoon fish sauce
    (optional)
¾ cup peanut butter
1 cup unsweetened coconut milk, or as needed
2 tablespoons sugar, or more to taste
2 tablespoons soy sauce
1 teaspoon fresh lime juice, or more to taste
1 tablespoon finely chopped cilantro
Coarse salt (kosher or sea) and freshly ground pepper

1 Heat the oil in a wok or saucepan over medium-high heat. Add the sliced garlic and cook, stirring, until golden, 2 minutes. Remove the garlic with a slotted spoon to paper towels to drain. Add the 2 cloves of minced garlic, the shallot, lemongrass, chile(s), and dried shrimp, if using, to the wok and cook over medium-high heat until fragrant and lightly browned, 2 minutes.

2 Stir in the peanut butter, coconut milk, sugar, soy sauce, fish sauce, if using (instead of the dried shrimp), lime juice, and ¾ cup water. Reduce the heat and gently simmer the sauce until it is thick but pourable, 5 to 8 minutes. Stir in the cilantro during the last 2 minutes of cooking.

3 Just before serving, stir in the fried garlic slices. If the sauce has gotten too thick and pasty, add a tablespoon or so of water. Taste and correct the seasoning, adding salt and pepper, and more sugar and lime juice if needed. The sauce should be richly flavored.

Singapore: Crossroads of Asian Grilling

What would you call a place where you could breakfast on grilled bread with coconut jam, lunch on *otak-otak* (Malaysian fish mousse grilled in banana leaves), dine on Indian tandoori, and midnight snack on Indonesian satés? Where *nonya* (grandmother) style stingray seasoned with garlic, chile, and lemongrass and grilled in banana leaves shares your plate with minced and grilled Chinese sweet pork jerky? The maps call it Singapore. The nearly five million people who make up this island nation at the tip of the Malaysian

> ## The maps call it Singapore. I call it a grilling nirvana.

peninsula call it home. I call it a grilling nirvana.

Established as a British colony by Sir Stamford Raffles in 1819, Singapore lies at Asia's strategic crossroads—Malaysia and Thailand to the north, Indonesia to the south, India far to the west, and China and Japan to the

northeast. Limited in size and natural resources, Singapore has always lived by trade. For two millennia, the island nation has been port of call for Chinese sampans, Arabian dhows, Indonesian *pinisi,* English merchant ships, and American clippers. The constant flow of peoples, comestibles, and food cultures have made Singaporean barbecue some of the most diverse in the world.

Singapore's government also helped. In Singapore, as throughout Southeast Asia, the best grilling (not to mention noodle dishes, soups, stir-fries, and the like) turns up not at restaurants, but at pushcarts and sidewalk cookshacks. In the 1970s the Singaporean government took the extraordinary step of registering and certifying all street vendors, relocating them to municipal hawker centers equipped with electricity, running water, and sanitation codes more stringent than those in the United States. Today, more than 10,000 street cooks—among them Singapore's top grill masters—ply their trade at 115 government-certified hawker centers, like the popular Newton Circus Hawker Centre, East Coast Lagoon Food Village, or Gluttons Bay. At almost any hour of the day or night, for a surprisingly affordable price, *this* is where the real Singapore eats. And so should you.

A Paradise of Hawker Centers

The Smith Street Hawker Centre in Singapore's Chinatown.

Fruit and flower garlands for sale as temple offerings in Singapore's Little India.

With Malaysia and Thailand to the north, Indonesia to the south, and India and China to the west and east, Singapore lies at the hub of some of the world's most thrilling grilling.

THE GRILLS: Most Singaporean grilling is done on long slender saté grills or larger charcoal grills. Chicken wings are roasted on charcoal-burning rotisseries.

Prawns grilled in the shells, heads and all, at the Newton Circus Hawker Centre.

THE FUEL: Natural lump charcoal—often made from mangrove wood or coconut shells

THE FLAVORINGS: As varied as Singapore's ethnically diverse population itself: Chinese grillers reach for soy sauce, oyster sauce, rice wine, ginger, scallions, and garlic. Malays use fragrant pastes of chiles, garlic, ginger, lemongrass, and coconut milk. Yogurt, coriander, and turmeric dominate Indian grilling, while *kejap manis* (sweet soy sauce) and chile sauce spice up Indonesian-style satés.

MUST TRY DISHES:

Bak kua: Chinese minced grilled pork jerky—salty with soy sauce and sweetened with sugar and hoisin sauce (see page 48 for a recipe)

Barbecued chicken wings: A favorite late-night snack: chicken wings marinated in Chinese seasonings and spit-roasted over charcoal. When properly prepared, the skin will be cellophane crisp and shiny and dark as polished wood.

Otak-otak: Sometimes written *otah-otah*, fish mousse enriched with coconut milk, candlenuts, and a dozen other Malaysian seasonings and grilled in fresh banana leaves (see page 448 for a recipe)

Satés: Tiny kebabs of chicken, beef, pork, or shrimp, sold by the fistful (page 32)

Stingray: Skate wings slathered with an aromatic Malaysian spice paste, wrapped in banana leaves, and grilled until golden (see page 450 for a recipe)

THE CONDIMENTS: Like all food in Singapore, barbecue comes with big-flavored condiments. *Sambal* refers to an almost endless variety of thick, fiery chile sauces and relishes, served in tiny bowls for dipping. Satés come with Indonesian-style peanut sauce, or sometimes with Peranakan-style pineapple and

Fanning the coals and basting the meat at a Singaporean grill stall.

chile sauce (Peranakans are Singaporeans of Chinese descent).

HOW TO EAT IT: Off a skewer, off a banana leaf, with chopsticks, or with your hands—any way you can. Satés often come with diced onion and cucumber. To eat the saté, you skewer a piece of onion and cucumber at the end of your skewer, swirl the meat in peanut sauce, and pop it into your mouth.

IF YOU CAN EAT AT ONLY ONE RESTAURANT: Forget restaurants. Go to one of the hawker centers. Gluttons Bay, located next to the Esplanade theater complex, has great satés, *otak-otak,* and grilled stingray that you can enjoy under the stars with a water view. In the words of Singapore food critic, K. F. Seetoh, whose *Makansutra* guidebook to street food is a must-read for anyone serious about food in Singapore, "Food tastes best with the moon overhead."

WHAT TO DRINK: Tiger beer. *Teh tarik*—"pulled tea," a sort of Singaporean cappuccino made with tea

THE MOST SINGULAR DISH IN THE REPERTORY: *Kaya* toast, a traditional Singaporean breakfast consisting of grilled or toasted bread served with a sweet coconut jam scented with pandanus (screwpine) leaf. Enjoy it with "sock" coffee—the beans are roasted in butter; the coffee brewed through a clean stocking.

Barbecue is always on the menu in Singapore.

~CHEF'S RECOMMENDATION~
BBQ Stingray
Butter Sea mantis
BBQ King Prawns
BBQ Lobster
Chilli / Black Pepper Crab
Butter Prawns
Fresh Oysters

Kebabs Around the World

Meat grilled on a stick was the first great technological leap forward in the evolution of the art of grilling. Today, the popularity of kebabs around Planet Barbecue attests to their universal appeal. Here's a gazetteer to help you travel the world of skewered grilled meats.

ANTICUCHOS: Peruvian beef heart kebabs served with a fiery pepper sauce .

BROCHETTE: A French kebab, usually lamb, *brochette* can feature beef, pork, chicken, or seafood. The term is also used in the former French colonies, such as Morocco and Mauritius Island.

ESPETADA: Literally "sword meat." Beef kebabs traditionally grilled on bay leaf branches—a specialty of the Portuguese island of Madeira.

KOFTA: The ground lamb kebabs of the Middle East.

KYINKYINGA: A popular street food in West Africa, these beef kebabs (pronounced chin-CHING-ga) owe their unique flavor and crunch to a crusting of peanut flour. They are usually made with steak, sometimes with liver.

LULA OR LYULYA: The ground lamb kebabs of the Caucasus Mountain region and former Central Asian republics of the Soviet Union.

PINCHOS: Small Spanish kebabs, often made with pork, served in tapas

Shashlik, *Russian pork kebabs, sear on a grateless grill called a* mangal.

bar-size portions; indeed, in some parts of Spain, *pinchos* is used as a generic term for tapas.

RAZNJICI: Pork, lamb, or mixed meat kebabs from the Balkans.

SATES: Tiny kebabs of chicken, pork, beef, or other meats grilled on bamboo skewers over a charcoal fire and traditionally served with peanut sauce. There are literally hundreds of styles of saté in Southeast Asia—Indonesia alone has more than one hundred varieties.

SEEKH KEBAB: India's version of the minced meat or vegetable kebab, cooked on a long vertical skewer in a tandoor.

SHASHLIK: The Russian and Baltic version of shish kebab, commonly made with pork, beef, or lamb and marinated in breath-wilting doses of onion.

SHIPUDIM: Kebabs Israeli style, made with everything from lamb to chicken to foie gras.

SHISH KEBAB: The most famous of the world's kebabs and a specialty of Turkey. Lamb is the most common meat—sometimes skewered in chunks, more often minced by hand and molded onto a flat skewer.

SOSATIE: Shish kebab Afrikaner style, enjoyed throughout South Africa. Traditionally made with pork or a combination of meats and skewered and flavored with fruits, such as apricots.

SOUVLAKI: Greek lamb shish kebabs, traditionally made with chunks of lamb and served on pita bread with yogurt.

SPIEDINI: Italian shish kebabs made with everything from pork to sausage to exotic game birds. Often sold preskewered and premarinated at Italian butcher shops.

SUYA: West African (especially Nigerian) kebabs flavored with ground peanuts and hot peppers. Traditionally made with beef, but other meats are used, too.

YAKITORI: Very small Japanese chicken kebabs, glazed with a sweet soy dipping sauce. Japanese grill masters use every imaginable cut of chicken, from white and dark meat, wings, and skin, to liver, gizzard, and embryonic eggs.

Peruvian Beef Kebabs

{ ANTICUCHOS }

No visit to Lima or Cuzco, or anywhere else in Peru, would be complete without sampling a kebab that's both an everyday snack and a national obsession: *anticuchos*. Peruvians from all economic classes eat these spicy kebabs dipped in fiery yellow chile sauce as a quick lunch on the go, a late night pick-me-up, and just about any time in between. There's only one stumbling block—from the North American point of view, at least: The traditional meat is beef heart.

When the conquistadores arrived in Peru, the Incas had been enjoying *anticuchos* for centuries. The name came from the Quechua word *anti-kuchu* (literally "mountain cut") or perhaps *anti-uchu* (mixture). The traditional meat was llama. The Spanish adopted the Inca kebabs, adding such European flavorings as vinegar, garlic, and cumin, and substituting the newly imported steer for the meat. The use of beef heart for *anticuchos* may have originated with the African slaves, who were brought to Peru to work the mines and plantations and fed the innards and other parts of the cattle the Spanish elite disdained to eat. **SERVES 6 AS AN APPETIZER, 4 AS A LIGHT MAIN COURSE**

4 cloves garlic, peeled

1 tablespoon cumin seeds, or 1 tablespoon ground cumin

¼ cup ají panca paste, 3 tablespoons Hungarian hot paprika, or 2 canned chipotle peppers with 1 tablespoon of their juices (see Note)

2 tablespoons red wine vinegar

About 2 tablespoons achiote oil or extra-virgin olive oil, plus oil for basting

Coarse salt (kosher or sea) and freshly ground black pepper

1½ pounds beef rib eye or sirloin, or 1½ pounds beef heart

Yellow Chile Peanut Sauce (optional, recipe follows)

YOU'LL ALSO NEED

Bamboo skewers; an aluminum foil grill shield (see page 611)

ADVANCE PREPARATION

2 to 4 hours for marinating rib eye or sirloin; 6 to 12 hours for marinating beef heart

THE SCOOP

WHERE: Peru

WHAT: Beef heart kebabs spiced up with fiery Peruvian chiles—have no fear: If beef hearts leave you cold, you can substitute beef rib eye steaks or sirloin.

HOW: Direct grilling

JUST THE FACTS: Beef hearts are much beloved by Peruvians and Bolivians (somewhat less so by everyone else). If you're feeling adventurous, you can likely find beef hearts at an ethnic meat market or special order them from your local butcher. One interesting alternative would be to use chicken hearts, which coincidentally, are wildly popular at Brazilian *churrascarias* (rotisserie restaurants, see page 538). If all this sounds a little too weird, a robust cut of beef, like sirloin, will give you the *anticucho* taste and texture. Of course, you could go uptown, with a more tender cut, like rib eye or even beef tenderloin.

1 Heat a dry cast-iron skillet over medium heat. (If your grill has a side burner, this is a good time to use it.) Add the garlic and cook until browned on all sides, 2 minutes per side, 6 to 8 minutes in all (you can also grill the garlic on a small skewer at a previous grill session). Transfer the garlic to a small bowl and let it cool.

2 Add the cumin seeds, if using, to the hot skillet and toast them over medium heat until the cumin is very fragrant and lightly browned, 2 to 4 minutes. Transfer the toasted cumin seeds to a small heatproof bowl and let them cool. Grind the cumin seeds to a fine powder in a spice mill or pound them in a mortar using a pestle. If you are using ground cumin, toast it in the skillet over medium heat until fragrant, 1 to 2 minutes.

3 Place the cooled garlic, ground toasted cumin, and *ají panca* paste (or paprika or chipotles) in a food processor and puree to a fine paste. Gradually work in the wine vinegar and enough achiote oil to make a thick paste. Season the marinade with salt and black pepper to taste; it should be highly seasoned.

4 If you are using beef hearts, cut them lengthwise into strips that are about 1½ inches wide. Cut each strip crosswise sharply on the diagonal to make pieces about 3 inches long, 1½ inches wide, and ¼ inch thick. If you are using steak, cut it into pieces of that size. Weave 3 pieces of meat back and forth onto each skewer so the flat side will be exposed to the fire.

5 Arrange the skewers in a nonreactive baking dish. Spread the marinade over the meat with a spoon, thickly coating both sides. If you are using steak, let it marinate in the refrigerator, covered, for 2 to 4 hours, turning it once or twice so that the meat marinates evenly. If you are using beef heart, let it marinate for 6 to 12 hours in the refrigerator, covered, turning it several times.

6 Set up the grill for direct grilling and preheat it to high.

7 When ready to cook, brush and oil the grill grate. Drain the *anticuchos,* discarding the marinade. Arrange the *anticuchos* on the hot grate, with the aluminum foil shield under the exposed ends of the skewers to keep them from burning. Grill the *anticuchos* until they are sizzling, golden brown, and cooked through, 3 to 4 minutes per side (*anticuchos* are generally eaten medium-well to well done). Baste the *anticuchos* on the grilled side with achiote oil after 3 minutes to keep the meat moist (you'll need about 2 tablespoons oil). Use the poke test to check for doneness (see the box on page 612). Serve the *anticuchos* sizzling hot off the grill with the Yellow Chile Peanut Sauce, if desired.

NOTE: The *ají panca* is a rust-red, medium-hot Peruvian chile that tastes like a cross between Hungarian hot paprika and Mexican chipotle. Either the paprika or chipotle can be used as a substitute—or a combination of the two. *Ají panca* and another Peruvian chile *ají amarillo* (literally yellow chile) are sold fresh in Peru and are available in North America in paste form, as well as frozen and dried. Look for them at Peruvian and Hispanic markets or via mail order (at www.tienda.com). If you use frozen chiles, you'll need ¼ cup. They will take about 1 hour to thaw at room temperature. You can also use dried chiles: Soak 3 in warm water to cover for 30 minutes, then drain them. Seed and chop frozen or soaked dried chiles before pureeing them. To substitute for *ají amarillo* use 1 grilled yellow bell pepper, peeled, cored, seeded, and diced, plus ½ teaspoon cayenne pepper.

Yellow Chile Peanut Sauce
{ AJI AMARILLO }

A fiery dip, made with *ají amarillo* (Peruvian yellow chiles), is the traditional sauce for *anticuchos*. Bolivians make a similar sauce, adding peanuts for extra richness, and that's the version you'll find here. *Huacatay* is an herb used widely throughout northern South America. A member of the marigold family, it has a flavor suggestive of parsley and mint. I've never seen it in the United States, but equal parts parsley and spearmint make a reasonable substitute. **MAKES ABOUT 1½ CUPS**

5 fresh, frozen, or dried ajís amarillos (Peruvian yellow chiles),
     or ¾ cup ají amarillo paste (see Note, facing page)
3 tablespoons smooth peanut butter
1 small bunch huacatay, chopped, or 2 tablespoons each finely
     chopped fresh flat-leaf parsley and spearmint
2 tablespoons extra-virgin olive oil
1 tablespoon fresh lime juice, or to taste
Coarse salt (kosher or sea)

1 If you are using frozen *ajís amarillos,* let them thaw at room temperature; this will take about 1 hour. If you are using dried *ajís amarillos,* soak them in water to cover for 2 hours, then drain. Stem the chiles and, if a milder sauce is desired, remove the seeds. Place the chiles, peanut butter, and ½ cup of water in a blender and puree until smooth. Blend in the *huacatay,* running the blender in short bursts.

2 Heat the olive oil in a saucepan over medium-low heat. Add the chile and peanut puree and cook, stirring often, until the sauce is thick, creamy, and richly flavored, 5 to 8 minutes. Lower the heat as needed; the sauce should simmer gently, not boil. Add the lime juice, if using, and season the sauce with salt to taste and more lime juice if needed; it should be highly seasoned and very hot. Serve the sauce warm or at room temperature. The sauce can be refrigerated, covered, for up to 3 days.

Pork Satés in the Style of Bangkok's Chinatown

Your grill master, aka me, strives to have competence in many areas, but fashion is not one of them. Fortunately, his wife, Barbara, stands ready to guide him. When we arrived in Bangkok, our first stop was a tailor shop named Mazzaro. Barbara came home with a suitcase full of swank clothes, and yours truly managed to score a perfectly fitting sports coat. But the real benefit of the visit was a trip to Chinatown to experience firsthand where Thai ladies, like shop owner Jutarat Phothisoontorni, lunch. Upon hearing about *Planet Barbecue!,* Jutarat whisked me away in her Mercedes to a nondescript storefront in Chinatown to sample the satés of Vichai Lumlerokit, who has cooked for the Thai royal family (you can read about him on page 43).

Satés are common currency in Thailand (as they are throughout Southeast Asia). The Chinese version starts with pork (no surprise there) and the flavorings run to turmeric and fish sauce, but not to the lemongrass and ginger associated with southern Thai grilling. If you're in

THE SCOOP

WHERE: Bangkok, Thailand

WHAT: Turmeric- and garlic-scented pork kebabs

HOW: Direct grilling

JUST THE FACTS:
As throughout Southeast Asia, these satés are cooked on a long, roaring-hot grill so slender that the exposed parts of the bamboo skewers hang off the edge and don't burn. If you are grilling on a large North American grill, you'll want to use an aluminum foil grill shield.

a hurry, you can skip the cucumber relish. **SERVES 6 TO 8 AS AN APPETIZER, 4 AS A MAIN COURSE**

FOR THE PORK AND MARINADE

1½ pounds trimmed pork tenderloin
    (2 to 3 tenderloins)
¼ cup sugar
1 tablespoon ground turmeric
1 teaspoon freshly ground white pepper
½ teaspoon coarse salt (kosher or sea)
2 cloves garlic, coarsely chopped
¼ cup Asian fish sauce or soy sauce
2 tablespoons vegetable oil, plus oil for basting

FOR THE RELISH (OPTIONAL)

2 small or Kirby cucumbers, or 1 full-size
    cucumber
2 shallots, or 1 small red onion, thinly sliced
2 tablespoons rice vinegar
2 tablespoons sugar
Coarse salt (kosher or sea)
Creamy Asian Peanut Sauce (page 18) or
    Fried Garlic Peanut Sauce (page 35)

YOU'LL ALSO NEED

Small bamboo skewers; an aluminum foil grill
    shield (optional; see page 611)

ADVANCE PREPARATION

1 to 4 hours for marinating the pork

1 Prepare the pork and marinade: Starting at the narrow end, cut each tenderloin sharply on the diagonal into thin slices, each about 3 inches long and ⅛ inch thick. Cut any wider strips in half lengthwise. Each piece should be about 1 inch wide. Place the pork in a nonreactive mixing bowl.

2 Place the sugar, turmeric, white pepper, salt, and garlic in a food processor and puree until smooth. Add the fish sauce and oil and process to a

smooth paste. Add the marinade to the pork and stir to coat. Let the pork marinate in the refrigerator, covered, for 1 to 4 hours; the longer it marinates, the richer the flavor will be.

3 Drain the pieces of pork, discarding the marinade. Weave the pork onto the skewers, leaving the bottom half of each skewer bare for a handle and ¼ inch exposed at the pointed end. The satés can be prepared several hours ahead to this stage and refrigerated, covered.

4 Make the relish, if serving: Partially peel the cucumbers in lengthwise strips to create a striped effect. Thinly slice small cucumbers crosswise; it is not necessary to remove the seeds. Cut a full-size cucumber in half lengthwise, remove the seeds, and thinly slice crosswise. Place the sliced cucumber, shallots, rice vinegar, and sugar in a mixing bowl and toss to mix until the sugar dissolves. Season with salt to taste.

5 Set up the grill for direct grilling and preheat it to high.

6 When ready to cook, brush and oil the grill grate. Arrange the satés on the hot grate with the aluminum foil shield under the exposed ends of the skewers to keep them from burning. Grill the satés until nicely browned on both sides, about 2 minutes per side, basting them with vegetable oil. Serve the satés at once with the cucumber relish, if using, and peanut sauce. Eat the cucumber relish off the point of the bamboo skewers.

Saté Chef to Kings

Everyone loves **VICHAI LUMLEROKIT'S** satés, including Thai royalty.

BANGKOK, THAILAND

Chong Kee restaurant may not be much to look at, but the cavernous dining room, located in the heart of Bangkok's Chinatown, attracts a high falutin' crowd—not just local business owners and ladies who do lunch, but even Thailand's royal family. Princess Srirasmi lunched here a few months earlier, and the restaurant's owner, Vichai Lumlerokit, has cooked for Thailand's revered King Bhumibol Adulyadej.

The reason is simple: For seventy years, Vichai Lumlerokit's family has turned out pork satés of such sizzling succulence and compellingly explosive flavor, they sell four to five thousand sticks a day. "Once we served one-hundred-thousand satés on a single occasion," the second-generation grill master recalls. Like all good Thai saté moguls, Lumlerokit's staff grills over coconut shell charcoal on troughlike braziers, each a yard long and kept screaming hot by an electric fan at one end.

Saté isn't all you'll find at Chong Kee. There are soulful soups ladled from mammoth stockpots, and all manner of Chinese-style barbecued duck, pork, and sausages hanging from racks in the window. Every few minutes a deliveryman departs, staggering under the weight of a carryout order for local business folk who can't come in person.

We sit down in the dining room amid photos of the royal family, and Lumlerokit demonstrates the proper way to eat saté. You take a bite of cucumber shallot relish, using the pointed end of your bamboo skewer as a fork. Then you swirl the grilled meat in a shallow dish of peanut sauce. Best of all, if you manage to eat one hundred satés, Mr. Lumlerokit will give you your meal for free. But be forewarned—only thirty people have managed this feat in seventy years.

Vichai Lumlerokit grills his trademark satés on a charcoal-burning saté grill. Note how the grate is raised in the center to help drain off the fat.

NAME: Vichai Lumlerokit

TERRITORY: Bangkok, Thailand

CLAIM TO FAME: Owner of a popular Bangkok saté parlor patronized by Thailand's royal family; Vichai once cooked for the king and queen of Thailand.

SPECIALTIES: Pork satés seasoned with turmeric and fish sauce

LUMLEROKIT SAYS:

▶ To keep the satés from drying out over the hot fire, baste them with coconut oil. For extra flavor, use a lemongrass basting brush.

▶ To avoid flare-ups, cook satés (or other foods) propped up so they slope slightly downward. That way the fat drains to the bottom of the grill, not directly onto the flames. (Vichai uses a grill with a raised bar in the center. On a North American grill, you could improvise an angled grate, using metal washers, stones, or a metal pipe to elevate the grate.)

Grilled Pork Skewers with Filipino Seasonings

Like Japanese yakitori and many Thai satés, this Filipino *inihaw* (barbecue) starts with a garlic-soy marinade. The twist comes in the addition of two unexpected ingredients: 7UP and banana ketchup. The 7UP lends a lemon-lime flavor and has a tenderizing effect on the meat, while the banana ketchup adds a fruity sweetness (many versions of pork kebabs use tomato ketchup in place of banana ketchup). Both ingredients let you know you're not in Bangkok (or Tokyo or Kuala Lumpur) any more. One thing: Do not confuse these kebabs with satés, says my Filipino grill buddy and guide to Pinoy grilling, Alex Paman. "We fill our skewers completely with pork—not half or a third of the way as they do in Southeast Asia." Duly noted. **SERVES 4**

1½ pounds trimmed pork tenderloin
   (2 to 3 tenderloins)
1 small onion, finely chopped
4 cloves garlic, minced
1 to 2 hot chile peppers, such as Thai chiles,
   seeded and finely chopped (for hotter
   barbecue, leave the seeds in)
½ cup soy sauce
¼ cup fresh lime juice (from about 2 limes)
¼ cup banana ketchup, or ¼ cup tomato ketchup
2 tablespoons brown sugar
1 to 2 teaspoons freshly ground black pepper
1 can (12 ounces) 7UP or Sprite
2 tablespoons vegetable oil, for basting
Banana leaves (optional), for lining a platter

YOU'LL ALSO NEED
8-inch bamboo skewers; an aluminum foil grill
   shield (optional; see page 611)

ADVANCE PREPARATION
4 hours to overnight for marinating the pork

1 Cut the pork sharply on the diagonal into ¼ inch-thick slices. Then, cut each slice lengthwise into strips that are 1 inch wide. Weave the pork strips onto bamboo skewers so that they look rippled or wavy. Arrange the pork kebabs in a nonreactive baking dish.

2 Place the onion, garlic, chile peppers, soy sauce, lime juice, banana ketchup, brown sugar, black pepper, and 7UP in a mixing bowl and whisk to mix. Pour the marinade over the pork, turning the skewers to coat evenly. Let the pork marinate in the refrigerator, covered, for at least 4 hours or more typically, overnight; the longer it marinates, the richer the flavor will be.

3 Drain the marinade off the pork kebabs through a strainer into a heavy saucepan, discarding the remaining solids. Boil the marinade over high heat until thick, flavorful, and reduced to about 1½ cups, 6 to 10 minutes. You'll use the reduced marinade as a basting mixture and sauce.

4 Set up the grill for direct grilling and preheat it to high.

5 When ready to cook, brush and oil the grill grate. Lightly brush each pork kebab on both sides with oil and arrange the kebabs on the hot grate. Grill the kebabs until the pork is sizzling, browned, and cooked through, 3 to 4 minutes per side. (You

may want to slide an aluminum foil shield under the exposed ends of the bamboo skewers to keep them from burning.) To test for doneness, pinch the meat between your fingers; it should feel firm to the touch. Using a clean brush, start basting the kebabs with the reduced marinade after 2 minutes, basting them several times.

6 Transfer the grilled pork kebabs to a platter (preferably one lined with banana leaves) or plates and serve them at once with the remaining reduced marinade in bowls to use as a dipping sauce.

Cheese Grilled Linguiça
{ LINGUICA CON QUESO }

When meat lovers in Porto Alegre, Brazil, get a carnivorous itch, they come to Na Brasa (literally "on the embers") to scratch it. Waiters emerge from the kitchen in endless succession, bearing swordlike spits of grilled meats they carve directly onto dinner plates. They won't cease fire until ordered to do so. That's where the green and red medallions on each table come in: Green means to keep serving; red means to stop. Believe it or not, this megarich grilled sausage with cheese would be served as a finger food in Brazil, washed down with a caipirinha, a daiquirilike drink made with cane spirits. **SERVES 6 TO 8 AS AN APPETIZER, 4 AS A MAIN COURSE (IF YOU DARE)**

1½ pounds linguiça or other cooked sausage
6 ounces coarsely grated mozzarella, Jack, Gouda, or other soft cheese (1½ cups)

YOU'LL ALSO NEED
Toothpicks, for serving

ADVANCE PREPARATION
None

1 Cut the *linguiça* in half lengthwise.

2 Set up the grill for direct grilling and

THE SCOOP

WHERE: Porto Alegre, Brazil

WHAT: A popular Brazilian appetizer and a cardiologist's nightmare— grilled *linguiça* sausage topped with melted cheese

HOW: Direct grilling

JUST THE FACTS: *Linguiça* (pronounced ling-GWEE-sa) is a lightly smoked Portuguese pork sausage flavored with garlic, cumin, and for a sweet touch, mace. Kielbasa would make a reasonable substitute. Choose the straightest links possible.

preheat it to medium-high. To be strictly authentic, you'd grill over charcoal.

3 When ready to cook, brush and oil the grill grate. Arrange the *linguiça,* cut side down, on the hot grate and grill until sizzling and golden brown, 3 to 5 minutes. Turn the *linguiça* and thickly sprinkle the cut side with the cheese. Close the grill lid.

Continue grilling the *linguiça* until browned on the uncut side and the cheese is melted and bubbling.

4 Using a spatula, carefully transfer the *linguiça* to a cutting board, keeping the cheese on top. Cut each piece crosswise into 1-inch sections. Stick a toothpick into each piece of *linguiça* and serve at once.

Hungarian Grilled Bacon
{ SOLINA SHUTESH }

There once was a time—perhaps it's true still—when Hungary had the highest per capita calorie intake of any country in Europe. Lard and goose fat undoubtedly helped Hungary achieve this distinction, but the real culprit was *solina shutesh*—grilled bacon. The preparation varies from griller to griller and from region to region. Some use chunks of slab bacon, for example, others thick slices of country-style bacon. Some grill the onion with the bacon; others slice it raw on the bread. Some grillers even add kielbasa and tomatoes. But every Hungarian agrees that *solina shutesh* just isn't complete until you serve it with slices of fire-warmed rye bread soaked with the dripping bacon fat. When they learned I was writing *Planet Barbecue!,* three people with Hungarian roots took the time to alert me to this dish: Ed Kish, Szabadtüzi Rend, and my Hungarian aunt, Judy Raichlen. It's *that* important. **SERVES 4 TO 6**

Solina shutesh (grilled bacon). No Hungarian barbecue is complete without it.

1 pound thickly sliced smokehouse bacon

2 medium-size white onions, peeled

Sweet or hot Hungarian paprika

1 loaf country-style rye bread, cut into
    ¾-inch-thick slices

1 ripe red tomato (optional)

YOU'LL ALSO NEED

Several 2-pronged grilling forks or long
    flat metal skewers; wood for building
    a fire (optional)

ADVANCE PREPARATION
None

1 Cut the bacon crosswise into 3-inch pieces. Cut 1 onion lengthwise into quarters. Break the onion quarters into individual layers. Skewer the pieces of bacon through the flat side onto the tines of the grilling forks or skewers, placing pieces of onion, between every 2 or 3 slices. Thickly season the outside of the bacon with paprika.

2 Set up the grill for direct grilling and preheat it to medium-high. Ideally, you'd grill over a wood or charcoal fire without a grill grate (see page 599 for instructions). But you can also cook the bacon on a gas grill. If you are using a gas grill, leave one section of the grill unlit for a safety zone.

3 Put the rye bread on a platter or plates and warm the bread by the fire. Although it's not strictly traditional, I like to lightly toast the bread on the grill. Thinly slice the remaining onion and the tomato, if using. Arrange some of the slices on each slice of bread.

Hungarian hot peppers—culinary
icon and indispensable seasoning.

4 When ready to cook, hold the forks or skewers of bacon over the fire or place them on the hot grate and grill the bacon until it is sizzling and browned on all sides, 5 to 8 minutes per side, 10 to 16 minutes in all. The dripping fat will cause flare-ups. That's OK—it's supposed to. Keep the fork moving to dodge them. From time to time, drip a little of the hot bacon fat over the onion-topped bread. When the bacon is done, unskewer it over the bread and eat it as an open-faced sandwich. Keep grilling bacon and topping the bread, onions, and tomatoes, if using, until everyone sinks into a food coma. The only known antidote to the lethargy caused by *solina shutesh* is massive doses of *palinka* (Hungarian brandy) and beer.

THE SCOOP

JUST THE FACTS: Your chief challenge will be finding the right bacon—the sort that's dark with wood smoke and thickly sliced or sold in slabs. Two good mail-order sources are www.nueskes.com and www.eurofoodmart.net. As for the seasoning, use imported Hungarian paprika, of course. Many supermarkets carry the Szeged brand (also available from www.eurofoodmart.net), or you can buy good-quality Hungarian paprika from www.penzeys.com. Hungarians would cook the bacon over a smoky wood fire. You'll need long-handled grilling forks or flat skewers. Sources for both are www.barbecuebible.com /store.

Grilled Pork Jerky
{ BAK KUA }

WHERE: Singapore, Macao, and other Chinese enclaves throughout Asia

WHAT: Sweet, salty squares of minced pork jerky served sizzling hot off the grill

HOW: Direct grilling

JUST THE FACTS: This recipe includes a few distinctly Asian ingredients. *Kejap manis* is a thick, sweet soy sauce. Look for it at Asian markets or mix equal parts regular soy sauce and molasses. *Shaoxing* is Chinese rice wine; sake or dry sherry will work just fine. Five-spice powder, a traditional Chinese seasoning, is a blend commonly made from star anise, fennel seeds, cinnamon, cloves, and white and/or Szechuan pepper. Hoisin sauce is a thick, sweet, anisey sauce made from soybeans, and you can find it in the international aisle of most supermarkets.

Kim Hock Guan left Fujian Province in southern China in 1905 to seek his fortune in the boomtown of Singapore. Like most immigrants, he came with little more than the clothes on his back, but he did have one intangible asset: a venerable family recipe for *bak kua*. A cross between a pork sausage patty and jerky, *bak kua* is a sizzling wafer of sweetened, spiced, cured, grilled minced pork. You find it at sidewalk grill stalls from Macao to Malaysia, not to mention at the red-fronted storefront on South Bridge Road in Singapore where Lim Sin Choon and Wilfrid Lim run the business founded by Lim Sin Choon's grandfather (Wilfrid's great-grandfather) more than a century ago.

I'll be frank with you: The following recipe is somewhat involved. You need to source a few exotic ingredients, roll out the pork, dry it in the refrigerator overnight, and prebake it before grilling (prepared to this stage, it will keep for several days in the refrigerator). But no survey of Planet Barbecue would be complete without these, sweet-salty, softly crisp squares of some of the best pork jerky in Southeast Asia. **MAKES EIGHTEEN TO TWENTY 3-INCH PIECES; SERVES 6 AS AN APPETIZER, 4 AS A SNACK**

Squares of bak kua (Singaporean pork jerky) sizzling on the grill.

Kim Hock Guan, serving Singapore's best bak kua since 1905.

2 pounds very coarsely ground pork
    (about 20 percent fat)
¾ cup firmly packed light brown sugar
2 teaspoons ground ginger
1½ teaspoons coarse salt (kosher or sea)
1 teaspoon freshly ground black pepper
½ teaspoon cayenne pepper
½ teaspoon Chinese five-spice powder
½ teaspoon MSG (optional)
2 tablespoons kejap manis (sweet soy sauce)
2 tablespoons hoisin sauce, preferably the
    Koon Chung brand
1 tablespoon Chinese rice wine (Shaoxing)
    or dry sherry
½ teaspoon rose water (optional, see Note)

YOU'LL ALSO NEED

Parchment paper or waxed paper; a rolling pin;
    a rectangular cake rack or metal grid about
    14 x 18 inches, lightly oiled

ADVANCE PREPARATION

The jerky is quick to grill, but you need at least 24 hours
    to cure and dry the meat in the refrigerator.

1 Place the pork, brown sugar, ginger, salt, black pepper, cayenne, five-spice powder, and MSG, if using, in a large mixing bowl and stir or knead to mix. Stir in the *kejap manis,* hoisin sauce, rice wine, and rose water, if using, and mix well.

2 Cut a sheet of parchment paper to fit an unrimmed baking sheet and dampen it. Place the dampened paper on the baking sheet and mound the pork on top, spreading it out into a rough rectangle.

Place another piece of damp parchment paper on top. Using a rolling pin, roll the pork mixture into a broad thin sheet about 12 x 16 inches and ¼ inch thick.

3 Peel off the top piece of parchment paper and place the oiled wire rack on top. Turn over the rack and the baking sheet with the pork on it. Remove the baking sheet and peel off the remaining piece of parchment paper. Place the rack with the pork on a rimmed baking sheet, then place everything in the refrigerator and let the pork air-dry for 24 hours.

4 Preheat the oven to 150°F. Bake the pork mixture on the rack until dry, about 1 hour. You can also do this on a grill set up for indirect grilling.

5 Let the pork mixture cool to room temperature, then cut it into approximately 3-inch squares. Store the squares of baked pork in a plastic bag in the refrigerator until ready to grill. They will keep for at least 3 days.

6 Set up the grill for direct grilling and preheat it to medium-high.

7 When ready to cook, brush and oil the grill grate. Grill the pork squares until sizzling and nicely browned, 2 to 4 minutes per side, turning with tongs. Serve the pork jerky hot off the grill as a snack.

NOTE: Rose water—optional here—adds a subtle floral flavor. It's sold at Asian and Middle Eastern markets and at specialty food shops.

South Korea: Fire It Up in the Land of Morning Calm

If you want to experience Korean barbecue in all its flame-charred glory, you have to get up pretty early. And be willing to stay out pretty late. And cover a lot of territory in the sprawling megalopolis that is Seoul, South Korea's capital. Take it from me, for I did nothing but eat barbecue—for breakfast, lunch, and dinner—during my last visit to the country, and I barely scratched the surface. Scratching the surface of Korea's barbecue culture could take years.

You probably know something about the grilling of the "Land of Morning Calm" already. Two dishes, *bool kogi* and *kalbi kui,* have made the leap from esoteric ethnic food to the American mainstream. *Bool kogi* is a rib eye steak sliced wafer-thin, glazed with a sweet-salty marinade, and grilled candy crisp over charcoal. *Kalbi kui* qualifies as one of the world's most ingenious rib dishes: beef short ribs sliced and butterflied in such a way that you can cook them by direct grilling. This transforms a tough, ornery rib that normally requires several hours of smoking,

Giant mussels shucked and ready for grilling.

into tender, incredibly flavorful beef you can grill in a couple of minutes.

But beef is only a start, for the Korean barbecue repertory is broad enough to include pork belly, oysters, clams, giant mussels, and eel glazed like lacquered mahogany. The way you eat Korean barbecue is equally remarkable—no monolithic hunk of meat burying your plate, as in Tuscany or Texas. Instead, it's a gustatory ballet that includes grilling meat and vegetables, done by a chopstick-wielding waitress in a classy restaurant or by you and your dining companions at more casual establishments, cutting what you have grilled into bite-size pieces using scissors, and wrapping and eating the result in lettuce leaves along with up to a dozen different flavorful condiments.

Night Life and Barbecue

Sandwiched between China and Japan, South Korea offers some of the most complex, vibrant grilling in Asia.

South Korea's capital, Seoul: land of anything but calm.

South Korea: where ancient traditions meet twenty-first-century Asia.

In many countries, barbecue is a summertime or warm weather affair, but Koreans like nothing better than to gather around the charcoal brazier set in the center of a table on a cold dreary day in the dead of winter. Yes, your eyes sting and your clothes get smoky, but that's part of the fun of eating Korean barbecue. And many establishments provide deodorizing sprays to help you remove the smoke smell before you leave the restaurant.

THE GRILL: At the heart of Korean barbecue—and at the center of the table—is a charcoal-burning brazier that looks like a large flower pot. Some restaurants use more conventional boxlike metal grills. Depending on the food, it's grilled either on a conventional wire grate or on what looks like an upside-down metal wok with holes or slits in it and a raised rim around the edge at the bottom that collects the juices, for dipping the meat.

THE FUEL: The traditional fuel is lump charcoal, lit outdoors and carried to the table in a brazier or metal box. Some South Korean chefs cook on gas grills, especially in big cities.

The Korean grill: a wire grate over blazing charcoal.

THE FLAVORINGS: Korean barbecue plays pinball on your taste buds. The marinades counterpoint the saltiness of soy sauce with the sweetness of sugar, Asian pear, and sometimes mirin (sweet rice wine). Sesame oil and sesame seeds provide a nutty element, one of the distinguishing flavors of Korean barbecue, while garlic and black pepper supply the aromatics. On the grill, the sugar and fruit juice cook to a candylike glaze. Koreans also like their barbecue spicy, using chile powder and hot bean paste to kick up the heat—especially with pork and seafood.

MUST TRY DISHES:
Barbecued eel (see page 478)

Bool kogi: Usually thinly sliced, sweet-salty grilled rib eye steak

Kalbi kui: Butterflied, thinly sliced, grilled beef short ribs

Sam gyeop sal: Thinly sliced pork belly seasoned with chile powder and grilled (see page 53)

Grilled clams: (see page 511), giant mussels, and oysters

THE CONDIMENTS: A small bowl of sesame salt is the basic seasoning for grilled meats, especially beef and pork. The traditional dipping sauce for beef contains soy sauce, sugar, Asian pear, garlic, scallion, and pepper. Grilled pork might be dipped in a fiery red chile sauce. Grilled seafood comes with *kochujang,* a sort of turbocharged cocktail sauce.

HOW TO EAT IT: A grilled dish becomes a whole meal at a typical Korean barbecue house. First, you slather a lettuce leaf with *doenjang,* Korean soybean paste. Then pile on some rice, *kimchi* (pickled cabbage, daikon, bok choy, or other vegetables), then the grilled meat, then grilled garlic, chiles, and scallions.

Steak and salad Korean-style: grilled meat wrapped and eaten in lettuce leaves by my friend Young-ho Moon.

Barbecued eel with panchan (Korean side dishes—see page 52).

Fold the ensemble into a bundle, dip it into Asian pear sauce and/or sesame salt, then pop it into your mouth. This is a feat which Koreans accomplish with perfect aplomb, using slippery stainless steel chopsticks.

IF YOU CAN EAT AT ONLY ONE RESTAURANT: In South Korea, you don't so much pick a barbecue restaurant as a particular grilled dish you want to eat. If you're craving *kalbi kui* or *bool kogi* in Seoul, head for a sprawling, popular, indoor-outdoor restaurant like Samwon Garden or Mae Chwi Soon, a restaurant chain with a name that means "plum drunk softly."

For grilled pork, try Choidaepo in Seoul's boisterous Mapo-gu district.

For grilled eel in a lovely riverfront setting, try Ilmijung in west Seoul.

WHAT TO DRINK: Plum wine, wild strawberry wine, rice wine, or cinnamon punch

THE MOST SINGULAR DISH IN THE REPERTORY: Blowfish *bool kogi*—yes, that's the same blowfish known as *fugu* in Japan that contains a deadly poison that must be removed by highly trained fish cutters. One famous place to try it is Cheol Cheol Globefish restaurant in the Jung-gu district of Seoul.

Korean Barbecue Accompaniments

No Korean meal, grilled or otherwse, would be complete without a massive onslaught of side dishes called *panchan* (sometimes transliterated as *banchan*). The bare minimum would include five or six items—pickles, salads, strong-flavored condiments, and lettuce leaves used as a wrap, like you'd use a tortilla. A particularly generous *panchan* might feature twenty dishes. The beauty of *panchan* is that it turns a single dish into a complete meal you can customize. (*Panchan* comes from the Chinese word for "accompaniment to rice.")

According to Jonathan Kim, owner of the online Korean grocery, www.koamart.com, *panchan* came into being after the Second World War and Korean War as a way for provision-deprived Koreans to give the illusion of bounty at tables largely devoid of meat.

Start with the lettuce leaves, then serve any or all of the following with any of the Korean grilled dishes in this book. The condiments and salads look great, taste even better, and are healthy to boot. You can also add some steamed rice to the table.

RED-LEAF, ROMAINE, AND OTHER LETTUCES: Broken into individual leaves, trimmed, rinsed, spun dry, and stacked on a plate, lettuce leaves—*ssang-chu*—are used for wrapping pieces of grilled meat or seafood along with the other *panchan* items.

DOENJANG: A thick, salty, tangy condiment made from cultured soybeans. *Doenjang* is available at Korean and Asian markets or at www.koamart.com.

KOCHUJANG: Korean chile pepper paste; a thick, salty, fiery condiment made from soybeans and Korean hot peppers.

KIMCHI: Korean pickles. The two most common kimchis are made from napa cabbage or daikon radish—both ignited with fiery Korean red pepper. Like sauerkraut or kosher pickles, kimchi tends to taste better when commercially manufactured than when made from scratch at home (unless you happen to be Korean). The good barbecue joints make their kimchi from scratch, often in earthenware pots buried in whatever outdoor space constitutes the backyard. You'll find kimchi at Korean and Asian markets and many supermarkets.

Replenishing the hot coals in the table grill. In South Korea, most of the grilling is done at your table.

CUCUMBER SALAD: The Korean version of the sweet-sour cucumber relishes found in Japan and Southeast Asia. To make a simple Korean cucumber salad, combine 1 tablespoon each of sugar and rice wine, 2 tablespoons of black or toasted white sesame seeds (see page 68 for toasting instructions), and 1 teaspoon of salt in a mixing bowl. Whisk until the sugar and salt dissolve. Stir in 2 peeled and thinly sliced baby or Kirby cucumbers or 1 medium-size cucumber.

MUNG BEAN SPROUT SALAD: Nutty and crisp, another great accompaniment to grilled meats. Blanch ½ pound of fresh mung bean sprouts in 2 quarts of rapidly boiling water for 15 seconds. Drain the mung beans well, rinse them under cold water to cool, and drain them again. Place the sprouts in a large mixing bowl and stir in 1 tablespoon of toasted sesame seeds (see page 68), 2 teaspoons each of soy sauce and Asian (dark) sesame oil, ½ teaspoon of freshly ground black pepper, and 1 clove of minced garlic.

WATERCRESS SALAD: Fresh, peppery, and perfect with grilled meats. Place 1 teaspoon each of salt and sugar and ½ teaspoon each of black pepper and minced peeled fresh ginger and garlic in a bowl and mash to a paste with the back of a wooden spoon. Whisk in 1 tablespoon each of rice vinegar and Asian (dark) sesame oil. Add a bunch of watercress that has been stemmed and torn into 1-inch sprigs and stir to mix.

Korean Grilled Pork Belly
{ SAM GYEOP SAL }

Paradoxically, *sam gyeop sal* is simultaneously the most simple and one of the most complex dishes in Korean barbecue. Simple, because the main ingredient, thinly sliced fresh pork belly, has no marinade, rub, or spice paste. Complex, because to get the full effect, you must season the grilled pork with sesame salt and Asian pear dipping sauce and serve it wrapped in lettuce leaves with grilled garlic and onion, chile paste, and steamed rice. Do all that and you'll be rewarded with pork that, while fatty, could almost qualify as barbecue health food—almost—thanks to the high ratio of crisp vegetables to meat. Here's how they make *sam gyeop sal* at Seoul's popular grilled pork house, Mapo Choidaepo. **SERVES 4**

FOR THE SESAME SALT

3 tablespoons coarse salt (kosher or sea)

3 tablespoons toasted sesame seeds
    (see page 68)

2 teaspoons freshly ground white pepper

FOR THE ASIAN PEAR DIPPING SAUCE

1 small or ½ large Asian pear or Bosc pear
    (about 12 ounces)

2 cloves garlic, coarsely chopped

2 slices (¼ inch thick) peeled fresh ginger,
    coarsely chopped

1 scallion, trimmed, white part coarsely
    chopped, green parts finely chopped

3 tablespoons sugar

1 teaspoon coarse salt (kosher or sea)

3 tablespoons Asian (dark) sesame oil

2 tablespoons rice vinegar

1 tablespoon Korean chile paste
    (optional, see box, facing page)

1 to 2 teaspoons Korean chile powder or
    hot paprika

1 tablespoon toasted sesame seeds
    (see page 68)

FOR THE SAM GYEOP SAL

8 cloves garlic, peeled and skewered on
    wooden toothpicks

1 medium-size onion, peeled and cut crosswise
    into ¼-inch slices

8 small hot green peppers, such as serrano
    peppers

1½ pounds pork belly, rind trimmed off,
    cut crosswise into ⅛-inch-thick slices

Your choice of Korean barbecue accompaniments
    (see facing page), for serving

YOU'LL ALSO NEED

A grilling grid, fish grate, or grill basket
    (optional); kitchen shears

ADVANCE PREPARATION

The seasoned salt and Asian pear dipping sauce
    can be prepared ahead.

THE SCOOP

WHERE: Seoul, South Korea

WHAT: One of Korea's national pork dishes—pork belly, thinly sliced, grilled dry, and served with grilled garlic, onion, sesame salt, and Asian pear dipping sauce

HOW: Direct grilling

JUST THE FACTS: *Sam gyeop sal* is uncured pork belly, the cut that North Americans turn into bacon. The name, literally "three-layered meat," refers to the pork's striped appearance, alternating layers of meat and fat. Since most American pork belly is destined for bacon (and most of the rest goes to chefs), you'll likely need to order it in advance from your butcher (partially freeze the pork belly to make it easier to slice). In a pinch you could substitute thinly sliced pork shoulder (are you listening, my friends in St. Louis?) or thinly sliced country-style ribs.

1 Make the sesame salt: Place the 3 tablespoons of salt, 3 tablespoons of sesame seeds, and the white pepper in a bowl and stir to mix. Divide the sesame salt among 4 tiny bowls.

2 Make the Asian pear dipping sauce: Place the pear, chopped garlic, ginger, scallion white, sugar, and salt in a food processor and puree to a smooth paste. Work in the sesame oil, rice vinegar, chile paste, if using, and hot pepper powder. Add the sesame seeds and the scallion greens and pulse the processor once or twice just to mix. Divide the sauce among 4 bowls for dipping. The dipping sauce can be made several hours ahead.

3 Set up the grill for direct grilling and preheat it to high. In Korea, they use a fine-mesh wire grate to keep the small pieces of pork from falling through the bars of the grate. An American wire grilling grid or fish grate will do the same and so will a grill basket. But you can use a regular grill grate if you're careful.

4 When ready to cook, brush and oil the grill grate. Arrange the skewered garlic, onion slices, and hot peppers on the hot grate and grill until the vegetables are browned, 2 to 4 minutes per side. Transfer the grilled garlic, onion, and peppers to a platter. Arrange the pork slices on the grate or grilling grid and grill until sizzling and browned, 2 to 4 minutes per side. Transfer the grilled pork to the platter with the garlic, onion, and peppers.

5 Set the table with the barbecue accompaniments of your choice, being sure to include lettuce leaves and chile paste. Using kitchen shears, cut the pork, garlic, onion, and hot peppers into bite-size pieces. To eat the *sam gyeop sal*, dip a piece of pork in the sesame salt. Next, dip it in the Asian pear dipping sauce. Spread a little chile paste on a lettuce leaf. Place pieces of the seasoned pork and some grilled garlic, onion, hot pepper, rice, and any other condiments, if using, on the lettuce leaf. Roll it up and pop it into your mouth.

Grilled Crocodile or Pork and Shrimp with Garlic Walnut Lime Sauce

THE SCOOP

WHERE: Nairobi, Kenya, and Johannesburg, South Africa

WHAT: Crocodile marinated in lime juice spiced with curry and a mixture of black, white, and cayenne pepper

HOW: Direct grilling

No, it doesn't taste exactly like chicken. And no, you probably won't find it at your local supermarket. But crocodile is grilled in Kenya, not to mention many other parts of Africa, and every ambitious griller should know how to prepare it.

The trick is to cut the meat in small pieces and marinate them in lime juice or another acidic liquid. This makes meat that you'd expect to be tough turn out to be surprisingly tender. Grilled crocodile is a specialty of the Carnivore restaurant, which has branches in Nairobi and Johannesburg. **SERVES 4**

1½ pounds trimmed crocodile meat, or
   1½ pounds pork shoulder, or 12 ounces
   each pork tenderloin and peeled and
   deveined shrimp
1½ teaspoons coarse salt (kosher or sea)
1½ teaspoons curry powder
½ teaspoon freshly ground black pepper
½ teaspoon white pepper, or more black pepper
¼ teaspoon cayenne pepper
2 cloves garlic, minced
¼ cup fresh lime juice
¼ cup vegetable oil, plus 1 to 2 tablespoons
   for basting
Garlic Walnut Lime Sauce (optional, recipe follows)

YOU'LL ALSO NEED
Flat metal or bamboo skewers

ADVANCE PREPARATION
2 to 4 hours for marinating the meat

1 Cut the crocodile into strips about 2 inches long, 1 inch wide, and ½ inch thick. Place the meat in a large nonreactive mixing bowl and sprinkle it with the salt, curry powder, black pepper, white pepper, and cayenne. Add the garlic and stir to mix. Stir in the lime juice and vegetable oil. Let the crocodile marinate in the refrigerator, covered, for 2 to 4 hours, stirring it once or twice so that it marinates evenly.

2 Drain the crocodile, discarding the marinade. Skewer the pieces of crocodile crosswise on flat skewers.

3 Set up the grill for direct grilling and preheat it to high.

4 When ready to cook, brush and oil the grill grate. Arrange the crocodile kebabs on the hot grate and grill them until golden brown and cooked through, 3 to 4 minutes per side. Once you have turned the kebabs, baste them with the oil. Serve the kebabs at once with the Garlic Walnut Lime Sauce, if desired.

Garlic Walnut Lime Sauce

At Carnivore they serve crocodile with a garlic potato sauce that may remind you of Greek *skordalia*. I've taken a few liberties with the recipe; bread gives you a lighter sauce than potatoes. The result is a sauce fragrant with fresh lime zest and lime juice coupled with earthy undertones of walnut. **MAKES ABOUT 1 CUP**

FOR THE SAUCE
4 slices white sandwich bread, crusts cut off
¼ cup walnuts or almonds, coarsely chopped
4 cloves garlic, coarsely chopped
½ teaspoon grated lime zest
3 tablespoons fresh lime juice
⅓ cup vegetable oil
2 tablespoons extra-virgin olive oil
Coarse salt (kosher or sea) and freshly ground
   white pepper

1 Place the slices of bread in a mixing bowl and add enough warm water to cover. Let the bread soak for 5 minutes, then drain it well in a strainer. Using your hands, squeeze the bread well to wring out any excess liquid.

2 Place the bread, walnuts, garlic, and lime zest in a food processor and puree to a smooth paste. With the processor running, gradually work in the lime juice, vegetable oil, and olive oil in a thin stream to obtain a smooth sauce. Season the sauce with salt and white pepper to taste; it should be highly seasoned.

The Ultimate Carnivore

Kenyan-born grill master **DANIEL KIPLAGAT** brings out the best in meat at Nairobi's most famous restaurant, Carnivore

NAIROBI, KENYA

It's a long way from a Kalenjin village in Kenya's Rift Valley to the popular Nairobi restaurant, Carnivore. Daniel Kiplagat made the journey as a young man and never looked back. Daniel remembers how as young as three years old, he would help his father slaughter one of the family buffalos for special occasions, or rabbits for more prosaic meals, to be grilled over bushwood fires. The seasonings were simple, if not wholly in keeping with Western tastes: salt, hot peppers, and buffalo bile. The flavor, he recalls, was out of this world.

Fast-forward twenty-seven years to the city where all ambitious villagers in Kenya eventually wind up: crowded, chaotic Nairobi. Daniel landed a job as a dishwasher at Carnivore. He didn't realize it at the time, but Carnivore—opened by the Kenya-based Tamarind Group in 1980—was the most famous restaurant in Africa. The sprawling 420-seat restaurant, with its 450-seat banquet hall and an outdoor concert venue that can accommodate 20,000, is a mandatory destination for tourists (not to mention a must-see on the safari circuit). But it also attracts enough locals to give you the feeling you're not just dining at a theme park.

So Daniel worked his way up from dishwasher to prep cook to line

Carnivore chef Daniel Kiplagat spit-roasts the meat to crusty perfection.

cook to sous chef. Today, he presides over a team of grill jockeys who man what may be the largest rotisserie on Planet Barbecue. Imagine a circular brick fire pit perhaps eighteen feet across with a continuous trough of embers and mechanized turnspits every few feet. In keeping with the general spirit, Kiplagat and company roast twenty-pound hams, monster beef sirloins, whole legs and racks of lamb, and so on until the exteriors are as crisp as pork cracklings and the insides are tender enough to cut with the side of a fork.

Once Daniel determines the meats are cooked, waiters wearing traditional African fabrics carve them off swordlike spits directly onto the diners' plate. The similarity to a Brazilian *churrascaria* is no accident: The idea for Carnivore was hatched in Brazil. In years gone by you could also eat your fill of impala, wildebeest, and other game—today protected species in Kenya. But they still serve crocodile and it still tastes like a cross between pork and shrimp.

"The key to our meats are the marinades," explains Daniel. "Traditionally, we Kenyans don't marinate our meat. The Carnivore way is better." So how do the seven guys grilling for five hundred people on a typical Friday night know when the various and constantly turning meats are ready? "By the color, feel, and taste," explains Daniel. "And that I learned in my village."

NAME: Daniel Kiplagat

TERRITORY: Nairobi, Kenya

CLAIM TO FAME: Runs the grill at the landmark Nairobi restaurant, Carnivore

SPECIALTIES: Spit-roasted lamb, beef, whole fresh ham, and crocodile

KIPLAGAT SAYS:

▶ The secret to moist meat is the marinade. Ours contain vegetable oil, soy sauce, and lime juice.

▶ To check for doneness, look at the meat juices. They should run clear, not red.

Grilled Israeli Spiced Foie Gras

Cross New York's Lower East Side with Belleville in Paris and you get the colorful populist Hatikva neighborhood in Tel Aviv. It was here that an Azeri immigrant named Avazi set up a pushcart with a grill that was destined to become a landmark restaurant. An unexpected place to find one of the world's most luxurious grilled foods, to be sure, but foie gras has been an Avazi specialty since the beginning. And so it remains, even though Israel outlawed foie gras production a few years ago (today, Avazi's foie gras comes from Eastern Europe). Foie gras, French for "fat liver," is the oversize liver of a specially raised goose. Sounds less than appetizing, right? Well, the process makes the goose liver as rich as butter. But why should you bother to grill foie gras? First, because the high dry heat of the grill accomplishes something that's very hard to do in a frying pan or in the oven: It gives you a crisp crust on the outside while cooking the foie gras through, without melting out too much of the fat. And second, because the Israeli spicing of cumin, turmeric, and pepper offsets the inherent richness of the foie gras in a way that is simultaneously exotic and familiar. **SERVES 6 AS AN APPETIZER, 4 AS AN UNBELIEVABLY RICH MAIN COURSE**

THE SCOOP

WHERE: Tel Aviv, Israel

WHAT: One of the best ways I know to cook foie gras, which is to say crusted with Israeli spices and seared over screaming-hot charcoal

HOW: Direct grilling

JUST THE FACTS: Buy foie gras, fattened goose or duck liver, by mail from a purveyor like D'Artagnan (www .dartagnan.com). To trim and devein it, cut the foie gras crosswise into ¾-inch-thick slices. Using tweezers, pull out and discard any red veins or blood spots. You can also make the dish with chicken livers; the result is very different, but you'll wind up with an interesting dish nonetheless.

1 tablespoon coarse salt (kosher or sea)

1 tablespoon sweet paprika

1 teaspoon ground turmeric

1 teaspoon ground cumin

1 teaspoon freshly ground black pepper

1 teaspoon freshly ground white pepper

½ teaspoon cayenne pepper

1½ pounds of foie gras

Pita bread (optional), for serving

YOU'LL ALSO NEED

Flat metal or bamboo skewers for grilling

ADVANCE PREPARATION

The foie gras can be trimmed and deveined several hours ahead (see Just the Facts, this page).

1 Place the salt, paprika, turmeric, cumin, and black and white peppers in a small bowl and stir to mix with a fork or your fingers. Set the rub aside.

2 Cut the foie gras into chunks that are 1½ by 1½ inches and ¾ inch thick. Skewer the chunks of foie gras on flat metal skewers through the thin side. Generously season each kebab on both sides with the rub.

3 Set up the grill for direct grilling and preheat it to high. If you are using a charcoal grill, follow the instructions for grateless grilling on page 599.

4 If you are using a charcoal grill, suspend the skewers of foie gras over the coals. If you are using a gas grill, brush and oil the grill grate, then turn off the gas and place the foie gras on the grill (see Note). Grill the foie gras until golden brown on the outside and just cooked inside, 3 to 5 minutes per side. If fat dripping on the coals causes flare-ups, and it likely will, move the skewers of the foie gras to another section of the grill.

5 Serve the grilled foie gras at once, using a pita bread or fork to slide the pieces of foie gras off the skewer. (Of course, you should eat the pita bread.)

NOTE: Dripping foie gras fat is highly flammable, especially on a gas grill. So I've developed a technique for grilling foie gras on a gas grill with a conventional metal grate. Preheat the grill to high, then turn the gas off and grill the foie gras on the still hot bars of the grate. Yes, the foie gras will sear and brown like you want it to. No, the dripping fat hitting the gas burners won't cause flare-ups. You saw it here first.

VARIATION

Grilled Foie Gras with Grenadine Onions: In keeping with his iconoclastic approach to cooking, when French grill master Laurent Mertz (see page 515) cooks foie gras, he uses his wood-burning grill and serves the foie gras with a sort of sweet-sour grenadine onion "jam."

To make it, melt 3 tablespoons of salted butter in a skillet over medium heat. Add 1 finely chopped sweet onion, such as a Vidalia, and cook it until it begins to brown, 8 to 12 minutes, stirring it often and lowering the heat to medium-low or low as necessary to keep the onion from burning. Stir in ¼ cup grenadine, 1 tablespoon balsamic vinegar, and ½ teaspoon finely grated lemon zest and let the onion cook until it is thick, jamlike, and richly flavored, 3 to 5 minutes longer. Season the jam with coarse salt and freshly ground black pepper to taste. The grenadine onions can be made ahead and refrigerated, covered, for at least three days (let it cool to room temperature before refrigerating it).

Let the grenadine onions warm to room temperature before serving. Grill the foie gras following the directions in Steps 2 through 4 on page 57 and this page (omit the rub and season the foie gras with salt and pepper). Serve the foie gras with the grenadine onions on the side.

Avazi co-owner, David Amrani, serves his Israeli spice-crusted grilled foie gras.

Salads

To many North Americans, the notion of a grilled salad is an oxymoron. After all, isn't the very essence of a salad its rawness—the refreshing cool crispness of the decidedly uncooked vegetables (lettuce, for example) that comprise it? Well, in many parts of the world salads are defined not by rawness but by the transformative powers of smoke and fire. Case in point, the roasted pepper salads of Morocco, Argentina, and Italy. Take a bite of an uncooked red bell pepper and you get a pleasant, if monodimensional, snappy sweetness. Char the same pepper over a wood fire, or roast it on the coals, and you get the haunting smoke and caramel flavors that are typical of complex wines.

Or consider chicken salad: In Guam, the commonplace boiled chicken and mayonnaise give way to a robust grill-smoked chicken invigorated with crisp coconut, fiery chiles, and fresh lime juice. It may well be the world's best chicken salad.

But the ultimate ingredient for grilled salads is eggplant, a staple not just in Central Asia, North Africa, and the Middle East, but as far east as Japan and the Philippines. So prized is the flavor of flame-charred eggplant that apartment dwellers in Athens and Tel Aviv who have no access to grills will roast eggplants directly on the gas or electric burners of their stoves to infuse the spongy flesh with the intense smoke flavor without which eggplant salads simply aren't worth lifting a fork for.

In this chapter, you'll find eight grilled salads from around Planet Barbecue. Sometimes, raw is good, but fired up is even better.

Previous page: In India, a vendor is surrounded by the freshest of vegetables, a bunch of just-picked cilantro in his hand.

Grilled Vegetable Salad
{ MANGAL SALATI }

THE SCOOP

WHERE: Russia

WHAT: Grilled vegetable salad as made in Russia and the Caucasus Mountains

HOW: Direct grilling

Grilled eggplants, tomatoes, and peppers turn up wherever grill masters light charcoal. They taste particularly spectacular in Russia and the Caucasus Mountains, where each vegetable is grilled on a grateless *mangal* grill just to the degree that suits it best. This flame-seared, smoke-scented salad is a great dish for people who have a tendency to burn food on the grill. You grill the vegetables until they are charred on all sides and tender inside. If the skins blacken too much, simply scrape off the burnt part. **SERVES 4 TO 6**

3 to 4 small or 2 medium-size eggplants
(about 1 pound total)

3 luscious, red ripe tomatoes

2 medium-size or 1 large green bell pepper,
3 Cubanelle or Anaheim peppers,
or 6 horn peppers

½ small sweet onion, finely chopped

4 to 6 purple or green basil leaves, thinly slivered
crosswise, plus 1 basil sprig for garnish

1 tablespoon chopped fresh dill

1 tablespoon chopped fresh cilantro,
or 1 more tablespoon dill

2 tablespoons vegetable oil, or more to taste

1 tablespoon red wine vinegar, or more to taste

Coarse salt (kosher or sea) and freshly
ground black pepper

Grilled bread for serving

ADVANCE PREPARATION

The vegetables can be grilled and the salad
prepped up to 24 hours ahead. If you make
this salad the same day, do so far enough
ahead for the grilled vegetables to cool to
room temperature. Then, be sure to adjust
the seasonings right before serving.

Roasting Vegetables in the Embers

The grilled peppers, tomatoes, and eggplants used in the salads throughout this chapter will taste even more delicious when roasted in the embers of a wood or charcoal fire. Just place them directly on top of the glowing embers—there's no need for a grill grate. Grill the vegetables until their skins are completely charred, then let them cool to room temperature. Scrape off the burnt skin before adding the vegetables to a salad.

1 Set up the grill for direct grilling and preheat it to high.

2 When ready to cook, brush and oil the grill grate. Arrange the eggplants, tomatoes, and peppers on the hot grate. Grill the eggplants until the skins are charred and blistered on all sides and the flesh is soft (the eggplants will be easy to pierce with a skewer), 3 to 4 minutes per side, 9 to 12 minutes in all. Grill the tomatoes until the skins are dark and blistered, about 2 minutes per side, 6 to 8 minutes in all. Grill the peppers until the skins are darkly browned and blistered, about 2 minutes per side, 6 to 8 minutes in all for medium-size bell peppers or Cubanelles; 3 to 4 minutes per side, 12 to 16 minutes in all for a large bell pepper; and 2 to 4 minute per side, 4 to 8 minutes in all for Anaheim or horn peppers. To ensure even cooking, turn the vegetables with tongs.

3 Transfer the grilled vegetables to a platter to cool to room temperature. Scrape off any burnt skin, discarding any stems. Cut the peppers in half, remove the cores, and scrape out the seeds. Cut the vegetables into ¼- to ½-inch dice (or as large as you like). Transfer the diced vegetables to a nonreactive mixing bowl.

4 Add the onion, basil, dill, cilantro, if using, and the oil and wine vinegar to the diced vegetables and stir to mix. Taste for seasoning, adding salt and black pepper to taste and more oil and/or vinegar as necessary. Serve the salad with a grilled bread on the side, for example, the Armenian "stick" bread, on page 96.

THE SCOOP

JUST THE FACTS: A salad this simple lives or dies by the quality of the ingredients. Near Eastern eggplants are smaller and sweeter than the large, bulbous eggplants sold in North American supermarkets. The best approximations are the 3- to 4-ounce eggplants (about 5 inches long and 2 inches wide) found in Italian produce markets and natural foods stores. If you are going to use conventional eggplants, choose the longest, most slender specimens you can find; they give you the highest ratio of charred skin to pulp. As for the tomatoes, they should be red and spectacularly ripe. The peppers can be green bell peppers, Cubanelles, or even hot peppers.

Moroccan Grilled Pepper Salad

WHERE: Morocco

WHAT: A smoky salad of grilled peppers and luscious, ripe red tomatoes with onion, lemon, and mint

HOW: Direct grilling

JUST THE FACTS: Moroccan peppers are sweeter than green bell peppers and milder than Mexican poblanos. You could use either or a mix of both. For a not strictly traditional but highly tasty version, use three red bell peppers (sweeter than green in the way that Moroccan peppers are sweeter than our bell peppers), plus three Anaheim or Cubanelle peppers. You'll need about four cups of roasted peppers in all.

Forget about the twelfth century Koutoubia Mosque or the Jemaa el Fna (the medieval city square). The real marvel of Marrakech is its salad. Or more precisely the array of salads—anywhere from a dozen to more than twenty served at the start of a traditional formal Moroccan meal. This one will pique the interest of grill lovers: a flame-roasted pepper salad flavored with cumin, onion, and mint. Normally I would tell you to grill all of the vegetables, but here I like the traditional Moroccan contrast of smoky grilled pepper and crisp raw onions and tomatoes. **SERVES 4 TO 6**

4 green bell peppers, 5 poblano peppers, or
    3 red bell peppers, plus 3 Anaheim or
    Cubanelle peppers
2 luscious, red ripe tomatoes, seeded and
    cut into ¼-inch dice
½ sweet onion, cut into ¼-inch dice
3 tablespoons chopped fresh mint, cilantro, or
    flat-leaf parsley (not too finely chopped)
½ teaspoon ground cumin
3 tablespoons extra-virgin olive oil
1 tablespoon fresh lemon juice, or more to taste
1 tablespoon red wine vinegar, or more lemon
    juice
Coarse salt (kosher or sea) and freshly ground
    black pepper

ADVANCE PREPARATION
The peppers can be grilled up to 48 hours ahead.

1 Set up the grill for direct grilling and preheat it to high. There is no need to brush or oil the grill grate.

2 Arrange the peppers on the hot grate and grill them until the skins are darkly browned and blistered on all sides, 3 to 4 minutes per side, 12 to 16 minutes in all, turning with tongs. Don't forget to grill the tops and bottoms of the peppers for 1 to 2 minutes. The idea is to char the skins completely. Transfer the grilled peppers to a cutting board and let them cool to room temperature. (No, you don't need to place them in a paper bag or bowl covered with plastic wrap. I've found no appreciable difference in ease of peeling.)

3 Using a paring knife, scrape the charred skins off the peppers. There's no need to remove every last bit; a few black spots will add color and flavor. Cut each pepper in half, remove the core, and scrape out the seeds. Cut each pepper into ¼-inch dice and place them in a nonreactive mixing bowl.

4 Add the tomato, onion, mint, cumin, olive oil, lemon juice, and wine vinegar, if using, and toss to mix. Season with salt and black pepper to taste; the salad should be highly seasoned. The salad can be prepared several hours ahead, but taste it for seasoning just before serving, adding more salt and/ or black pepper as necessary.

Morocco: Ancient Land of Grill Culture and Cuisine

They're all here—the snake charmers and fortune tellers, the hustlers, touts, and tourists from six continents—assembled in a vast square you could call North Africa's antechamber (to paraphrase Napoléon's description of St. Mark's Square in Venice). They gather here for a nightly ritual that dates back to the Middle Ages, a kaleidoscopic cacophony of sounds, scents, and colors that makes this one of the world's most spectacular backdrops for savoring meat hot off the grill. The scene is all the more remarkable for the fact that none of the dozens of open-air restaurants, with their colorful kebabs and blazing grills, were here a few hours earlier. They're erected from scratch every evening. Welcome to the Jemaa el Fna square: "Barbecue Central" for Marrakech—and the world.

Kebabs hot off the grill at a street-side grill parlor.

As it is throughout the Arab world, lamb is king in Morocco, but just how you get it depends on your mood, socioeconomic status, and the occasion. The wealthy feast on tender lamb shoulder or loin kebabs at an upscale restaurant, like Dar Fassi, located just outside Marrakech's old city walls and run by women from Fez. The not so wealthy might settle for grilled heart or kidneys or fatty *merguez* sausage from an itinerant street vendor. (Talk about resourceful: One vendor I met fashioned his grill from the metal coolant coil of a scavenged refrigerator.) An everyday hunger is satisfied by dropping into one of the casual grill parlors that line Bani Sadr Street for *brochette* (shish kebab) or *kofta,* grilled ground lamb eaten with tomato relish and Moroccan bread. For a wedding or other special occasion, Moroccans order a *méchoui,* a spectacular whole lamb roasted in an underground pit similar to a Turkish *tandir* or Iranian *tanoor* and brought, ready to eat, to their doorstep.

Of course, there's a lot more to Moroccan barbecue than lamb.

Grilling Where Desert Meets Sea

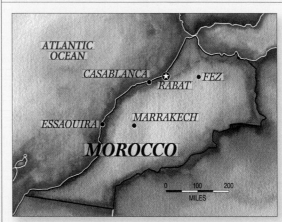

Morocco has it all: the Atlas Mountains, the Sahara Desert, and a fish-rich coastline stretching from the Atlantic Ocean to the Mediterranean Sea.

A spice market in the souk. Moroccan grilling is defined by its bold seasonings.

A familiar sight in Morocco: skewering the meat for kebabs.

Carving *méchoui, Moroccan pit-roasted whole lamb.*

Grill masters in seaside towns like Tangier and Essaouira grill whiting, bass, sardines, squid, and other Mediterranean seafood. Beef is popular inland—sometimes seasoned with a ginger, paprika, and cardamom-scented spice paste favored by the Berbers in the Atlas Mountains. Chicken comes spatchcocked, served with coarse salt and cumin or a fiery Moroccan hot sauce called *harissa*. As for grilled vegetables, they do double duty—as ingredients for salads and seared on skewers over the fire to accompany kebabs. It's all in a day's work when you fire the grill in Morocco.

THE GRILLS: Moroccans grill on just about everything from conventional table grills to *mangal*-style grateless box grills to charcoal burning rotisseries. There's also a traditional ceramic brazier (it looks like an oversize flower pot) called a *kanoun.*

Moroccans grill on a grateless charcoal burning brazier similar to a Russian mangal.

THE FUEL: Natural lump charcoal

THE FLAVORINGS: Moroccan grillers keep flavorings simple: salt and cumin here; chopped garlic and parsley there, used with ground meats and offal. Fancier restaurants might add saffron, turmeric, and mint. Chunk lamb and beef tend to be grilled plain, with seasonings applied at the table. Fish is also grilled without seasoning. Chicken is often marinated with lemon and hot peppers.

MUST TRY DISHES:

Brochette: The generic term for shish kebab (as in most North African countries, French is widely spoken in Morocco). *Brochette d'agneau* is a lamb kebab; *brochette de poulet* is a chicken kebab; *brochette de boeuf* is a beef kebab.

Kofta: The Arabic word for a ground meat kebab or patty, *kofta* is often lamb but can also be made from ground beef or chicken (you'll find a recipe on page 328).

Méchoui: Whole lamb or leg of lamb spit roasted or roasted in an underground pit. See page 272 for a recipe.

Merguez: A spicy Moroccan lamb sausage

THE CONDIMENTS: Sit down for barbecue at a typical Moroccan grill joint and you'll be served a plate of marinated olives, small bowls of salt and ground cumin, a luscious relish made from ripe tomatoes and shallots or onions, the fiery red pepper *harissa* sauce (see page 282 for a recipe), and Moroccan bread.

HOW TO EAT IT: The traditional way to eat *kofta* is to sprinkle the meat with salt and cumin, then make a sandwich with the relish, *harissa,* and bread.

Essential gear in Moroccan grill joints: a set of scales for portioning the meat.

IF YOU CAN EAT AT ONLY ONE RESTAURANT: Haj Brik in Marrakech. You'll know it when you see it: It's the busiest restaurant on the block.

WHAT TO DRINK: Mint tea—Morocco has the best.

THE MOST SINGULAR DISH IN THE REPERTORY: Lamb spleen grilled with garlic, parsley, and onion. I wish I could say it tastes better than it sounds. It doesn't. You probably have to be Moroccan to enjoy it.

Roasted Bell Pepper Salad with Anchovies and Garlic

La Brigada, in the San Telmo district, is one of the obligatory stops on a beef eater's pilgrimage through Buenos Aires, and if with each passing year the tourists seem to displace a few more of the locals, most *porteños* (the citizens of Buenos Aires) still give its grilled grass-fed beef a big thumbs up. But while you're overdosing on red meat, save room for the grilled pepper salad. This is about as elaborate as an Argentinean vegetable dish gets; the salty tang of anchovies, the pungency of garlic, and the sweet smoky flavor of flame-roasted peppers make this a compelling combination. **SERVES 4 TO 6**

4 large red bell peppers
1 can (2 ounces) anchovy fillets, drained
1 to 2 cloves roasted (see facing page) or
    raw garlic, minced
2 to 3 tablespoons fruity extra-virgin olive oil
2 tablespoons finely chopped flat-leaf parsley
Coarse salt (kosher or sea) and freshly ground
    black pepper

ADVANCE PREPARATION
The peppers can be grilled up to a day ahead.

1 Set up the grill for direct grilling and preheat it to high. There is no need to brush or oil the grate.

2 Arrange the bell peppers on the hot grate and grill them until darkly browned and blistered on all sides, 3 to 4 minutes per side, 12 to 16 minutes in all, turning with tongs. Don't forget to grill the peppers on the tops and bottoms for 1 to 2 minutes. The idea is to char the skins completely. Transfer the charred peppers to a cutting board and let them cool to room temperature. (No, you don't need to place them in a paper bag or bowl covered with plastic wrap. I've found no appreciable difference in ease of peeling.)

3 Using a paring knife, scrape the charred skins off the peppers. There's no need to remove every last bit; a few black spots will add color and flavor. Cut each pepper in half, remove the core, and scrape out the seeds. Cut each pepper half in half again lengthwise.

4 Arrange the pieces of pepper on a platter or plates. Arrange the anchovy fillets in a decorative pattern on top. Sprinkle the peppers with chopped garlic and drizzle olive oil over them. Sprinkle the parsley over the peppers (this is essential to neutralize the pungency of the garlic) and season them with salt and black pepper to taste, taking into account that the anchovies are quite salty already. Serve at once.

How to Roast Garlic

Roasted garlic is one of those equations in which one plus one equals three. You take a single ingredient: garlic. You apply a single cooking technique: roasting, which can be done on the grill using the indirect method, or in the oven. You wind up with something so richly and deeply flavorful, you can scarcely believe it comes from a single ingredient. Roasting garlic mutes its nose-jarring pungency while intensifying and caramelizing its natural sweetness. It's the sort of stuff you want to keep on hand in the refrigerator (in a jar with just enough olive oil to cover the garlic), so you can spread it on bruschetta or on a grilled veal chop at a moment's notice.

To roast garlic, set up the grill for indirect grilling and preheat it to medium (350°F). Place a whole head of garlic with its skin intact in the center of the grill away from the heat and cover the grill. Roast the garlic until the skin is lightly browned and the cloves feel squeezably soft, about 30 minutes. Alternatively, you can roast the garlic indoors on a piece of aluminum foil in an oven preheated 350°F. You can also roast individual cloves of garlic (again, with their skins intact); the cooking time will be about 15 minutes.

When you want to use the garlic, simply peel off the papery skin or cut the top off and squeeze out the roasted garlic (it's rather like squeezing a tube of toothpaste).

Bell Pepper Salad with Capers and Pine Nuts

{ PEPERONI AI FERRI CON CAPPERI E PINOLI }

Roasted peppers loom so large on America's culinary landscape now, it's hard to believe there was a time when we ignored their very existence. I didn't get my first taste until a trip through the southern half of Italy. (I was trying to retrace the path of the Crusades during a postgraduate research grant to study medieval cooking.) Today, everyone roasts peppers, but until you've done it on the grill—and in particular, until you've roasted the peppers caveman style, directly on the embers—you haven't fully experienced how much burning (and I mean burning) a food can broaden and deepen its flavor. **SERVES 4 TO 6**

THE SCOOP

WHERE: Italy

WHAT: A sweet-sour salad of flame-charred bell peppers with currants for sweetness, capers for tang, and pine nuts for crunch

HOW: Direct grilling

Giorgina Mazero, chef at Da Ivo in Venice, drizzles extra-virgin olive oil over a grilled pepper salad. Italian grilling is simplicity raised to the level of art.

JUST THE FACTS:
In the Italian countryside, the bell peppers would be roasted on a charcoal grill. In the city, most people roast the peppers directly on a stove burner. My personal favorite method for roasting the peppers (decidedly un-Italian) is to place them directly on the embers—without the grill grate. When it comes to imparting a smoky flavor to the peppers, nothing beats roasting in the embers.

4 large bell peppers (I like a mix of colors: red, yellow, orange, and/or green)

2 to 3 tablespoons best-quality extra-virgin olive oil

1 tablespoon best-quality balsamic vinegar

3 tablespoons pine nuts, toasted golden brown (see box)

3 tablespoons currants

1 tablespoon capers (optional), drained

1 tablespoon finely chopped flat-leaf parsley (optional)

Coarse salt (kosher or sea), preferably, and freshly ground black pepper

ADVANCE PREPARATION

The peppers can be grilled up to a day ahead.

1 Set up the grill for direct grilling and preheat it to high. There is no need to brush or oil the grate.

2 Arrange the bell peppers on the hot grate and grill them until darkly browned and blistered on all sides, 3 to 4 minutes per side, 12 to 16 minutes in all, turning with tongs. Don't forget to grill the peppers on the tops and bottoms for 1 to 2 minutes. The idea is to char the skins completely. Transfer the charred peppers to a cutting board and let them cool to room temperature. (No, you don't need to place them in a paper bag or bowl covered with plastic wrap. I've found no appreciable difference in ease of peeling.)

3 Using a paring knife, scrape the charred skins off the peppers. There's no need to remove every last bit; a few black spots will add color and flavor. Cut each pepper in half, remove the core, and scrape out the seeds. Cut each pepper lengthwise into ¼-inch strips (or into whatever shape you fancy).

4 Arrange the peppers in a shallow bowl or on a platter. Drizzle the olive oil and balsamic vinegar over the peppers. Sprinkle the pine nuts and currants and the capers and parsley, if using, on top. The salad can be prepared to this stage up to 2 hours ahead.

5 Right before serving, season the salad with salt and black pepper to taste. You do this at the last minute so you get to bite into the salt crystals before they completely dissolve.

How to Toast Nuts and Seeds

Toasting brings out a richer flavor in nuts and seeds. There are two easy ways to do this: Set a dry skillet over medium heat (do not use a nonstick skillet for this). Add the nuts or seeds and heat them until lightly toasted and aromatic, 3 to 5 minutes, shaking the skillet occasionally. Keep an eye on them—you don't want the nuts or seeds to burn. Transfer the toasted nuts or seeds to a heatproof plate to cool.

You can also toast nuts and seeds in a preheated 350°F oven. Spread them out on a rimmed baking sheet and bake them until lightly browned, five to ten minutes. Again, watch carefully to avoid burning.

This works equally well for almonds, walnuts, pine nuts, sesame seeds, and the like, as well as for bread crumbs.

HOW TO PREPARE A GRILLED PEPPER

1. *Place the pepper on the grate or directly on the coals and grill until the skin is charred and blackened on all sides.*

2. *Scrape off the burned skin with a paring knife. It's not necessary to remove every last bit. A few black spots add color and flavor.*

3. *Cut out and discard the stem end.*

4. *Cut open the pepper, lay it flat, and scrape out the seeds.*

5. *Using a paring knife, cut out the veins.*

6. *Cut the peppers into ¼-inch strips.*

Bell Pepper Salad with Capers and Pine Nuts (page 67): simple ingredients, bold flavors.

Grilled Eggplant Salad
{ MELITZANOSALATA }

Visit a Greek *taverna* (a sort of cross between a bar and a café) at the end of the day and you'll find an eye-popping array of dips, salads, fritters, and other appetizers served with glasses of ouzo or Greek wine. Welcome to mezes, the Greek answer to Spanish tapas or Italian *cicchetti*. And at least one of those mezes tastes best grilled: *melitzanosalata*, eggplant salad scented with fresh dill and mint. Grilled eggplant salads turn up across

THE SCOOP

WHERE: Greece

WHAT: Baba ghanoush Greek-style—grilled chopped eggplant with lemon, fresh dill, and mint

HOW: Direct grilling

JUST THE FACTS:
Choose long slender eggplants, which give you the highest ratio of charred skin—and thus smoke flavor—to flesh. The small oval eggplants sold in Italian markets (3 to 4 ounces each) most closely resemble the ones used in Greece.

To get the full effect of this salad, you must use fresh dill and fresh mint.

Planet Barbecue, especially in the Mediterranean basin and Middle and Near East. There's a simple reason for their universal appeal: The eggplant has a sort of built-in smoker—all you need to do is char it in the skin. This can be done on a grill grate, on a bed of glowing embers, or even on one of the burners of your stove. The spongy eggplant flesh readily absorbs the ensuing smoke flavors, resulting in flavors as bold as Greek cuisine itself.

SERVES 4

1 pound eggplant (ideally, small slender eggplants)

1 clove garlic, minced

Coarse salt (kosher or sea) and freshly ground black pepper

1 tablespoon finely chopped fresh dill

1 tablespoon finely chopped fresh mint

1 tablespoon finely chopped flat-leaf parsley, or more dill or mint

1 scallion, both white and green parts, trimmed and minced

3 tablespoons extra-virgin olive oil, preferably Greek, plus oil for the pita breads

1 tablespoon fresh lemon juice, or more to taste

1 tablespoon red wine vinegar

4 pita breads, for serving

Lemon wedges, for serving

A produce seller on Milos in the Cyclades Islands in Greece.

ADVANCE PREPARATION
None, however, the eggplants can be grilled up to a day ahead.

1 Set up the grill for direct grilling and preheat it to high.

2 When ready to cook, brush the grill grate. Arrange the eggplants on the hot grate and grill them until the skins are completely charred (they should be crisp and black), 3 to 4 minutes per side, 9 to 12 minutes in all, depending on the size of the eggplants. Transfer the eggplants to a baking sheet to cool.

3 Using a paring knife, scrape the charred skin off each eggplant. Don't worry about removing every last bit of black skin; a few specks will add color and flavor. Coarsely or finely chop the eggplant.

4 Place the garlic, ½ teaspoon of salt, and ¼ teaspoon of pepper in the bottom of a nonreactive mixing bowl and mash to a paste with the back of a wooden spoon. Add the chopped eggplant, dill, mint, parsley, and scallion and stir to mix. Stir in 2 tablespoons of the olive oil and the lemon juice and wine vinegar. Taste for seasoning, adding more salt, pepper, and/or lemon juice as necessary; the eggplant salad should be piquant and highly seasoned.

5 Transfer the salad to a serving bowl and drizzle the remaining 1 tablespoon of olive oil over the top. Serve the salad with pita and lemon wedges (if you like, brush the pita with olive oil and grill it as described on page 91).

Grilled Eggplant Salad with Jerusalem Flavors

After a day prowling the grill stalls and *shawarma* parlors around Jerusalem's Mahane Yehuda market, you begin to crave a proper restaurant with white tablecloths and a bona fide chef. Head for Arcadia, one of the pioneers of what might be termed the "new" Israeli cuisine. Some call the food here Israeli-French fusion; I call it a tasteful reinvention of traditional Israeli and Middle Eastern cuisines. You enter Arcadia through a narrow alley that leads to a courtyard with a canopy of trees. There you can dine as did the ancient Hebrews, Romans, Christians, Arabs, and other conquerors of Jerusalem—in the open air under the stars. Of course, this being the Middle East, even highfalutin restaurants have wood-burning grills, and while you couldn't ask for more succulent grilled lamb or fresher grilled seafood (don't miss the sweet, mild John Dory if it's available), what really makes me miss Arcadia is a deceptively simple-sounding appetizer called "eggplant carpaccio." You'll recognize it as a deconstructed, reconstructed version of the grilled eggplant dips and salads prevalent throughout the region—fire-charred eggplant counterpointed by smoky tomato sauce, nutty tahini (sesame seed paste), creamy yogurt, and crunchy walnuts. Think of it as the Middle East on a salad plate. **SERVES 4**

The fruit of the vine and grilled meat: Two biblical gifts from the Holy Land.

Vegetable stalls at the Mahane Yehuda market in West Jerusalem, Israel.

GRILLED EGGPLANT SALAD WITH JERUSALEM FLAVORS | page 71

4 small eggplants (3 to 4 ounces each)

2 luscious, red ripe tomatoes

2 tablespoons extra-virgin olive oil

3 tablespoons fresh lemon juice, or more
    to taste

Coarse salt (kosher or sea) and freshly ground
    black pepper

½ clove garlic, minced

¼ cup tahini

½ cup plain thick Greek or Middle Eastern-style yogurt

¼ cup walnuts, lightly toasted (see page 68) and coarsely
    chopped

¼ cup coarsely chopped flat-leaf parsley

Pita bread, for serving (see page 91)

ADVANCE PREPARATION

The eggplants and tomatoes can be grilled several hours ahead.

1 Set up the grill for direct grilling and preheat it to high.

2 When ready to cook, brush and oil the grill grate. Arrange the eggplants and tomatoes on the hot grate and grill them until the skins are blackened; 3 to 4 minutes per side, 9 to 12 minutes in all for the eggplants and about 2 minutes per side, 6 to 8 minutes in all for the tomatoes. The eggplants should be cooked all the way through (they will be easy to pierce with a skewer). The tomatoes should be charred on the outside but remain raw inside. Transfer the grilled eggplants and tomatoes to an aluminum foil pan to cool to room temperature.

3 Using a paring knife, scrape any really burned skin off the tomatoes; a few black spots will add flavor. Puree the tomatoes in a food processor. Add the olive oil and 1 tablespoon of lemon juice. Taste for seasoning, adding salt and pepper to taste and more lemon juice as necessary; the sauce should be highly seasoned. Set the tomato sauce aside.

4 Place the garlic and ¼ teaspoon of salt in a mixing bowl and mash to a paste with the back of a wooden spoon. Add the tahini and whisk to mix. Whisk in ¼ cup of water (the sauce will thin), followed by 2 tablespoons of lemon juice (the sauce will thicken). Taste for the seasoning, adding more lemon juice and/or salt as necessary. Set the tahini sauce aside.

5 Using a paring knife, scrape any really burned skin off the eggplants and cut the flesh into ½-inch dice. Season the eggplant with salt and pepper to taste.

6 To assemble the salad, spoon pools of tomato sauce on 4 plates or a platter. Mound the eggplant in the center. Spoon circles (puddles) of tahini sauce on the tomato sauce around the eggplant. Spoon the yogurt over the eggplant and top it with the walnuts and parsley. Serve at once with pita bread—it's the Middle East on a plate.

A traditional Middle Eastern street café in the holy Israeli city of Safed.

Israel: From the Biblical to the Modern Grill

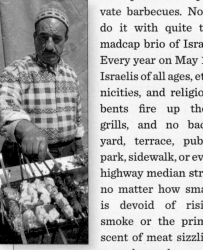

Many countries celebrate their independence day with public and private barbecues. None do it with quite the madcap brio of Israel. Every year on May 14, Israelis of all ages, ethnicities, and religious bents fire up their grills, and no backyard, terrace, public park, sidewalk, or even highway median strip, no matter how small, is devoid of rising smoke or the primal scent of meat sizzling over charcoal.

Take your pick from a variety of kebabs offered by street grillers in the Old City, Jerusalem.

Israeli barbecue has certainly been a long time in the making. Animal sacrifice (roasting whole carcasses over wood fires) abounded in biblical times. According to the Roman historian Flavius Josephus, Jerusalem's Jews sacrificed more than 250,000 lambs during a twelve-month period around A.D. 70. The Old Testament offers precise instructions on the best beast to sacrifice for a particular occasion (the roster includes cattle, sheep, goats, pigeons, and even turtledoves); the preferred cut of meat and seasoning (the Almighty seems to have had a

penchant for kidney fat and flank fat seasoned with sea salt), and even the proper wood for building the fire.

Many of our most often-told Bible stories involve live fire. Cain's troubles started, for example, when he offered God the first fruits from his garden (Jehovah preferred a fatted beast from Abel's flock). When Noah found dry land on which to dock his ark, he thanked God with a sacrificial grill session. Abraham's sacrifice of his first-born son, Isaac, was prevented when a ram conveniently appeared and was killed and roasted on the pyre instead. To this day, lamb remains the preferred grilled meat of many Israelis.

What you grill in Israel depends on where your parents or grandparents came from and, as almost everyone in Israel is an immigrant or is

The Mediterranean Grill's Eastern Outpost

Israel has been home to dozens of civilizations. Here are the remains of an early Roman viaduct.

Israel—grilling at the eastern edge of the Mediterranean.

Jerusalem and the Dome of the Rock. A holy place for Muslims, Christians, and Jews, who would probably get along better if they debated barbecue instead of religion.

descended from immigrants, Israeli barbecue is some of the most diverse in the world. Russian Jews relish *shashlik* (onion-blasted shish kebab; see page 248); Moroccan Jews make *méchoui* (spit-roasted lamb, page 272), Bulgarian Jews devour cumin- and onion-scented burgers. Arab Israelis crank up the heat for *kofta* (mincemeat kebabs), *shish toufic* (cinnamon-scented chicken kebabs), and pita bread grilled with *za'atar* (wild thyme and sesame).

Cooking pita bread in a traditional wood-fired oven at the Abulafia bakery in Jaffa, Israel.

Men grill meat at a festival honoring Rabbi Baba Sali in Netivot in the Negev, Israel.

Some dishes have transcended their ethnic roots to become national specialties, like *shawarma*—spiced lamb, chicken, or turkey roasted on a vertical rotisserie and thinly sliced onto pita (you can read all about it on page 409). Grilled John Dory and other Mediterranean fish turn up at Tunisian restaurants in Tel Aviv's old port district, Jaffa, and at the waterfront restaurants on Lake Tiberias. And no trip to Tel Aviv is complete without sampling another unique Israeli specialty, invented by a grill master from Azerbaijan and served at the landmark restaurant, Avazi: grilled foie gras.

THE GRILLS: The basic Israeli grill is the *mangal*—a rectangular metal box with charcoal at the bottom and flat metal skewers or grill baskets stretched across the open top. *Shawarma* is cooked on a vertical rotisserie similar to the device used by Greeks to cook a gyro.

THE FUELS: Natural lump charcoal is the fuel of choice, but some people use propane.

THE FLAVORINGS: Visit an open air food market, like Tel Aviv's Ha'Carmel, and you'll see just how serious Israelis are about their barbecue spices. The most popular is a sort of Yemeni rub called *hawaij*. The formula varies from vendor to vendor; the main ingredients are turmeric, cumin, and black pepper. Onion, garlic, lemon, mint, cumin, coriander, and sumac figure prominently in Israeli Arab grilling.

MUST TRY DISHES:

Baba ghanoush: Flame-charred eggplant dip

Kofta: Ground meat kebab

Shawarma: The Israeli version of a Greek gyro or Turkish doner: thin slices of lamb, chicken, or turkey cooked in a large roast on a vertical spit.

Shipardim is the generic Hebrew term for shish kebab. Many Israelis of Russian or Balkan descent use the Russian term, *shashlik*.

Grilled fish from the Mediterranean or Lake Tiberias (aka the Sea of Galilee)

Grilled spring chicken, spatchcocked and seasoned with Yemeni grilling spices

THE CONDIMENTS: Traditional accompaniments to Israeli barbecue include lemon wedges; sumac; onion and parsley relish (see page 319); and a variety of salads and pickles, especially pickled eggplants and cucumber. Tahini (sesame seed paste) is enjoyed by Israelis who keep kosher, as they're not supposed to serve yogurt or other dairy products with meat. *Z'hûg*, a fiery Yemenite chile sauce, supplies the heat.

HOW TO EAT IT: Piled on pita bread with all of the aforementioned salads and condiments

THE MOST SINGULAR DISH IN THE REPERTORY: The smoked egg pâté served at the Auberge Shulamit in Rosh Pina overlooking the Sea of Galilee. You can read about it on page 13.

Filipino Grilled Eggplant Salad

THE SCOOP

WHERE: Philippines

WHAT: Vegetable salad Manila style—made with grilled eggplant, peppers, and shrimp paste

HOW: Direct grilling

JUST THE FACTS: There are two ways to approach the salad. To be authentic, you'd use three somewhat exotic ingredients, described in the box on the facing page, that are available at Asian markets in North America. The other way is to make it using substitute ingredients that are readily available and within your comfort zone. Either will give you a salad with an astonishing range of flavors.

Grilled eggplant salads are a constant on the barbecue trail (for some more examples, see pages 69 and 71). The reason is simple—only one other vegetable tastes this good when you burn it (that would be peppers, another ingredient in this salad). I like to think of this salad as a Filipino-grilled Caesar: Like a Caesar salad, it contains egg (one-hundred-year-old egg, to be precise); like a Caesar it contains a salty fish product (shrimp paste instead of anchovies); and like a Caesar it offers a panoply of textures and flavors. But, unlike a Caesar, you can make it ahead of time. Here's how this explosively flavorful salad is prepared by Manila chef Mike Profeta.

SERVES 4 TO 6

1 pound Asian eggplants (see Note)
2 Anaheim peppers, or 1 poblano pepper
2 green or ripe mangoes
One 100-year-old egg, or 2 hard-cooked eggs
    (optional)
1 large or 2 medium-size luscious, red ripe
    tomatoes, seeded and cut into
    ¼-inch dice
½ medium-size sweet onion, cut into
    ¼-inch dice
1 to 2 small hot chiles, such as Thai bird chiles,
    seeded and minced (for a hotter salad,
    leave the seeds in)
¼ cup vegetable oil
3 cloves garlic, thinly sliced crosswise
1 teaspoon bagoong (Filipino shrimp paste,
    see box, facing page; optional), or 2 anchovy
    fillets (also optional)
2 tablespoons fresh lime juice, or more
    to taste
1 tablespoon rice vinegar, or more lime juice
½ cup loosely packed chopped fresh cilantro
Coarse salt (kosher or sea) and freshly ground
    black pepper (a lot)

Asian eggplants: their long slender shape maximizes the surface area exposed to the fire.

ADVANCE PREPARATION

The vegetables can be grilled and the salad prepped up to a day ahead.

1 Set up the grill for direct grilling and preheat it to high.

2 When ready to cook, brush and oil the grill grate. Arrange the eggplants and pepper(s) on the hot grate. Grill the eggplants until the skins are charred and blistered on all sides and the flesh is soft (the eggplants will be easy to pierce with a skewer), about 2 minutes per side, 6 to 8 minutes in all. Grill the peppers until the skins are darkly browned and blistered, about 2 minutes per side, 6 to 8 minutes in all. To ensure even cooking, turn the vegetables with tongs as they grill.

3 Transfer the grilled vegetables to a platter to cool. Scrape off most of the burnt skin, discarding any stems. Cut the peppers in half, remove the core, and scrape out the seeds. Cut the vegetables into ¼-inch dice. Transfer the diced vegetables to a nonreactive mixing bowl.

4 Peel the mangoes. Cut the flesh off the pits, then cut it into ¼-inch dice. Cut the egg(s), if using, into ¼-inch dice. Add the diced mango, egg, tomato(es), onion, and chile(s) to the diced eggplant and peppers.

5 Heat the oil in a small skillet over medium heat. Add the garlic and cook until lightly browned, 1 to 2 minutes. Using a skimmer, transfer the fried garlic to a plate lined with paper towels to drain. Remove 2 tablespoons of garlic oil from the pan and place it in a small heatproof bowl to cool. Add the shrimp paste or anchovies, if using, to the oil remaining in the skillet and cook until fragrant and browned, about 1 minute. Transfer the shrimp paste or anchovies to the paper towels to drain. Discard the oil in the pan.

6 To assemble the salad, add most of the garlic chips to the bowl with the eggplant. Add the 2 tablespoons of garlic oil, the lime juice, rice vinegar, and most of the cilantro and stir to mix. Season with salt and black pepper to taste; the salad should be highly seasoned. Transfer the salad to an attractive serving bowl. Sprinkle the remaining cilantro and garlic chips on top. Crumble the fried shrimp paste or anchovies on top, if using. Serve the salad at once.

NOTE: Asian eggplants are longer and skinnier than their western cousins, which makes them ideal for charring in the skins. Look for them at Asian markets and many supermarkets.

A Taste of Asia

Green mango adds a welcome crunch and tartness to the Filipino Grilled Eggplant Salad. You can find green mangoes at Asian markets, however, the musky fruitiness of ripe mango gives you an equally remarkable result.

Hundred-year-old eggs are preserved duck eggs: black on the outside, sulfurous in flavor (in a good way, the way a well-aged cheese might be) and "rubbery" in a manner that complements the crunch, chew, and moistness of the other ingredients in this salad. No, they're not really one hundred years old, they just look that way after curing for a month in lime. A regular hard-boiled egg would work fine.

Bagoong is fermented shrimp paste, a salty, fishy condiment related to Thai *trasi* and Malaysian *belacan,* that tastes better than it smells. Sure, it sounds weird for salads—until you pause to think about the anchovies we add to Caesar salad. Anchovies make an interesting substitute. However, it's fine to omit the shrimp paste or anchovies entirely.

Grilled Chicken Salad with Chiles and Coconut

{ KELAGUEN }

THE SCOOP

WHERE: Guam, Saipan, and other islands in the South Pacific

WHAT: Not your usual chicken salad: flame-seared diced chicken with shredded fresh coconut, spiced up with chiles, scallions, and lemon

HOW: Direct or indirect grilling

JUST THE FACTS: Traditionally the chicken is grilled. One day, I smoked it instead and what started as an excellent salad to begin with became a phenomenon—one of the top ten dishes I've tasted on Planet Barbecue.

Guam—where the sun first rises on American barbecue. That's the motto of the Guam Bar-B-Q Federation and it serves as a reminder that, while Kansas City or the Texas Hill Country grab the headlines for their ribs and smoked brisket, the world of American barbecue extends to the opposite side of the earth. Here's a chicken salad from Guam barbecue expert Steven Cruz that's definitely not like what you grew up with—unless you grew up on this tiny tropical island in the South Pacific. There are just two main ingredients: grilled chicken and freshly grated coconut, along with vivifying doses of lemon juice and chiles. But unless the chicken is freshly grilled, the coconut is freshly grated, and the lemon freshly squeezed, you won't get the full mouth-blasting pleasure of smoke, crunch, and tartness. **SERVES 4**

Grilled chicken salad with shredded fresh coconut, chiles, and lime.

1 chicken (3½ to 4 pounds, for 2½ to 3 cups of shredded cooked meat)

Coarse salt (kosher or sea) and freshly ground black pepper

1 ripe (hard) coconut, shredded, (for about 2½ cups shredded coconut, see the box on the facing page)

2 scallions, both white and green parts, trimmed and thinly sliced crosswise

2 to 6 fresh hot red chiles, such as Thai chiles or red serrano peppers, thinly sliced crosswise

½ cup fresh lemon juice, or more to taste

2 large or 4 small flour tortillas, warmed on the grill or in the oven and cut into wedges

YOU'LL ALSO NEED

2 cups wood chips, soaked for 1 hour in water to cover, then drained

ADVANCE PREPARATION

While the chicken can be grilled or smoked up to a day ahead, you'll get the best flavor if you grill it only a few hours before serving.

1 Spatchcock the chicken (see page 370) or cut it in half lengthwise. Season the chicken generously all over with salt and black pepper.

2 To grill: You have a couple of options here. On Guam, they traditionally grill the chicken using the direct method and to be authentic, you'd use charcoal. The indirect method is less prone to flare-ups and the chicken is less likely to burn. You can also smoke the chicken in a smoker; follow the manufacturer's instructions.

If you are using the direct method, set up the grill for direct grilling and preheat it to medium. When ready to cook, brush and oil the grill grate. If you are using a charcoal grill, toss the wood chips or chunks on the coals. If you are using a gas grill, add the wood chips or chunks to the smoker box or place them in a smoker pouch under the grate (see page 603). Place the chicken on the hot grate skin side down and grill it until nicely browned and cooked through, 15 to 20 minutes per side, moving the chicken as needed to dodge any flare-ups.

How to Shred Fresh Coconut

First, you want to be sure the coconut you buy is fresh. Shake it to hear if the water sloshes around inside. A dry coconut is often rancid.

Open the coconut following Steps 1 to 3 in the photo instructions on this page. (You can save the coconut water for cocktails.) Using a hammer, break the coconut into pieces. Using a blunt butter knife or clean screwdriver, pry the coconut from the shell pieces. Using a vegetable peeler, remove the brown skin from the meat, then shred the coconut in a food processor fitted with a coarse shredding disk.

Sound too complicated? Buy a coconut grater at an Indian or Asian market. It looks like a citrus reamer with a crank handle (see photos, Step 4). I know this sounds like a lot of work, but believe me, the sweet crunch of fresh coconut is eminently worth it.

HOW TO OPEN A COCONUT

1. Tap the coconut around its circumference with the back of a cleaver, working over a bowl.

2. Once the shell cracks, ease it open to drain out the liquid inside.

3. Pull apart the coconut halves.

4. Grate the white coconut meat out of the shell, turning the crank of a rotary coconut grater.

If you are using the indirect method, set up the grill for indirect grilling, place a drip pan in the center, and preheat the grill to medium. When ready to cook, if you are using a charcoal grill, toss the wood chips or chunks on the coals. If you are using a gas grill, add the wood chips or chunks to the smoker box or place them in a smoker pouch under the grate (see page 603). Arrange the chicken skin side up in the center of the grate over the drip pan and away from the heat. Cover the grill and grill the chicken until browned and cooked through, about 40 minutes.

3 To check for doneness, use an instant-read meat thermometer, inserting it into the thickest part of a thigh but not touching the bone. When done, the internal temperature should be about 165°F.

4 Transfer the grilled chicken to a cutting board and let it cool to room temperature. Remove the crisp brown chicken skin and eat it when no one is looking. Cut the chicken meat off the bone and shred or finely dice it. Place the chicken in a large nonreactive mixing bowl. The recipe can be prepared to this stage up to 24 hours ahead. Refrigerate it, covered, until ready to use.

5 Add the shredded coconut to the chicken followed by the scallions, chiles, and lemon juice and toss to mix. Taste for seasoning, adding salt and black pepper to taste and more lemon juice as necessary; the salad should be highly seasoned.

6 Transfer the salad to an attractive platter or bowl and serve at once, with the tortilla wedges for scooping.

Grilled Breads

Given the staunchly carnivorous appetites of our prehistoric ancestors (there's a reason they were known as hunter-gatherers), you may be surprised to learn that one of the first documented freestanding barbecue pits was actually used to cook bread. The year was 2600 B.C.E. (give or take a few centuries); the place, the Ganganagar district in Rajasthan, India; the device, a tall, urn-shaped, charcoal-burning clay cooker that looked remarkably like a modern Indian tandoor. Thanks to its unique thermodynamics, dough slapped on its thick clay walls was cooked by both radiant and direct heat in a matter of seconds. The result: puffy, smoky flatbreads that were soft and moist in the center and crisp at the edges—the sort of bread we know and love today as Indian naan.

To most North Americans the notion of grilled bread may seem peripheral to barbecue, if not downright strange—until you stop to think about some of the world's great breads and bread dishes. Consider Italian bruschetta, fire-toasted bread rubbed with cut garlic, for example, which takes its name from *bruscare,* Italian for to burn (although burning is *not* what you want to do when you make it). Or Colombian *arepas,* South African *rooster brood* from the Cape Peninsula, Catalan *pa amb tomàquet* (tomato bread), or German Obersteiner "filet mignon" (grilled rye bread with herb butter). These are but a few of the world's

CLOCKWISE FROM TOP LEFT: *Rolling dough for Indian flatbread; Uzbek bread baking in a wood-burning oven; hot out of the tandoor; Vietnamese breakfast on a stick: grilled with butter and sugar; Indian naan, hot from the tandoor.*

great bread dishes, and no self-respecting local would cook them anywhere else but on the grill.

In this chapter, you'll learn how to make simple yeast doughs, the starting point for *pide* (Turkish flatbread and the etymological cousin of Middle Eastern pita), as well as for the Indian naan and *lachha paratha.* You'll also learn how to use the grill as a sort of primal toaster to make Italian crostini, Vietnamese sweet toast, and grilled cheese sandwiches from South Africa.

Dough on the fire. Bread on the grill. We're just warming up on Planet Barbecue.

Previous page: Toting an armload of fresh tandoor-baked naan in India.

Tuscan Grilled Toasts
{ CROSTINI AND BRUSCHETTA }

Grilled bread turns up all along the world's barbecue trail, often served as an appetizer, almost always hot off the grill. Italy has two great grilled bread appetizers: crostini and bruschetta. Crostini come with toppings; bruschetta tends to be served by itself (contrary to the way bruschetta is served in North America).

Crostini

Here are two crostini toppings from the heartland of Italian grilling, Tuscany. On page 85 you'll find a recipe for bruschetta. **MAKES 16 CROSTINI, 8 FOR EACH TOPPING**

TOPPING #1: CAVOLO NERO

2 bunches of kale, preferably black kale (about 1 pound)

3 tablespoons extra-virgin olive oil

2 cloves garlic, finely chopped

Coarse salt (kosher or sea) and freshly ground black pepper

TOPPING #2: PATE DI FEGATO

2 tablespoons (¼ stick) unsalted butter, or 2 tablespoons olive oil

1 shallot, or ¼ medium-size onion, finely chopped

4 tablespoons finely chopped fresh flat-leaf parsley

½ pound chicken livers, trimmed of any sinew, fat or green spots

Freshly ground black pepper and perhaps a little fine sea salt

½ cup dry white wine

1 tablespoon drained capers

1 anchovy fillet (optional), finely chopped

FOR THE CROSTINI

8 slices of Italian bread (½ inch thick), cut in half crosswise, or 16 slices of baguette (½ inch thick)

ADVANCE PREPARATION

The toppings can be prepared several hours ahead and refrigerated, covered.

1 Make *Topping #1: Cavolo nero:* Rinse the kale. Cut out and discard the thick stems. Pile the kale leaves on top of one another, a half dozen leaves at a time, and starting at the side, roll them up tightly. Using a chef's knife, cut the kale crosswise into ¼-inch-wide strips. Open the strips up with your fingers.

Heat the extra-virgin olive oil in a large skillet over high heat. Add the garlic and cook until fragrant but not brown, about 1 minute. Stir in the kale and cook it until soft but not mushy, 2 to 4 minutes. Season the kale with salt and pepper to taste; it should be highly seasoned. Set the *cavolo nero* aside.

Bread, olives, and olive oil—staples of the Italian good life.

Make *Topping #2: Pâté di fegato*: Melt the butter in a large skillet over medium heat. Add the shallot and 2 tablespoons of the parsley and cook until the shallot begins to brown, about 3 minutes. Season the chicken livers with pepper to taste and perhaps a little salt (remember, the capers and anchovy, if any, will be salty).

Increase the heat to high, add the chicken livers to the skillet, and cook them until they are done to rare, 3 to 5 minutes, turning them with a wooden spoon. Add the white wine, capers, and anchovy, if using, and let boil until most of the wine has evaporated, about 3 minutes. Remove the pan from the heat and let the liver mixture cool to room temperature.

Coarsely puree the liver mixture in a food processor, running the machine in short bursts. Taste for seasoning, adding more salt and/or pepper as necessary.

2 Make the crostini: Set up the grill for direct grilling and preheat it to medium-high.

3 When ready to cook, brush and oil the grill grate. Arrange the slices of bread on the hot grate and grill them until toasted and golden brown, 1 to 2 minutes per side. Watch the bread carefully; it can burn quickly.

4 Spread the topping of choice on each slice of toasted bread. Sprinkle the liver crostini with the remaining 2 tablespoons of parsley. Serve at once.

Bruschetta

Bruschetta (pronounced bru-SKET-ta) is the granddaddy of garlic bread. (*Bruscare* is Italian for to burn.) A traditionalist in Tuscany would be perplexed by the toasts topped with tomato salad that masquerade as bruschetta in North America. The authentic version consists of saltless Tuscan bread toasted on the grill, rubbed with pungent cut raw garlic, drizzled with fruity olive oil, and sprinkled with crunchy crystals of sea salt. Simple? Yes. But, done right, this becomes one of the world's great grilled breads. **MAKES 8 SLICES**

8 slices of bread (½ inch thick), preferably saltless Tuscan bread (see Note)
4 cloves garlic, cut in half crosswise
4 to 6 tablespoons of the best Tuscan extra-virgin olive oil money can buy, in a cruet
Coarse crystals of sea salt, such as French fleur de sel, in a small bowl

ADVANCE PREPARATION
None

1 Set up the grill for direct grilling and preheat it to medium-high. In the best of circumstances, you'll be grilling over wood embers; the wood imparts a delicate smoke flavor (see page 601 for instructions).

2 When ready to cook, brush and oil the grill grate. Arrange the slices of bread on the hot grate and grill them until toasted and golden brown, 1 to 2 minutes per side. Watch the bread carefully; it can burn quickly.

3 To eat, rub each slice of grilled bread with the cut side of a half garlic clove, drizzle olive oil over the bread, then sprinkle it with salt. Take a bite—sometimes, nothing beats complex flavors like simplicity.

NOTE: Tradition calls for grilling saltless Tuscan bread, a loaf that will strike you as a mistake on the part of the baker, until you taste it grilled and crusted with sea salt. Look for Tuscan bread at Italian markets or use regular Italian bread and less salt.

Grilled Greek Bread with Oregano

THE SCOOP

WHERE: The Greek
island of Kea in the
Cyclades

WHAT: The Greek
version of bruschetta—
bread grilled with olive
oil and oregano

HOW: Direct grilling

JUST THE FACTS:
If you live in an area with
a large Greek community,
you can find Greek white
bread, recognizable by
its sesame seed–dotted
hard crust. Italian bread
or semolina bread would
make a good substitute.

Dried Greek oregano
has a lemony tang and
an aromatic sweetness;
look for it at Greek
markets, where it's
generally sold in bunches.
Rub the bunch between
the palms of your hands
over a large bowl to shake
off the leaves. You can
also buy high-quality
dried Greek oregano
from such specialty
grocers as Dean & Deluca
(www.DeanDeLuca.com).

Grilled bread turns up throughout Europe—see the crostini on page 83, Obersteiner "Filet Mignon" on page 88, and the *pa amb tomàquet* on page 90. Here's the Greek rendition, traditionally served with *païdakia* (grilled lamb chops) and spit-roasted whole hog. I first tasted it on the island of Kea. The contrast of fragrant oregano and smoky grilled bread is a knockout. **SERVES 8**

1 large or 2 small loaves of Greek bread or crusty
   sesame bread
¼ cup extra-virgin olive oil, preferably Greek
¼ cup crumbled dried Greek oregano
Coarse salt (kosher or sea) and freshly ground
   black pepper

YOU'LL ALSO NEED
A grill basket (optional)

ADVANCE PREPARATION
None

1 Set up the grill for direct grilling and preheat it to medium-high.

 2 Cut the bread crosswise into ½-inch-thick slices. Lightly brush each slice on both sides with the olive oil. Season each slice of bread on both sides with the oregano and salt and pepper to taste.

3 When ready to cook, brush and oil the grill grate. Arrange the slices of bread on the hot grate and grill them until toasted and golden brown, 1 to 2 minutes per side. (If you're working on an open fire without a grate, you can grill the bread in a grill basket.) Watch the bread carefully; it can burn quickly. Serve the bread at once.

Approaching the island of Kea in the Greek Cyclades.

Grilled Breads Around the World

What do Colombian *arepas,* Italian bruschetta, Indian naan, and Spanish *pa amb tomàquet* have in common? All are breads cooked in a barbecue pit or directly over the fire on the grill. Grilled bread may seem like a relatively new concept in North America, but the act of cooking bread directly over live fire is almost as old as barbecue—and dare I say—humanity itself.

The first breads were simple flour and water flatbreads cooked on flame-heated stones next to a fire, a technique that survives today in Indian *chapati* (a whole wheat flour flatbread). Next came yeasted breads cooked directly on the walls of an urn-shaped clay vessel that has been used in what is now India, Afghanistan, Iran, and Iraq for at least five thousand years. That was the original purpose of the tandoor—to cook bread—and what makes Indian *naan* so extraordinarily flavorful is that it's actually grilled on both sides at once: the bottom on the fire-heated clay walls of the tandoor; the top by the radiant heat of the coals.

The history of grilled bread also takes us to Italy, or more precisely to ancient Rome, where grilling took place on a sort of indoor raised hearth called a *focus.* Breads were roasted on the hot stones on the *focus;* today we call their lingustic descendants *focaccia.*

The grill was the original toaster and there isn't an electric toaster that can beat it for imparting a crusty, smoky flavor to toast. Here are some of the grilled breads you'll encounter as you travel around Planet Barbecue (there are also recipes for many of them in this chapter).

AREPAS: Flat, round cornmeal cakes grilled over charcoal fires in Colombia, Venezuela, and elsewhere in South America. Stuffed with cheese or slathered with salsa, *arepas* are a popular Colombian street snack and restaurant side dish.

BRUSCHETTA: Fire-toasted slices of saltless Tuscan bread rubbed with garlic and salt and drizzled with olive oil.

GRILLED PIZZA: Pioneered by the restaurant Al Forno in Providence, Rhode Island, and today enjoyed across North America and beyond: To make grilled pizza, you cook the dough directly on the grill grate, not on a pizza stone, then add the toppings.

NAAN AND LACHHA PARATHA: Indian flatbreads roasted on the walls of a tandoor. Naan, a simple bread made with flour, yeast, milk, and eggs, comes in a distinctive teardrop shape. *Lachha paratha* is a fire-roasted flatbread that owes its flaky layered consistency to a complex process of folding and rolling the dough.

OBERSTEINER "FILET MIGNON": Germany's grilled rye bread topped with herb butter

PAPADOM: A spicy Indian lentil flour flatbread toasted over charcoal braziers in Mumbai. You've probably had the fried version at Indian restaurants in North America.

QUESADILLA: Mexico's cheese-stuffed tortilla "sandwich," cooked on a *comal,* a flame-heated griddle, or directly over the coals.

PA AMB TOMAQUET: Catalan grilled tomato bread: Sliced grilled bread that is rubbed with garlic and fresh tomato, then drizzled with olive oil and sprinkled with salt. More elaborate versions come with anchovies, eggs, and/or sliced country ham.

ROOSTER BROOD: South African grilled bread—in some regions *rooster brood* consists simply of small, dinner roll–like knots of dough cooked on the grill. Elsewhere, it becomes a grilled cheese sandwich (literally) flavored with chutney, tomato, and onion.

Naan, *hot off the grill.*

Obersteiner "Filet Mignon"

Barbecue sparks fierce rivalries. In the sister towns of Idar-Oberstein, the grill-obsessed people in Idar believe their *spiessbraten*—onion-stuffed, spit-roasted pork (see page 206) to be vastly superior to what people in the neighboring town take off the grill. (The Obersteiners feel the same in reverse.) Rivalries require put-downs, and what better way to insult someone in this meat-loving part of Germany than to give the name of Obersteiner "Filet Mignon" to a humble slice of grilled bread? Well, there's grilled bread and there's grilled bread, and when you toast a slice of dark rich *bauernbrot* (rye bread—literally peasant bread) over a smoky beech wood fire and slather it with garlic-onion-parsley butter, you just might not miss the meat. **MAKES 8 SLICES**

½ clove garlic
1 tablespoon sweet onion, minced fine as dust
1 tablespoon minced fresh dill
1 tablespoon minced fresh flat-leaf parsley, or
    more dill
6 tablespoons (¾ stick) salted butter,
    at room temperature
Freshly ground white pepper
8 slices of dense rye bread (½ inch thick)

ADVANCE PREPARATION
The herb butter can be made up to a day ahead.

1 Crush the garlic in a garlic press or mince it, then mash it to a paste with the side of a knife. Place the garlic, onion, dill, parsley, if using, and butter in a mixing bowl and whisk until well combined. Season with white pepper to taste. Place the garlic herb butter in 4 ramekins for serving.

2 Set up the grill for direct grilling and preheat it to medium-high.

3 When ready to cook, brush and oil the grill grate. Arrange the slices of bread on the hot grate and grill them until toasted and browned, 1 to 2 minutes per side. Watch the bread carefully; it can burn quickly. Serve the grilled bread at once, hot off the grill with the garlic herb butter.

VARIATION
Steven's Version: Before grilling, spread the garlic herb butter on both sides of the slices of bread. Arrange the slathered bread on the hot grate and grill it until the butter is sizzling and the bread is toasted and browned, about 2 minutes per side.

Catalan "Bruschetta"

The French call it *convivialité*—the particular kind of comfort, warmth, and hospitality you experience when you dine at a restaurant like L'Hostalet de Vivès. You know, the sort of place where hungry eaters crowd around rustic wooden tables piled with oversize platters brimming with meats grilled in a centuries-old manorial fireplace. The sort of place where you can't help but talk to your neighbors, where wine bottles pass back and forth, and where even a modest lunch means you won't have to eat again until tomorrow. Located in a farmhouse in the hamlet of Vivès (near the artist town of Céret in southwestern France), L'Hostalet is a fifteen-minute drive from the Spanish border. You feel the Catalan influence everywhere—in the grilled lamb and rabbit topped with mega-garlicky aioli (garlic mayonnaise), in the stunningly rich Catalan cream for dessert (see page 586), and especially in this singular, plate-burying appetizer, which could double for a light lunch: grilled bread topped with grilled peppers, eggplant, and anchovies. **MAKES 4 SLICES**

2 red bell peppers

2 long slender eggplants (8 ounces each), or
    2 green bell peppers or additional red bell
    peppers

4 large slices of crusty country-style bread
    (about 8-inches long and ½-inch thick)

1 clove garlic, cut in half crosswise

1 luscious, red ripe tomato, cut in half crosswise

About 20 good-quality oil-packed anchovy fillets,
    drained and blotted dry

The best quality extra-virgin olive oil you can find

Coarse sea salt and freshly ground black pepper

2 tablespoons chopped fresh flat-leaf parsley

ADVANCE PREPARATION

You can certainly grill the peppers and eggplants ahead of time.

1 Set up the grill for direct grilling and preheat it to high. There is no need to brush or oil the grate.

2 Arrange the bell peppers on the hot grate and grill them until darkly browned and blistered on all sides, 3 to 4 minutes per side, 12 to 16 minutes in all, turning with tongs. Don't forget to grill the peppers on the tops and bottoms for 1 to 2 minutes. The idea is to char the skins completely. If you are using green bell peppers instead of the eggplant, grill them the same way. Transfer the charred peppers to a cutting board and let them cool to room temperature. (No, you don't need to place them in a paper bag or bowl covered with plastic wrap. I've found no appreciable difference in ease of peeling.) Leave the fire burning.

3 Arrange the eggplants on the hot grate and grill them until the skins are completely charred (they should be crisp and black), 3 to 4 minutes per side, 9 to 12 minutes in all. Transfer the grilled eggplants to the platter with the peppers.

4 Using a paring knife, scrape the charred skins off the bell peppers. There's no need to remove every last bit; a few black spots will add color and flavor. Cut each pepper in half, remove the core, and scrape out the seeds, then cut the peppers into ½-inch-wide strips. When the eggplants are cool, scrape off the charred skin and cut the flesh into strips the same size as the bell pepper strips. The recipe can be prepared several hours ahead up to this stage.

5 Just before you are ready to serve, set up the grill for direct grilling and preheat it to medium-high.

6 When ready to cook, brush and oil the grill grate. Arrange the slices of bread on the hot grate at a diagonal to the bars and grill them until darkly toasted on both sides, 1 to 2 minutes per side. Watch the bread carefully; it can burn quickly.

7 Transfer the grilled bread to a cloth-covered cutting board or plate (the cloth will absorb the steam, preventing the bread from becoming soggy). Rub each slice of bread on the top with the cut side of a half garlic clove, then with the cut side of a tomato half, pressing the tomato onto the bread so it absorbs the juices.

8 Top each slice of bread with alternating rows of bell pepper, eggplant, and anchovy; the more colorful the arrangement, the better. Drizzle extra-virgin olive oil on top and season the toasts with salt and black pepper to taste. Sprinkle the parsley on top and serve at once.

VARIATIONS

Pa Amb Tomàquet: This simple Catalan tomato bread is a fantastic dish to serve at a barbecue; let each guest assemble his or her own. To make *pa amb tomàquet,* prepare the Catalan "Bruschetta," omitting the bell peppers, eggplants, and anchovies. That is, grill the bread, then have everyone rub the toasted slices with cut garlic and tomato, drizzle extra-virgin olive oil on top, and season them with salt and black pepper to taste. Eat the *pa amb tomàquet* at once.

Catalan Grilled Bread with Country Ham: Here's another popular variation on Catalan grilled bread. Prepare the Catalan "Bruschetta," substituting paper-thin slices of *jamón ibérico,* or other Spanish cured ham, for the anchovies and vegetables. After the bread has been grilled, rubbed with garlic and tomato, drizzled with extra-virgin olive oil, and seasoned with salt and black pepper, carpet the slices with the ham.

Catalan "Bruschetta": Grilled bread topped with fire-roasted vegetables and anchovies.

Pita Bread Grilled Two Ways

While reading the headlines, you might think that all Jews and Palestinians do is fight, yet they often coexist peacefully in Israel—especially in the presence of a lit barbecue grill. The popular Tel Aviv restaurant, Abu-Nassar-Hinnawi, was founded by an Arab butcher turned restaurateur, and the open-air eatery has been a popular gathering spot—for Israelis of all faiths—in the predominantly Arab neighborhood of Jaffa for more than half a century. It was there that I learned a great trick for oiling a grill grate using an onion half dipped in oil and stuck on the end of a barbecue fork. It was also there that I tasted two versions of grilled pita—one the Middle Eastern version of garlic bread; the other a sort of grilled herb flatbread. **MAKES 8 PITA BREAD HALVES**

VERSION #1:

GRILLED GARLIC PITA

2 cloves garlic, peeled and cut in half

¼ cup extra-virgin olive oil, in a small bowl

4 pita breads

2 tablespoons sesame seeds

ADVANCE PREPARATION

None

1 Using a garlic press, squeeze the garlic into the olive oil. Don't have a garlic press? Smash the garlic cloves with the side of a cleaver or chef's knife on a cutting board and stir them into the oil.

2 Set up the grill for direct grilling and preheat it to medium-high.

3 When ready to cook, brush and oil the grill grate. Gently tear each pita

bread in half through the side; the idea is to have 2 flat halves. Brush each pita half on both sides with some of the garlic oil and sprinkle it with sesame seeds. Arrange the pita halves cut side up on the hot grate and grill them until toasted and brown, 1 to 2 minutes per side. Watch the pita carefully; it can burn quickly. Serve the grilled pita at once.

VERSION #2:

GRILLED HERB PITA

4 pita breads

3 to 4 tablespoons extra-virgin olive oil

¼ cup za'atar (recipe follows)

1 Set up the grill for direct grilling and preheat it to medium-high.

2 When ready to grill, brush and oil the grill grate. Gently tear each pita

THE SCOOP

WHERE: Israel

WHAT: The Middle Eastern version of grilled bread. One version features pita bread swabbed with garlic oil; the other is pita grilled with a fragrant herb blend called *za'atar*.

HOW: Direct grilling

JUST THE FACTS: *Za'atar* is a blend of Middle Eastern herbs and spices. The recipe varies from region to region, but it usually includes oregano, sweet marjoram, and thyme. Sometimes ground sumac is added for tartness and sesame seeds for crunch. Most people buy *za'atar* ready made— and you can find it at Israeli, Lebanese, Middle Eastern, and Greek markets. There's a recipe on page 92 for a rough approximation if you wish to make your own.

Sumac can be ordered from www.penzeys.com.

bread in half through the side; the idea is to have 2 flat halves. Brush each pita half on both sides with some of the olive oil. Arrange the pita halves torn side down on the hot grate and grill them until toasted and brown, 1 to 2 minutes. Turn the pita halves over, sprinkle each half with about 1½ teaspoons of *za'atar*, and grill the second side the same way. Watch the pita carefully; it can burn quickly. Serve the grilled pita at once.

Middle Eastern Herb Blend
{ ZA'ATAR }

Most grillers in the Middle East use ready-made *za'atar*, and in North America you can find it at Middle Eastern markets. Here's a quick recipe if you want to make your own. It makes a great seasoning for fish and poultry. **MAKES 1 CUP**

¼ cup dried oregano
¼ cup dried marjoram
¼ cup dried thyme
3 tablespoons lightly toasted sesame seeds
 (see page 68)
2 tablespoons coarse salt
 (kosher or sea)
1 tablespoon ground sumac (optional)

Combine the oregano, marjoram, thyme, sesame seeds, salt, and sumac, if using, in a mixing bowl and stir to mix. Store in a sealed jar away from heat and light. The *za'atar* will keep for several months.

Vietnamese Grilled Bread

Her name was Hang Hon and she squatted over a charcoal brazier not much smaller than she was. A bread half on a stick was ready for grilling in one hand and a straw fan was in her other to fan the flames. A black wool cap on her head kept her warm in the Hanoi winter. Behind her: the Hanoi Botanical Gardens, where you can take in a unique Hanoi spectacle—a water puppet show at an open-air theater. (Water puppetry is a Vietnamese theatrical art, where the "stage" is a sort of shallow swimming pool and the puppets move around it with great splashing and shouting.) All around, Hang Hon's customers lined up for a quick breakfast or snack of bread grilled with butter and sugar. Think of this as barbecue for breakfast—a sort of cinnamon bread, without the cinnamon, on the grill. Come to think of it, cinnamon would make a nice—if not strictly traditional—Vietnamese touch. And to drink? Sweet Vietnamese coffee: espresso-strength drip coffee sweetened with condensed milk. **MAKES 8 HALF ROLLS**

4 soft, lightly crusted French rolls
4 tablespoons (½ stick) unsalted butter, melted
½ cup sugar

YOU'LL ALSO NEED
Long bamboo skewers (optional)

ADVANCE PREPARATION
None

1 Set up the grill for direct grilling and preheat it to medium-high.

2 Cut each French roll in half lengthwise through the side. Stick each half roll on a skewer (this is optional, but it makes a convenient way to eat the bread).

3 Brush each half roll with some of the melted butter, brushing most of it on the cut side. Sprinkle each half roll with about 1 tablespoon of sugar, again most of it on the cut side.

4 When ready to cook, brush and oil the grill grate. Arrange the half rolls cut side down on the hot grate and grill them until toasted and brown, 1 to 2 minutes per side. Watch the bread carefully; it can burn quickly. Serve the grilled bread at once.

VARIATION
Vietnamese Cinnamon Toast: Sprinkle the rolls with 2 teaspoons of ground cinnamon along with the sugar.

WHERE: Hanoi, Vietnam

WHAT: French bread grilled with butter and sugar

HOW: Direct grilling

JUST THE FACTS: Vietnamese French bread is a bit softer and puffier than a traditional French baguette. French-style sandwich rolls work great for this dish.

Hanoi breakfast: Butter- and sugar-grilled French bread. Note the use of a straw fan to fire up the coals.

Vietnam: Where Barbecue Is a Meal in One, and That's a Wrap

One doesn't normally think of Vietnam as a mecca of barbecue, and yet the Vietnamese grill everything: bread, oysters, pork, chicken, beef, shellfish, bananas, and even eggs in the shell. Vietnamese grill masters build complex layers of flavor into each dish, using herbs not just as seasonings but as grilling papers and even as skewers. Consider a dish like *gà nướng lá chanh,* chicken marinated in turmeric and lemongrass and grilled wrapped in lemon leaves; you don't actually eat the leaves, but the lemon oils perfume the chicken. And *chao tom,* shrimp mousse grilled on sugarcane. One bite takes you through the briny shrimp mousse to the sweet, wet crunch of the sugarcane—an orgy of textures, flavors, and even temperatures in a single mouthful.

Vietnamese fruit market on Phu Quoc Island.

As in Texas, the most famous dish in Vietnam's barbecue repertory is beef. But the contrast between a Lone Star State brisket and Vietnamese *bo bun* speaks volumes about the difference between the cultures of West and East. In Texas, you'd get beef seasoned mainly with salt, pepper, and wood smoke, cooked half a day, and dished out in such gargantuan proportions that a single serving could feed a family of six in Hanoi. In Vietnam, the beef comes sliced paper-thin, marinated in an electrifying mixture of Asian herbs and condiments, flash grilled for a matter of minutes if not seconds, and served with a pyrotechnic assortment of chiles, vegetables, herbs, nuts, rice noodles, and dipping sauces, all wrapped together in rice paper (another sort of noodle). Each bite offers a contrast of mild and spicy, of meat, vegetables,

Master Grillers of Southeast Asia

Vietnam—a seafood griller's paradise, with 1,859 miles of coastline stretching from China to the South China Sea.

Good morning, Vietnam. A billboard amid the rice patties.

Bananas bound for market on a motorized rickshaw.

HANOI

GULF OF TONKIN

VIETNAM

HUE

0 50 100 150
MILES

NHA TRANG

HO CHI MINH CITY

SOUTH CHINA SEA

and starches—in short, a whole meal in a single dish. Vietnamese grilled pork, poultry, and seafood are served in a similar manner, always as part of an ensemble that includes all the elements of a meal.

Grilling at the Quan An Ngon food court in Hanoi. Note the pile of charcoal in the bottom left corner. Once lit, the embers will be raked out for grilling.

Squeeze the lime juice into the salt and pepper to make a dipping sauce.

THE GRILL: The traditional Vietnamese grill is a charcoal brazier that looks like an oversize flower pot. Your waitress sets it up on your table so she or you can grill the meat to the degree of doneness you like. Larger restaurants and resorts use table grills and rotisseries.

Do-it-yourself grilling at Lac Canh restaurant in Nha Trang.

THE FUEL: Natural lump charcoal

THE FLAVORINGS: The Vietnamese create symphonically complex flavors, using a wide range of Southeast Asian spices and herbs. Most marinades start with garlic and lemongrass, with ginger, galangal, or fresh turmeric added for extra pungency. Fish sauce provides the salt; lime juice, acidity; sugar, a touch of sweetness. Lemon, basil, and *la lot* leaves are often used as wrappers for grilling.

MUST TRY DISHES:

Bo bun: Lemongrass-scented grilled beef served with rice noodles, rice paper, and vegetables (see page 177 for the recipe)

Bo goi la lot: Garlicky chopped beef grilled in aromatic *la lot* leaves

Chao tom: Shrimp mousse grilled on sugarcane

Gà nuóng lá chanh: Turmeric-marinated chicken grilled in lemon leaves (see page 386 for the recipe)

Thit bò kho: Grilled beef jerky, cured with lemongrass, sugar, and salt

Grilled baguette with butter and sugar: A popular street snack (see page 93 for the recipe)

Vietnamese grilled squid with sweet chile sauce for dipping.

THE CONDIMENTS: Vietnamese condiments are remarkable in their simplicity, stunning in their flavor. Case in point: salt-and-pepper grilled shellfish. You get a small dish with neat piles of sea salt and ground white pepper. You squeeze a lime or two over these seasonings and mix them with the tip of a chopstick to make a bracingly piquant dipping sauce.

Vietnam's other "barbecue" sauce (and general table sauce) is *nuoc cham,* a thin, topaz-colored, delicate, mildly sweet, mildly sour sauce made with fish sauce, shredded carrot, and sugar.

HOW TO EAT IT: Vietnamese grilling is very much a do-it-yourself/build-it-yourself affair. Grilled meats and seafood come with lettuce leaves and rice paper for wrappers

to which you add rice noodles, mung bean sprouts, sliced tomatoes, cucumbers, and chiles, not to mention fresh sprigs of cilantro, mint, and Asian basil.

IF YOU CAN EAT AT ONLY ONE RESTAURANT: Grilling is so ubiquitous and democratic in Vietnam, served from humble street stalls and at fancy restaurants, it's hard to cite a single must-try restaurant. In Hanoi, I would go to Quan An Ngon, an upscale food court specializing in street-style grilling and other street foods, but with the amenities of refrigeration and running water. If you are in the beach resort town of Nha Trang on the central coast, be sure to visit the Lac Canh restaurant.

WHAT TO DRINK: Vietnamese iced coffee, sweetened with sweetened condensed milk. Salted lemonade or sweet lemonade. Milk shakes made from durian, a malodorous but exquisite fruit.

THE MOST SINGULAR DISH IN THE REPERTORY: Eggs grilled in the shell and served in lettuce leaves with chiles, cilantro, and mint

Armenian Stick Bread

Armenian bread, grilled shish kebab style on a skewer.

This singular bread comes from the landlocked Republic of Armenia in the Caucasus Mountains. But if you ever spent time as a Boy Scout or a Girl Scout, you'll probably recognize the method of cooking it: You mold the soft dough onto flat metal skewers and grill it shish kebab style next to the fire. Cool, you may say, but why bother? The fire gives the bread a soft, puffy interior, crackling crust, and an unexpected smoke flavor—not to mention a novelty factor that's off the charts. Here's how it's made by Onik Kauckchan, chef of the popular Yerevan restaurant in Moscow, named after the Armenian capital. **MAKES 8 BREADS**

1 envelope active dry yeast (2½ teaspoons)
1 tablespoon sugar
1 tablespoon plus 1½ cups warm water
3 tablespoons milk
4 cups unbleached all-purpose flour, or more as
    needed, plus flour for kneading and rolling
2 teaspoons coarse salt (kosher or sea)
3 tablespoons vegetable oil, plus oil for the bowl
    and basting

YOU'LL ALSO NEED
Flat metal skewers; 2 bricks

ADVANCE PREPARATION
2 to 4 hours for making the dough
    and letting it rise

1 Place the yeast, sugar, and the 1 tablespoon of warm water in a small bowl and mix with a fork. Let the yeast mixture stand until foamy, 5 to 10 minutes; this activates the yeast. Combine the remaining 1½ cups of warm water with the milk.

2 Place the flour and salt in a food processor fitted with a metal blade or dough blade. With the processor running, add the yeast mixture, the milk and water mixture, and the oil. Run the processor in short bursts to mix and knead the dough until it comes away from the side of the processor bowl in a smooth ball, 3 to 5 minutes. The dough should be very soft and pliable but not quite sticky. Add additional flour as needed. (You can also use a stand mixer fitted with a dough hook to make the dough; see box, facing page.)

3 Turn the dough out onto a lightly floured work surface. Flour your hands and knead the dough for a minute or two until it is smooth (although I use a food processor for kneading, I always like to give the dough a human touch). Transfer the dough to a large, lightly oiled mixing bowl, turning it to coat all sides with the oil. Cover the bowl with plastic wrap, place it in a warm draft-free spot, and let the dough rise until doubled in bulk, 1 to 1½ hours.

HOW TO PREPARE ARMENIAN STICK BREAD

1. *Roll the dough into 2-inch balls. Have flat metal skewers ready for grilling.*

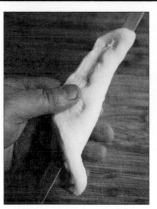

2. *Shape each ball into an oblong about 8 inches long and 4 inches wide. Fold it over a flat metal skewer and pinch the edges to secure it.*

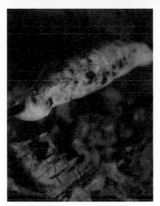

3. *Position the skewered dough at the edge of the fire and grill until puffed and browned on both sides. No grill grate needed.*

4. *Armenian Stick Bread served with sliced pickled peppers.*

4 Punch the dough down and turn it out onto a work surface. Divide the dough into 8 equal pieces. Roll each piece between the cupped palms of your hands to form a smooth ball. Arrange the balls of dough on a lightly floured baking sheet about 2 inches apart. Cover the balls of dough with plastic wrap, then a clean dish towel. Let the dough balls rise until doubled in bulk, about 30 minutes.

5 Set up the grill for direct grilling so that only one side of the grill is preheated to high. If you are using a charcoal grill, rake the coals out over only one half of the grill. If you are using a gas grill, light only one side. Arrange 2 bricks on the grate at the front and back of the grill so that they are next to but not over the heat source. Each skewer will be positioned with the ends of the skewer on the bricks.

6 Mold a ball of dough onto a flat metal skewer (see photo number 2, above). Suspend the skewer between the bricks and grill the bread until it is puffed and golden on the bottom, 3 to 4 minutes lightly basting it with oil. Turn the bread over and grill the bread until the second side is puffed and golden 3 to 4 minutes more. Using grill mitts, transfer the skewer to a platter, slide off the bread, and serve it. Continue skewering and grilling the breads until all of the balls of dough have been used.

VARIATION

Armenian Flatbread: Here's how to grill the Armenian Stick Bread dough directly on the grill grate. After the balls of dough have risen in Step 4, working on a lightly floured work surface, roll out each ball of dough to form a flat disk about 6 inches in diameter. Using a basting brush, brush off any excess flour.

Set up the grill for direct grilling and preheat it to medium-high. When ready to cook, brush and oil the grill grate. Lightly brush the tops of each circle of dough with vegetable oil, then arrange them oiled side down on the hot grate. Working in batches, if necessary, grill the breads until they are puffed and golden, about 2 minutes per side, lightly brushing the top of the breads with oil before turning. Serve the breads at once.

Mixing It Up

You can make and knead the bread doughs either in a food processor or using a stand mixer fitted with a dough hook. If you want to use a mixer, run it until the dough comes away from the sides of the mixing bowl in a smooth ball; this will take 6 to 8 minutes.

Indian "Puff Pastry"
{ LACHHA PARATHA }

Naan (Indian flatbread) was the first food cooked in a tandoor, and to this day, it accompanies any Indian barbecued meat, fish, or vegetarian dish. Basic naan starts as a yeast, flour, and water dough enriched with milk or yogurt, sugar, and sometimes an egg. Here's a twist (literally) on naan—a flaky, buttery, multilayered flatbread that, thanks to an ingenious folding technique, recalls French puff pastry. The recipe was inspired by the bread of the baker at the Moti Mahal restaurant in Old Delhi. It's quite simple, but for an even easier Indian grilled flatbread, you can turn the dough into naan; you'll find the instructions on page 100. **MAKES 12 BREADS**

THE SCOOP

WHERE: India

WHAT: Naan with a difference—buttered, rolled, folded, grilled Indian-style flatbread

HOW: Direct grilling

JUST THE FACTS: This and all Indian bread recipes in this chapter should bring out the showman in you, as they are best rolled and grilled to order. The grill of choice would be a tandoor, of course, but highly credible naan can be grilled directly on a conventional charcoal or gas grill. If you own a Big Green Egg, or other ceramic cooker, you can cook the naan Indian style, using the pizza stone provided with most models.

1 envelope active dry yeast (2½ teaspoons)
3 tablespoons sugar
1½ cups warm water
4½ cups unbleached all-purpose flour, or more as needed, plus flour for kneading and rolling
2 teaspoons coarse salt (kosher or sea)
3 tablespoons plain yogurt
1 tablespoon vegetable oil, plus oil for the bowl
4 tablespoons (½ stick) unsalted butter, melted, or more oil

ADVANCE PREPARATION
2 to 4 hours for making the dough and letting it rise

1 Place the yeast, sugar, and ¼ cup of the warm water in a small bowl and mix with a fork. Let the yeast mixture stand until foamy, 5 to 10 minutes; this activates the yeast.

2 Place the flour and salt in a food processor fitted with a metal blade or dough blade. With the processor running, add the yeast mixture, the yogurt, oil, and the remaining 1¼ cups of warm water. Run the processor in short bursts to mix and knead the dough until it comes away from the side of the processor bowl in a smooth ball, 3 to 5 minutes. The dough should be very soft and pliable but not quite sticky. Add additional flour as needed. (You can also use a stand mixer fitted with a dough hook to make the dough.)

3 Turn the dough out onto a lightly floured work surface. Flour your hands and knead the dough for a minute or two until it is smooth (although I use a food processor for kneading, I always like to give the dough a human touch). Transfer the dough to a large, lightly oiled mixing bowl, turning it to coat all sides with the oil. Cover the bowl with plastic wrap, place it in a warm draft-free spot, and let the dough rise until doubled in bulk, 1 to 1½ hours.

4 Punch the dough down and turn it out onto a work surface. Divide the dough into 12 equal pieces. Roll each piece between the cupped palms of your hands to form a smooth ball. Arrange the balls of dough on a lightly floured baking sheet about 2 inches apart. Cover the balls of dough with plastic wrap, then a clean dish towel. Let the dough balls rise until doubled in bulk, about 30 minutes.

5 Set up the grill for direct grilling and preheat it to medium-high.

6 Meanwhile, roll and fold the balls of dough. In India, this would be done right next to the tandoor. I like to do it at grill side; I bring a cutting board and rolling pin outside and work on a table next to the grill. Working on a lightly floured work surface, roll out a ball of dough to form a flat disk about 6 inches in diameter. Using a pastry brush, brush off any excess flour. Using a second pastry brush, brush the top of the disk with some of the melted butter. Starting at the end closest to you, fold the dough up like an accordion; each pleat should be about 1 inch wide. You will end up with a flat rectangle of dough. Now, starting at one end, roll up the rectangle into a circle; from the top it will look spiraled, like a sticky bun. Finally, using a rolling pin and adding a little more flour to the work surface, if necessary, roll out the dough to form a flat disk about 6 inches across. Lightly brush the top with butter. Repeat with the remaining balls of dough.

7 When ready to cook, brush and oil the grill grate. Arrange the breads, buttered side down, on the hot grate, a few at a time (don't crowd the grate). Grill the bread until the bottom is crusty and browned and the top is puffed and blistered, 2 to 4 minutes. Lightly brush the top of the bread with a little more butter, then turn it over and grill the second side until lightly browned, 2 to 4 minutes longer. Lightly brush each bread with more butter as it comes off the grill. Serve the bread piping hot, whole or the traditional way, cut into 3 wedges.

INDIAN "PUFF PASTRY"

VARIATION

Traditional Naan: Traditional naan is to Indian barbecue what pita bread is to Middle Eastern grilling (or for that matter, a slab of white bread is to the barbecue of the American South)—an indispensable accompaniment to the grilled meat or vegetables. You can use the Indian "Puff Pastry" dough to make naan. Here's how:

Prepare the recipe through Step 5. Roll a ball of dough into a flat disk about 6 inches in diameter, then gently slap the disk from one hand to the other to stretch it into an elongated 7- to 8-inch oblong with one narrow end like a teardrop. Lightly brush both sides with butter, then grill the naan as described in Step 7, 2 to 4 minutes per side. Lightly brush the naan with more butter and serve at once, repeating the process until all of the balls of dough have been grilled.

I get a lesson in cooking naan in a tandoor at a bakery in Old Delhi.

Naan Crusted with Pumpkin, Poppy, and Nigella Seeds

THE SCOOP

WHERE: New Delhi, India

WHAT: Flatbread Indian-style with a difference—grilled with pumpkin, poppy, and nigella seeds, to name a few

HOW: Direct grilling

JUST THE FACTS: Use any or all of the seeds listed for crusting the naan. Nigella seeds, also known in India as *kalonji*, are a black, earthy, mildly oniony spice used in Indian cooking. Look for them in Indian markets or via mail order from www.ethnicfoods.com or www.chefshop.com.

An Indian barbecue without naan would be like a Carolina pig pickin' without the sesame seed–topped hamburger buns. I mean that more than figuratively speaking; here's a naan from New Delhi that's grilled with a colorful crunchy, nutty crust, a mixture of sesame, poppy, pumpkin seeds, and more. **MAKES 12 BREADS**

1 envelope active dry yeast (2½ teaspoons)
2 tablespoons sugar
1 cup warm water
4½ cups unbleached all-purpose flour, or more as needed, plus flour for kneading and rolling
2 teaspoons salt
1 teaspoon baking powder
½ cup plain whole milk Greek-style yogurt or plain yogurt
1 tablespoon vegetable oil, plus oil for the bowl

1 egg, beaten with a pinch of salt to make an egg glaze
1 cup of any or all of the following seeds, mixed: hulled pumpkin, sesame, poppy, and/or nigella seeds
3 tablespoons unsalted butter, melted, or more oil

ADVANCE PREPARATION
2 to 4 hours for making the dough and letting it rise

1 Place the yeast, sugar, and ¼ cup of the warm water in a small bowl and mix with a fork. Let the yeast mixture stand until foamy, 5 to 10 minutes; this activates the yeast.

2 Place the flour, salt, and baking powder in a food processor fitted with a metal blade or dough blade. With the processor running, add the yeast mixture and the yogurt, oil, and the remaining ¾ cup of warm water. Run the processor in short bursts to mix and knead the dough until it comes away from the side of the processor bowl in a smooth ball, 3 to 5 minutes. The dough should be very soft and pliable but not quite sticky. Add additional flour as needed. (You can also use a stand mixer fitted with a dough hook to make the dough; see box, page 97.)

3 Turn the dough out onto a lightly floured work surface. Flour your hands and knead the dough for a minute or two until it is smooth (although I use a food processor for kneading, I always like to give the dough a human touch). Transfer the dough to a large, lightly oiled mixing bowl, turning it to coat all sides with the oil. Cover the bowl with plastic wrap, place it in a warm draft-free spot, and let the dough rise until doubled in bulk, 1 to 1½ hours.

4 Punch the dough down and turn it out onto a work surface. Divide the dough into 12 equal pieces. Roll each piece between the cupped palms of your hands to form a smooth ball. Arrange the balls of dough on a lightly floured baking sheet about 2 inches apart. Cover the balls of dough with plastic wrap, then a clean dish towel. Let the dough balls rise until doubled in bulk, about 30 minutes.

5 Set up the grill for direct grilling and preheat it to medium-high.

6 Meanwhile, roll and fold the balls of dough. (I like to do it at grill side.) Working on a lightly floured work surface, roll out a ball of dough to form a flat disk about 6 inches in diameter. Roll and stretch one end to make the traditional teardrop shape. Using a pastry brush, brush off any excess flour. Using a second pastry brush, brush the top of the bread with the egg glaze. Sprinkle the top of the bread with about 1½ tablespoons of the mixed seeds. Repeat with the remaining balls of dough.

7 When ready to cook, brush and oil the grill grate. Arrange the breads, seed side up, on the hot grate, a few at a time (don't crowd the grate). Grill the bread until the bottom is crusty and browned and the top is puffed and blistered, 2 to 4 minutes. Lightly brush the top of the bread with a little more butter, then turn it over and grill the second side until lightly browned, 2 to 4 minutes longer. Lightly brush each bread with more butter as it comes off the grill. Serve the bread piping hot, whole or the traditional way, cut into 3 wedges.

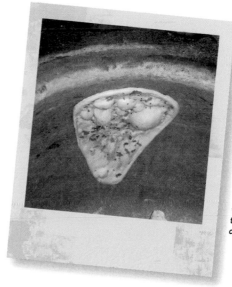

Naan cooking on the walls of a tandoor. Notice how the dough blisters when exposed to the heat of the charcoal.

India: Ancient Realm of Fire and Spice

Five thousand years ago, an ingenious potter in what is now northern India threw a tall urn-shaped pot and lit some lump charcoal in the bottom. Thanks to the unique thermodynamics of the vessel, with air that rushed into a vent hole at the bottom and out the round inwardly sloping opening in the top, a relatively small amount of charcoal produced a blast-furnace heat. The contraption was ideal for "baking" flatbreads on its fiery clay walls and roasting meats on the spits placed inside it. Thus was born one of the world's most unique and efficient barbecue pits, the tandoor, and one of the world's most unique styles of grilling, tandoori.

Forming naan at Ganesh restaurant in New Delhi.

Today, barbecue is enjoyed throughout India, especially in the north—not to mention from New Caledonia to Newcastle to New York. You'd never guess that the current tandoori craze (and it has become a craze) is of relatively new coinage, the result of the political upheavals associated with India's independence from Britain in 1947. Independence brought Partition,

the separation of primarily Hindu India from Muslim Pakistan, and Partition saw the resettling of large numbers of Kashmiris in New Delhi, India's capital. Kashmir, a northern province bitterly claimed by both India and Pakistan (the same Kashmir famed for its soft wool), has long been the epicenter of Central Asian barbecue. Kashmiri grill masters opened a new sort of dining establishment in the capital—a restaurant where not just breads but meats were grilled in the tandoor,

and served not just to the British ruling class, but to Indians as well.

If the tandoor is part of what makes Indian grilling unique on Planet Barbecue, equally important are the seasonings, without a doubt the most flavorful and complex in the world. Indian barbecue involves a four-step seasoning process: first, a sharply acidic marinade tenderizes the meat; second, a marinade of the distinctive Indian spices provides flavoring. Next comes a basting mixture—melted butter, lemon

The Birthplace of Tandoori

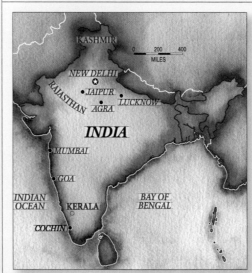

A cashmere trader's daughter sits demurely at her wedding, henna-painted hands on display.

Bordered by the Himalayas to the north and the Bay of Bengal and Indian Ocean to the south, India has been a barbecue hotspot for more than 5,000 years.

The Taj Mahal, Agra, India—built in the seventeenth century as an emperor's memorial to a favorite wife.

juice, and sometimes sesame seeds and cilantro—applied to the meat as it emerges hot from the tandoor. Finally, a chutney or relish is served in the way North Americans would use barbecue sauce.

In centuries gone by, villagers would gather in the center of town to cook their family meals in a communal tandoor, a ritual known as *sanjha chulna,* the "evening brazier." Today, the tandoor continues to bring Indians and non-Indians alike together in a tradition that's almost as old as barbecue itself.

Indian naan, one of the best grilled breads on Planet Barbecue.

THE GRILL: Indian barbecue is cooked on two kinds of grill: the tandoor and the *sigri.* Because tandoors operate at between 900° and 1,200°F, they are typically housed in concrete-filled metal boxes or barrels. This makes them too big, heavy, and expensive to use in the average home (at least the average Indian home). For this reason, when most Indians crave tandoori, they typically go to restaurants.

The *sigri* is an open-fire grill similar to Russia's and Central Asia's *mangal* (see page 605). Meats, seafood, cheese, and/or vegetables are skewered on flat metal skewers positioned front to back over the coals.

THE FUEL: The traditional fuel for tandoors and *sigris* is lump charcoal (deep in the countryside dried cow patties are also used). In the big cities, gas-fired tandoors have gained popularity, but the pros still insist on charcoal.

THE FLAVORINGS: As you'd expect of a country that is both a major spice producer and former way station on the legendary Silk and Spice Routes, India's *kebabi-wallahs* (grill masters) make profligate use of seasonings, often adding a dozen or more spices to a single marinade. A single dish might contain garlic water as a cleansing agent; a tenderizing acid, like yogurt or *amchur* (green mango); and intricate blends of aromatics and spices to build complex layers of flavors.

Marinade ingredients range from the familiar—ginger and garlic pounded to a paste in a stone mortar with a pestle—to such exotics as nigella, black onion seeds, and *ajwain,* a seed similar in flavor to caraway. Many marinades contain a thickening agent, like *besan,* chickpea flour, often used for seafood (see the Tandoori Grilled Kingfish on page 432), which gives the finished barbecue a batterlike crust. Indian barbecue is as much about the seasoning as what is being seasoned.

MUST TRY DISHES: India's barbecue repertory is huge, starting with grilled breads, like naan and *lachha paratha* (see page 98). The basic meats are *murgh,* chicken; *gosht,* lamb; *machhi,* fish; and *jhinga,* shrimp. If you are a vegetarian, India is probably the best grilling destination on Planet Barbecue. Look for fabulous tandoori made from *gobi,* cauliflower; *aloo,* potatoes; and *paneer,* cheese.

Here are some other useful Indian barbecue terms:

Raan: Refers to a whole roasted leg of baby goat or lamb

Seekh: Kebabs made from minced meat

India's tandoor is a tall urn-shaped clay barbecue pit—here without its final housing.

Tikka: Meats cut into bite-size pieces and grilled

THE ACCOMPANIMENTS: Tandoori is always served with sliced onions, fresh cilantro, naan, lemon wedges, and some sort of *chatni*—chutney—generally a piquant and electrifying, although not terribly fiery, green mixture of yogurt, lemon juice, spinach, cilantro, and other fresh herbs.

IF YOU CAN EAT AT ONLY ONE RESTAURANT: Karim in Old Delhi for a more populist experience; Bukhara at the ITC Maurya for a more upscale ambience.

HOW TO EAT IT: With the fingers of your right hand

WHAT TO DRINK: *Lassi,* a thick yogurt drink that can be sweet—flavored with rose water—or salty. Beer—one good Indian brand is Kingfisher.

THE MOST SINGULAR DISH IN THE REPERTORY: *Tandoori ghia,* a gourd stuffed with spiced vegetables and cheese and cooked in a tandoor.

Mumbai spice market: Spices are the soul of Indian barbecue.

South African Grilled Rolls
{ ROOSTER BROOD #1 }

Die Strandloper is a funky glorified fishing camp where mussels, rock lobsters, and South African fish, like snook, are grilled with the utmost simplicity over driftwood fires. And where simple country-style white bread comes piping hot out of a wood-burning oven (in this case, constructed from an old iron boiler pipe)—when the dough isn't tied into knots and cooked directly on the grill. Crusty on the outside, soft and steamy inside, imbued with a subtle smoke flavor, *rooster brood* is the sort of bread you'll remember long after the fire has burned out. For the full effect, serve it with sweet butter and gooseberry jam as they do in South Africa. **MAKES 16 ROLLS**

1 envelope active dry yeast (2½ teaspoons)
3 tablespoons sugar
1 tablespoon plus 1½ cups warm water
4 cups unbleached all-purpose flour, or more as
    needed, plus flour for rolling
2 teaspoons salt
Vegetable oil, for the bowl
2 to 3 tablespoons salted butter, melted,
    plus butter, for serving
Jam, for serving

ADVANCE PREPARATION

2 to 4 hours for making the dough
and letting it rise

1 Place the yeast, 1 tablespoon of the sugar, and the 1 tablespoon of warm water in a small bowl and mix with a fork. Let the yeast mixture stand until foamy, 5 to 10 minutes; this activates the yeast.

2 Place the flour, the remaining 2 tablespoons of sugar, and the salt in a food processor fitted with a metal blade or dough blade. With the processor running, add the yeast mixture, the oil, and the remaining 1½ cups of warm water. Run the processor in short bursts to mix and knead the dough until it comes away from the side of the processor bowl in a smooth ball, 3 to 5 minutes. The dough should be very soft and pliable, but not quite sticky. Add additional flour as needed. (You can also use a stand mixer fitted with a dough hook to make the dough; see box, page 97.)

3 Turn the dough out onto a lightly floured work surface. Flour your hands and knead the dough for a minute or two until it is smooth (although I use a food processor for kneading, I always like to give the dough a human touch). Transfer the dough to a large, lightly oiled mixing bowl, turning it to coat

Rooster brood on the grill. Turn the rolls often so they brown evenly.

all sides with the oil. Cover the bowl with plastic wrap, place it in a warm draft-free spot, and let the dough rise until doubled in bulk, 1 to 1½ hours.

4 Punch the dough down and turn it out onto a work surface. Divide the dough into 16 equal pieces. Roll each piece into a rope about 8 inches long and ½ inch in diameter. Tie each rope in a simple knot. Arrange the knotted dough on a lightly floured baking sheet about 2 inches apart. Cover the baking sheet with plastic wrap, then a clean dish towel. Let the knots of dough rise until doubled in bulk, about 30 minutes.

5 Set up the grill for two-zone grilling (see page 611). Preheat one zone to medium and one zone to low. Leave one section fire-free for a safety zone.

6 Lightly brush each knot of dough with melted butter and arrange it on the hot grate. Grill the rolls until puffed and golden brown on the outside and cooked through, 3 to 4 minutes per side. If the outsides start to burn before the dough is cooked through, move the rolls to a cooler part of the grill. Serve the rolls at once with butter and jam.

VARIATION

South African Bread in Loaves: To grill the bread in loaves, after it has risen the first time, punch the dough down, divide it in half, and place it in two tall, well-oiled loaf pans, 8½ by 4½ by 2½ inches (South African loaf pans are a bit taller than those in North America). Let the loaves rise a second time, covered, until puffed and soft, about 30 minutes. Brush the top of each loaf with oil.

Set up the grill for indirect grilling and preheat it to medium-high. To approximate the smoke flavor of a wood-burning oven, you can use 2 cups of unsoaked wood chips or chunks.

When ready to cook, if you are using a gas grill, add the wood chips or chunks to the smoker box or place them in a smoker pouch under the grate (see page 603). If you are using a charcoal grill, toss the wood chips or chunks on the coals. Place the loaf pans in the center of the grate away from the heat and cover the grill. "Bake" the breads until the loaves are puffed, browned, and crusty (when tapped, they'll sound hollow), 40 to 50 minutes. Turn the loaves out on a cake rack to cool. Serve the bread with butter and jam.

South African Grilled Cheese Sandwiches

{ ROOSTER BROOD #2 }

Say you're a guy or gal embarking on South Africa's national pastime—*braaing* (barbecuing). The meal will take at least four hours to grill and eat. While you're waiting for the larger cuts—your leg of lamb or haunch of springbok to grill—you need something to keep your mouth occupied. The answer? Another form of *rooster brood*, this time a grilled cheese sandwich unlike any you'll experience anywhere else on Planet Barbecue. The contrast of sweet chutney and salty cheese is quintessentially South African. **SERVES 4**

THE SCOOP

WHERE: South Africa

WHAT: Grilled cheese sandwiches Afrikaner style—with cheddar cheese and fruit chutney

THE SCOOP

HOW: Direct grilling

JUST THE FACTS:
None, but to experience the sandwich at its best, use homemade chutney (page 272) and an aged (two-year-old) cheddar. This recipe calls for direct grilling the sandwiches on a conventional grill, but you can also cook them on a panini grill.

8 slices of white sandwich bread

4 tablespoons (½ stick) butter, melted

½ cup fruit chutney (a good commercial one, such as Major Grey's)

8 ounces sharp orange cheddar cheese, thinly sliced

1 large or 2 medium-size tomatoes, thinly sliced

½ medium-size sweet onion, sliced paper-thin

ADVANCE PREPARATION
None

1 Lightly brush 4 slices of the bread with melted butter on one side and place them buttered side down on a work surface. Spread the top of each slice with about 2 tablespoons of chutney. Place slices of cheese on top of the chutney, followed by slices of tomato and onion. Place the remaining slices of bread on top to make sandwiches. Brush the top of each sandwich with the remaining melted butter.

2 Set up the grill for direct grilling and preheat it to medium-high.

3 When ready to cook, brush and oil the grill grate really thoroughly. Arrange the sandwiches on the hot grate at a diagonal to the bars and grill them for 1 minute. Then, slide a spatula under each sandwich and give it a quarter turn to create a handsome crosshatch of grill marks (this is optional but it sure looks cool). Grill the sandwiches until they are browned on the bottom, 2 to 4 minutes. Then, using a spatula, carefully turn the sandwiches over and grill the second side until the bread is browned and the cheese is melted, 2 to 4 minutes longer. Serve the sandwiches hot off the grill.

VARIATION

Truffled Cheese Sandwiches with Onion: Once you make the leap from grilling cheese sandwiches in a frying pan to toasting them on the grill, there's no limit to the variations. Here's an Italian-inspired twist on the South African grilled cheese sandwiches, made with *caciotta al tartufo,* an Italian cheese flavored

HOW TO MAKE SOUTH AFRICAN GRILLED CHEESE SANDWICHES

1. *Brush the bread slices with melted butter.*

2. *Spread each bread slice with fruit chutney and top with sharp cheddar cheese.*

3. *Shingle fresh tomato slices on top of the cheese followed by onion slices.*

4. *Rooster brood: It may just be the best grilled cheese sandwich on Planet Barbecue.*

with small pieces of black truffles. Sweet-sour onion jam makes a perfect counterpoint to the cheese. You can make truffled cheese sandwiches by following the recipe on the facing page and substituting 8 slices of whole wheat bread for the white bread and 8 ounces of sliced *caciotta al tartufo* for the cheddar (if you can't find *caciotta al tartufo* locally, one good online source is Marky's, www.markys.com). Use ½ cup of onion jam in place of the chutney and onion—either the balsamic vinegar–glazed onions from page 180 (follow the instructions in Steps 1 and 2 to make it) or a good commercial brand. Don't forget the tomato slices.

Turkish Puff Bread
{ PIDE }

P*ide* belongs to an extended family of Middle and Near East flatbreads cooked on the grill or in a wood-burning oven and served with grilled meats. No Turkish barbecue would be complete without these soft, puffy, wood oven–cooked pillows of dough, and while technically the cooking process is closer to baking than grilling, a grill top pizza stone produces excellent *pide*. The dough is easy to make, but allow yourself enough time for both the sponge—a sort of dough starter that adds extra lift and flavor—and the dough to rise. Roll out and bake the breads when other people are gathered around the grill—it's really fun to see the *pide* puff on the grill. **MAKES 8 BREADS**

THE SCOOP

WHERE: Turkey

WHAT: The Turkish version of pita bread—a soft puffed pillow of dough that is traditionally cooked in a wood-burning oven

HOW: Direct grilling

Turkish pide accompany lamb and vegetable kebabs.

FOR THE SPONGE
1 envelope active dry yeast (2½ teaspoons)
2 teaspoons sugar
½ cup warm water
½ cup all-purpose unbleached flour

TO FINISH THE PIDE
3 cups unbleached all-purpose flour, or more as needed, plus flour for rolling
½ cup whole wheat flour
2 teaspoons table salt
2 tablespoons extra-virgin olive oil, plus oil for the bowl

1¼ cups warm water
2 tablespoons toasted sesame seeds or nigella seeds (see Note)

YOU'LL ALSO NEED
2 cups unsoaked oak or other wood chips or chunks

ADVANCE PREPARATION
2 to 4 hours for making the sponge and letting the dough rise

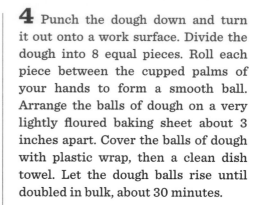

JUST THE FACTS: Unlike most of the grilled breads in this book, *pide* is cooked on a stone positioned on top of the grill grate; you won't get the proper puff without the stone. If you own a Big Green Egg, you're in luck because the Egg comes with its own ceramic pizza stone. Alternatively, many companies, including Sur la Table and Williams-Sonoma, sell baking stones for the grill. To simulate the delicate wood-smoke flavor you get in a wood-burning oven, toss a handful of unsoaked wood chunks on the coals. As for nigella seeds, imagine a sesame seed with a mild onion flavor and you'll get an idea of how they taste.

1 Make the sponge: Place the yeast, sugar, and the ½ cup of warm water in a small bowl and stir to mix. Stir in the ½ cup of all-purpose flour. Cover the bowl with plastic wrap and let the mixture rise for 30 minutes.

2 Make the *pide:* Place the all-purpose and the whole wheat flours, salt, and oil in a food processor fitted with a metal blade or dough blade. With the processor running, add the sponge and the 1¼ cups of warm water. Run the processor in short bursts to obtain a soft and sticky dough, 3 to 5 minutes. The dough will be a little wetter than that of most flatbreads; you need the moisture for it to puff. However, if the dough is really sticky, add a little more flour.

3 Turn the dough out onto a very lightly floured work surface. Flour your hands and knead the dough for a minute or two until it is smooth (although I use a food processor for kneading, I always like to give the dough a human touch). Transfer the dough to a large, lightly oiled mixing bowl, turning it to coat all sides with the oil. Cover the bowl with plastic wrap, place it in a warm draft-free spot, and let the dough rise until doubled in bulk, 1 to 1½ hours.

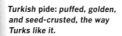

Turkish pide: puffed, golden, and seed-crusted, the way Turks like it.

4 Punch the dough down and turn it out onto a work surface. Divide the dough into 8 equal pieces. Roll each piece between the cupped palms of your hands to form a smooth ball. Arrange the balls of dough on a very lightly floured baking sheet about 3 inches apart. Cover the balls of dough with plastic wrap, then a clean dish towel. Let the dough balls rise until doubled in bulk, about 30 minutes.

5 Set up the grill for direct grilling and preheat it to high. Place a grill-safe pizza stone on the grate and preheat it as well.

6 Using a rolling pin, roll out each dough ball to form an oblong about 4 by 8 inches. Using your fingertips, dimple the top of each oblong in a lengthwise row, then sprinkle a generous ½ teaspoon of sesame seeds on top of each.

7 When ready to cook, if you are using a gas grill, add the wood chips or chunks to the smoker box or place them in a smoker pouch under the grate (see page 603) and run the grill until you see smoke. If you are using a charcoal grill, toss the wood chips or chunks on the coals. Arrange the breads, seed side up, on the hot pizza stone, a few at a time (don't crowd the stone). Cover the grill and cook the breads without turning until puffed and browned, 5 to 8 minutes. Serve at once.

NOTE: Nigella seeds are available at East Indian markets or by mail order from www.chefshop.com.

Grilled Corn Cakes with Salsa

{ AREPAS CON SALSA }

Cross polenta with pita bread and you get one of Colombia's national snacks—a street food, side dish, and culinary treasure: *arepas*. (Think Mexico's tortillas on steroids.) During my stay in Colombia, I sampled at least eight different varieties of *arepa*, some as crisp as soda crackers, others as softly creamy inside as cornmeal mush. The toppings varied, too—salsa, hot sauce, butter, and cheese, for example. There's even a sweet version doused with butter and cinnamon sugar. Many types of *arepas* split naturally in the center as they grill, so you can stuff them the way you would pita bread. **MAKES 7 AREPAS**

THE SCOOP

WHERE: Colombia

WHAT: A grilled white cornmeal cake served with cilantro-scented salsa

HOW: Direct grilling

JUST THE FACTS: *Arepas* are made with boiled, hulled, dried corn, a bit like North American grits cakes. A proper Colombian grill master knows how to make several varieties from scratch. For the sake of simplicity, I call for ready-made *arepas*, which are available in the dairy case at many supermarkets and Latino markets. (You can buy frozen *arepas* at www.arepasonline .com; look for the *Arepa Antioqueña medio telón*.)

FOR THE SALSA

½ medium-size sweet onion, very finely diced (see Note)
½ green bell pepper, cored, seeded, and very finely diced (see Note)
½ red bell pepper, cored, seeded, and very finely diced (see Note)
1 clove garlic, minced (see Note)
⅓ cup finely chopped fresh cilantro (see Note)
2 tablespoons distilled white vinegar
1 tablespoon fresh lime juice, or more as needed
Coarse salt (kosher or sea)

FOR THE AREPAS

7 arepas, thawed if frozen
3 tablespoons unsalted butter, melted

ADVANCE PREPARATION

The salsa can be made several hours ahead.

1 Make the salsa: Place the onion, green and red bell peppers, garlic, cilantro, vinegar, and lime juice in a mixing bowl. Toss to mix, then season the salsa with salt to taste, adding more lime juice as necessary; the salsa should be highly seasoned. You will have about 1½ cups of salsa. Set the salsa aside: it can be made several hours ahead.

2 Grill the *arepas:* Set up the grill for direct grilling and preheat it to high.

3 When ready to cook, brush and oil the grill grate especially well. *Lightly* brush each of the *arepas* on both sides with some of the melted butter. Arrange the *arepas* on the hot grate and grill them until toasted and browned on both sides, about 2 minutes per side, turning with a spatula or tongs.

4 Transfer the *arepas* to a platter or plates. Brush them with any remaining butter. Top each *arepa* with some of the salsa and serve at once.

NOTE: The salsa ingredients can be chopped in a food processor and then combined; run the machine in short bursts.

PLANET   BARBECUE

Colombia: The Grilling Rival of Argentina

For months, I had been hearing about Colombia's legendary *lomo al trapo*—beef tenderloin thickly crusted with salt, wrapped in a cloth, and roasted right on the embers. What results looks like a burnt log, but when the crust is cracked off, the meat inside is the ultimate in primal grilling (see page 123 for the recipe). Did someone say *primal?* The next thing I knew, I was on a flight bound for Bogotá, where my Colombian contacts Andres and Marta Reyes took me on a barbecue crawl that would have overwhelmed Gargantua himself.

Colombia? Barbecue crawl? Wasn't this the place where herbs run to coca leaves and hot zones are guerrilla encampments in the jungle? Well, it turns out Colombia may be the best-kept barbecue secret in South America—with grilled meats that rival those of Argentina, grilled corn cakes that rival Mexico's tortillas and Italy's polenta, and grill restaurants that stretch whole city blocks and that will serve you and two thousand other hungry carnivores on a typical Saturday night.

A dancer entertains at a festival in Cartagena.

You find grilling everywhere: on the coast, in the perfectly preserved colonial city of Cartagena, for example, where street vendors serve up cheese-crusted grilled corn and intricate shish kebabs (curiously, you don't find much grilled seafood here). In the Llano district, Colombia's cattle country in the northwest, where cowboys roast hunks of *mamona* (six-month-old veal) on sticks in front of a campfire. And of course, in Bogotá, where chophouses draw chic crowds for monster portions of what will strike North Americans as amazingly inexpensive *bife de chorizo* (New York strip) and *lomos* (filets mignons) seared over wood- or charcoal-burning fires.

If you love beef, you're going to love Colombia, because the Brahmin

The Northernmost Realm of South American Grilling

CARIBBEAN SEA
BARRANQUILLA
CARTAGENA

MEDELLÍN
CHÍA
BOGOTÁ

COLOMBIA

0   100   200   300
MILES

Human puppets on stilts performing at a street festival, Bogotá, Colombia.

Colombians grill bananas at every degree of ripeness.

With one coast on the Caribbean and one coast on the Pacific, Colombia offers some of the most diverse grilling in South America.

cattle found here have a lot more flavor than the grass-fed Herefords and Angus you find farther south. But even if you don't, Colombian grill masters work wonders with pork, poultry (often marinated in mustard), and fire-roasted bananas and plantains.

Here I am at the entrance to Andrés Carne de Res, the most famous restaurant in Colombia.

THE GRILL: Colombians use two basic models of grill: the *parrilla*, a conventional grill typically outfitted with a grate hung from chains that can be lowered or raised with a flywheel; and an *hogao*, a campfire or fireplace grill, where meats are roasted on sticks in front of the fire.

THE FUEL: Wood, especially oak, favored around Bogotá, and eucalyptus, used in the nothern Llanos district

THE FLAVORINGS: Colombians tend to season their beef simply with coarse salt and black pepper, although many Bogotá chophouses marinate lean meats like beef tenderloin in marinades of stock and wine.

Arepas grilled over charcoal.

MUST TRY DISHES (TO MENTION A FEW):

Arepas: Cornmeal cakes

Bife de chorizo: New York strip steak

Lomito: Butterflied filet mignon

Lomo al trapo: Beef tenderloin packed with salt, wrapped in a cotton cloth, then roasted in the embers (you'll find a recipe on page 123)

Pinchos: Colorful vegetable and meat shish kebabs

Sobrebarriga: Brisket—boiled or braised first, then grilled with cheese

THE CONDIMENTS: Colombian grilled meats typically come with two condiments: *ají* and guacamole. *Ají* is a hot sauce, a puree of hot peppers, garlic, salt, and vinegar or lime juice; think of it as Colombia's version of salsa. Colombian guacamole is smoother and wetter than its Mexican cousin—a sauce, rather than a dip.

IF YOU CAN EAT AT ONLY ONE RESTAURANT: Andrés Carne de Res: The most famous restaurant in Colombia, it serves four thousand people on a typical weekend (you can read about it on page 136).

WHAT TO DRINK: In addition to the predictable beer and wine, Colombians serve two highly distinctive beverages with barbecue:

Refajo is the Colombian version of a shandy— beer mixed with a sweet Colombian soft drink. *Chicha* is a sweet, purple, ciderlike beverage fermented from corn.

THE MOST SINGULAR DISH IN THE REPERTORY: *Chiguiro*— capybara—a large furry mammal that looks like an oversize guinea pig. The flavor is mild and luscious, rather like a well-marbled pork shoulder. *Chiguiro* is traditionally roasted on sticks over a eucalyptus fire.

A street vendor prepares pinchos de chorizo (sausage kebabs) on a pushcart grill.

José Andrés' Grilled Bread with Chocolate

THE SCOOP

WHERE: Spain

WHAT: A sandwich unique in the annals of barbecue: grilled bread with chocolate, salt, and olive oil

HOW: Direct grilling

JUST THE FACTS: When a recipe is this simple, you need the best ingredients money can buy: Spanish country-style bread; a dark bitter chocolate; the highest quality extra-virgin olive oil; and coarse crunchy crystals of sea salt.

Yes, you've read this right—grilled bread with chocolate. Sounds weird and yet, bread with chocolate is a venerable European tradition. France has *pain au chocolat,* a rectangle of croissant dough with a bar of dark chocolate baked in the center, the traditional after-school snack of French children (adults enjoy it, too, for *petit déjeuner*). Then there's the film *Bread and Chocolate* by Franco Brusati, chronicling the bittersweet existence of *gastarbeitern,* guest workers, in Switzerland. And now my friend, Spanish-born culinary wunderkind José Andrés, owner of the Café Atlantico and minibar in Washington, D.C., and a TV star in Spain, adds his own version: a crusty sandwich of grilled bread, dark chocolate, and olive oil—a combination that is at once smoky, sweet, fruity, and pleasantly bitter. Have all the ingredients ready at grill side, so the chocolate melts when you put it on the hot bread. After all, how many grilled dishes can you serve with equal aplomb for breakfast, as a snack, and for dessert? **SERVES 4**

Spanish barbecue the way God meant you to eat it—outdoors.

Toast the Spanish way—browned on the grill.

8 thin slices of Spanish-style white bread
(¼-inch thick, see Note)
Extra-virgin olive oil
4 thin rectangles of bittersweet chocolate
(each about 3 ounces and 2 by 5 inches)
Coarse sea salt

ADVANCE PREPARATION
None

1 Set up the grill for two-zone grilling (see page 611). Preheat one zone to medium-high and one zone to medium.

2 Lightly brush the slices of bread with olive oil. Sandwich each piece of chocolate between 2 pieces of bread with the oiled side out.

3 When ready to cook, brush and oil the grill grate. Arrange the chocolate "sandwiches" on the hot grate and grill them until the bread is toasted and the chocolate is melted, 2 to 4 minutes per side. Watch the bread carefully; it can burn quickly. Move the sandwiches to the medium zone if they start to burn.

4 Transfer the grilled sandwiches to a platter or plates, drizzle a little more olive oil over them, sprinkle them with salt, and serve at once. The chocolate sandwiches taste as outrageous as they are unexpected.

NOTE: Spanish bread has a crisp crust and a puffy but firm white interior. You can also use an Italian-style bread, like *ciabatta*.

Beef,
Veal, and
Game

Sixteen thousand or so years ago, anonymous artists painted the walls of a cave in what is now Lascaux, France, with magnificent herds of equines, stags, and bison—more than two thousand images in all. But none has the power and mouthwatering majesty of the four aurochs (black bulls), ancestors of the modern steer and a meat prized by prehistoric pit masters as much as beef is by our own.

Travel the world's barbecue trail and you'll find every imaginable cut of grilled beef, from Tuscany's *bistecca alla fiorentina,* a plate-burying porterhouse, to the smoky briskets of the Texas Hill Country. From the sesame-grilled short ribs in Seoul, to the spicy beef satés in Singapore, to the ham- and mushroom-stuffed cheese steaks in Split, Croatia.

When it comes to beef, many of the world's grill masters take a less is more approach. Indeed, a half-dozen recipes in this chapter contain little more than beef and salt. But thanks to innovative grilling techniques, Spain's *chuleton* (salt-grilled rib steak) tastes completely different from Uruguay's *colita de cuadril* (salt-grilled tri-tip) or Colombia's magisterial *lomo al trapo* (beef tenderloin covered in salt, wrapped in a cotton cloth, and roasted directly in the embers).

Other grillers take a more intricate approach, seasoning the beef with complex marinades such as those in Malaysia's *nonya* steaks or fiery spice pastes like Peru's cumin- and chile-blasted *anticuchos.* And no survey of the world's great beef dishes would be complete without Russia's veal chops grilled with garlic and dill.

So whether you like your steer big and smoky or bite-size and shish kebabed, grilled as steak, spit roasted on the rotisserie, or even roasted caveman style, in the embers or in front of a bonfire, Planet Barbecue has you covered.

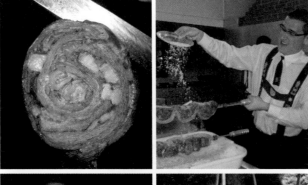

CLOCKWISE FROM TOP LEFT: Matambre *(rolled, stuffed flank steak) ready for slicing;* Sprinkling coarse sea salt on Brazilian *picanha (flat-capped top sirloin);* Mamona *(Colombian veal) roasts on sticks over a eucalyptus fire; The world's biggest beef rib, cooked by a* fogo de chão *(bonfire).*

Previous page: Tri-tip on the grill in Tucson, Arizona.

Hill Country Brisket

The perfect brisket is the holy grail of barbecue—often pursued, rarely attained. The basic principle for cooking brisket can be summed up in a single sentence: You smoke this tough ornery cut low and slow until it's tender enough to cut with the side of a fork. Then, you spend the next decade mastering the fine points. Your goal is a thick moist slab with a crusty "bark," a vivid smoke ring, and meat so smoky, you're inclined to measure your consumption in pounds not ounces. What follows is a synthesis of my favorite Hill Country briskets. You don't need a sauce, but if you want one, the Bourbon-Brown Sugar Barbecue Sauce on page 229 hits the spot. **SERVES 8 TO 12**

1 beef brisket flat (6 to 8 pounds) with—very important—a cap of fat at least ¼ inch thick
3 tablespoons dry mustard
3 tablespoons coarse salt (kosher or sea)
3 tablespoons cracked or coarsely ground black pepper
3 tablespoons Worcestershire powder (optional, see Note)

YOU'LL ALSO NEED

6 to 8 cups oak or hickory chips or chunks, soaked for 1 hour in water to cover, then drained; a heavy-duty aluminum foil pan

ADVANCE PREPARATION

4 hours to overnight for curing the brisket (optional), then allow 8 to 9 hours for smoking the brisket *and* ½ hour for it to rest.

1 Trim the brisket so as to leave a ¼-inch cap of fat. (Any less and the brisket will dry out, any more and the fat will prevent the rub from seasoning the meat.)

2 Place the the mustard, salt, pepper, powdered Worcestershire sauce, if using, in a bowl and mix them with your fingers. Sprinkle the rub on the brisket on all sides, rubbing it onto the meat. If you have time, wrap the brisket in plastic wrap and let it cure in the refrigerator for at least 4 hours or as long as overnight.

3 To grill: *If you are using a smoker,* set it up following the manufacturer's instructions and preheat it to 275°F. When ready to cook, place the brisket fat side up in the smoker. Add wood chips or chunks to the smoker every hour, following the manufacturer's instructions.

If you are using a charcoal grill, set up the grill for indirect grilling, place a large drip pan in the center, and preheat the grill to low (275°F). To achieve this low temperature, use only half as much charcoal as normal. When ready to cook, toss about 2 cups of wood chips or chunks on the coals. Place the brisket on the hot grate over the drip pan, fat side up, and cover the grill. You'll need to add fresh coals and

THE SCOOP

WHERE: Texas, U.S.A.

WHAT: Brisket crusted with spices and slow smoked over oak and hickory—simply some of the most righteous beef on Planet Barbecue

HOW: Smoking or indirect grilling over charcoal

JUST THE FACTS: A brisket is comprised of three parts: a lean rectangular flat, a fibrous point, and a fatty cap called the deckle. The three are encased in and connected by a thick sheath of waxy fat. This recipe calls for the flat (sometimes called the center cut) a six- to eight-pound slab of lean muscle with a quarter inch–thick layer of fat on top. Normally, brisket flats are what you find at the supermarket, but it's a good idea to order one ahead of time to make sure that you get a full flat and that they leave the fat intact.

PREPARING THE BRISKET

1. Trim the excess fat off the top of the brisket, leaving a layer at least ¼-inch thick.

2. Rub the seasonings into the meat with the palm of your hand. Hey, that's why they call it a rub.

3. After rubbing, but before wrapping, place the brisket in the smoker.

4. Wrap the partially cooked brisket in aluminum foil.

5. Use an instant-read meat thermometer to check for doneness: the internal temperature should be about 195°F.

more wood chips or chunks to each side of the grill every hour for the first 4 hours.

4 Smoke or grill the brisket until a dark "bark" (outside crust) forms and the internal temperature of the meat is about 150°F, 4 to 5 hours; use an instant-read meat thermometer to test for doneness. Then, tightly wrap the brisket in a couple of layers of aluminum foil, crimping the edges to make a hermetic seal. Return the brisket to the smoker or grill and continue cooking until the brisket is very tender, but not soft, and the internal temperature is about 195°F, about 4 hours longer.

5 Remove the wrapped brisket from the smoker or grill and place it in a warm spot. Let the brisket rest for about 30 minutes. This resting period is very important; during that time, the brisket will reabsorb its juices.

6 To serve, unwrap the brisket and thinly slice it. Spoon any juices over the brisket and get ready for some of the most extraordinary smoked beef on Planet Barbecue.

NOTE: Worcestershire powder is available by mail order through www.spicebarn.com. If unavailable, add 1 tablespoon more of dry mustard.

Brisket the way they like it in Texas Hill Country—with a dark bark (crust) on the outside and moist, tender meat inside.

Montreal Smoked Meat: Canadians do an interesting variation of Texas brisket.

Served at Jewish delicatessens in Montreal, it starts with the same cut of beef and the same process of curing with a spice rub (note the pastrami overtones). **SERVES 8 TO 12**

3 tablespoons dark brown sugar
3 tablespoons sweet or smoked paprika
2 tablespoons coarse salt (kosher or sea)
1 tablespoon cracked black peppercorns
1 tablespoon mustard seeds
2 teaspoons coriander seeds
2 teaspoons fennel seeds
2 teaspoons celery seeds

1 teaspoon cumin seeds
1 beef brisket flat (6 to 8 pounds) with a cap of fat at least ¼ inch thick

Place the brown sugar, paprika, salt, peppercorns, mustard seeds, coriander seeds, fennel seeds, celery seeds, and cumin seeds in a mixing bowl and mix well, breaking up any lumps in the brown sugar with your fingertips. Sprinkle the rub on the brisket on all sides, rubbing it onto the meat. Wrap the brisket in plastic wrap and let it cure in the refrigerator for at least 6 hours or as long as overnight. Cook the brisket following the instructions in Steps 3 through 6 on page 117. Serve the brisket hot or cool on rye bread slathered with mustard.

Brazilian Spit-Roasted Beef Tenderloin
{ FILET MIGNON NO ESPETO }

Nothing says magnanimity at a barbecue like a whole beef tenderloin smokily charred on the grill. And if you think it's good grilled using the direct method, wait until you try it spit roasted. In the best Brazilian steak house style, you would bring the tenderloin to the table on the spit and carve it right onto everyone's plate, providing each guest with a miniature set of tongs to grab the beef as you're carving it. Each paper-thin slice would be crusty on the outside, sanguine and moist inside, and tender enough to cut with the side of a fork. The drawback to this method of serving is that you, the grill master, will need to make several trips between the rotisserie and the table to recook the tenderloin after each carving, so you can always serve an end cut. It's far easier to remove the whole tenderloin from the spit, then carve it crosswise into slices. In either case, the beef is seasoned with nothing more than coarse salt and served with nothing more elaborate than a simple tomato-onion salsa. Here's how they do it at Grimpa, the celebrated *churrascaria* (grill house) in Curitiba, Brazil. **SERVES 6 TO 8**

THE SCOOP

WHERE: Brazil

WHAT: A whole beef tenderloin spit roasted and served with a tomato-onion salsa

HOW: Spit roasting

JUST THE FACTS: Pinecones were traditionally used in this part of Brazil to start a fire, imparting an extra layer of flavor. (You'll find a similar grilling technique in Nuremberg, Germany, where they grill bratwurst over pinecones.) If you have access to pinecones, add them to the charcoal.

FOR THE TOMATO-ONION SALSA

1 large luscious, red ripe tomato

½ sweet white onion, peeled and cut into ¼-inch dice

1 small or ½ large yellow bell pepper, cut into ¼-inch dice

3 tablespoons finely chopped fresh flat-leaf parsley or cilantro

½ cup vegetable oil, or extra-virgin olive oil, or a combination of the two

3 tablespoons fresh lime juice or red wine vinegar, or more to taste

Coarse salt (kosher or sea) and freshly ground black pepper

FOR THE BEEF TENDERLOIN

1 beef tenderloin, trimmed (3 to 4 pounds; see Note)

About 1 tablespoon extra-virgin olive oil (optional)

About ¼ cup rock salt or very coarse sea salt

Cracked black peppercorns

ADVANCE PREPARATION

None

1 Make the tomato-onion salsa: Not more than 1 hour before serving, remove the stem ends from the tomato, then cut the tomato into ¼-inch dice. Combine the diced tomato, onion, bell pepper, parsley, ½ cup of oil, and the lime juice in an attractive nonreactive serving bowl and toss to mix. Season with salt and black pepper to taste and more lime juice as necessary; the salsa should be highly seasoned.

2 Set up the grill for spit roasting, following the manufacturer's instructions, and preheat the grill to high.

3 Thread the tenderloin lengthwise onto the rotisserie spit. Start by weaving the narrow "tail" back and forth onto the skewer, then skewer the spit directly through the center of the "head" end. Bunch up the tail end of the tenderloin slightly; this will not only make it fit on the spit but make it thicker so the meat cooks evenly. Place the tenderloin on a baking sheet and, if desired, lightly brush it on all sides with the olive oil (this isn't often done in Brazil, but it helps the salt adhere to the

Turn Up the Heat

In Brazil they spit roast beef tenderloins over charcoal, a fuel that has the advantage of producing a more intense heat than that of the rotisserie on most gas grills. If you own a charcoal kettle grill, it's easy to outfit it with a rotisserie: The Weber-Stephen Products Company sells a rotisserie collar and motor attachment that fits right over the grill. You'll want to put coals on both sides of the grill, the way you would when grilling using the indirect method: To get the right ratio of crisp crust to juicy meat you need to spit roast at a high temperature.

If you use a gas grill rotisserie, get it screaming hot. To boost the heat, you can light the outside grill burners, as you would for indirect grilling, thereby providing two heat sources in one: the lateral heat from the rotisserie burner and the indirect heat from the outside burners under the grate. In a pinch, you could also grill the tenderloin using the direct method, in which case you'll need about four to six minutes per side (assuming four sides).

meat and gives you an extra layer of flavor). Season the tenderloin *very* generously on all sides with the salt and some cracked peppercorns; Brazilians like their meat salty.

4 When ready to cook, attach the spit to the grill and turn on the motor. Spit roast the tenderloin until crusty and brown on the outside and cooked to taste, about 25 to 30 minutes for rare; 35 to 40 minutes for medium-rare. Use an instant-read meat thermometer to test for doneness, inserting it deep into the thickest part of the meat but not touching the metal spit. When cooked to rare the internal temperature will be about 125°F; medium-rare will be about 145°F.

5 *To serve the tenderloin Brazilian style,* bring the spit to the table. Holding it vertically over a plate to catch any drippings and using a large, sharp knife, carve the meat in downward strokes into thin slices, inviting each eater to grab a slice with tongs. If you reach a core of meat that's too rare, return the spit to the rotisserie to continue cooking.

To serve the tenderloin North American style, place it on a cutting board, remove the spit, and let the meat rest for 5 minutes, loosely tented with aluminum foil. Slice the tenderloin crosswise into ½-inch-thick slices (or whatever thickness you desire).

6 Serve the tomato-onion salsa alongside the tenderloin.

NOTE: The beef tenderloin should be trimmed of the silverskin and most of its fat. If possible, leave intact a ¼-inch layer of fat.

VARIATION

Italian Spit-Roasted Beef Tenderloin: For a killer Italian version of this dish, thread the tenderloin onto the rotisserie spit, brush it with olive oil and season it with salt and cracked peppercorns as described in Step 3. Sprinkle 3 minced cloves of garlic and 3 tablespoons of finely chopped fresh rosemary or sage or a mixture of the two over the tenderloin. Drizzle a little more oil on top and pat the seasonings onto the meat. Spit roast the tenderloin as described in Step 4. After you carve the tenderloin, drizzle a little of the best extra-virgin olive oil you can buy over it. *Benissimo!*

A Brazilian churrasqueiro (waiter-griller) is responsible for both roasting and serving the meat.

Brazilian Grilled Flank Steak

If you've spent any time at the grill, I'm sure you've grilled flank steak. What you may not realize is how delectable it is spit roasted. The lateral heat and slow rotation crisp the meat fibers, producing a flank steak that is simultaneously crusty and moist. Here's how *fraldinha,* a cut that roughly corresponds to North American flank steak, is prepared at a *churrascaria* (Brazilian steak house). **SERVES 4**

1 large flank steak (about 1½ pounds; see Note)
3 tablespoons rock salt or very coarse sea salt
Freshly cracked or coarsely ground black pepper
Tomato-Onion Salsa (page 120)

1 Set up the grill for spit roasting, following the manufacturer's instructions, and preheat the grill to high.

2 Thread the flank steak onto the spit lengthwise, so the spit runs down the center. Insert the prongs into the meat at each end to hold the steak. Alternatively, you can use a flat rotisserie basket (available at www.thebbqdepot.com).

3 When ready to cook, sprinkle it all over with salt and pepper. Attach the spit to the grill and turn on the motor. Spit roast the flank steak until crusty and brown on the outside but still medium-rare inside, 15 to 20 minutes.

4 To serve, thinly slice the steak across the grain and serve the tomato-onion salsa alongside.

NOTE: Pick the fattiest flank steak you can find. The fat will melt out during the spit roasting, crisping the meat fibers while keeping the meat moist.

Salt-Crusted Beef Tenderloin Grilled in Cloth

{ LOMO AL TRAPO }

Beef tenderloin holds a singular place in the world of barbecue—it's one of the costliest and most prestigious cuts of meat, but paradoxically, one of the least flavorful. Remember: In North America, it's the cheap lowbrow cuts, like spareribs and brisket, that have achieved barbecue cult status. So when I heard that Colombian grill masters had figured out a way to give beef tenderloin drama and taste, I couldn't board an Avianca flight fast enough to try it. *Lomo al trapo* (literally "tenderloin in cloth") is a beef tenderloin wrapped in a salt-packed cotton cloth and roasted in the embers. It's cool as all get out and ridiculously quick and easy to make. It looks positively prehistoric when it's done (a guaranteed showstopper) and, damn, if it isn't the best way I've found to grill a beef tenderloin. Here's how they make *lomo al trapo* at the legendary Andrés Carne de Res restaurant. The Brazilian Rotisserie Onions on page 537 would be good served alongside. **SERVES 2**

1 center cut piece of beef tenderloin,
    meticulously trimmed of all fat and silverskin
    (about 6 inches long and 12 to 16 ounces)
About 2 cups table salt
1 tablespoon dried oregano

YOU'LL ALSO NEED

1 piece of clean cotton cloth approximately
    16 inches square, dipped in cold water and
    wrung out slightly; butcher's string

ADVANCE PREPARATION
None

1 Arrange the cotton cloth on a work surface on the diagonal (like a diamond), so that one corner points down toward you. Spread the salt out on top of the cloth to form a layer ¼ inch thick that extends to within 1 inch of the bottom edges of the cloth. Sprinkle the oregano evenly over the salt.

2 Arrange the beef tenderloin crosswise on top of the salt about 4 inches up from the point of the cloth closest to you; the tenderloin should be parallel to your shoulders. Starting at the corner closest to you, roll the tenderloin up in the cloth and salt. The idea is to make a compact roll. Now take the points of cloth at each end of the resulting cylinder and tie them together on top of the tenderloin. Tuck in any loose ends. The goal is to form a tight cylinder. (If necessary, tie the center of the cylinder with butcher's string to secure it.) You should roll up the tenderloin just prior to grilling.

THE SCOOP

WHERE: Bogotá, Colombia

WHAT: Beef tenderloin crusted with perhaps a half a pound of salt, wrapped in a cotton cloth, and charred on a bed of fiery embers

HOW: A popular dish to cook in the fireplace in Colombian homes, *lomo al trapo* is prepared using the oldest of the five methods of live-fire cooking: roasting in the embers. You place the wrapped roast on a bed of hot coals long enough to burn the cloth wrapping, but briefly enough to cook the meat inside until it's tender and medium-rare. If you have a gas grill, preheat it to screaming hot and char the *lomo* (beef tenderloin) on the grate. This won't look quite as dramatic as yanking the burnt roll out of the embers, but you'll still get a great flavor.

JUST THE FACTS: You need a beef tenderloin that has been completely trimmed of all fat and silverskin. This is easy, if a little time consuming; you may want to ask your butcher to do it. You'll also need a clean white cotton cloth about 16 inches square (a clean cotton dishcloth or cotton napkin works well).

HOW TO MAKE A SALT-CRUSTED BEEF TENDERLOIN

1. *Sprinkle the salt over a clean, damp cotton cloth.*

2. *Spread out the salt in a ¼ inch-thick layer over the cloth to within 1 inch of the edges.*

3. *Place the beef tenderloin on the diagonal at one corner of the cloth. Note the dried oregano sprinkled over the salt.*

4. *Starting at the corner, bring the cloth and salt over the tenderloin.*

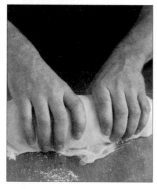

5. *Roll the tenderloin in the cloth and salt until it is completely encased.*

6. *Bring the ends of the cloth together and tie into a tight knot.*

7. *Grill the cloth-wrapped tenderloin directly on the charcoal. Turn using tongs.*

8. *Crack open the salt crust with the back of a large, heavy chef's knife or cleaver to reveal the beef inside.*

3 To grill: *If you are using a charcoal grill,* light the coals in a chimney starter and rake them out in an even layer at the bottom of the grill. You will not need a grill grate. Place the wrapped tenderloin right on the coals, knotted side up, and grill it for about 9 minutes. Using long-handled tongs, gently turn the tenderloin package over and grill it for about 8 minutes longer. Do not be alarmed if the cloth burns; it's meant to. In fact, the whole package should look about as appetizing as a fire-charred log.

If you are using a gas grill, preheat it as hot as it will go; you need a "2 Mississippi" fire (see page 610). There is no need to oil the grill grate. Place the wrapped tenderloin on the hot grate, knotted side up, and grill it for about 9 minutes. Using long-handled tongs, gently turn the tenderloin package over and grill it for about 8 minutes longer. You may need a little more cooking time and the crust won't burn as black when charcoal grilled but the tenderloin will still turn out pretty tasty.

4 Use an instant-read meat thermometer to test the tenderloin for doneness, inserting it through the cloth into the center of the meat. When cooked to rare, the internal temperature will be about 125°F; to medium-rare, 140° to 145°F.

5 Transfer the charred tenderloin to a metal platter or rimmed sheet pan and let it rest for 2 minutes. Lift the tenderloin with tongs and tap it hard with the back of a large, heavy chef's knife (you may need to tap it several times). The burnt shell should crack and come off. Using a pastry brush, brush any excess salt off the tenderloin. Transfer the tenderloin to a clean platter, cut it into 2 to 4 pieces and serve at once.

Santa Maria Tri-Tip

Santa Maria, California: It was here, in this ranching turned agricultural town between Los Angeles and San Francisco that the meat synonymous with barbecue in southern California came into being—the Santa Maria tri-tip. When grilled, this boomerang-shaped cut, the tip of the sirloin, has two genial properties: It slices like brisket but has the rich beefy flavor of steak. And if it weren't for Bob Schutz, Californian butchers might still be grinding it up to make hamburger. Schutz was a singularity himself, a one-armed butcher working at an old Safeway store in Santa Maria. One day in 1952, already in possession of more hamburger meat than he needed, Schutz had the idea to spit roast tri-tip on the rotisserie. Seasoned with salt and garlic powder and thinly sliced across the grain like London broil or brisket, tri-tip prompted whistles of admiration from the moment people first tasted it. Over time, the rotisserie gave way to wood-burning grills that have grates you raise and lower with a flywheel (the local red oak became the preferred fuel). The Mexican ranchers, who first settled the area in the 1800s, provided a one-two punch of flavor: cumin seeds and fresh cilantro, as well as the accompaniments: salsa and stewed pinquito beans. **SERVES 4**

THE SCOOP

WHERE: Southern California, U.S.A.

WHAT: Wood grilled tri-tip with garlic, cilantro, and cumin

HOW: Direct grilling

JUST THE FACTS: If you live in California (and on the West Coast in general), you will likely find tri-tip at your local supermarket. If not, you can order it by mail from Lobel's (www.lobels.com).

1 beef tri-tip (about 2 pounds)

Coarse salt (kosher or sea) and freshly ground black pepper

1 teaspoon cumin seeds or ground cumin

3 cloves garlic, minced

¼ cup minced fresh cilantro

1 to 2 tablespoons extra-virgin olive oil

Pico de Gallo (page 130)

YOU'LL ALSO NEED

Unsoaked wood logs, chips, or chunks (optional)

ADVANCE PREPARATION

None

1 Place the tri-tip on a sheet pan or roasting pan. Very generously season it on both sides with salt and black pepper, and the cumin, garlic, and cilantro. Drizzle the olive oil over the tri-tip on both sides and rub it and the spices into the meat with your fingertips. Let the tri-tip marinate in the refrigerator, covered, while you light the grill.

2 Set up the grill for two-zone grilling (see page 603). Preheat one zone to medium-high and one zone to medium. Ideally, you'd grill over a wood fire (see page 603 for instructions). Alternatively, you can use wood chips or chunks to add a smoke flavor.

3 When ready to cook, brush and oil the grill grate. If you are using a charcoal grill, toss the wood chips or chunks on the coals. If you are using a gas grill,

add the wood chips or chunks to the smoker box or place them in a smoker pouch under the grate (see page 603). Place the tri-tip on the hot grate, over the medium-high zone, and grill it until it is crusty and brown on the outside and cooked to taste, 6 to 8 minutes per side for medium-rare. Use an instant-read meat thermometer to test for doneness, inserting it into the thickest part of the meat. When cooked to medium-rare the internal temperature will be about 145°F. If the tri-tip begins to brown too much, move it to the medium zone.

4 Transfer the tri-tip to a cutting board and let it rest for 3 minutes. Thinly slice the meat across the grain and serve at once with *pico de gallo* on the side.

Salt-Crusted Tri-Tip

WHERE: Uruguay and southern Brazil

WHAT: Beef tri-tip thickly crusted with—make that buried under—rock salt and slow roasted over a wood fire

HOW: The traditional cooking method combines direct and indirect grilling. As in direct grilling, the tri-tip is positioned on a grate directly over the embers. (More accurately speaking, the embers are raked under the meat.) But, as in indirect grilling, the meat is cooked low and slow—for 45 minutes to 1 hour, to be precise.

For years, I'd been hearing about a singular method of grilling beef: Crust it with enough salt to give half the population of Uruguay hypertension. Grill it to the color of coal on the outside, leaving the inside cherubic pink, then whack it with a knife to knock off the salt just before you serve it. I chalked up the description to the sort of hyperbole that runs rampant in barbecue circles. But lo and behold, there's a Montevideano griller, Diego Seckback, who does just that. It's another one of those South American meat recipes that contains only two ingredients—beef and salt—but the crusty texture is highly satisfying and the flavor is utterly unique. **SERVES 6**

1 beef tri-tip (about 2 pounds)
¾ cup rock salt or very coarse sea salt

YOU'LL ALSO NEED
2 cups oak chips or chunks, soaked for 1 hour in water to cover, then drained

ADVANCE PREPARATION
None, but allow an hour for grilling the tri-tip.

1 Place the tri-tip fat side up on a rimmed baking sheet. Gently pour the rock salt over it, pressing the salt into the top of the meat with the palm of your hand. The layer of salt should be at least ¼ inch thick.

2 Set up the grill for direct grilling and preheat it to low. Ideally, you'd grill over oak wood embers as they do in South America (see page 603 for instructions on grilling over a wood fire). Alternatively, you can use wood chips or chunks to add a smoke flavor.

3 When ready to cook, brush and oil the grill grate. If you are using a charcoal grill, toss the wood chips or chunks on the coals. If you are using a gas grill, add the wood chips or chunks to the smoker box or place them in a smoker pouch under the grate (see page 603). Place the tri-tip on the hot grate, working gently so as not to dislodge the salt. Grill the tri-tip until the bottom is crusty and a dark golden brown, 40 to 50 minutes.

4 Increase the heat to medium, either by raking the coals into a mound or by turning up the gas burner control.

5 Turn the tri-tip over and place it salt side down over the heat. Grill the tri-tip until the second side is crusty and brown, 5 to 10 minutes longer. Use an instant-read meat thermometer to test for doneness, inserting it into the thickest part of the meat. When cooked to medium-rare the internal temperature will be about 145°F.

6 Turn the tri-tip over again and tap the top with the back of a knife a few times to dislodge the salt. Transfer the tri-tip to a cutting board and let it rest for a few minutes, then thinly slice it across the grain.

Uruguayan Salt-Crusted Tri-Tip

Mexican Grilled Beef

{ CARNE ASADA }

Most cultures have a barbecued street food, a dish that's simultaneously nutritional, varied, and filling enough to serve as a full meal. Mexico's version is *carne asada*—literally grilled meat—and as elsewhere on Planet Barbecue, the simple name doesn't begin to do the dish justice.

Carne asada starts with, no surprise here, a thin, cheap, flavorful cut of beef from the steer's underbelly or loin. Some grill masters marinate the meat in chiles, oregano, or lime juice; more often it is seasoned simply with salt and perhaps garlic powder and black pepper. However it's seasoned, the meat is always grilled fresh to order, ideally over glowing

WHERE: Mexico

WHAT: Flame-charred beef served on fire-warmed tortillas with salsas, fresh and grilled vegetables, sour cream, and cheese

HOW: Direct grilling

JUST THE FACTS: The traditional cut for *carne asada* is *arrachera*—flap meat, a thin, flavorful muscle from the underbelly of the steer. Look for it at a Mexican butcher. Good alternatives include skirt steak (*fajita*), flank steak, hanger steak, or thin slices of top or bottom round or sirloin, all of them thin, flavorful, and cheap.

oak or mesquite embers, but charcoal and even propane are used, too. And because such flavorful, economical beef cuts tend to be tough, the meat is always chopped or cut into bite-size pieces before serving to shorten the length of the tough meat fibers.

The wrapping is equally important: corn or flour tortillas, preferably freshly made, brushed with meat drippings, and warmed on the grill. To round things out, you add vegetables—grilled scallions or onions perhaps, or thinly sliced fresh cabbage, chiles, radishes, cucumbers, and/or avocado. And because we're in Mexico, you need salsa: *pico de gallo* (a simple tomato, onion, and jalapeño salsa) at bare minimum, or a *salsa verde* ("green" tomatillo salsa), *salsa de chile chipotle* (smoked jalapeño salsa), or *salsa de chile de árbol* (Sinaloan grilled tomato salsa piqued with fiery *chiles de árbol*). At a good *carne asada* joint, you'll find a half dozen salsas or more.

But you're not done yet, because where there's fire in Mexico, there's generally ice (or at least something cool and creamy) for a counterpoint—a spoonful of guacamole, for example, or a dollop of sour cream. And to gild the lily, as it were, there will likely be a sprinkling of grated salty cheese. You can take all of this into your mouth in a single bite if you have the agility that comes with years of practice. The result is the gustatory equivalence of a full symphony orchestra in a package the size of your iPod.

What follows is not so much a recipe as a broad blueprint. Follow it to the letter if you're feeling ambitious, or make the bare minimum—grilled beef, tortillas, and a salsa—if you're in a hurry. **SERVES 4**

FOR GRILLING

2 poblano peppers, or 4 banana peppers or other large, moderately hot chiles

1 bunch scallions, trimmed

1 sweet onion, cut crosswise into ¼ inch–thick slices

1½ pounds beef flap meat, skirt steak, hanger steak, or another thin (¼ inch) cut of beef

Coarse salt (kosher or sea)

Garlic powder (optional)

Freshly ground black pepper (optional)

20 to 24 corn tortillas, preferably freshly made at a Mexican tortilla shop or market, or 12 small (6 inch) flour tortillas

Meat drippings (see Notes) or vegetable oil (optional)

FOR SERVING (SEE NOTES)
One or more of these accompaniments:

1 small head green cabbage (about 1 pound), cored and sliced paper-thin

1 large or 2 small cucumbers, thinly sliced

1 bunch radishes, stemmed and thinly sliced

2 ripe avocados, pitted, peeled, cut into wedges or diced, and sprinkled with fresh lime juice to keep it from discoloring

1 cup sour cream

1 cup coarsely grated queso blanco or Cotija or Jack cheese

3 limes, quartered

One or more of these salsas:
Pico de Gallo (recipe follows)
Salsa Verde (page 130)
Salsa de Chile Chipotle (page 131)
Mexican Guacamole (page 131)

YOU'LL ALSO NEED
3 cups unsoaked wood chips or chunks (optional)

ADVANCE PREPARATION
None for marinating the meat, but allow yourself an hour or so for making the various salsas and assembling all of the condiments.

1 Set up the grill for direct grilling and preheat it to high. Ideally, you'll grill over a wood fire (see page 603 for instructions), but you can achieve a similar effect by using dry wood chips on a charcoal or gas grill (the chips should be unsoaked, because you want a light wood smoke flavor).

2 When ready to cook, brush and oil the grill grate. If you are using a charcoal grill, toss the wood chips or chunks on the coals, if using. If you are using a gas grill, add 2 cups of wood chips, if using, or chunks to the smoker box or place them in a smoker pouch under the grate (see page 603). If you are using poblano peppers or banana peppers, arrange them on the hot grate and grill them until the skins are darkly browned, 3 to 4 minutes per side, 12 to 16 minutes in all (banana peppers will take a little less time than poblanos). Arrange the scallions and onion on the grate and grill them until golden brown on both sides, 2 to 4 minutes per side. Place the scallions or onion on the grate for about 6 minutes after the peppers have grilled.

3 Transfer the grilled vegetables to a chopping block or cutting board. Leave the fire burning. Cut the poblanos into strips, discarding the seeds. Cut the scallions and onion into 2-inch pieces. Arrange the grilled vegetables on a serving platter.

4 Generously season the beef on both sides with salt and garlic powder and pepper, if using. Add the remaining wood chips, if using. Arrange the meat on the hot grate and grill until cooked to taste, 3 to 4 minutes per side for medium. (Mexicans prefer their *carne asada* medium to medium-well done.) Use the poke test to check for doneness (see the box on page 147). Transfer the grilled beef to a chopping block or cutting board, reserving any of the meat drippings, if desired. Leave the fire burning.

5 Lightly brush the tortillas with meat drippings or oil, if desired (this is not necessary but does make the tortillas a little richer and moister). Arrange the tortillas on the hot grate and grill them just long enough to warm them, about 15 seconds per side.

MEXICAN CARNE ASADA | page 127

6 Chop or thinly slice the beef across the grain. To eat the *carne asada,* place a few slices of beef on a warm tortilla, then pile on the grilled vegetables, raw vegetables, sour cream, cheese, and salsa(s) of your choice and add a squeeze of lime, if desired.

NOTES: Before you light the grill, set everything you will need for serving out on the table. Place the salsas in attractive serving bowls. Arrange your selection of cabbage, cucumber, radishes, and/or avocado on a platter or in serving bowls. Place the sour cream, your choice of cheese, and/or the lime quarters in serving bowls. And be sure you have spoons ready for serving.

Save the meat drippings that accumulate in the pan you use to transfer the grilled beef to the cutting board and the drippings from the cutting board and you can brush them on the tortillas before you heat them on the grill.

Queso blanco is a mild, salty cow's milk cheese; it sort of squeaks against your teeth when you take a bite. Cotija is a bit sharper (like feta). For a Californian touch, you could use Jack or pepper Jack cheese.

Pico de Gallo

Literally translated as "rooster beak," *pico de gallo* is the most basic Mexican salsa, found in one version or another from Sonora to Chiapas. Perhaps the salsa takes its name from its pugnacious bite. Because there's no cooking, this salsa lives or dies by the quality of the raw materials. **MAKES ABOUT 1½ CUPS**

1 large or 2 medium-size luscious, red ripe tomatoes, diced
½ medium-size sweet onion, finely diced
1 to 3 jalapeño peppers, seeded and finely diced
    (for a hotter salsa, leave the seeds in)
½ cup coarsely chopped fresh cilantro
3 tablespoons fresh lime juice, or more to taste

Combine the tomato(es), onion, jalapeño(s), cilantro, and lime juice in a mixing bowl and gently stir to mix. Taste for seasoning, adding more lime juice as necessary. You can chop the ingredients ahead of time but the salsa tastes best mixed within 15 minutes or so of serving. The salsa will be quite moist.

Salsa Verde

Mexico's ubiquitous "green salsa," *salsa verde* is made with a ground cherrylike fruit called tomatillo that's prized for its refreshing tartness (it's available in most supermarkets). Tradition calls for the tomatillos to be roasted on a *comal* (flat skillet) or boiled, but you'll get even more flavor if you grill them. **MAKES ABOUT 2 CUPS**

1 pound fresh tomatillos, papery husks removed
2 to 4 jalapeño or serrano peppers, or 1 poblano pepper
½ medium-size onion, cut in half, each half skewered on a
    wooden toothpick
3 cloves garlic, peeled and skewered on a wooden toothpick
½ cup loosely packed chopped fresh cilantro
1½ tablespoons lard or olive oil
½ cup chicken stock or vegetable stock
½ teaspoon sugar, or more to taste
Coarse salt (kosher or sea) and freshly ground black pepper

1 Set up the grill for two-zone grilling (see page 611). Preheat one zone to high and one zone to medium.

2 When ready to cook, brush and oil the grill grate. Place the tomatillos and peppers on the hot grate and grill them until darkly browned, even blackened, and blistered on all sides, about 2 minutes per side. Place the onion on the grate and grill it until darkly browned and tender, about 3 minutes per side. Position the garlic over the cooler zone of the grill so it browns without burning, about 2 minutes per side. Transfer the grilled vegetables to a plate.

3 Seed the peppers and scrape off the charred skin; don't worry about a few black specks of skin—they'll add color and flavor. Remove and discard the toothpicks from the onion and garlic. Puree the tomatillos, peppers, onion, garlic, and cilantro in a food processor or blender until thickish but pourable (like the consistency of cream of tomato soup).

4 Heat the lard or oil in a large saucepan. Add the tomatillo puree and cook over high heat until the mixture is thick, slightly darkened, and highly aromatic, 3 to 5 minutes. Whisk in the stock and let the salsa boil until it is thick and flavorful, about 5 minutes. Whisk in the sugar. Taste for seasoning, adding salt and pepper to taste and more sugar as necessary; the *salsa verde* should be highly seasoned.

Salsa de Chile Chipotle

This salsa comes from the north of Mexico, where jalapeño peppers are smoked—originally this was done to preserve them, today it's done for flavor. Chipotles are one of the rare instances where I prefer a canned product to fresh. Canned chipotles come in a tangy vinegar and oregano sauce called *adobo,* so they have more flavor. **MAKES ABOUT 2 CUPS**

1 pound luscious, red ripe tomatoes (see Note)
½ medium-size onion, cut in quarters, each quarter skewered
    on a wooden toothpick
3 cloves garlic, peeled and skewered on a wooden toothpick
2 to 5 canned chipotle chiles with their juices
    (they're hot suckers; don't use more than you mean to)
¼ cup loosely packed chopped fresh cilantro
1 teaspoon dried oregano, preferably Mexican
Coarse salt (kosher or sea)

1 Set up the grill for two-zone grilling (see page 611). Preheat one zone to high and one zone to medium.

2 When ready to cook, brush and oil the grill grate. Place the tomatoes on the hot grate and grill them until darkly browned, even blackened, and blistered on all sides, about 2 minutes per side. Place the onion on the grate and grill it until darkly browned and tender, about 3 minutes per side.

Position the garlic over the cooler zone of the grill so it browns without burning, about 2 minutes per side. Transfer the grilled vegetables to a plate.

3 Scrape the charred skin off the tomatoes; don't worry about a few black specks of skin—they'll add color and flavor. Remove and discard the toothpicks from the onion and garlic. Puree the tomatoes, onion, garlic, chipotles, cilantro, and oregano in a food processor or blender until thickish but pourable (like the consistency of cream of tomato soup). Season the salsa with salt to taste.

NOTE: The salsa can also be made with 1 pound of tomatillos. Remove the papery husks before grilling.

Mexican Guacamole

Most Americans are so used to thinking of guacamole as a dip that we forget its usefulness as a salsa, making a cool and creamy contrast to crusty, sizzling hot beef and the more fiery of the salsas. To make the guacamole as they do in Mexico you'd use a *molcajete,* a lava stone mortar. **MAKES ABOUT 2 CUPS**

½ medium-size sweet onion, finely diced
1 to 4 jalapeño or serrano peppers, seeded and finely diced
    (for a hotter guacamole, leave the seeds in)
1 clove garlic, minced
1 teaspoon salt, or more to taste
2 medium-size ripe avocados (see Note), pitted, peeled,
    and coarsely chopped
½ cup loosely packed coarsely chopped fresh cilantro
3 tablespoons fresh lime juice, or more to taste
Freshly ground black pepper

***Molcajete* method** Place half of the onion and pepper(s) and the garlic and salt in the stone bowl and mash it to a coarse paste using the pestle. Add the avocado and coarsely mash it. Work in the remaining onion and pepper(s) and the cilantro and lime juice. Taste for seasoning, adding more salt and/or lime juice as necessary and black pepper to taste; the guacamole should be highly seasoned. Don't overmash the guacamole; it should be quite coarse in consistency.

Food processor method Place the onion, pepper(s), garlic, salt, and avocado in a food processor and run the machine in short bursts to coarsely mix the ingredients. Add the cilantro and lime juice, and pulse just to mix. Taste for seasoning, adding more salt and/or lime juice

and black pepper to taste; the guacamole should be highly seasoned. Don't overprocess the guacamole; it should be quite coarse in consistency. Alternatively, if your avocado is quite ripe, you can place the ingredients in a large bowl and mash them with a wooden spoon or fork.

NOTE: The avocado should be ripe and soft, but not squishy. You're looking for Charmin-like squeezability. You may want to buy the avocado a day or two ahead and let it ripen at room temperature.

Santander Cheese Steak
{ LOMO SANTANDEREANO GRATINADO }

THE SCOOP

WHERE: Bogotá, Colombia

WHAT: Wine-marinated butterflied grilled beef tenderloin topped with tomatoes and melted cheese

HOW: Direct grilling

JUST THE FACTS: The recipe here calls for beef tenderloin, but it would also work well with a less expensive cut, like New York strip steak or skirt steak. You could even use slices of smoked brisket. (As you will see, the brisket comes the closest to the dish's origins.) Colombian cheese is difficult to find in the United States, but Jack cheese or a mild white cheddar will give you the right effect.

Who says "kill all the lawyers"? (Actually, it was Shakespeare in *Henry VI, Part 2,* but never mind.) The legal profession has done at least one positive thing to advance the art of grilling: It gave us Carlos Gómez. A tax lawyer by training, with a passion for barbecue in his private life, Gómez founded Bogotá's popular Lomos restaurant in 1986. (Talk about an appropriate name—*lomo* means "beef tenderloin.") For two decades, local writers, artists, politicians, and embassy types have come here for hypercarnivorous Colombian specialties as *lomo al trapo* (tenderloin crusted with salt and grilled in cloth, see page 123), *bife de chorizo* (New York strip steak), and this Santander cheese steak. Lomos makes its cheese steak with grilled boiled sliced brisket. As boiling brisket is not something we normally do in North America (or in the Raichlen household), I've grafted the tomato cheese topping on to another Lomos specialty: red-wine marinated grilled beef tenderloin. I haven't heard any complaints. Why Santander? It's a department in western Colombia that was once reputed to be the site of the legendary El Dorado. **SERVES 4**

1 center cut piece of trimmed beef tenderloin
    (about 6 inches long and 1½ pounds), or 4 thin New York
    strip steaks or skirt steaks (each about ½ inch thick
    and 6 to 8 ounces)
1 cup beef broth, preferably homemade
1 cup dry red wine
3 tablespoons extra-virgin olive oil
2 cloves garlic, minced
2 bay leaves
1 teaspoon dried or fresh thyme
Coarse salt (kosher or sea) and freshly ground black pepper
1 large or 2 medium-size luscious, red ripe tomatoes,
    thinly sliced crosswise
6 to 8 ounces Gruyère, Jack cheese, or mild or sharp cheddar
    cheese, cut into broad, thin slices
1 teaspoon dried oregano

ADVANCE PREPARATION
1 to 2 hours for marinating the beef

1 Cut the tenderloin completely in half lengthwise, then cut each half completely in half again lengthwise. You shuold have 4 broad pieces of meat.

2 Place the beef steaks in a nonreactive baking dish just large enough to hold them in a single layer. Put the beef broth, red wine, olive oil, garlic, bay leaves, thyme, and salt and pepper to taste in a large nonreactive mixing bowl and whisk them to mix. Pour the marinade over the beef and let it marinate in the refrigerator, covered, for 1 to 2 hours, turning the pieces several times.

3 Set up the grill for direct grilling and preheat it to high. Leave one section of the grill fire free for a safety zone.

4 When ready to cook, brush and oil the grill grate. Drain the beef steaks well, discarding the marinade. Season the beef on both sides with salt and pepper. Arrange the steaks on the hot grill at a diagonal to the bars. Grill the beef until it is browned on the bottom, about 3 minutes. Transfer the steaks to the safety zone, arranging them cooked side up. Top each steak with tomato slices and cheese and sprinkle with the oregano.

5 Slide the steaks back over the hot zone of the grate and grill the steaks until the bottoms are browned, the cheese is melted, and the steaks are cooked to taste, 2 to 3 minutes longer for medium-rare. Transfer the steaks to a platter or plates and serve at once.

Chilean Steak with Pepper Sauce
{ ENTRANA CON PEBRE }

Chile is the forgotten stepchild in South American barbecue, eclipsed by its showier neighbors, like Argentina and Peru. In fact, I'd venture to say that most North Americans would be hard-pressed to name a single Chilean grilled dish. But, Chileans are grill obsessed, too, and unlike their neighbors, they take great pride in making their own charcoal. The grill repertory may be more limited, but no tour of Planet Barbecue

THE SCOOP

WHERE: Chile

WHAT: A thin beef belly steak seared over charcoal and served with pepper sauce

HOW: Direct grilling

THE SCOOP

JUST THE FACTS:
If you live in an area with a large South American community you may be able to buy a flat, thin, flavorful Chilean steak known as *entraña*. Alternatively, you can use the equally tasty and readily available skirt steak.

Nancy Loseke (my assistant) stands next to a traditional Chilean horno de barro (mud oven used for burning wood into charcoal).

Chile's asado al disco, a grill fashioned from the metal disks of a harrow, here used to cook chorizo.

would be complete without sampling *entraña con pebre*. *Entraña* is a flat, fibrous, robustly flavorful steak cut from the beef diaphragm (don't worry, the taste is more inviting than the description). *Pebre* (pronounced pe-vreh) is the south-ernmost member of a family of fresh salsas that includes Colombian *ají* (see page 185) and Brazilian *molho à campanha* (page 155). **SERVES 4**

2 luscious, red ripe tomatoes
1 poblano pepper, or 2 Anaheim peppers
2 scallions, both white and green parts, trimmed
½ cup chopped fresh cilantro
½ cup extra-virgin olive oil, preferably Chilean
Juice of 1 lemon, or more to taste
Coarse salt (kosher or sea) and freshly ground
    black pepper
1½ pounds entraña or skirt steak
Garlic salt (optional)

ADVANCE PREPARATION
None, but you can make the *pebre* up to 4 hours ahead.

1 Cut each tomato in half and wring out the pulp and seeds. For a milder *pebre,* seed the pepper(s); personally, I'd leave them in. Very finely chop the tomatoes, pepper(s), and scallions. A Chilean would do this by hand, but you can also use a food processor, running the machine in short bursts. If you use a processor, cut the vegetables into 1-inch pieces before processing.

2 Transfer the chopped vegetables to a mixing bowl and stir in the cilantro, olive oil, and lemon juice. Taste for seasoning, adding salt and black pepper to taste and more lemon juice as necessary; the *pebre* should be highly seasoned. You can make the *pebre* up to 4 hours ahead; taste it for seasoning before serving, adding more salt and/ or pepper as necessary.

3 Set up the grill for direct grilling and preheat it to high.

4 When ready to cook, brush and oil the grill grate. Season the steaks on both sides with salt and black pepper; a Chilean might not use garlic salt, however, it works nicely with the *pebre*. Arrange the steaks on the hot grate at a diagonal to the bars. Grill the steaks until cooked to taste, 3 to 5 minutes per side for medium. Use the poke test to check for doneness (see page 612). If desired, give each steak a quarter turn on each side after 1½ minutes to create a hand-some crosshatch of grill marks.

5 Transfer the steaks to a platter or plates. Spoon a little *pebre* on top and serve the rest on the side. As Santiagan grilling enthusiast Francisco Ortiz notes, you don't need salads, vegetable side dishes, starches, or desserts (although he does allow for the presence of a hard roll). It's all about the *pebre* and the meat.

Romanian Garlic Steak
{ FLEICA }

Romanians lunge for their steak knives at the sight of *fleica* and if you like garlic (and what Romanian doesn't?), this steak gives you enough to ward off a legion of vampires. How convenient, for Bram Stoker based his Dracula on a medieval Romanian ruler with the sympathetic name of Vlad the Impaler. And garlic, of course, was one of the few antidotes powerful enough to ward off the undead. (You can visit the ruins of Vlad's castle, a few hours drive from Bucharest.) **SERVES 4**

1½ pounds skirt steak or flank steak

Coarse salt (kosher or sea) and cracked or
freshly ground black pepper

1 to 2 tablespoons sweet paprika

6 to 8 cloves fresh garlic, minced fine as dust

⅓ cup minced fresh flat-leaf parsley

2 tablespoons vegetable oil

Romanian Pickled Peppers (optional, page 542),
for serving

ADVANCE PREPARATION

1 to 4 hours for marinating the steak

1 Arrange the steak in a nonreactive baking dish. If you are using flank steak, score both sides in a crosshatch pattern with a sharp knife (the cuts should be ⅛ inch deep and ¼ inch apart). Generously season the meat on both sides with salt, pepper, and paprika. Sprinkle the garlic and all but 2 tablespoons of the parsley on both sides of the steak. Drizzle the oil over both sides of the steak and pat the spices and oil into the meat with your fingertips. Let the steak marinate in the refrigerator, covered, for 1 to 4 hours; the longer it marinates, the richer the flavor will be.

2 Set up the grill for direct grilling and preheat it to high.

3 When ready to cook, brush and oil the grill grate. Arrange the steak on the hot grate at a diagonal to the bars. Grill the steaks until cooked to taste, 3 to 5 minutes per side for medium for skirt steak, 1 to 2 minutes longer per side for flank steak. Use the poke test to check for doneness (see page 147). If desired, give the steak a quarter turn on each side after 1½ minutes to create a handsome crosshatch of grill marks.

4 Transfer the steak to a platter or plates and sprinkle the remaining 2 tablespoons of parsley on top. Serve the steak with the pickled peppers, if desired.

NOTE: You must start with fresh whole cloves of garlic. Prechopped garlic or minced garlic in oil just won't give you the right flavor.

The Chief of Beef

ANDRES JARAMILLO.
A grill master with the fame of a rock star.

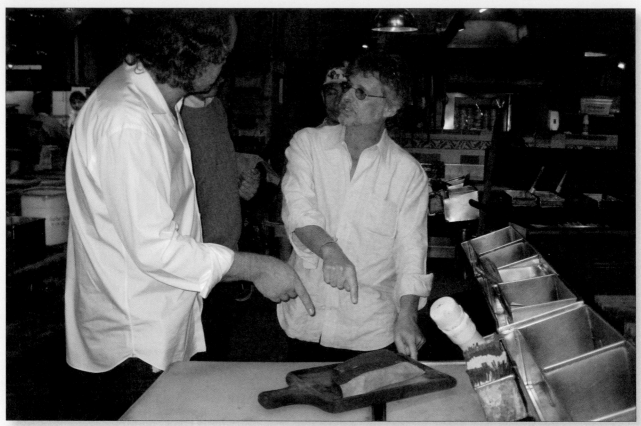

Andrés Jaramillo (left) shows me (right) a punta de anca (fat-capped top sirloin—Colombia's version of Brazil's picanha—see page 153). The thick cap of fat gives the steak its unique richness.

CHIA, COLOMBIA

If grill masters were rock stars, Andrés Jaramillo would be Rod Stewart. Or Bob Dylan. Or Bono. Or Bruce Springsteen. Or all four rolled into one. There isn't a Colombian you meet in Miami, in Paris, anywhere in the world, who *hasn't* heard of—and likely been to—his eponymous restaurant, Andrés Carne de Res (literally, Andrés beef; a name that rhymes in Spanish).

To come to Bogotá, Colombia's capital, situated more than a mile above sea level, and not take the forty-five minute drive to the mercifully congestion-free village of Chia would be a little like visiting the Louvre in Paris and bypassing the *Mona Lisa*. I use an art metaphor on purpose, for if Jaramillo owes his inclusion in *Planet Barbecue* to his remarkable restaurant, he's as celebrated in Colombia for his art as for his food. (As an artistic side note, the Colombian artist, Fernando Botero once paid for his meal at the restaurant by drawing a picture on the bill.)

To see Andrés Carne de Res in action on a typical Saturday—three thousand meat-hungry revelers packed into a string of dining rooms that stretch a square city block—you'd never guess that the venture began as a six-table eatery, opened in 1982 by a visual arts student and autodidact born in Medellín. Or that the seed money for the restaurant came from severance pay from a bulldozer company where Andrés had worked, and that his Argentinean sister-in-law taught him how to grill.

Over the years, Andrés added tables, then more dining areas, then satellite kitchens to service them, filling every square inch of the walls with paintings and sculptures, found objects, and antiques. Imagine Frida Kahlo crossed with Salvador Dalí and Grandma Moses and you'll get an idea of the decor. Andrés Carne de Res may be the world's only grill restaurant to have its own art department—a warehouse-size studio that employs two-dozen artisans to create the one of a kind tables, chairs, wall decorations, and *objets d'art* that fill the dining room.

Each morning, Andrés (recognizable by his swept back hair and two-day-old beard) walks through the dining room, notebook in hand, jotting down pictures to be hung, fixtures to be changed, and art works to be added or rotated. A similar attention to detail pervades his open kitchen, with a military-strength charcoal-burning grill. The *arepas* (cornmeal cakes) are patted by hand; the salsas are chopped fresh before the meal service; and each steak and chop is custom seared over screaming hot charcoal.

As for the house specialty, *lomo al trapo,* it's not until the order comes in that one of the grill chefs wraps a long strip of beef tenderloin in salt, oregano, and a cotton cloth, securing the ends with a square knot, and places the resulting bundle directly on the embers.

NAME: Andrés Jaramillo

TERRITORY: Colombia

CLAIM TO FAME: Chef-owner of Andrés Carne de Res in Chia, Colombia

SPECIALTIES: *Pincho mlxto,* Colombian shish kebab; *punta de anca,* fat-capped sirloin steak; *churrasco* with *ají criollo,* New York strip with fiery salsa; *lomo al trapo,* beef tenderloin crusted with salt, wrapped in cloth, and grilled in the embers; *tomates rellenos con puré de patatas,* mashed potato–filled tomatoes; and *plátanos asados,* cheese and guava–stuffed roasted plantains

JARAMILLO SAYS:

▶ Grilling plays to all the senses.

▶ People think of me as an artist, but we time the cooking of our *lomo al trapo* to the second using digital clocks. (*Lomo al trapo* is the house specialty; see page 123.)

▶ The customer is not always right.

▶ Sure, the meat, the fire, the grilling tactics are important. But here, at Andrés Carne de Res, what really matters is heart.

Left: A dining room at Andrés Carne de Res—a study in visual overload. Every piece of art and furniture is custom-made for the restaurant. Right: Andrés Jaramillo

Nonya-Style Flank Steak

THE SCOOP

WHERE: Kuala Lumpur, Malaysia

WHAT: Flank steak Malaysian "grandmother" style—marinated with oyster sauce and anise and topped with fried garlic

HOW: Direct grilling

JUST THE FACTS: There are several options for steaks to use in this dish, ranging from uptown rib eyes or New York strips to down-home sirloin or flank steak. Whichever cut you choose, serve it thinly sliced, which is how steak is enjoyed not just in Malaysia, but throughout Southeast Asia. By the way, Malaysians like their steaks cooked all the way through.

Does barbecue promote ethnic harmony? I like to think so. Malays, Indians, and Chinese—in other words, Muslims, Hindus, and Buddhists—all call the slender Malaysian peninsula home. All have managed to maintain their cultural and religious traditions, not to mention their cuisines. Visit a hawker center like Jalan Alor, the aptly nicknamed "24-Hour Food Street" in Kuala Lumpur and you'll find Chinese-style pork being grilled at stalls next to Malay beef kebabs and Indian tandoori. Indeed, there's even a unique style of barbecue based on cultural fusion, the result of marriages between Malay women and the Chinese laborers who came to Malaysia to work the rubber and coconut plantations. Named for the Malay term for grandmother, *nonya* describes a style of cooking that incorporates Chinese ingredients, like soy sauce and oyster sauce, with traditional Malay flavorings like turmeric and coconut milk. Here's how a *nonya* makes steak that explodes with flavor. **SERVES 4**

1½ pounds flank steak
3 tablespoons vegetable oil
3 cloves garlic, thinly sliced
3 tablespoons oyster sauce
2 tablespoons soy sauce
2 tablespoons sugar
2 teaspoons aniseed or Chinese five-spice powder
1 teaspoon ground turmeric
1 teaspoon freshly ground black pepper
Coarse salt (kosher or sea)
Nonya Sauce (recipe follows), for serving

ADVANCE PREPARATION
1 to 4 hours for marinating the flank steak

1 Using a sharp knife, lightly score the flank steak on both sides in a cross-hatch pattern. The cuts should be about ⅛ inch deep and ¼ inch apart.

Place the steak in a nonreactive baking dish just large enough to hold it.

2 Heat the oil in a small skillet over medium heat. Add the garlic and cook until golden brown, about 1 minute. Transfer the garlic to a plate lined with paper towels to drain. Pour the garlic flavored oil into a heatproof mixing bowl and let cool to room temperature.

3 Add the oyster sauce, soy sauce, sugar, aniseed, turmeric, and pepper to the garlic oil. Season with salt to taste. Pour the marinade over the flank steak, turning it to coat both sides. Let the steak marinate in the refrigerator, covered, for 1 to 4 hours, turning it once or twice.

4 Set up the grill for direct grilling and preheat it to high.

5 When ready to cook, brush and oil the grill grate. Drain the flank steak, discarding the marinade. Arrange the steak on the hot grate at a diagonal to the bars. Grill the steak until cooked to taste, 3 to 5 minutes per side for medium-rare. Use the poke test to check for doneness (see page 147). If desired, give the steak a quarter turn on each side after 1½ minutes to create a handsome crosshatch of grill marks.

6 Transfer the grilled flank steak to a platter or cutting board and let it rest for 2 to 3 minutes. Thinly slice the steak and serve it with the fried garlic slices sprinkled on top and the Nonya Sauce alongside for dipping.

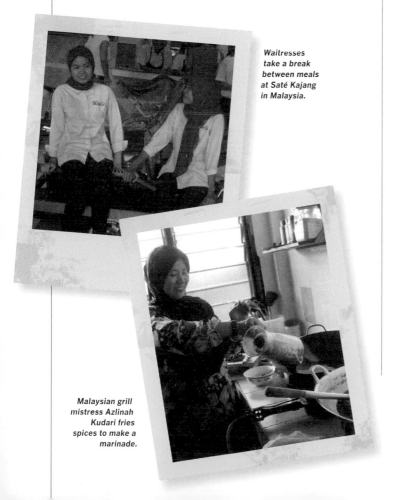

Waitresses take a break between meals at Saté Kajang in Malaysia.

Malaysian grill mistress Azlinah Kudari fries spices to make a marinade.

Nonya Sauce

Sweet-and-sour sauces are a constant on the world's barbecue trail. Here's the *nonya* version, sweetened with palm sugar (made from date palm sap and very similar in texture and color to light brown sugar), soured with lime juice, and enriched with coconut milk. **MAKES ABOUT 1 CUP**

3 tablespoons vegetable oil
4 cloves garlic, minced
1 shallot, minced (about ¼ cup)
1 to 2 hot chiles, such as Thai chiles or serrano peppers, seeded and finely chopped (for a hotter sauce, leave the seeds in)
2 tablespoons Asian chile paste, such as sambal ulek (see the box on page 374)
2 tablespoons Asian fish sauce or soy sauce
2 tablespoons fresh lime juice
1 tablespoon palm sugar or light brown sugar, or more to taste
½ teaspoon freshly ground black pepper
¼ cup unsweetened coconut milk or water, or more as needed

Heat the oil in a wok or small frying pan over medium heat. Add the garlic, shallot, and chile(s) and cook until golden brown, about 2 minutes, stirring often. Stir in the chile paste, fish sauce, lime juice, palm sugar, and black pepper and cook until thick, 4 to 6 minutes. Stir in the coconut milk and let the sauce simmer until it is mellow and thick but pourable, 3 to 5 minutes. If the sauce has thickened too much, add a little more coconut milk. Taste for sweetness, adding more palm sugar if necessary. Let the sauce cool to room temperature, then transfer it to small individual bowls for dipping. The sauce can be refrigerated, covered, for several days; let it return to room temperature before serving.

Brazilian Matambre

WHERE: Porto Alegre, Brazil

WHAT: The coolest thing to come off a rotisserie since the Brazilian spit-roasted pineapple on page 578—a butterflied, rolled flank steak stuffed with vegetables, ham, and cheese

HOW: Spit roasting or direct grilling

JUST THE FACTS: Traditionally, Brazilians cook *matambre*, like everything else, on the rotisserie: The slow and gentle rotation is ideal for crisping the exterior while basting the meat. Argentinean and Uruguayan grill masters make a similar dish that they grill in aluminum foil, using the direct method. I give instructions for both options here.

The name says it all: "hunger-killer." That's what *matambre* means in Portuguese and Spanish. This monster roll—a sort of Brazilian braciole—turns up throughout southern South America, where it pairs the salty tang of ham and cheese with the sweetness of peppers and onions. What Brazil adds to the mix is the *churrasquiera* (industrial-strength rotisserie). Spit roasting gives you a texture and flavor that's very different from grilling the *matambre* in foil as is done in Argentina. This recipe comes from Schneider, a Germanically decorated grill house near Porto Alegre that pays tribute to the Teuton roots of much of the population in this part of Brazil. **SERVES 8 AS AN APPETIZER, 4 AS A MAIN COURSE**

1 flank steak (1½ to 2 pounds, the larger the better)
Coarse salt (kosher or sea) and freshly ground black pepper
3 ounces thinly sliced cheese, such as Provolone
3 ounces thinly sliced smoked ham
2 tomatoes, cut crosswise into ¼-inch slices
1 medium-size onion, peeled and cut crosswise into very thin slices
1 green bell pepper, seeded and cut into flat slices
2 carrots, peeled and cut lengthwise into very thin slices
4 slices of thick-cut country-style bacon (about 4 ounces)

YOU'LL ALSO NEED
Butcher's string

ADVANCE PREPARATION
The beef roll can be assembled several hours ahead. Allow at least 1 hour for grilling the *matambre*.

1 Butterfly the flank steak: Place the flank steak at the edge of a cutting board. Place one hand on top to hold it flat. Using a sharp, slender knife, cut through the long side of the steak to butterfly it, cutting to but not through the opposite side; stop cutting about ¼ inch from the edge. As you cut, fold open the top of the flank steak to help you see what you're doing. Open up the flank steak like a book.

2 Place the butterflied flank steak between 2 pieces of plastic wrap. Using a meat mallet, scaloppine pounder, or the side of a heavy cleaver, pound the meat to a thickness of ¼ inch. Transfer the flank steak to a large cutting board and season it generously on both sides with salt and black pepper.

3 Arrange the slices of cheese and ham in one layer on top of the meat. Arrange the slices of tomato, onion, and bell pepper on top of the cheese and ham. Arrange the slices of carrot on top

Matambre, *proudly displayed on its spit.*

lengthwise (parallel to the grain of the meat). Then roll up the flank steak tightly like a jelly roll.

4 Place a slice of bacon lengthwise on the top, bottom, and each side of the stuffed flank steak. Tie the rolled flank steak crosswise every inch or so with butcher's string. The *matambre* can be prepared up to this stage several hours ahead and refrigerated, covered.

5 To grill: *If you are using a rotisserie,* set up the grill for spit roasting and preheat it to medium-high. Position a drip pan under the spit where the *matambre* will turn. Skewer the *matambre* on the spit so that it is perpendicular to the spit, securing the *matambre* with the rotisserie forks. When ready to cook, attach the spit to the grill and turn on the motor. Spit roast the *matambre* until it is sizzling and dark brown on the outside and cooked through, about 1 hour. Use an instant-read meat

Seven Myths About Grilling a Steak

The perfect steak is one of the "high holies" of the grill. So let's dispel some common myths to help you nail the perfect steak every time.

MYTH #1: A steak is a steak is a steak.
FACT: Not all steaks are created equal and each requires its own special way of grilling. Thin ones, like skirt and flank steaks, should be grilled quickly over a hot fire. Thick steaks, like a porterhouse or T-bone, require a two-zone fire—the hot zone for searing, the medium hot zone for cooking the meat through. Tough, fibrous steaks, like flank steaks, should be scored on the top and bottom to tenderize them and thinly sliced across the grain when served. Lean steaks, like filet mignon, require added fat, either in the form of an oil-based marinade or a wrapping of pancetta or bacon.

MYTH #2: You should bring a steak to room temperature before grilling.
FACT: Leaving meat out at room temperature is a formula for disaster and there isn't a respectable steak house in the world that does it. Steaks (indeed, any meat) should be kept ice-cold—and bacteria free—until the moment they go on the grill. (When you're working over a 600° to 800°F fire, it takes mere seconds to take the chill off the meat.)

MYTH #3: Salt toughens steak. Don't apply it before grilling.
FACT: A generous sprinkling of salt (kosher or coarse sea salt) and cracked black peppercorns applied just prior to grilling gives you the savory crust and robust flavor characteristic of the best steak house steaks. Grill masters from Florence to Florianópolis back me up on this. Season steaks right before they go on the grill. Just don't season them hours ahead or the salt will draw out the meat juices and make the steaks soggy.

MYTH #4: A barbecue fork is the proper tool for turning a steak.
FACT: Stabbing a steak with a fork serves only to puncture the meat and drain out the juices. Turn your steaks with tongs.

MYTH #5: Turn the steaks often while grilling.
FACT: If you watch really top steak masters from around the world, you'll notice they turn a steak only once. Why? This produces a better crust.

MYTH #6: The best way to check a steak for doneness is to cut into it with a knife.
FACT: Again, cutting the meat releases the juices. The best way to check for doneness is to poke a steak with your finger (the poke test is explained in full on page 147). A rare steak is soft and squishy; a medium-rare steak is yielding; medium is gently yielding; medium-well is firm; and well-done is hard and springy.

MYTH #7: Steak tastes best sizzling hot off the grill.
FACT: Like most grilled meats, a steak hot off the grill will taste leathery and dry. You need to let it rest for a few minutes on a warm plate before serving. This allows the meat to "relax," making for a juicier, more tender steak.

Finally, for flavor, sheen, and succulence, don't forget to drizzle a little extra-virgin olive oil, melted butter, or beef fat over your perfectly grilled steak before serving. Think of it as the varnish on your masterpiece.

thermometer to test for doneness, inserting it into the center of the *matambre* but not touching the spit. When done the internal temperature will be about 190°F. In Brazil, they'd carve the *matambre* into thin slices right off the spit onto plates. You may find it easier to transfer the *matambre* to a cutting board and remove the spit. Let the *matambre* rest for 5 minutes.

If you are using the direct method, set up the grill for direct grilling and preheat it to medium-low. Tightly wrap the *matambre* in heavy-duty aluminum foil, twisting the ends like a Tootsie Roll.

When ready to cook, place the *matambre* on the hot grate and grill it until the meat is cooked through, 1 to 1½ hours, turning often with tongs. Use an instant-read meat thermometer to test for doneness, inserting it into the center of the *matambre* but not touching the spit. When done the internal temperature will be about 190°F. Transfer the *matambre* to a cutting board and let it rest for about 5 minutes before removing the foil.

6 Carve the *matambre* crosswise (against the grain) into thin (¼-inch-thick) slices and serve.

Hanger Steak with Marchand de Vin (Wine Merchant) Sauce

THE SCOOP

WHERE: France

WHAT: Grilled hanger steak with a tangy red wine and shallot sauce

HOW: Direct grilling

JUST THE FACTS: Hanger steak is a long, thin, fibrous steak cut from the underbelly of the steer. It "hangs" from the diaphragm near the kidney, rather than being connected to a bone, hence the name. (For more information on hanger steak, including where to buy it, see the box on page 144.) If hanger steak is unavailable, skirt steak and flank steak make good substitutes.

I first discovered hanger steak, known in France as *onglet,* during my student days in Paris. I loved its juicy, fibrous texture and its rich, meaty, almost sanguine flavor. I loved its price; as it was one of the few steaks I could afford on a student budget. Hanger steak was a bistro and neighborhood café favorite and always came with some variation on a shallot sauce. The trick was to thinly slice the steak across the grain to shorten the meat fibers and make the meat tender. American chefs discovered this budget cut meat during the last economic downturn, and while hanger steak is no longer the bargain it used to be, it rewards you with a fabulous flavor for a fraction of the price of one of the more prestigious steaks. **SERVES 4**

½ teaspoon cornstarch

3 cups dry red wine, such as Burgundy

3 tablespoons unsalted butter, at room temperature

1 strip bacon, cut crosswise into ¼-inch slivers

2 to 3 shallots, finely chopped (about ½ cup)

1 clove garlic, minced

1 large mushroom, finely chopped (optional)

1 cup beef stock, preferably homemade

¼ cup fresh flat-leaf parsley, finely chopped

Coarse salt (kosher or sea) and freshly ground black pepper

1 tablespoon extra-virgin olive oil or vegetable oil

1½ pounds hanger steak, trimmed

HANGER STEAK WITH MARCHAND DE VIN (WINE MERCHANT) SAUCE

1 Place the cornstarch and 1 tablespoon of the wine in a small bowl and stir to blend. Set the mixture aside.

2 Melt 1 tablespoon of the butter in a heavy saucepan over medium heat. Add the bacon and cook 2 minutes to render some of the fat. Add the shallots, garlic, and mushroom, if using, and cook until the ingredients begin to brown, about 5 minutes. Add the remaining wine, the stock, and 1 tablespoon of the parsley to the saucepan. Increase the heat to high, and boil the mixture until it's reduced to about 1 ½ cups, about 15 minutes.

3 Stir the cornstarch mixture to reblend it, then whisk it into the boiling sauce to slightly thicken the sauce. (If this book was about classic French cuisine, you'd strain the sauce. I prefer it with the bits of bacon, shallots, and mushroom, so I don't bother.) Whisk in the remaining 2 tablespoons butter and 2 tablespoons of the parsley and season with salt and pepper. The sauce should be highly seasoned. Keep warm or on a corner of the grill (see Note).

4 Set up the grill for direct grilling and preheat it to high.

5 When ready to cook, brush and oil the grill grate. Place the steak on the hot grate and grill until cooked to taste; it tastes best served rare or medium-rare, about 2 minutes per side for rare; 3 minutes per side for medium-rare. Use the poke test to test for doneness (see the box on page 147).

6 Transfer the grilled steak to a platter or plates. Slice the steak sharply on the diagonal. Spoon the sauce over the steak and sprinkle the remaining 1 tablespoon of parsley on top.

NOTE: If you are preparing the sauce more than 15 minutes ahead, do not add the final butter and parsley. Instead, bring the sauce to a boil right before serving and whisk them in at the last minute.

Hanger Steak

The world of barbecue is full of formerly "trash" cuts of meat that have become pricy delicacies. Fifty years ago, for example, you could scarcely give away a rack of baby back ribs in Memphis. Or a brisket in Texas. Or a skirt steak in northern Mexico or the American Southwest. Today all three are icons of American barbecue.

The latest member to join the nouveau riche club is the hanger steak, known in French as *onglet,* in Italian as *lombatello,* and in Spanish as *solomillo de pulmón.* The hanger steak takes its name from its anatomical position—it "hangs" from the steer's diaphragm near the skirt steak and flank steak. (Unlike many of the most popular steaks, it's not connected to a bone.)

The hanger steak's proximity to the kidneys gives it a rich, meaty flavor. This flavor, coupled with the steak's former obscurity and relative lack of a commercial market, led it to be nicknamed the "butcher's steak" or "butcher's tenderloin." Butchers would keep this flavorful but unknown cut for their families, so the story went, rather than sell it to be ground up as hamburger.

The hanger steak comprises two long slender strips of muscle connected by a tough vein (usually removed by the butcher). It weighs between one and one and a half pounds; there is only one hanger steak per steer. Like skirt and flank steak, the meat is highly fibrous, so you need to cook it quickly and slice it thinly across the grain.

Hanger steaks are seldom seen at the supermarket, but you can order them from your local butcher shop. You can also buy them online from New York's celebrity butcher shop, Lobel's (www.lobels.com).

The Real Bistecca alla Fiorentina

Picture in your mind's eye your fantasy Tuscan grill house. The building would be old—hewn from stones quarried in Michelangelo's day. It would be cavernous enough to accommodate large parties of hungry meat eaters and with a ceiling high enough to absorb the noise. Lined with frescoes (or at least paintings), its barrel arches would make you feel like you're dining in a Renaissance home. Of course, there'd be beef—loins so long that the butcher bends his back bringing them into the restaurant. And in the center of it all there should be a grill on a raised hearth—a *focolare* in Italian (from *focus,* the Latin word for "hearth," which also gives us the word focaccia). Monster porterhouse steaks would be grilled there, over charcoal or wood, to the Tuscan notion of perfection. That means crusty and dark on the outside and not too far from still mooing within. If such is your vision, take it to the boisterous basement Florentine restaurant called Buca Lapi, where the porterhouses come as thick as the *Decameron* and are served with such Machiavellian machismo that they don't even bother to spice up the meat with olive oil. However, for those of you who crave a counterpoint, you can add a salsalike Tuscan bean salad. Pour yourself a glass of Brunello di Montalcino or Vino Nobile di Montepulciano and get ready for an orgy of meat. **SERVES 2 TO 3**

THE SCOOP

WHERE: Florence, Italy

WHAT: Porterhouse steak like only the Florentines know how to make it: salted, grilled, and with olive oil optional

HOW: Direct grilling

JUST THE FACTS: The beef of choice in Italy is Chianina—full-flavored, wine-dark beef from an ancient Italian breed of cattle. Dry-aged prime beef would be the closest equivalent in the United States. To be strictly authentic, you'd use a steak that's at least two inches thick.

1 really big porterhouse steak
(about 2 inches thick and 2 pounds)
About ½ cup rock salt
Tuscan Bean Salad (recipe follows)

ADVANCE PREPARATION
None

1 Set up the grill for direct grilling and preheat it to medium-high. Ideally, you'll grill over a bed of embers, using natural charcoal lumps.

2 When ready to cook, brush and oil the grill grate. Arrange the steak on the hot grate at a diagonal to the bars. Dump a fistful of rock salt (about ¼ cup) on top. Grill the steak until it is crusty and browned on the bottom, 5 to 8 minutes.

3 Turn the steak over and dump another fistful of salt on top. Continue grilling the steak until the second side is crusty and browned and the meat

Two Tuscan Steaks
{ BISTECCA ALLA FIORENTINA AND TAGLIATA }

No survey of Planet Barbecue would be complete without at least one Tuscan steak, and while I've written extensively about *bistecca alla fiorentina* in previous books, each time I visit Florence I appreciate something new about this iconic dish. What's the difference between *bistecca* and *tagliata?* In a nutshell, how they're served. Both come from the beef loin. Depending on where the cut is made, the steak would correspond to an American porterhouse or T-bone. The thickness of the cut might range from a

modest 1¼ inches (for one or two people) to a massive 3 inches (for three to four people). Traditionally, *bistecca* is presented whole, then carved off the bone into a strip steak and filet mignon. (The T-shaped bone is returned to the grill for searing.) *Tagliata* (from the Italian verb *tagliare,* to slice) takes the process one step further; once the bone is removed, the steaks are cut into ¼-inch-thick slices. This has two advantages: It facilitates divvying up the steak for multiple eaters and it allows you to coat more of

the beef with extra-virgin olive oil and meat juices. As a rule, Tuscan steak is served by itself. The notion of a sauce (beyond a drizzle of olive oil) would strike most Tuscans as sacrilege. However, sometimes salsalike salads turn up with the steak—on the same table, at least, if not on the same plate. So here's the basic *bistecca alla fiorentina,* with a separate recipe for *tagliata* on page 150. For those who like their beef with a bit more embellishment, I've included a simple bean salad (below) and a grape tomato salad (page 150).

is cooked to taste, 5 to 8 minutes longer, about 10 minutes in all for rare; 14 to 16 minutes in all for medium-rare. Use the poke test to test for doneness (see the box on the facing page).

4 Lift the porterhouse with tongs and hold it upright over the grill. Using the back of a large knife, whack it on both sides to knock off the excess salt. Transfer the steak to a cutting board, let it rest a couple of minutes, then take it to the table.

5 With guests watching and as much ceremony as you can muster, cut the New York strip portion of the porterhouse (the larger, elongated steak) off the T-bone. Then cut the tenderloin (the rounder steak on the other side) off the bone. At most Tuscan grill houses, the meat would be thinly sliced (see the *tagliata* on page 150), but at Buca Lapi, they place the whole steaks on a platter or plates, with the T-bone standing upright like an obelisk. If the meat on the bone is too rare—even for an Italian—you can return it to the grill for additional charring.

NOTE: At most Tuscan steak houses, they drizzle the best quality Tuscan extra-virgin olive oil over the cooked steak. I do this at home and I certainly recommend it. At Buca Lapi, they don't bother.

Tuscan Bean Salad

Italians have a greater appreciation (higher tolerance?) for simplicity than most North Americans do. (Certainly more than I do.) Here's a Tuscan salsalike salad you can serve next to *bistecca,* this one made with the region's beloved cannellini beans. If you're feeling ambitious, cook dried beans from scratch. But good canned beans will give you a highly agreeable salad, too. If you are starting with dried beans, be sure to leave enough time for them to soak overnight. **SERVES 2 TO 3 AND CAN BE MULTIPLIED AS DESIRED**

¾ cup dried cannellini beans, or 1½ cups canned cannellini
   beans (from one 15-ounce can)
1 onion slice (about ¼ inch thick; see Note)
1 bay leaf (see Note)
½ clove garlic
3 fresh sage or basil leaves, thinly slivered
2 tablespoons of the best Tuscan extra-virgin olive oil,
   or more to taste
Coarse salt (kosher or sea) and freshly ground black pepper

1 *If you are using dried beans,* soak them in the refrigerator overnight in 3 cups of cool water (enough to cover them). The next day, drain the beans well and place them in a pot with the onion slice, bay leaf, and 4 cups of water. Bring the beans to a boil over high heat. Reduce the heat to a gentle simmer, cover the pan, and cook the beans until tender (you should be able to crush one easily between your thumb and forefinger), 40 to 60 minutes, depending on the freshness of the dried beans. Drain the beans well in a colander and let cool to room temperature.

If you are using canned beans, place the beans in a colander and rinse well with cold water (this removes the excess salt). Drain the beans well.

2 Rub the inside of an attractive serving bowl with the cut side of the garlic. Place the cooked beans in the bowl and add the sage and olive oil and season with salt and pepper to taste. Toss the beans to mix at the last minute. Taste for seasoning, adding more salt and/or olive oil to taste. Serve the bean salad at once.

NOTE: If you are using canned beans, omit the onion and bay leaf.

The Doneness of Steak

How do you like your steak? Rare? Medium? And just exactly what is meant by the various degrees of doneness? Here are the terms referenced by grill masters around the world. Use them to order a steak that will be cooked just the way you like it.

AMERICAN ENGLISH

Rare: Meat that is red and warm but not hot in the center. Soft and squishy when poked. Internal temperature of 120° to 125°F.

Medium-rare: Meat that is red *and* hot in the center. Yielding but not quite squishy when poked. Internal temperature of 140° to 145°F.

Medium: Meat that is pink and hot in the center. Gently yielding when poked. Internal temperature of 155° to 160°F.

Medium-well: Meat that has a grayish center with just a trace of pink. Firm with just the slightest yield when poked. Internal temperature of 170° to 175°F.

Well-done: Meat that has a gray center with no trace of pink. Firm when poked. Internal temperature of 185° to 190°F.

Pittsburgh rare: The exterior will be charred black and the interior so rare it's still mooing. The description harks back to when Pittsburgh was a steel town. You need a grill with blast furnace heat to achieve this result.

SPANISH

The Spanish tend to eat their steaks a little more rare than we Americans do.

Jugoso **(literally juicy):** Very rare meat with a warm red center.

A punto: Medium-rare meat with a hot red center.

Cocido **(literally boiled):** Medium to medium-well done meat with a hot pink center.

FRENCH

The French also tend to eat their steaks a bit more rare than we Americans do.

Bleu **(literally blue):** Extremely rare—blood red meat that's cool in the center.

Saignant **(literally bloody):** Very rare—blood red meat that's warm in the center.

A point: Corresponds to the American medium-rare. Red or reddish pink meat that's hot in the center.

Bien cuit **(literally well cooked):** Corresponds to the American medium-well or well done.

PLANET BARBECUE

Italy: Focus on Grilling

Italian grilling. Where do I begin? In Venice, where supernaturally fresh, bread crumb–crusted Laguna prawns sizzle over olive wood charcoal? In Rome, where herb-scented, spatchcocked whole chickens grill under the weight of a brick perched right on the bird on the grill grate? In Tuscany, where slices of salt-less bread are toasted in a fireplace, rubbed with garlic, and drizzled with olive oil to make *bruschetta,* an appetizer the whole world has adopted (and often bastard-ized)? Or on the island of Sardinia, where olive oil–basted artichokes achieve wafer crispness over live fire, and metal mattress springs are transformed into giant grill grates.

Aged beef loin about to be cut into Florentine porterhouse steaks.

For my money, the best start-ing point, the most visceral, the most exuberantly carnivorous, is without a doubt, the Tuscan capital, Florence—home of the *bistecca alla fiorentina.* Imagine a porterhouse steak as thick as a Roman phone book, encrusted with rock salt, charred over glowing embers until almost black on the outside and yet still almost raw at the bone, carved at the table, and served with no more ceremony or condiment than a drizzle of fresh Tuscan olive oil. And that's if you're feeling fancy. At many Florentine steak houses, like the popular Perseo or Buca Lapi, even the olive oil is considered superfluous. It's really all about the beef.

Italians have been grilling for a long time. Apicius, author of what's considered to be the first cookbook, included recipes for barbecued cow's udder and grilled dormice in his *De Re Coquinaria (On Things Culinary),* written in the fifth cen-tury A.D. The ancient Romans did their grilling on a raised hearth called a *focus*—the "focal" point of the home then, as now. Two thou-sand years later, Italians still grill in the fireplace. Indeed, Italy is one of the few countries on Planet Barbecue where the onset of cold weather inspires people to fire up the grill.

2,500 Years of Great Grilling

Italians grill from the Alps in the north to the beaches of Sicily and Sardinia—outdoors in summer and indoors in winter.

Sweet red bell peppers ready for the grilled pepper salad on page 62.

The typical Italian outdoor grill replicates a fireplace with a chimney.

The rolling hills of Tuscany—home to some of the most soulful grilling in Italy.

THE GRILLS: Italy's most unique contribution to the world of grills is the Tuscan grill, a cast-iron grill grate about 16-inches square mounted on 6-inch legs. You position it on your hearth or in your fireplace or wood-burning oven and rake the embers beneath it. It's that simple and it's equally well suited to grilling both indoors and out. Italians also use conventional grills (although rarely with lids) and rotisseries. In fact, the most spectacular rotisserie ever depicted—it's two stories tall—appears in *The Satyricon,* Frederico Fellini's 1969 masterpiece film based on the first century B.C. novel attributed to Gaius Petronius. (If you haven't seen the film, order it from Netflix immediately. The novel is worth reading, too, featuring what's perhaps the most extravagant banquet scene in western literature: Trilmachio's Feast.)

THE FUEL: Wood (preferably oak) and natural lump charcoal.

THE FLAVORINGS: Italians paint with a simple palate: sea salt, black pepper, garlic, fresh rosemary, and perhaps sage. Some grill masters kick up the heat with hot pepper flakes.

MUST TRY DISHES:

Bistecca alla fiorentina: Tuscan T-bone or porterhouse. *Tagliata* refers to a grilled steak that's served sliced, usually drizzled with olive oil.

Cialdo (pronounced chi-AL-do): Two thin, tortilla-sized cracker breads sandwiched with cheese and fresh greens and cooked over an open fire using special long-handled tongs.

Crostini and *bruschette:* Both are grilled breads—*crostini* are lavished with liver pâté or other toppings; *bruschette* are traditionally rubbed with garlic and drizzled with olive oil.

Polenta ai ferri: Yes, Italians even grill polenta. *Ai ferri* literally means on the irons—as in on the hot iron bars of the grill grate.

Pollo alla diavola and *coniglio alla diavola:* *Alla diavola* translates as "devil's style"—in this case chicken or rabbit grilled over wood or charcoal and seasoned with hot peppers.

Pollo al matone: Chicken grilled under a brick.

Porceddu: Rosemary-and-garlic scented, spit-roasted suckling pig.

THE CONDIMENTS: As utterly simple as the rest of Italian cooking: A squeeze of fresh lemon. A splash of extra-virgin olive oil. The closest Italians come to barbecue sauce is *salsa verde*—a simple sauce made of chopped garlic, parsley, anchovies (optional), and olive oil (see page 130).

HOW TO EAT IT: In general, Italian grilled entrees are served by themselves. The vegetable accompaniments are served as a separate course.

Cooking "music paper" flatbreads in a wood-burning oven in Sardinia.

IF YOU CAN EAT AT ONLY ONE RESTAURANT: Da Delfina outside Florence for wood-grilled meats and game birds cooked on a wood-burning rotisserie.

WHAT TO DRINK: The wine of the region.

THE MOST SINGULAR DISH IN THE REPERTORY: *Fagioli al fiasco:* Tuscan beans "baked" with garlic and herbs in a glass bottle in the fireplace. Like the mythical unicorn, it's often described and even pictured in books, but despite much effort on numerous trips to Italy, I've never actually been able to find one in the flesh (or flask).

Bistecca alla fiorentina (Florentine porterhouse) on a Tuscan grill over an oak fire.

Grilled T-Bone Steak with Grape Tomato Salad

{ TAGLIATA CON INSALATA DI POMODORO }

THE SCOOP

WHERE: Venice, Italy

WHAT: About as fancy as steak gets in Italy—a grilled T-bone or New York strip served with a salad of baby tomatoes

HOW: Direct grilling

JUST THE FACTS: One secret to a great *tagliata* is to start with a thick steak, at least 1¼ inches—thick enough so that you can sear the outside without overcooking the center. There are several options for steak: the T-bone, a New York strip (the larger half of the aforementioned steak), or even a rib steak. I've called for T-bones here.

Tagliata (from the Italian word *tagliare,* to slice) refers to an Italian-style steak cooked *al ferri* (literally on the iron, as on the metal bars of the grill grate) and sliced before serving. Slicing serves two purposes: It enables you to serve a single steak to more than one person and it allows you to coat more of the beef with the meat juices and the extra-virgin olive oil traditionally used to sauce Italian beef. This particular version, from our friends at Da Ivo in Venice, is about as elaborate as Italian steak gets, served as it is with a sort of "salsa" made with indecently tiny grape tomatoes and baby leeks. **SERVES 2 HUNGRY EATERS**

FOR THE TOMATO SALAD

1 pint ripe grape tomatoes or baby cherry
  tomatoes
1 baby leek, or 1 scallion, both white and
  green parts, finely chopped
2 teaspoons finely chopped fresh oregano leaves
2 tablespoons extra-virgin olive oil
1 tablespoon balsamic vinegar
Coarse salt (kosher or sea) and freshly
  ground black pepper

FOR THE STEAK

2 T-bone steaks (each about 1¼ inches thick
  and 12 to 14 ounces)
Coarse sea salt (must be coarse)
Freshly ground or cracked black pepper (optional)
Extra-virgin olive oil, for serving
1 tablespoon chopped fresh rosemary

ADVANCE PREPARATION

None, although the tomato salad can be prepared
  up to 2 hours ahead of time and tossed at the
  last minute.

1 Make the tomato salad: If you are using soft, ripe grape tomatoes, leave them whole. Otherwise, cut the tomatoes in half lengthwise. Place the tomatoes in an attractive serving bowl. Add the leek, oregano, olive oil, and the balsamic vinegar. Do not toss the salad; you'll do this at the last minute. Season the salad with salt and pepper to taste when you toss it.

2 Set up the grill for two-zone direct grilling (see page 611). Preheat one zone to high and one zone to medium.

3 Prepare the steaks: Generously— and I mean generously—season the steaks with salt and pepper, if using. When ready to cook, brush and oil the grill grate. Arrange the steaks on the hot grate over the high-heat zone and at a diagonal to the bars. Grill the steaks until the outside is crusty and browned and the inside is cooked to taste, 3 to 4 minutes per side for rare, 5 to 6 minutes per side for medium-rare. Use the poke test to test for doneness (see page 147). (Italians almost never eat their beef more cooked than medium-rare.) If the steak starts to burn, move it to the medium zone.

4 Transfer the steaks to a deep baking dish and let them rest for 2 minutes. Cut the steaks off the bone and, holding your knife upright, cut the meat into strips ¼ inch wide and 3 inches long. Douse the slices with a few tablespoons of olive oil, sprinkle the rosemary on top, and spoon the juices that accumulate in the dish over the meat. Serve the steaks at once with the tomato salad on the side.

Caveman T-Bones with Hellfire Hot Sauce

Somewhere between 2 million and 800,000 years ago, a human ancestor called *Homo erectus* became the first animal to cook. This recipe pays homage to that first caveman barbecue—with steaks grilled directly on the embers. Of course, the "wow" factor is off the charts (and I've amazed more than a few people when I've demonstrated Caveman T-Bones at Barbecue University and on the *Today* show), but there's a lot more to this dish than mere showmanship. Roasting the steaks on the embers gives the meat a surface charring and smoke flavor you just can't duplicate on a conventional grill. To that add a sizzling sauce of pan-fried jalapeños, cilantro, and garlic, and you've got T-bones that roar off the plate with flavor—guaranteed to awaken the caveman in all of us. **SERVES 4 HUNGRY EATERS (AND ALL CAVEMEN ARE HUNGRY EATERS)**

FOR THE STEAKS

4 T-bone steaks (each about 1¼ inches thick and 12 to 14 ounces)

Coarse salt (kosher or sea) and cracked black peppercorns

FOR THE HELLFIRE HOT SAUCE

¾ cup extra-virgin olive oil

10 jalapeño peppers, thinly sliced crosswise

10 cloves garlic, thinly sliced

¾ cup loosely packed fresh cilantro leaves, coarsely chopped

YOU'LL ALSO NEED

An 8 to 10–inch cast-iron skillet

ADVANCE PREPARATION

None: The beauty of this dish is its spontaneity.

1 Grill the steaks: Build a charcoal fire and rake the coals into an even layer (leave the front third of the grill coal free). When the coals glow orange, fan them with a newspaper or hair dryer to blow off any loose ash.

THE SCOOP

WHERE: Primordial and universal

WHAT: The ultimate primal grilling—T-bone steaks charred directly on the embers and topped with an incendiary sauce of jalapeños, cilantro, and garlic

HOW: Roasting in the embers

JUST THE FACTS: To get the full effect, you must cook the steaks on a bed of charcoal or wood embers. No, you don't use a grill grate. If you don't own a charcoal grill, you should. But if you're firmly wedded to propane, you can achieve acceptable results by preheating your grill screaming hot before you put on the steaks.

★
Build your fire with natural lump charcoal or wood.

★
Just prior to putting on the steaks, fan the embers to blow off any loose ash.

★
Use the longest possible tongs and heavy grill gloves to protect your hands.

★
When you turn the steaks and when they're fully cooked, hold each on its side with tongs and shake it to dislodge any glowing embers.

★
Put the steaks on a heatproof platter. Use a natural bristle brush to dislodge ash from the steaks.

★
Use the longest-handled cast-iron frying pan you can find for cooking the sauce.

CAVEMAN T-BONES WITH HELLFIRE HOT SAUCE | page 151

2 Generously, and I mean generously, season the steaks on both sides with salt and cracked pepper. Place the steaks directly on the embers about 2 inches apart. Grill the steaks until cooked to taste, 4 to 6 minutes per side for medium-rare, turning with tongs. Use the poke test to check for doneness (see page 147).

3 Using tongs, lift the steaks out of the fire, shaking each to dislodge any embers. Using a basting brush, brush off any loose ash and arrange the steaks on a platter. Cover the steaks loosely with aluminum foil and let them rest while you make the sauce.

4 Make the hellfire hot sauce: Heat the olive oil in a cast-iron skillet directly on the embers, on the side burner of a gas grill, or on the stove. When the oil is hot, add the jalapeños, garlic, and cilantro. Cook the sauce over high heat until the jalapeños and garlic begin to brown, about 2 minutes. Immediately pour the sauce over the steaks and go for it.

Spit-Roasted Rump Steak with Country Salsa
{ PICANHA }

Most countries have a dish that epitomizes the local grill culture (and for that matter, the greater culture at large). In the United States, it's the rib (or T-bone steak if you live in Texas). In Italy, it's *bistecca alla fiorentina;* in South Africa, *boerewors;* in Indonesia, the saté. In Brazil, a land where a typical *churrascaria* (grill restaurant) might serve more than a dozen varieties of spit-roasted meat, one stands out as iconic and indispensible: *picanha.* The mere sight of *picanha,* with a graceful curl of sizzling fat atop a sanguine swathe of meat, is visual poetry. To this add a piquant "country" salsa and *farofa* (bacon-spiked toasted manioc flour) and the result is simply carnivorous heaven on earth.

Picanha starts as fat-capped sirloin (the top part of a top sirloin) that is cut into three inch–wide slices that are skewered with the ends curled under. The roast is sliced paper-thin to guarantee tenderness. The result: lean rare beef with a luscious, crisp edge of fat. Traditionally, the *picanha* is spit roasted to take full advantage of the basting properties of the melting fat. (Sorry to be harping on the fat, folks. It's what gives this otherwise

THE SCOOP

WHERE: Native to the state of Rio Grande do Sul in southern Brazil, *picanha* is enjoyed today in Brazilian steak houses all over the world

WHAT: The most popular beef dish in meat-obsessed Brazil: fat-capped top sirloin spit roasted and thinly sliced

HOW: Spit roasting

JUST THE FACTS:
A dish that contains two ingredients (one of them beef, the other salt) is pretty straightforward. But, you do need to locate the right cut of beef. *Picanha* (pronounced pee-KAHN-ya) is defined on Wikipedia as rump cover steak—a wonderfully descriptive term that will likely leave your butcher scratching his head in puzzlement. The "rump" in question is top sirloin (cut from the rump of the steer) and the "cover" is a ½ to 1 inch–thick cap of hard, white fat that sits atop the meat. In the United States *picanha* is the top part of a top sirloin, but to achieve the authentic flavor, you must get it with the fat. Your best option would be to buy it at a Brazilian or Argentinean market (the Spanish name is culote).

lean cut of meat its moistness and flavor.) You can also grill the *picanha* using the direct method, a technique employed by grill masters in neighboring Argentina and Uruguay. More and more South Americans have discovered the virtues of grilled rump steak. I hope North Americans won't be far behind. **SERVES 4**

1½ pounds beef top sirloin with a thick cap
    of fat on top
Coarse sea salt
Country Salsa (optional, recipe follows),
    for serving
Farofa (toasted cassava flour; optional, page 217),
    for serving

ADVANCE PREPARATION
None

1 Set up the grill for spit roasting, following the manufacturer's instructions, and preheat the grill to high. (To be strictly authentic, you'd spit roast over charcoal with some of the coals raked under the spit for a very hot fire.)

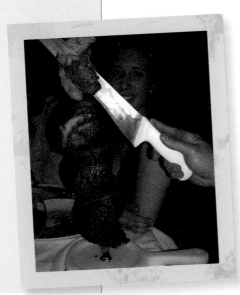

Straight off the spit—proper slices of picanha include a strip of fat with the meat.

2 Cut the top sirloin crosswise, across the grain, into slices each about 3 inches thick. Skewer each slice on the spit through the ends so that the fat forms a rounded curve on the outside, arranging the slices next to each other; you should have a row of 2 or 3 slices. Generously, and I mean generously, season (crust) the meat on all sides with salt.

3 When ready to cook, attach the spit to the grill and turn on the motor. Spit roast the meat until darkly browned on the outside but still rare to medium-rare inside, 10 to 15 minutes. Use an instant-read meat thermometer to test for doneness, inserting it into the center of the meat. When cooked to medium-rare the internal temperature will be 140° to 145°F.

4 Let the meat rest for a few minutes before slicing. To serve *picanha* Brazilian-style, carry the spit to the table and carve the meat into thin slices onto each person's plate—a tricky endeavor. Alternatively, you can transfer the *picanha* to a cutting board, let it rest for a couple of minutes then, thinly slice it across the grain and sharply on the diagonal, including a bit of fat in each slice. Serve the Country Salsa on the side, along with the *farofa* (for soaking up the juices), if desired.

VARIATION
Grilling *Picanha* Using the Direct Method: Here's how *picanha* is grilled in Brazilian homes, not to mention in grill joints in neighboring Uruguay and Argentina.

1 Cut the top sirloin across the grain into slices that are 1½ inches thick.

2 Set up the grill for direct grilling with a fire-free area as a safety zone. Preheat the grill to high.

3 When ready to cook, brush and oil the grill grate. Arrange the slices of meat, fat side down, on the hot grate and grill until the fat is partially rendered, crisp, and brown, 2 to 4 minutes, moving the meat as needed to dodge flare-ups. Turn each piece of meat on its side and grill until browned, 2 minutes per side. If the fat starts to burn before the meat is cooked, move the *picanha* to a cooler part of the grate. Grill the fatless side the same way. Use the poke test to check for doneness (see page 147).

4 Transfer the *picanha* to a cutting board, fat side up, and let it rest for a couple of minutes. Carve the *picanha* into thin slices across the grain, including a bit of fat and a bit of meat in each slice.

Country Salsa
{ MOLHO A CAMPANHA }

This vibrant condiment is one of myriad salsas served with grilled meats in Latin America. Unlike familiar Mexican salsas, it contains no hot chiles or cilantro. **MAKES ABOUT 2 CUPS**

3 tablespoons red wine vinegar, or more to taste
Coarse salt (kosher or sea) and freshly ground black pepper
½ green bell pepper, cored, seeded, and cut into ¼-inch dice
½ red bell pepper, cored, seeded, and cut into ¼-inch dice
½ yellow bell pepper, cored, seeded, and cut into ¼-inch dice
½ sweet onion, cut into ¼-inch dice
3 tablespoons finely chopped fresh flat-leaf parsley
3 tablespoons vegetable oil

Place the wine vinegar, 1 teaspoon of salt, and ½ teaspoon of black pepper in a nonreactive mixing bowl and whisk until the salt dissolves. Add the bell peppers, onion, parsley, and oil and stir to mix. Taste for seasoning, adding more salt, black pepper, and/or vinegar as necessary.

Croatian "Cheesesteak"
{ PUNJENI RAMSTEK }

Nostromo is the premier fish restaurant in Split, Croatia, with a series of whitewashed, nautically themed rooms where impeccably fresh Dalmatian coast shrimp, squid, lobster, and fish come scorching hot off a charcoal-burning grill. So why am I writing about steak? Because pristine as the fish here is (and Split's colorful fish market is but a few steps away), it's grilled with such simplicity (a sprinkle of salt, a squeeze of lemon), there's nothing to write about it—except that you shouldn't miss it when you're in Split. Nostromo's steak, on the other hand, comes pounded and tenderized with a mallet, stuffed with smoky ham, Croatian cheese, and mushrooms and is smokily seared on the grill. It takes all of about five minutes to assemble,

THE SCOOP

WHERE: Split, Croatia

WHAT: Grilled steak stuffed with mushrooms, cheese, and smoked ham

HOW: Direct grilling

JUST THE FACTS: Thin slices of rump steak (top round) would be used in Croatia. Another good cut is sirloin; ask your butcher to cut thin slices on a meat slicer.

and the flavor is out of this world. Mustard isn't traditional, but I like the way it rounds out the flavor.

Split is one of the most fascinating cities in Croatia, built around the palace of the third century A.D. Roman emperor Diocletian (there's a fabulous hotel, the Vestibul Palace, built right into the palace walls), with a charming medieval district, waterfront, and ferry service to the islands off the Dalmatian coast. **SERVES 4**

4 broad, thin top round, sirloin, or thinly sliced New York strip steaks (each about 8 inches long, 4 inches wide, ¼ inch thick and 6 to 8 ounces)

Coarse salt (kosher or sea) and freshly ground black pepper

2 tablespoons Dijon mustard (optional)

4 slices (⅛ inch thick, 6 ounces total) smoked cooked ham

4 slices (⅛ inch thick, 6 ounces total) full-flavored cheese, such as Edam or Gruyère

4 to 6 large button or cremini mushrooms, thinly sliced

2 tablespoons vegetable oil, for basting

YOU'LL ALSO NEED

Small bamboo skewers or large wooden toothpicks

ADVANCE PREPARATION

None—the beauty of this dish is that it's stuffed and grilled to order.

1 Pound each steak with a mallet or meat tenderizer to flatten and tenderize it (the steaks will wind up about 2 inches longer after pounding). Season the top of each steak with salt and pepper. Spread the meat with the mustard, if using.

2 Place a slice of ham on the lower half of a steak. Place a slice of cheese and a couple of slices of mushroom on top. Fold the top half of the meat over the bottom to make a sort of turnover. Pin the edge shut with bamboo skewers or toothpicks. Fill the remaining steaks the same way.

3 Set up the grill for direct grilling and preheat it to high.

4 When ready to cook, brush and oil the grill grate. Place the steaks on the hot grate and grill until nicely browned on the first side, 3 to 5 minutes. Turn the steaks and brush the grilled sides with some of the vegetable oil. Grill the second side until the steaks are nicely browned all over and the cheese is melted, 3 to 5 minutes more for medium. (Croatians prefer to eat this stuffed steak medium to medium-well done.) Use the poke test to check for doneness (see page 147). Transfer the grilled steaks to a platter or plates, remove the skewers, and serve.

Traditional Croatian grill—a raised stone hearth surmounted by metal gridirons.

An open-air market in Dubrovnik, Croatia. Simply grilled vegetables play a cardinal role in Balkan grilling.

Buenos Aires "Heart-Stopper"

{ BUTTERFLIED NEW YORK STRIP WITH BACON AND EGGS }

The French Paradox grabs all the headlines, but the one that really puzzles me might be called the Argentinean Paradox. How does this nation of relentless carnivores manage to stay so trim? Argentineans eat meat an average of ten to twelve times a week (that's meat for dinner daily and for lunch as often as possible). Yet Argentineans generally look fit and slender, and the kind of obesity so rampant in the United States is virtually unknown there. If such is the Argentinean Paradox, here's its apotheosis—butterflied grilled strip steak topped with bacon and fried eggs. It's a specialty of the lively Buenos Aires grill joint El Pobre Luis. **SERVES 1 AND CAN BE MULTIPLIED**

1 New York strip steak (about 1 ¼ inches thick
    and 12 ounces)
1 tablespoon vegetable oil, or more as needed
4 slices of country-style bacon
2 large eggs
Coarse salt (kosher or sea) and freshly ground
    black pepper (pepper optional)
The Real Chimichurri sauce (recipe follows)

ADVANCE PREPARATION
None

1 Butterfly the strip steak; place the steak on a cutting board. Starting at the narrow end, cut it almost in half through the side, cutting to but not through the wide end; it helps to hold your knife parallel to the cutting board with one hand and place your other hand flat on the top of the steak. Open the steak up like a book.

2 Set up the grill for direct grilling and preheat it to high.

3 If your grill has a side burner, set it on medium-high and heat the oil in a skillet. If not, you'll have to cook the bacon in a skillet directly on the grill or on your stove indoors. Cook the bacon until crisp, 2 to 4 minutes per side. Drain the bacon on paper towels on a plate and keep it warm. Set the skillet aside.

4 When ready to cook, brush and oil the grill grate. Season the steak with salt and pepper and arrange it, opened out, on the hot grate at a diagonal to the bars. Grill the steak until cooked to taste, 2 to 3 minutes per side for medium-rare. Use the poke test to test for doneness (see page 147). Transfer the steak to a plate and keep warm.

5 Meanwhile, if you like bacon fat (and Lord knows, I do), crack the eggs into the skillet in which you cooked the bacon. If you don't like bacon fat,

BUENOS AIRES "HEART-STOPPER" (BUTTERFLIED NEW YORK STRIP WITH BACON AND EGGS) | page 157

pour it off, add 2 more tablespoons of oil, and cook the eggs in that. Cook the eggs sunny-side up, 2 to 3 minutes, or over easy, 2 to 3 minutes on the bottom and 1 minute on the top.

6 Arrange the eggs side by side on top of the steak and place 2 strips of fried bacon beside each egg. Serve at once with the *chimichurri* sauce on the side.

Brushing the grill grate with salt water at La Cabaña restaurant in Buenos Aires.

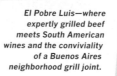

El Pobre Luis—where expertly grilled beef meets South American wines and the conviviality of a Buenos Aires neighborhood grill joint.

The Real Chimichurri

Argentina's national "steak sauce," *chimichurri* is actually more like a vinaigrette, and if you've tasted more elaborate versions in North America (some flavored with fresh cilantro or even mint), you may be surprised—and momentarily underwhelmed—by the real McCoy. Many versions don't even contain fresh parsley. But when you stop to consider the origins of *chimichurri,* among the rough gauchos (cowboys) of the Pampas, the simplicity of the sauce and the use of dried herbs makes sense. This *chimichurri* is pretty intense stuff; Argentineans use it sparingly.

As to how *chimichurri* got its name, the story generally involves an English cattle trader or merchant named Jim who asked his Argentinean hosts for some curry sauce. Over time, "Jimmy's curry" became *chimichurri.* Hmmm.

One of our "Up in Smoke" newsletter subscribers, Nelida Bernal, proposes another theory. Born in Argentina, Bernal has lived in the United States for forty years. She cites a word in the Basque language, *tximitxurri,* loosely translated as "a mixture of several things in no particular order." The Basques have always been highly nomadic, settling in many corners of North and South America. Indeed, Basque fishermen are sometimes credited with being the first Europeans to have discovered the Americas. **MAKES ABOUT ½ CUP; SERVES 2 TO 4**

3 cloves garlic, minced

1 teaspoon coarse salt (kosher or sea), or more to taste

½ teaspoon freshly ground black pepper

1 tablespoon dried oregano

1 to 2 teaspoons hot red pepper flakes

2 tablespoons red wine vinegar, or to taste

A few drops of fresh lemon juice

¼ cup extra-virgin olive oil or vegetable oil

¼ cup finely chopped fresh flat-leaf parsley (optional)

Place the garlic, salt, and black pepper in a mixing bowl and mash to a paste with the back of a wooden spoon. Add the oregano, hot pepper flakes, wine vinegar, and lemon juice and whisk to mix. Whisk in the olive oil in a thin stream, followed by the parsley, if using. Taste for seasoning, adding more salt and/or vinegar as necessary. You can serve the *chimichurri* right away but if you let it stand for an hour or so, the flavors will be better blended and richer.

NOTE: To make a red *chimichurri,* stir in 1 tablespoon tomato paste.

Cambodian Steak
with Salads and Condiments

THE SCOOP

WHERE: Siem Reap, Cambodia

WHAT: Sirloin or strip steak served with a table-burying array of Cambodian salads and condiments

HOW: Direct grilling

JUST THE FACTS: You'll need to know about one special distinctive ingredient here, and honestly, I mention it with some trepidation: It's called *pra hok*—fish paste—and it's a malodorous (that's putting it mildly) condiment made from fermented freshwater fish. One Western chef I know working in Siem Reap calls it "Cambodian cheese." The analogy is apt, as it really does smell and taste like a very ripe cheese. To smell *pra hok* is not to love it, unless you were born in Cambodia or Laos, and unlike the fish sauces of neighboring Thailand and Vietnam, it has not made its way into the Western kitchen. However, if you're willing to bend the rules a little, you could substitute Asian fish sauce, soy sauce, or my favorite substitute, Japanese miso. You'll still get a remarkable rendition of Cambodian steak.

What do you do if you're young and restless on a hot steamy night in Siem Reap? (Of course, they're all hot steamy nights in Siem Reap.) Or if you want to feed a posse of friends or a family of six and still get change from a 50,000 riel banknote (about $12)? Head for the restaurant Nana, where flames leap from a charcoal brazier out front, where the chiles are fiery, and the Angkor beer is always icy cold. As elsewhere in Asia, steak plays a subservient role in the main course. You eat it thinly sliced, wrapped in lettuce, with a farmers' market array of crisp fresh vegetables, and dipped in a bone-rattlingly pungent sauce. As a result, the steak that would normally serve one person in the western parts of Planet Barbecue feeds a whole table in Cambodia. But the accompaniments are so flavorful that not for a moment do you crave more meat. The fact is, most of the steak in Asia (at least outside of fancy hotels for Westerners) is so tough and ornery, you wouldn't want a 24 ouncer anyway. But eaten in small quantities with lots of accompaniments, it becomes a rich, satisfying meal in itself.

The only complicated thing about this recipe is reading through the list of ingredients. Most components need only to be arranged on the platter. The actual time spent cooking is less than twenty minutes. **SERVES 4**

Cambodian steak hot off the grill at Nana restaurant in Siem Reap.

FOR THE STEAK AND MARINADE

3 cloves garlic, minced

1 piece (2 inches) fresh ginger, peeled and minced

4 scallion whites, minced (set the green parts aside for
the condiment tray)

2 to 4 small hot red chiles, such as Thai chiles
or serrano peppers, seeded and finely chopped
(for hotter Cambodian steak, leave the seeds in)

⅓ cup fresh lemon juice

¼ cup Asian fish sauce or soy sauce

3 tablespoons vegetable oil

¼ cup finely chopped dry-roasted peanuts (see Notes)

1 teaspoon ground turmeric

½ teaspoon freshly ground black pepper

1 to 1½ pounds thinly sliced sirloin steak
(¼ to ½ inch thick; see Notes)

FOR THE SALAD PLATTER

1 large or 2 small heads Boston lettuce, broken
into whole leaves (16 to 20 leaves), rinsed,
and spun dry

1 bunch watercress, torn into 2-inch sprigs

2 cups thinly sliced napa cabbage

1 cup fresh Thai basil leaves or regular basil leaves

½ pound long beans or green beans, cut into 2-inch pieces

2 to 3 carrots, peeled and cut sharply on the diagonal into
⅛-inch slices

1 medium-size cucumber, peeled and thinly sliced

2 medium-size tomatoes, cut in half and thinly sliced

FOR THE CONDIMENT TRAY

½ cup sugar

3 stalks lemongrass, trimmed and sliced paper-thin crosswise

½ cup finely chopped dry-roasted peanuts (see Notes)

2 to 4 small hot red chiles, such as Thai chiles
or serrano peppers, thinly sliced crosswise

Green parts of 4 scallions, thinly sliced sharply on the diagonal

4 limes, cut into ovals or wedges, for squeezing

FOR THE DIPPING SAUCE

1 cup pra hok, or 1 cup Asian fish sauce, or 1 cup white miso

ADVANCE PREPARATION

1 to 4 hours for marinating the steak

1 Prepare the steak and marinade: Place the garlic, ginger, scallion whites, Thai chiles, lemon juice, fish sauce or soy sauce, the oil, peanuts, and the turmeric, and black pepper in a large nonreactive mixing bowl and stir to mix. Add the steak and stir to coat the beef well. Let the steak marinate in the refrigerator, covered, for 1 to 4 hours; the longer it marinates, the richer the flavor will be.

2 Prepare the salad platter shortly before serving: Arrange the lettuce, watercress, cabbage, basil, beans, carrots, cucumber, and tomatoes on a serving platter by kind and in an attractive pattern.

3 Prepare the condiment tray: Place the sugar, lemongrass, peanuts, chiles, and scallion greens in separate small bowls. Arrange the bowls and the limes on a platter and provide a spoon for each bowl.

4 Finally, prepare the dipping sauce: Divide the *pra hok* among 4 small bowls. Add enough water (2 to 4 tablespoons) to each bowl to obtain a thinnish, pourable sauce; it should be about the consistency of heavy cream (the water also serves to dilute the sauce's primal pungency).

5 Set up the grill for direct grilling and preheat it to high.

6 When ready to cook, brush and oil the grill grate. Drain the steak, discarding the marinade. Place the steak slices on the hot grate and grill until cooked to taste, 3 to 4 minutes per side for medium. (Cambodians prefer their steaks medium to medium-well done.) Use the poke test to check for doneness (see page 147). Transfer the grilled steak to a cutting board and let it rest for 2 minutes, then using a chef's knife or a cleaver, slice each piece of steak crosswise into ¼-inch-wide slivers. Transfer the steak to a platter.

7 Here's how you eat Cambodian steak: First, prepare your dipping sauce by placing sugar, lemongrass, peanuts, sliced chiles, scallion greens, and freshly squeezed lime juice to taste in your bowl of *pra hok*. Stir to mix with chopsticks. Next, dip a couple slices of steak into the dipping sauce, swirling it around to coat well, then place the steak on a lettuce leaf. Finally, put some watercress, cabbage, basil, beans, carrot, cucumber, tomato, and scallion greens on top of the meat. Roll the whole thing up, dip it again in the sauce, if you like, and eat it like a taco. This may be about the most glorious and complex set of steak flavors ever.

NOTES: A portion of steak for a Cambodian would be 3 to 4 ounces per person. A Westerner might feel more fulfilled with 5 to 6 ounces. I've called for sirloin here, but you could also use skirt steak or flank steak. When I make this dish at home, I use my personal favorite steak, New York strip.

Chop the peanuts in a food processor, running the machine in short bursts.

Spruce-Grilled Steak

THE SCOOP

WHERE: Quebec, Canada

WHAT: One of the simplest, tastiest, and downright coolest ways there is to grill steak—flash smoked on fresh spruce branches

HOW: Direct grilling

JUST THE FACTS: You need one uncommon ingredient—fresh spruce branches. You could also use fresh pine branches. Not available or you're an inveterate city dweller? You could achieve some of the explosive aromatic effect (although with a somewhat milder flavor) by substituting a bunch of fresh rosemary, thyme, or mint.

Canada doesn't have much of an indigenous grilling tradition, but there's one dish—a steak—that could come from nowhere else. Created by my friend and the editor of my French-Canadian books, Pierre Bourdon, it consists of a "Spencer" steak (what Canadians call a rib eye) grilled on spruce or pine branches, one of those simple, brilliant ideas you come up with after a bottle or two of wine around a campfire. It is not as crazy as it sounds—after all, the minty resins in spruce used to be a flavoring in chewing gum and soft drinks. And on page 513, you'll find a French recipe for grilling mussels on pine needles. Besides, any dish that shatters a myth about grilling—in this case, that you should never use a softwood, like spruce, or pine—has a place in my book. A powerful, aromatic red wine, like a Cahors or Côtes-du-Rhône would make a great accompaniment. **SERVES 2 AND CAN BE MULTIPLIED AS DESIRED**

2 rib eye steaks (each at least 1¼ inches thick and 8 to 10 ounces)
Coarse salt (kosher or sea) and freshly ground black pepper

YOU'LL ALSO NEED
2 small fresh spruce or pine branches (branches of the feathery needled leaves should be just slightly larger than the steaks)

ADVANCE PREPARATION
None

SPRUCE-GRILLED STEAK

1 Set up the grill for direct grilling and preheat it to high.

2 When ready to cook, brush and oil the grill grate. Very generously season the steaks on both sides with salt and pepper. Arrange the steaks on the hot grate at a diagonal to the bars. Grill the steaks until the outside of each is crusty and browned and the inside is cooked to taste, about 3 minutes per side for rare, 4 to 5 minutes per side for medium-rare. Use the poke test to check for doneness (see page 147). If desired, give each steak a quarter turn on each side after 1½ minutes to create a handsome crosshatch of grill marks.

3 Right before the steaks are done, place the spruce branches under them and grill them until smoky and aromatic (if you see flames, even better)—maybe 15 to 30 seconds—just long enough to perfume the steaks with spruce smoke. Serve the steaks at once.

Basque Country
Salt-Crusted Rib Steaks

THE SCOOP

WHERE: Tolosa, Spain

WHAT: A steak as thick as a leather-bound copy of *Don Quixote* crusted with a ¼ inch of rock salt and charred over charcoal

HOW: Direct grilling

JUST THE FACTS: To be strictly authentic, you'd use steaks cut from mature grass-fed steers. At Casa Julián, the beef is grilled over charcoal.

How far would you go for a great steak? Would you drive the back roads of Spain's Basque Country, an hour from San Sebastián, to wind up at a restaurant so well hidden, you have to grab a passerby by the arm and ask him to show you the door? Would you dine in a dungeonlike dining room that's actually an old garage filled with bric-a-brac that seems to go back a half century? Would you patronize a restaurant that has no menu and only one main dish to speak of—and that dish is steak grilled with a ¼-inch crust of sea salt? Of course you would, and when you stagger out of Casa Julián two hours later, you'll already be planning a return visit. This steak is ridiculously simple to make, but there's something about flame charring the salt crust that gives the beef a colossal flavor. It's one of those instances where one plus one equals a great deal more than two. Serve the steaks with a well-aged Rioja and get ready for some of the best steak you've ever tasted. **SERVES 4**

Matias Gorrochatequi: master of Spanish grilled beef.

4 bone-in beef rib steaks (each about 1¼ inches thick and
12 ounces to 1 pound)
2 cups rock salt or very coarse sea salt

ADVANCE PREPARATION
None

1 Set up the grill for direct grilling and preheat it to medium-high.

2 When ready to cook, brush and oil the grill grate. Arrange the steaks on the hot grate and sprinkle the tops with a ¼-inch-layer of salt. Grill the steaks until they are darkly browned on the bottom and beads of blood start to form on the top, about 5 minutes.

3 Turn the steaks over (some of the salt will fall into the fire; it's supposed to). Sprinkle another ¼ inch-layer of salt on top of the steaks. Continue grilling until the second sides are darkly browned and the steaks are cooked to taste, 4 to 5 minutes longer for medium-rare. Use the poke test to check for doneness (see page 147). At Casa Julián, they serve the steaks blood rare.

4 Using tongs, turn each steak on its side and whack it with the back of a knife to knock off the excess salt. Transfer the steaks to a cutting board and let them rest for 2 minutes. Cut the meat off the bone. Return the bones to the grill to char them, then serve them separately.

5 Cut the boneless steaks crosswise and slightly on the diagonal into ½ inch-thick strips.

Filets Mignons with Whisky Mushroom Sauce

There's fantasy and there's reality. Grilled filet mignon with mushroom sauce turns up at steak houses throughout Uruguay. More often than not, the sauce contains canned mushrooms and starchy thickeners that leave it with a consistency more akin to library paste than sauce. The canned mushrooms are even more perplexing, for if you drive from Montevideo to José Ignacio in the spring, you'll see wild mushroom vendors lined up every few hundred yards by the side of the road. So here's the mushroom sauce I would like to have been served with Uruguay's fine grilled beef tenderloin. The bacon helps keep the normally lean filets mignons moist as they grill. **SERVES 4**

THE SCOOP

WHERE: Montevideo, Uruguay

WHAT: Filets mignons wrapped and grilled in bacon and served with mushroom cream sauce

HOW: Direct grilling

JUST THE FACTS:
For the best results, use wild or exotic mushrooms. There are lots of candidates, including chanterelles, porcini, or morels. In the farmed mushroom category, you could use shiitakes, small portobellos, oyster mushrooms, or creminis. Better still, use a mixture.

FOR THE SAUCE

12 ounces chanterelle, porcini, or other wild or exotic mushrooms, or in a pinch, shiitake or button mushrooms

2 tablespoons (¼ stick) butter, salted or unsalted—it doesn't matter

1 shallot, thinly sliced

2 teaspoons all-purpose flour

1 cup beef stock, preferably homemade

¼ cup heavy (whipping) cream

2 tablespoons Scotch whisky

2 teaspoons Dijon mustard

½ teaspoon finely grated lemon zest

Coarse salt (kosher or sea) and freshly ground black pepper

FOR THE STEAKS

4 filets mignons (each 1½ inches thick and 6 to 8 ounces)

4 slices of country-style bacon (4 to 6 ounces)

8 bay leaves (optional)

YOU'LL ALSO NEED

Butcher's string

ADVANCE PREPARATION

None, but the mushroom sauce can be made several hours ahead.

1 Make the sauce: Trim the stems off the mushrooms and wipe the caps clean with a damp paper towel. Thinly slice the mushrooms. Melt the butter in a pan over medium heat. Add the shallot and cook until translucent but not brown, about 2 minutes. Add the mushrooms and increase the heat to high. Cook the mushrooms, stirring often, until tender and most of the liquid has evaporated, about 3 minutes. Stir in the flour and cook, stirring, until the flour evenly coats the mushrooms, about 1 minute. Stir in the beef stock and cream and bring to a boil, stirring well. Reduce the heat and let the sauce gently simmer until it is slightly reduced and richly flavored, 3 to 5 minutes, stirring often. Stir in the whisky, mustard, and lemon zest and cook, stirring, until blended, about 2 minutes, then season with salt and pepper to taste. The sauce can be prepared up to 1 hour ahead and kept warm.

2 Prepare the steaks: Wrap a slice of bacon around the side of each filet mignon, sandwiching 2 bay leaves, if using, between the bacon and beef on opposite sides of the steak. Tie the bacon in place with butcher's string. Season the top and bottom of the steaks with salt and pepper.

3 Set up the grill for direct grilling and preheat it to high. To be strictly authentic, you'd grill over oak or eucalyptus embers (see page 603 for instructions on grilling over a wood fire).

4 When ready to cook, brush and oil the grill grate. Arrange the filets mignons on the hot grate and grill until cooked to taste, 4 to 6 minutes per side for medium-rare. Use the poke test to test for doneness (see page 147). Don't forget to grill the steaks on their sides to brown the bacon.

5 Transfer the filets mignons to a platter or plates. Cut and remove the strings. Spoon the mushroom sauce over the steaks and serve at once.

Gaucho-Style Beef Ribs
{ COSTELAS DE BOI }

Visit the iconic Brazilian steak house Fogo de Chão (with branches throughout Brazil and North America), and the first thing you'll see is the namesake campfire with racks of ribs roasting on upright metal stakes around it. (You can read more about Fogo de Chão on page 170.) That's the traditional way to cook beef ribs gaucho (Brazilian cowboy) style, and if you have a big enough backyard and several hours to do the cooking, you'll find instructions below on how to do it. But excellent Brazilian beef ribs can be made on a rotisserie, on a charcoal grill using the indirect method, and yes, even on a gas grill. Whatever method you use, you'll get ribs with a sizzling salty crust on the outside and tender succulent meat inside—a Brazilian's idea of nirvana, and mine, too. **SERVES 4**

2 racks (7 bones each) beef long ribs
    (each 2½ to 3 pounds), or 1 large rack
    (6 to 8 pounds)
Coarse (and I mean really coarse) sea salt
Cracked black peppercorns
    (optional; Brazilians don't use it,
    but I like the way it rounds out the flavor)

YOU'LL ALSO NEED

2 cups oak or other hardwood chips
    (optional; see Note)

ADVANCE PREPARATION

None, but allow yourself a couple of hours to
    cook the ribs.

1 Remove the thin, papery membrane from the back of each rack of ribs: Turn a rack of ribs meat side down. Insert a sharp implement, such as the tip of a meat thermometer, under the membrane (the best place to start is on one of the middle bones). Using a dishcloth, paper towel, or needle-nose pliers to gain a secure grip, pull off the membrane. Repeat with the remaining rack of ribs, if using.

2 Right before grilling, very generously season the ribs on both sides with salt and pepper, if desired.

3 To grill: Grilling with a rotisserie produces beef ribs that are closest to those served at Fogo de Chão. (The campfire ribs are largely for show.)

If you are using a rotisserie, thread the ribs onto the rotisserie spit: Using a sharp, slender knife, make starter holes in the center of the meat between every two ribs. Twist the knife blade to widen the holes; this will make it easier to insert the spit. Use an over and under weaving motion to thread the spit through the holes in the racks of ribs. Two racks will fit on a large rotisserie, otherwise you'll have to cook one at a time. Set up the grill for spit

roasting, following the manufacturer's instructions, and preheat the grill to medium-high. Attach the spit to the rotisserie mechanism, turn on the motor, and cover the grill.

If you are using the indirect method, set up the grill for indirect grilling, place a drip pan in the center, and preheat the grill to medium. When ready to cook, if you are using a charcoal grill, toss the wood chips on the coals. If you are using a gas grill and want a smoke flavor, add the wood chips to the smoker box or place them in a smoker pouch under the grate (see page 603). Place the racks of ribs, meaty side up, in the center of the grate over the drip pan and away from the heat and cover the grill.

4 Cook the ribs until they are well browned, tender, and cooked through, 1 to 1½ hours for smaller racks, 2 to 2½ hours for a large one. When the ribs are done, the meat will have shrunk back from the ends of the bones by about ½ inch. If you like, during the last half hour, baste the ribs with any fat in the drip pan. If you are using a charcoal grill, you will need to replenish the coals after 1 hour.

5 Transfer the grilled ribs to a cutting board, carefully removing the spit, if necessary. Cut the ribs into 1- or 2-bone sections and serve at once.

NOTE: I've made the wood chips optional. If you want a light smoke flavor, use unsoaked chips. For a more intense smoke flavor, soak the wood chips for 1 hour in water to cover, then drain them.

VARIATION

Grilling Ribs Over a Campfire: Build a brisk campfire. Using wire, attach the racks of ribs to a vertical metal stake (like a rotisserie spit) and stand them in front of the fire so they are 12 to 18 inches away from it, starting with the fatty side facing the fire. Grill the ribs until they are well browned, tender, and cooked through, 1 to 2 hours per side depending on the size of the ribs. Add fresh logs to the fire periodically and turn the ribs halfway through so the other side grills the same way. When the ribs are done, the meat will have shrunk back from the ends of the bones by about ½ inch.

Beef ribs Fogo de Chão-style, roasted on upright rotisserie spits in front of an open fire.

A gaucho-size beef rib ready for carving.

The Bonfire Brothers

Inspired by an American president, **JAIR AND ARRI COSER,** have built an empire of sixteen restaurants across the United States called Fogo de Chão. The name means campfire, and that's how their style of cooking was originally done.

BRAZIL

In 1996, claim Jair Coser and his brother Arri, they received a challenge they couldn't resist. "Come to Texas," said former American president, George Herbert Walker Bush, who was dining at one of their restaurants in São Paolo. Talk about bringing coals to Newcastle—a Brazilian steak house in the epicenter of America's beef culture. But six months later, the brothers opened the first Fogo de Chão (pronounced fo-go dje shaow), in Dallas. Today, they have sixteen restaurants across the United States, with more to come.

Not bad for two brothers of Italian descent who grew up on a farm in a flyspeck of a town called Revaldo in southern Brazil. The family farm lay in the heart of Brazil's cattle country and it was there that the young Jair and Arri first experienced *fogo de chão*—roasting meats the gaucho way, on sticks in front of a wood campfire.

When the brothers finally opened a restaurant of their own, in Porto Alegre in 1979, they remembered the gaucho campfire. They named the place Fogo de Chão and installed a wood fire pit in the front of the restaurant where huge racks of beef ribs roasted in front of the fire. Most of the cooking was done on a wood-burning rotisserie featuring flat spits that had to be turned by hand.

They still carve the meats, fifteen varieties in all, directly on to guests' plates.

Fogo de Chão founders Jair and Arri Coser.

Fogo de Chão has evolved a lot since then—with mammoth motorized rotisseries that turn 108 spits at a time. The campfire in the front of the restaurant has become largely ceremonial—the beef is still cooked the traditional way, seasoned with only fistfuls of coarse sea salt. The *churrasqueiros* (grill chef-waiters) still wear the red neckerchiefs, blousy white shirts, *bombacha* pants, and black leather boots of their gaucho predecessors. And they still carve the meats, fifteen varieties in all, directly on to guests' plates until the guests turn over a green-and-red medallion specially provided for the purpose of instructing the *churrasqueiros* to stop.

At an American steak house customers have a monolithic experience, explains Jair. They order a particular steak (a filet mignon or a flank steak, for example) grilled to a particular degree of doneness (rare or medium); the cooking and serving are done by different people. "At our restaurants, each guest gets to taste all fifteen meats," Jair says. "It's the *churrasqueiro*'s job to make sure that each skewer has some rare meat, some medium meat, and some crisp crust.

NAME: Jair and Arri Coser

TERRITORY: Brazil and the United States

CLAIM TO FAME: Built a single Brazilian steak house into a restaurant chain spanning two continents. Introduced Americans to *fogo de chão* (gaucho campfire cooking) and *churrasco* (Brazilian spit roasting).

SPECIALTIES: *Picanha* (fat cap sirloin), *alcatra* (top sirloin), *fraldinha* (bottom sirloin or flank steak), *bife ancho* (rib eye steak), and other meats spit roasted Brazilian style over charcoal and carved right onto your plate

THE COSER BROTHERS SAY:

► You can buy the best meat in the world, but if you don't build the right fire and cook at the right temperature it won't taste like anything special.

► We like competition. It means you're doing something right.

► The most important ingredient for great barbecue? Passion. If you love what you do, it will show in your food.

Butterflied Sesame-Grilled Beef Short Ribs

{ KALBI }

THE SCOOP

WHERE: Korea

WHAT: Beef short ribs thinly sliced, marinated with Asian pear and sesame oil, and grilled over charcoal

HOW: Direct grilling, unusual for beef ribs

JUST THE FACTS: You'll need to butterfly the ribs in this recipe: With a bone end facing you, and using a small, sharp knife, cut the meat away from the top of the bone, almost to the side edge. Fold out the meat; one side should still be attached to the bone. Cut through the meat flap two thirds of the way down its thickness, again almost to the edge, and open up this flap. Then make a final cut through the thicker section of meat, again almost to the edge, and open up this last flap. Repeat with the remaining ribs.

No survey of world barbecue would be complete without Korea's *kalbi*. I've written about these thin-sliced, direct-grilled beef short ribs many times before, but on my last trip to Seoul, I discovered some new twists. So how did *kalbi* begin? Youngho Moon, communications director at one of Korea's agricultural ministries, has an interesting theory. Starting five hundred years ago, a huge cattle fair took place in Suwon—a freestanding city at the time, today part of the sprawling megalopolis that is Seoul. Farmers would bring their livestock there from all over the region. A lively hospitality business arose to accommodate the out-of-town vendors and take advantage of their bovine merchandise. Over time the seasonings evolved from simple salt and sesame seeds to complex marinades flavored with Asian pear, sesame oil, and soy sauce. The restaurant Hwachunok in Suwon serves one of the more unusual versions of *kalbi:* The marinade contains no soy sauce. "We do this to preserve the bright red color of the beef," says the restaurant's owner and lifelong grill master, Kim Su Kyong. I say that any dish that allows you to combine beef, sesame, and Asian pear is worth firing up the grill for. For a side dish, try the Korean Barbecue Accompaniments. We're talking oceans of flavor here, but if you'd like a dipping sauce, use the one on page 179. **SERVES 4**

1 small or ½ large Asian pear, peeled and
    seeded, or ½ cup pear nectar

3 cloves garlic, coarsely chopped, plus 8 cloves
    garlic, peeled and skewered on toothpicks

1 tablespoon finely chopped peeled fresh ginger

1 tablespoon toasted sesame seeds
    (see page 68), plus 1 tablespoon for garnish

2 tablespoons sugar

2 teaspoons coarse salt (kosher or sea)

½ teaspoon freshly ground black pepper

1 teaspoon Asian (dark) sesame oil

2 pounds of beef short ribs, cut into 2-inch
    lengths

Korean Barbecue Accompaniments (see page 52)

1 bunch scallions, both white and green parts,
    trimmed

YOU'LL ALSO NEED

Kitchen shears

ADVANCE PREPARATION

1 to 4 hours for marinating the meat

1 Puree the Asian pear, chopped garlic, ginger, 1 tablespoon of sesame seeds, sugar, salt, and pepper in a food processor. Work in the sesame oil.

2 Score the meat in a crosshatch pattern with a sharp knife (the cuts should be ⅛ inch deep and ⅛ inch apart). Butterfly the ribs as described in Just the Facts on page 171. Arrange them in a single layer in a nonreactive baking dish. Pour the pear marinade over the ribs, turning them to coat both sides. Let the ribs marinate in the refrigerator, covered, for 1 to 4 hours; the longer they marinate, the richer the flavor will be.

3 Make the Korean side dish sampler.

4 Set up the grill, preferably a hibachi, for direct grilling and preheat it to high.

5 When ready to cook, brush and oil the grill grate. Drain the ribs, discarding the marinade. Arrange the skewered garlic, the scallions, and the beef ribs with the meat spread out on the hot grate and grill until the garlic is browned and tender, 3 to 4 minutes per side; the scallions are browned, 2 to 4 minutes per side; and the beef is sizzling and browned, 2 to 4 minutes per side. (Koreans prefer their meat medium to medium-well done.) Use the poke test to test for doneness (see the box on page 147).

6 Transfer the grilled beef to a warm platter and, using kitchen scissors, cut it into bite-size pieces. Cut the garlic cloves in half and cut the scallions into 1-inch pieces. To eat the *kalbi,* dip a piece of beef in the sesame salt. Spread a little chile paste on a lettuce leaf. Place pieces of beef, garlic, and scallion on the lettuce leaf. Roll it up and pop it into your mouth.

Cartagena Beef Kebabs

{ PINCHOS DE BIFE CARTAGENOS }

THE SCOOP

WHERE: A popular street snack in Cartagena and elsewhere in Colombia

WHAT: Beef kebabs marinated in mustard, lemon, tomato sauce, and hot paprika, then flash charred on the grill

HOW: Direct grilling; charcoal is the traditional fuel

There's one in every city in Latin America—a street corner grill jockey whose kebabs fill the skewer a little more generously, whose grill sizzles a little louder, and whose stall or pushcart is busier than everyone else's. In the colonial city of Cartagena, this go-to guy is Piedro "Peter" Goncales. For more than a quarter century, Goncales has dished up amazingly cheap and spectacularly flavorful beef kebabs, using a square of cardboard to fan the embers hot enough to apply the right char to the meat. Every evening you'll find his pushcart at the corner of the Calle de Ayos and the Calle de los Santos de Piedra. Warning: Go early. When Piedro sells out of beef, he goes home. **SERVES 4**

2 tablespoons tomato paste

2 tablespoons Dijon mustard

2 tablespoons fresh lime juice

2 tablespoons vegetable oil

1 tablespoon hot or sweet paprika

1 teaspoon ground cumin

1 teaspoon sugar

1 clove garlic, minced

Coarse salt (kosher or sea)

½ teaspoon freshly ground black pepper

1½ pounds beef sirloin, bottom round, or rib eye, cut into ¾-inch cubes

8 tiny new potatoes (each about 1 inch in diameter)

1 medium-size onion, broken into layers and cut into 1-inch squares

1 green bell pepper, cored, seeded, and cut into 1-inch squares

YOU'LL ALSO NEED

Bamboo or metal skewers

ADVANCE PREPARATION

2 to 6 hours for marinating the beef

1 Place the tomato paste, mustard, lime juice, oil, paprika, cumin, sugar, garlic, 1½ teaspoons of salt, and the black pepper in a large nonreactive bowl and whisk to mix. Stir in the beef. Let the meat marinate in the refrigerator, covered, for 2 to 6 hours; the longer it marinates, the richer the flavor will be.

2 Place the potatoes in a large saucepan and add water to cover by 3 inches. Add salt to taste. Bring the potatoes to a boil and boil until almost tender, about 5 minutes. When cooked, the potatoes should be relatively easy to pierce with a bamboo skewer. Drain the potatoes in a colander, rinse them with cold water until cool, then drain them well again.

3 Drain the cubes of beef, discarding the marinade. Thread the beef onto bamboo skewers, placing a piece of onion or bell pepper between every 2 pieces of beef. The last ingredient to go on each skewer should be a potato. The kebabs can be prepared up to 24 hours ahead to this stage and refrigerated, covered with plastic wrap.

4 Set up the grill for direct grilling and preheat it to high.

5 When ready to cook, brush and oil the grill grate. Arrange the beef kebabs on the hot grate and grill until cooked to taste; in Colombia the beef would be served medium to medium-well, 3 to 5 minutes per side for each kebab, 6 to 10 minutes in all. Use the pinch test to test for doneness (see page 147).

6 Transfer the kebabs to a platter or plates or do as they do in Cartagena— eat the kebabs right off the stick while standing around the grill.

JUST THE FACTS: Grill master Piedro Goncales uses a special cut of beef he calls *masa del frente*, cut from the inside of a steer's thigh. In North America, you could use top or bottom round or sirloin, or even a more tender prestige cut, like beef rib eye (that's what I use when I make this dish). In Colombia, you'd cap each kebab with a *papa criolla*, a small, rich-flavored, creamy-textured "Creole" potato. A small new potato will do the trick.

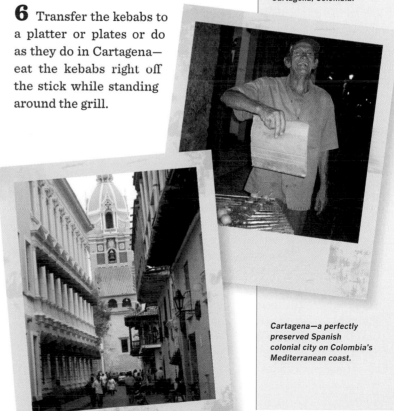

Piedro "Peter" Goncales fans his sidewalk grill in Cartagena, Colombia.

Cartagena—a perfectly preserved Spanish colonial city on Colombia's Mediterranean coast.

PLANET BARBECUE

Argentina: World's Champion Beef Eaters

The stats are in and the winner is . . . Argentina. No other country consumes more beef. Last year, Argentineans consumed an average of 154 pounds per person—compared to 89.8 pounds in the U.S.

Argentina's love affair (I use the term deliberately) with beef began with the gauchos, rugged cowboys who settled the Pampas to tend vast herds of cattle, the descendants of steers brought here by conquistadors in 1536. Gaucho life was primitive, and so was gaucho barbecue: whole lambs, pigs, and racks of beef ribs stuck on T-shaped metal stakes in front of a roaring bonfire. Seasonings were limited to salt or perhaps such dried herbs as you could find at a country general store. And the herbs were moistened with a little vinegar—the origin of Argentina's table sauce, *chimichurri*. The gaucho's *asado* (literally, "roast") remains one of the world's most authentic and heroic live-fire cooking experiences, popular throughout rural Argentina and even in major cities.

A gaucho (Argentinean cowboy) prepares a traditional asado (meat roasted on a vertical stake in front of a bonfire).

By the early twentieth century, beef had made Buenos Aires one of the wealthiest cities in the western hemisphere. Refrigerated freighters, their holds brimming with meat, steamed down the Plata River destined for New York, Europe, and beyond. Beef fortunes transformed Buenos Aires from a cultural backwater into the "Paris of South America."

Over time, the rustic *asado* of the gauchos evolved into sophisticated steak houses distinguished by their broad menus, with dishes grilled to order on industrial-strength *parrillas* (grills). The preparation remains simple—salt, fire, and perhaps a *chimichurri* for serving. The focus stays on the beef.

Where Beef Is King

ARGENTINA
CÓRDOBA
MENDOZA
THE PAMPAS
BUENOS AIRES
PATAGONIA
ATLANTIC
OCEAN

0   500   1000
MILES

Dramatic Cerro Torre in Los Glaciares National Park, Patagonia.

Chimichurri, country salsa, and other Argentinean sauces for grilled meats.

Argentina stretches from Brazil's barbecue heartland, Rio Grande do Sul, to pristine Patagonia. From one end of the country to the other, Argentineans are obsessed with two things above all else—meat and fire.

THE GRILLS: The basic Argentinean grill, the *parrilla,* consists of a stone platform or metal box or table with a grill grate positioned over the embers. At the center of the grill, or to one side, there's a firebox where logs or charcoal are burned down to embers. The *asador* (grill master) rakes these coals under the meat to control and maintain the fire. One distinctive feature of the Argentinean grill grate is that it slopes upward from front to back, enabling the grill master to control the heat by moving the food closer to or farther away from the fire. The second is that on many Argentinean grills the bars of the grate are V-shaped to channel off the dripping fat. Not that the fat goes to waste—it's used for basting the meat.

The other live-fire cooking set-up is the *asado,* basically a campfire with large hunks of meat or whole animals impaled on stakes in front of it. The heat is controlled by positioning the food closer to or farther away from the fire.

Frequent basting with meat drippings or oil keeps the grilled beef sizzling and succulent.

THE FUEL: Wood (preferably oak) or natural lump charcoal. Never, ever, propane.

THE FLAVORINGS: Most Argentinean beef is grass fed. At first bite, the meat may seem to lack the luscious, fatty mouthfeel of American corn-fed beef. With time, you come to appreciate its forthright natural flavor, and in particular, the distinctive flavor of each cut of beef. Grass-fed beef

also has decided health and environmental advantages: It contains more omega-3 fatty acids and less saturated fat than corn-fed beef. And because grass is a steer's natural diet, Argentinean beef is much less likely to be treated with antibiotics.

MUST TRY DISHES: In Argentina you can order your meat *jugoso* (literally "juicy," which is to say rare) or *a punto* (medium). Argentineans tend to eat their meat somewhat more well done than do Europeans.

Here are some of the individual cuts and meats:

Asado: Gaucho (cowboy)–style barbecue, made by roasting whole lambs, pigs, and sections of beef ribs in front of a campfire. This is generally done at the *estancias* (ranches) of the Pampas, but also at restaurants in Buenos Aires.

Asado de tiro: cross-cut beef short ribs, cut ½-inch thick and in a way that gives you a long, slender steak that hangs off the plate

Bife de chorizo: New York strip steak

Mollejas: Grilled sweetbreads

Tapa de ojo: A singular and spectacularly delectable cut of beef unique to Argentina— imagine cutting a rib eye steak in half crosswise. The meatier (less fatty) half is the *tapa de ojo.*

THE CONDIMENTS: The traditional sauce spooned over grilled meat in Argentina is *chimichurri,* a sort of vinaigrette made with olive oil, wine vinegar, and herbs (you can read about the origin of this iconic condiment on page 159). At its simplest, *chimichurri* consists of dried oregano, salt, hot pepper flakes, and vinegar. A more elaborate version might feature chopped fresh flat-leaf parsley and garlic. There's also a red *chimichurri*— created at the legendary Buenos Aires chophouse, La Cabana—made with tomato sauce and anchovies.

Ready to cook with one of the grill chefs at the popular El Pobre Luis in Buenos Aires.

HOW TO EAT IT: As simply as possible

IF YOU CAN EAT AT ONLY ONE RESTAURANT: In a country that boasts great steak houses in every neighborhood, almost on every block, it's hard to single out one. I always enjoy the beef—and the buzz—at El Pobre Luis in Buenos Aires (check out the Buenos Aires "Heart-Stopper" on page 157). In Mendoza, don't miss Francis Mallmann 1884, named for South America's most famous grill master (you can read about him on page 576), located in the Bodega Escorihuela in the heart of Argentina's wine country and home of what may be the most humongous beef rib on Planet Barbecue.

WHAT TO DRINK: An Argentinean malbec or cabernet sauvignon

THE MOST SINGULAR DISH IN THE REPERTORY: *Choto* or *chinculines:* coiled grilled sheeps' intestines or grilled sheeps' chitlins. They taste better than they sound.

Buenos Aires
Garlic Butter Beef Roulades

THE SCOOP

WHERE: Buenos Aires, Argentina

WHAT: Thin rolls of beef tenderloin stuffed with garlic-parsley butter and grilled shish kebab style

HOW: Direct grilling, preferably over charcoal

JUST THE FACTS: The sheer extravagance of stuffing filet mignon with herb butter speaks loudly for itself.

Overkill as only Argentineans know how to do it—imagine if chicken Kiev had originated not in the Ukraine, but in Buenos Aires. The chicken would be beef; it would be grilled instead of deep-fried; and chances are it would be served on a skewer. Well, just such a dish exists at the hyper-popular restaurant La Cabrera in the trendy Palermo district of Buenos Aires. The butter helps moisten an intrinsically lean cut of beef, like tenderloin (a trick used to great advantage also at North American steak houses), while adding an insidiously good flavor of its own. **SERVES 4**

FOR THE HERB BUTTER

8 tablespoons (1 stick) salted butter, at room temperature
1 clove garlic, minced
3 tablespoons finely chopped fresh flat-leaf parsley
2 teaspoons Worcestershire sauce
2 teaspoons fresh lemon juice
½ teaspoon grated lemon zest

FOR THE BEEF

1 center cut beef tenderloin (1½ pounds), trimmed
Coarse salt (kosher or sea) and freshly ground black pepper

YOU'LL ALSO NEED

Long bamboo or metal skewers

ADVANCE PREPARATION

1 hour for preparing and freezing the butter; the beef roulades can be stuffed and skewered up to 6 hours ahead.

1 Make the herb butter: Place the butter, garlic, parsley, Worcestershire sauce, lemon juice, and lemon zest in a mixing bowl and whisk to mix. Transfer the herb butter to a plate lined with plastic wrap. Mold the butter into a rectangle about 6 inches long, 1½ inches wide, and ½ inch thick. Freeze the herb butter until hard, about 1 hour.

2 Meanwhile, prepare the beef: Cut the tenderloin crosswise into ¾-inch-thick steaks. Place a steak between 2 pieces of plastic wrap or a resealable plastic bag and, using a meat mallet, scaloppine pounder, or the side of a heavy cleaver, pound it to form an oval about 4 inches long, 3 inches wide, and ¼ inch thick. Repeat with the remaining pieces of tenderloin.

3 Place the butter on a cutting board and slice it into ½ x 2-inch pieces. Arrange a piece of butter at the edge of a short side of each piece of beef. Starting at that edge, roll up the beef around the butter. Thread the rolls crosswise onto skewers, 3 rolls to a skewer. The roulades can be prepared several hours ahead to this stage and refrigerated, covered with plastic wrap.

4 Set up the grill for direct grilling and preheat it to high.

5 When ready to cook, brush and oil the grill grate.

Season the beef rolls on both sides with salt and pepper. Place the skewers on the hot grate and grill the beef rolls until the beef is sizzling and brown on the outside and the butter is melted and bubbling, 3 to 4 minutes per side. Move the kebabs as needed to dodge any flare-ups. Remove the skewers and serve at once.

Lemongrass-Grilled Beef with Noodles and Salad
{ BO BUN }

"**B**arbecue—the new health food." It's not a claim you often hear in the brisket- and rib-loving American heartland. But in many parts of Asia, barbecue is served in a manner consistent with the latest nutritional wisdom; moderate portions of grilled meat are paired with fresh vegetables and explosive spices. In short, a description of Vietnam's national grilled beef dish, *bo bun*—thin shavings of lean beef marinated in a pungent mixture of lemongrass, fish sauce, and garlic, then seared on a charcoal brazier.

What turns this simple dish into a feast are the accompaniments: a mountain of snowy, cool, hair-thin rice noodles; a plate of lettuce leaves; platters of fiery chiles, crisp bean sprouts, sliced cucumbers, and fresh basil, cilantro, and mint leaves. You wrap the ingredients in lettuce leaves and dip them into a sweet-sour-salty, completely fat-free "barbecue" sauce called *nuoc cham*. What you get is the meat, starch, and salad course all rolled into one. And because the ingredients are so intensely flavorful, you don't even miss the fat. Everyone at the table assembles *bo bun* to taste. The sheer activity—grilling the meat, selecting and piling on the ingredients, rolling everything up—makes this a great dish for parties. Set up a couple of hibachis in the center of a table outside on a fireproof surface, like an inverted rimmed sheet pan, and have your guests grill their own *bo bun*.

Don't be intimidated by the length of the recipe. It's really just a series of simple steps, most of which can be done ahead of time. **SERVES 4**

THE SCOOP

WHERE: Vietnam

WHAT: Thinly shaved beef flavored with lemongrass and flash charred over a brazier— a whole meal in a single dish hot off the grill

HOW: Direct grilling

JUST THE FACTS: You'll need to know about a few Vietnamese ingredients to make this. Rice "vermicelli" (*bun*) are noodles made from rice flour. They come fully cooked from the factory; all you need to do is rehydrate them by soaking them. They're available at Vietnamese and Asian markets and at many supermarkets.

FOR THE MARINADE AND BEEF

2 cloves garlic, coarsely chopped

2 stalks fresh lemongrass, trimmed and thinly sliced, or
    3 strips lemon zest (each ½ x 2 inches), removed with
    a vegetable peeler and coarsely chopped

1 large or 2 small shallots, coarsely chopped

1 piece (1 inch) fresh ginger, peeled and coarsely chopped

2 small hot chiles, such as Thai chiles or serrano or
    jalapeño peppers, stemmed, seeded, and
    coarsely chopped

3 tablespoons sugar

1 teaspoon freshly ground black pepper

½ teaspoon coarse salt (kosher or sea), or more to taste

¼ cup Asian fish sauce or soy sauce

¼ cup Asian (dark) sesame oil or vegetable oil

2 tablespoons fresh lemon or lime juice

1 tablespoon sesame seeds

1½ pounds beef (tenderloin, tenderloin tips, sirloin, or top
    round; see Note), sliced paper-thin across the grain

FOR THE NOODLES

8 ounces rice vermicelli

FOR THE SALAD PLATE

1 large or 2 small heads Boston lettuce, separated into
    whole leaves, rinsed, and spun dry

1 medium-size or 2 small cucumbers, peeled and
    thinly sliced (it's not necessary to seed the cucumber)

2 to 4 Thai chiles, jalapeño peppers, or other hot chiles,
    thinly sliced

2 to 3 cups mung bean sprouts

1 bunch fresh Thai basil, rinsed, dried, and torn into sprigs

1 bunch fresh mint, rinsed, dried, and torn into sprigs

1 bunch fresh cilantro, rinsed, dried, and torn into sprigs

FOR SERVING

½ cup finely chopped salted roasted peanuts, in a
    serving bowl

Vietnamese Dipping Sauce (recipe follows)

YOU'LL ALSO NEED

Bamboo skewers (optional); an aluminum foil grill shield
    (optional, see page 611)

ADVANCE PREPARATION

1 to 2 hours for marinating the beef and soaking the
    rice noodles

1 Prepare the marinade and beef: Place the garlic, lemongrass, shallot, ginger, chiles, sugar, black pepper, and salt in a heavy mortar and pound to a paste with a pestle, then work in the fish sauce, sesame oil, and lemon juice. Stir in the sesame seeds. If you don't have a mortar and pestle, puree the garlic, lemongrass, shallot, ginger chiles, sugar, black pepper, and salt in a food processor, then work in the fish sauce, sesame oil, and lemon juice. Add the sesame seeds and pulse the processor once or twice to mix. Taste for seasoning, adding more salt if necessary.

2 Arrange the beef in a large nonreactive baking dish. Spoon the marinade over the beef, turning the pieces to coat both sides. Let the beef marinate in the refrigerator, covered, for 1 to 2 hours, turning the pieces once or twice so that they marinate evenly.

3 Place the rice vermicelli in a large bowl and add hot water to cover by 3 inches. Let the vermicelli soak until pliable, about 30 minutes. Drain the vermicelli of any excess water, fluff the noodles with your fingers, transfer them to a bowl or onto a platter, and cover them with a slightly damp dish towel or paper towel to keep them soft. Alternatively, mound the vermicelli in 4 wide serving bowls.

4 Prepare the salad plate: Arrange the lettuce, cucumber, chiles, bean sprouts, basil, mint, and cilantro on a salad plate or platter. Cover the salad with a damp dish towel or paper towel to keep it crisp and fresh. The salad can be refrigerated, covered, for up to 2 hours.

5 Drain the beef, discarding the marinade. To grill the beef kebab style, thread it onto bamboo skewers across the grain, weaving it back and forth on the skewer so that the flat side will be stretched out and exposed to the fire. You may be able to thread more than 1 piece of beef on a skewer. You can also grill the beef in individual pieces.

6 Just prior to serving, set up the grill for direct grilling and preheat it to high (I like to use a hibachi).

7 When ready to cook, brush and oil the grill grate. Arrange the beef on the hot grate and grill it until golden brown on both sides, 1 to 3 minutes per side. (If you are using bamboo skewers, you may want to slide an aluminum foil shield under the exposed ends to keep them from burning.) Transfer the grilled beef to a platter or plate.

8 To eat *bo bun,* spread out a lettuce leaf and arrange some rice vermicelli, cucumber, sliced chiles, bean sprouts, basil, mint, and cilantro on it. Place a piece of grilled beef on top (pull out the skewer, if using) and sprinkle it with peanuts. Roll everything into a tight cylinder. Dip the *bo bun* into the dipping sauce and pop it into your mouth.

NOTE: The Vietnamese would use a tough, robust cut, like sirloin or top round; at home I like a more upscale cut, like beef tenderloin or tenderloin tips. In either case, the beef should be sliced paper-thin; partially freezing the meat facilitates slicing. While 3 to 4 ounces of beef would be a reasonable serving per person for a Vietnamese person, a Westerner will probably want more like 6 ounces per person.

Vietnamese Dipping Sauce
{ NUOC CHAM }

Quick, list the characteristics of a great barbecue sauce. Sweet? Sour? Salty? Spicy? And no stinting on the garlic. But before you unscrew a bottle of Kansas City–style barbecue sauce, you should know that Vietnam's ubiquitous dipping sauce, *nuoc cham,* possesses very nearly the same flavor profile, although it's a lot more subtle and delicate. This dipping sauce is the traditional—and perfect—condiment for Vietnamese grilled beef. **SERVES 4**

1 carrot, peeled
2 tablespoons sugar
1 clove garlic, minced
¼ cup fresh lemon or lime juice, or more to taste
¼ cup rice vinegar
¼ cup Asian fish sauce, or more to taste
1 tiny hot red or green chile, cut crosswise into
   the thinnest possible slices
1 tablespoon finely chopped salted roasted peanuts
   (optional)

1 Using a vegetable peeler, cut 4 paper-thin strips of carrot. Pile these one on top of the other and, using a sharp chef's knife, cut them lengthwise into hair-thin threads. Place these in a small bowl. Stir in 1 tablespoon of sugar and let stand for about 10 minutes. The carrot threads will soften.

2 Place the garlic and the remaining 1 tablespoon of sugar in a nonreactive mixing bowl and mash to a paste with the back of a spoon. Add the lemon juice, rice vinegar, and fish sauce and stir until the sugar dissolves. Stir in the sugared carrot threads and enough water (4 to 5 tablespoons) to make a mellow, well-balanced sauce. Taste for seasoning, adding more lemon juice and/or fish sauce as necessary; the sauce should be sweet, sour, salty, and aromatic.

3 Divide the sauce among 4 small serving bowls. Sprinkle the chile and peanuts, if using, over each serving.

Grilled Veal Chops with Sweet-and-Sour Onions

THE SCOOP

WHERE: Florence, Italy

WHAT: Grilled veal chops topped with a sort of marmalade made with onions, balsamic vinegar, and honey

HOW: Direct grilling

JUST THE FACTS: I first tasted this dish made with veal loin chops (aka veal T-bones), but you could also use rib chops. Select chops that are 1 to 1¼ inches thick.

'Round about your fifth day of dining on the Italian barbecue trail you may find yourself tiring of the noble ideals of understatement, simplicity, and less is more. After all, you can eat only so much perfectly grilled but utterly unadorned steak. And even the most sweet, tender, delicately grilled veal chop becomes dull after a while for want of a sauce. Well, here's the antidote: a specialty of Florence's subterranean temple of simple grilled meats, Buca Lapi (for more on Buca Lapi, see page 145). It's a grilled veal chop as thick as *War and Peace* served with onions glazed in balsamic vinegar, honey, and red wine. The contrast of smokily grilled veal and sweet-and-sour onions will take your breath away. **SERVES 4**

1 pound small torpedo onions, cipollinis, pearl
    onions, or shallots (see Note)
2 cups dry red wine
1 cup balsamic vinegar, or more to taste
1 cup honey, or more to taste
4 tablespoons (½ stick) unsalted butter
Coarse salt (kosher or sea) and freshly ground
    black pepper
4 thick loin or rib veal chops (each 1 to 1¼
    inches thick and 12 to 14 ounces)
1 tablespoon chopped fresh flat-leaf parsley
    (optional)

ADVANCE PREPARATION

None, but allow yourself at least 1 hour to make
    the Sweet-and-Sour Onions.

1 Peel the onions, leaving most of the stem end intact; this helps hold the onions together as they cook. Place the onions in a large, deep saucepan, add the red wine, balsamic vinegar, honey, and 3 tablespoons of the butter and bring to a boil over high heat.

2 Reduce the heat to medium and cook the onions until tender—they'll be easy to pierce with a skewer—12 to 15 minutes. If all goes well, the wine, vinegar, and honey will cook down to a syrupy glaze at precisely the same moment the onions are tender. If not, using a slotted spoon, transfer the onions to a plate and continue boiling the sauce until it is thick and syrupy. Return the onions to the pan, if necessary and taste for seasoning, adding salt and pepper to taste and more vinegar and/or honey as necessary; the onions should be a little sweet, a little sour, and very flavorful. If you add more vinegar and/or honey, return the pan to the heat to let the liquid cook down. You should wind up with about 1¼ cups. The onions can be cooked several hours, or even a day, ahead and reheated just before serving.

GRILLED VEAL CHOPS WITH SWEET-AND-SOUR ONIONS

3 Set up the grill for direct grilling and preheat one zone to high.

4 When ready to cook, brush and oil the grill grate. Generously season the chops on both sides with salt and pepper. (OK, I know they add the salt *after* grilling in Tuscany and they don't bother with pepper. But I still maintain you get a better crust when you season the meat just prior to grilling.) Arrange the veal chops on the hot grate at a diagonal to the bars. Grill the chops until nicely browned on the outside and cooked through, 5 to 6 minutes per side for medium. Use the poke test to test for doneness (see page 147). Give each chop a quarter turn after 2½ minutes on each side to create a handsome crosshatch of grill marks.

5 Transfer the chops to a platter or plates and let them rest while you reheat the onion mixture.

Just before serving, stir in the remaining 1 tablespoon of butter. Spoon the onions over the chops and sprinkle the parsley, if using, on top. Serve the chops at once.

NOTE: Baby torpedo onions (elongated red onions), cipollinis (small, flat, round onions), pearl onions—or any small whole onions or shallots will all work well here. Exotic onions are available from Melissa's (www.melissas.com). Although it's not strictly traditional, a few years ago I took to grilling the onions before simmering them in the wine and balsamic vinegar. This takes a little more time (although you can grill the onions at a previous grill session), but it gives the sauce an incredible depth of flavor. Brush the onions with oil, season with salt and pepper, and grill over a hot fire until browned on the outside but still firm inside, 4 to 6 minutes per side.

Baby Veal Chops with Garlic, Dill, and Russian "Ketchup"

{ TELYACHYA KOREJKA NA GRILE }

THE SCOOP

WHERE: Moscow, Russia

WHAT: Veal chops scented with the hallmark Russian seasonings of garlic and fresh dill, grilled until golden and crusty

HOW: Direct grilling

If you've ever fantasized about experiencing the imperial cuisine of Catherine the Great's Russia, Ermak is the place to do it. This sprawling timber and stucco edifice modeled on an eighteenth-century Russian fort is a Moscow landmark, equally popular with locals and tourists. Presiding over the kitchen is a great bear of a chef named Valery Arseev. He's the sort of guy who serves two kinds of borscht, five kinds of *piroshki,* and every imaginable sort of smoked fish as a prelude to lunch. Like most Russian grill masters, Arseev cooks on a grateless charcoal-burning grill called a *mangal.* His veal chops are the stuff of legend, seasoned with blasts of garlic and fresh dill and smokily charred over charcoal. By way of a sauce, Arseev riffs on a tomato-, coriander-, and dill-based condiment from the Republic of Georgia in the Caucasus Mountains. You could think of it as Russian ketchup. These are the sort of veal chops you want to lift to your mouth with your hands and gnaw right off the bone. **SERVES 4**

FOR THE CHOPS

4 thick rib or loin veal chops (each about 1 to
    1¼ inches thick and 12 to 14 ounces)
Coarse salt (kosher or sea) and freshly ground or
    cracked black peppercorns
2 cloves garlic, minced
2 tablespoons chopped fresh dill
2 tablespoons vegetable oil

FOR THE RUSSIAN KETCHUP

¾ cup canned tomato sauce
2 tablespoons fresh lemon juice
1 clove garlic, minced
2 tablespoons finely chopped fresh dill or
    cilantro
1 teaspoon ground coriander
Coarse salt (kosher or sea) and freshly ground
    black pepper

ADVANCE PREPARATION

1 hour for making the sauce and marinating
    the veal

1 Prepare the veal chops: Place the chops in a baking dish and season them generously on both sides with salt and pepper. Sprinkle the chops on both sides with the minced garlic and of chopped dill. Drizzle the oil over the chops, patting the garlic and dill onto the meat with a fork. Let the veal marinate in the refrigerator, covered, while you make the Russian ketchup.

2 Make the Russian ketchup: Place the tomato sauce, lemon juice, minced garlic, finely chopped dill, and the coriander in a nonreactive mixing bowl and whisk to mix. Whisk in enough water (⅓ to ½ cup) to thin the sauce to a pourable consistency. Season the ketchup with salt and pepper to taste; it should be highly seasoned.

3 Set up the grill for direct grilling and preheat it to high.

4 When ready to cook, brush and oil the grill grate. Arrange the veal chops on the hot grate at a diagonal to the bars. Grill the chops until nicely browned on the outside and cooked through, 5 to 6 minutes per side for medium. Use the poke test to test for doneness (see page 147). Give each chop a quarter turn after 2½ minutes on each side to create a handsome crosshatch of grill marks.

5 Transfer the grilled veal chops to a platter or plates and let them rest for 2 minutes. Serve the chops with the Russian ketchup on the side.

Pickle, spice, and sauce vendor at a Moscow food market. Moscovites prefer homemade or family barbecue sauces to commercial condiments.

Eucalyptus-Grilled Veal Roast with Colombian Salsas

{ MAMONA ASADO CON AJI Y GUACAMOLE }

WHERE: Bogotá, Colombia

WHAT: A veal roast cooked on a stick in front of a eucalyptus wood campfire; the traditional condiments include *ají,* a fresh hot pepper sauce, and guacamole, a pourable Colombian version of the popular Mexican dip.

HOW: The traditional way to cook *mamona* is on sticks over a campfire, a preparation similar to Argentinean *asado* (see page 175), but excellent results can be achieved by spit roasting or indirect grilling.

There's an old saying in the Llano, Colombia's cattle-raising district in the north central part of the country:

La mamona solo lleva
Sal y candela.
If it's veal you desire
All you need is salt and fire.

That pretty much sums up one of the most singular styles of barbecue in South America, roasting over a eucalyptus wood campfire. The seasonings are simple: salt and wood smoke. The fireworks come from the crackling crust and haunting smoke flavor, not to mention from a creamy guacamole sauce and fiery *ají.* Best of all, you don't even need to travel to the Llano to enjoy it, for grill master Juan Jairo Mojica Ayo has brought the meats and techniques—fire pit and all—to his popular Bogotá restaurant, Llano y Mamona. House specialties include *mamona* (six-month-old veal), *nouilla* (two-year-old Brahmin beef), and *chiguiro* (capybara, see Just the Facts), all imported from the Llano region. Here are three ways to grill this savory roast: on a rotisserie, using the indirect method, or over a campfire. **SERVES 6**

1 veal shoulder or loin roast (about 3 pounds)
Coarse salt (kosher or sea)
Cracked black peppercorns (optional)
Colombian Chile Sauce (recipe follows)
Colombian Guacamole (page 186)

YOU'LL ALSO NEED
3 cups eucalyptus wood chips or chunks, or
   1 bunch dry eucalyptus leaves, soaked for
   1 hour in water to cover, then drained
   (see Note)

ADVANCE PREPARATION
None, but be sure to allow yourself 1 to 1½ hours for the roasting.

1 Very generously season the veal roast all over with salt and cracked pepper, if using.

2 To grill: *If you are using a rotisserie,* set up the grill for spit roasting, following the manufacturer's instructions, and preheat the grill to medium-high. Thread the roast on the rotisserie spit, using the forked prongs to hold it in place. When ready to cook, if you are spit roasting on a charcoal grill, toss the eucalyptus wood chips, chunks, or leaves on the coals. If you are spit roasting on a gas grill, add the eucalyptus wood chips, chunks, or leaves to the smoker box or place them in a smoker pouch under the grate (see page 603). Attach the spit to the grill and turn on the motor.

If you are grilling using the indirect method, set up the grill for indirect grilling, place a drip pan in the center, and preheat the grill to medium-high. When ready to cook, if you are using a gas grill, add the eucalyptus wood chips, chunks, or leaves to the smoker box or place them in a smoker pouch under the grate (see page 603). If you are using a charcoal grill, toss the wood chunks, chips, or leaves on the coals. Place the roast in the center of the grate, fat side up, over the drip pan away from the heat, and close the lid.

3 Grill the veal until it is crusty and dark brown on the outside and cooked to taste, 1 to 1½ hours for medium. (Colombians like their veal cooked with a blush of pink in the center.) Use an instant-read meat thermometer to test for doneness, inserting it deep into the thickest part of the roast but not touching the spit, if using. When cooked to medium the internal temperature should be about 150°F for veal with a blush of pink in the center.

4 To serve, transfer the veal roast to a cutting board and let it rest for 5 minutes. Cut the roast in half lengthwise, then cut each half crosswise into 2-inch pieces. The idea is to give everyone a piece with some crusty outside and moist inside. Serve the veal with bowls of Colombian Chile Sauce and Colombian Guacamole on the side.

NOTE: Eucalyptus leaves can be ordered by mail from www.amazon .com.

VARIATION
Traditional *Mamona*: Here's how to cook *mamona* the way they do in the Llano. Build a campfire, preferably with eucalyptus logs (there is no need to soak the logs). Let the fire burn down to embers but keep adding fresh logs. Impale the veal roast on a long slender stick and stand it next to and leaning slightly over the fire, but not too close. You may wish to support the stick holding the veal with a smaller forked stick. The meat should be 12 to 18 inches away from the embers. Grill the veal until it is crusty and dark brown on the outside, turning it on the stick as needed. Total cooking time will be 2 to 3 hours. If using eucalyptus chunks, chips, or leaves, soak and drain them before tossing them on the fire. Check for doneness as described in Step 3.

Colombian Chile Sauce
{ A J I }

Aⱼí belongs to an extended family of salsas and chile sauces served with grilled meats throughout South America (for another, see the the Peruvian *ají amarillo* sauce on page 40). Even in Colombia, the recipe varies widely from pit master to pit master. Colombians use a variety of chiles. The best approximation in North America would be jalapeño or serrano peppers with a Scotch bonnet or two thrown in for aromatics and heat. **MAKES ABOUT 1¼ CUPS**

4 jalapeño peppers, or 8 serrano peppers, stemmed, seeded, and coarsely chopped

1 green or yellow Scotch bonnet chile or habañero pepper, stemmed, seeded, and coarsely chopped (optional)

½ medium-size sweet onion, such as a Vidalia, coarsely chopped (about ½ cup)

1 scallion, both white and green parts, trimmed and coarsely chopped

½ cup coarsely chopped fresh cilantro

1 teaspoons coarse salt (kosher or sea), or more to taste

3 tablespoons distilled white vinegar or fresh lime juice, or more to taste

Place the jalapeños, Scotch bonnet (if using), onion, scallion, cilantro, and salt in a food processor and finely chop them, running the processor in short bursts. Work in the vinegar and about ½ cup of water, adding enough to make a thick but pourable sauce. Taste for seasoning, adding more vinegar and/or salt as necessary.

You can also make the *ají* in a blender: Place all of the ingredients, including the vinegar and water, in the blender and run it in short bursts. Do not overblend; the sauce should be a little chunky.

Colombian Guacamole
{ SALSA DE AVOCATE }

Yes, Colombians eat guacamole, and yes, they make it with ripe avocados and cilantro. But they also add mayonnaise—heresy in other parts of Latin America—and they normally serve the guacamole as a sauce, not a dip. **MAKES ABOUT 1¼ CUPS**

1 ripe avocado

1 serrano or other chile pepper, stemmed, seeded, and minced

¼ cup chopped fresh cilantro

¼ cup finely chopped sweet onion

2 tablespoons mayonnaise, preferably Hellmann's

½ teaspoon salt, or more to taste

1 tablespoon fresh lime juice, or more to taste

Peel and seed the avocado. Cut the avocado into 1-inch dice and place it in a food processor along with the serrano pepper, cilantro, onion, mayonnaise, and salt. Run the machine in short bursts until a smooth puree forms. Add the lime juice and enough water (2 to 4 tablespoons) to obtain a thick but pourable sauce. Taste for seasoning, adding more salt and/or lime juice as necessary.

Roasting mamona (veal) the traditional way—on sticks over a eucalyptus wood fire.

Hunters' Kebabs

{ FRIGARUI VANATOREȘTI }

Like most Europeans, Romanians have a deep nostalgia for the countryside. Even if they live in the heart of Bucharest. Especially if they live in the heart of Bucharest. To assuage that primal longing, the owners of the Terasa Doamnei have filled their lively restaurant with the stags' heads, antique farm implements, and straight-backed pine chairs you'd find at a Carpathian country inn. Of course, there's live music, amplified by an industrial-strength sound system and danced to by folk dancers clad in white. Come summertime, the action spills out onto a courtyard terrace. Game is the house specialty—bear from the Carpathian Mountains, or the more commonplace wild boar and venison. While none of these will win any tenderness contests, they're definitely more interesting than chicken or pork, especially when marinated with garlic, marjoram, and wine. **SERVES 4**

THE SCOOP

WHERE: Romania

WHAT: Wild game kebabs with peppers and onions

HOW: Direct grilling

JUST THE FACTS: If you hunt, you may have the ingredients for these kebabs in your cooler or freezer, and if you don't, you can buy farm-raised game (admittedly oxymoronic) at a specialty meat market or via mail order from a purveyor such as D'Artagnan (www.dartagnan.com) or www.exoticmeats.com. Beef and pork will give you tamer (but also tasty) kebabs. The Romanian Grilled Peppers on page 546 would make a good accompaniment.

FOR THE KEBABS

- 1½ pounds boneless venison, wild boar, or bear, or a combination of all three
- 1 sweet onion, peeled
- 2 green bell peppers, cored and seeded
- 2 red bell peppers, cored and seeded
- ¼ pound thick-sliced country-style bacon, cut into 1-inch pieces

FOR THE MARINADE

- 1½ teaspoons coarse salt (kosher or sea)
- ½ teaspoon freshly ground black pepper
- ¾ cup dry white wine
- 3 cloves garlic, crushed with the side of a cleaver
- 3 to 4 sprigs fresh marjoram, or 2 teaspoons dried marjoram
- 3 to 4 sprigs fresh thyme or 2 teaspoons dried thyme
- ¼ cup vegetable oil, plus oil for basting

YOU'LL ALSO NEED

Small bamboo skewers

ADVANCE PREPARATION

2 to 4 hours for marinating the kebabs

1 Make the kebabs: Cut the meat into pieces that are 1 inch square and ½ inch thick. Cut the onion in half crosswise, then cut each half in quarters. Break the quarters into layers. Finely chop the center pieces of the onion and set them aside for the marinade. Cut the bell peppers into 1-inch squares, discarding the seeds and pith. Finely chop the scrap pieces of the bell peppers and set them aside for the marinade.

2 Thread the pieces of meat onto skewers, alternating pieces of onion, bell pepper, and bacon between the pieces of meat. Place the kebabs in a nonreactive baking dish large enough to hold them in a single layer.

3 Make the marinade: Place the salt, black pepper, and white wine in a mixing bowl and whisk until the salt dissolves. Add the reserved chopped onion and bell pepper and the garlic, marjoram, thyme, and oil, and stir to mix. Pour the marinade over the kebabs and let them marinate in the refrigerator, covered, for 2 to 4 hours, turning the kebabs several times.

4 Set up the grill for direct grilling and preheat it to high.

5 When ready to cook, brush and oil the grill grate. Drain the kebabs, discarding the marinade. Arrange the kebabs on the hot grate and grill them until they are golden brown on the outside and cooked to taste (game is served well done at Terasa Doamnei), 2 to 3 minutes per side, 8 to 12 minutes in all. Use the pinch test to check for doneness (see page 147). Start basting the kebabs with vegetable oil after they have grilled for a couple of minutes. Serve at once.

Kangaroo Kebabs with Grilled Olive Tzatziki

If you happen to be reading this recipe in Australia, the main ingredient will neither shock nor surprise you. In fact, you can probably find it in the meat section of your local supermarket. However, if you live just about anywhere else on Planet Barbecue, you may need some reassurance. The ingredient is kangaroo and it's no more uncommon for an Australian to eat it than, say, venison or buffalo would be in the United States. Here's how Melbourne grill master Stavros Abougelis prepares this indigenous Australian meat at his landmark Albert Park restaurant, Stavros Tavern. Like all good Greek Australians, Stavros burns only charcoal in his grill and he takes his obsession with barbecue to the extreme of grilling the olives for the *tzatziki* (yogurt sauce). If you like conventional beef shish kebab, these sizzling, garlic-rosemary kebabs, served with creamy grilled-olive yogurt sauce will take you to a whole new level. **SERVES 4**

1½ pounds kangaroo meat, beef, lamb, or veal,
    cut into 1-inch pieces
1 tablespoon chopped fresh rosemary or mint
1 tablespoon dried oregano, preferably Greek
1½ teaspoons coarse salt (kosher or sea)
½ teaspoon cracked black peppercorns
3 cloves garlic, peeled and crushed with the side of a knife
¼ cup extra-virgin olive oil
¾ cup dry red wine, preferably an Australian shiraz
1 medium-size sweet onion
1 red bell pepper, cored, seeded, and cut into
    1-inch squares
1 green bell pepper, cored, seeded, and cut into
    1-inch squares
Grilled Olive Tzatziki (recipe follows)

YOU'LL ALSO NEED
Flat bamboo skewers

ADVANCE PREPARATION
4 hours to overnight for marinating the meat

1 Place the kangaroo meat, rosemary, oregano, salt, peppercorns, and garlic in a nonreactive bowl and stir to mix. Stir in the olive oil and red wine. Let the meat marinate in the refrigerator, covered, for at least 4 hours or as long as overnight; the longer it marinates, the richer the flavor will be.

2 Cut the onion in half crosswise, then cut each half into quarters. Break the quarters into layers. Stir any small onion pieces into the marinade with the kangaroo.

3 Drain the kangaroo through a strainer set over a saucepan. Discard the other solids, then set aside the marinade. Thread the kangaroo chunks onto skewers alternating the meat with the onion and bell pepper pieces.

4 Bring the reserved marinade to a rolling boil and let boil for 3 minutes. Let the marinade mixture cool to room temperature. You'll use it for basting the kebabs.

Shish kebabs, Aussie style, made with kangaroo instead of beef.

Stavros Abougelis, the Greek grill master of Melbourne, Australia.

5 Set up the grill for direct grilling and preheat it to high.

6 When ready to cook, brush and oil the grill grate. Arrange the kebabs on the hot grate and grill them until cooked to taste, 2 minutes per side, 8 minutes in all for medium-rare (the way Stavros serves them); 3 minutes per side, 12 minutes in all, for medium. Use the pinch test to check for doneness (see page 147). Start basting the kebabs with the boiled marinade after 4 minutes, basting them several times.

7 Transfer the grilled kebabs to a platter or plates and serve with generous dollops of Grilled Olive Tzatziki.

Grilled Olive Tzatziki

A creamy white condiment, tart with yogurt and lemon juice, pungent with garlic, and crunchy with diced cucumber, *tzatziki* turns up whenever Greeks put meat to fire. The Aussie twist here is the grilled olives—adding smoke to salt, as it were. You can grill the olives just before you put on the kangaroo kebabs or at a previous grill session. Greek yogurt has the consistency of sour cream. One good brand, Fage, is available at most natural foods stores and some supermarkets. **MAKES 1½ CUPS**

16 pitted kalamata olives
1 clove garlic, minced
½ teaspoon coarse salt (kosher or sea), or more to taste
1 cup plain whole-milk Greek yogurt
1 small cucumber, peeled, seeded, and cut into ½-inch dice
1 tablespoon chopped fresh mint
1 tablespoon fresh lemon juice, or more to taste

YOU'LL ALSO NEED
Flat bamboo skewers

1 Set up the grill for direct grilling and preheat it to high.

2 When ready to cook, brush and oil the grill grate. Skewer the olives onto the bamboo skewers and place them on the hot grate. Grill the olives until toasted and smoky, about 2 minutes per side. Transfer the grilled olives to a cutting board and let cool. Remove the skewers and cut the olives into ¼-inch dice.

3 Place the garlic and salt in the bottom of a mixing bowl and mash to a paste with the back of a wooden spoon. Stir in the diced olives, yogurt, cucumber, and mint, then stir in the lemon juice. Taste for seasoning, adding more salt and/or lemon juice, as necessary; the *tzatziki* should be highly seasoned.

Pork

While the Chinese get to celebrate the Year of the Pig only once a decade, happily for most citizens of Planet Barbecue a celebration of the hog comes around daily. If grilled, smoked, or spit-roasted pork is your idea of barbecue heaven, you'll find paradise literally all around the world. The short list of iconic pork dishes includes Mexico's *poc chuc* (grilled pork with grilled pickled onions); Brazil's wine-marinated spit-roasted baby back ribs; Serbia's *punjena vešalica* (cheese- and bacon-stuffed grilled pork tenderloin); and Greece's *kandosouvle* (hot pepper spit-roasted pork chunks). And that doesn't begin to address the central role pork plays in traditional American barbecue, from North Carolina's pulled pork to Kansas City's barbecued ribs.

What makes pork such a popular meat for the grill? First, there's its unique flavor—at once mild, sweet, and robust. Pork possesses a particular affinity for spice, smoke, and fruit flavors. It marries particularly well with sweet spices and condiments (case in point: the nutmeg-scented *schwenkbraten* on page 218). But pork goes equally well with any of the olive oil, lemon, and oregano flavors of the Mediterranean and the chile hellfire of Southeast Asia and Mexico.

Then there's the sheer diversity and versatility of the various pork cuts. You want lean? Pork loin contains less fat than skinless, boneless chicken breasts. You want rich? It's hard to imagine a more luscious, generously marbled meat than baby-back ribs. You want uptown? Pork tenderloin has all the

CLOCKWISE FROM TOP LEFT: Schweinshaxen *(Bavarian spit-roasted ham hocks); The Prince of Tutul-Xiu, birthplace of Yucatán poc chuc; Jerk pork at Bloomie's Jerk Centre in Yallahs, Jamaica; Shashlik (Russian shish kebab) grills on a mangal in Moscow.*

finesse of beef tenderloin at a fraction of the price. (Remember the old expression "eating high off the hog?" That's what you do whenever you grill a cut like pork loin or tenderloin.) You want to get down and dirty? You can't beat the rib or whole hog recipes, where the meat tastes best when eaten with your bare hands.

Finally, pork is one of the most economical meats in the market, costing fewer dollars per pound than most other proteins. Even premium pork breeds, like the Berkshire, sometimes sold under its Japanese name, *kurobuta,* are affordable luxuries. And, given its rich, primal flavor—the way pork used to taste and should taste, in the words of more than one grill master—spending a few dollars more gives you a giant dividend in flavor.

Previous page: Grilling at a Christmas market in Eastern Europe.

Keith Allen's North Carolina Pork Shoulder

First, the bad news. Unless you have a firebox for burning oak logs down to glowing embers and a brick pit seasoned with decades of wood smoke and hog drippings, you will not be able to duplicate Keith Allen's astonishing pork shoulder. This is not all bad. It gives you an excuse to travel to Allen & Son Barbeque, the cinder block box that houses his restaurant, to sample the quintessential Carolina pork shoulder—meat simultaneously tender, moist, and crusty, with just the right proportion of vinegar sauce to counterbalance the unctuousness of the pork fat. Add the eiderdown softness of a sesame bun (precisely four and a half inches across, insists Allen) and the crunch of a mayonnaise- and vinegar-based country slaw, and you get a pork sandwich so perfect an ancient Greek philosopher would have called it the Platonic ideal of barbecue. So what's the good news? If you have a charcoal grill (and if you don't, you should go out and get one), you can come very close to Allen's original. **MAKES ABOUT 12 SANDWICHES; ENOUGH TO SERVE 6 TO 12**

FOR THE PORK

1 Boston butt (bone-in pork shoulder roast;
   6 to 7 pounds with ample fat)
Coarse salt (kosher or sea) and freshly
   ground black pepper

FOR THE VINEGAR SAUCE

2 cups distilled white vinegar
2 tablespoons sugar
4 teaspoons coarse salt (kosher or sea)
4 teaspoons hot paprika
1 tablespoon hot red pepper flakes (optional)
1 teaspoon freshly ground black pepper

FOR THE COUNTRY SLAW

¾ cup mayonnaise (Allen swears by Duke's;
   see Note)
3 tablespoons sugar

3 tablespoons distilled white vinegar, or more
   to taste
1 small head green cabbage (about 1 pound),
   cored and finely chopped in a food processor
Coarse salt (kosher or sea) and freshly ground
   black pepper
12 sesame seed buns, for serving

YOU'LL ALSO NEED

About 5 cups hickory chips or chunks,
   soaked for 1 hour in water to cover,
   then drained

ADVANCE PREPARATION

None, but allow yourself 4 to 5 hours for grilling
   the pork. And, the country slaw can be made
   several hours in advance.

1 Set up the grill for indirect grilling, place a drip pan in the center, and preheat the grill to medium. Ideally you'll grill the pork shoulder over charcoal. You won't get as much smoke flavor on a gas grill.

2 Grill the pork: When ready to cook, brush and oil the grill grate. Generously season the pork shoulder on all sides with salt and black pepper. Add ¾ cup of wood chips or chunks to each mound of coals. If you are using a gas grill, add the wood chips or chunks to the smoker box or place them in a smoker pouch under the grate (see page 603). Place the pork shoulder, fat side up, in the center of the grate over the drip pan and away from the heat and cover the grill. Grill the pork shoulder until crusty and dark golden brown and the meat reaches an internal temperature of 190° to 195°F, 4 to 5 hours. Use an instant-read meat thermometer to check for doneness, inserting it deep into the thickest part of the meat but not touching any bones. Another test for doneness is to pull on the ends of any bones; they should pull out easily. There's no point in rushing the process: If you don't get to the desired temperature, the pork won't chop properly. Add ¾ cup of wood chips or chunks to each mound of coals after the first and second hours. There's no need for wood chips after that. You will need to add fresh coals to each side every hour.

3 Meanwhile, make the vinegar sauce: Place the vinegar and 1 cup of water in a nonreactive mixing bowl. Add the sugar, salt, the red pepper, hot pepper flakes, if using, and the black pepper and whisk until the salt dissolves. Alternatively, place the ingredients in a large jar with a tight-fitting lid and shake to mix. Set the vinegar sauce aside.

4 Make the country slaw: Place the mayonnaise in a large mixing bowl. Add the sugar and vinegar and whisk to mix. Stir in the cabbage, then taste the slaw for seasoning, adding salt and black pepper to taste and more vinegar as necessary; the slaw should be highly seasoned. The slaw can be made several hours in advance and refrigerated, covered. If it has been kept for more than 2 hours, taste for seasoning, adding more salt, black pepper and/or vinegar as necessary.

5 When the pork is done, transfer it to a large cutting board or chopping block, loosely tent it with aluminum foil, and let it rest for 10 minutes. Pull out any bones and discard any really large chunks of fat, but remember, you need some fat to keep the pork moist. Using a cleaver or a large knife, coarsely chop the pork; the pieces should be between ¼ and ½ inch in size.

6 Transfer the chopped pork to a large mixing bowl and stir in enough vinegar sauce to give the pork a terrific flavor and keep it moist but not soupy. You'll need about 1 cup.

7 To serve, place about ¼ pound (¾ cup) of chopped pork on each bun. Top the pork with slaw and serve at once with the remaining vinegar sauce on the side.

NOTE: To check the availability of Duke's Mayonnaise in your state, go to www.dukesmayo.com.

Allen & Son Barbeque—home of some of the best pork sandwiches in North Carolina.

The Curmudgeon of Chapel Hill

KEITH ALLEN of Allen & Son Barbeque is a member of an endangered species— grill masters who still burn wood.

CHAPEL HILL, NORTH CAROLINA

Keith Allen has been hard at work since the small hours of the morning. He feels like hell and looks it, with a complexion the color of wood ash, a blue T-shirt plastered to his torso, hands sheathed in electrician's gloves, and an apron darkly stained with pork fat. When I catch up with him, he's wildly swinging two massive meat cleavers, reducing a half-dozen 16-pound pork shoulders to a mound of crusty hash. It's a cinematic performance, all right, but the star that comes to mind is Anthony Perkins as Norman Bates in Alfred Hitchcock's 1960 thriller *Psycho*.

Guys like Allen used to be found in every hamlet and village in North Carolina. Today, they're an endangered species. The vast majority of North Carolina's pit masters have switched to gas or—even worse electric cookers, which require no more creativity than setting a thermostat and flipping a switch. Allen still burns wood in a pit blackened with wood smoke, as he has since he opened the restaurant in 1970. Decades of heat have warped the metal bars of the grate. It takes him about nine hours to turn thirty pork shoulders into hundreds of meltingly tender, crusty, subtly smoky

Keith Allen cooks his pork the old-fashioned way—in a wood-burning pit seasoned with decades of use.

Carolina-style pork sandwiches. "I must be stupid to make a living this way," he says.

Maybe not: Cars jam the parking lot of the green cinder block building that houses his restaurant, located on a country road outside Chapel Hill. I remember the first time I had lunch at Allen & Son Barbeque. The pulled pork sandwich, piquant with vinegar sauce; crunchy with shards of dark crust; creamy with a generous proportion of pork fat; and crowned with crisp, vinegary North Carolina coleslaw, was so remarkable, I returned to the restaurant that evening for dinner to make sure I wasn't dreaming.

There are actually two Allen & Son Barbeques in Chapel Hill (it's a long story). The one you want is located at 6203 Millhouse Road; telephone (919) 942-7576.

NAME: Keith Allen

TERRITORY: North Carolina

CLAIM TO FAME: Chef-owner of Allen & Son Barbeque

SPECIALTIES: Pork sandwich. Hush puppies. Coleslaw. Pie. Period.

ALLEN SAYS:

▶ The secret to great barbecue? That's easy. Wake up at 3 A.M. Split and haul a quarter ton of hickory logs each morning and burn them in a brick pit you built yourself. Roast the pork shoulders over the embers—not burning wood, mind you, embers—for four to five hours per side. Chop the pork shoulders by hand with a meat cleaver and douse them with vinegar sauce. That's all there is to it.

▶ Sorry, if you don't use real wood, it's not barbecue.

Puerto Rican Pork Shoulder
{ LECHON ASADO }

For years I had been trying to re-create a *lechon* (spit-roasted hog) I tasted in a village on the way to El Yunque rain forest in Puerto Rico—a pork shoulder as remarkable for its steamy, tender, garlic- and oregano-scented meat as for its spectacularly crisp skin. (This was back in the days before I wrote about barbecue.) Then Steve Cannon e-mailed me a description of the very dish I'd wanted to reconstruct for so long. The secret, it turns out, is simple: You remove the skin, season and oil the meat underneath it, then tie the skin back in place with butcher's string. Spit roasting crisps the skin the way deep-frying would, and if you cut the skin with a sharp knife right away, you'll get perfect diamonds of one of the glories of Puerto Rican gastronomy: *chicharrones,* crackling crisp pork rind. **SERVES 10 TO 12**

1 pork shoulder ham (6 to 7 pounds bone-in and
    with skin on, see Note)
3 cloves garlic, cut into ¼-inch slivers
1 bunch fresh oregano, broken into sprigs
2 tablespoons coarse salt (kosher or sea)
2 tablespoons dried oregano
2 tablespoons granulated garlic
1 tablespoon freshly ground black pepper
2 teaspoons dried sage
2 tablespoons extra-virgin olive oil
½ cup vegetable oil
¼ cup annatto seeds (optional)
Sparkling Barbecue Sauce (optional,
    recipe follows)

YOU'LL ALSO NEED
Butcher's string or bamboo skewers; about
    5 cups oak chips or chunks (optional), soaked
    for 1 hour in water to cover, then drained

ADVANCE PREPARATION
None, but allow yourself 3 hours or so for grilling.

1 Carefully remove the skin from the pork shoulder ham and set it aside. Using the tip of a paring knife, make a series of cuts in the pork, each about ½ inch deep, ½ inch wide, and spaced 2 inches apart. Place a sliver of garlic and a sprig of fresh oregano in each slit.

2 Combine the salt, dried oregano, granulated garlic, pepper, and sage in a bowl and stir with your fingers to mix. Sprinkle the rub all over the pork shoulder. (You may not need all of the rub; it keeps well in an airtight jar and is good to have on hand for an impromptu grill session.) Drizzle the olive oil over the seasoned pork and rub it into the meat.

3 Put the pork skin back on the roast and tie it in place with butcher's string or pin it in place with bamboo skewers.

THE SCOOP

WHERE: Puerto Rico

WHAT: One of the best pork shoulders you'll ever taste (with all due respect to North Carolina), studded with garlic and oregano under the skin, basted with annatto oil, and spit roasted to such crackling crispness, people will hear you when you take a bite

HOW: Spit roasting or indirect grilling

JUST THE FACTS: This pork shoulder owes its golden color to annatto oil, made by frying the aromatic, rust-colored Caribbean spice annatto in vegetable oil. Annatto seeds (often sold by their Spanish name, *achiote*) can be found at any Hispanic market, and I venture to say at your local supermarket. In a pinch you can make an aromatic orange oil by frying sweet paprika or turmeric; you'd need about one tablespoon of either in place of the annatto seeds called for here.

4 Make the annatto oil, if using, by heating the vegetable oil in a small saucepan over medium heat. Add the annatto seeds and cook until fragrant and brown and the oil turns bright orange, 2 to 4 minutes. Immediately strain the oil into a heat-proof bowl. Discard the annatto seeds.

5 To grill: Ideally you'll grill the pork shoulder over charcoal. If you want a smoke flavor, charcoal will give you the most pronounced result.

If you are using a rotisserie, set up the grill for spit roasting, following the manufacturer's instructions, and preheat the grill to medium-high. Thread the pork shoulder onto the rotisserie spit, using the forked prongs to hold it in place. When ready to cook, if you are spit roasting on a charcoal grill and want a smoke flavor, toss 1½ cups of wood chips or chunks on the coals. If you are using a gas grill, add the wood chips or chunks to the smoker box or place them in a smoker pouch under the grate (see page 603). Attach the spit to the grill and turn on the motor.

If you are grilling using the indirect method, set up the grill for indirect grilling, place a drip pan in the center, and preheat the grill to medium. When ready to cook, if a smoke flavor is desired and you are using a gas grill, add the wood chips or chunks to the smoker box or place them in a smoker pouch under the grate (see page 603). If you are using a charcoal grill, toss 2 cups of the wood chips or chunks on the coals. Place the pork shoulder, skin side up, in the center of the grate over the drip pan and away from the heat and cover the grill.

6 Grill the pork shoulder until dark golden brown on the outside and completely cooked through. If you spit roast the pork shoulder with the rotisserie covered, it will take 2 to 2½ hours; grilling with the rotisserie uncovered will take a little longer. If you are grilling using the indirect method it will take about 4 hours. Use an instant-read meat thermometer to test for doneness, inserting it into the thickest part of the meat but not touching any bones or the spit. When the pork is done the internal temperature will be 190° to 195°F. Start basting the pork with the annatto oil, if using, or with plain vegetable oil after the pork has grilled for 30 minutes, if spit roasting, or after 1 hour of indirect grilling. Continue basting every 30 minutes. If you are using a charcoal grill, add 1½ cups of wood chips or chunks after the first and second hours. Add fresh coals to each side of the grill every hour.

7 Transfer the pork shoulder to a cutting board. Remove the skin and cut it into 1-inch squares. It will crisp into cracklings as it cools. Thinly slice the pork and serve it with the cracklings and the Sparkling Barbecue Sauce, if desired.

NOTE: To maximize the ratio of crisp skin to meat, buy the shank end of the pork shoulder, sometimes called a shoulder ham or picnic ham. A pork chop version of this dish appears on page 224.

Sparkling Barbecue Sauce

Barbecue sauces based on soft drinks turn up all across Planet Barbecue, and whether they owe their popularity to the sweet-sour flavor dynamic or simply to the convenience and whimsy of using a beverage to flavor the meat, I can't say. What I can say is that you'll find them throughout the Spanish-speaking world. **MAKES 1½ CUPS**

1 cup lemon-lime soda, such as 7UP
1 cup ketchup
1 cup of your favorite sweet red barbecue sauce
½ teaspoon liquid smoke
½ teaspoon freshly ground black pepper

Place the soda, ketchup, and barbecue sauce in a saucepan and whisk to mix. Bring the sauce to a simmer over medium heat and let it simmer gently until thick and richly flavored, 10 to 15 minutes.

The Real Jamaican Jerk Pork

Industrial espionage? I don't normally buy recipes: I count on the good will of pit masters around the world to share their knowledge with their barbecue brethren. But even after an hour-long interview, Mickey Burke, owner of the popular Mickey's Jerk Center in Boston Beach, wasn't talking. So when his half-brother, Mark Whyte, pulled me into a room and offered to share the recipe for a . . . er . . . financial gesture of appreciation, let's say he had my attention. As the details came into focus, I realized what was missing from my previous jerk seasoning recipes—or more precisely, what they had in overabundance: white sugar, brown sugar, and rum. Mickey's jerk seasoning is ornery stuff without the least gentility of sweeteners. It's a salty, hot (just shy of unbearable) mixture of Scotch bonnet chiles and dry seasonings, with just the right aromatic touch of pimento (allspice), ginger, and thyme. What's remarkable is the ability of this jerk seasoning to utterly transform commonplace pork without overpowering it. This recipe makes about a quart of jerk seasoning—more than you'll need for one pork shoulder—but the excess keeps almost indefinitely.

This isn't the first jerk recipe I've published, so what makes it different from all the others? Well, besides a new jerk seasoning, this version features a distinctively Jamaican and, for me at least, interesting new technique: boning the pork and making a series of cuts accordionlike that maximize the surface area of the meat exposed to the spice, smoke, and fire. By way of accompaniments, you might serve *festivals* (Jamaican hushpuppies) or chunks of breadfruit roasted in the embers. **SERVES 10 TO 12**

Jamaican jerk pork cooked over smoldering spice wood on an allspice wood grate—just as it's been cooked for centuries.

THE SCOOP

WHERE: Boston Beach, near Port Antonio, Jamaica

WHAT: Jamaica's national dish: deeply scored pork, marinated in a fiery paste of Scotch bonnet chiles, thyme, and allspice (and many other ingredients), and smoke-grilled over a pimento wood fire

HOW: Direct grilling

JUST THE FACTS: In Jamaica you'd start with a whole hog, which you'd bone and butterfly, making parallel rows of accordion cuts to spread open the pork in a thin flat sheet. You'd place it on a wooden grate with bars of fragrant pimento (allspice) wood and grill it over equally fragrant embers of the same wood. You'd work over a very low heat, covering the pork with a sheet of corrugated tin, cooking the meat until it shines like polished ebony and is tender enough to rip apart with your fingers. What you'll find here is my best approximation of how to prepare a pork shoulder Jamaican jerk style on a North American grill.

1 pound Scotch bonnet chiles, stemmed and cut in half
  (½ pound seeded Scotch bonnets for the tender
  of tongue)
1 green bell pepper, cored and seeded
1 bunch scallions, both white and green parts, trimmed
  and cut into 1-inch pieces
1 small onion, coarsely chopped
2 shallots, coarsely chopped
3 cloves garlic, coarsely chopped
1 piece (2 inches) fresh ginger, peeled and coarsely
  chopped
2 teaspoons fresh thyme leaves,
  or 1 teaspoon dried thyme
3 giant thyme leaves (Spanish thyme),
  or 1 additional teaspoon fresh thyme leaves,
  or ½ teaspoon dried thyme
6 fresh basil leaves, or 1½ teaspoons dried basil
1 tablespoon ground allspice, or more to taste
2 teaspoons ground cinnamon

2 teaspoons freshly ground black pepper
½ cup coarse salt (kosher or sea)
¼ cup vegetable oil
1 tablespoon soy sauce, or more to taste
1 Boston butt (bone-in pork shoulder roast; 6 to 7 pounds,
  with ample fat)

YOU'LL ALSO NEED

1½ cups oak or apple wood chips; ½ cup whole
  allspice berries

ADVANCE PREPARATION

2 to 4 hours for marinating the pork shoulder

1 Place the Scotch bonnets, bell pepper, scallions, onion, shallots, garlic, ginger, thyme, basil, ground allspice, cinnamon, and black pepper in a food processor fitted with a metal blade and puree to a smooth paste, running the machine in bursts.

Jamaican Seasonings

The Scotch bonnet ranks among the world's most fiery chiles, so using one pound of them to make a quart of seasoning for Jamaican jerk pork may seem like overkill to the point of sadism. However, this is how they do it in Jamaica, and the combination of a long marinating time and prolonged cooking over a low, slow heat really does temper the virulence of the jerk seasoning. I suppose you could moderate the heat somewhat by seeding the Scotch bonnets or by using a half pound instead of the full pound.

The Jamaican jerk pork recipe here calls for two types of thyme: conventional, small-leaf thyme and a large variegated-leaved thyme, sometimes called Spanish thyme or Cuban

Jamaican firepower—Scotch bonnet chiles at a roadside stand in Port Antonio.

oregano. It has an aromatic flavor that lies halfway between that of thyme and fresh basil. Assuming you won't be able to find the large-leaf thyme, I've upped the quantity of regular thyme and added some fresh basil in this jerk recipe.

As for the cinnamon and allspice, in Jamaica both would come whole—curls of bark in the case of the cinnamon; dried berries in the case of the allspice. And because they'd be so fresh, they'd be softer and more aromatic than their American spice-rack counterparts. In my jerk recipe I've increased the quantities to compensate for preground cinnamon and allspice.

Jamaicans also use a variety of premixed commercial seasonings: "chicken spice," for example, and seasoned salt, meat seasoning, and so on. These are added to the jerk in small quantities; given the ferociousness of the Scotch bonnets and the intensity of the salt, their absence will not be missed in this jerk dish.

Work in the salt, oil, and soy sauce. Add enough water (about ¼ cup) to obtain a thick but pourable paste. Taste for seasoning, adding more allspice and/or soy sauce, as necessary; the mixture should be very salty and very flavorful. You should have about 2¼ cups—perhaps a little more than you need, but any excess keeps well in the refrigerator. Store it in a glass jar and place a piece of plastic wrap between the top of the jar and the lid, so the pepper fumes and salt don't corrode the lid.

2 Cut through one side of the pork shoulder to the bone. Cut around the bone and keep cutting to within an inch of the other side of the shoulder. Do not cut all the way through. Open the pork shoulder like a book. Cut under the bone and remove it. Pound the pork with a meat mallet or rolling pin until it is about 1½ inches thick. Holding the knife parallel to the short edge of the pork rectangle, make a series of parallel cuts ½ inch deep and 2 inches apart from one edge to the other. Turn the pork over and make parallel cuts on the other side, working so that the cuts on the second side are midway between the cuts on the first side. These "accordion" cuts are a signature of Jamaican jerk masters and help the marinade and smoke flavors penetrate the meat.

3 Spread half of the jerk marinade in the bottom of a nonreactive roasting pan or aluminum foil pan. Place the butterflied pork on top. Spread the remaining jerk paste over it. Let the pork marinate in the refrigerator, covered, for 2 to 4 hours.

4 Mix the wood chips and allspice berries and soak them in water for 1 hour. Drain just before using.

5 Drain the pork, scraping off the excess jerk seasoning; it's OK to leave a little on.

6 To grill: Technically Jamaicans grill jerk pork using the direct method, but the low heat and corrugated tin cover they use produces an effect similar to indirect grilling. And, indirect grilling requires less attention than direct grilling here. Take your choice.

If you are grilling using the indirect method, set up the grill for indirect grilling and preheat it to medium. When ready to cook, if you are using a gas grill, add the wood chips and allspice berries to the smoker box or place them in a smoker pouch under the grate (see page 603). If you are using a charcoal grill, toss the wood chips and allspice berries on the coals. Arrange the butterflied pork, fat side up, in the center of the grate over the drip pan and away from the heat and cover the grill.

If you are grilling using the direct method, set up the grill for direct grilling and preheat it to medium-low. When ready to cook, if you are using a charcoal grill, toss half of the wood chips and allspice berries on the coals. If you are using a gas grill, add the wood chips and allspice berries to the smoker box or place them in a smoker pouch under the grate (see page 603). Arrange the butterflied pork, fat side up, on the hot grate and cover the grill. Toss the remaining wood chips and allspice berries on the coals when you turn the pork; keep the grill covered.

7 Grill the pork until it is darkly browned and very tender, 40 to 60 minutes using the indirect method; about 20 minutes per side using the direct method. Use an instant-read meat thermometer to test for doneness, inserting it through the side of the pork. When done the internal temperature should be about 190° to 195°F.

8 To serve, transfer the jerk pork to a cutting board and let it rest, loosely covered with aluminum foil, for 10 minutes. Using a cleaver, whack the pork into bite-size pieces. Traditionally, jerk pork is served on waxed paper to be eaten with your fingers.

Jamaica: Where Smoke and Fire Meet the Caribbean

When it comes to barbecue, Jamaica has only one trick up its sleeve. But, oh, what a trick. I'm talking, of course, about Jamaica's national dish—and cultural icon—jerk. Once you've tasted this fiery smoke-

Jamaican jerk served the traditional way— on butcher paper. No plate needed.

Jerk represents a fusion of peoples and cultures.

roasted pork, sweet with allspice, fragrant with island thyme, and above all, electrified with more Scotch bonnet chiles than you'd ever thought humanly possible to consume, well, a trick becomes a miracle and that sleeve a rich brocade.

Like so much West Indian cuisine, jerk represents a fusion of peoples and cultures: indigenous Caribbean ingredients, an ancient Taíno Indian cooking technique, an African penchant for highly spiced foods, and even an act of political rebellion. The native ingredients include pimento (allspice) berries, Scotch bonnet chiles, and a local green onion called *escallion*. The cooking technique involves roasting meats on a spicewood grate over a low smoky fire. As for the political rebellion, the Maroons, runaway slaves in the mountains of Jamaica who became the first black freedom fighters in the western hemisphere, nourished their troops on this salty, smoky, fiery meat.

Jerk has very likely been on Jamaica's menu since before the arrival of the first European colonists. Here's how one seventeenth century visitor from England, Hans

Make Mine Jerk

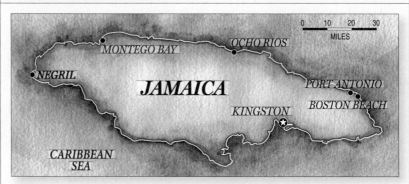

Jamaica—birthplace of jerk and epicenter of West Indian barbecue culture. Where pork, chicken, fish, and even lobster come smoked with fiery Scotch bonnet chiles.

A typical Jamaican jerk shack. It's about the food, not the ambiance.

Visitors come for Jamaica's stunning beaches; they return home with a hunger for jerk.

Sloane, described an early version: "Swine . . . pierced through with lances, cut open, the Bones taken out, and the Flesh is gash'd on the inside into the Skin, fill'd with Salt and expos'd to the Sun, which is call'd jirking." The word *jerk* may come from the Quechua Indian term *ch'arki*, the origin of our word *jerky*, or it may have originated from the Jamaican patois, where *jook* means to stab or pierce.

Today, you can buy jerk chicken, jerk fish, even jerk lobster, but the ur-jerk remains pork, more specifically, a whole hog, meticulously boned, butterflied, and cut into accordion pleats to maximize the surface area of the meat exposed

to the spice and fire. In the 1930s the great Afro-American writer Zora Neale Hurston summed up jerk this way: "It is hard to imagine anything better than pork the way the Maroons jerk it." (And if you haven't read Hurston's fabulous novel, *Their Eyes Were Watching God,* run, don't walk, to your local bookstore to pick up a copy.)

Smokey Joe—one of the legions of itinerant jerk vendors in Jamaica.

THE GRILLS: In 1526, a Spanish explorer named Gonzalo Fernández de Oviedo y Valdés (see page xvii) described the barbecue grills used by the Taíno Indians—a frame of wooden branches positioned over a smoky fire. Five centuries later, Jamaican jerk masters still cook meat on pimento wood grates. The bars of the grate scorch during the half day needed to jerk a hog and impart a unique flavor. Such are the barbecue pits you find at the jerk houses of Boston Beach. Elsewhere, Jamaicans grill on half 55-gallon steel drums.

A jerked (butterflied, seasoned) hog cooks on a traditional Jamaican grill—an allspice wood grate over a smoky allspice wood fire.

THE FUEL: The traditional fuel, like the grill grate itself, is pimento wood; it both smokes and cooks the meat. In cities and towns, however, grill jockeys use lump charcoal.

THE FLAVORINGS: At first taste, Jamaican "seasonin'" will strike you as sadistically fiery, but behind the pyrotechnics

there is great gustatory complexity, ranging from sweet (allspice and cinnamon) to aromatic (thyme, chives, and scallions) to pungent (onion and garlic) to bracingly and assertively salty. The first bite may hurt, but jerk quickly becomes addictive.

MUST TRY DISHES: Jerk pork, chicken, fish, lobster, and sausage

THE CONDIMENTS: Jerk pork is so intensely flavorful, you don't really need condiments. You can certainly douse jerk chicken and fish with one of the homemade Scotch bonnet–based hot sauces restaurants provide for those who are gluttons for additional punishment.

The traditional accompaniments to jerk include *festivals* (cornmeal fritters) and breadfruit roasted in the embers.

HOW TO EAT IT: On butcher paper with your fingers

IF YOU CAN EAT AT ONLY ONE RESTAURANT: Go to Boston Beach, a former fruit-packing transit port, named for the Boston Fruit Company and today a local beach hangout and the epicenter of Jamaica's jerk culture. The road to the beach is lined with jerk joints—pick one that looks crowded and where the jerk pork is sliced fresh to order. If you happen to be in Ocho Rios, check out the Jerk Centre, founded in 1983. In Montego Bay, take a taxi to Scotchie's.

WHAT TO DRINK: Red Stripe beer, Ting (grapefruit soda), or tamarind water, or another of the fruit drinks sold by itinerant drink vendors in Boston Beach

THE MOST SINGULAR DISH IN THE REPERTORY: "Steam" fish—whole scorpion fish slathered with jerk seasoning and other spices, wrapped in foil, and roasted in the embers (for a recipe see page 467)

Jelly coconuts—the juice and custardy sweet flesh are a popular drink and dessert rolled into one.

Pepper-Spiced Spit-Roasted Pork
{ KANDOSOUVLE }

Think of Greek barbecue and what comes to mind? I bet you'll say lamb. So you may be as surprised as I was to learn of the prominent role pork plays in Hellenic grilling. The short list of Greek grilled specialties includes pepper-crusted pork ribs, a whole hog spit roasted with oregano (see page 259), and even charcoal-grilled pork belly. But my hands-down favorite is a dish little known outside of Greece called *kandosouvle,* rotisserie-grilled chunks of pork marinated with hot peppers and served glistening and crusty hot off the spit. *Kandosouvle* originated in northern Greece, but the best I ever tasted came from a casual grill joint called Yammas on the island of Kea in the Cyclades. If you like your pork crusty as cracklings, tender enough to pull apart with your fingers, and spicy as a swig of Tabasco, this one has your name on it. **SERVES 8**

1 pork shoulder roast (4 to 5 pounds,
   if boneless; 6 to 7 pounds if bone in)
1 large onion, peeled and cut in half
   crosswise
2 luscious, ripe red tomatoes, cut in half
   crosswise
2 tablespoons coarse salt (kosher or sea)
2 tablespoons hot paprika, or 1 tablespoon
   hot red pepper flakes
1 tablespoon dried oregano, preferably Greek
1 tablespoon freshly ground black pepper
2 tablespoons tomato paste dissolved in
   2 tablespoons hot water
2 green bell peppers, cored, seeded, and
   cut into 2-inch squares
¼ cup extra-virgin olive oil, preferably Greek,
   for basting
Crusty bread, for serving

ADVANCE PREPARATION
4 to 6 hours for marinating the pork

1 Cut the pork into 3-inch chunks. Try to include some fat on each chunk; it will keep the pork moist as it spit roasts. Place the pork in a large mixing bowl.

2 Grate the onion halves over the pork through the largest holes of a box grater. Grate the tomato halves over the pork, discarding the tomato skins. Or, remove and discard the tomato skins, then puree the onion and tomatoes in a food processor. Add the salt, paprika, oregano, black pepper, and the tomato paste and water mixture to the pork and stir to mix. Let the pork marinate in the refrigerator, covered, for 4 to 6 hours; the longer it marinates, the richer the flavor will be.

3 Drain the marinade off the pork, discarding the marinade. Thread the pork chunks onto the rotisserie spit, placing a piece of bell pepper between each.

4 Set up the grill for spit roasting, following the manufacturer's instructions, and preheat the grill to high.

5 When ready to cook, attach the spit to the grill and turn on the motor. Spit roast the pork until the meat is sizzling, darkly browned, and cooked through, 30 to 40 minutes. Start basting the pork with olive oil after it has cooked for 20 minutes and baste it every 5 minutes after that. Use an instant-read meat thermometer to test for doneness, inserting it into the thickest part of meat, but not touching any bones or the spit. When the pork is done the internal temperature will be 190°F. (Greeks prefer their pork well-done.)

6 Transfer the pork to a platter and remove the spit. If there are drippings in the drip pan, spoon them over the pork. Serve the pork with crusty bread for dunking in the juices.

VARIATION

***Kandosouvle* Grilled Directly Over the Fire:** You can also grill *kandosouvle* using the direct method. Thread the pork chunks onto large, flat metal skewers. Set up the grill for direct grilling and preheat it to medium-high. When ready to cook, brush and oil the grill grate. Grill the pork until it is sizzling, darkly browned, and cooked through, 8 to 12 minutes per side, 16 to 24 minutes in all. (When done, it will register about 190°F on an instant-read meat thermometer. Start basting the *kandosouvle* with olive oil after 4 minutes.

Onion-Stuffed, Spit-Roasted Pork Shoulder
{ SPIESSBRATEN }

"You know the rule," Dietmar says. "You don't turn, you don't drink." Tourism guide and grill maniac Dietmar Brunk has kindly agreed to initiate me into the art of Obersteiner *spiessbraten*. The "turn" refers to a stint at the hand-cranked rotisserie in the *spiessbratenhaus* in his backyard. The drink is a glass of crisp, honeyed riesling, the wine for which the nearby Nahe wine region is famous. A *speissbratenhaus* (loosely translated as "grill hut") is the first thing any self-respecting resident of the barbecue-obsessed twin towns of Idar and Oberstein in western Germany looks for when purchasing a new home. Dietmar's is a handsome cabin, the focal point of which is a fire pit formed from an antique washing machine tumbler.

The task at hand is turning a *spiessbraten,* a pork shoulder roast stuffed with onion and garlic, over a smoky beech wood fire, and if you don't take a turn cranking the rotisserie, not only don't you drink—you don't eat.

Spiessbraten, a specialty of the state of Rhineland-Palatinate, is one of the world's truly great grilled pork dishes. The ingredients are simple: pork, onion, and sometimes garlic. The seasonings are even simpler: salt and pepper. But the process of spit roasting the roast over a beech wood fire (not embers, but a smoky fire) transforms these ingredients into some of the most unforgettable barbecued pork you'll taste on the planet. I use the word *barbecue* here on purpose, for although the pork is cooked over an open fire, not in a pit, the slow roasting in the beech wood smoke produces the subcutaneous layer of red that any American pit master would proudly recognize as a smoke ring. **SERVES 8**

1 boneless pork shoulder roast or loin
   (4 to 5 pounds)
Coarse salt (kosher or sea) and freshly ground
   black pepper
1 medium-size onion, thinly sliced crosswise
3 cloves garlic (optional), thinly sliced
Icicle Radish Salad (recipe follows), for serving

YOU'LL ALSO NEED
Butcher's string; about 2 cups beech wood, oak,
   or other hardwood chips or chunks, soaked
   for 1 hour in water to cover, then drained

ADVANCE PREPARATION
None, but be sure to allow yourself at least
   1½ hours for spit roasting.

1 Butterfly the pork: Place the pork roast on a cutting board. Starting at a long side and holding the knife blade parallel to the cutting board, cut the roast almost in half to the other side. Open up the pork roast as you would a book. Place the pork between 2 pieces of plastic wrap and, using a meat mallet, scaloppine pounder, or the side of a heavy cleaver, pound both halves of the butterflied pork to lightly flatten it.

2 Generously season the inside of the pork with salt and pepper. Arrange the onion slices on top of one side of the roast. Arrange the garlic, if using, on top of the onion. Fold the other side over the onion to return the roast to its original cylindrical shape. Using butcher's string looped around the roast crosswise, tie it into a tight cylinder.

3 To grill: You can spit roast the *spiessbraten* (the traditional method) or you can use the indirect method. Indirect grilling is less interactive, but it produces an excellent *spiessbraten*— especially on a charcoal grill.

THE SCOOP

JUST THE FACTS: Germans use a cut of pork called *schweinekamm*—a cylindrical roast cut from the neck and forward part of the loin. It's a bit more generously marbled (actually, a lot more generously marbled) than a North American pork loin. Pork shoulder probably comes the closest in fat content and texture, but you'll have to cut around and remove the bone before you can butterfly the meat. So, pork loin makes an easier alternative.

As the spit turns: roasting spiessbraten the traditional way—perpendicular to the spit and over a beech wood fire.

Deitmar and Anna Brunk take turns cranking the spit. As they say in Idar-Oberstein, "If you don't turn, you don't eat."

HOW TO MAKE GERMAN SPIESSBRATEN

1. *Make a deep cut along one side of the pork loin almost to but not through the other side.*

2. *Open the loin like a book.*

3. *Flatten the butterflied pork with a rolling pin. The plastic wrap prevents sticking.*

4. *Stuff the pork with sliced onions and garlic.*

5. *Close the roast and tie it into a tight cylinder with butcher's string.*

6. *Pull the end of the string through the loops to make a butcher's knot.*

7. *Thread the roast onto the skewer for spit roasting. Tradition calls for the roast to be skewered perpendicular to the spit (ideal for charcoal and wood grills), but on a gas grill you may need to skewer it lengthwise as shown above.*

8. *Spiessbraten cut crosswise into ¼-inch slices for serving. Note the smoke ring at the edges—produced by the smoke from the beech wood.*

If you are using a rotisserie, set up the grill for spit roasting, following the manufacturer's instructions, and preheat the grill to medium-high. Thread the pork roast crosswise or lengthwise onto the rotisserie spit, using the forked prongs to hold it in place. When ready to cook, if you are spit roasting on a charcoal grill, toss the wood chips on the coals. If you are using a gas grill, add the wood chips to the smoker box or place them in a smoker pouch under the grate (see page 603). Attach the spit to the grill and turn on the motor.

If you are using the indirect method, set up the grill for indirect grilling, place a drip pan in the center, and preheat the grill to medium. When ready to cook, if you are using a charcoal grill, toss the wood chips on the coals. If you are using a gas grill, add the wood chips to the smoker box or place them in a smoker pouch under the grate (see page 603). Place the pork roast in the center of the grate over the drip pan and away from the heat and cover the grill.

4 Cook the pork roast until crusty and browned on the outside and the internal temperature reaches about 190°F, 1¼ to 1¾ hours. Use an instant-read meat thermometer to test for doneness, inserting it into the thickest part of the meat but not touching any bones or the spit. If you are using a charcoal grill, you will need to add fresh coals and more wood chips or chunks after 1 hour.

5 Transfer the *spiessbraten* to a cutting board and let it rest for 5 minutes. Remove and discard the butcher's string, then carve the roast crosswise into ¼ inch-thick slices. Admire the smoke ring. Serve the *spiessbraten* with the Icicle Radish Salad.

Icicle Radish Salad

This earthy radish salad is what German grill masters serve with *spiessbraten*. It belongs to a family of slaws found in virtually every corner of Planet Barbecue (*sla* is the Dutch word for salad). There are even radish slaws in Korea), but to the best of my knowledge, this is the world's only slaw made with icicle radishes. The soft crunch of the pungent radish and the creamy dressing make a perfect foil for the smoky, meaty chew of *spiessbraten*. **MAKES 2 TO 3 CUPS**

1 pound icicle radishes (see Note)
2 tablespoons mayonnaise, preferably Hellmann's
2 tablespoons vegetable oil, such as sunflower oil
1 to 2 tablespoons distilled white vinegar
Coarse salt (kosher or sea) and freshly ground black pepper

Peel the radishes and coarsely grate them into a mixing bowl. Add the mayonnaise, oil, and vinegar and stir to mix. Season with salt and pepper to taste and additional vinegar as necessary; the salad should be highly seasoned.

NOTE: The icicle radish is a long, pale green root with a crisp white flesh; it looks a bit like an Asian black radish. Look for it in a store with a good produce section or substitute red radishes or daikon radishes.

Serbian Stuffed Pork Loin
{ PUNJENA VESALICA }

Don't try to do official business in Belgrade on a Friday afternoon. Chances are, the government officials you need to see are busy stretching lunch into dinner at a restaurant like Dva Jelena (the Two Stags). If it's 4 P.M., the dining room, with its ceiling timbers, massive stone walls, and tables with white cloths and crimson undercloths, will be jamming. As for dinner, "We Serbs like to eat until ten or eleven P.M.," says proprietor Tomislav Ivanivic. "We drink until we keel over." Ivanivic hails from Pec, Kosovo, as does his pit master, Velisic Blagoje. Both came to Belgrade, Serbia, as refugees of the war that led to Kosovo's independence. This history lesson has some bearing on barbecue, as the people of Pec are reputed to

THE SCOOP

WHERE: Kosovo via Serbia

WHAT: Butterflied grilled pork loin stuffed with bacon, cheese, and smoked ham

HOW: Direct grilling

JUST THE FACTS:
Kosovars and Serbs use a very heavily smoked bacon and don't bother to precook it. If you are using typical American bacon, brown it lightly before using.

You'll find a description of *kajmak* (Balkan sour cream) in the Note on page 248. Although it's not done at Dva Jelena, elsewhere in Belgrade grill masters spread the inside of the pork with mustard.

rank among the best grill masters in the region. All peoples in these parts work with a common palette of flavors—smoky bacon, piquant cheese, fiery chiles—but you can discern subtle differences: the spiciness of Bosnian grilling, the smoky, soulful flavors of Kosovo, and so on. All of which is a lengthy prologue to a dish that is as remarkable for its platter-carpeting heft as for its great depth of flavor: a whole pork loin stuffed with cheese, ham, and bacon and traditionally charred over mild plum wood charcoal. (Thanks to the robust stuffing, you'll get plenty of flavor grilling the pork loin on a gas grill, too.) Unlike most butterflied pork loins, this one is traditionally cut open from the end, not the side. **SERVES 4 VERY GENEROUSLY, SERVES 6 WITH LOTS OF SIDE DISHES**

Serbian grill master Velisic Blagoje holds open a butterflied flattened pork loin.

3 ounces (3 to 4 slices) smoky country-style bacon

1 piece of center cut pork loin (about 2 pounds)

Coarse salt (kosher or sea) and freshly ground black pepper

3 tablespoons Dijon mustard (optional)

3 ounces thinly sliced smoked ham

2 ounces piquant cheese, such as Edam, Gouda, or Provolone, coarsely grated or thinly sliced

¾ cup kajmak, clotted cream, mascarpone, or sour cream (optional), for serving

Sour Cream Cucumber Salad (recipe follows), for serving

YOU'LL ALSO NEED

Wooden toothpicks, small bamboo skewers, or butcher's string (optional)

ADVANCE PREPARATION

None, but you can assemble the roast several hours ahead.

1 Cook the bacon in a frying pan over medium heat until lightly browned and just beginning to crisp, about 2 minutes per side. Drain the bacon on paper towels and set aside.

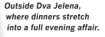

Outside Dva Jelena, where dinners stretch into a full evening affair.

2 Butterfly the pork loin: Place the pork loin on a cutting board. If you'd like to do it as they do in Serbia, starting at a narrow end and holding the knife blade parallel to the cutting board, cut the pork loin almost in half to the other end (see Note). Open up the pork loin as you would a book. Place the pork between two pieces of plastic wrap and, using a meat mallet, scaloppine pounder, or the side of a heavy cleaver, pound both loin halves into a flat sheet about ½ inch thick. Remove and throw away the plastic wrap.

3 Generously season the inside of the pork loin with salt and pepper and spread the mustard, if using, over it. Arrange the bacon over the bottom half of the open pork loin. Place the slices of ham on top, followed by the cheese. Fold the top half of loin back over the bottom piece. Season the outside of the loin with salt and pepper. If you like, secure the edges with toothpicks or skewers or tie the loin with butcher's string. (Velisic doesn't bother with this, but he's had lots of experience turning pork roasts without them falling apart.)

4 Set up the grill for direct grilling and preheat it to medium-high.

5 When ready to cook, brush and oil the grill grate. Arrange the stuffed pork loin on the hot grate at a diagonal to the bars. Grill the pork loin until well browned and cooked to medium; the cheese should be melted and sizzling, 6 to 8 minutes per side. If desired, give the loin a quarter turn after 4 minutes on each side to create a handsome crosshatch pattern. Use an instant-read meat thermometer to test for doneness, inserting it into the thickest part of the meat. The internal temperature should be about 160°F.

6 Transfer the grilled pork loin to a platter and remove the toothpicks, skewers, or string, if using. Cut the loin crosswise and top each serving with a spoonful of *kajmak,* if desired. Serve the cucumber salad on the side.

NOTE: It may be easier to butterfly the pork loin the way most of us are used to doing—starting at one long side and cutting to, but not through, the other long side.

Sour Cream Cucumber Salad
{ TARATOR }

Cucumber salads turn up often around Planet Barbecue. The Kosovar-Serb version goes by the name *tarator* (not to be confused by a Middle Eastern sesame sauce, which is also called *tarator*) and features a sour cream dressing.

MAKES ABOUT 2 CUPS

2 medium-size cucumbers
1 clove garlic, minced
Coarse salt (kosher or sea)
2 tablespoons distilled white vinegar
½ cup sour cream
¼ large red onion, finely diced
2 tablespoons finely chopped fresh flat-leaf parsley
   or dill
Freshly ground black pepper

1 Using a vegetable peeler, remove the cucumber peel in lengthwise strips, leaving thin strips of skin intact (the overall effect will be striped). Cut the cucumbers in half lengthwise and scoop out the seeds with a melon baller or spoon. Cut each cucumber half crosswise into ¼ inch-thick slices.

2 Place the garlic and ½ teaspoon of salt in the bottom of an attractive serving bowl and mash to a paste. Add the vinegar and stir until the salt dissolves. Stir in the sour cream, followed by the cucumber slices, onion, and parsley. Season with more salt and pepper to taste; the salad should be highly seasoned. Refrigerate until ready to serve.

"Shepherd's Tacos"
{ TACOS AL PASTOR }

Like many totemic dishes on Planet Barbecue, the *tacos al pastor* stems from multiple peoples, cultures, and continents. *Pastor* means shepherd, the nickname Mexicans gave to Lebanese merchants who immigrated to the Yucatán and to Mexico City in the early decades of the last century. Among the Middle Eastern comfort foods these immigrants brought to Mexico was *shawarma*—thin slices of lamb roasted on a vertical rotisserie to be sliced wafer-thin and served on pita bread. Local grill masters recognized the ingenuity of the preparation and, over time, made it their own. Pork came to replace the lamb, chiles and achiote replaced the olive oil and Middle Eastern herbs, and the whole shebang came to be served on tortillas instead of pita.

Perhaps the most breathtaking innovation of all was sandwiching the meat between fresh pineapple slices; the pineapple offers a sweet, fruity counterpoint to the chiles (and marries exceptionally well with pork). In addition, some people claim that an enzyme in pineapple called bromelain serves to tenderize the meat. Given that paper-thin slices of well-done pork are fork-tender to begin with, this may be a case of retrofitting science to justify taste. *Tacos al pastor* are served all over Mexico. Here's how they're made at El Fogon, a great grill joint in Carmen del Playa on the Yucatán coast. **SERVES 6 TO 8**

4 ounces guajillo chiles (20 to 24 chiles), or ½ cup pure chile powder (see Notes)

1 pork loin (about 3 pounds)

2 medium-size sweet onions, peeled and cut crosswise into ¼-inch slices

¼ cup distilled white vinegar

3 tablespoons achiote paste (optional, see Notes)

3 tomatillos, or 1 ripe tomato, coarsely chopped

2 cloves garlic, coarsely chopped

2 bay leaves, crumbled

1 tablespoon coarse salt (kosher or sea)

2 teaspoons freshly ground black pepper

2 teaspoons ground cinnamon

2 teaspoons dried oregano

1 teaspoon ground cumin

1 teaspoon anise seed

1 teaspoon dried thyme

1 fresh ripe pineapple, peeled and cut crosswise into ¼ inch slices

20 to 24 corn tortillas (see Notes)

1 bunch fresh cilantro, rinsed, dried, stemmed, and placed in an attractive serving bowl

Your favorite salsa (optional)

ADVANCE PREPARATION

3 to 6 hours for marinating the pork

1 If you are using guajillo chiles, place them in a bowl with 4 cups of warm water and let them soak for 1 hour.

2 Using a very sharp knife, cut the pork loin across the grain into paper-thin round slices. Arrange half of the onion slices in a large mixing bowl or roasting pan. Arrange the sliced pork over the onion slices, then place the remaining onion slices on top.

3 Drain the soaked guajillo chiles, if using, setting aside 1 cup of soaking liquid. Tear open each chile and scrape out and discard the seeds. Coarsely chop the chiles and place them in a blender with the vinegar and the reserved 1 cup of chile soaking liquid, then puree until smooth. If you are using chile powder, place it and ¾ cup of water in the blender along with the vinegar. Add the achiote paste, if using, and the tomatillos, garlic, bay leaves, salt, pepper, cinnamon, oregano, cumin, aniseed, and thyme and process to a smooth, pourable puree. Alternatively, you can puree the ingredients in a food processor, but in this case, puree the solid ingredients (the chiles, tomatillos, garlic, and so on) first, then add the liquids.

4 Pour the marinade over the pork and onions, turning them to coat both sides (They don't have to stay in layers). Let the pork marinate in the refrigerator, covered, for 3 to 6 hours; the longer it marinates, the richer the flavor will be.

Carving the pork for tacos al pastor. *Note the pineapple at the top of the spit.*

5 Set up the grill for direct grilling and preheat it to high.

6 When ready to cook, brush and oil the grill grate. Drain the pork and onion slices, discarding the marinade. Place the pineapple slices on the hot grate and grill until golden brown, 3 to 5 minutes per side. Keep the grilled pineapple warm on the side of the grill or on a platter. Place the pork and onion slices on the grate and grill until golden brown, 2 to 4 minutes per side.

7 Transfer the pork, onion, and pineapple to a cutting board, stacking several slices of pork with a slice of onion and pineapple. Thinly slice them crosswise.

8 Warm the tortillas on the grill for about 30 seconds per side. Place some sliced pork, onion, and pineapple on a tortilla. Top the filling with cilantro and salsa, if desired, to taste. Fold the tortilla in half and eat.

NOTES: The guajillo chile is an elongated, smooth-skinned, reddish brown dried chile with a bright earthy-fruity flavor, natural sweetness, and gentle heat. Guajillos are available in the Mexican food sections of many supermarkets and via mail order at www.americanspice.com. In a pinch, you could use a pure Mexican chile powder (the main ingredient of which is likely chile guajillos).

Achiote paste is made from the aromatic, rust-colored seed of a tropical shrub; it is available from www.amazon.com.

If you can find freshly made corn tortillas, by all means use them. They're available at Mexican markets.

Mexico: Fire and Smoke From Coast to Coast

I'm sitting under a *palapa* (a thatched open-air hut) at La Casa del Tikin Xik on Isla Mujeres off the Yucatán coast, eating *sierra* (king mackerel) spiced with *recado rojo* (the electric orange annatto, garlic, and vinegar marinade of the region), grilled over a driftwood fire, and served with hand-formed tortillas and tongue-blistering habañero salsa. I'm wondering what all this was like when this beachfront fish shack opened in 1940—back before the dive and T-shirt shops, before the skyscraper hotels rose from the sugary sands of the Cancún beaches off on the horizon.

I imagine there were Mayans, who built the angular stone pyramids that dot the Yucatán Peninsula at sites like Chichen Itza and Uxmal. I imagine there were fishermen, whose descendants still sail forth in colorful wooden boats from the colonial city of Campeche. But most of all, I imagine there was barbecue—dishes with exotic Mayan names like *tikin xik* and *poc chuc*—fruits of the fire given to the inhabitants of the region by whatever the equivalent to Prometheus was among the fierce gods of the Maya.

Three civilizations—Mayan, Aztec, and Spanish—called Mexico home and helped make it one of world's most vibrant and complex barbecue cultures. The Mayans gave Mexico the *pib,* a stone-lined barbecue pit still used to prepare the Yucatán's famous *cochinita pibil* (spice slathered pork cooked in banana leaves). The Aztecs fire roasted such indigenous New World foods as turkey, corn, and chiles, charring vegetables on the fire to make salsas, perfecting complex sauces of nuts, fruits, and chiles—the ancestors of Oaxacan *molé.* (What you get when you order the dish today depends on where in Mexico you are.) The Spanish added a whole new set of ingredients and cooking technologies to Mexico's melting pot, from the steer and lamb, to such seasonings as cumin and the Seville orange, to the art of distillation (what would Mexican barbecue be without tequila?) and the all-important metal gridiron for grilling. Today, there isn't a

A squeeze of fresh lime juice brings carne asada (Mexican grilled beef) alive.

South of the Border

Grilling takes place in every Mexican province, from the *carne asada* of Mexico's cattle country to the *barbacoa* of Oaxaca, and the superlative grilled seafood of Mexico's coasts.

0   200   400
MILES

JUAREZ

MONTERREY

GULF OF MEXICO

MEXICO

ISLA MUJERES
CANCÚN

MEXICO CITY ★

CAMPECHE

YUCATÁN

PACIFIC OCEAN

OAXACA

Tacos al pastor *on a charcoal-buring rotisserie.*

Mexican city so big or a pueblo so small that your nose won't lead you to the primal aroma of meat or fish roasting over charcoal.

Elsewhere in Latin America, grill masters make a virtue of simplicity (think of the salt—and salt only—grilled steaks of Argentina and Uruguay). Mexican grill masters build layer upon layer of flavor, marinating meats in spice pastes and soulful chile and vinegar marinades; wrapping and grilling them in aromatic leaves, like avocado and maguey cactus; and searing them over hardwood fires. Equally complex is the way you eat Mexican barbecue: on freshly made tortillas, with fiery salsas, often topped with crisp vegetables, sour cream, and piquant cheese.

Beachfront dining at the Casa del Tikin Xik on the Isla Mujeres in the Yucatán.

THE GRILLS: As befits a country obsessed with barbecue, Mexicans cook on every imaginable type of grill from the *tambor,* an ember-filled half steel drum, to the *pib,* the underground barbecue pit of the Yucatán; from wood-burning rotisseries to the open fire pits used in Monterey to roast *cabrito*—baby goat; from conventional grills with grill grates to campfires on the beach, perfect for grilling snapper or lobster on a stick; even to car wheel rims filled with charcoal for improvised grill sessions.

Cooking tortillas the traditional way, on a fire-heated comal (iron griddle).

THE FUEL: Lump charcoal or wood; mesquite in Sonora; oak in the Yucatán

THE FLAVORINGS: Mexican grill masters use a full barrage of flavors: *naranja agria* (the aromatic juice of the sour or Seville orange), *adobos* (chile-based marinades), *recados* (red, green, and black spice pastes in the Yucatán), and golden glazes made from *achiote* (annatto seed) to be brushed on sizzling meats—to mention just a few.

MUST TRY DISHES:

Barbacoa: The etymological descendant of the *barbacoa* of the Taíno Indians (for the full story on the birth of barbecue, see page xvi). What you get when you order the dish depends on where in Mexico you are. In Mexico City, for example, the term refers to a quarter or half lamb swaddled in maguey cactus leaves and roasted in a wood-fired brick barbecue pit. In the Oaxaca region, you'd get spice-slathered goat smoke roasted over a pot of vegetables and broth, which become the evening's soup.

Cabrito: Roast baby goat or kid—the most famous comes from Monterey, where it's roasted on stakes in front of a fire

Carne asada: The general term for thin slices of grilled beef, chopped or thinly sliced and served on tortillas with grilled scallions and other vegetables, guacamole, sour cream, and *pico de gallo* or other salsas

Cochinita pibil: Yucatán-style pork shoulder or whole hog, marinated with achiote (annatto) and other spices, wrapped in banana leaves, and roasted in an underground pit

Poc chuc: A Yucatán specialty: thin slices of wood-grilled pork served with grilled onions marinated in sour orange juice, diced avocado, and an incendiary habañero salsa

Tacos al pastor: "Shepherd's Tacos" (see page 212) are thin slices of spiced pork and pineapple roasted on a vertical rotisserie, then thinly shaved and served on tortillas

Tikin xik: Yucatán-style fish (snapper or kingfish), split through the back, marinated in *recado rojo* (red spice paste), and grilled over wood

THE CONDIMENTS: When it comes to saucing their barbecue, Mexicans pull out all the stops. The short list of popular condiments includes:

Pico de gallo: Literally rooster's beak—a simple salsa of tomato, onion, jalapeño peppers, and cilantro. Sometimes a bowl of chopped onions and cilantro is served instead.

Salsa borracha: A "drunken" salsa made from dried chiles and pulque (cactus spirits)

Salsa de chile chipotle: A fiery salsa made from smoked jalapeño peppers

Salsa verde: A piquant "green" salsa made from boiled or flame-roasted tomatillos

Xni pec "dog's snout": A tongue-blistering salsa made from grilled habañeros.

IF YOU CAN EAT AT ONLY ONE RESTAURANT: If you're willing to travel long, hard, and deep into the Yucatán (it's a three hour drive from Mérida), you won't find a more perfect grilling experience than lunch at the open-air El Príncipe Tutul Xiú in the hamlet of Maní, birthplace of *poc chuc.*

WHAT TO DRINK: *Sangrita* (chile juice- and grapefruit-spiked tomato juice); margaritas; pulque; or any of Mexico's excellent beers

THE MOST SINGULAR DISH IN THE REPERTORY: The northern Mexican (and southwestern Texas) version of *barbacoa,* a steer's head roasted underground in a wood-fired pit, then shredded and served on tortillas

Pork Tenderloin Grilled with Bacon and Prunes with Farofa

Sweet and salty is one of the hallmark flavor profiles of Latin America, incarnated here in a pork tenderloin stuffed with prunes, wrapped in smoky bacon, and grilled. The mustard is my own contribution—you can certainly omit it. You can also make an appetizer version of this dish with bite-size pieces of pork tenderloin. The recipe was inspired by the sprawling Churrascaria Schneider in São Leopoldo, Brazil, and I dare say, the triple whammy of grilled pork, sweet prunes, and smoky bacon is tough to top. **SERVES 4**

1½ pounds trimmed pork tenderloin
(2 to 3 tenderloins)
Coarse salt (kosher or sea) and freshly ground
black pepper
2 tablespoons Dijon mustard (optional)
8 ounces (2 cups) pitted prunes
½ pound smoky bacon slices
Toasted Cassava Flour (optional,
recipe follows)

YOU'LL ALSO NEED
Butcher's string

ADVANCE PREPARATION
None, but the pork rolls can be stuffed several
hours ahead.

1 If you will be spit roasting the pork tenderloins, cut each one in half cross-wise. (If you're direct grilling, leave the tenderloin whole.) Cut a deep pocket in the long side of each whole pork tenderloin or pork tenderloin half. The pocket should extend almost to but not through each tenderloin and to within ½ inch of each end. Spread open the pockets and season the meat with salt and pepper. Spread mustard, if using, in the pockets, and fill the pockets with the prunes. Season the outside of the tenderloins with salt and pepper.

2 Press one slice of bacon onto the bottom of each tenderloin or tenderloin half. Press additional slices of bacon on the sides and tops of the tenderloins and tie them in place with butcher's string in three or four places.

3 To grill: *If you are grilling using the direct grilling method,* set up the grill for direct grilling and preheat it to medium-high. When ready to cook, brush and oil the grill grate. If you are using a charcoal grill, leave one section of the grill fire-free for a safety zone. Arrange the pork tenderloins on the hot grate and grill them until they are golden brown on all sides and cooked through, 3 to 4 minutes per side, 12 to

16 minutes in all. If the dripping bacon fat causes a flare-up, move the tenderloins to the safety zone.

If you are using a rotisserie, thread the stuffed pork tenderloin halves onto the spit, crosswise. Set up the grill for spit roasting, following the manufacturer's instructions, and preheat the grill to high. When ready to cook, attach the spit to the grill and turn on the motor. Spit roast the tenderloins until they are golden brown on the outside and cooked through, 20 to 30 minutes.

4 Use an instant-read meat thermometer to test for doneness, inserting it through the fat end of the tenderloin but not touching the spit, if any. When done to medium the internal temperature of the pork should be about 160°F.

5 Transfer the grilled tenderloins to a cutting board and let them rest for 2 to 3 minutes. Remove and discard the butcher's string. Cut the tenderloins crosswise into ½-inch-thick slices and serve at once with the Toasted Cassava Flour, if desired.

Toasted Cassava Flour
{ FAROFA }

Look at the menu of a *churrascaria* in southern Brazil and you may find a strange phrase: *com farinha,* literally, "with flour." No, this doesn't mean white powder from a sack of King Arthur; it refers to a sort of coarsely ground meal made from *mandioca* (cassava root) and roasted or sautéed with bacon and onions. Much the way

we might soak up meat juices with bread in North America, Brazilians—particularly in the southern part of the country—like to sprinkle juicy meats with *farofa.* **MAKES ABOUT 2½ CUPS**

4 tablespoons (½ stick) salted butter
2 thick slices of smoky bacon, cut into ¼-inch dice
4 scallions, both white and green parts, trimmed and thinly sliced crosswise
¼ cup finely diced red or yellow bell pepper
¼ cup finely chopped fresh flat-leaf parsley
2 cups cassava flour (see Note), toasted bread crumbs, or matzo meal

1 Melt 1 tablespoon of the butter in a large skillet over medium-high heat. Add the bacon and cook until golden brown, about 3 minutes. Transfer the bacon to a plate lined with paper towels to drain and discard all but 2 tablespoons of fat from the skillet.

2 Melt the remaining 3 tablespoons of butter in the skillet over high heat. Add the scallions, bell pepper, and parsley and cook until lightly browned, about 3 minutes. Stir in the drained bacon and the cassava flour and cook until the flour is lightly browned and the mixture is fragrant, 3 to 5 minutes, stirring with a wooden spoon. Serve the *farofa* warm (the way I like it) or at room temperature. The *farofa* will keep for several days.

NOTE: You can buy cassava flour at Brazilian markets.

Cassava root and cassava flour—the base of Brazil's beloved farofa.

"Swinging" Pork Steaks
{ SCHWENKBRATEN }

"**C**ome over for some *schwenken*" (literally, this means "swinging"). No, it's not an invitation for German wife swapping but an evening of barbecue Saarbrüken style. This lively city on the Saar River, a stone's throw from the French border, has one of the most distinctive grilling methods in Europe, and one of its best kept barbecue secrets. And it all starts with a *schwenker*—a swinging, or more accurately, both swinging and rotating, grill. A *schwenker* ("swinger") is also a person (usually male) who has perfected the art of grilling *schwenkbraten,* the pork steak cooked on this singular grill. *Schwenken* is the meal and the evening's entertainment that has the unique dish as its focal point. And no one does it better than Klaus Marx, owner of what is likely the most amazing grill shop in Germany: Eisen Marx (Iron Marx); you can read more about Klaus on page 221. What you need to know here is that by marinating pork steaks in paprika, onions, and fresh herbs, and grilling them over beech wood, you wind up with some of the most spectacular grilled meat in Europe. A crisp white wine from the Nahe or Mosel River areas makes a great beverage. **SERVES 4**

Klaus Marx builds a fire in one of his high-tech swinging grills.

¼ cup table salt

¼ cup sweet paprika

4 teaspoons freshly ground white pepper

½ teaspoon ground allspice

½ teaspoon ground nutmeg

½ teaspoon ground ginger

4 pork steaks cut from the neck or shoulder (each about 1 inch thick and 8 to 10 ounces), or 1½ pounds thick-cut country-style ribs

1 large sweet onion, thinly sliced

2 cloves garlic, peeled and lightly crushed with the side of a knife

½ cup chopped mixed fresh herbs, including parsley, rosemary, sage, and/or thyme

¼ cup vegetable oil, such as sunflower oil

YOU'LL ALSO NEED

2 cups beech wood or oak chips or chunks (optional),
   soaked for 1 hour in water to cover, then drained,
   or beech wood logs for building a fire

ADVANCE PREPARATION

2 to 4 hours for marinating the pork

1 Place the salt, paprika, white pepper, allspice, nutmeg, and ginger in a bowl and stir to mix. This makes a little more rub than you need for this recipe but what's left over keeps well stored in an airtight container away from heat and light and will always come in handy for a future grill session. You can use the rub on pork, chicken, or beef.

2 Arrange the pork steaks in a baking dish just large enough to hold them in a single layer and season them generously on both sides with the rub. Add the onion, garlic, mixed herbs, and oil and turn the pork several times to coat it on both sides with the seasonings and oil. Let the pork marinate in the refrigerator, covered, for 2 to 4 hours; the longer it marinates, the richer the flavor will be.

3 Set up the grill for direct grilling and preheat it to medium-high. Ideally you'll grill over a beech wood fire (see page 603 for instructions on grilling over a wood fire). Alternatively you can use wood chips or chunks to add a smoke flavor. If you are using a gas grill, add the wood chips or chunks to the smoker box or place them in a smoker pouch under the grate (see page 603).

4 When ready to cook, brush and oil the grill grate. Drain the pork steaks well, discarding the marinade (it's OK if a few onion rings cling to the meat). If you are using a charcoal grill, toss the wood chips or chunks on the coals. Arrange the steaks on the hot grate and grill them until they are nicely browned and cooked through, 4 to 6 minutes per side, turning once or twice. Use the poke test to check for doneness, (see the box on page 147). Serve the grilled pork steaks at once.

VARIATION

Spiessbraten **Grilled on a** *Schwenker:* It's linguistically confusing, but in Idar-Oberstein they not only call grilled pork neck roast *spiessbraten* (see page 206 for the recipe), but when they grill the thick pork steaks cut from that pork neck, they call those *spiessbraten,* as well. And they grill these pork steaks over a wood fire using the swinging *schwenker* grill. The most famous *spiessbraten* steaks in Idar-Oberstein come from the restaurant Im Haag, where grill master Otmar Schönhofen has spent the last forty years perfecting his technique. The thick juicy steaks are seasoned with salt, pepper, onion, and—for a touch of sweetness—nutmeg. Then they are smokily charred over a raging beech fire. (You can also grill pork chops and country-style ribs this way.) **SERVES 4**

½ cup table salt

2 tablespoons freshly ground white pepper

1 tablespoon freshly ground black pepper

2 teaspoons ground nutmeg

4 pork steaks cut from the neck (each about 1 inch thick and
   8 to 10 ounces), or 4 large, thick loin or rib pork chops,
   or 1½ pounds country-style ribs

Garlic powder

Onion powder

Icicle Radish Salad (page 209), for serving

Thinly sliced bauerbrot ("farmers bread") or German
   rye bread (optional), for serving

Herb Butter (page 176), for serving

YOU'LL ALSO NEED

2 cups beech wood, oak, or other hardwood chips or chunks,
   soaked for 1 hour in water to cover, then drained, or beech
   wood logs for building a fire

1 Place the salt, white pepper, black pepper, and nutmeg in a bowl and stir to mix.

2 Place the pork on a baking sheet and season each piece generously on both sides with the salt and pepper mixture. You'll have more rub than you need for the pork. It's good with any cut of pork (ribs, for example), not to mention with lamb or

chicken, and keeps well stored in an airtight jar away from heat and light.

3 Sprinkle the garlic and onion powder generously all over the pork. (This may seem redundant, but double spicing occurs in many places on Planet Barbecue; it adds an extra layer of flavor.)

4 Set up the grill for direct grilling and preheat it to medium. When ready to cook, brush and oil the grill grate. If you are using a charcoal grill, toss the wood chips on the coals. If you are using a gas grill, add the wood chips to the smoker box or place them in a smoker pouch under the grate (see page 603). Arrange the pork on the hot grate and grill until browned on the outside and cooked through, 10 to 15 minutes (a little less for country-style ribs). Turn each piece of pork several times as it grills. Use the poke test to check for doneness (see the box on page 612).

5 Serve the grilled pork with the Icicle Radish Salad and *bauerbrot* and Herb Butter, if desired, on the side.

Schwenkbraten *(marinated pork steaks) cook on a "swinging grill" over a beech wood fire.*

The Iron Man of the German Grill

KLAUS MARX has turned his grill factory retail shop into a fiefdom of fire and smoke. His laser-cut, precision-welded, stainless steel grills are the stuff of dreams.

SAARBRUCKEN, GERMANY

Most of the grill masters profiled in *Planet Barbecue* run restaurants or grill palaces. Klaus Marx is here on account of his ability to bend metal. Marx, whose nickname, "Eisen," means iron, runs Germany's largest grill and barbecue shop, but his real gift is designing and manufacturing *schwenkbraten—* barbecue grills. Of course, there are grills and then there are grills, and Marx's masterpieces have the sleek design and high performance of another German dream machine: the Porsche.

Marx grew up near the historic steel manufacturing capital, Saarbrücken, a region that lay

> Marx's masterpieces have the sleek design and high performance of another German dream machine: the Porsche.

in ruins after World War II. "We couldn't buy grills, so people built their own with scavenged metal," Marx recalls. "For that matter, you couldn't buy charcoal, so people grilled over wood from the nearby forests." Wood gives you what Marx calls a "nervous" fire—unpredictable, full of hot spots and cool spots. To compensate, the locals designed a grill unique on Planet Barbecue: a firebox surmounted by a circular

grate hanging from a tripod or from the roof of the fireplace. By swinging and rotating the grate, the griller could turn an erratic fire into a steady heat source. Thus was born Germany's distinctive *schwenker* (swinging grill).

A few years ago Marx opened a grilling school, where dinners are served in a barrel-vaulted wine room and washed down with vintages from the nearby Nahe and Rhine.

"Around here, we learn to grill before we learn to walk," says Marx. It's not quite clear whether he's talking about his family, his business, or Saarbrücken—quite likely all three.

NAME: Klaus Marx

TERRITORY: Germany and beyond

CLAIM TO FAME: Grill manufacturer and owner of a barbecue shop called Eisen Marx

SPECIALTIES: Venison steaks with plum chutney. Veal burgers stuffed with foie gras. Hot-smoked duck breasts. *Schwenkbraten* (swinging grilled pork steak). *Schweinshaxen* (spit-roasted ham hocks). *Spanferkel* (spit-roasted whole hog).

MARX SAYS:

▶ Make friends with your butcher. There's no better way to assure you get the best meat.

▶ Keep the seasoning subtle. You don't want to camouflage the original taste of the meat.

▶ There's nothing worse than trying to cook for a crowd on too small a grill.

Klaus Marx grills schwenkbraten (pork steaks) on one of his swinging grills. (Note: the rising hot air turns the fan, which in turn spins the grill grate.)

Uruguayan Pork "Skirt Steak" with Mustard Plum Barbecue Sauce

Ah, the redemptive powers of barbecue. What do the fajita, *vacillo*, and *matambre* have in common? All are made from thin, flat, fibrous muscles from the underbelly of the steer that overcompensate in flavor what they may lack in tenderness. Well, there's a new budget steak on the block, and it comes not from beef, but pork. Uruguayans and Argentineans call it *matambrillo*, and if you see it on a menu in those countries, don't miss it. As to exactly where it comes from, anatomically speaking, grill masters rarely agree. My best guess is the thin, top outer layer of meat and fat on a rack of spareribs, discarded by most American butchers, but richly rewarding when grilled. As for the distinctive Uruguayan sauce for the pork, like most of the world's great barbecue sauces, it manages to be simultaneously sweet, sour, and spicy—the result of combining two totally unexpected ingredients: prune preserves and mustard. I give two versions here; the first is a little spicier, the second a little sweeter. If you want to try this dish in its birthplace, check out the La Perdiz grill house in Montevideo, Uruguay. **SERVES 4**

1½ pounds pork steaks
Coarse salt (kosher or sea) or garlic salt
Freshly ground black pepper
Mustard Plum Barbecue Sauce
   (recipe follows)

YOU'LL ALSO NEED
2 cups oak chips or chunks (optional, see Note)

ADVANCE PREPARATION
The sauce can be prepared several
   hours ahead.

1 Set up the grill for direct grilling and preheat it to high. Ideally you'll grill over an oak wood fire (see page 603 for instructions on grilling over a wood fire). Alternatively you can use wood chips or chunks to add a smoke flavor.

2 When ready to cook, brush and oil the grill grate. Generously season the pork steaks on both sides with salt and pepper. If you are using a charcoal grill, toss the wood chips or chunks on the coals. If you are using a gas grill, add the wood chips or chunks to the smoker box or place them in a smoker pouch under the grate (see page 603). Place the pork steaks on the hot grate and grill them until sizzling, brown, and cooked through, 3 to 4 minutes per side. Use the poke test to check for doneness (see the box on page 612).

3 Transfer the grilled pork steaks to a platter or plates and serve them with a little Mustard Plum Barbecue Sauce spooned over each steak and the remainder of the sauce on the side.

NOTE: The fuel of choice in Uruguay is oak. If a wood-burning grill is not an option, at the very least add some wood chips or chunks to the coals or the smoker box of your gas grill.

Although they don't do it in Uruguay, for a stronger smoke flavor, soak the wood chips or chunks for 1 hour in water to cover and drain them before using.

Mustard Plum Barbecue Sauce

The flavors of this sauce—sweet, spicy, a little tart—will be recognizable to any North American barbecue buff. But Uruguayans get there a different way, using plum preserves and dried plums for sweetness (instead of the usual North American ketchup), mustard for spice, and red wine for acidity. It probably began as British Cumberland sauce and acquired a Uruguayan accent somewhere along the way. This makes more sauce than you need for the pork steaks, but you'll want to have a jar in the refrigerator for later use. It's great with any grilled meat, especially pork or poultry. **MAKES ABOUT 3 CUPS**

VERSION #1: HOT AND SPICY

1 cup plum or prune preserves
½ cup Dijon mustard
1 cup dry red wine
3 tablespoons fresh orange juice (from ½ large orange)
1 tablespoon triple sec or other orange-flavored liqueur
2 ounces (½ cup) pitted dried prunes
Coarse salt (kosher or sea) and freshly ground black pepper

Place the preserves, mustard, red wine, orange juice, triple sec, and prunes in a heavy nonreactive saucepan and gradually bring to a boil over medium-high heat, whisking to mix. Reduce the heat to medium and let the sauce simmer gently until it is reduced and flavorful and the prunes are soft, 8 to 12 minutes. Season with salt and pepper to taste; the sauce should be highly seasoned. Let the sauce cool to room temperature, then cover and refrigerate it if not serving it immediately. Let the sauce return to room temperature before serving; it can be made several days ahead.

VERSION #2: MELLOW AND SWEET

2 cups dry red wine
1½ cups plum or prune preserves
¼ cup Dijon mustard
¼ cup fresh orange juice (from 1 large orange)
2 tablespoons triple sec or other orange-flavored liqueur
2 ounces (½ cup) pitted dried prunes
2 tablespoons light brown sugar
Coarse salt (kosher or sea) and freshly ground black pepper

Place the red wine, preserves, mustard, orange juice, triple sec, prunes, and brown sugar in a heavy nonreactive saucepan and gradually bring to a boil over medium-high heat, whisking to mix. Reduce the heat to medium and let the sauce simmer gently until it is reduced and flavorful and the prunes are soft, 8 to 12 minutes. Season with salt and pepper to taste; the sauce should be highly seasoned. Let the sauce cool to room temperature, then cover and refrigerate it if not serving it immediately. Let the sauce return to room temperature before serving; it can be made several days ahead.

Puerto Rican Grilled Pork Chops

Here's a version of the Puerto Rican Pork Shoulder (page 197) made with pork chops and quick enough to be prepared on a weeknight. There are several options for the pork chops—thick rib chops, pork "porterhouses" (loin chops with both loin and tenderloin attached by a T-bone), and even country-style ribs, which are elongated chops cut from the pork shoulder. **SERVES 4**

4 pork chops (each 8 to 10 ounces and 1 inch thick)
1 tablespoon extra-virgin olive oil or vegetable oil
2 teaspoons coarse salt (kosher or sea)
2 teaspoons dried oregano
2 teaspoons granulated garlic
1 teaspoon freshly ground black pepper
1 teaspoon dried sage
¼ cup vegetable oil
2 tablespoons annatto seeds (optional)
Sparkling Barbecue Sauce (optional, page 198)

1 Arrange the pork chops in a baking dish just large enough to hold them in a single layer. Lightly brush the chops on both sides with the olive oil.

2 Combine the salt, oregano, granulated garlic, pepper, and sage in a bowl and stir with your fingers to mix. Sprinkle the rub over the pork chops on both sides, patting the spices onto the meat with your fingers. Let the chops cure in the refrigerator, covered, for 15 to 30 minutes.

3 Make the annatto oil, if using, by heating the vegetable oil in a small saucepan. Add the annatto seeds and cook until fragrant and brown and the oil turns bright orange, 2 to 4 minutes. Immediately, strain the oil into a heat-proof bowl. Discard the annatto seeds.

4 Set up the grill for direct grilling and preheat it to high.

5 When ready to cook, brush and oil the grill grate. Arrange the chops on the hot grate at a diagonal to the bars. Grill the chops until browned on the outside and cooked through, 4 to 6 minutes per side. Give each chop a quarter turn on each side after 2 minutes to create a handsome crosshatch of grill marks. Start basting the chops with the annatto oil, if using, or with the vegetable oil after 1 minute, basting them several times on both sides.

6 Transfer the chops to a platter or plate. Serve at once, with the Sparkling Barbecue Sauce, if desired, although the chops are so flavorful, you don't really need a sauce.

Mayan Pork Chops
{ POC CHUC }

Deep in the heart of the Yucatán, past Mayan temple complexes and dusty villages, down bone-jarring country roads, in the proverbial middle of nowhere, stands the restaurant El Príncipe Tutul Xiú. Much to my surprise, when I finally got there, the parking lot was full. Founded in 1973, named for a fifteenth century Mayan prince, and housed in a sort of giant *palapa* (open-air thatched hut), El Príncipe Tutul Xiú has achieved world renown for a single dish: *poc chuc*. And what a dish—thin slices of brined pork grilled over oak, pumped up with pickled grilled onions, and cooled down with cool fresh vegetables, and blasted with an incendiary Yucatán hot sauce. The restaurant uses pork tenderloin, but it struck me that this would be a great way to prepare another cut of meat that tends to dry out on the grill: pork chops, particularly thin pork rib chops. The chops acquire the crusty edges characteristic of good *poc chuc,* and of course, it's always agreeable to gnaw the meat off the bone. To be strictly authentic, you'd grill the pork over oak. (*Poc* means "grilled" in Mayan; *chuc* means "embers.") This recipe may sound complicated, but you prepare it in stages. And it does give you a whole meal on a plate. To simplify matters, you can grill and pickle the onions ahead of time, and the salsa is optional. **SERVES 4**

THE SCOOP

WHERE: Mexico

WHAT: Some of the best pork chops you've ever tasted—lightly brined, wood grilled, and served with grilled onions, fresh vegetables, and sour orange juice— a whole summertime meal on a single plate, and a good-looking one at that

HOW: Direct grilling

JUST THE FACTS: To be strictly authentic, you need *naranja agria*, sour orange juice, from a fruit that looks like an orange, but tastes more like a tart fresh lime. You'll find it at supermarkets that cater to Hispanic communities.

Deep in Mayan country: the magnificent temple at Uxmal.

Grilling poc chuc (brined pork) over oak at the restaurant El Príncipe Tutul Xiú in the hamlet of Maní in the Yucatán.

2 pounds thin bone-in pork chops, or 1½ pounds pork
     tenderloin

Coarse salt (kosher or sea)

1 large white onion, quartered from tip to root
     (leave the skin and root intact)

¾ cup naranja agria (sour orange) juice, or 6 tablespoons
     each fresh orange juice and fresh lime juice

1 tablespoon fresh lime juice, or to taste

½ small green cabbage, quartered, and thinly sliced crosswise

1 large or 2 small avocados, peeled, pitted, and thinly sliced
     (see Note)

1 bunch red radishes, rinsed, stemmed, and thinly sliced
     crosswise

¼ cup coarsely chopped fresh cilantro, plus ¼ cup fresh
     cilantro leaves

Salsa (optional), such as: xni pec (Fiery Habañero Salsa,
     page 465) or chiltomate (Grilled Tomato Habañero Salsa,
     page 459)

YOU'LL ALSO NEED

2 cups unsoaked oak chips or chunks (optional)

ADVANCE PREPARATION

None

1 Make a small cut in the side of each pork chop to prevent it from curling during grilling. Arrange the pork in a baking dish just large enough to hold it in a single layer and season it very generously all over with salt; you'll need about 2 tablespoons of salt in all. Add enough water just to cover the pork (about 1 cup) and let it marinate in the refrigerator, covered, for 15 to 30 minutes.

2 Set up the grill for two-zone grilling (see page 611). Preheat one zone to high and one zone to medium. Ideally, you'll grill over a wood fire (see page 603). If you like, add some unsoaked oak chips or chunks to the charcoal or place them in the smoker box or in a smoker pouch of a gas grill (see page 603).

3 When ready to cook, place the onion quarters on the hot grate and grill them until well browned on all sides, 3 to 4 minutes per side, 9 to 12 minutes

in all. It's OK if the skin burns—it will add flavor. If the onion itself starts to burn, move it to the cooler part of the grill. Transfer the onions to a cutting board and let them cool to room temperature. Trim off the root end and burnt skin and thinly slice the onion quarters crosswise. Place the onion slices in a nonreactive mixing bowl and stir in the sour orange juice and lime juice. Season with salt to taste; the mixture should be highly seasoned.

4 Line a platter with the sliced cabbage.

5 Drain the pork well, dry it with paper towels, and place it on the hot grate. Grill the pork until it is sizzling and browned on the outside and cooked through, 3 to 4 minutes per side for pork chops; about 8 minutes per side, 16 minutes in all, for pork tenderloin. Use an instant-read meat thermometer to test for doneness, inserting it through the side of the meat but not touching the bone, if any. When done, the internal temperature should be about 160°F.

6 If you are using pork chops, leave them whole; if using pork tenderloin, let rest then thinly slice it sharply on the diagonal across the grain. Arrange the grilled pork on top of the cabbage. Arrange the avocado and radish slices on top of the pork. Stir the chopped cilantro into the grilled onion mixture and spoon it over the pork and vegetables. Sprinkle the cilantro leaves on top and serve at once, with the salsa on the side, if desired.

NOTE: Sprinkle the avocado slices with a little sour orange juice or lime juice to keep them from discoloring.

VARIATION

Beef _Poc Chuc_: The other house specialty of El Príncipe Tutul Xiú is beef tenderloin grilled, sliced, and served the same way as the pork. You'll need 1½ pounds of tenderloin tips. Grill the beef to taste, thinly slice it on the diagonal, and serve it on the cabbage, topped with the pickled grilled onions.

Kansas City–Style Spareribs

One of the things I like best about barbecue is its spirit of individuality—the fact that in our homogenized age, with a fast food outlet on every street corner, barbecue remains some of the last truly regional food in America. I love the fact that *barbecue* means something different in Lexington, North Carolina, than it does in Lubbock, Texas, or Owensboro, Kentucky. That there are still pit masters independent (or ornery) enough to stake their reputations on dry rubs versus wet rubs (or vice versa), on hickory versus oak, on spareribs versus baby backs, and so on.

And all of these polemics come together in a city that was founded relatively late in American history (compared with Jamestown or Boston, for example), but that caught the true religion of smoke and fire early—a metropolis that came by its barbecue obsession thanks to the unexpected confluence of a river, a trail, and a ballpark. The river is the Missouri, and in the waning years of the nineteenth century, a southerner schooled in the art of roasting meat over hickory sailed up it. He was a paddleboat cook and porter named Mr. Henry Perry, and he opened one of the first commercial barbecue joints in the United States. The trail bore the name of Chisholm, and it was along this timeworn path that Texas cowboys drove cattle from the ranches around Fort Worth to the packing houses of Kansas City, which enabled Missouri to become one of the centers of the American meat industry. As for the ballpark, it was the old Municipal Stadium, and it was here that the old-time sportswriters came to discover, popularize, and evangelize Kansas City barbecue.

In the process, the meaty pork ribs, smoked to dusky perfection in pits fueled by slow-smoldering hickory and slathered with a thick sweet, smoky, tomato-based barbecue sauce (typified by KC Masterpiece, a commercial sauce invented by another native son, Dr. Rich Davis) became the very epitome of American barbecue itself. All of which is a lengthy prologue to the one rib recipe that should be part of every grill master's repertory: pork spareribs crusted with a spice rub, sprayed with apple juice and bourbon, and slathered with a brown sugar and bourbon barbecue sauce. Yes, I've written before about Kansas City ribs, but this all-new version will knock it out of the park every time. **SERVES 4 EXCEEDINGLY HUNGRY EATERS, 6 TO 8 MORE MODEST APPETITES**

THE SCOOP

WHERE: Kansas City, U.S.A.

WHAT: One of America's barbecue icons, not to mention the dish that made Kansas City famous—spareribs rubbed with spices, sprayed with apple cider and whiskey, and sizzled with a sweet and smoky barbecue sauce

HOW: Smoking or indirect grilling

JUST THE FACTS: The traditional rib in Kansas City is the pork sparerib—meaty and richly flavorful, although somewhat tougher and slower to cook than the currently more popular baby back. I call for spareribs here. You can use baby backs, but shorten the cooking time by about 30 percent.

2 racks spareribs (each 3 to 4 pounds)

5 tablespoons sugar

4 tablespoons sweet paprika

3 tablespoons coarse salt (kosher or sea)

2 tablespoons lemon pepper

1 tablespoon granulated garlic

¾ cup apple cider

¼ cup bourbon

Bourbon-Brown Sugar Barbecue Sauce (recipe follows)

YOU'LL ALSO NEED

A spray bottle and a funnel; 4½ to 5 cups of hickory or other hardwood chips or chunks if you are smoking the ribs, or 3 cups if you are grilling them using the indirect method. Soak the chips or chunks in water for 1 hour, then drain them; a rib rack (optional)

ADVANCE PREPARATION

2 to 12 hours for curing the ribs (optional)

1 Remove the thin, papery membrane from the back of each rack of ribs, following the instructions in photo number 1 on page 235.

2 Place the sugar, paprika, salt, lemon pepper, and granulated garlic in a bowl and stir with your fingers to mix. Generously sprinkle the rub on both sides of the ribs, rubbing the seasonings onto the meat. (This rub is called a 5-4-3-2-1 rub, making it easy to remember the proportions of the ingredients.) You can cook the ribs right away, but you'll get a richer, more complex flavor if you let the ribs cure in the refrigerator, covered, for at least 2 hours, or as long as overnight.

3 Using a funnel, pour the cider and bourbon into a spray bottle. Shake the bottle to mix.

4 *If you are using a smoker* (see Note), set it up following the manufacturer's instructions and preheat it to low (225° to 250°F). When ready to cook, place the racks of ribs in the smoker bone side down. Smoke the ribs until cooked through, 4 to 5 hours. Add about 1½ cups of wood chips or chunks every hour for the first 3 hours. Start spraying

the ribs with the cider and bourbon mixture after 1 hour and spray them once an hour after that.

If you are grilling using the indirect method, set up the grill for indirect grilling, place a drip pan in the center, and preheat the grill to medium (325°F). When ready to cook, if you are using a charcoal grill, toss 1½ cups of the wood chips or chunks on the coals. If you are using a gas grill, add the wood chips or chunks to the smoker box or place them in a smoker pouch under the grate (see page 603). Place the racks of ribs, bone side down, in the center of the grate over the drip pan and away from the heat and cover the grill. (If your grill has limited space, you can use a rib rack to stand the racks of ribs upright.) Cook the ribs until well browned and cooked through yet tender enough to pull apart with your fingers, 1½ to 2 hours. Start spraying the ribs with the cider and bourbon mixture after 30 minutes and spray them again every 30 minutes until they are done. After 1 hour, if you are using a charcoal grill, replenish the coals and add another 1½ cups of wood chips or chunks.

5 When the ribs are done, the meat will have shrunk back from the ends of the bones by about ½ inch and will be tender enough to pull apart with your fingers. The exterior will be dark, almost black, but not burned.

6 Transfer the racks of ribs to a large platter or cutting board and cut the racks in half or into 2 or

Kansas City ribs—dark bark, sweet meat, and smoky as you could wish for. Serve the Bourbon Brown Sugar Barbecue Sauce on the side.

3 bone portions. Serve the ribs with the Bourbon-Brown Sugar Barbecue Sauce on the side.

NOTE: Using a smoker is the true Kansas City way to cook barbecue low and slow, so that the meat acquires a remarkable tenderness and a deep flavor synonymous with smoke. However, grilling ribs using the indirect method is well suited to people who have a charcoal grill, not a smoker. You get ribs with a good "bark" (crust); a visible smoke ring—a pinkish tinge just below the surface of the meat; a pronounced smoke flavor; and a somewhat meatier, chewier texture than with smoking. While I urge you to get a charcoal grill for smoking, you can use wood chips or chunks on a gas grill, you just won't get as pronounced a wood flavor. One more advantage to the indirect method: You're ready to eat after a couple of hours.

How Sweet It Is

If you like ribs with a sweet glaze, you'll want to brush them with Bourbon-Brown Sugar Barbecue Sauce toward the end of their cooking time. If you are using a smoker, brush the racks with some of the barbecue sauce during the last 30 minutes of smoking. If you are grilling the ribs using the indirect method, brush the racks with some sauce during the last 5 minutes of smoking, then move the ribs directly over the fire and grill them until the sauce sizzles and browns. Personally, I like to serve the ribs unadorned in all their smoky glory, with the barbecue sauce passed separately.

Bourbon-Brown Sugar Barbecue Sauce

Describe the perfect barbecue sauce. Well, if you come from North Carolina, you'll probably evoke a thin sauce based on vinegar and hot peppers. If Decatur, Alabama, is your home, your dream barbecue sauce probably contains cider vinegar and mayonnaise. But if you belong to the great ranks of "unaffiliated" barbecue lovers (that is, those not bound by the tradition of your micro-region), you'll probably hunger for a sauce that is thick, sweet, and tomatoey, with only the faintest hint of acid and a potent whiff of wood smoke to reinforce the smoke flavor of the meat. In short, the sort of barbecue sauce Kansas City pit masters have been swabbing on ribs for decades. **MAKES ABOUT 2 CUPS**

1 cup ketchup
¼ cup firmly packed brown sugar
¼ cup bourbon
3 tablespoons cider vinegar, or more as needed
3 tablespoons molasses
2 tablespoons Worcestershire sauce
1 tablespoon Dijon mustard
1½ teaspoons liquid smoke (see Note)
1 teaspoon hot sauce, such as Tabasco
½ teaspoon onion powder
½ teaspoon garlic powder
½ teaspoon freshly ground black pepper

1 Combine the ketchup, brown sugar, bourbon, cider vinegar, molasses, Worcestershire sauce, mustard, liquid smoke, hot sauce, onion powder, garlic powder, and pepper in a nonreactive saucepan and whisk to mix.

2 Gradually bring the sauce to a simmer over medium heat and let simmer until thick and flavorful, 8 to 10 minutes. Taste for seasoning, adding more cider vinegar if necessary; the sauce should be highly seasoned. Transfer the sauce to a bowl or clean jars and let cool to room temperature. Refrigerate the sauce, covered, until serving time; let it return to room temperature before using. The sauce can be refrigerated for several weeks.

NOTE: Contrary to popular belief, liquid smoke is a natural product, made from distilled wood smoke and water.

The USA: E Pluribus Barbecue

A Pacific Northwest Indian salmon roast on the Makah Indian Reservation, Olympic Peninsula, Washington State.

Long before the United States was a country (before there were even states to be united), its inhabitants loved barbecue. Indians of the Pacific Northwest butterflied whole salmon through the belly, pinned them to cedar stakes, and roasted the fish in front of bonfires. Early settlers found a land teaming with game, with rivers and bays brimming with seafood, and with vast forests of hickory and oak to provide fuel for smoking and grilling. Spanish *vaqueiros* (cowboys) migrating north from Mexico grilled steaks over mesquite and spit-roasted goats over campfires. And, in what would become the American South, whole hogs were roasted over ember-filled trenches—the original pit barbecue.

One of the first laws promulgated in the colony of Virginia forbade the discharge of firearms at a barbecue; even back then, we were a nation obsessed by smoked meat

Home on the Range

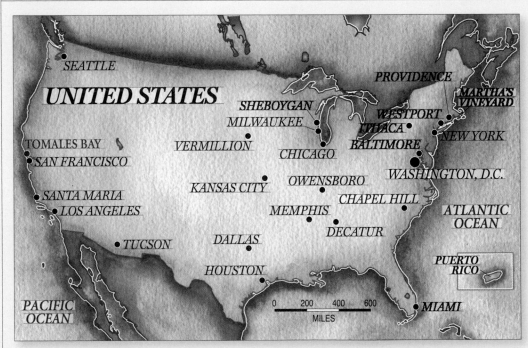

SEATTLE

UNITED STATES

PROVIDENCE

MARTHA'S VINEYARD

SHEBOYGAN

MILWAUKEE

WESTPORT

ITHACA

NEW YORK

TOMALES BAY

VERMILLION

BALTIMORE

SAN FRANCISCO

CHICAGO

KANSAS CITY

OWENSBORO

WASHINGTON, D.C.

SANTA MARIA

CHAPEL HILL

LOS ANGELES

MEMPHIS

ATLANTIC OCEAN

TUCSON

DALLAS

DECATUR

HOUSTON

PUERTO RICO

0   200   400   600
MILES

MIAMI

PACIFIC OCEAN

For most people, Planet Barbecue begins at home. We Americans are no different. America is blessed with an incredibly rich barbecue culture. Many countries grill. Some smoke. But only one—the United States—has a deep, rich, and highly evolved tradition of both barbecuing (smoking) and grilling.

Southern barbecue at its roots—whole hogs being smoke roasted over an ember-filled pit.

and smoking guns. In his diaries George Washington wrote often about barbecues. When Abraham Lincoln's parents married, the wedding feast was a barbecue. It was an American—Henry Ford (yes, *that* Henry Ford)—who pioneered the charcoal briquette. An American, George Stephen, an employee of the Weber Brothers Metal Works in Illinois, who attached legs and fitted vents to a half-round nautical buoy to invent one of the world's most popular grills: the Weber kettle.

Most of the world grills; in some countries they smoke; but only the United States has highly developed traditions for both. Grilled specialties range from California tri-tip to Texas T-bones to Sheboygan "brats" (grilled bratwurst in Wisconsin). The hamburger, served at Delmonico's restaurant in New York City as early as 1834, sold for the princely price of 10 cents—twice the cost of roast beef. The American culinary revolution of the 1980s brought wood-burning grills to upscale restaurants, ushering in new grilled classics, from grilled artichokes to oysters to pizza.

True barbecue, meats cooked low and slow over a smoky fire, is America's greatest gift to the world of live fire cooking. The short list includes Carolina pulled pork, Texas brisket, Memphis baby backs, and Kansas City smoked spareribs and beef ribs. Each region has its own way of serving: Carolina pork is shredded or finely chopped and doused with a thin peppery vinegar sauce; Memphis ribs are thickly crusted with spices; Alabama barbecued chicken is dipped twice in a white sauce made from mayonnaise and vinegar that's found virtually nowhere else on the planet. Who else but an American could have dreamed up beer-can chicken? Or barbecued cabbage or *huli huli* (spit-roasted) pineapple? Or that campfire classic now found deconstructed and reconstructed at some of our most fashionable restaurants: the s'more?

Beale Street by night. Memphis, Tennessee, is home of some of the most singular ribs on Planet Barbecue.

THE GRILLS: More than 84 percent of American families own grills; more than 40 percent own multiple grills; and at least 54 percent of us grill all year round—even in the coldest winter. Last year, we fired up our grills more than three *billion* times. Americans cook on everything from the Sputnik-shaped charcoal kettle grill to stainless steel gas supergrills that cost in excess of $10,000. In the South, Texas, and the Midwest, we smoke in stone or metal pits that maintain a low temperature (around 250°F) for a long time (up to sixteen hours). Grill masters in Santa Maria, California, use oak-burning grills with grates raised and lowered by flywheels to cook roast tri-tip.

The bigger the grill, the better the barbecue—here a well-loaded grate holds enough for a community summer celebration in Pontiac, Michigan.

Among the more distinctive grills are the offset barrel smoker, originally manufactured with steel oil pipe in the petroleum fields of Texas; the heat-efficient ceramic *kamado* cookers, best typified by the Big Green Egg; and pellet smokers, like the Traeger, that burn pellets of hardwood sawdust. At the Memphis in May World Championship Barbecue Cooking Contest, you'll see smokers in the shape of airplanes, tea kettles, and even tractor trailer–size pigs.

There's no limit to what a Texan will grill—even pancakes.

THE FUEL: Propane, charcoal, and wood, which is used for both grilling and smoking. Wood smoke is the soul of true barbecue and the most popular species include mesquite, used in Texas; hickory, used in the South; oak, used in Texas and California; apple, used in the Midwest; maple, used in New England); and kiavi, a thorny hardwood similar to mesquite used in Hawaii.

THE FLAVORINGS: As rich and varied as our multiethnic population itself. The basic all-purpose barbecue seasoning

American icons: a pick-up truck parked outside a barbecue joint on Route 66 in Texas.

consists of equal parts of salt, pepper, paprika, and brown sugar. South Carolinians would add mustard powder (to go with their mustard barbecue sauce); Texans, chili powder and cumin (and likely cut back the sugar); in Miami, they add cumin, oregano, and garlic powder.

MUST TRY DISHES:
The Big Four

Kansas/Missouri: Kansas City wet ribs (sweet and smoky) or burnt edges (brisket trimmings)

North Carolina: Pulled pork shoulder (or the whole hog version served at a "pig pickin")

Tennessee: Memphis dry rub ribs

Texas: Smoke-roasted brisket and clod

Texas clod, a smoke-roasted beef shoulder.

Here are some regional barbecue specialties:

Alaska: Reindeer sausage—the bratwurst of our northernmost state

California: Barbecued oysters—topped with chipotle barbecue sauce and grilled on the half shell in Tomales bay

Connecticut: Planked shad—nailed to oak boards and roasted in front of a bonfire

Hawaii: *Huli huli* chicken—honey-soy glazed and spit roasted

Maine: Bean-hole beans

Maryland: Baltimore pit beef—thinly sliced beef round grilled and served on a kaiser roll with horseradish sauce

New York: Cornell chicken—invented by a poultry scientist at Cornell University in Ithaca. Grilled chicken halves basted with an egg, oil, and poultry seasoning glaze.

Rhode Island: Grilled pizza—yes, the dough is cooked directly on the grill grate. Popularized at the restaurant Al Forno in Providence.

South Dakota: Corn cob–smoked spareribs—a little known but meritorious specialty of the city of Vermillion

Texas, Southern California, and the Southwest: Carnitas—Mexican-style, thinly sliced grilled beef served on tortillas with guacamole, salsa, and *pico de gallo*

Wisconsin: Grilled bratwurst served on hard rolls with German-style mustard

THE CONDIMENTS: For most Americans, barbecue just isn't complete without sauce. But what constitutes barbecue sauce depends on where you live. Here are some regional favorites:

In eastern North Carolina you'll find a thin, red peppery vinegar sauce. In the western part of the state they redden and sweeten the sauce with a little ketchup. In South Carolina you'll find a sweet, vinegary mustard sauce. In northern Alabama the sauce is white barbecue, based on mayonnaise and vinegar. In Kansas City, barbecue sauce comes thick, sweet, and smoky, while in Tennessee sauce is tomato-based. In Owensboro, Kentucky, they make a black barbecue sauce with Worcestershire sauce and melted butter. In Miami, Florida, *mojo*, a fried garlic, cumin, and lime juice sauce is popular with Florida's Hispanics.

With barbecue, Americans also like to serve: baked beans—sweet and smoky in New England and the Midwest; semisweet and semispicy in California; and spicy and not sweet at all in Texas. And coleslaw: mustardy in the South; creamy in the Northeast and Midwest. Hush puppies, cornmeal fritters, and cornmeal flat cakes are popular in the South.

IF YOU CAN EAT AT ONLY ONE RESTAURANT: It's impossible to pick just one, but here are some good choices cross-country:

Allen & Son in Chapel Hill, North Carolina, for pulled pork; Charles Vergo's Rendezvous in Memphis, Tennessee, birthplace of the dry rub baby back rib; Oklahoma Joe's Barbecue in Kansas City, for Kansas City–style spareribs; Cooper's Old Time Pit Bar-B-Que in Llano; Kreuz Market in Lockhart, Goode Co.; in Houston, and the original Sonny Bryan's Smokehouse in Dallas (all four in Texas—of course) for Texas-style brisket (note you must visit the original Sonny Bryan's restaurant near Love Field); Big Bob Gibson Bar-B-Q in Decatur, Alabama, for chicken with white barbecue sauce; The Hog Island Oyster Company in Marshall, California, for barbecued oysters; Tillicum Village on Blake Island, near Seattle, for a Pacific Northwest salmon bake.

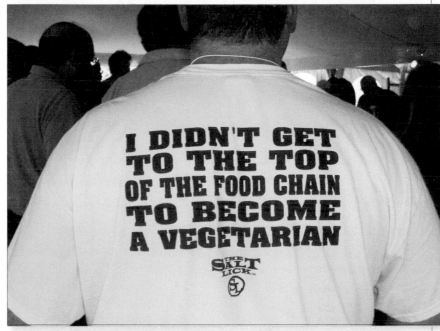
Telling it like it is—obviouisly a heartfelt message.

Big Bob Gibson's: World pork champion and home of the world's only smoked chicken with white mayonnaise-based barbecue sauce.

THE NEW YORK CITY BARBECUE CRAWL OPTION: The last decade has seen the rise of a number of excellent barbecue restaurants in New York City. Visitors to this country with limited time can feast their way around America's barbecue trail—without leaving Manhattan. Some good stops: Blue Smoke, Daisy May's BBQ USA, Hill Country, RUB BBQ, and Virgil's Real Barbecue.

WHAT TO DRINK: Microbrew beer or wine from California, Oregon, or Washington State—when you're not drinking a sweet red soda called Cheerwine in North Carolina.

THE MOST SINGULAR DISHES IN THE REPERTORY: Rocky Mountain oysters, sometimes called prairie oysters—grilled bull testicles—a specialty of Texas and Colorado. Or barbecued mutton (yes, big gamy mutton, not delicate lamb) grilled in Owensboro, Kentucky.

Caribbean Pineapple Baby Back Ribs with Pineapple Barbecue Sauce

THE SCOOP

WHERE: Trinidad and Tobago

WHAT: Baby back ribs rubbed with West Indian spices, sprayed with pineapple juice, smoked with allspice berries, and sizzled with pineapple barbecue sauce

HOW: Indirect grilling

JUST THE FACTS: I like to mist the ribs with pineapple juice as they smoke. To do this you'll need a spray bottle, available at hardware stores. You can also apply the pineapple mixture with a barbecue mop.

Barbecue—both the technique of smoke roasting and the word itself—originated in the Caribbean (on page xvii, you can read how it was done in the sixteenth century) by the Taíno Indians in what is now the Dominican Republic. Columbus managed to miss it (at least he never mentioned it in his journals), but he did encounter several New World ingredients that became staples for the world's grill masters, among them the chile pepper, allspice, and pineapple. All three come together in a dish of Trinidadian inspiration—baby back ribs glazed and sauced with pineapple. Here's how my assistant, Nancy Loseke, experienced it on her last trip to the West Indies. Think of these ribs as the apotheosis of spice, smoke, and fruit. **SERVES 4**

2 tablespoons coarse salt (kosher or sea)

1 tablespoon light brown sugar

1 teaspoon freshly ground black pepper

1 teaspoon granulated garlic

½ teaspoon onion powder

½ teaspoon ground allspice

½ teaspoon chili powder

¼ teaspoon ground cinnamon

2 racks baby back pork ribs (each 2 to 2½ pounds)

1 cup pineapple juice

3 tablespoons distilled white vinegar

2 tablespoons Worcestershire sauce

Pineapple Barbecue Sauce (recipe follows)

YOU'LL ALSO NEED

A clean spray bottle; 2 cups wood chips or chunks, preferably apple or other fruitwood, soaked for 1 hour in water to cover, then drained; 20 whole allspice berries (optional); a rib rack (optional)

ADVANCE PREPARATION

1 to 4 hours for curing the meat

1 Place the salt, brown sugar, pepper, granulated garlic, onion powder, ground allspice, chili powder, and cinnamon in a small bowl and mix them with your fingers, breaking up any lumps.

2 Remove the thin, papery membrane from the back of each rack of ribs (see photo number 1, facing page).

3 Sprinkle the rub over both sides of the ribs, rubbing it onto the meat. Cover the ribs with plastic wrap and let them cure in the refrigerator for at least 1 hour or as long as 4; the longer the ribs cure, the richer the flavor will be.

4 Meanwhile, combine the pineapple juice, vinegar, and Worcestershire sauce in a clean spray bottle and shake to mix.

5 Set up the grill for indirect grilling, place a drip pan in the center, and preheat the grill to medium. I urge you to get a charcoal grill for smoking. You can use wood on a gas grill, but you just won't get as pronounced a smoke flavor.

6 When ready to cook, brush and oil the grill grate. If you are using a charcoal grill, toss the wood chips and the allspice berries, if using, on the coals. If you are using a gas grill, add the wood chips or chunks and the allspice berries, if using, to the smoker box or place them in a smoker pouch under the grate (see page 603). Place the racks of ribs, bone side down, in the center of the grate over the drip pan and away from the heat and cover the grill. (If your grill has limited space, you can use a rib rack to stand the racks of ribs upright.) Cook the ribs for about 45 minutes.

7 Spray the ribs on both sides with some of the pineapple spray. Cover the grill again and continue cooking the ribs until they are well browned, cooked through, and tender enough to pull apart with your fingers, 30 to 45 minutes longer, 1¼ to 1½ hours in all. When the ribs are done, the meat will have shrunk back from the ends of the bones by about ¼ inch. Spray the ribs once or twice more. If you are using a charcoal grill, you will need to replenish the coals after 1 hour.

8 Just before serving, brush both sides of the ribs with some of the Pineapple Barbecue Sauce. Move the ribs directly over the fire and grill them until the sauce is sizzling and browned, 1 to 3 minutes per side. Be careful not to let the ribs burn.

9 Transfer the ribs to a platter or cutting board. Let the ribs rest for 3 minutes, then cut the racks in half or into individual ribs. Serve at once with the remaining Pineapple Barbecue Sauce.

PREPARING BABY BACKS

1. *Remove the papery membrane from the back of the ribs.*

2. *Season the ribs with the rub, rubbing the spices into the meat.*

3. *Add soaked, drained chips to the fire to generate wood smoke.*

4. *Spray the ribs with pineapple juice to keep them moist and to add an extra layer of flavor.*

5. *Brush the pineapple barbecue sauce on the ribs a few minutes before you're finished cooking and sizzle directly over the fire.*

Caribbean Pineapple Baby Back Ribs glazed with Pineapple Barbecue Sauce.

Pineapple Barbecue Sauce

Here's a tasty sauce that's sweet, fruity, and smoky—just like a traditional North American barbecue sauce—but the Scotch bonnets, rum, and allspice let you know you're not in Kansas anymore. **MAKES ABOUT 2 CUPS**

1 tablespoon vegetable oil

1 medium-size onion, diced (about 1 cup)

2 cloves garlic, minced

2 teaspoons minced peeled fresh ginger

1 to 2 Scotch bonnet chiles, seeded and minced

2 cups pineapple juice, or more as needed

1 cup finely diced fresh or canned pineapple

¼ cup dark rum, or more to taste

⅓ cup dark brown sugar, or more to taste

¼ cup distilled white vinegar

1 tablespoon Worcestershire sauce

½ teaspoon coarse salt (kosher or sea), or more to taste

½ teaspoon freshly ground black pepper

¼ teaspoon ground allspice, or to taste

3 tablespoons fresh cilantro leaves

1 Heat the oil in a large nonreactive saucepan over medium heat. Add the onion, garlic, ginger, and Scotch bonnet(s) and cook until soft, about 5 minutes. Do not let them brown.

2 Add the pineapple juice, pineapple, rum, brown sugar, vinegar, Worcestershire sauce, salt, black pepper, and allspice. Briskly simmer the sauce until richly flavored and reduced by one third, 8 to 12 minutes, stirring often.

3 Remove the sauce from the heat. Place 1 cup of the sauce in a blender along with the cilantro. Pulse until blended. Return the cilantro mixture to the saucepan and cook the sauce over low heat until the flavors are well blended, about 5 minutes. If the sauce seems too thick, add more pineapple juice. Taste for seasoning, adding more brown sugar, rum, salt, and/or allspice as necessary. If you are not using the sauce immediately, refrigerate it, covered. The sauce can be made up to 3 days ahead. Let it return to room temperature before serving.

Ginger, Garlic, and Honey Grilled Baby Back Ribs

THE SCOOP

WHERE: Siem Reap, Cambodia

WHAT: Baby back ribs spiced with garlic and ginger and served with lime dipping sauce

HOW: Direct grilling

Ribs, like wine, reflect strong regional and cultural influences. The vast ranch lands and forests of the New World led to American-style barbecue, with its mammoth slabs of spareribs slow roasted in a smoker for the better part of a day. Asians adopted a different strategy, cooking small cuts or single ribs on tiny grills engineered for fuel efficiency. The flavor comes not from wood smoke (Asians didn't have wood to burn by the cord) but from the intensely flavorful seasonings indigenous to the region, like

GINGER, GARLIC, AND HONEY GRILLED BABY BACK RIBS

JUST THE FACTS:
There once was a time when baby back ribs really were "baby." They came from Denmark, and the racks were so tender and small (three quarters to one pound), you could grill them directly, like pork chops. This is the sort of baby backs you find in Cambodia. You can also grill full-size American baby backs this way, but cut each rack in half before grilling.

lemongrass, ginger, and fish sauce. These Cambodian-style ribs are a specialty of Sarun Pich, chef and culinary instructor at the Amansara resort in Siem Reap, Cambodia. If you're interested in learning about Khmer cuisine, there's no better way to get an immersion in Cambodian culture than by booking a private cooking class with Sarun, taught in a traditional Cambodian stilt house overlooking lake Srah Srang. **SERVES 4**

FOR THE RIBS AND SPICE PASTE

4 racks true baby back ribs (each ¾ to 1 pound),
    or 2 racks American baby back ribs
    (each 2 to 2½ pounds)
6 cloves garlic, coarsely chopped
1 piece (2 inches) fresh ginger, peeled and
    coarsely chopped
1 tablespoon sugar
1 tablespoon coarse salt (kosher or sea)
2 teaspoons freshly ground black pepper
2 tablespoons honey
1 tablespoon soy sauce
1 tablespoon Asian fish sauce or more soy sauce

FOR THE DIPPING SAUCE

4 teaspoons coarse salt (kosher or sea)
4 teaspoons white pepper
4 juicy limes, cut in half

ADVANCE PREPARATION

1 to 4 hours for marinating the ribs

1 Prepare the ribs and spice paste: If necessary, remove the thin, papery membrane from the back of each rack of ribs (see photo number 1, page 235)—some stores sell baby backs with the membrane removed. If you are using the larger racks of ribs, cut each rack in half. Place the ribs in a nonreactive baking dish just large enough to hold them in a single layer.

2 Place the garlic, ginger, sugar, 1 tablespoon of salt, and the black pepper in a mortar and pound to a paste with a pestle. If you do not have a mortar and pestle, puree these ingredients in a food processor. Work in the honey, soy sauce, and fish sauce. Spread the spice paste over the baby back ribs on both sides. Let the ribs marinate in the refrigerator, covered, for 1 to 4 hours; the longer the ribs marinate, the richer the flavor will be.

3 Prepare the ingredients for the dipping sauce: Place 1 teaspoon of salt and 1 teaspoon of white pepper in neat mounds side by side in each of 4 tiny bowls for the dipping sauce. Place 2 lime halves next to each bowl.

4 Set up the grill for direct grilling and preheat it to medium.

5 When ready to cook, brush and oil the grill grate. Place the ribs, bone side down, on the hot grate and grill until golden brown and cooked through, 8 to 12 minutes per side, a little longer for full-size ribs. Watch for flare-ups. Should they occur, move the ribs to another section of the grill. When the ribs are done, the meat will have shrunk back from the ends of the bones by about ¼ inch.

6 Transfer the racks of ribs to a cutting board and cut them into individual ribs, then arrange them on a platter or plates for serving. Just before eating, instruct your guests to squeeze 1 to 2 tablespoons of lime juice into their bowls of salt and white pepper and stir them with chopsticks until mixed. Dip the ribs in the sauce before eating.

Nuri's Ribs: Grilled Baby Backs with Sweet Soy Glaze

For every rule, there is an exception. If I had a dollar for every time I have preached *never* to boil ribs, I'd be floating on a yacht in the Sea of Siam. Yet here I am at a lively restaurant called Naughty Nuri's Warung in Ubud, Bali, sipping icy martinis with a motley crowd of expats, backpackers, and local yuppies, watching the flames dance at the grill, and I'm about to devour a dish I spent years disparaging: ribs that have been boiled prior to grilling. Of course, they're glazed in *kejap manis,* the sweet, syrupy soy sauce that's a staple in Indonesia, and they're so sweet, so crusty, so succulent, I just have to reach for another. And another. It just can't be. I'm actually eating boiled ribs.

The Nuri of Naughty Nuri's is Isnuri Suryatmi, who visited Bali from the Javanese city of Yogyakarta one day and decided she had landed in paradise. That was more than a decade ago, and she calls her thriving restaurant a "dream come true." So what's a purist to do? I could lie to you and tell you the ribs weren't boiled before grilling, or I could take the moral high road and tell you that Nuri boils her ribs, but you needn't and shouldn't—that the requisite tenderness can be achieved by indirect grilling or smoking (indeed, the purist will find instructions on how to do this in the recipe that follows). But that's not what you'd eat at Nuri's. So, here's a pretty compelling rib for all you folks who say you like your ribs so tender that the meat falls off the bones. **SERVES 2 TO 4**

FOR THE RIBS

1 cup Indonesian sweet soy sauce (kejap manis), or ½ cup each regular soy sauce and molasses

½ cup sugar

1 tablespoon minced, peeled fresh ginger

2 cloves garlic, minced

1 large shallot, minced

Freshly ground black pepper

¼ teaspoon freshly ground white pepper, or more to taste

2 racks baby back pork ribs (each 2 to 2½ pounds)

Coarse salt (kosher or sea)

Garlic powder

YOU'LL ALSO NEED

2 cups fruit wood chips or chunks (optional), soaked for 1 hour in water to cover, then drained; a rib rack (optional)

ADVANCE PREPARATION

Allow yourself 1½ hours for precooking the ribs if you are making Nuri's version.

THE SCOOP

WHERE: Bali, Indonesia

WHAT: Pork ribs Balinese style—glazed with sweet soy sauce and ginger

HOW: Direct or indirect grilling

JUST THE FACTS: *Kejap manis* (sometimes spelled *kecap manis*) is a thick, sweet Indonesian soy sauce, and if the name reminds you of another barbecue condiment (one you'd slather on hamburgers), it's no coincidence. Our bright red sauce and the Indonesian soy sauce share a common ancestor (a sauce British mariners discovered on voyages to Malaysia in the eighteenth century). A lot of Southeast Asian barbecue, like these ribs, acquires its sweet-salty, lacquerlike glaze from the Indonesian sweet soy sauce. The sauce is available at Asian markets and via mail order from www.importfood.com (you'll find it there as *kecap manis*). Or substitute equal parts regular soy sauce and molasses.

1 Place the sweet soy sauce, sugar, ginger, garlic, shallot, ¼ teaspoon of black pepper, the white pepper, and 3 tablespoons of water in a heavy saucepan over high heat and bring to a boil. Let the glaze boil until thick and syrupy and reduced to about 1⅓ cups, 4 to 6 minutes, stirring often. If the glaze becomes too thick, add 1 to 3 additional tablespoons of water. The sweet soy glaze can be made several hours ahead of time and refrigerated, covered. Let it come to room temperature before using.

2 Remove the thin, papery membrane from the back of each rack of ribs (see photo number 1, page 235). Season the ribs generously on both sides with salt, black pepper, and garlic powder.

3 Set up the grill for indirect grilling, place a drip pan in the center, and preheat the grill to medium. I urge you to get a charcoal grill for smoking, but you can use wood on a gas grill; you just won't get as pronounced a wood flavor.

4 When ready to cook, if you are using a charcoal grill, toss the wood chips or chunks, if using, on the coals. If you are using a gas grill, add the wood chips or chunks, if using, to the smoker box or place them in a smoker pouch under the grate (see page 603). Brush and oil the grill grate. Place the racks of ribs bone side down in the center of the grate over the drip pan and away from the heat. (If your grill has limited space, you can stand the racks of ribs upright in a rib rack.) Cover the grill and cook the ribs until tender, 1¼ to 1½ hours. When the ribs are done, they'll be handsomely browned and the meat will have shrunk back from the ends of the bones by about ¼ inch. If you are using a charcoal grill, you will need to add fresh coals after 1 hour.

5 During the last 10 minutes of grilling, brush the ribs on both sides with the sweet soy glaze. When the ribs have grilled for about 5 minutes after being glazed, move them directly over the fire. Brush the ribs on both sides with glaze again and grill them until the glaze is sizzling, 1 to 3 minutes per side.

6 Transfer the ribs to a large platter or cutting board and cut the racks into individual ribs. Pour any remaining glaze over the ribs and serve at once.

Nuri's Version

Nuri's Version: To prepare baby back ribs the way Nuri does, by boiling them first, you'll need these ingredients in addition to the ones on page 239:

1 onion, quartered

1 piece (2 inches) fresh ginger, peeled, cut crosswise into ¼-inch slices, and flattened with the side of a cleaver

2 cloves garlic, peeled and flattened with the side of a cleaver

2 stalks lemongrass, trimmed and flattened with the side of a cleaver

1 Several hours, or even a day ahead, remove the papery membrane from the back of each rack of ribs, (see photo number 1, page 235). Then, place the ribs in a large pot with cold water to cover by 4 inches. Bring the ribs to a boil over medium heat, skimming off any foam that rises to the surface.

2 Add the onion, ginger, garlic, and lemongrass to the pot with the ribs. Let the ribs return to a gentle simmer and cook them until the meat is very tender and has shrunk back from the ends of the bones by about ¼ inch, about 1 hour. Transfer the ribs to a platter and let cool to room temperature, then refrigerate them until you are ready to grill. For even moister ribs, let the ribs

and cooking liquid cool to room temperature separately, then put the ribs back in the cooking liquid and refrigerate them together. The ribs can be boiled up to 24 hours ahead of time.

3 When you are ready to grill, drain the ribs if necessary, discarding the cooking liquid or setting it aside for another use in a soup or stew. Grill the ribs, bone side down, using the direct method until they are sizzling hot and darkly browned, 3 to 5 minutes per side. Baste the ribs generously and repeatedly with the sweet soy glaze, serving any extra glaze on the side as a sauce.

THE SCOOP

ORIGIN: Bali, Indonesia

WHAT: Pork ribs Nuri's way

HOW: Direct grilling

JUST THE FACTS: A Raichlen barbecue heresy—ribs boiled prior to grilling.

Naughty Nuri's— an institution in Ubud, Bali.

Indonesia: The Large and the Small of It

Does size really matter? In the West, we assume that bigger is better. In Asia, good things tend to come in small packages. I'm talking about barbecue, of course, and while we Westerners like our hogs whole and our steaks bible-thick and plate-burying, Asians appreciate the finesse of yakitori and other grilled foods you can eat in one or two bites. Then there's Indonesia—a nation of dizzying ethnic and cultural diversity, where grilling is a national obsession (not to mention a daily ritual for eating) and where the barbecue comes both petite and larger-than-life.

Sweets on the street in Indonesia.

On the macro end, you find *babi guling*, the legendary roast pig of Bali, where hogs the size of small horses are stuffed with fragrant pastes of chiles, lemongrass, turmeric, galangal, and other spices, then skewered on log-size turnspits and roasted for a half day or so over coconut-shell charcoal, to be hewn apart with terrifyingly huge meat cleavers. Then, plates are piled high with pork meat, crisp skin, Balinese rice, vegetables, salads, and

17,508 Islands and About as Many Ways to Grill

Indonesia, where Muslims grill lamb, Hindus grill pork, and barbecue is a religious experience for everyone.

Barbara and I with Balinese dancers at a dance prelude to a barbecue in Ubud.

Rice paddies near Papuan in Bali. Rice is the preferred starch to serve with barbecue on this part of Planet Barbecue.

incendiary *sambals* (raw and cooked chile-based relishes). Not the least remarkable thing about this extraordinary pork dish is that it originated in the world's largest Muslim country.

On the micro end, there's the saté, a tiny kebab born in Indonesia,

where it has morphed into hundreds of different varieties, from Madura's *saté lalat,* "fly saté," so named because this minced beef and coconut kebab isn't much bigger than a housefly, to Java's *saté kalong,* literally "flying fox saté," sold by vendors who come out at dusk—the same time of day as when flying foxes (a sort of squirrel actually), take to the air to sail from tree to tree. The saté itself takes its name from a Sumatran word meaning to stab or to pierce—a reference to the act of skewering meat. In terms of sheer numbers consumed (it's not uncommon for an Indonesian to eat twenty or thirty at a single meal), saté is probably the most widely enjoyed kebab on Planet Barbecue.

Indonesian barbecue comes in all sizes, to suit all appetites and ethnic dispositions: whole grilled fish and mammoth prawns, spatchcocked chickens, barbecued ducks, even racks of baby back ribs sizzled with sweet soy glaze and served at expat watering holes in Kuta and Ubud, Bali.

Grilling satés over coconut-shell charcoal in Indonesia's capital, Jakarta.

THE GRILL: Indonesian grills come in two basic models: a long slender saté grill, with one or two center bars running the length of the grill to the skewers; and a charcoal-burning rotisserie with log spits for roasting whole hogs.

THE FUEL: Coconut-shell charcoal

THE FLAVORINGS: Indonesia was once called the Spice Islands, so it should come as no surprise that fiery chiles, exotic herbs such as tamarind and curry leaves, and pungent rhizomes and roots, like ginger, galangal, and lesser and greater turmeric, should dominate Indonesian grilling. Most dishes start with some sort of *bumbu*—an intensely flavorful marinade or spice paste. Other dishes are grilled on lemongrass stalks or wrapped and flame roasted in aromatic leaves.

MUST TRY DISHES:

Babi guling: Balinese herb-stuffed, spit-roasted whole hog

Saté age: Ground beef and coriander saté from Solo in Central Java

Ibu Oka: Turn in here for the best babi guling *(roast pig) in Ubud.*

Saté ayam: Chicken saté served with peanut sauce and sweet soy sauce

Saté babi manis: Pork saté served with sweet soy sauce

Saté buntel: Ground lamb and coriander saté served with tamarind sauce

Saté lilit: Seafood, chicken, or duck mousse saté grilled on lemongrass stalks

Saté tusuk: Goat saté with sweet soy and pineapple

THE CONDIMENTS: Indonesian condiments are designed to play pinball on your taste buds, from the sweet garlicky peanut sauce traditionally served with chicken saté to a huge family of *sambals*, some merely hot, others ferociously fiery, and all designed to electrify each bite.

HOW TO EAT IT: Satés are often served with dishes of *kejap manis* (sweet soy sauce), chile sauce, sliced shallots, and fried garlic. You stir them together with the end of one saté and use the resulting sauce as a dip for the remainder.

IF YOU CAN EAT AT ONLY ONE RESTAURANT: Satés are served from market pushcarts and casual storefront and open-air restaurants all over Indonesia. The best place to try *babi guling* is Ibu Oka ("Grandma Oka") in Ubud, Bali.

THE MOST SINGULAR DISH IN THE REPERTORY: *Bebek tutu,* a Balinese delicacy consisting of a whole duck wrapped in palm fronds (or other aromatic leaves) and smoke roasted over the fire.

A saté sampler with peanut sauce. Note the lemongrass skewers on the left.

Rotisserie Baby Back Ribs with Garlic and Wine

THE SCOOP

WHERE: Brazil

WHAT: Garlic and wine-marinated baby back pork ribs spit-roasted *churrascaria* (Brazilian steak house) style

HOW: Spit roasting

JUST THE FACTS: To be the most true to the original, you'd work on a wood or charcoal burning rotisserie. You can also cook the ribs by the indirect method; you'll find instructions on the facing page. Because the spicing is minimal, this would be a great recipe to try with a really rich-tasting pork, like Berkshire, sometimes referred to by its Japanese name, *kurobuta.* You'll find it at www.allenbrothers.com or www.lobels.com.

If there's one cut of meat that captures a culture's grilling aesthetic, it's ribs. Here in the United States, we like our ribs sweet, smoky, and tender (some might say soft). But in many countries, ribs aren't about the smoke or barbecue, but the pristine flavor of the meat. Prime example: Brazil. *Churrasqueros,* as grill masters are called in Brazil, cook ribs on the rotisserie (a great technique for achieving maximum tenderness with minimal fat), keeping the flavorings in the savory (salty) realm. Here's how they prepare baby backs at Brazil's famous steak house, Fogo de Chão (you can read about it on page 170): crusty on the outside; meaty to gnaw; and focused on the primal taste of the pork. **SERVES 2 TO 4**

2 racks baby back pork ribs
   (each 2 to 2½ pounds)
Coarse salt (kosher or sea) and
   freshly ground black pepper
Lemon pepper seasoning
1 medium-size onion, finely chopped
3 cloves garlic, finely chopped
½ cup finely chopped fresh flat-leaf parsley
½ cup dry white wine
¼ cup vegetable oil
Country Salsa (optional, page 155), for serving

ADVANCE PREPARATION
4 to 6 hours for marinating the ribs

1 Remove the thin, papery membrane from the back of each rack of ribs (see photo number 1, page 235).

2 Place the ribs in a nonreactive baking dish or roasting pan and season them very generously on both sides with salt, pepper, and lemon pepper.

Sprinkle the ribs on both sides with the onion, garlic, and parsley. Pour the wine over the ribs, followed by the oil, turning them several times to coat both sides. Let the ribs marinate in the refrigerator, covered, for 4 to 6 hours, turning them several times.

3 Drain the ribs, discarding the marinade. Using a sharp, slender knife, make starter holes in the center of the meat between every 2 ribs in one of the racks. Twist the knife blade to widen the holes; this will make it easier to insert the spit. Repeat with the remaining rack of ribs. Use an over and under weaving motion to thread the spit through the holes in the racks of ribs.

4 Set up the grill for spit roasting, following the manufacturer's instructions, and preheat the grill to medium-high. Place a large drip pan in the center of the grill directly under the spit.

5 When ready to cook, attach the spit to the rotisserie mechanism, turn on the motor, and cover the grill. Spit roast the ribs until they are well browned, tender, and cooked through, 40 minutes to 1 hour. When the ribs are done, the meat will have shrunk back from the ends of the bones by about ¼ inch. If you like, during the last half hour of grilling, baste the ribs with any fat in the drip pan.

6 Transfer the spit with the ribs to a cutting board. Carefully remove the spit and cut the ribs into 1- or 2-bone pieces. Serve the ribs as is or, if desired, with the Country Salsa on the side.

Indirect Grilling Method: Indirect grilling will give you ribs similar in texture and flavor to spit roasting (although not quite as crusty). And because Brazilians don't use wood smoke in their grilling, this is a good candidate for a gas grill. (Of course, if you do like smoke, you can toss a couple of handfuls of drained, soaked hardwood chips on the coals.)

Set up the grill for indirect grilling, place a drip pan in the center, and preheat the grill to medium. Grill the ribs, bone side down, until they are well browned and cooked through, yet tender enough to pull apart with your fingers, 1¼ to 1½ hours. If you are using a charcoal grill, you will need to replenish the coals after 1 hour.

Spit-Roasted Ham Hocks
{ SCHWEINSHAXEN }

I call it "barbecue whiplash." You're walking along the street and you catch sight of some live-fire cooking so compelling, your head whips around for a closer look. It might be a mammoth *shawarma* spinning on a vertical spit in a storefront in Israel, or a whole hog being reduced to crisp bites by a cleaver-wielding pit mistress in Bali. My whiplash moment in Germany took place in the old market quarter of Munich, where rows of sizzling, glistening, spice-crusted *schweinshaxen* (fresh ham hocks) spun on a military-strength rotisserie. And although I had already eaten one dinner, I was obliged to stop in for another meal. The place was a landmark Munich restaurant called Haxenbauer (literally Farmer Ham Hock), where since 1915 locals and tourists alike have come to stretch their jaws, and jazz their taste buds with succulent, crusty, meaty *schweinshaxen* that literally dwarf the plate. If you're looking for a new way to cook pork, these formidable *schweinshaxen* are your ticket. And to drink? A good *Münchener* beer. **SERVES 4 REALLY HUNGRY GERMANS, 6 TO 8 PEOPLE WITH NORMAL APPETITES**

THE SCOOP

WHERE: Germany

WHAT: Bliss on a spit—whole ham hocks seasoned with juniper and mugwort and spit roasted over charcoal

HOW: Spit roasting

JUST THE FACTS:
Your first challenge will be finding fresh ham hocks, which is a good reason to make friends with your local butcher. (You should *always* make friends with your local butcher.) Given the choice, you want hocks from the hindquarters; each should be one and a half to two pounds. You must use fresh, not smoked ham hocks. If these are unavailable, you could spit roast a pork shoulder in the same manner. You won't get quite the same high ratio of crisp skin to sizzling meat, but you will leave the table full and happy.

2 tablespoons juniper berries (see Note)

2 tablespoons coarse salt (kosher or sea)

2 tablespoons dried marjoram

1 tablespoon freshly ground black pepper

1 tablespoon dried mugwort or dried sage (see Note)

4 fresh (raw) ham hocks (each 1½ to 2 pounds), or 1 pork shoulder (6 to 7 pounds, preferably from the shank end and with the skin)

FOR SERVING

Sauerkraut

Rye bread

ADVANCE PREPARATION

2 to 12 hours for curing the ham hocks, and be sure to allow 1 to 1½ hours for spit roasting.

1 Lightly crush the juniper berries between your fingers to release the oils. Place the juniper berries in a bowl with the salt, marjoram, pepper, and mugwort or sage. Stir to mix.

Haxen (fresh ham hocks) roasted crackling-crisp and fork-tender on an ingenious upright charcoal rotisserie and sold by the kilogram.

2 Arrange the ham hocks in a roasting pan and season them on all sides with the rub, rubbing the seasonings onto the meat. Let the ham hocks cure in the refrigerator, uncovered, for 2 to 12 hours (more time equals richer flavor).

3 Set up the grill for spit roasting, following the manufacturer's instructions, and preheat the grill to medium-high. (To be strictly authentic, you'd fuel your rotisserie with beech wood charcoal.)

4 When ready to cook, thread the ham hocks lengthwise onto the rotisserie spit; the spit should run parallel to the leg bones. (If you are using pork shoulder, thread it on the spit, using the forked prongs to hold it in place.) Attach the spit to the grill and turn on the motor. Spit roast the ham hocks until they are crusty and golden brown on the outside and very tender inside, 1 to 1½ hours. (If you are using pork shoulder, the spit roasting time will be 2½ to 3 hours.) Use an instant-read meat thermometer to test for doneness, inserting it into the thickest part of the meat but not touching any bones or the spit. When done the internal temperature should be about 190°F.

5 Transfer the ham hocks to a platter or plates, removing the spit, and serve with sauerkraut and rye bread.

NOTE: Two ingredients are unique to the rub: juniper berries and mugwort (*beifuss*). The juniper berries are blackish-blue berries used as a flavoring for gin. They add a fresh piney aromatic note. You can find the berries in the spice rack of many supermarkets. Mugwort is a pungent, pleasantly bitter herb in the wormwood family traditionally used as a flavoring for pork and goose in Germany and rice cakes in the Far East. You may be able to find mugwort at an herbalist.

(Please note that according to the American Cancer Society, women who are pregnant or breast feeding should not eat mugwort.) Sage makes a suitable substitute.

Pork Kebabs "Dacho"

I've eaten a lot of kebabs on the world's barbecue trail, but I've never quite seen the technique featured here used anywhere else. The "rub" is a sort of paprika-flavored cornmeal (the same cornmeal used to make Serbian cornmeal dumplings) and the kebabs are dredged in the mixture when they are three-fourths of the way cooked, then returned to the grill and drizzled with oil. What results is the sort of crunchy crust you get on Wiener schnitzel, but it's grilled instead of fried. Here's how they make it at Dacho (see page 5), a landmark restaurant in Belgrade done up like a country farmhouse. To complete the scene you need *rakija* (fruit brandy), served in tiny pear-shaped flasks. Yes, you empty the flask in one gulp. **SERVES 4**

FOR THE CORNMEAL RUB

1 cup fine yellow cornmeal
¼ cup sweet paprika
1½ teaspoons coarse salt (kosher or sea)
1½ teaspoons freshly ground black pepper

FOR THE KEBABS

1½ pounds pork shoulder
1 medium-size onion
6 ounces very smoky thick-sliced country-style
    bacon, cut crosswise into 1 inch-long
    pieces
Coarse salt (kosher or sea)
Vegetable oil in a squeeze bottle
1 cup kajmak, clotted cream, mascarpone, or
    sour cream (optional, see Note), for serving

YOU'LL ALSO NEED

Small bamboo or metal skewers; an aluminum
    foil grill shield (optional, see page 611)

ADVANCE PREPARATION
None

1 Make the cornmeal rub: Place the cornmeal, paprika, salt, and pepper in a shallow bowl or pan and stir to mix.

2 Assemble the kebabs: Cut the pork into 1 inch cubes. Cut the onion in half crosswise, then cut each half in quarters. Break the quarters into layers.

THE SCOOP

WHERE: Belgrade, Serbia

WHAT: Pork kebabs crusted and grilled with paprika and cornmeal

HOW: Direct grilling

JUST THE FACTS: Serbian pork is amazingly flavorful, the result of being raised on small farms and not in industrial processing facilities. The nearest equivalent in the United States would be an heirloom variety like Berkshire pork. But the real standout ingredient is Serbian bacon, which is intensely smoky— about ten times more smoky than American bacon. Use a naturally smoked, farmhouse-style slab bacon. One good brand is Nueske's (www.nueskes.com).

3 Thread the pieces of pork onto the skewers, placing a piece of bacon and a piece of onion between each. You can pretty much fill up the skewers, but leave 2 inches at the end as a handle.

4 Set up the grill for direct grilling and preheat it to medium-high.

5 When ready to cook, brush and oil the grill grate. Season the kebabs with salt and place them on the hot grate. Grill the kebabs until they are three-quarters of the way cooked, 2 to 3 minutes per side, 8 to 12 minutes in all. (If you are using bamboo skewers, you may want to slide an aluminum foil shield under the exposed ends to keep them from burning.)

6 Dredge the kebabs in the cornmeal rub, turning to coat all sides and shaking off the excess. Drizzle a little oil over each kebab, turning to coat all sides. Continue grilling the kebabs until the crust is golden brown and the kebabs are cooked through, 1 to 2 minutes longer per side, 4 to 8 minutes in all. Use the pinch test to check for doneness (see page 612).

7 Serve the grilled kebabs at once with *kajmak* or other suggested creamy topping, if desired.

NOTE: Serbian grilled meats are traditionally served with a thick clotted cream (sometimes sweet, sometimes sour) called *kajmak*. Look for it in Balkan, Slavic, and even Middle Eastern markets. Sour cream, clotted cream, and mascarpone taste quite different, but get you in the ballpark.

Russian Onion and Pork Kebabs

{ SHASHLIK }

Shashlik is to Russia (and the former Soviet Republics) what shish kebab is to Turkey. They even mean the same etymologically: "sword meat"—in other words, meat grilled on a swordlike metal spit. The meat in question here is pork, marinated in grated onion and charred over charcoal. If you ever visit a *dacha* (weekend villa) in the countryside around Moscow on a weekend, you'll smell *shashlik* before you actually see or taste it, for everyone seems to be grilling some in the backyard. Here's how *shashlik* is prepared by my friend Nikolai Baratov, editor of *BBQ,* Russia's first barbecue magazine. (If you read Russian, or you just want to look at cool pictures, check out Nikolai's website: bbqmag.ru.) **SERVES 4**

1½ pounds pork shoulder, cut into
    1-inch cubes
1½ teaspoons coarse salt (kosher or sea)
1½ teaspoons ground coriander
1 teaspoon freshly ground black pepper
1 large white onion, peeled and quartered
Russian-style black bread, for serving
Russian "Ketchup" (page 183), for serving

YOU'LL ALSO NEED
Long flat metal skewers

ADVANCE PREPARATION
2 hours or as long as overnight for marinating
    the pork

1 Place the cubes of pork in a large mixing bowl. Sprinkle the salt, coriander, and pepper over them and stir well to coat.

2 Grate the onion over the pork using the large holes of a box grater. You can also finely chop the onion in a food processor and spoon it over the pork. Stir to mix. Tightly cover the bowl with a couple of layers of plastic wrap to keep the onion scent from permeating your refrigerator. Let the pork marinate in the refrigerator for at least 2 hours or as long as overnight, stirring it a couple of times so it marinates evenly. The longer the pork marinates, the richer the flavor will be. (As far as most Russians are concerned, you can never have enough onion.)

3 Drain the pork well, discarding the marinade, and thread the pork onto the skewers.

4 Set up the grill for direct grilling and preheat it to high.

KEBABS AROUND PLANET BARBECUE

★ *BROCHETTE:* France and North Africa

★ *KYINKYINGA:* West Africa

★ *KOFTA:* Middle East

★ *LULA:* Near East and Central Asia

★ *PINCHO:* Spain

★ *RAZNJICI:* Balkans

★ *SATE:* Southeast Asia

★ *SEEKH KEBAB:* India

★ *SHASHLIK:* Russia and the former Soviet Republics; Israel

★ *SOSATIE:* South Africa

★ *SPIEDINI:* Italy

★ *SOUVLAKI:* Greece

★ *YAKITORI:* Japan

5 When ready to cook, brush and oil the grill grate. Arrange the kebabs on the hot grate and grill the pork until it is sizzling, nicely browned on all sides, and cooked through, 2 to 3 minutes per side, 8 to 12 minutes in all.

6 Using tongs, slide the pieces of pork off the skewers onto plates or a platter. Serve the pork with Russian black bread (grilled if you like) and one of the suggested sauces.

South African Shish Kebabs

{ SOSATIES }

Travel the world's barbecue trail and you'll find meat on a stick almost everywhere. South Africa's version goes by its Afrikaner name: *sosatie*. Like all good Cape Malay meat dishes, it contains fruit and curry—the fruit (usually apricots) interspersed with the meat on the skewers; the curry used to flavor the marinade and sauce. Cape Malay refers to the descendants of Javanese and Malaysian slaves and indentured workers brought to Cape Town to work in shipbuilding and farming during the seventeenth through nineteenth centuries.

The *sosaties* here are based on C. Louis Leipoldt's classic version. Leipoldt was South Africa's preeminent twentieth-century food writer. You can read more about him in the box on the next page. I've made the heavy cream optional. It will give you richer *sosaties* and sauce, but the cream has an odd way of clotting until you cook it, which you may find disconcerting. Personally, I add the cream, but you'll get excellent *sosaties* without it. **SERVES 4**

A sosatie with its mix of apricot, onion, and bacon nestled between cubes of pork.

THE SCOOP

WHERE: Native to the Cape Malays of Cape Town and today enjoyed throughout South Africa

WHAT: Shish kebab South African style, which means meat with dried fruit and curry

HOW: Direct grilling

JUST THE FACTS: The traditional recipe calls for both pork and lamb. However, excellent *sosaties* can be made with either meat alone.

1 pound pork tenderloin, cut into 1-inch cubes

½ pound lamb shoulder or leg, cut into 1-inch cubes,
    or ½ pound more pork

3 to 4 tablespoons dark brown sugar

1 tablespoon plus ½ teaspoon curry powder

2 teaspoons coriander seeds

2 teaspoons black peppercorns

Coarse salt (kosher or sea)

2 cups dried apricots

1 medium-size onion, thinly sliced, plus 1 onion, peeled

4 strips orange zest (each ½ by 2 inches) removed with
    a vegetable peeler

1½ cups dry red wine

½ cup red wine vinegar

¼ cup extra-virgin olive oil

½ cup plus 2 tablespoons heavy (whipping) cream
    (optional, see Note)

3 slices of bacon, cut into 1-inch pieces

2 tablespoons (¼ stick) butter

2 tablespoons apricot jam, or more to taste

YOU'LL ALSO NEED

Flat metal or bamboo skewers; an aluminum foil grill shield
    (optional, see page 611)

ADVANCE PREPARATION

2 hours to overnight for marinating the meat

1 Place the pork and lamb in a large nonreactive bowl or baking dish. Sprinkle 2 tablespoons of the brown sugar, the 1 tablespoon of curry powder, and the coriander seeds, peppercorns, and 1½ teaspoons of salt over the meat and stir to coat. Add the apricots, the sliced onion, and the orange zest, red wine, wine vinegar, and olive oil and stir to mix. Stir in the ½ cup of cream, if using. Let the meat marinate in the refrigerator, covered, for 2 to 4 hours, turning it several times so it marinates evenly. The longer the meat marinates, the richer the flavor will be (for an even stronger wine flavor, marinate the meat overnight).

2 Meanwhile, cut the peeled onion in half crosswise, then cut each half in quarters. Break the quarters into layers.

Sosaties

"There is perhaps no other single dish that can be regarded as more genuinely Afrikaans," wrote the South African food writer C. Louis Leipoldt. Active in the 1930s and 1940s, Leipoldt was to Afrikaner cuisine what James Beard or M.F.K. Fisher were to our own. His 1945 essay on the *sosaties* prepared by his grandmother Liesbet stands as some of the finest writing on barbecue anywhere. (You can read it in English translation in his book, *Food and Wine*.) In short order he describes the ideal place to marinate the meat for *sosaties* (in the shadow of a mulberry tree), the ideal coriander to add to the marinade (weevil free), and the best type of skewers to use (hand-whittled green bamboo). Like all great food writers, Leipoldt dispensed not recipes, but the wisdom gleaned from considering cooking as a manifestation of a culture.

3 Drain the marinated meat in a large, fine-meshed strainer over a large saucepan. Remove the meat and apricots from the strainer and discard the remaining solids. Set the marinade aside. Thread the meat, apricots, onion layers, and pieces of bacon onto the skewers, alternating the ingredients and beginning and ending with a cube of meat. Refrigerate the kebabs, covered, until ready to cook.

4 Place the saucepan with the marinade over high heat, let the marinade come to a boil, and boil until thick and reduced by about one-third, 5 to 8 minutes. Whisk in the butter, apricot jam, 1 tablespoon of brown sugar, and the remaining ½ teaspoon of curry powder. If you used heavy cream in the marinade, add the remaining 2 tablespoons of cream to the sauce. Let the sauce continue to boil, whisking it until thick and richly flavored, 2 to 4 minutes longer. Taste for seasoning, adding up to 1 tablespoon more brown sugar and more apricot jam and/or salt as necessary; the sauce should be a little sweet. Pour one-quarter of the sauce into a small bowl for basting.

5 Set up the grill for direct grilling and preheat it to high.

6 When ready to cook, brush and oil the grill grate. Place the kebabs on the hot grate and grill until browned on the outside and the meat is cooked through, about 2 minutes per side, about 8 minutes in all. (If you are using bamboo skewers, you may want to slide an aluminum foil shield under the exposed ends to keep them from burning.) Use the pinch test to check for doneness (see page 612). After 4 minutes, start basting the *sosaties* with the sauce set aside for that purpose.

7 Serve the *sosaties* at once. Unskewer the kebabs onto plates and spoon some of the remaining sauce on top, serving the rest in a bowl on the side.

NOTE: In the old days, Afrikaners would add sour milk or heavy cream to the marinade for extra richness. Most younger grill masters omit it. I've made the cream optional, but I like the richness it adds.

South African Springbok or Pork Kebabs with Monkey Gland Sauce

What would South Africa be without springbok? Recognizable by its tan back, white belly, and a sort of black racing stripe running along its flank, springbok is one of the numerous varieties of gazelle you see bounding across the savannah at game reserves like Kruger National Park. The graceful creature is so popular in South Africa it has been adopted at one time or another as an emblem for South Africa's air force, national airline, and rugby team. In Cape Town or Johannesburg, bringing home springbok requires nothing more strenuous than a trip to the local butcher shop. The meat cooks to the color of pork, with a flavor that's meaty and mouth filling, but not what you'd call funky or gamey. Given the robustness of the marinade and the Monkey Gland Sauce, you could certainly substitute pork for the springbok—hence the recipe's place in the pork chapter—and still wind up with kebabs that pack a wallop of flavor. **SERVES 4**

THE SCOOP

WHERE: South Africa

WHAT: A shish kebab for game fanatics with a sweet-sour beer-based barbecue sauce reminiscent of chutney. Don't be put off by the sauce's outrageous name: Its ingredients are completely innocuous.

HOW: Direct grilling

JUST THE FACTS:
Springbok, a kind
of gazelle, is South
Africa's preferred game
meat—lighter in flavor
than venison, but more
robust than pork or veal.
All three would make
reasonable substitutes.
You can use the antelope
raised on Broken Arrow
Ranch in Texas, which can
be ordered online from
www.brokenarrowranch
.com.

FOR THE SPRINGBOK AND MARINADE

1½ pounds springbok, pork, or veal,
    cut into 1-inch cubes
2 large sweet onions
2 bay leaves
1 tablespoon black peppercorns
1 tablespoon coriander seeds
½ cup dry white wine
¼ cup extra-virgin olive oil
2 yellow bell peppers, cut into 1-inch squares
6 ounces shiitake or other flat-capped
    mushrooms, stems removed
6 ounces thick-sliced country-style bacon,
    sliced crosswise into 1-inch pieces
Monkey Gland Sauce (recipe follows)

YOU'LL ALSO NEED
Bamboo or metal skewers

ADVANCE PREPARATION
2 to 4 hours for marinating the meat

1 Place the springbok in a nonreactive mixing bowl or baking dish. Cut one of the onions in half and grate it on the large holes of a box grater or puree it in a food processor. Strain the resulting puree through a wire strainer over the springbok, pressing on the onion to extract the juices. Add the bay leaves, peppercorns, coriander seeds, white wine, and olive oil and stir to mix. Let the springbok marinate in the refrigerator, covered, for at least 2 hours or as long as overnight. The longer the meat marinates, the richer the flavor will be.

2 Cut the remaining onion in half crosswise and cut each half in quarters. Break the quarters into individual layers. Finely chop the smaller onion pieces and add them to the marinating springbok. Set the remaining pieces of onion aside.

3 Drain the cubes of meat, discarding the marinade. Thread the springbok onto skewers, alternating the cubes of meat with the pieces of onion, bell pepper, mushrooms, and bacon.

4 Set up the grill for direct grilling and preheat it to high.

5 When ready to cook, brush and oil the grill grate. Arrange the kebabs on the hot grate and grill them until golden brown on the outside and cooked to taste, 2 minutes per side, 8 minutes in all for medium-rare; 3 minutes per side, 12 minutes in all for medium. Start basting the kebabs with the Monkey Gland Sauce during the last 4 minutes of grilling. Serve the grilled kebabs at once with the remaining Monkey Gland Sauce on the side.

Monkey Gland Sauce

Do not be afraid. There are no monkey parts (glands or otherwise) in this piquant, fruity, sweet-salty condiment—a sort of liquid fruit chutney. Invented at a luxury hotel in Cape Town in the 1950s, so the story goes, and named to achieve the maximum shock value, Monkey Gland Sauce is a staple at South African *braais* (barbecues). **MAKES 1¼ CUPS**

1 tablespoon unsalted butter
1 small or ½ medium onion, diced (about ½ cup)
1 clove garlic, minced
1 teaspoon piri-piri sauce (see page 22) or
    hot paprika, or to taste
½ cup tomato sauce
3 tablespoons Worcestershire sauce

2 tablespoons Dijon mustard

1 tablespoon commercial steak sauce, preferably A.1. or
    Best of Barbecue Steak Sauce

½ cup firmly packed dark brown sugar

1 bottle (330 milliliters; about 12 ounces) lager-style beer,
    preferably a South African brand, such as Castle Lager

1 cup beef or veal stock, preferably homemade

Coarse salt (kosher or sea) and freshly ground black pepper

1 Melt the butter in a medium-size nonreactive saucepan over medium heat. Add the onion and cook until translucent but not brown, about 3 minutes, stirring with a wooden spoon. Stir in the garlic and cook for 30 seconds. Stir in the *piri-piri* sauce, tomato sauce, Worcestershire sauce, mustard, steak sauce, and brown sugar. Let the mixture simmer gently over medium heat until thick, 3 to 5 minutes.

2 Stir in the beer, increase the heat to high, and cook the sauce until it is reduced by about half, 8 to 12 minutes, stirring with the wooden spoon. Stir in the beef stock and continue cooking the sauce until it is thick and richly flavored, 4 to 6 minutes longer. Season with salt and pepper. The sauce should be highly seasoned. The sauce will keep for at least 1 week, covered, in the refrigerator.

Bacon Cheese Pork Roulade

{ ROLOVANI PUNJENI RAZNJICI }

Most grill masters enjoy their work. Some burn with such passion, their faces light with pleasure every time they approach the grill. Milica Perunovic, the Montenegrin-born chef-owner of the popular Chubura restaurant in Belgrade's old Turkish quarter (you can read more about her on page 257) has this fire. To watch her is to observe the culinary equivalent of a perpetual motion machine: lightning fast, laser focused, and able to grill a dozen dishes at once without skipping a beat. The skewers here combine two of Montenegro's favorite dishes: *rolovani* (meat roulades) and *ražnjići* (Balkan-style shish kebabs). The cheese stuffing and bacon wrapping keep even a relatively lean meat like pork tenderloin from drying out on the grill. And the bacon, cheese, pickles, and onion imbue the roulades with more flavor in a single dish than most of us hope for in a whole meal. **SERVES 4**

THE SCOOP

WHERE: Serbia

WHAT: Bacon-wrapped, cheese-filled, pork scaloppine grilled shish kebab style

HOW: Direct grilling

JUST THE FACTS: I first tasted these roulades made with pork tenderloin, but they're equally common and every bit as tasty made with butterflied chicken thighs. The closest equivalent to Serbian cheese available in North America would be Dutch Edam or Gouda. Gruyère or white cheddar would also work well.

1½ pounds pork tenderloin

Coarse salt (kosher or sea) and freshly ground black pepper

6 ounces mildly tangy cheese, such as Edam, Gouda, or
   Gruyère, cut into sticks 2 inches long and ¼ thick and wide

1 medium-size onion, thinly sliced crosswise, each slice cut in
   half then separated into layers

12 to 16 whole cornichons, or 3 to 4 sour dill pickles, each cut
   into 4 lengthwise strips

8 ounces thinly sliced smoky bacon, cut into 4-inch pieces

1 cup kajmak, clotted cream, mascarpone, or sour cream
   (optional, see Notes), for serving

YOU'LL ALSO NEED

Long flat bamboo or metal skewers

ADVANCE PREPARATION

None, but the roulades can be assembled and skewered
   up to 4 hours ahead.

1 Thinly slice the pork tenderloin sharply on the diagonal to obtain pieces that are about 3 inches long, 2 inches wide, and ⅛ inch thick; it helps to partially freeze the meat before slicing (see Notes). Season each piece of pork generously with salt and pepper.

2 Place a slice of pork on a work surface and arrange a cheese stick, a few pieces of onion, and a cornichon or some pickle strips along one of the short edges, then roll it up to form a roulade. Repeat with the remaining slices of pork, cheese, onion, and cornichons. Wrap a piece of bacon crosswise around each roulade. Skewer the roulades crosswise on flat skewers, 4 to 6 roulades to a skewer, pinning the bacon to the roulades.

3 Set up the grill for direct grilling and preheat it to medium-high. Leave one section of the grill fire-free for a safety zone.

4 When ready to cook, brush and oil the grill grate. Arrange the roulades on the hot grate and grill until the bacon and pork are browned on the outside, the meat is cooked through, and the cheese is melted, 4 to 6 minutes per side. Because you're grilling bacon, you'll likely get flare-ups. If this occurs, move the pork rolls to the safety zone.

5 Transfer the grilled roulades to a platter or plates. Remove the skewers, spoon *kajmak* over the roulades, if desired, and serve at once.

NOTES: Pound the pork slices between sheets of plastic wrap with a meat pounder or rolling pin to obtain an ⅛-inch thickness.

Kajmak is a sort of Balkan clotted cream—substitute English clotted cream, Italian mascarpone, or North American sour cream.

HOW TO PREPARE BACON CHEESE PORK ROULADE

1. *Roll the pork around the cheese, then roll the bacon around the pork.*

2. *Thread the pork roll onto the skewer, pinning the bacon to the meat.*

3. *Place the skewered rolls on the grill grate.*

4. *Grill the pork rolls until darkly browned on both sides.*

FIRE STARTERS
The Montenegrin Hurricane

BELGRADE, SERBIA

Call her "The Hurricane." That's how Milica Perunovic is known to her family, staff, and customers. Spend a half hour or so with her in the white-tiled kitchen of her busy restaurant, Chubura, and you'll see how she earned her nickname. In rapid succession Milica turns out three orders of *ćevapčići* (Serbia's fabled ground veal and pork patties—see page 322), *teleči ražnjići* (bacon-grilled veal kebabs), and *muckalica* (a fiery stew of grilled meat and Balkan pepper paste), not to mention her awe-inspiring *chubura* (a towering Serbian mixed grill platter). She does this in less than thirty minutes, a smile on her lips, and she never breaks a sweat.

Opened in 2000 and located in Belgrade's old Turkish quarter, Chubura has a rustic forty-eight-seat dining room decorated with baskets hanging from the rafters in the style of a Balkan farmhouse. Like all good Serbian grill parlors, there are two trellised terraces where you can dine outdoors in the summer. But the heart and soul of the restaurant is the grill—a sort of raised indoor fireplace, where Milica, aided by two female assistants, grills every imaginable cut of pork, veal, and Serbian forcemeat.

Born in Nikšić, Montenegro, Milica attended culinary school as a young woman, finishing her training in Belgrade. "My family loves to eat," she quips. "What other choice did I have but to learn to cook?" Chubura was her idea, and while her husband, sons, and their spouses help run the restaurant, it's clear that the marching orders come from Milica.

Working within a simple range of flavors—smoky bacon, salty ham, piquant cheese, and fiery peppers—the Montenegrin creates dishes of deep and symphonic flavor. "Everything at our restaurant is *à la carte* and *à la minute*," says Milica. "We grind our *ćevapčići* daily. We cut and stuff the meats and assemble each kebab to order. Everything we serve is fresh and local." When asked what makes a great grill master, Milica repeated a single word three times—practice. "Do what you love," she says, "and love what you do."

Milica Perunovic. Laser focused, lightning fast, and single-minded about grilling.

NAME: Milica Perunovic

TERRITORY: Born in Montenegro. Lives and works in Serbia.

CLAIM TO FAME: Chef-owner of the popular Chubura restaurant in Belgrade

SPECIALTIES: *Cevapčići,* skinless spiced mincemeat sausages. *Pljeskavica,* Balkan burgers. *Rolovani ćevapčići,* rolled mincemeat sausages stuffed with garlic, pepper, and cheese. *Rolovani punjena veśalica,* ham and cheese pork rolls. *Muckalica,* a fiery stew of grilled meat and Balkan pepper paste. And of course, the eponymous *chubura,* a towering six-meat mixed grill meant to be shared by the whole table.

PERUNOVIC SAYS:

▶ Grilling is very intuitive. You have to "feel" the fire.

▶ Know your meats. Each animal, each cut, grills differently.

▶ Be consistent. Try to build your fire, regulate your heat, and grill your meats the same way every time.

▶ Don't substitute one meat for another. Respect the integrity of the original dish.

Belgian Pork Rolls with Chutney, Mint, and Bacon

Here's a dish of stunning simplicity, requiring few ingredients to achieve flavor that roars off the plate. The recipe comes from Belgium's haute grill restaurant, Elckerlijc in Maldegem (more about the restaurant and its owner on page 430). The contrast of sweet and salty—chutney and bacon—is simultaneously universal and utterly unique. **SERVES 4 AS A MAIN COURSE**

1½ pounds pork tenderloin
Coarse salt (kosher or sea) and freshly ground
    black pepper
About ¾ cup mango chutney
1 bunch fresh mint, rinsed, shaken dry,
    and stems removed
½ pound smoky bacon, cut crosswise into
    4-inch strips

YOU'LL ALSO NEED
Wooden toothpicks

ADVANCE PREPARATION
None

1 Thinly slice the pork tenderloin crosswise sharply on the diagonal into pieces that are about 3 inches long, 2 inches wide, and ⅛-inch thick (see Note). The meat will be easier to slice if it is partially frozen first. Generously season each slice of pork with salt and pepper on both sides.

2 Spread the top of each slice of pork with some of the mango chutney. Place a mint leaf on top. Tightly roll up each pork slice, starting from one of the wider sides. Wrap a strip of bacon around each pork roll and secure it with a toothpick.

3 Set up the grill for direct grilling and preheat it to medium-high. Leave one section of the grill fire-free for a safety zone.

4 When ready to cook, brush and oil the grill grate. Place the pork rolls on the hot grate and grill them until nicely browned on the outside and cooked through, 2 to 4 minutes per side. Because you're grilling bacon, you're likely to get flare-ups. If this occurs, move the pork rolls to the safety zone to keep them from burning. Transfer the pork rolls to a platter or plates and serve.

NOTE: If necessary, pound the pork slices between sheets of plastic wrap with a meat pounder or rolling pin to obtain an ⅛-inch thickness.

Whole Hog in the Style of a Greek Island

Some food experiences are so remarkable, they stay with you forever. Such was my first bite of the spit-roasted young hog at the Phillipas Taverna on the Greek island of Kea. Phillipas Maroulis is a farmer who turned pit master for the sole reason that he wanted to ensure that the pigs and lambs from his family farm would be cooked in a way that does them justice. I'm writing these words three days after my visit so I can still conjure up the experience: the skin of the pig, normally so tough, transformed into dark, buttery wafers of crystalline crispness; the meat deeply flavorful in the way an heirloom breed like Berkshire pork is flavorful and tender enough to cut with the edge of a dinner plate (which I've actually seen done); with a faint whiff of Greek oregano, a presence you surmise more than actually taste. Then there's the fat: most of it melted out during the four hours of roasting, but there's enough left to give you the pleasure of licking something akin to hog-flavored butter off your fingertips. And so the cycle goes—wafer-crisp skin, soulful meat, buttery pork fat—until you stagger away from the table in a state of bliss, unable (but regretfully so) to eat another bite. **SERVES 18 TO 24 (THAT COMES TO 6 TO 8 OUNCES OF COOKED MEAT PER PERSON)**

Phillipas Maroulis sews a whole hog to the rotisserie spit—essential for even roasting.

Whole hogs and lambs turn on the spit at a typical Greek hasapotaverna (butcher's taverna).

⅓ cup coarse salt (kosher or sea)

⅓ cup crumbled dried Greek oregano

¼ cup coarsely ground or cracked black peppercorns

1 cup extra-virgin olive oil, preferably Greek

1 cup dry white wine, preferably Greek

1 small pig (25 to 30 pounds), gutted and dressed

2 lemons, cut in half, seeds removed, plus 4 lemons
    cut into wedges, for serving (optional)

6 bay leaves

Grilled Greek Bread with Oregano (optional, page 86),
    for serving

YOU'LL ALSO NEED

Trussing needle and heavy cotton string; baling wire or single-
    strand picture wire (optional); pliers; 20 to 30 pounds of
    charcoal; a large rotisserie; several disposable aluminum
    foil drip pans; a grill or garden hoe for raking the coals; a
    work table large enough to hold the grilled pig; and most
    important, a helper

ADVANCE PREPARATION

None, but it will take you 30 minutes or so to secure
    the pig to the spit and 5 to 6 hours to do the spit roasting.

1 Place the salt, oregano, and pepper in a small bowl and mix them well with your fingers.

2 Place the olive oil, white wine, and 2 table-spoons of the oregano rub in a deep pot or bowl and whisk to mix. Set the olive oil mixture aside; you'll use it for basting.

3 Generously season the inside of the pig with about a third of the remaining oregano rub. Place the lemon halves and bay leaves in the cavity. Season any exposed parts of the meat, like the throat, with some of the oregano rub. Secure the pig to the spit, and sew it up tight, using a trussing needle and butcher's string or wire (see the instructions, page 262). Using butcher's string or wire, tightly tie the legs to the pig, looping the string around the spit. Pig skin is tough, so a pair of pliers will help you pull the needle through.

How to Tie a Surgeon's Lock Knot

Grilling may not be brain surgery (to paraphrase a popular expression), but a lot of preparations on Planet Barbecue call for trussing birds, tying roasts into tight cylinders, fastening bacon to tenderloins, or otherwise securing with string foods that will be grilled. There are several traditional butcher's knots that are easy to use, but hard to explain. A few years ago, one of my students, Dr. John Wiley from Virginia, showed me a quick and easy surgeon's lock knot, and I've been using it ever since.

1. Loop the string over the food to be tied. Loop one end of the string over the other as though you were starting to tie your shoe.

2. Loop the same end of the string over the other end a second time—again, as though you were tying your shoe.

3. Pull the ends tight. The second loop will lock the string in place so you can make any final adjustments to the meat and achieve the tension you want.

4. Finally, tie off the two ends of the string as you would to seal a package. Cut the excess string off the ends with scissors and you're ready to go.

4 Light the charcoal and let it burn to glowing embers. Start the first batch of charcoal in a chimney starter, then add more charcoal to the fire as needed.

5 Set up the rotisserie or grill for spit roasting following the manufacturer's instructions. Place a row of aluminum foil drip pans down the center of the grill under and parallel to the spit. Arrange a row of lit charcoal on both sides of the foil pans. Mound the coals a little deeper where the shoulders and hams will be and a little shallower in the center. Note: On some rotisseries, like the SpitJack "Beast," you mound the coals on one side only.

6 When ready to cook, attach the spit to the rotisserie; this is a two-person job. Turn on the motor and spit roast the pig until the skin is a dark golden brown and crackling crisp and the meat is cooked through. Use an instant-read meat thermometer to check for doneness. The internal temperature should be 190° to 195°F in the deepest part of the shoulder and ham, but not touching the bone. Add fresh coals as needed to keep the fire going. If you are using natural lump charcoal, you can add it directly to the fire. If you are using briquettes, light them in a chimney starter first. Mound, rake out, or move the coals, using a grill hoe or a garden hoe, as needed to assure even cooking. The cooking time will vary depending on your particular pig, rotisserie, altitude, and the weather. Normally, 5 to 6 hours will do it.

7 Start basting the pig with the olive oil mixture after 1½ hours; then, baste it every 30 minutes. You can also baste the pig with the pork drippings. Sprinkle some of the oregano rub on the outside of the pig as it cooks, using about half of what remains.

8 Arrange several large cutting boards on the worktable or spread the table with butcher paper or aluminum foil. Transfer the cooked pig to the worktable, remove the spit, and let the meat rest, loosely tented with aluminum foil, for about 20 minutes. If you plan to serve the Greek Grilled Oregano Bread with the pork, this is a good time to grill it.

9 Carve the pig as described on page 263, or chop it into 2-inch chunks using a cleaver. Season the meat with the remaining oregano rub; you may not need all of it. Make sure each serving includes both meat and skin. Serve the pork with lemon wedges, if desired, and the grilled bread on the side, also if desired.

NOTE: Philippas removes the feet; I've made that optional.

Two More Ways to Go Whole Hog

Both the Germans and the Indonesians are known for grilling whole hogs. Here are their equally different but equally spectacular versions. To grill a 5 to 7 pound pork shoulder the same way, reduce the rest of the ingredients by one-third and follow the directions for spit roasting pork shoulder as detailed on pages 205 through 207. **BOTH SERVE 18 TO 24**

German Whole Hog

The *summum bonum* of German barbecue, *spanferkel* is a whole hog slathered with a spice-scented seasoning paste, spit roasted over wood, and glazed with three ingredients near and dear to any German's heart: dark, malty German beer, honey, and ginger—the flavorings in Nuremberg's beloved *lebkuchen* (gingerbread).

FOR THE WET RUB AND HOG

2 tablespoons coarse salt (kosher or sea)
2 tablespoons ground ginger
2 tablespoons curry powder
2 tablespoons ground coriander
2 tablespoons dried marjoram
2 tablespoons freshly ground black pepper
½ teaspoon cayenne pepper
¾ to 1 cup vegetable oil
1 small pig (25 to 30 pounds), gutted and dressed

FOR THE HONEY AND BEER GLAZE

8 tablespoons (1 stick) salted butter
3 tablespoons minced peeled fresh ginger
1 cup honey
1 cup dark beer

Make the wet rub by combining the salt, ground ginger, curry powder, coriander, marjoram, black pepper, and cayenne pepper in a bowl and stirring

How to Secure a Whole Hog or Lamb to a Rotisserie Spit

One of the first steps when spit roasting a whole hog (or lamb or other four-footed animal)—and the only step that's remotely tricky—is securing the animal to the spit. This is important, because a whole hog is basically hollow. If you don't secure it tightly to the spit, it will flop around. The skin will crack and the whole grilling process will look amateurish and undignified. Here's how to attach the hog to the spit securely.

1. Pass the spit through the mouth of the hog, through the cavity, and out the other end. Be sure to have one set of prongs on the spit before you pass the spit through the animal.

2. Sew the animal to the spit using a trussing needle and heavy cotton string (like butcher's string).

Starting just below the neck, push the needle through the skin on one side of the backbone into the cavity. Loop the string around the spit and push the needle back through the meat and skin and out the other side of the backbone, lining it up with the first hole. As the skin can be tough, it helps to use pliers to push and pull the needle.

3. Tightly tie off the ends of the string, pulling the meat to the spit and using a lock knot (see page 260) to secure the string.

4. Make another loop 1 inch down from the first and then another inch farther down, repeating the process until you have sewn to the spit the length of the backbone that is accessible through the cavity.

5. Place whatever flavorings you are using in the cavity of the hog. Using the trussing needle and string or wire, tightly sew the cavity closed. This seals in the flavorings and helps the hog roast more evenly.

6. Place the other set of prongs on the spit and tighten the set screws with pliers. Your beast is now ready for spit roasting.

NOTE: You can use baling wire or single-strand picture wire to secure the hog to the spit, but with wire, you need to poke holes through the skin with a needle, feed the strand of wire through the holes, then clip and twist the wire closed with pliers to secure it.

in enough oil to obtain a thick, fragrant paste. Place one-third of the wet rub in the cavity of the pig and spread it with a spatula. Spread the remaining wet rub all over the outside of the pig. (If possible, let the pig marinate in the refrigerator, covered, or in an ice-filled cooler for 12 to 24 hours.)

Shortly before you are ready to spit roast, make the glaze: Melt the butter in a heavy saucepan over medium heat. Add the fresh ginger and cook until fragrant but not brown, about 2 minutes. Stir in the honey and beer and let the mixture boil until bubbly and glazy, about 2 minutes. Set the honey and

beer glaze aside. You may need to rewarm it if the butter gets too hard.

Attach the pig to the spit and roast it as described in Steps 3 through 7 on pages 260 to 261. Start basting the pig with the honey and beer glaze after about 1½ hours, then baste it every 30 minutes. When done, transfer the pig to a worktable and remove the spit. Let the pig rest, loosely tented with aluminum foil for about 20 minutes, before carving it as described on the facing page or slicing or chopping it. Serve any remaining honey and beer glaze drizzled over the pork.

Whole Hog with Balinese Spices

Here's the roast pork that made Ibu Oka ("Grandma Oka") famous. More than thirty-five years ago, Ms. Oka started cooking *babi guling* (Balinese roast pig) in the courtyard of her home, and selling it to her neighbors. Today her granddaughter runs the business, which has morphed into an internationally renowned open-air restaurant. Home-raised hogs are seasoned with a fragrant paste of lemongrass, ginger, galangal, and turmeric. *Babi guling* is traditionally served with an aromatic long bean salad.

16 cloves garlic, coarsely chopped

8 shallots, coarsely chopped

8 stalks lemongrass, trimmed and coarsely chopped

8 to 16 small Asian chiles, such as Thai chiles, or 4 to 8 red serrano peppers, seeded and coarsely chopped

1 piece (3 inches) fresh ginger, peeled and coarsely chopped

1 piece (3 inches) fresh galangal, or more fresh ginger, peeled and coarsely chopped

¼ cup coarse salt (kosher or sea)

2 tablespoons freshly ground black pepper

1 piece (2 inches) fresh turmeric, peeled and coarsely chopped, or 1½ tablespoons ground turmeric

1 small pig (25 to 30 pounds), gutted and dressed

1 cup vegetable oil (in Bali, they'd use coconut oil)

Balinese Salad (optional, recipe follows), for serving

Place the garlic, shallots, lemongrass, chiles, ginger, galangal, if using, salt, black pepper, and turmeric, in a food processor and puree to a coarse paste. Add enough water (1 to 2 cups) to obtain a wet paste; the spice paste should have the consistency of sour cream.

Attach the pig to the spit and roast it as described in Steps 3 through 7 on pages 260 to 261, spooning some of the spice paste into the cavity of the pig and spreading the rest over any exposed meat, like the throat. Start basting the pig with the oil after about 1½ hours, then baste it every 30 minutes. You can also baste the pig with the drippings.

How to Carve a Whole Hog

To carve a small pig (25 to 30 pounds), use a chef's knife or cleaver to cut under and around each front leg to the joint and remove it from the body. Cut the leg in half (into a thigh and calf section) through the joint. Cut the meat off the bone and slice it across the grain. Next, cut off the rear legs. Cut each leg in half, then cut and slice the meat as you did the front legs. Using a cleaver, cut the body in half and then Greek-style into 2-inch sections.

To carve a larger hog, run the knife down the back on either side of the backbone, cutting through the skin and meat to the bone. Lift the skin and remove the loin. Cut it crosswise into slices. Remove the legs and carve them as described above. Cut the ribs into two-rib sections.

No matter what the size of your hog, be sure to cut the crisp skin into squares and serve it, too.

When done, transfer the pig to a worktable and remove the spit. Let the pig rest, loosely tented with aluminum foil for about 20 minutes, before carving it as described in the box above or chopping it into 2-inch chunks using a cleaver. Make sure each serving includes both meat and skin. Serve the pork with rice and the Balinese Salad, if desired.

Carrying a Balinese spit-roasted hog through the streets of Ubud, Bali, from the pit to the restaurant.

Balinese Salad

A crisp, aromatic salad traditionally accompanies *babi guling*. Jackfruit is a tropical fruit with a brassy, apricotlike flavor. Apricots make a good substitute. Long beans look like twenty-inch green beans—they're available at Asian markets, or you can use string beans or haricots verts. **SERVES 12 TO 16**

3 cups dried apricots, or 1½ pounds jackfruit
Coarse salt (kosher or sea)
1½ medium-size green or savoy cabbages
1½ pounds long beans
3 cups shredded unsweetened coconut, preferably fresh
   (see page 79)
6 to 18 Thai chiles or serrano or jalapeño peppers
1½ cups fresh lime juice, or more to taste
Generous ½ cup vegetable oil
Freshly ground black pepper

1 If you are using apricots, place them in a large bowl and add hot water to cover. Let the apricots soak for about 20 minutes, then drain them well and blot them dry with paper towels. Cut the apricots into ¼-inch-wide strips and place them in a large nonreactive mixing bowl.

If you are using jackfruit, remove the peel and any seeds and thinly slice them. Place the jackfruit in a large nonreactive mixing bowl.

2 Trim off the ends of the long beans and cut the beans into 2-inch lengths. Cook them in a large pot of rapidly boiling salted water until just tender, 4 to 6 minutes. Drain the beans in a colander, then rinse under cold running water until cool. Drain again, then pat dry with paper towels. Add them to the bowl with the apricots.

3 Core the cabbages and thinly slice them crosswise. Add it to the bowl with the fruit and long beans. Add the coconut, chiles, lime juice, and oil, but do not toss the salad. The salad can be made several hours ahead to this stage and refrigerated, covered.

4 About 15 minutes before serving, toss the salad. Taste for seasoning, adding salt and pepper to taste and more lime juice as necessary; the salad should be highly seasoned.

Lamb and Goat

In much of North America, pork rules the barbecue circuit. Among South American *asadores,* beef reigns supreme. So it may take you by surprise to learn that on any given evening, probably more fires are lit around Planet Barbecue to grill lamb (and goat) than any other meat. The grilled-lamb zone begins in West Africa, stretches east along the north and south of the Mediterranean to the Middle and Near East, through the Caucasus Mountains to Central and South Asia, then on to China, Southeast Asia, Indonesia, and all the way to Australia and New Zealand. In the New World, you find barbecued lamb in Mexico, Argentina, Brazil, and, yes, Owensboro, Kentucky (home of the world's only barbecued mutton), not to mention the Caribbean, where the lamb's nimble cousin, the goat, has been the meat of choice for generations of pit masters.

Thus, a lamb lover could literally eat his or her way around Planet Barbecue, feasting on *méchouie,* cumin- and garlic-scented roast leg of lamb, in Morocco; *brochettes d'agneau à la pâte d'arachide,* lamb kebabs grilled with peanut flour, in Burkina Faso; *Païdakia,* baby lamb chops, in Greece; and *Lucknowi champ,* mustard-scented lamb chops in India. Are you hungry yet? How about chipotle-spiced lamb *"churrasco,"* spit-roasted leg, from Sydney, Australia, or lamb chops grilled on a shovel over a campfire the way they do in the Aussie bush.

Goat may not top the charts of American grill masters (although it's definitely gaining in popularity), but the ability of this sure-footed animal to thrive in rocky, mountainous, and arid regions has endeared it to grill masters from Mexico to Bali. In the following pages, you'll find recipes for South African fruit-stuffed leg of kid and pineapple-scented goat satés from Indonesia.

Americans have long lagged behind the rest of the world in lamb consumption, eating less than three pounds per person per year. As you grill your way through this chapter, you can help improve our national average.

CLOCKWISE FROM TOP LEFT: *Grilling lamb in the Jema al Fna in Marrakech; Lamb on a shovel from the Australian outback; The "Medicine Man" (roving bartender) at Carnivore restaurant in Nairobi; Indonesian goat satés.*

Previous page: Jema al Fna—Marrakech's popular, bustling marketplace.

Spit-Roasted Lamb or Goat with Garlic and Mint

The English colonial roots of this spit-roasted leg of lamb are obvious, but Kenyans have toned down the sweetness of the traditional mint jelly, playing up the aromatic punch of garlic and mint. Here's how lamb and goat are prepared by Daniel Kiplagat, born into the Kalenjin tribe in Kenya's Great Rift Valley and today head grill master at the Carnivore in Nairobi (for more about this outrageous restaurant, see page 56). **SERVES 6 TO 8**

1 bone-in leg of lamb or young goat (4 to 5 pounds)
⅔ cup soy sauce
⅔ cup fresh lime juice
⅔ cup vegetable oil
2 teaspoons plus 1½ tablespoons coarse salt (kosher or sea)
2 teaspoons plus 1½ tablespoons cracked peppercorns or freshly ground black pepper
About 4 tablespoons (½ stick) salted butter, melted
4 cloves garlic, minced
¼ cup dried mint
Sweet-Sour Mint Sauce (optional, recipe follows), for serving

ADVANCE PREPARATION

4 hours or as long as overnight for marinating the lamb; about an hour for grilling time.

1 Prick the lamb on all sides with a fork; the holes should be about ½ inch deep (this helps the meat absorb the marinade). Place the lamb in a nonreactive baking pan just large enough to hold it.

2 Place the soy sauce, lime juice, oil, the 2 teaspoons of salt, 2 teaspoons of the cracked peppercorns, and ⅔ cup of water in a nonreactive mixing bowl and whisk to mix. Pour the marinade over the lamb, turning the leg to coat it on all sides. Let the lamb marinate in the refrigerator, covered, for at least 4 hours or as long as overnight, turning it several times so it marinates evenly. The longer the lamb marinates, the richer the flavor will be.

3 Drain the lamb, discarding the marinade. Blot the lamb dry with paper towels. If you are spit roasting the lamb, starting at the fatter end, thread the leg lengthwise on the rotisserie spit, parallel to the leg bone, using the forked prongs of the spit to hold it in place. Brush the lamb on all sides with some of the melted butter and thickly crust it with the garlic, and the mint, the remaining 1½ tablespoons of salt, and the remaining 1½ tablespoons of cracked peppercorns, pressing them onto the meat.

SPIT-ROASTED LAMB OR GOAT WITH GARLIC AND MINT | page 267

4 To grill: *If you are using a rotisserie,* set up the grill for spit roasting, following the manufacturer's instructions, and preheat the grill to medium-high. When ready to cook, attach the spit to the grill and turn on the motor.

If you are using the direct method, set up the grill for indirect grilling and preheat it to medium-high. Place the leg of lamb in the center of the grate, fat side up, over the drip pan and away from the heat and cover the grill.

5 Cook the lamb until it is crusty and darkly browned on the outside, 1 to 1¼ hours for medium-rare. Use an instant-read meat thermometer to test for doneness, inserting it into the thickest part of the leg but not touching the bone or the spit, if any. When cooked to medium-rare the internal temperature will be about 145°F. Baste the lamb often with butter and, if desired, the drippings from the lamb.

6 Transfer the grilled lamb to a platter. Loosely tent the leg with aluminum foil and let it rest for 5 to 10 minutes, then carve it. Serve the lamb with Sweet-Sour Mint Sauce, if desired.

Roasting lamb at Carnivore restaurant in Nairobi.

Sweet-Sour Mint Sauce

For generations the English have served (afflicted?) lamb with mint jelly, and while the mint oils help to neutralize the gamy flavor of mature lamb (not a problem with the mild young lamb sold in North America), the jelly has a sugary cloy that many lamb lovers find off-putting. So here's a sweet-sour mint sauce for grown-ups, jazzed up with fried garlic, ginger, and fresh mint and not in the least bit cloying. **MAKES ABOUT 1½ CUPS**

2 tablespoons (¼ stick) unsalted butter
2 cloves garlic, minced
1 tablespoon minced fresh ginger
1 tablespoon finely chopped fresh or dried mint
½ cup distilled white vinegar, or more to taste
1 cup mint jelly
1 to 2 tablespoons Worcestershire sauce
Coarse salt (kosher or sea) and freshly ground black pepper

Melt the butter in a heavy saucepan over medium-high heat. Add the garlic, ginger, and mint and cook until just beginning to brown, about 3 minutes. Increase the heat to high, add the vinegar, and let boil until reduced by half, 3 to 5 minutes. Whisk in the mint jelly and Worcestershire sauce and let the sauce simmer until thick and richly flavored, about 3 minutes. Season the sauce with salt and pepper and more vinegar as necessary; the sauce should be highly seasoned.

Fruit-Stuffed Leg of Kid, Lamb, or Impala

WHERE: South Africa

WHAT: One of the best ways I know to enjoy kid, lamb, or game for that matter—a leg stuffed with dried fruits and served with fruit chutney

HOW: Direct grilling or indirect grilling

JUST THE FACTS: Kid is baby goat, remarkable for its tender meat and mild flavor. You could also use young lamb or even a mild game meat, like impala. If you live in an area with a large Muslim or West Indian community, you should be able to find kid at a local butcher shop. Otherwise you can order it online at www.elkusa.com, or use baby lamb. (Impala are the small antelopes that you see scattering in all directions over the savannah when you're on safari. As game goes, the meat is mild and sweet.)

No trip to South Africa is complete without a bush *braai*. And one of the most luxurious places to experience this South African–style barbecue is at the Singita Lebombo Lodge in Kruger National Park. A Land Rover grinds over a bone-jarring dirt road to a sort of natural amphitheatre ringed by huge boulders and illuminated by flickering torchlight. Belying this rustic setting are the tables draped with white cloths and set with china plates and wineglasses. Afrikaner chef Nico Pretorius has been working for hours grilling both game and domestic meats. The fare coming off his charcoal-burning barrel grill may not be better than what you'd get at any first-rate South African *braai*—it just tastes that way, seasoned by the fresh air and enjoyed in this primal setting. Like much South African barbecue, the following dish reflects the Afrikaners' fondness for mixing sweet and savory flavors, fruit and meat—first in the dried fruit stuffing, then in the chutney served by way of a sauce. After dinner, locals and staff gather around a huge campfire to sing the sort of a cappella music popularized by groups like Ladysmith Black Mambazo. It's a night on Planet Barbecue you'll not soon forget. **SERVES 6 TO 8**

1 tablespoon butter

3 slices of bacon (about 3 ounces), cut crosswise into ¼-inch strips

¾ cup diced dried apricots (¼-inch dice)

¼ cup diced dried apples (¼-inch dice)

¼ cup diced dried pears, or more dried apples (¼-inch dice)

3 tablespoons raisins or currants

¾ cup dried bread crumbs, preferably homemade

½ to 1 cup chicken stock, preferably homemade

Coarse salt (kosher or sea) and freshly ground black pepper

1 bone-in leg of kid, young lamb, or impala (3 to 4 pounds), butterflied and boned (see Note)

3 tablespoons extra-virgin olive oil, for basting

Apricot Chutney (recipe follows)

YOU'LL ALSO NEED
Butcher's string

ADVANCE PREPARATION
None, but allow an hour or so for making the stuffing and grilling the meat.

1 Melt the butter in a large skillet over medium-high heat. Add the bacon and cook it until golden brown, 3 to 5 minutes, stirring often. Pour off all but 2 tablespoons of fat. Add the apricots, apples, pears, and raisins to the skillet and cook until lightly browned, about 3 minutes. Stir in the bread crumbs and cook until lightly browned, about 3 minutes. Add ½ cup of chicken stock, or enough stock to make the stuffing moist. Cook the stuffing until it is thick enough to hold together, 5 to 8 minutes. Season the stuffing with salt and pepper to taste; it should be highly seasoned. Let it cool to room temperature.

2 Place the butterflied leg on a work surface and open it up. Generously season the inside of the leg with salt and pepper. Spoon the stuffing on top of one side and fold the other half over the stuffing to reform the leg. Tie the leg closed with butcher's string. Generously season the outside of the leg with salt and pepper.

3 To grill: There are two options for grilling the leg: the direct method, as is done at Singita Lebombo Lodge, and the indirect method.

If you are grilling using the direct method, set up the grill for two-zone grilling (see page 611). Preheat one zone to medium and one zone to medium-low. When ready to cook, brush and oil the grill grate. Place the stuffed leg on the hot grate, fat side down, and grill it until the outside is brown and crusty and the inside is cooked to taste, about 1 hour for medium-rare; about 1½ hours for medium. Turn the leg halfway through grilling, or as needed. If it is browning too quickly, move it to the cooler side of the grill.

If you are grilling using the indirect method, set up the grill for indirect grilling, place a large drip pan in the center, and preheat the grill to medium. When ready to cook, place the stuffed leg, fat side up, in the center of the grate over the drip pan and away from the heat. Cover the grill and cook the leg until it is cooked to taste, about 1 hour for medium-rare, 1½ hours for medium. With indirect grilling, there is no need to turn the leg as it grills.

4 Use an instant-read meat thermometer to test for doneness, inserting it deep into the thickest part of the leg. When cooked to medium-rare the internal temperature should be about 145°F; medium will be about 160°F. Start basting the meat with olive oil after 20 minutes and baste it every 10 to 15 minutes.

5 Transfer the grilled leg to a cutting board, tent it loosely with aluminum foil, and let it rest for 10 minutes. Remove and discard the string and cut the leg crosswise into ¼-inch-thick slices and serve it with the Apricot Chutney.

NOTE: Butterflying means cutting open the leg of kid (or lamb, or impala) lengthwise through the side to remove the bone. To butterfly the leg, place it flat on a cutting board and, holding your knife so the blade is parallel to the cutting board, cut through one side to the bone. Then cut around the bone, cutting almost to the other side. Open the leg like a book and remove the bone. You can also ask the butcher to do this for you.

Larger than life: safari sight in South Africa.

Apricot Chutney

The Portuguese, Dutch, and English settlers of South Africa had at least one thing in common gastronomically speaking—a love of fruit preserves, jams, and chutneys. Even today, no South African *braai* would be complete without a spread of fruit jams and jellies served as condiments for the meats. This recipe makes more chutney than you'll need for the kid, but it keeps well and will definitely go to use at another barbecue with other grilled meats. **MAKES ABOUT 4 CUPS**

2 tablespoons vegetable oil

3 cloves garlic, thinly sliced crosswise

1 small onion, diced

1 tablespoon minced peeled fresh ginger or
    1 tablespoon minced candied ginger

1 tablespoon chopped fresh rosemary

½ teaspoon curry powder, or more to taste

12 ounces dried apricots, diced

1 can (14½ ounces) good-quality diced tomatoes,
    with their juices

¼ cup firmly packed brown sugar, or more to taste

¼ cup red wine vinegar, or more to taste

1 tablespoon Worcestershire sauce, or more to taste

1 bay leaf

1 Heat the oil in a small saucepan over medium heat. Add the garlic and cook until golden brown, about 2 minutes; do not let it burn. Pour the garlic oil through a strainer into a large nonreactive saucepan. Drain the fried garlic on paper towels and set it aside.

2 Add the onion, ginger, rosemary, and curry powder to the saucepan with the garlic oil and cook over medium heat until the onion is lightly browned. Stir in the apricots, tomatoes with their juices, brown sugar, wine vinegar, Worcestershire sauce, bay leaf, and 1 cup of water. Let the chutney simmer until thick and jamlike, about 30 minutes, stirring often with a wooden spoon. Add more water as needed to keep the mixture moist. You can start cooking the chutney at a higher heat to evaporate the excess liquid. As the chutney thickens, you'll need to lower the heat to medium, then to low; do not let the chutney burn. Taste for sweetness adding more brown sugar, wine vinegar, Worcestershire sauce, and/or curry as necessary; the chutney should be sweet, sour, and highly aromatic. Remove and discard the bay leaf, then transfer the chutney to clean sterile jars. The South African way to serve the chutney at a barbecue is with a spoon right out of the jar.

Méchoui of Lamb or Goat with Berber Spices

Call him Mr. Mayor. Almost everyone else in Marrakech and Fez does if they are even remotely involved with the food or hospitality business. I'm talking about Rafih Benjelloun, the Fez-born chef with a bigger than life personality who runs the Imperial Fez and Ibiza restaurants in Atlanta, Georgia. Rafih was my go-to guy when I planned my research trip to Morocco, and if you read about Moroccan "sliders" (page 317), chicken kebabs in the style of Fez (page 394), or the Marrakech grill master, Haj Brik (page 276), well, Rafih was the guy who made sure I visited the right place at the right time. So when it comes to the big kahuna, the pièce de résistance of Moroccan grilling, barbecued lamb, I can think of no better guide than Rafih. In keeping with his Fez roots, he takes a two-step approach, studding the lamb with onion, garlic, and ginger then basting it with what he calls the "mother of all Moroccan sauces": a sort of garlic, cumin, and cilantro vinaigrette called *charmoula*. Here's how Rafih prepares lamb at his farm outside Marrakech. There, of course, he'd probably roast a whole lamb. **SERVES 8 TO 10**

FOR THE LAMB

1 bone-in leg of lamb or young goat (4 to 5 pounds)

1 medium-size white onion, cut in half crosswise, each half into 3 wedges

4 cloves garlic, peeled and cut lengthwise into 4 or 5 slices

1 piece (1 inch) fresh ginger, peeled and cut crosswise into thin slices, each slice cut in half

Coarse salt (kosher or sea) and freshly ground black pepper

FOR THE CHARMOULA

1 medium-size onion, coarsely chopped

3 cloves garlic, coarsely chopped

1 piece (2 inches) fresh ginger, peeled and coarsely chopped

½ cup finely chopped fresh cilantro or flat-leaf parsley

3 tablespoons sweet or smoked paprika

2 teaspoons coarse salt (kosher or sea), or more to taste

2 teaspoons ground cumin

1 teaspoon freshly ground black pepper, or more to taste

1 cup extra-virgin olive oil

YOU'LL ALSO NEED

2 cups oak chips or chunks (optional), soaked for 1 hour in water to cover, then drained

ADVANCE PREPARATION

None, but allow a couple of hours of grilling time.

1 Prepare the leg of lamb: Using a sharp chef's knife, deeply score the leg of lamb on all sides in a crosshatch pattern. The cuts should be about 1 inch deep and 2 inches apart. Break the onion wedges into individual layers. Insert the pieces of onion and the slices of garlic and ginger into the cuts made by the scoring, pushing each in as deeply as possible. Generously season the leg of lamb on all sides with salt and pepper.

2 Make the *charmoula:* Place the chopped onion, garlic, and ginger in a heavy mortar and pound them to a paste with a pestle. Add the cilantro, paprika, salt, cumin, and pepper and pound them into a paste. Work in the olive oil and enough water to obtain a thick but pourable sauce (about 1½ cups). If you don't have a mortar and pestle, puree the onion, garlic, and ginger in a food processor, followed by the cilantro, paprika, salt, cumin, and pepper, then work in the olive oil and water. Taste the *charmoula* for seasoning, adding more salt and/or pepper as necessary; it should be highly seasoned. Transfer the *charmoula* to a saucepan and let it simmer over medium heat until richly flavored, about 5 minutes.

3 To grill: *If you are grilling using the indirect method,* set up the grill for indirect grilling, place a large drip pan in the center, and preheat the grill

HOW TO MAKE MECHOUI

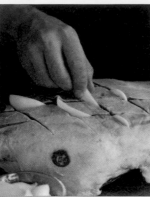

1. *Score the leg of lamb by making a series of deep incisions in a crosshatch pattern.*

2. *Insert onion, garlic, and ginger slices into the cuts, pushing them deep into the meat.*

3. *Baste the lamb with the charmoula as it roasts on the rotisserie.*

Mechoui of lamb the way we like it, spice-blasted, crusty, and moist.

to medium. When ready to cook, if you are using wood chips or chunks, toss them on the coals of a charcoal grill or, if you are using a gas grill, add the chips or chunks to the smoker box or place them in a smoker pouch under the grate (see page 603). Place the leg of lamb, fat side up, in the center of the grate over the drip pan and away from the heat. Cover the grill and cook the lamb until it is sizzling and dark golden brown, depending upon the grill and the size of the leg of lamb, 1½ to 2¼ hours.

If you are using a rotisserie, set up the grill for spit roasting, following the manufacturer's instructions, and preheat the grill to medium-high. Place a large drip pan under the spit. Starting at the fatter end, thread the leg of lamb lengthwise on the rotisserie spit, parallel to the leg bone, using the forked prongs of the spit to hold it in place. When ready to cook, attach the spit to the grill and turn on the motor. Spit roast the lamb until it is sizzling and dark golden brown, depending on the grill and the size of the leg of lamb, 1¼ to 2 hours.

4 Use an instant-read meat thermometer to test for doneness, inserting it into the thickest part of the leg but not touching the bone or the spit, if any. When cooked to well-done the internal temperature should be 190° to 195°F. (Moroccans prefer their lamb well-done.) After 30 minutes, start basting the lamb all over with the *charmoula,* basting it every 20 minutes. If you are using a charcoal grill, you'll need to add fresh coals after the lamb has grilled for an hour.

5 Transfer the grilled lamb to a platter. Loosely tent the leg with aluminum foil and let it rest for 5 to 10 minutes. Strain the lamb drippings into what remains of the *charmoula* sauce. Bring the *charmoula* to a boil and let boil until slightly thickened and richly flavored, 3 to 5 minutes.

6 Carve the lamb so that each person gets pieces with both meat and the outside crust. Spoon the *charmoula* on top and serve at once.

MECHOUI OF LAMB OR GOAT WITH BERBER SPICES | page 272

FIRE STARTERS

Father Barbecue

HASSAN BIN BRIK— a legend of Moroccan grilling.

MARRAKECH, MOROCCO

The locals call him "grand-father," as in the grandfather of Marrakech grilling. Hassan Bin Brik—known respectfully as Haj Brik—is the wizened man with a white skullcap you'll find behind the cash register, overseeing the flaming grill, scurrying waiters, and jostling customers, just as he has for the last sixty years. Welcome to the epicenter of Marrakech grilling on Bani Marine Street, just outside the old city walls.

> "There isn't a grill cook in Marrakech who didn't learn his craft directly or indirectly from Haj Brik."

Like many of the grill masters profiled in *Planet Barbecue!*, Haj Brik got his start behind a pushcart. The year was 1946; Morocco was just starting to recover from the war; and Haj Brik's *merguez,* grilled, spicy Moroccan sausage, found a ready clientele among the French and the locals. He saved a few dirhams each day and a decade later, he was able to acquire a storefront on Bani Marine Street. He lined the tiny dining room, also called Haj Brik, with blue-and-white tiles, installing additional seating in the mezzanine as business grew. To keep priorities straight, he hung the meats in the window and positioned his charcoal-burning grill in a brick hearth in the front of the restaurant, right by the entryway for everyone to see.

Now, as in the old days, the lamb, beef, or ground meat for each order is weighed on an old-fashioned balance scale. Now, as then, each *kofta* (ground meat patty) or *brochette* is seasoned and hand shaped to order. The restaurant still reverberates with the thump, thump of the heavy meat cleaver used to pound lamb chops to the thickness of poker chips. The grill jockeys, dressed in white jackets and caps, still oil the wire grates with a lump of beef fat. The tomato salad and onion-parsley relish continue to be made fresh several times each mealtime.

Haj Brik is the sort of place where you eat elbow to elbow with strangers at communal tables set with brown cloths, bowls of spicy black olives, and baskets of Moroccan bread. Each guest receives tiny bowls of cumin and salt for seasoning the meat, plus *harissa,* a Moroccan sauce hot enough to measure your tolerance for chile hellfire. If the formula sounds familiar, don't be surprised: According to the man sitting next to me, a regular here for twenty years, "There isn't a grill cook in Marrakech who didn't learn his craft directly or indirectly from Haj Brik."

Haj Brik, grandfather of Moroccan grilling, stands at his charcoal-fired brick hearth.

NAME: Hassan Bin Brik

TERRITORY: Marrakech, Morocco

CLAIM TO FAME: Founder of the first grill parlor in Marrakech

SPECIALTIES: *Kofta,* lamb burgers; *brochettes,* shish kebab; *côtelettes d'agneau,* wafer-thin, crusty grilled lamb chops

BIN BRIK SAYS:

▶ What does it take to succeed in the barbecue business? Cleanliness. Confidence. Hard work. And of course, the grace of Allah.

▶ Don't cook by eyeballing. Here at Haj Brik, we measure each portion of meat to the gram.

Australian Chipotle-Glazed Lamb "Churrasco"

ustralian grilling embraces literally dozens of international influences and nowhere is this more apparent than at Sydney's stunning restaurant Wildfire. Where else would you find a South American–style *churrascaria* (chophouse) that specializes in Australian meats and seafood electrified with New Mexican seasonings, and grilled or spit roasted over blazing wood in a harbor-front setting that will take your breath away? (The Sydney Opera House looms on the horizon almost close enough to touch.) No surprise here: Wildfire originated with American Southwestern culinary visionary Mark Miller, of Coyote Cafe and Red Sage fame, which explains the smoky heat of this spit-roasted lamb, marinated with chipotle chiles, toasted cumin, and sherry vinegar. It's a long way from Santa Fe to Sydney, but this crusty, smoky, spice-scented lamb warrants the journey. You need a big wine to stand up to this baby: An Australian shiraz from the Barossa Valley would be terrific. **SERVES 6 TO 8**

THE SCOOP

WHERE: Sydney, Australia

WHAT: Leg of lamb spit roasted with a fiery paste of chipotle chiles, grilled garlic, and sherry vinegar

HOW: Spit roasting or indirect grilling, plus direct grilling for the peppers and garlic

JUST THE FACTS: You have two options for the lamb: You can use a bone-in leg, which looks great for carving but is a little difficult to put on the spit, or a butterflied boned leg of lamb, which you can roll into a cylindrical roast and carve into round slices.

2 poblano peppers

8 unpeeled garlic cloves, skewered on wooden toothpicks

1 teaspoon Szechuan peppercorns

1 teaspoon cumin seeds

1 teaspoon caraway seeds

1 bunch fresh thyme

2 to 3 canned chipotle peppers with their juices

½ cup sherry vinegar or red wine vinegar

Coarse salt (kosher or sea) and cracked black pepper

1 bone-in leg of lamb (4 to 5 pounds), or 1 butterflied (boneless) leg of lamb (3 to 4 pounds)

3 to 4 tablespoons extra-virgin olive oil for basting

YOU'LL ALSO NEED
Butcher's string

ADVANCE PREPARATION
4 hours or as long as overnight for marinating the lamb and allow 20 minutes for grilling and preparing the poblano peppers and 1 to 1½ hours for grilling the lamb.

1 Set up the grill for direct grilling and preheat it to high.

2 When ready to cook, brush and oil the grill grate. Place the poblanos on the hot grate and grill them until charred and black on all sides, 3 to 4 minutes per side, 9 to 12 minutes in all, turning with tongs. Transfer the grilled poblanos to a cutting board and let them cool.

3 Place the garlic on the hot grate and grill it until the skins are charred and the garlic is partially cooked, about 2 minutes per side. Transfer the grilled garlic to the cutting board and let it cool.

4 Scrape the burned skin off the poblanos, seed them, and cut them into 1-inch pieces. Don't worry about removing every last bit of black skin; a few burnt bits will add color and flavor. Peel the garlic. You can grill the poblanos and garlic a day ahead of time.

5 Heat a dry cast-iron skillet on the grill or over medium heat on the stove (do not use a nonstick frying pan). Toast the Szechuan peppercorns, cumin seeds, and caraway seeds until fragrant, about 3 minutes, shaking the pan. Do not let them burn. Transfer the toasted spices to a heatproof bowl to cool, then grind them to a fine powder in a spice mill.

6 Strip about 1 tablespoon of leaves from the bunch of thyme and add them to the ground toasted spices. Using butcher's string, tie the remaining thyme into a bunch to make a basting brush and set it aside.

7 Place the grilled poblanos and garlic, the ground spices and thyme, and the chipotles with their juices in a food processor and process to a smooth paste. Work in the sherry vinegar, then season with salt and black pepper to taste; the spice paste should be highly seasoned.

8 Using the tip of a paring knife, make a series of slits in the leg of lamb on all sides, each about ½ inch deep x ½ inch wide, and 1 inch apart. Place the lamb in a large nonreactive roasting pan just large enough to hold it and spread the spice paste over it on all sides, forcing the paste into the slits in the meat. Let the lamb marinate, in the refrigerator covered, for at least 4 hours or as long as overnight; the longer it marinates, the richer the flavor will be.

9 If you are using a butterflied leg of lamb, roll it into a tight cylinder and tie it with butcher's string.

10 To grill: *If you are using a rotisserie,* set up the grill for spit-roasting, following the manufacturer's instructions, and preheat to medium-high. If you are grilling a bone-in leg of lamb, starting at the fatter end, thread the leg lengthwise onto the rotisserie spit, parallel to the leg bone. If you are grilling a butterflied leg of lamb, thread it lengthwise onto the spit. Use the forked prongs of the spit to hold the leg in place. When ready to cook, attach the spit to the grill and turn on the motor.

If you are grilling using the indirect grilling method, set up the grill for indirect grilling, place a large drip pan in the center, and preheat the grill to medium. When ready to cook, place the leg of lamb, fat side up, in the center of the grate over the drip pan and away from the heat and cover the grill.

11 Cook the lamb until it is crusty and darkly browned on the outside and done to taste, 1 to 1¼ hours for medium-rare, 1½ hours for medium for a bone-in leg of lamb; about 1 hour for medium-rare, about 1¼ hours for medium for a butterflied leg of lamb. Use an instant-read meat thermometer to test for doneness, inserting it into the thickest part of the leg but not touching the bone or spit, if any. When done to medium-rare the internal temperature will be about 145°F; medium lamb will be about 160°F. Baste the lamb often with olive oil, using the bunch of thyme as a basting brush. If you are using a charcoal grill, you'll need to add fresh coals after the lamb has grilled for an hour.

12 Transfer the lamb to a platter. Loosely tent the leg with aluminum foil and let rest for 5 to 10 minutes, then carve it.

Beer-Marinated Lamb Steaks Grilled over Herbs and Spices

Ifirst met Peter De Clercq at SPOGA, the giant barbecue and outdoor living trade show held annually in Cologne, Germany. The next thing I knew, I was dining in his restaurant, Elckerlijc, in Maldegem, Belgium. For despite the fact that I couldn't think of a single Belgian grilled dish—traditional or otherwise—I was convinced I would be in the hands of a master. Peter lived up to my expectations, leaving no fire unlit or meat unmarinated or unbasted in his quest to harness live fire to boost flavor. The following recipe is pure Peter: Start with traditional Belgian flavorings, like mustard and beer, then borrow a technique from a neighboring grill culture, like France (in this case, the practice of tossing dried herbs on the fire), to create a dish equally striking for its simplicity and bold flavors. Depending on the dish he is preparing, Peter might toss olive pits, grapevines, wood chips, or grilling spices on the embers: whatever it takes to create a fragrant smoke to flavor the meat. (You can read more about Peter on page 430.) **SERVES 4**

1½ pounds lamb steaks, or 2 pounds rib lamb chops (½ to ¾ inch thick)
¼ cup whole-grain mustard
¼ cup finely chopped onion
2 cloves garlic, minced
2 tablespoons chopped fresh rosemary
1 cup wheat beer (see Note)
2 tablespoons fresh lemon juice
3 tablespoons extra-virgin olive oil
1½ cups veal or beef stock, preferably homemade
½ cup heavy (whipping) cream
Coarse salt (kosher or sea) and freshly ground black pepper
Fire Spices (recipe follows)

ADVANCE PREPARATION
At least 4 hours or as long as overnight for marinating the lamb.

Belgian grill master Peter De Clercq in front of one of his charcoal paintings.

1 Arrange the lamb in a nonreactive baking dish just large enough to hold it in a single layer.

2 Place the mustard, onion, garlic, and rosemary in a mixing bowl and whisk to mix. Gradually whisk in the beer, lemon juice, and 2 tablespoons of the olive oil. Pour the marinade over the lamb, turning it a couple of times to coat. Let the lamb marinate in the refrigerator, covered, for at least 4 hours or as long as overnight; the longer it marinates, the richer the flavor will be.

3 Remove the lamb from the marinade and dry with paper towels. Place the marinade in a large heavy saucepan and bring it to a boil over high heat. Let the marinade boil until only ¼ cup of liquid remains, 5 to 8 minutes. Add the veal stock and cream and let boil until the mustard and beer sauce is reduced by half, 5 to 8 minutes. Season the sauce with salt and pepper to taste; it should be highly seasoned. Strain the sauce into a bowl for serving and set it aside.

4 Set up the grill for direct grilling and preheat it to high.

5 When ready to cook, brush and oil the grill grate. Brush the lamb steaks with the remaining 1 tablespoon of olive oil and season them generously with salt and pepper. Toss the Fire Spices on the grill and immediately arrange the steaks on the hot grate. Grill the lamb until cooked to taste, 3 to 4 minutes per side for medium-rare, giving each steak a quarter turn after 1½ minutes to create a handsome crosshatch of grill marks. Use the poke test to check for doneness (see page 612).

6 Transfer the grilled lamb to a platter or plates and serve it at once with the mustard-beer sauce on the side for spooning on top.

NOTE: Wheat beer (*witbier* in Flemish; *bière blanche* in French) is a refreshing, mild-flavored brew made with a significant percentage of malted wheat. It's especially popular in Belgium in the spring and summer. One good brand is Hoegaarden. You could certainly substitute a *weissbier* from Germany or the United States.

Fire Spices

Inspired by the Provençal practice of tossing rosemary bunches or fennel fronds on the fire when French grill jockeys grill fish, Peter De Clercq contrived a spice blend unique in the annals of grilling. It's unique because you put the seasonings on the fire, not on the meat, which creates an aromatic smoke that subtly perfumes the food. Here's a homemade version of a commercial blend Peter sells in Europe. **MAKES 1½ CUPS**

¼ cup coriander seeds
¼ cup juniper berries
¼ cup dried rosemary
¼ cup crumbled bay leaves
¼ cup dried oregano
¼ cup dried thyme

Combine the coriander seeds, juniper berries, rosemary, bay leaves, oregano, and thyme in a large bowl and stir to mix. Transfer the mixed spices to a 1 pint jar with a secure lid. The Fire Spices will keep stored away from heat and light for several months. To use the Fire Spices, toss a couple of handfuls directly on the coals, or on the flavorizer bars, ceramic bricks, or lava stones of a gas grill, immediately prior to putting on the meat, adding more when you turn the meat.

Mentioning the Unmentionables

Spend enough time on the world's barbecue trail and you'll see just about everything cooked on the grill, including many foods you likely won't find in North America. Here are some of the odder dishes I have experienced on Planet Barbecue.

ARGENTINA AND URUGUAY

Choto: Coiled grilled lamb small intestines

Chinchulin: Grilled chitterlings

Morcilla: Grilled blood sausage

GREECE

Kokoretsi: Sheep liver, lungs, spleen, heart, and so on, all wrapped in the small intestines of the lamb and spit roasted on the rotisserie

MOROCCO

Rate: Sheep spleen, stuffed with garlic and parsley and then grilled

PHILIPPINES

Sisig: Pig's nose, ears, and cheeks first boiled in water, then grilled over coals until darkly browned. Everything is chopped small and simmered in a sauce of onions, lemons and chiles, then served on a sizzling hot plate.

Here are some dishes you'll find at Filipino street corner grill stalls. All are grilled on and eaten off bamboo skewers and served with a vinegar-soy dipping sauce like the one found on page 356.

"Adidas": Grilled chicken feet

"Betamax": Grilled rectangles of cooked chicken blood

"Helmets": Grilled chicken heads

"IUDs": Grilled chicken's intestines; their coiled shape is said to resemble a birth control device

"PAL": Short for Philippines Airlines, "PALS" are grilled chicken wings

"Walkman": Grilled pig ears

Wrapping skewered lamb innards to make the strangest dish on Planet Barbecue: Greek kokoretsi.

Moroccan Lamb Chops with Harissa and Cumin

Order a mixed grill at a typical Marrakech grill joint and you'll be treated to lamb's lights (lungs), liver, kidney, heart, and yes, lamb chops. I'm betting you'll push the organ meats around your plate with your fork. The chops are another story, however, pounded thin with a heavy cleaver and grilled sizzling and crisp over a screaming-hot fire. The result is more akin to a lamb crackling than to the thick, meaty, rare or pink lamb chops we like to serve in North America, chops just perfect for dipping in the fiery Moroccan tomato sauce called *harissa*. Here's how they grill lamb chops at Marrakech's landmark grill parlor Haj Brik (you can read more about the

THE SCOOP

WHERE: Marrakech, Morocco

WHAT: Lamb chops pounded thin, grilled until crisp, and served with a fiery, Moroccan fresh tomato sauce

HOW: Direct grilling

JUST THE FACTS:
Moroccans would use thin, well-marbled chops cut from the lamb neck. Rib chops come the closest to these in North America. Preserved lemon is a sort of pickle made by curing the fresh fruit in salt. Taste it once and you will always want to keep some of this tart, salty, and incredibly potent condiment on hand. You can buy preserved lemon in jars at specialty food shops and North African markets or make your own following the simple recipe on this page; you'll need to allow one week for the lemons to pickle.

restaurant on page 276). When you eat the chops, it's customary to season the lamb again with salt and cumin from tiny spice bowls at the table before you take a bite. **SERVES 4**

FOR THE HARISSA

2 large or 3 medium-size luscious,
 ripe red tomatoes
1 tablespoon minced preserved lemon
 (optional, recipe follows)
1 to 3 teaspoons red hot pepper flakes or
 hot paprika
¼ teaspoon ground cumin
2 tablespoons vegetable oil
Coarse salt (kosher or sea) and freshly
 ground black pepper

FOR THE LAMB

1½ pounds thin lamb shoulder chops or
 rib chops (about ½ inch thick)
Coarse salt (kosher or sea) and freshly
 ground black pepper
Ground cumin
2 tablespoons vegetable oil, for basting

ADVANCE PREPARATION
The harissa can be prepared up to
 4 hours ahead.

1 Make the *harissa:* Cut each tomato in half widthwise. Starting with the cut side, grate the tomatoes on the coarse holes of a box grater into a large mixing bowl. Discard the skin. Stir in the preserved lemon, if using, and the hot pepper flakes, cumin, and 2 tablespoons of oil. Season the *harissa* with salt and black pepper to taste (you won't need much salt if you are using preserved lemon. You should have 1½ to 2 cups. The *harissa* can be made up to 4 hours ahead of time and refrigerated, covered. Let the *harissa* come to

room temperature before serving, then divide it among 4 small bowls.

2 Prepare the lamb: Using the side of a heavy cleaver or a scaloppine pounder, pound the meat of each lamb chop to a thickness of ¼ inch. Season the lamb on both sides with salt, black pepper, and cumin.

3 Set up the grill for direct grilling and preheat it to high.

4 When ready to cook, brush and oil the grill grate. Arrange the lamb chops on the hot grate and grill them until nicely browned and crisp on the outside and cooked to medium to medium-well done, 2 to 4 minutes per side, basting them with oil. (Moroccans prefer their lamb medium to medium-well done.) Use the poke test to check for doneness (see page 612).

5 Transfer the grilled lamb chops to a platter or plates. To eat, sprinkle the lamb chops with more salt and cumin, then dip them in the *harissa* or spoon the *harissa* over them.

Preserved Lemon

Preserved lemon is one of the most intense flavors on Planet Barbecue. Cross a fresh lemon with a cornichon or a really strong dill pickle and you'll start to get the idea. It's hard to think of a marinade, sauce, relish, salad, or other dish that wouldn't benefit from its addition. **MAKES 1 PINT**

2 large or 3 medium-size juicy lemons
½ cup coarse salt (kosher or sea)

LAMB AND GOAT 283

1 Scrub each lemon with a brush under hot water. Cut each lemon in half crosswise and cut each half in quarters. Remove any seeds with a fork.

2 Place the lemons and salt in a nonreactive mixing bowl and toss to mix. Transfer the mixture to a clean sterile canning jar, scraping the salt and juices into it with a spatula.

3 Let the lemons pickle in the refrigerator for 1 week, stirring them every day or so to make sure all of the pieces are coated with salt. Preserved lemons will keep for several months in the refrigerator—if, of course, they stay around that long.

Australian Lamb on a Shovel

I first heard about this singular dish in an irate e-mail—the sort you normally dispose of in your junk box. It was sent by a barbecue buff from a country better known for the civility of its public discourse, Australia. The author, however, had a valid point: In all of the writing I've done about grilling around the world, I've never mentioned a technique used by generations of Australians living and cooking in the bush: grilling meats on a shovel over an open campfire. The meat sizzles on the metal blade, a little like a South American *chapa* (a flat piece of cast iron; see page 365), perfumed by the fragrant swirls of wood smoke. The seasonings are kept to a bare minimum: salt, maybe pepper. That's it. The outdoor setting, the picturesque technique, the fresh air and wood smoke are considered condiments enough. Of course, when it comes to grilling lamb, garlic and rosemary are never out of place, so I give you the option of including them. As for the lamb, well, you could do far worse than the sweet, mild-flavored lamb for which Australia is so rightfully famous. **SERVES 4**

1½ pounds thick-cut rib or loin lamb chops (1 to 1½ inches thick)

1 to 2 tablespoons extra-virgin olive oil, plus olive oil for serving (optional)

Coarse salt (kosher or sea) and cracked black pepper

3 cloves garlic, finely chopped (optional)

1 to 2 tablespoons finely chopped fresh rosemary (optional)

Lemon wedges (optional), for serving

YOU'LL ALSO NEED
Logs, wood chips, or wood chunks (for a more pronounced smoke flavor, soak the wood chips or chunks in water to cover for 30 minutes, then drain them)

ADVANCE PREPARATION
None

1 Lightly brush the lamb chops on both sides with olive oil. Season them very generously on both sides with salt and pepper and the garlic and rosemary, if desired.

2 Set up the grill for direct grilling and preheat it to high. If you are using a charcoal grill and want to use logs, place them on the coals.

How to Grill Lamb on a Shovel

Here's how to grill lamb chops the way they do in the Outback. First of all, you'll need a clean metal shovel. Then, build a wood campfire with a good base of glowing embers. Feed fresh logs to the fire from time to time to generate plenty of wood smoke. Heat the shovel blade in the fire. This serves two purposes: It helps clean and sterilize the cooking surface and preheats the metal, so it will sear the meat.

After brushing the lamb chops with olive oil and seasoning them with salt, pepper, and garlic and rosemary, if desired, arrange the chops on the hot shovel blade, leaving an inch between each. Don't overcrowd the shovel—it's OK to work in several batches. Remember, in Australia grilling isn't just about getting a meal to the table, it's a whole evening's entertainment. Thrust the shovel over the fire or lay it on the embers. Cook the chops until done to taste, 4 to 6 minutes per side for medium-rare, turning them with tongs. Don't forget to burn the fat and juices off the shovel when you're finished.

3 When ready to cook, if you are using a charcoal grill and wood chips or chunks, toss them on the coals. If you are using a gas grill, add the wood chips or chunks to the smoker box or place them in a smoker pouch under the grate (see page 603). Brush and oil the grill grate. Arrange the lamb chops on the hot grate and grill them until done to taste, 4 to 6 minutes per side for medium-rare. Use the poke test to check for doneness (see page 612).

4 Transfer the grilled chops to a platter or plates. If desired, drizzle a little more olive oil over the chops and serve them with lemon wedges.

Indispensible for a Down Under grill session: Heat Beads, Australia's top-selling charcoal.

THE SCOOP

JUST THE FACTS: To be strictly authentic, you'd cook the lamb on the blade of a clean metal shovel over a wood fire. The wood smoke subtly flavors the lamb and the preparation looks outrageously cool. If this setup is not an option, then the next best thing would be to grill the chops on a wood-burning grill or over charcoal with wood chips or chunks. As a last resort, you can use a gas grill with wood chips in the smoker box. If you happen to live in wine country, for even more flavor you could toss an armful of grapevine trimmings on the fire.

Russia: Grilling in the Former Land of Czars

As the sun rose over a bend in the Moskva River, three masters lit their grills. The first, an Uzbek wearing the embroidered cotton skullcap of Russia's Muslims, was about to prepare cumin-scented ground lamb kebabs called *lula* (see page 330). The second, a huge bear of a chef (he would have looked at home in Cossack boots and a fur hat and coat) would soon grill garlic and dill flavored veal chops (see page 182) and ham and cheese stuffed fish from his native Siberia. The third—yours truly—had rigged up a smoker to

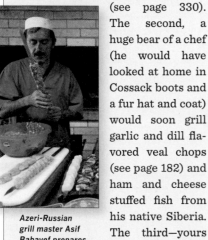

Azeri-Russian grill master Asif Babayef prepares lula, minced lamb kebabs.

cook baby back ribs and Carolina-style pork shoulder. We gathered in the gardens of Moscow's Yermak restaurant for a grill festival hosted by *BBQ*, Russia's premier barbecue magazine.

Grill festival? Russian barbecue magazine? Huh? Isn't this the country that, when I was young, was infamous for its chronic meat shortages and bread lines? Isn't this where the temperature drops below freezing eight months a year and

where the summer grilling season comes and goes almost before you can say *shashlik?* And just exactly how does barbecue fit into a cuisine best known for its steaming borscht and buttery *pelmeni* (dumplings)?

Well, if this is your notion of Russia, it's time to take a fresh look. Grilling in the former realm of czars and commissars is alive and well, thank you, and Russians are every bit as smoke and fire obsessed as their counterparts in North America. Russian grilling is expansive enough to include Armenian grilled bread,

Azeri sturgeon kebabs, Georgian-spiced game hens, and Uzbek *lula*. You can eat your way around the republics of the former Soviet Union virtually within the shadow of the Kremlin. Cold and dreary, indeed, is the day when the skies around Moscow aren't filled with the aroma of meat roasting over charcoal.

At the heart of Russian barbecue is *shashlik*—shish kebab—and depending on your ethnic background (and socioeconomic status), the main ingredient might be beef or more likely pork (popular among

Grilling Where Fire Meets Ice

Russia: Where Uzbek *lula*, Azeri *tandir*, Armenian *mangalsalat*, and Georgian *tkemali* meet *shashlik* (Russian shish kebab).

The quintessential symbol of Russia—matryoshka, nesting dolls.

Another symbol of Russia—St. Basil's Cathedral in Moscow's Red Square.

Christians), lamb (preferred by Muslims), or poultry (often spiced and marinated in wine in the style of the Caucasus Mountains). Everyone loves grilled vegetables, which range from eggplants, tomatoes, and peppers to potatoes, grilled whole, in pieces, or even mashed.

Assembling shashlik at the popular Moscow Georgian restaurant, Kabanchik.

THE GRILL: The traditional Russian grill is the *mangal* (see page 605), a rectangular metal box with charcoal at the bottom and no grill grate. The food is threaded on flat metal skewers or placed in a grill basket and suspended from the front to the back of the grill over the fire.

THE FUEL: Lump charcoal, preferably from fruit trees

THE FLAVORINGS: Onion is the primary flavoring in Russian grilling, sometimes chopped, more often grated, and as a rule, the more you use, the better. Predictably, garlic and dill are popular seasonings, and so are vegetable oil and lemon. As you move east in Russia and through the former Soviet republics, ground meats are spiced with cumin and coriander and enriched with chopped or ground lamb tail fat. Russians of all ethnic persuasions buy Georgian grilling spices—fragrant blends of coriander, cumin, cinnamon, paprika, ground marigold petals, and a half dozen other spices—the way Americans would purchase a can of Memphis- or Kansas City–style barbecue rub.

MUST TRY DISHES:

Lula **(sometimes spelled *lyulya*):** Central Asian–style minced lamb kebabs. These can also be made with ground chicken, turkey, or sturgeon.

Uzbek lamb kebabs grilled with fresh rosemary.

Shashlik: Russian shish kebab: onion-blasted and typically made with pork, beef, or lamb

THE CONDIMENTS: Barbecue sauce in Russia means *tkemali* (pronounced kay-mal-ee), a tart, cranberry-colored sauce from the Republic of Georgia based on sour plums and flavored with garlic, dill, and cilantro. Another popular sauce is *satsibili*, a sort of Caucasus "ketchup" brewed from tomatoes, cilantro, and ground coriander; no, it's not in the least bit sweet. Perhaps there are commercial versions of these sauces, but everyone I know buys them from a favorite stall at their local food market.

Grilled meats and kebabs come with bread, sometimes grilled, often baked in a wood-burning oven. It ranges from paper-thin lavash and spit-roasted rolls at Armenian restaurants to bialy-shaped breads crusted with sesame seeds at Uzbek restaurants. At Caucasus restaurants colorful platters of fresh herbs, sliced radishes and cucumbers, tomatoes, lettuce leaves, and other vegetables invariably accompany grilled meats.

HOW TO EAT IT: Ground meat kebabs are rolled in lavash with herbs and vegetables, then doused with plum or tomato sauce or yogurt. As in the Middle and Near East, sumac, a tart powder made from a purplish berry, is often sprinkled over meat.

IF YOU CAN EAT AT ONLY ONE RESTAURANT: If you have time for only one restaurant, go to Uzbekistan, decorated like a Silk Road caravanserai and located in the heart of downtown Moscow.

WHAT TO DRINK: Vodka or *kvass,* a fermented bread drink, at a Russian restaurant.

Wine, often Georgian, at a Caucasus restaurant. Some variation of *doh,* an unsweetened yogurt drink, at Central Asian restaurants.

MUST DOS: Go with a crowd. The larger your party, the bigger the selection of kebabs you can eat. And if you can manage to wrangle an invitation to a private barbecue at someone's *dacha* (country villa), don't miss it. The ambience will be uniquely Russian.

Musicians add ambiance at a typical Russian grill restaurant.

THE MOST SINGULAR DISH IN THE REPERTORY: Lamb or veal loin pounded paper-thin, sandwiched in thin sheets of lamb tail fat, rolled into a log, cut crosswise into pinwheels, and grilled shish kebab style

Onion and Coriander Brined Lamb Chops

THE SCOOP

WHERE: Uzbekistan and Russia

WHAT: Lamb chops of striking simplicity and succulence—marinated with onion and coriander and seared over charcoal

HOW: Direct grilling

JUST THE FACTS: To be strictly authentic, use spring water in the brine.

Moist and savory, these lamb chops are Uzbekistan's best seller. I'm talking about the restaurant Uzbekistan in Moscow, not the former Soviet republic located in Central Asia. But the authentic food of the country Uzbekistan is the specialty of the restaurant. I was surprised to learn what the "secret" ingredient in these lamb chops was: water. "We have our own spring sixty meters below the restaurant," the manager explained. Normally, water diminishes flavor, not boosts it, but when combined with salt and coriander, as it is here, the marinade becomes a sort of brine. By the process of osmosis (remember your high school chemistry?) some of the brine is drawn into the chops, which explains why these simple Uzbek-style lamb chops are so incredibly flavorful and moist. **SERVES 4**

FOR THE BRINE AND LAMB CHOPS

1 small or ½ medium-size sweet onion, such as Vidalia
1 cup spring water
1 tablespoon coarse salt (kosher or sea)
2 teaspoons ground coriander
1 teaspoon freshly ground back pepper
12 thin-cut rib lamb chops (each ½ to ¾ inch thick, about 1¾ pounds total)

FOR SERVING

1 luscious, red ripe tomato, thinly sliced crosswise
1 small or ½ medium-size sweet onion, such as Vidalia, thinly sliced crosswise
Lavash
Minced flat-leaf parsley, for garnish

YOU'LL ALSO NEED

Aluminum foil; a grill basket (optional)

ADVANCE PREPARATION

1 hour for marinating the lamb

1 Make the brine: Using the large-holed side of a box grater, grate the onion into a mixing bowl. You can also finely chop the onion in a food processor, running the machine in short bursts. Add the water, salt, coriander, and pepper and whisk until the salt dissolves.

2 Arrange the lamb chops in a nonreactive baking dish just large enough to hold them in a single layer. Pour the brine over the chops and let them marinate in the refrigerator, covered, for about 1 hour, turning once or twice.

3 Drain the chops well, discarding the brine. Wrap the exposed parts of the rib bones in aluminum foil, shiny side out, to keep them from burning. If you like, place the lamb chops in a grill basket.

4 Set up the grill for direct grilling and preheat it to high.

5 When ready to cook, brush and oil the grill grate. Arrange the lamb chops on the hot grate and grill them until nicely browned on the outside and cooked to taste, 2 to 3 minutes per side for medium-rare; 3 to 4 minutes per side for medium. (Uzbeks prefer their lamb cooked to medium.) Use the poke test to check for doneness (see page 612).

6 Transfer the chops to a platter or plates and serve them at once with the tomatoes and sliced onion sprinkled with parsley, and the lavash. To eat, cut the meat off the bone and eat it wrapped in lavash with some of the tomato and onion slices. Of course, don't forget to gnaw on the bones.

Serve the grilled Uzbek lamb chops on lavash bread with sliced onion and tomato.

HOW TO BRINE LAMB CHOPS

1. Add spring water to grated onion and coriander to make the brine.

2. Pour the brine over the lamb chops and marinate for 1 hour.

3. Wrap the exposed rib bones with foil to keep them from charring.

4. Drain the chops well on a wire rack before grilling.

5. Place another wire rack on top of the chops to make a sort of grill basket (useful when grilling on a grateless Uzbek grill).

6. Grill the chops until browned on both sides. The beauty of a grill basket is that you turn it, not the individual chops.

FIRE STARTERS
120 Kebabs and Counting

ASIF BABAYEF makes kebabs that are so good, they melt in your mouth like chocolates.

MOSCOW, RUSSIA

Asif Babayef claims to know how to make 120 different types of *shashlik*. I'm not about to dispute it. Not when I walk into his kitchen unannounced and, in less than an hour, he demonstrates eight different Azeri shish kebabs for me—each more innovative than the next. He works seemingly without thinking and definitely without breaking a sweat. "His kebabs are so good, they melt in your mouth like chocolates," says his admiring sous-chef.

Babayef presides over the kitchen at Moscow's lively Azeri restaurant Yhznaya Notch (Southern Nights). He looks a little like the old sitcom character Dobie Gillis. Born in Baku, the capital of the oil-rich former Soviet Republic of Azerbaijan, Babayef comes from a family of grill masters. He serves forty-six different kebabs at the restaurant, and his skills are in such demand that he commands what in Russia is the impressive salary of $3,000 a month. "At this restaurant we're the bosses," he quips. "Not the owners."

I watch as the wiry grill master butterflies a veal tenderloin, tops it with a paper-thin sheet of lamb tail fat, rolls it into a tight cylinder, then cuts and grills it in pinwheels. I watch as Babayef reduces a prehistoric-looking sturgeon into buttery steaks to be grilled with oil and tomato paste. I watch as he grinds boiled potatoes and lamb fat together and molds the resulting mixture onto a flat skewer to make a first for this writer: grilled mashed potatoes.

I'd still be watching if, right in the middle of this furious grill session, we hadn't stopped for a time-honored Azeri ritual of hospitality—steaming glasses of tea served with baklava.

For Babayef, great grilling begins with whole lambs, which he butchers fresh each morning. No part of the animal goes to waste. (If ever you were tempted to order grilled lamb kidneys or testicles, this is the place to try them.) Years of grilling have toughened Babayef's hands to the point where he can lift a hot metal skewer without a grill mitt.

Like most Azeris, Babayef is a devout Muslim, but sometimes his work in Moscow requires him to grill pork. "When I get home, I wash before I pray," he says. "A man has to make a living."

Ancient tradition. New friends. Me and Azeri grill master Asif Babayef.

NAME: Asif Babayef

TERRITORY: Born in Azerbaijan; works in Russia

CLAIM TO FAME: Grill master of the popular Azeri restaurant Yhznaya Notch in Moscow

SPECIALTIES: All manner of *lula* (ground lamb kebabs). Sturgeon kebabs. Grilled veal and lamb fat kebabs. Mashed potato kebabs.

BABAYEF SAYS:

▶ The most important thing for any aspiring grill master is to observe. Watch the meat. Watch the fire. Observe tradition, but don't be afraid to innovate.

▶ The best lamb for grilling comes from an animal that weighs twenty-five pounds.

▶ Freshness counts. We chop our lamb by hand with a large knife not more than an hour before grilling. When making sturgeon kebabs, we grind the fish to order.

▶ Don't make onion relish too early. When a cut onion is exposed to air, the taste becomes strong and bitter. [Onion relish is an indispensable accessory to any Azeri grilled dish; Asif cuts and makes his onion relish to order.]

Lucknowi Lamb Chops
{ LUCKNOWI CHAMP }

How far would you go to make what are arguably the world's best lamb chops? Are you willing to make a special trip to an Indian grocery store to pick up a few esoteric ingredients you probably won't find at your local supermarket? Are you willing to marinate the meat in two stages, one of which requires procuring either green papaya or a papaya-based meat tenderizer, like Adolph's? If so, read on, because these Lucknowi lamb chops, named for an ancient Mogul city in northeastern India and a specialty of the überposh Amanbagh resort in Rajasthan, will redefine your very notion of grilled lamb. Traditionally, the chops would be roasted in a tandoor; conventional direct grilling produces equally excellent results. Not that you need accompaniments, but the Green Herb Chutney on page 398 and the *lachha paratha* bread on page 98 will turn a remarkable dish into a remarkable meal. **SERVES 4**

the Green Herb Chutney on page 398 and the *lachha paratha* bread on page 98

3 cloves garlic, coarsely chopped

1 piece (2 inches) fresh ginger, peeled and coarsely chopped

¼ cup coarsely grated peeled green papaya, or 2 teaspoons Adolph's unseasoned meat tenderizer (optional, if you use really tender lamb, you can skip it)

2 teaspoons hot paprika

Coarse salt (kosher or sea)

3 tablespoons vegetable oil

16 loin or rib lamb chops (each about ¾ inch thick; 2 pounds total)

1 cup strained yogurt

1 cup mustard oil, or ¾ cup vegetable oil and ¼ cup Dijon mustard

3 tablespoons fresh lemon juice

2 teaspoons ground coriander

1 teaspoon ground cumin

½ teaspoon ground fenugreek (optional)

3 to 4 tablespoons salted butter, melted, for basting

1 lemon, cut into wedges, for serving

YOU'LL ALSO NEED

Long metal skewers (optional)

ADVANCE PREPARATION

4 to 6 hours for marinating the lamb

1 Place the garlic and ginger in a heavy mortar and pound with a pestle, adding 2 to 4 tablespoons of water as needed to obtain a smooth paste. If you don't have a mortar and pestle, place the garlic, ginger, and water in a blender or spice mill (a food processor does not work particularly well for this) and puree to a smooth paste. Transfer half of the garlic-ginger paste to a large nonreactive mixing bowl and set aside.

2 Add the papaya, paprika, and 1 teaspoon of salt to the remaining garlic-ginger paste and pound or blend until smooth. Work in the oil.

THE SCOOP

WHERE: Lucknow, capital of the northern Indian state of Uttar Pradesh

WHAT: Grilled lamb chops that deliver a one-two punch of flavor in the form of a garlic and ginger wet rub and a mustard-yogurt marinade

HOW: Direct grilling

JUST THE FACTS: This recipe isn't difficult, but it does require some ingredients that may not be in your cupboard. (I do suggest readily available substitutes.) Strained yogurt is thick and unflavored. The Greek-style yogurt sold under the Fage brand makes an excellent stand-in. Fenugreek powder, known in India as *methi,* is a Central Asian spice with an aromatic, pleasantly bitter flavor. I've made fenugreek optional— you'll still get highly flavorful chops without it. The third is mustard oil, which adds the richness of oil and the heat of freshly ground mustard seed. Both fenugreek powder and mustard oil are available online at www.kalustyans.com.

3 Arrange the lamb chops in a nonreactive baking dish and, using a spatula, spread the garlic-ginger-papaya mixture over them on both sides. Cover the chops with plastic wrap and let marinate in the refrigerator, for 1 hour.

4 Add the yogurt, mustard oil, lemon juice, salt, to taste, coriander, cumin, and fenugreek, if using, to the remaining garlic-ginger paste in the mixing bowl and whisk to mix. Pour this mixture over the lamb chops, turning the chops to coat both sides. Let the chops marinate in the refrigerator, covered, for 3 to 5 hours.

5 Set up the grill for direct grilling and preheat it to high.

6 When ready to cook, brush and oil the grill grate. Remove the chops from the marinade and drain them well, discarding the marinade. If desired, thread the chops diagonal to the bone on metal skewers, leaving 1 inch between each chop; this is the way they'd be grilled in India. Or you can grill the chops unskewered. Arrange the chops on the hot grate and grill until golden brown on the outside and cooked through, 4 to 6 minutes per side for medium. (Indians prefer their lamb medium to medium-well done.) Use the poke test to check for doneness (see page 612). Once you've turned the chops once, start basting them with the melted butter, basting each side a couple of times before serving.

7 Transfer the grilled lamb chops to a platter or plates and remove the skewers, if any. Drizzle any remaining butter over the chops and serve at once with the lemon wedges.

MAURITIUS GRILLED LAMB CHOPS

Mauritius Grilled Lamb Chops

For days I had been puzzling over the "secret ingredient"—the flavor that gave Mauritian barbecue its uniqueness, a taste that was sweet but also a little acidic, with an aromatic herbaceous quality you don't find anywhere else on earth. With a forehead-slapping "duh," I realized the answer lay all around me, in the sugarcane fields that stretch from one end of this island nation to the other. Obviously, sugarcane juice is sweet, but it also possesses a grassy acidity that offsets the sweetness. The locals call it "honey" and no Mauritius barbecue is complete without it. Here's how a grill mistress named Sanjeev Kissoandoyal marinates and grills lamb chops on a pushcart near the village of Balaclava. **SERVES 4**

⅓ cup Chinese oyster sauce

¼ cup soy sauce

2 tablespoons Asian fish sauce, or additional soy sauce

2 tablespoons vegetable oil

¼ cup plus 2 tablespoons chopped fresh cilantro or flat-leaf parsley

1 tablespoon minced peeled fresh ginger

2 cloves garlic, minced

½ teaspoon fresh thyme

½ teaspoon freshly ground black pepper

½ teaspoon MSG (optional)

2 pounds rib lamb chops (½ to ¾ inch thick)

1 cup sugarcane juice

ADVANCE PREPARATION

2 to 4 hours for marinating the lamb

1 Place the oyster sauce, soy sauce, fish sauce, oil, the ¼ cup of cilantro, and the ginger, garlic, thyme, pepper, MSG, if using, and ⅔ cup of water in a large nonreactive bowl and whisk to mix. Add the lamb chops and stir to coat. Let the lamb marinate in the refrigerator, covered, for 2 to 4 hours.

2 Set up the grill for direct grilling and preheat it to high.

3 When ready to cook, brush and oil the grill grate. Drain the lamb chops well, discarding the marinade. Arrange the chops on the hot grate and grill them until sizzling and browned on the outside and cooked through or to taste, 3 to 5 minutes per side for medium. (Mauritians prefer their lamb medium to medium-well done.) Halfway through the grilling, start basting the lamb chops with the sugarcane juice and baste them again just before serving. Sprinkle on the remaining cilantro and serve.

NOTE: To make lamb kebabs Mauritius island style, marinate 1½ pounds lamb shoulder cut into 1-inch cubes in the marinade prepared in Step 1. Make kebabs, interspersing the lamb with 1-inch squares of onion, fresh pineapple, and red and green bell peppers. Grill and baste with the sugarcane juice as described in Step 3.

Three Generations of Grill Masters

A family affair: **DELFINA, CARLO**, and **RICCARDO CIONI**—keeping the fires burning at Da Delfina for more than half a century.

ARTIMINO, ITALY

By the time you get to Da Delfina, you probably know that the restaurant began as a private canteen for hunters and that the cook was Delfina Cioni. That Delfina happened to have married the last gamekeeper at the Villa Ferdinanda, a Medici estate, perched on a hillside in the hamlet of Artimino, a thirteen-mile drive from Florence. That in the 1950s, the diminutive cook turned the canteen into a small trattoria in one of the villa's stables, which quickly became the go-to spot for Tuscan intellectuals and foodies. That she moved the restaurant to an old olive oil mill in 1975, and that *USA Today* called Da Delfina's terrace one of the most beautiful outdoor dining spots in Italy.

What you may not know is that Delfina herself worked in the kitchen until the age of ninety-nine

Delfina Cioni—in her younger days. The grill—behind her—awaits her touch.

Delfina herself worked in the kitchen until the age of ninety-nine

(she lived to be one hundred and one years old), and that the restaurant is currently run by her son, Carlo, and grandnephew, Riccardo. The heart and soul of Da Delfina is the massive stone wood-burning combination rotisserie/grill. Each year, the family burns eight hundred *quintales* (nearly a ton) of sweet-scented Tuscan oak to fire that rotisserie/grill. "There aren't many of us left who still cook over wood," says Carlo, sighing. "The tradition is dying out."

From this wood-burning rotisserie come Delfina's astonishingly moist pancetta-wrapped, rosemary-stuffed pheasants, not to mention another house specialty: *coniglio allo spiedo*—rabbit stuffed with garlic, sage, and pork belly, and spit roasted wrapped in stalks of wild fennel. From the grill come *costolette scottadito*—bay leaf–stuffed lamb chops served so sizzling hot, their name (*scottadito*) literally means "finger burners." And of course, a *bistecca alla fiorentina,* served the traditional way—doused, after cooking, with extra-virgin olive oil—that would be the envy of many a grill master in Florence. Incidentally, there's one dish you should try that

does *not* come hot off the grill: *ribollita,* which means "reboiled." It's a thick pan-fried Tuscan bean and bread "soup" that tastes like vegetable hash.

When asked what his six decades at Da Delfina have taught him about grilling, Carlo speaks of patience, attention, and love. "Maintain a brisk fire and feed it with oak, not resinous softwoods. Position your food the proper distance from the embers. Keep the seasonings simple, so the focus is on the fire and meat. And don't try to serve more than sixty or eighty people at once."

NAME: The Cioni family

TERRITORY: Tuscany, Italy

CLAIM TO FAME: Owners of Da Delfina, one of the most famous restaurants in Tuscany—and one of the few places Florentines will leave Florence to dine at

SPECIALTIES: *Fegatelli di maiale allo spiedo,* pork liver and herbs wrapped in caul fat and grilled on a spit; *costolette scottadito di capretto giovane,* wood-grilled baby goat chops; *coniglio allo spiedo,* spit-roasted rabbit

THE CIONIS SAY:

▶ Use a big fire. Grilling and spit roasting need power.

▶ Add the salt after grilling—never before.

▶ Herbs before cooking, yes. Marinating, no. With high-quality meat that's all the seasoning you need.

Baby (and I Mean Baby) Lamb Chops with Greek Oregano

{ PAIDAKIA }

Grilled lamb chops are served in many countries, but no one does it better than the Greeks. There: I've said it. I'm sure that hordes of Australians, New Zealanders, Moroccans, French, and of course, a few Americans, will be ready to clobber me, but if you've been to Greece, you know what I mean. It may come as a surprise because the recipe for *païdakia* calls for only four ingredients starting with the lamb, salt, and pepper. (That's three, right?) The fourth is *origanon,* fragrant, pungent Greek oregano, and not every grill master uses it. Order *païdakia* at a serious grill joint, and the chops will be cut to order (by hand with a heavy meat cleaver, not on a meat saw). They're always grilled in a grill basket, and they're typically sold by the pound—heaped high on a platter to be munched with the sort of abandon you'd bring to a bowl of bread sticks or potato chips. Crusty on the outside, meaty and buttery inside, with the mildest imaginable lamb flavor, they're perfection on a rib bone. Like most Greek barbecue, *païdakia* are served without sauce. You do get lemon halves to squeeze over the chops, however, and the lemon juice helps cut the fat. **SERVES 4**

½ cup coarse salt (kosher or sea)

3 tablespoons freshly ground black pepper

3 tablespoons dried oregano, preferably Greek

2 pounds of the smallest, youngest rib lamb chops you can find (each about ½ inch thick)

Lemon wedges, for serving

YOU'LL ALSO NEED

A grill basket (optional)

ADVANCE PREPARATION

None

1 Place the salt, pepper, and oregano in a small bowl and stir to mix. Coat the lamb chops all over with the rub. (This makes more rub than you'll need for one batch of chops. Any leftover rub will keep well in a sealed jar for several weeks. It's not only great on grilled lamb but also with chicken and seafood.)

2 Set up the grill for direct grilling and preheat it to high.

3 When ready to cook, brush and

THE SCOOP

WHERE: Greece

WHAT: Baby lamb chops seasoned with salt, pepper, and Greek oregano and grilled over a hot fire—simply the best lamb chops in the world

HOW: Direct grilling

JUST THE FACTS: Greeks like to eat lamb when it's one to two months old, so the chops are incredibly tiny, mild in flavor, delicate in texture, and so generously marbled, it's almost like eating lamb-flavored butter. Your best shot is to buy your lamb at a Greek or halal market in the springtime (halal meat has been slaughtered according to Muslim law). If you live in the Manhattan area, go to the epicenter of Greek culture in New York, the Astoria neighborhood in Queens. A great mail-order source for baby lamb chops is Jamison Farm in Latrobe, Pennsylvania (www.jamisonfarm.com). Otherwise, use the smallest lamb rib chops you can find.

For information on Greek oregano, see page 86.

oil the grill grate. Arrange the lamb chops in the grill basket, if using, and place it on the hot grate. If you are not using a grill basket, arrange the chops directly on the grate. Grill the chops until darkly browned on the outside and cooked through, 3 to 5 minutes per side for medium. (Greeks prefer their chops medium to medium-well done.) Use the poke test to check for doneness (see page 612). You may get flare-ups from the dripping lamb fat. If you do, move the chops to another section of the grill.

4 Transfer the chops to a platter or plates and sprinkle a little additional rub over them. This double seasoning is characteristic of Greek grilling. Serve the chops at once with lemon wedges.

On the barbecue trail in the Plaka, Athens, Greece.

Lamb cut to order at a typical Greek butcher shop.

Greek Lamb Chops

It's a sight you see throughout Greece: the brick red and pearl white carcasses of baby lambs hanging in butcher shop windows and restaurant kitchens. It's a sound you hear at restaurants and *hasapotavernas* (butchers' taverns) from Macedonia to the Peloponnese: the thunk, thunk, thunk of a meat cleaver cutting sides of lamb into chops not much bigger than Popsicles.

Greeks have raised the act of grilling and eating chops to the level of art, and it all starts with a meat already celebrated in Homer's day—baby lamb. Elsewhere in the Middle and Near East, not to mention in Central Asia, grill masters prize the ripe, gamy flavor of full-grown lamb. But in Greece, baby lamb is king. I'm not kidding when I say young.

The best lamb chops come from an animal dispatched at one to two months. The tender age means three things: tiny ribs; candy-striped meat, thanks to alternating layers of meat and fat in roughly equal proportion; and a flavor so mild, so delicate, even people who feel neutral about lamb will enjoy it.

So where do you find Greek-style baby lamb chops in Greece? At butcher shops, meat markets, and restaurants on virtually every street corner. And outside of Greece? The short answer is you don't. It's something to look forward to the next time you travel to Greece. The somewhat longer answer is that if you live in an area with a large Greek community, like Astoria in Queens, New York, you may be able to find baby lamb and

baby lamb chops at a Greek butcher shop. The best time to look for it is in the spring.

There are three other things you need to know about Greek lamb chops:

▶ Greek lamb chops are cut to order and cut thin, just shy of ½ inch thick. This maximizes the surface area exposed to the fire and guarantees maximum crust and crispness.

▶ Greeks like their lamb chops well-done. Don't dream of asking for them (or getting them) rare or pink.

▶ Greek lamb chops are fatty. They're supposed to be fatty. That's what makes them so luscious and crisp.

Peanut-Crusted Lamb Kebabs in the Style of Burkina Faso
{ BROCHETTES D'AGNEAU A LA PATE D'ARACHIDE }

Her name was Sala Ouedraogo and she drove a taxi in Paris. Our talk turned to barbecue, as it often does when I ride in a cab. The reason is simple: In most places taxi drivers come from somewhere else, sometimes from countries I have not visited, which have barbecue traditions I don't know firsthand. Ms. Ouedraogo, for example, comes from the tiny West African nation of Burkina Faso, and while the grilled meat varies, it's always seasoned with a unique ingredient ubiquitous in West Africa—peanut meal (*pâte d'arachide* in French). Peanut meal adds a sweet nutty crunch to the local shish kebab. You find variations on this dish, known locally as *kyinkyinga* and pronounced "chinchinga," as far north as Senegal and as far south as Benin. Serve the kebabs with plenty of Castle Lager or other African beer. **SERVES 6 TO 8 AS AN APPETIZER, 4 AS A MAIN COURSE**

1½ pounds lamb, preferably shoulder, and fatty shoulder at that

1 small onion, minced

1 tablespoon minced peeled fresh ginger

1½ teaspoons coarse salt (kosher or sea)

1 teaspoon freshly ground black pepper

½ teaspoon ground allspice or French Quarter épices

½ teaspoon cayenne pepper, or to taste

1 to 2 tablespoons vegetable oil

1 cup peanut meal, or 1¼ cups dry-roasted peanuts

YOU'LL ALSO NEED

Small bamboo skewers; an aluminum foil grill shield (see page 611)

ADVANCE PREPARATION

15 minutes to 1 hour for marinating the lamb

1 Cut the lamb into ¾-inch cubes and place them in a large nonreactive mixing bowl. Sprinkle the onion, ginger, salt, black pepper, allspice, and cayenne over the lamb and stir to mix well. Add the oil and mix well. Let the lamb marinate in the refrigerator, covered, for 15 minutes to 1 hour.

2 If you are using peanuts, place them in a food processor fitted with a metal blade and grind them to the finest possible powder. The best way to do this is to run the machine in short bursts; do not overprocess or you'll make peanut butter. Place the ground peanuts in a shallow bowl.

3 Thread the lamb chunks onto the bamboo skewers, alternating fatty pieces with lean pieces.

4 Set up the grill for direct grilling and preheat it to high.

5 When ready to cook, brush and oil the grill grate. Working at grillside, dip each kebab in the ground peanuts, rolling it to coat the lamb on all sides and lifting and shaking the kebabs over the bowl to knock off the excess ground peanuts. Arrange the kebabs on the hot grate with the aluminum foil shield under the exposed ends of the skewers to keep them from burning.

6 Grill the lamb kebabs until golden brown on the outside and cooked to taste, 1½ to 2 minutes per side, 6 to 8 minutes in all, for medium. Use the pinch test to check for doneness (see page 612). Serve the kebabs at once.

Yogurt-Marinated Lamb Tenderloin Kebabs

THE SCOOP

WHERE: Istanbul, Turkey

WHAT: The most tender, delicate part of the lamb—the tenderloin—marinated in yogurt and tomato paste, crusted with paprika and salt, and grilled

HOW: Direct grilling

JUST THE FACTS: There once was a time when you found lamb tenderloin only at high-end restaurants. Today, you can buy this delicate cut at natural foods stores or butcher shops. Lamb chops, leg of lamb, or even lamb ribs could be prepared the same way. For the best results, use imported Turkish or Greek tomato paste and thick yogurt.

Hamdi is the sort of restaurant your hotel concierge will happily steer you to—a glass-enclosed ziggurat that looks out onto Istanbul's glittering waterfront. But because this is an Istanbul institution, not just a tourist trap, you'll find kitchens lined with blazing charcoal grills manned by seasoned grill masters, turning out *adana* and *sogar* kebabs of the strictest authenticity. It's the sort of place where the *kibbe*—Turkish lamb tartar—is prepared at tableside and the grilled meats come out sizzling and smoky. But what really keeps me awake at night are memories of the grilled lamb tenderloin kebabs with Turkish yogurt, sweet tomato paste, and aromatic Turkish paprika. **SERVES 4**

3 tablespoons thick (Turkish- or Greek-style) plain yogurt

2 tablespoons tomato paste, preferably Turkish

1 tablespoon fresh lemon juice

3 cloves garlic, crushed with the side of a knife

2 teaspoons Aleppo pepper, or 1 teaspoon hot red pepper flakes (optional)

1 teaspoon dried oregano

½ teaspoon freshly ground black pepper

⅓ cup extra-virgin olive oil

1½ pounds lamb tenderloin or shoulder

Sweet or hot paprika, preferably Turkish

Coarse salt (kosher or sea)

Lavash

Onion and Parsley Relish (page 319)

YOU'LL ALSO NEED
Metal skewers

ADVANCE PREPARATION
4 hours to overnight for marinating the lamb

1 Place the yogurt, tomato paste, lemon juice, garlic, Aleppo pepper, oregano, and black pepper in a large nonreactive mixing bowl and whisk to mix. Gradually whisk in the olive oil.

2 If you are using lamb tenderloins, cut them crosswise into 1½-inch pieces. If you are using lamb shoulder, cut it into 1½-inch chunks. Add the lamb to the bowl with the marinade and let it marinate in the refrigerator, covered, for 4 hours or as long as overnight; the longer it marinates, the richer the flavor will be.

3 Drain the lamb, discarding the marinade. Then thread the pieces of lamb onto skewers, skewering them crosswise if you are using lamb tenderloin. Place the skewers on a baking dish with raised sides, so the meat is suspended in midair. Very generously sprinkle the kebabs on all sides with paprika and salt. The meat should be crusted with spice.

4 Set up the grill for direct grilling and preheat it to high. Ideally, you'll set up your grill for grateless grilling (see page 599).

5 When ready to cook, if you are using a grill grate, brush and oil it. Arrange the kebabs on the hot grate and grill them until the lamb is sizzling and browned and cooked through, 4 to 6 minutes per side, 8 to 12 minutes in all for medium. (Turks prefer their lamb medium to medium-well done.) Use the pinch test to check for doneness (see page 612).

6 Transfer the grilled lamb to a platter or plates and unskewer it. Serve the lamb with Onion and Parsley Relish and lavash to wrap it all up.

YOGURT-MARINATED LAMB TENDERLOIN KEBABS

PLANET BARBECUE

Turkey: Grilling Where East Meets West

Quick: Name the most popular grilled dish in the world. You probably chose a version of shish kebab. Meat on a stick is universal and nowhere do they make it better than in the land that gave it its name. *Şiş* (pronounced shish) means sword in Turkish; *kebab* means meat. In former times, so the story goes, Turkish warriors would pause from their cavalcades just long enough to roast chunks of meat on their sabers over a campfire. From these primitive beginnings, Turks have evolved some of the most sophisticated grilling on Planet Barbecue.

Turkey stands at many strategic crossroads: between Europe and Asia, Russia, and North Africa, Greece and the Middle and Near East. The legendary Silk and Spice Road (from China and India through Afghanistan, Iraq, and Iran) had its terminus in Istanbul. Each successive culture—the Greeks, Romans, Byzantines, and Ottomans—added its ingredients to Turkey's barbecue melting pot. If you want to get an idea of what is available to Turkish grill masters, just take a stroll through

Musa Dagdeviren, master griller and chef-owner of the restaurant Çiya in Istanbul.

the food bazaar in the ancient Silk Road way station of Gaziantep, a city in southeast Turkey said to produce the nation's best grill masters. Aleppo pepper, sumac, supernaturally green pistachio nuts, crab apples, quince, and pomegranate molasses all find their way into the local kebabs.

To most North Americans, shish kebab means chunks of meat

and vegetables on a skewer, but the vast majority of Turkey's kebabs are made from minced meat, not chunks. The mincing is done with a huge, scimitar-shaped knife called a *zirh*, hours, if not minutes, before grilling. Often minced lamb is interspersed with fruits or vegetables, such as eggplant, onions, apricots, medlars, or quinces.

Unlike in North America, Turks

Birthplace of Shish Kebab

With Europe to the west, Asia to the east, Russia to the north, and the Middle East to the south, Turkey offers some of the best grilling on Planet Barbecue.

Fire-roasted tomatoes. When Turks make shish kebab, each vegetable is grilled on a separate skewer.

Istanbul's spectacular skyline: the Hagia Sophia Mosque with the Bosporus behind it.

grill pieces of meat and vegetables on separate skewers, a technique that guarantees that each will be cooked to the proper degree of doneness. Most Turks would not look kindly on the shish kebab I grew up with—the meat chunks soggy, the onions still raw, the tomatoes so soft they fall into the embers.

THE GRILL: Turks do most of their grilling on a *mangal*, a troughlike metal or stone box filled with embers. There is no grill grate: Flat metal skewers are stretched across the coals.

There's also a Turkish version of pit barbecue, *tandir*, where whole lambs or lamb quarters roast in a wood- or charcoal-burning underground clay ovens—the Turkish answer to an Indian tandoor.

THE FUEL: Natural lump charcoal

THE FLAVORINGS: Lamb is the cornerstone of Turkish barbecue. But if you're used to the mild-flavored lamb sold in North America, your first taste of Turkish lamb will make you sit up and take notice. It's full flavored, almost gamy, with a fat content that may send a typical American rushing for his Lipitor. Turks love the waxy white fat found just at the tail of Near Eastern sheep breeds—so much so that they add 30 to 40 percent of the fat to the minced meat.

Turks season with a relatively restrained palate: salt, pepper, onion, garlic, flat-leaf parsley for ground meat kebabs; marinades based on yogurt, tomato paste, and olive oil. One ingredient that may be new for you is *antep biberi* (Gaziantep pepper), better known in the West by its Syrian name, Aleppo pepper (see Just the Facts on page 393).

MUST TRY DISHES:

Adana kebab: A fiery, chile-laced minced lamb kebab from the southern Turkish city of Adana

Ali nazik kebab: Literally "Gentle Al" kebab, named for a grill master from Bursa, who had the genial idea to serve a grilled minced lamb kebab over a puree of fire-charred eggplant

Çöp şiş: Little chunks of lamb tenderloin or loin grilled on a skewer

Doner kebab: Turkey's version of Greek gyro or Middle Eastern shawarma, grilled on a charcoal-burning rotisserie and sliced paper-thin to order.

Doner kebab: Turkey's version of Greek gyro or Middle Eastern *shawarma*—a huge roast cooked on a vertical spit, then thinly sliced to order onto a pita bread and topped with a variety of Turkish salads and yogurt. *Yaprak doner* features thin slices of lamb meat, while *kiyma doner* is made with minced lamb.

Iskender kebab: "Alexander" kebab, thinly shaved grilled ground lamb served over creamy tomato sauce with thick Turkish yogurt

Köftesi: The Turkish version of a hamburger, a grilled patty of ground beef, bread, and onion made famous by a landmark Istanbul restaurant called Sultanahmet Köftecisi (see page 312)

Tavuk şiş: Chicken kebabs

THE CONDIMENTS: Grilled meats are typically served with hot *pide* (Turkey's version of pita bread) and *sogan piyaz* (a fresh onion, flat-leaf parsley, and sumac relish). Often grilled meats are drizzled with a thick sweet-sour syrup made from boiled-down pomegranate juice (pomegranate molasses). As in the Middle East, Turks often sprinkle grilled meats with sumac powder.

HOW TO EAT IT: Wrap the meat, onion relish, and pomegranate molasses and/or sumac in lavash or *pide*.

IF YOU CAN EAT AT ONLY ONE RESTAURANT: In a city like Istanbul, which has literally thousands of grill joints, it's impossible to single out one. For upscale barbecue, check out the *Köşebaşi* chain. For Turkish grilling with great views of the Bosporus, book a terrace table at Hamdi. Beyti near the airport attracts Istanbul's TV and media crowd, while Mabeyin occupies a former Ottoman country palace. For a more intimate, casual, Kurdish-style grilling experience, visit Zübeyir, located in Istanbul's colorful Beyoglu district.

WHAT TO DRINK: Start your meal with *raki*, Turkey's anise-flavored liquor (add water until it turns white). *Ayran* is a refreshing, if strange, drink made with yogurt, salt, and sparkling water.

Turkish food writer Engin Akin, at a bar specializing in a Turkish fermented millet drink called boza.

THE MOST SINGULAR DISH IN THE REPERTORY: Grilled lamb kidneys with Kurdish seasonings; it's a specialty of the aforementioned Zübeyir restaurant.

Baby Goat or Lamb Satés with Pineapple and Sweet Soy

THE SCOOP

WHERE: Bali, Indonesia

WHAT: Tiny kebabs of goat or lamb marinated in pineapple and sweet soy sauce, served with a peanut-hoisin dipping sauce

HOW: Direct grilling

JUST THE FACTS: This recipe is easy to make, but it does call for a few unusual ingredients. Kid (baby goat) has a delicate flavor that's a cross between veal and lamb. Don't be put off by the notion of baby goat—it's considerably milder than the lamb. If it's unavailable or unappealing, lamb makes a good substitute. *Kejap manis* is Indonesian soy sauce, thick and sweet, like molasses. It's available at Asian markets and many supermarkets, and I also tell you here how to make an excellent substitute at home. Hoisin sauce is a thick, sweet, aniselike Chinese condiment available at most supermarkets.

Warung Muselman isn't the sort of place you'd notice roaring down the main drag in the spiritual, artistic, and commercial city of Ubud in Bali, Indonesia. There's nothing remarkable about this storefront grill shop, except perhaps, three legs of young goat in various states of dissection, hanging unrefrigerated in the window. Or the slender charcoal saté grill on rickety legs, ventilated by an electric fan, by the front door. It's a scene you'd see in ten thousand other places in Indonesia. But if you have an itch for the Muslim-style satés typical of Java or Sumatra, this is a great place in primarily Hindu Bali to scratch it. And despite the bare-bones surroundings, these tiny kebabs boast an incredible depth of flavor—first from a pineapple and sweet soy marinade (the acid in the pineapple helps tenderize the meat), then from a dipping sauce mixed on the spot with peanut sauce, hoisin sauce, and fresh shallots. **SERVES 4**

FOR THE MEAT AND MARINADE

1½ pounds leg or shoulder of kid or lamb
½ cup kejap manis (sweet Indonesian soy sauce),
    or ¼ cup soy sauce plus ¼ cup molasses
8 ounces peeled and cored fresh pineapple,
    pureed in a food processor (see Note)

FOR THE PEANUT-HOISIN DIPPING SAUCE

1 cup Fried Garlic Peanut Sauce (page 35) or
    Creamy Asian Peanut Sauce (page 18) or
    your favorite commercial brand
¼ cup hoisin sauce
2 shallots, sliced crosswise paper-thin
2 tablespoons vegetable oil for basting
    (in Bali they use coconut oil)

YOU'LL ALSO NEED

8-inch bamboo skewers; an aluminum foil grill
    shield (see page 611)

ADVANCE PREPARATION

15 to 30 minutes for marinating the satés

1 Prepare the satés: Cut the kid into ½-inch cubes and thread them onto bamboo skewers. Leave the bottom half of the skewers exposed as a handle. Arrange the satés in a nonreactive baking dish.

2 If using soy and molasses, place them in a small bowl and mix well. Drizzle the *kejap manis* or the soy and molasses mixture over the satés, turning each skewer to coat the meat. Pour the pureed pineapple over the satés, turning them to coat. Let the satés marinate in the refrigerator, covered, for 15 to 30 minutes.

3 Make the peanut-hoisin dipping sauce: Pour 3 tablespoons of the peanut sauce into each of 4 small shallow bowls or dishes. Pour 1 tablespoon of hoisin sauce in the center of each bowl. Place some shallot slices on top. The sauce can be prepared ahead to this stage.

4 Set up the grill for direct grilling and preheat it to high.

5 When ready to cook, brush and oil the grill grate. Arrange the satés on the hot grate, with the aluminum foil shield under the exposed ends of the skewers to keep them from burning. Grill the satés until cooked to taste, 1 to 2 minutes per side, 2 to 4 minutes in all for medium. (Indonesians prefer their kid medium to medium-well done.) Use the poke test to check for doneness (see page 612). Baste the satés with oil as they grill.

6 Serve the satés hot off the grill or transfer them to plates or a platter. To eat, use the first saté to stir together the ingredients for the peanut-hoisin dipping sauce. Eat the satés dipped in a little of the sauce.

NOTE: In a pinch you can use a drained 8-ounce can of unsweetened pineapple plus 2 tablespoons of fresh lime juice in place of the fresh pineapple.

Piri-Piri Goat Kebabs

Jojo occupies a bare-bones storefront in Soweto (short for Southwest Township—the birthplace of the African National Congress). But, it offers the sort of grilling experience you find throughout South Africa—a do-it-yourself barbecue that consists of buying your meat at a butcher, then cooking it out front on the grill provided by the butcher. The butcher in question here is a shy woman recognizable by her red headscarf and a smile that illuminates her face like a floodlight. Jojo (she prefers not to be identified by her last name) makes a virtue of the privations of her neighborhood. Yes, the meat comes from the less-expensive cuts. Yes, the seasonings come in commercial packets. But Jojo provides an electrifying *chacalaka* (tomato relish) to kick up the overall flavor. She'll even lend you a tin plate to carry your meat to the grill (a half 55-gallon steel drum filled with blazing charcoal). I first had this preparation with thinly sliced deckle (the fatty cap on a brisket), but it goes amazingly well with another popular African meat, young goat. The peppery *piri-piri* seasoning and piquant tomato relish will give you a whole new perspective on a meat that's well worth discovering: goat. **SERVES 4**

1½ pounds leg or shoulder of young goat or lamb

1 large sweet onion

1 tablespoon sweet paprika

2 teaspoons coarse salt (kosher or sea)

2 teaspoons ground coriander

1 to 3 teaspoons cayenne pepper

1 teaspoon onion powder

1 teaspoon garlic powder

1 teaspoon freshly ground black pepper

2 tablespoons vegetable oil for basting

Spicy Tomato Relish (Chacalaka, optional), recipe follows

YOU'LL ALSO NEED

Metal or bamboo skewers

ADVANCE PREPARATION

None needed, but the goat will be more flavorful if you let it marinate in the refrigerator for 30 to 60 minutes before grilling.

1 Cut the goat into 1-inch cubes. Cut the onion in half widthwise and cut each half into quarters; separate the quarters into individual layers. Thread the kid and onion onto skewers, alternating pieces of onion with the meat cubes. Arrange the kebabs on a large platter or plate.

2 Place the paprika, salt, coriander, cayenne pepper, onion powder, garlic powder, and black pepper in a bowl and stir to mix (see Note). Generously season the kebabs all over with the *piri-piri* rub, then drizzle them with oil, turning the kebabs to coat all sides. Let the kebabs marinate in the refrigerator, covered, while you make the *chacalaka* and build your fire.

3 Set up your grill for direct grilling and preheat it to high.

4 When ready to cook, brush and oil the grill grate. Arrange the kebabs on the hot grate and grill until sizzling brown on all sides, and cooked through, 2 to 3 minutes per side, 8 to 12 minutes in all for medium. (South Africans like their goat medium to medium-well done.) Use the pinch test (page 612) to check for doneness. Serve at once with the tomato relish.

NOTE: This will make more rub than you need for this recipe. The excess stores well in a sealed jar and can be used as a rub for meat kebabs and steaks.

Spicy Tomato Relish
{ CHACALAKA }

Chacalaka belongs to a broad family of tomato salads and relishes that are served with grilled meats in virtually every corner of Planet Barbecue. (Think of it as South African salsa.) The cool moist tomatoes are meant to counterpoint the hot crusty meat.

1 large or 2 medium-size ripe red tomatoes, cored

1 medium-size or ½ large sweet onion

1 to 2 serrano or jalapeño peppers

1 tablespoon fresh lemon juice, or to taste (optional)

1 teaspoon coarse salt (kosher or sea), or to taste

Cut the tomatoes (with their skins and seeds), onion, and chiles into ¼-inch dice (for a milder salsa, seed the peppers). Place the tomatoes and their juices in a mixing bowl and add the onion, pepper(s), lemon juice, and salt, but do not toss until a few minutes before serving. After tossing, correct the seasoning, adding salt or lemon juice to taste.

Ground
Meat

July 4th. Independence Day. More Americans will fire up their grills on this day than on any other day of the year. And the dish they're most likely to grill is a culinary icon, not to mention one of America's favorite foods: the hamburger. No surprise here, but what you may not realize is just how many grill cultures around Planet Barbecue are obsessed by grilled ground meat.

In the burger family alone, you find *köftesi* (a grilled ground beef and onion patty) served at a century-old restaurant in the shadow of the Hagia Sophia in Istanbul, Turkey. Or *bifteki,* a grilled ground beef and veal patty popular on Santorini and elsewhere in Greece. Or *pljeskavica,* a Balkan garlic- and chile-spiked grilled meat patty that has the distinction of being the largest burger on Planet Barbecue.

Of course, on much of the world's barbecue trail grilled ground meat takes the form of sausage. Consider *boerewors,* South Africa's cinnamon- and nutmeg-scented beef sausage, or *currywurst,* Germany's veal sausage slathered with curry-scented tomato sauce (on page 344 you can read about the invention of this curious dish). Closer to home, there's grilled chorizo, Latin America's vinegar- and paprika-piqued pork sausage grilled on skewers the way they do it in Cartagena, Colombia. And no sausage survey would be complete without Wisconsin's beloved bratwurst, here smoke roasted

CLOCKWISE FROM TOP LEFT: Merguez (Moroccan sausage) on the grill in Marrakech, Morocco; Mici (Romanian "sliders"); Serb grill mistress Jelena Stuparevic with a sampler of her grilled ground meats; Pljeskavica, the brobdingnagian burger of the Balkans.

on the grill and served in simmering beer and onions.

Sausage normally comes in a casing, but on large swaths of Planet Barbecue, grill masters simply mold the ground meat onto flat metal skewers to be grilled on a grateless grill called a *mangal.* Moroccan *kofta,* Turkish *adana kebab,* and Uzbek *lula* all give you the crusty succulence of grilled sausage without the task of stuffing the meat into a casing.

So what's the secret to superlative grilled ground meat patties or sausages? I hate to say it in these nutritionally correct times, but it's fat: 15 to 20 percent fat for burgers; as high as 40 percent for such skinless grilled sausages as *kofta* and *lula.* OK, I know this flies in the face of modern convention (that's putting it mildly; as I write I can feel the disapprobation of my dietician stepdaughter, Betsy). Try the following recipes without anxiety—and with authentic levels of fat. As the late, great Julia Child used to say: Enjoy all things in moderation.

Previous page: Uzbek grill master Stalic Khankishiev (see page 333) prepares *lula* kebabs.

The Paul Newman Burger

How far would you go to make the perfect burger? Would you take the time to source organic grass-fed beef (better for flavor and better for the planet)? Would you custom grind the meat, going so far as to freeze the grinder parts to keep the fat sufficiently cold for the optimum texture? Michel Nischan would and he did so for a very demanding client. His late boss, Paul Newman, insisted that their Westport, Connecticut, restaurant, Dressing Room, serve the best burger in North America. Nischan and Newman spent several months creating and sampling burgers, varying the meat, fat content, size, weight, and shape of the patty, the fuel, cooking technique, and garnishes. It took thirty contenders to determine the winner.

So what constitutes the perfect burger? You'll know the moment you bite into it. Your teeth will sink through a softly crisp smoky crust into a rich, meaty, lasciviously moist interior. Of course, you should smell wood smoke and the beef should taste, well, like beef. In short, it will be the sort of burger that doesn't need ketchup or mustard or a lot of fancy garnishes but that benefits from a few judiciously chosen accompaniments. So what's the secret? Well, actually there are twenty and you'll find them in the box on page 309. Who said perfection was easy? **MAKES 4 BURGERS; SERVES 4**

2 pounds (32 ounces) ground beef, ideally 14 ounces brisket and 18 ounces chuck, with a fat content of 22 percent

Coarse salt (kosher or sea) and freshly ground black pepper

4 teaspoons unsalted butter at room temperature, plus 1 to 2 tablespoons for buttering the buns

4 freshly baked buns (3½ inches across), preferably brioche

4 Boston or Bibb lettuce leaves, preferably organic

1 luscious, red ripe tomato, preferably an heirloom organic, thinly sliced

4 thick slices of smokehouse bacon (about 4 ounces, optional), cut in half crosswise and cooked until crisp

YOU'LL ALSO NEED

2 cups oak or fruitwood wood chips or chunks, soaked for 1 hour in water to cover, then drained

ADVANCE PREPARATION

None, but allow enough time to grind the beef, if you don't have the butcher do it. The burgers can be formed up to 4 hours ahead.

1 Divide the beef into 4 even portions. Lightly wet your hands with cold water and mold each portion into a patty about 1 inch thick and 1 inch larger in diameter than the buns. Work with a light touch, handling the meat as little as possible. Make a shallow depression in the center of each patty with your thumb (the patties should be slightly concave; this helps them cook evenly). You can form the patties up to 4 hours ahead. Place them on a plate lined with plastic wrap and refrigerate them, covered, until you are ready to grill.

2 Set up the grill for direct grilling and preheat it to high. Ideally you'd grill over a wood fire (see page 603 for instructions). Alternatively you can use wood chips or chunks to add a smoke flavor.

3 When ready to cook, brush and oil the grill grate. Toss the wood chips or chunks on the coals of a charcoal grill or, if you are using a gas grill, add the chips or chunks to the smoker box or place them in a smoker pouch under the grate (see page 603). If you are using a gas grill, wait until you see smoke, about 5 minutes, before putting on the burgers. Generously season the tops of the burgers with salt and pepper. Place the burgers on the hot grate and grill them until the bottoms are browned, 2 to 3 minutes. Using a spatula, turn the burgers over and season the tops with salt. Continue grilling the burgers until cooked to taste, 4½ to 5 minutes in all for rare, 6 to 7 minutes for medium-rare, 8 to 9 minutes for medium. Unless you're absolutely sure about the purity of your meat, you should cook the burgers to medium. Insert an instant-read meat thermometer through the side of a burger; when cooked to medium the internal temperature will be about 160°F.

4 Transfer the burgers to a warm plate. Place a teaspoon of butter on top of each. Let the burgers rest for about 2 minutes.

5 Meanwhile, butter the buns and toast the cut sides until golden brown, 30 seconds to 1 minute. Watch the buns; they can burn quickly.

6 To assemble the burgers, place a lettuce leaf on the bottom half of a bun. Place a burger on top and top it with tomato, bacon, if using, and the top half of the bun. Repeat with the remaining buns and burgers.

VARIATION

The Paul Newman Cheeseburger: To make these you'll need 4 slices, each about 1 ounce, of aged cheddar cheese. Place a slice on each burger during its last 2 minutes on the grill.

Chef Michel Nischan with late boss Paul Newman.

The Perfect Burger

Michel Nischan did extensive kitchen testing to develop the ultimate burger for the Dressing Room, the restaurant he opened along with the late Paul Newman in Westport, Connecticut. Here are the twenty secrets to grilling the perfect burger:

1. Use grass-fed beef. It tastes better, poses less risk of bacterial contamination, and is healthier for the planet.

2. Grind the beef from a combination of brisket and chuck (beef shoulder clod) in a ratio of 45 to 55 percent. The brisket provides the richness; the chuck, a rich beefy flavor.

3. Keep the fat content at 22 percent; according to Michel Nischan, this is the single most important taste factor. Sorry folks: You'll have to cut back on your fat intake somewhere else.

4. Grind the meat twice through the coarse plate of a meat grinder. Freeze the grinder parts before grinding the meat to minimize the heat generated by friction. Heat softens the fat, which makes for an inferior burger.

5. The perfect weight for a full-size burger is 9 ounces. Make the patty at least 1 inch thick and at least 1 inch larger in diameter than the bun. That way, when the burger cooks down, it will be about the same size as the bun.

6. When forming the burger, work quickly and with a light touch, packing the meat as loosely as possible. You get a lighter texture and less shrinkage if you don't pack the meat.

7. Make a slight depression in the center of each patty. Burgers shrink more at the edges than in the center, so the indentation in the center will give you a patty of a more even thickness when the meat is cooked.

8. If you form the burgers ahead of time (and you can), store them in the refrigerator in a single layer so as not to crush the meat.

9. For the best flavor, grill the burgers over the embers of a hardwood fire. Nischan uses a blend of Connecticut hardwoods, like apple, cherry, and ash.

10. Immediately prior to putting the burgers on the grill, salt the tops with thin-flaked Maldon sea salt from England. Salt the other side when you turn the burgers.

11. Use a spatula for turning the burgers but never, *ever* press the tops with the spatula. Pressing the burgers serves only to squeeze out the juices.

12. The total cooking time will be 4½ to 5 minutes for a rare burger; 6 to 7 minutes for medium-rare. By using grass-fed beef that is custom ground for the restaurant, Nischan is able to serve rare or medium-rare burgers without a food safety risk. At home, you should go for medium—8 to 9 minutes total.

13. Turn the burgers only once. This gives you the best crust.

14. "Temper" the burgers—that is, let them rest on a warm plate for two minutes after grilling before serving them. This "relaxes" the meat, making it more juicy, while simultaneously keeping the juices in the patty, not spilling out into the bun.

15. Place a "thumbnail" (about 1 teaspoon) of unsalted butter on top of each hot burger while it rests for extra moistness and richness.

16. Buy your buns at a bakery or make them at home. Nischan uses home-baked brioche buns, which he toasts on the grill before assembling the burgers. (Brioche is made from a French dough rich in eggs and butter.)

17. Shop at your local farmers' market. Nischan uses locally raised lettuce and organic tomatoes, ideally heirlooms.

18. If you like a bacon cheeseburger, use a good smokehouse bacon, like Nueske's. Nischan cures his own bacon. For cheese, he uses a farmhouse cheddar from Grafton, Vermont.

19. Think seasonal. In the winter, Nischan forgoes tomatoes for caramelized onions.

20. Make a contribution. Paul Newman funded and Nischan runs the Wholesome Wave Foundation (www.wholesomewave.org), which among many other good works, doubles the value of food stamps to help their users be able to shop at farmers' markets.

"Kobe" Beef Sliders

Kobe beef sliders began turning up a few years ago at marquee restaurants in New York City and Los Angeles. The irony of this was not lost on anyone who has eaten a "slyder" at one of the sixty-plus White Castle burger joints around the United States. Imagine small, thin, gray, square patties of ground beef, "steam grilled" (griddled) with onion and served on equally diminutive soft buns. The term *slyder,* coined shortly after the first White Castle opened in Wichita, Kansas, in 1921, was said to refer to the ease with which the burger slid out of its signature white cardboard box (or perhaps it had something to do with the way it slid down your gullet). Something about the burger's iconic shape and role in American popular culture (rhapsodized by, among others, the Beastie Boys) struck the fancy of a new generation of American chefs. The humble slider went upscale, with top-grade meat, caramelized shallots, and a brioche bun. Here's a slider you truly cook on the grill and that definitely will lend style and substance to your next grill session. **MAKES 12 SLIDERS; SERVES 4**

FOR THE CARAMELIZED SHALLOTS

2 tablespoons (¼ stick) unsalted butter
1 tablespoon extra-virgin olive oil, or more butter
1 pound shallots, peeled and thinly sliced crosswise
Coarse salt (kosher or sea) and freshly ground black pepper

FOR THE SLIDERS

1½ pounds ground wagyu or Kobe-style beef, ideally with a fat content of 15 to 20 percent
Coarse salt (kosher or sea) and freshly ground black pepper
12 small brioche rolls or Parker House rolls
2 tablespoons (¼ stick) unsalted butter, melted
Sliced dill pickles or sweet pickles (optional)

ADVANCE PREPARATION

None, but the shallots can be caramelized a day ahead.

1 Make the caramelized shallots: Melt the butter in the olive oil in a heavy saucepan over medium heat. Add the shallots and cook until the shallots have been reduced to a dark, thick, sweet paste, 15 to 25 minutes; you will have to stir the shallots often. Lower the heat as needed to keep the shallots from burning. Season the shallots with salt and pepper to taste. The shallots can be caramelized several hours or even a day ahead and refrigerated, covered. Let them return to room temperature before using.

2 Make the sliders: Lightly wet your hands with cold water and divide the beef into 12 portions, then form each portion into a square patty about 2 inches square and ½ inch thick. Place the beef patties on a plate lined with plastic wrap and refrigerate them, covered, until you are ready to grill.

3 Set up the grill for direct grilling and preheat it to high. Ideally you'd grill over oak or another hardwood fire (see page 603 for instructions).

4 When ready to cook, brush and oil the grill grate. Generously salt and pepper the beef patties and place them on the hot grate. Grill the sliders until cooked to taste, 2 to 3 minutes per side for medium, turning them with a spatula.

5 Brush the cut sides of the rolls with the melted butter and grill them until golden brown, 2 minutes. Watch the buns; they can burn quickly.

6 To assemble the sliders, place a spoonful of caramelized shallots on the bottom half of each bun. Top each with a slider, a slice of pickle, if desired, and the top of the bun and serve at once.

Wagyu to Go

Pronounced ko-bay, Kobe (more accurately, "Kobe-style") is one of the most widely misunderstood terms for American beef eaters. Kobe is a coastal city in Japan renowned for its beef, specifically for a particular breed of Japanese cattle, *wagyu*, that is raised with a meticulous care that includes a special diet and grooming. This does not, contrary to popular myth, include baths in beer or sake and massages to redistribute the fat (if this were truly possible, we wouldn't need liposuction). The result is beef with a prodigious marbling of fat. (I first sampled Kobe beef in Tokyo in 1995, and I can still remember today how its melting richness felt on my tongue.) Despite Kobe's reputation (and name recognition), many other cattle districts in Japan—Saga, for example—are equally revered for their beef.

In 1976 a handful of *wagyu* cows were brought to the United States, launching a superpremium beef industry that supplies steak houses with Kobe-style beef. (Sorry, if it doesn't come from Kobe, Japan, it's not Kobe beef.) Unfortunately, there are no precise industry standards for diet, marbling, or aging that dictate just what constitutes *wagyu* or Kobe-style beef, with the result that, while some of the beef is good, much of it is extremely ordinary and price is no indication of quality.

Turkish "Meatball" Burgers
{ KOFTESI }

In the early years of the last century, a pious young man from eastern Tajikistan set off to make *haji,* the Muslim pilgrimage to Mecca. Mehmet Tezçakin got as far as Istanbul when the First World War broke out. Stranded in the big city, he did what innumerable grill masters have done: He set up a *mangal*—a grateless grill—and three tables in a storefront no wider than a closet and began selling tiny rectangular ground beef patties called *köftesi.* (Yes, they're related etymologically to the ground meat kebabs of the Middle East known as *kofta.*) To bring in a little extra cash, he moonlighted selling charcoal. Business boomed; soon he had eight tables, then a proper dining room, then a new restaurant in the lively Sultanahmet neighborhood in the shadow of Istanbul's most famous mosque. Today, the tiny shop he founded, Tarihi Sultanahmet Köftecisi, is an Istanbul institution, with a 270-seat dining room run by Tezçakin's grandchildren and great grandchildren. Now, as then, the house specialty remains a sort of square burger made from only five ingredients: beef, bread, onion, salt, and pepper, ground and mixed daily to produce burgers with a finer, spongier texture than an American burger—a sort of grilled meatball. Served on lavash or pita with pickled peppers, it's Turkey's answer to the burger. **MAKES 8 KOFTESI; SERVES 4**

6 slices stale white bread, crusts cut off

1½ pounds ground sirloin or chuck, not too lean, about 20 percent fat

1 small sweet onion, minced fine as dust (about ¾ cup)

1 clove garlic (optional, see Note), minced

1½ teaspoons coarse salt (kosher or sea)

½ teaspoon freshly ground black pepper

2 large or 4 small pieces of lavash, or 4 large pita breads, halved to form pockets, for serving

1 cup sliced pickled peppers, for serving

Lemon wedges, for serving

ADVANCE PREPARATION
The burgers can be made up to 3 hours ahead.

1 Place the stale white bread in a bowl and add enough lukewarm water to cover it. Let the stale bread soak until very soft, about 5 minutes. Drain the bread well and, working in 2 or 3 batches, squeeze it between your fingers to wring out the water.

2 Place the soaked bread, beef, onion, garlic, if using, and the salt and pepper in a bowl and mix with your fingers until smooth. Knead the beef mixture for 3 to 5 minutes; this gives it a spongy texture much prized by Turks. Divide the beef mixture into 8 equal portions and form each into a square patty about 3 inches across and ½ inch thick. Place the patties on a plate lined with plastic wrap and refrigerate them, covered, until you are ready to grill.

3 Set up the grill for direct grilling and preheat it to high.

4 When ready to cook, brush and oil the grill grate. Place the patties on the hot grate and grill them until nicely browned and cooked through, 4 to 6 minutes per side for medium to medium-well.

5 Transfer the grilled patties to a platter or plates and serve them with lavash or in half pita bread pockets with pickled peppers and a squeeze of lemon juice.

NOTE: Garlic is not in the original formula, but I like the way it rounds out the flavor.

Köftesi, Turkish "meatball" burgers with grilled hot peppers.

Will the Real Hamburger Stand Up

I'm standing in the kitchen of a homey *taverna* called Kallisti in the village of Pyrgos on the stunning Greek island of Santorini. I'm watching a grill master named Mustaffa prepare *bifteki,* which appears to be a hamburger. Like an American burger, it's made with ground meat, which is shaped by hand into a patty. Like an American burger, it's flavored with chopped onion and charred over charcoal until crusty and brown. But there the similarity ends. The meat is a mixture of beef and veal to which half a loaf of bread, crusts removed, bread soaked in water and wrung out, has been added, producing a patty that tastes halfway between an American burger and a Swedish meatball.

Now I'm standing beside a grill (charcoal burning, of course) in the restaurant Don—more a truck stop really—in an industrial neighborhood in Belgrade, Serbia. The pit mistress here, a slight woman named Jelena Stuparevic, demonstrates how to make a Serbian version of a burger called *ćevapčići.* She mixes three parts of ground veal with one part ground pork, adding chopped hot pepper and some slivers of garlic (to order, mind you). She forces this mixture through a sort of oversize funnel into four touching parallel tubes, each about 3 inches long and ¾ inch wide. The result is a sort of deeply ridged, square patty, which Jelena sears over glowing charcoal. Like *bifteki,* the *ćevapčićis* are served without a bun.

Round three takes place in a renowned grill restaurant called Karim in Old Delhi, India, where a turbanned grill jockey combines ground lamb with chopped cilantro, ginger, cumin, nutmeg, chiles, and a half dozen other ingredients into a mixture he'll grill on a wide flat metal skewer over embers fired by a small electric fan. The dish is called *seekh kabab*—yet another member of a burger family that is much vaster than many Americans realize.

The fact is, as you travel the barbecue trail, grilled ground meat patties turn up everywhere. But what goes into them, and how they're seasoned and shaped, varies as much as the language and culture of the countries where they're enjoyed. The short list of burgers on Planet Barbecue include *pljeskavica* from Bosnia and Herzegovina, *mititei* from Romania, *chapli kabab* from Pakistan, *kufteh* from Bulgaria, and *lula* from Azerbaijan.

Even the burger we know and love may not be quite as American as you think. Our beloved patty takes its name, not surprisingly, from Hamburg, Germany. In the eighteenth century, Hamburg was the largest port in Europe and thus something of a culinary melting pot. German seafarers, the story goes, acquired a taste for the seasoned chopped raw beef known as steak tartare popular in trading ports in Russia. Tartary was the name given to the steppes of Central Asia, where marauding Mongol horsemen made the original ground beef patty, again so the story goes, by tenderizing tough slabs of meat under their saddles.

Obviously, there are some gaps in the story. First, who first had the idea to cook steak tartare instead of serving it raw? Second, did they really eat hamburgers in Hamburg (and how come they are not part of traditional German cooking?), and how did the dish come to the United States? Many places claim to be the birthplace of the hamburger. Few defend the title more fiercely than Louis' Lunch in New Haven, Connecticut. According to the owner of this tiny redbrick building, patronized by generations of Yalies (like my late friend Michael Male), the hamburger was invented in 1898 by Louis Lassen, a Danish blacksmith turned preacher and lunch counter operator, whose frugality made it painful for him to discard any leftover scraps of beef. So he ground them into patties, which he broiled over an open flame and slapped between two slices of toast. Louis felt his burgers were so remarkable that they shouldn't be camouflaged under ketchup or mustard. To this day, these condiments are eschewed at Louis' Lunch.

It's an interesting theory, but the historical record suggests the hamburger reached America in the early nineteenth century. By 1834, "hamburger steaks" were listed on the menu of the legendary Delmonico's in New York. Curiously, they sold for ten cents an order—twice the price of a veal cutlet or a slab of roast beef!

My own belief is that there is no one ur-hamburger—that like language or law, it was a great idea that occurred in many parts of the world simultaneously.

Really Big Bosnian Burgers
{ PLJESKAVICA }

Sure, there are larger burgers in the record books—monstrosities like the 8,266 pound hamburger created at the Burger Fest in Seymour, Wisconsin, on August 4, 2001. But when it comes to the largest burger served day in and day out to ordinary folks, the prize goes to *pljeskavica*, a grilled beef and veal patty from the Eastern European region once known as Yugoslavia. Every new country in this ancient land of grilling and religious tension has a version, but even hard-liners of opposing political camps will go out of their way to eat a *pljeskavica* made by a Bosnian grill master. Traditionally, the burger is eaten with a knife and fork and with bread on the side, but you can certainly serve it on a pita bread as a sandwich. **MAKES 4 BURGERS; SERVES 4**

12 ounces ground beef, ideally chuck and with a
    fat content of 15 to 20 percent
12 ounces ground veal, or more ground beef
½ medium-size onion, minced
2 cloves garlic, minced
1 to 2 serrano peppers, stemmed, seeded,
    and minced (for a hotter pljeskavica leave
    the seeds in), or 1 tablespoon hot red
    pepper flakes
¼ cup finely chopped fresh flat-leaf parsley
1½ teaspoons coarse salt (kosher or sea)
½ teaspoon freshly ground black pepper
Grilled pita bread (optional, page 91),
    for serving
Tomato slices (optional), for serving
Lemon wedges (optional), for serving

ADVANCE PREPARATION
30 minutes to 1 hour for refrigerating the meat

1 Place the beef, veal, onion, garlic, serrano pepper(s), parsley, salt, and black pepper in a large mixing bowl and knead them gently with your hands until thoroughly blended. Cover the bowl with plastic wrap and refrigerate the beef mixture for 30 minutes to 1 hour.

2 Divide the meat mixture into 4 equal portions and place these on a metal baking sheet. Mold each portion into a large flat disk shaped like a pita bread. Each *pljeskavica* should be 6 to 8 inches across and ¼ inch thick.

3 Set up the grill for direct grilling and preheat it to high.

4 When ready to cook, brush and thoroughly oil the grill grate. Loosen the *pljeskavicas* from the baking sheet by sliding a slender metal spatula or carving knife under them and then

THE SCOOP

WHERE: Enjoyed throughout the former Yugoslavia; this—the spiciest version—comes from Bosnia and Herzegovina

WHAT: The world's biggest burger, a plate-size beef- and veal-patty spiced up with garlic, onion, and hot peppers

HOW: Direct grilling

JUST THE FACTS: The easiest way to form a *pljeskavica* is to mold it on a hard, cold flat work surface, like a steel table or marble slab, then pry it loose with a slender metal spatula or carving knife.

HOW TO MAKE REALLY BIG BOSNIAN BURGERS

1. *Add the minced onion and garlic to the beef and veal mixture.*

2. *Knead the ingredients together with your fingers.*

3. *Divide the meat mixture into four equal portions.*

4. *Form the mixture into large flat burgers shaped like pita breads.*

5. *Use a long metal spatula to loosen the meat from the work surface.*

6. *Grill the pljeskavicas until browned on both sides and cooked through.*

Pljeskavica with traditional accompaniments: pita, tomato, and lemon.

carefully transfer them to the hot grill grate. Grill the *pljeskavicas* until cooked through, 2 to 3 minutes per side for medium to medium-well, using a wide spatula to turn them. (Bosnians prefer their grilled meat medium to medium-well done.)

5 Transfer the grilled *pljeskavicas* to a platter or plates and serve them at once with pitas, tomato slices, and lemon wedges, if desired.

Moroccan "Sliders"

You know the scene: In every barbecue capital there's one street with grill restaurants lined up one after another. Four or five will have a handful of customers and one will have standing room only. Welcome to Haj Brik, located at the epicenter of the Marrakech grill scene: Bani Marine Street. Since 1947, this tiny storefront has been packing them in for *kofta* (ground lamb kebabs), Marrakech mixed grill, and the Moroccan equivalent of sliders. You sit down for lunch at Haj Brik and the grill man shapes and cooks your sliders to order. They come off the grill crusty on the outside; the succulence comes from the tomato-olive relish and the Onion Relish. (For more on Haj Brik, see page 276.) **MAKES 12 SLIDERS; SERVES 4**

THE SCOOP

WHERE: Marrakech, Morocco

WHAT: Cumin-scented, grilled ground beef or lamb patties served with a tomato and olive salad and onion relish

HOW: Direct grilling

JUST THE FACTS: The ground meat shouldn't be too lean— 15 to 20 percent fat is ideal.

1½ pounds ground beef or lamb, or a mixture of both, not too lean

1 small onion, finely chopped

¼ cup chopped fresh flat-leaf parsley

1½ teaspoons coarse salt (kosher or sea)

½ teaspoon freshly ground black pepper

½ teaspoon ground cumin

2 luscious, red ripe tomatoes

½ cup black olives, preferably Moroccan dry-cured olives

3 tablespoons coarsely chopped fresh flat-leaf parsley

1 lemon, cut into wedges

Coarse salt (kosher or sea) and freshly ground black pepper

Moroccan bread or pita bread

Onion Relish (see page 337)

ADVANCE PREPARATION
None

1 Place the beef, chopped onion, ¼ cup parsley, salt, pepper, and cumin in a mixing bowl and mix them together with your fingers. Lightly wet your hands with cold water and form the meat mixture into 12 patties that are about 2 inches across and ½ inch thick. Place the patties on a baking sheet lined with plastic wrap and refrigerate them, covered, until you are ready to grill.

Moroccan "sliders" on the grill at Haj Brik.

Barbara and I enjoy a traditional formal Moroccan meal at a riad (garden mansion) in Marrakech.

2 Place the tomatoes, olives, and 3 tablespoons of parsley in a nonreactive bowl and toss to mix. Squeeze in the juice of one or two lemon wedges. Place the remaining lemon wedges in a dish and set them aside for serving. Season the tomato-olive relish with salt and pepper to taste; it should be highly seasoned.

3 Set up the grill for direct grilling and preheat it to high.

4 When ready to cook, brush and oil the grill grate. Place the patties on the hot grate and grill them until crusty and brown and cooked through, 2 to 4 minutes per side for medium to medium-well. (Moroccans prefer their meat medium to medium-well done.)

5 Transfer the grilled patties to a platter or plate. To eat, place a patty on a piece of bread. Squeeze some lemon juice on top and spoon some tomato-olive salad and Onion Relish over the patty.

Veal and Beef Burgers
{ BIFTEKI }

THE SCOOP

WHERE: Santorini, Greece

WHAT: A Greek beef and veal "hamburger"

HOW: Direct grilling

JUST THE FACTS: Because the burger mixture is soft, consider grilling the *bifteki* in a grill basket. Like many of the burgers in the Balkans, Greek *biftekis* are not traditionally served on a bun but with bread on the side.

Marry a Swedish meatball with an American hamburger and you wind up with Greek *bifteki*. The etymology of this singular dish is as convoluted as its description. The name comes from the French *bifteck,* a transliteration of the English beefsteak. There's nothing remotely steak-like about Greek *bifteki;* it's really more of a burger made with a mixture of ground veal, beef, and bread. If American burgers are characterized by their meatiness and chew, Greek *bifteki* are prized for a light consistency that could almost be described as airy. A paradoxical effect, to be sure, and the way you achieve it is by lightening the veal and beef mixture with white bread softened in water. Here's how *bifteki* is made by an Egyptian grill master named Mustaffa at the homey *taverna* Kallisti on the main square in the village of Pyrgos on the island of Santorini. **MAKES 8 BURGERS; SERVES 4**

Grill the bifteki *until crusty and brown on both sides.*

FOR THE BURGERS

1 chunk (4 to 5 inches) country-style white bread,
    or 4 thick slices of white bread, crusts removed
1 pound coarsely ground veal
½ pound coarsely ground beef, ideally with a fat content
    of 15 to 20 percent
¼ red onion, finely chopped (about 3 tablespoons)
3 tablespoons chopped fresh flat-leaf parsley
1½ teaspoons coarse salt (kosher or sea)
½ teaspoon freshly ground black pepper

FOR THE ONION AND PARSLEY RELISH

½ medium-size red onion, or 1 large shallot, thinly sliced
¼ cup coarsely chopped fresh flat-leaf parsley

Lemon halves or wedges, for serving

YOU'LL ALSO NEED

Grill basket (optional)

Taverna Kallisti owners, Nektarios and Nikki Fitros.

ADVANCE PREPARATION

None, however the patties can be made several hours ahead.

1 Make the burgers: Place the bread in a bowl and add enough lukewarm water to cover it. Let the bread soak until very soft, about 5 minutes. Drain the bread well and, working in 2 or 3 batches, squeeze it between your fingers to wring out the water.

2 Place the soaked bread, veal, beef, onion, parsley, and the salt and pepper in a shallow bowl or on a metal tray, as they do in Greece, and mix with your fingers until smooth. (The motion is rather like kneading bread; mix with your fingers and push with the heel of your hand.) Divide the meat mixture into 8 equal portions. Mold each portion into a patty about 3 inches across and ½ inch thick. Place the patties on a plate lined with plastic wrap and refrigerate them, covered, until you are ready to grill.

3 Make the onion and parsley relish: Combine the sliced onion and ¼ cup of parsley in a small bowl and refrigerate the relish, covered, until you are ready to serve.

4 Set up the grill for direct grilling and preheat it to high.

5 When ready to cook, if you are not using a grill basket, brush and oil the grill grate. If you are using a grill basket, spray it with cooking oil spray, arrange the burgers in the basket, and close it. Place the burgers on the hot grate and grill them until nicely browned and cooked through, 2 to 4 minutes per side for medium to medium-well. If you are not using a grill basket, use a spatula to turn the burgers.

6 Transfer the grilled burgers to a platter or plates and serve them with the Onion and Parsley Relish and lemon.

Serbia: Meat Meets Fire on the Banks of the Danube

I must confess, as I landed in Belgrade, I felt no small apprehension. After all, wasn't this the place where just a decade ago Serb nationalists ignited one of the bloodiest civil wars in Europe? Imagine my surprise to find a city of stately old buildings and a people with old-fashioned manners, where men doff their hats to strangers and stand up when a lady comes to the table. I also found a country obsessed with grilling, where no restaurant is too fancy—or too humble—to do without a charcoal-burning grill and where a carnivore (and everyone is a carnivore in Serbia) can look forward to meats bursting with smoky primal flavors; where chickens and pigs are still raised on farms and not in factories.

Kalemegdan Fortress in Belgrade on the Danube (Dunav) River, Serbia.

One measure of the Serbian passion for grilling is that gas grills are virtually nonexistent. Charcoal is king; a lot of Serbs make their own and over it they grill all manner of beef, pork, lamb, poultry, and peppers, often to be served at a single meal. As you'd expect of a country once occupied by the Ottoman Turks, shish kebab enjoys great popularity. It's known locally as *ražnjići,* and as in Turkey, Serbs completely fill the skewers with meat. Serbs also love meats that are stuffed and/or rolled, like *pileći paketići* ("little bundles"), chicken legs stuffed with onions and Serbia's supernaturally smoky bacon, or *rolovani,* small rolls of pork or veal cutlets stuffed with ham and cheese.

Ground meats achieve the level of a fetish in Serbian barbecue, grilled in short, stubby skinless sausages known as *ćevapčići* (think of a cross between a hamburger and bratwurst), for example, or as *pljeskavica,* a large, flat, thin, mixed ground meat patty spiced up with garlic and fresh hot peppers that may qualify as the world's biggest burger. Some grill masters gild the lily, as it

Both Truck Stops and Fancy Restaurants Have Grills

Fresh hot peppers electrify Balkan grilling.

SERBIA

BELGRADE

LESKOVAC

0   25   50   75
MILES

S erbia, home of *ćevapčići, pljeskavica, ražnjići,* and other Balkan grilling.

Outdoor cafes on Kneza Mihailova a popular pedestrian boulevard in Belgrade.

were, by stuffing the *pljeskavica* with onions, bacon, and cheese. The largest *pljeskavica* on record, created at the barbecue festival in Leskovac, weighed 48 kilograms—105 pounds.

The best way to enjoy Serbian barbecue is to "ride a Leskovac train," an orgy of meat eating named for a city in southern Serbia, where you stop at every outdoor grill stall at one of the city's popular street festivals, eating every imaginable grilled meat in a single meal. Every September, Leskovac hosts an annual barbecue contest. Contestants compete in four categories: *pljeskavica*, *vesalica* (pork steaks), *mučkalica* (mixed meats), and innovation. The winner of the contest the year I visited Serbia was a woman named Bojana Mirkovic.

THE GRILL: Serbs grill on a conventional metal grate, generally positioned on a raised stone hearth or in a fireplace.

THE FUEL: Natural lump charcoal

THE FLAVORINGS: Serbs season with a bold hand, using such salty, strong-flavored ingredients as bacon, mustard, and cheese to counterpoint the grilled meat. As you move east and south in Serbia and in the former Yugoslavia, the meats get spicier, thanks to the addition of garlic and fiery green or red chiles. Many restaurants smoke their own meats on the premises.

MUST TRY DISHES:

Cevapčići: Pronounced che-VAP-chee-chee, *ćevapčići* is a sort of small stubby skinless sausage made from a mixture of pork, veal, and sometimes lamb. See page 322 for a recipe.

Serbian mixed grill (left to right): Cevapčići (Balkan bratwurst), pileći paketići (chicken bundles), and pljeskavica (Balkan Burgers).

Dimljena vesalica: Smoked pork cutlets

Mešana mesto: A Serbian mixed grill

Pileći paketići: "Little bundles"—grilled stuffed chicken thighs; you'll find a recipe on page 388.

Pljeskavica: A large, flat, grilled ground meat patty you could call the hamburger of the Balkans. Often *pljeskavica* is flavored with garlic, hot peppers, and bacon; see page 315 for a recipe.

Ražnjići: Balkan shish kebab

Rolovani: A rolled meat, such as a pork or veal cutlet, often stuffed with bacon, onions, or cheese—there's a pork version on page 255.

Seoski cekić: "Village hammers"—cheese-stuffed, bacon-grilled prunes; see page 5 for a recipe.

Vesalica: Pork steaks

Musicians at a Belgrade restaurant: part of the Serb barbecue experience.

THE CONDIMENTS:

Kajmak: A sort of clotted cream much prized by Serbs to spoon over grilled meats. Some versions are mild and sweet, like Italian mascarpone; others are fermented and bitter—a taste you have to be Serbian to love.

Tarator: A cucumber and sour cream salad often served with grilled meat

My guide, Uros Markovic, demonstrates the proper way to drink slivovitz (plum brandy)—from a flask in one gulp.

IF YOU CAN EAT AT ONLY ONE RESTAURANT: Dacho, decorated like a Serbian farmhouse, is an obligatory stop on Belgrade's small, but growing tourist circuit. If you're feeling adventurous (or you want to go local), check out Chubura in Belgrade's former Turkish quarter, run by a colorful grill mistress named Milica Perunovic (you can read more about her on page 257).

WHAT TO DRINK: No Serbian meal, grilled or otherwise, would be complete without a few vivifying shots of slivovitz (plum brandy), *viljamovka* (pear brandy), *pelinkovac* (a sort of Serbian absinthe), and/or Lav, Jelen, or Jagodinsko beer.

THE MOST SINGULAR DISH IN THE REPERTORY: *Mučkalica*, a peppery dish that starts with grilled meat (one version calls for pork neck meat, calf testicles, pig liver, and pig testicles) and finishes in a pot as a fiery stew.

Balkan Grilled Veal and Pork "Burgers"
{ CEVAPCICI }

THE SCOOP

WHERE: This recipe comes from Serbia, but ćevapčići are enjoyed throughout the Balkan world.

WHAT: A sizzling grilled ground veal and pork skinless sausage flavored with onion, hot pepper, and garlic

HOW: Direct grilling

JUST THE FACTS: Serb grill masters use a sort of wide-mouthed metal funnel to squeeze the ground meat mixture into short stubby sausages for grilling. You can buy the funnels at a Balkan market. Although not traditional, a pastry bag fitted with a round ¾-inch tip will give you the same effect. Or you can shape the patties by hand.

Cross a North American hamburger with a German bratwurst and you get an idea of one of the world's great grilled ground meat patties—ćevapčići (pronounced che-VAP-chee-chee). Popular throughout the Balkans, ćevapčići is a staple and a fast food from Bosnia to Bulgaria, from the Danube to the Black Sea (there's even a Turkish version called köftesi, see page 312). Cevapčići starts with ground meat, usually a two-to-one mixture of veal and pork, although in some places the ratio changes or flips, or other meats, like lamb or beef, are added. The flavorings range from diced onion and garlic to hot peppers or paprika, usually mixed into the meat to order. The meat mixture is squeezed through a funnel to form sausage-shaped strips that are three to four inches in length. These are positioned snugly side by side, resulting in a sort of square patty that looks a little like a White Castle burger. The "burger" goes on the grill whole and, when browned on both sides, is cut into individual sausages to finish grilling. (This comes in handy when you're grilling a few hundred ćevapčići for lunch.) You can serve ćevapčići with rolls on the side (most common) or sandwich style on a roll or bun. Here's the basic model with some common variations for flavorings. Note that four individual ćevapčići make a serving. **SERVES 4**

FOR THE CEVAPCICI
1 pound ground veal
½ pound ground pork
1 small onion, finely chopped
Coarse salt (kosher or sea) and freshly ground
    black pepper

**FOR THE FLAVORINGS,
ANY OF THE FOLLOWING**
1 to 2 cloves garlic, minced
1 to 2 hot peppers, seeded and minced
    (for hotter ćevapčići, leave the seeds in)
1 to 2 slices of smoky bacon (1 to 2 ounces),
    cut into thin slivers

1 to 3 teaspoons mild or hot paprika, Aleppo
    pepper, or hot red pepper flakes

FOR SERVING
Thinly sliced onion (optional)
Thinly sliced hot peppers, such as Anaheim
    peppers (optional)
Crusty rolls

ADVANCE PREPARATION
None, most Serb grill masters form, flavor, and
    grill the ćevapčići to order

1 Make the *ćevapčići:* Place the veal, pork, chopped onion, about 1½ teaspoons of salt, and about ½ teaspoon of pepper in a large bowl and mix with your hands or a wooden spoon. Many Balkan grill masters mix the meat right on the work surface. Mix in your choice of any of the flavorings.

2 If you have a sausage funnel or pastry bag, squeeze the ground meat mixture into short, stubby sausage shapes, each about 4 inches long and 1 inch wide. Arrange four next to and touching each other on a work surface or a plate lined with plastic wrap to form a square patty. Repeat until all of the meat mixture is used up. Alternatively, oil your hands with vegetable oil and form the sausages and then the patties by hand.

3 Set up the grill for direct grilling and preheat it to high.

4 When ready to cook, brush and oil the grill grate. Slide a metal spatula or long slender knife under the *ćevapčići* to loosen them from the work surface and transfer them directly to the grill.

5 Arrange the *ćevapčići* on the hot grate and grill them until about three quarters cooked, 2 to 3 minutes per side; the outside will begin to brown and the ground meat will be sizzling. Cut each patty into individual sausages and continue grilling until browned and cooked through, 1 to 2 minutes longer. Serve the *ćevapčići* at once with sliced onion and peppers on top, if desired, and crusty rolls.

Cevapčići *(top) and* pljeskavica *(bottom)—two iconic Balkan burgers.*

From Fire Chef to Iron Chef

BOBBY FLAY— from delivering pizzas to grilling for the President of the United States

NEW YORK, NEW YORK

He has grilled for the President of the United States. He's defeated an Iron Chef in Tokyo. Millions of people watch him on the Food Network and *The Early Show* on CBS. And dine in his restaurants in New York, Las Vegas, and at the Atlantis in Nassau, the Bahamas. His name is Bobby Flay and he's had a profound influence on the way America grills.

"Grilling makes everyone loosen up and enjoy the party."

Many Americans came to know Bobby through his first Food Network show, *Grillin' & Chillin'*. Here was a guy who made grilling look tough and cool—even on a gas grill. Subsequent shows included *Hot Off the Grill with Bobby Flay, Boy Meets Grill, Throwdown! with Bobby Flay,* and *Grill It!* Not bad for a kid whose first jobs in food were delivering pies for a pizza parlor and scooping ice cream at Baskin-Robbins. And not wholly unexpected for a guy who trained in classical French cuisine at the French Culinary Institute in New York City.

Flay's grilling is eclectic enough to include the chile hellfire

Chief Grill Master and Commander in Chief: Bobby Flay grills for President Obama.

of the Southwest, the specialty of the Mesa Grill in New York, and the bold flavors of Asia, where he battled—and defeated—Japanese Iron Chef Masaharu Morimoto. He's equally at home serving delicate tasting plates of Spanish-style tapas (a specialty of his *New York Times*–acclaimed, former Manhattan restaurant, Bolo) and hamburgers, the theme of Flay's growing chain of burger joints, Bobby's Burger Palace.

"I don't know of any other style of cooking that lends itself so easily to good times," says Flay. "Grilling makes everyone loosen up and enjoy the party." According to Flay, you don't need a lot of fancy equipment.

"I rely on a good strong pair of tongs, a sturdy spatula, brushes for sauces and glazes, a few heavy-duty pot holders, and a strong wire scraper to keep the grates of the grill clean," he says. "Don't spend your money on a hundred different gadgets that promise to make you an expert griller. You will become an expert with practice."

NAME: Bobby Flay

TERRITORY: United States

CLAIM TO FAME: Chef-owner of the Mesa Grill, Bar Americain, Bobby Flay Steak, and Bobby's Burger Palace. Food Network TV host and Iron Chef

SPECIALTIES: Grilled shrimp with smoked chile butter and tomatillo salsa; coffee-rubbed filet mignon with ancho mushroom sauce; grilled lamb porterhouse chops with mustard barbecue sauce; grilled sweet corn and goat cheese quesadillas with fresh tomato-basil salsa

FLAY SAYS:

▶ Fat is where the flavor is. A great-tasting burger needs at least 20 percent fat.

▶ Don't press a burger with your spatula—unless you want to squeeze the flavorful juices onto the fire.

▶ Keep it simple. It's perfectly acceptable just to brush the food with olive oil and season it with salt and pepper. I save the real blast of flavor for later, using bold-flavored condiments, such as fruit and vegetable-based vinaigrettes, sauces, relishes, and salsas.

Bobby Flay's Cheyenne Burgers

Here's a first—a cheeseburger you make with ground turkey from a guy's guy grill master—throwdown, anyone? To reinforce the smoke flavor, Flay serves it with barbecue sauce and smoked cheddar cheese. Flay tops the burgers with shoestring onion rings, or you can use the caramelized shallots on page 310. The double-smoked bacon is optional. It's a cheeseburger that would satisfy the most diehard barbecue fanatic. MAKES 4 BURGERS; SERVES 4

1½ pounds ground turkey

Coarse salt (kosher or sea) and freshly ground black pepper

4 thin slices smoked sharp cheddar cheese (3 to 4 ounces in all)

4 sesame seed hamburger buns, split

2 tablespoons (¼ stick) melted butter, or 2 tablespoons extra-virgin olive oil

4 slices of country-style smoked bacon (about 4 ounces in all), cut in half crosswise and browned in a skillet (optional)

¼ cup your favorite smoky barbecue sauce

Dill pickle slices (optional)

Shoestring onion rings (see box, page 326) or caramelized shallots (optional, see page 310)

1 Divide the turkey into 4 even portions. Lightly wet your hands with cold water and loosely form each portion into a patty that is about 3 inches across and ¾ inch thick. Make a shallow depression in the center of each patty with your thumb (the patties should be slightly concave; this helps them cook evenly). Place the patties on a plate lined with plastic wrap and refrigerate them, covered, until you are ready to grill.

2 Set up the grill for direct grilling and preheat it to high. Ideally you'd grill over an oak or other hardwood fire (see page 603 for instructions).

3 When ready to cook, brush and oil the grill grate. Generously salt and pepper the patties and place them on the hot grate. Grill the burgers until the bottoms are sizzling and browned, 3 to 5 minutes. Using a spatula, turn the burgers and grill them for another 3 to 4 minutes for medium. During the last minute of grilling, place a slice of cheese on each burger. Cover the grill and continue grilling until the cheese is melted. To test for doneness, insert an instant-read meat thermometer through the side of a burger; when cooked to medium the internal temperature will be about 170°F.

4 Meanwhile, brush the cut sides of the buns with melted butter and grill them, buttered side down, until golden brown, about 30 seconds to 1 minute. Watch the buns; they can burn quickly. Warm the slices of bacon, if using, on the grill.

THE SCOOP

WHERE: The United States of America

WHAT: Turkey burgers pumped up with smoked cheese and barbecue sauce

HOW: Direct grilling

JUST THE FACTS: One good barbecue sauce option is the Bourbon-Brown Sugar Sauce on page 229. Or use your favorite commercial brand.

5 To assemble the burgers, place a spoonful of barbecue sauce on the bottom half of a bun. Place a burger on top and top it with the pickle slices and bacon, and shoestring onion rings or caramelized shallots, if using, and the top half of the bun. Repeat with the remaining buns and burgers. Serve the burgers at once.

Shoestring Onion Rings

To make shoestring onion rings, heat 1 quart of peanut oil to 360°F in a deep heavy pot. Dredge thinly sliced Vidalia onion rings in flour seasoned with salt, black pepper, and cayenne. Dip the onion rings in buttermilk seasoned with salt and black pepper, then dredge them in more flour. Fry the onion rings until golden brown, turning them once or twice, about 4 minutes. Drain the fried onion rings on paper towels, then season them with salt.

Bazaar Burgers
{ SEYHMUZ KEBAB }

THE SCOOP

WHERE: Istanbul, Turkey

WHAT: Burgers with a twist—lamb piqued with garlic and hot peppers, served with a fiery tomato salad

HOW: Direct grilling

JUST THE FACTS: You can get pomegranate molasses (see page 328) at Middle Eastern groceries or online at www.spicehouse.com.

Ibrahim Usta minces lamb with his trademark zirh (crescent-shaped chopper) several times a meal.

The Grand Bazaar has served as Istanbul's mercantile and cultural heart for half a millennium. Ibrahim Usta has been chopping and grilling lamb since 1975, and his restaurant, Seyhmuz, located in a homey storefront a few blocks from the main entrance of the bazaar, stands as a haven for hungry merchants, shoppers, and the occasional tourist in search of flavor-blasted food at moderate prices. You can't miss Usta—he's the guy with the giant *zirh*, a crescent-shaped chopper, which he uses to reduce just the right ratio of bright red lamb meat and fat to mincemeat—the base of his burgers and kebabs. The *zirh* appears through the lunch service, for unless the meat is chopped every fifteen minutes, Usta doesn't consider it properly fresh. His *seyhmuz* kebabs (kebab simply means "meat" in Turkish)—spiced up with hot peppers, tomato, and garlic—are lamb burgers with an attitude. Serve them with grilled horn peppers and tomatoes and *pide* (puffy Turkish flatbread), if desired. **MAKES 4 LARGE OR 8 SMALL BURGERS; SERVES 4**

1½ pounds ground or finely chopped lamb, with a fat content
    of 20 to 25 percent

1 red ripe tomato, seeded and finely diced

1 to 2 hot peppers, such as horn peppers or jalapeños, seeded
    and finely chopped (for hotter lamb burgers, leave the
    seeds in)

2 cloves garlic, minced

¼ cup finely chopped fresh flat-leaf parsley

1½ teaspoons coarse salt (kosher or sea)

½ teaspoon freshly ground black pepper

8 long slender green peppers, such as horn peppers,
    or 1 to 2 poblano peppers

2 medium-size red ripe tomatoes, quartered

Spicy Turkish Tomato Salad (recipe follows) or Tomato Salad
    with Walnuts and Pomegranate Molasses (page 328),
    for serving

Onion Relish (optional, page 337), for serving

Turkish Puff Bread (page 107), lavash, or pita bread, for serving

1 cup Turkish- or Greek-style plain yogurt (optional), for serving

Lemon wedges, for serving

YOU'LL ALSO NEED
Flat metal skewers

ADVANCE PREPARATION
None, however the burgers can be made up to 2 hours ahead.

1 Place the lamb, diced tomato, chopped peppers, garlic, parsley, salt, and pepper in a shallow bowl or on a metal tray and mix them with your fingers until well blended. Form the meat mixture into 4 large or 8 small patties, each about ½ inch thick. Place the patties on a plate lined with plastic wrap and refrigerate them, covered, until you are ready to grill.

2 Skewer the slender green peppers and tomato quarters crosswise on flat metal skewers.

3 Set up the grill for direct grilling and preheat it to high.

4 When ready to cook, brush and oil the grill grate. Place the skewered peppers and tomatoes on the hot grate and grill them until brown and tender,

4 to 6 minutes per side. Place the lamb patties on the grate and grill them until nicely browned and cooked through, 3 to 5 minutes per side for medium to medium-well.

5 Transfer the grilled burgers, peppers, and tomatoes to a platter or plates and serve them with one of the tomato salads, the Onion Relish, if desired, bread, yogurt, and lemon wedges. The lamb burgers are generally eaten with knife and fork, not on the bread like a sandwich.

Spicy Turkish Tomato Salad

Tomato salads like this one accompany grilled meats throughout Turkey—you could think of them as Turkish salsa. Here's the salad Usta serves with his lamb burgers.

2 luscious, red ripe tomatoes, cut into ¼-inch dice,
    with their juices

½ small sweet onion, cut into fine dice (about ¼ cup)

1 to 2 hot green peppers, such as horn peppers or jalapeños,
    seeded and cut into fine dice (for a hotter salad,
    leave the seeds in)

¼ cup finely chopped fresh flat-leaf parsley

1 tablespoon Aleppo pepper, 1 tablespoon Turkish pepper paste
    (see Note), or 1 to 2 teaspoons hot red pepper flakes

2 tablespoons olive oil or vegetable oil

1 tablespoon fresh lemon juice

Coarse salt (kosher or sea) and freshly ground black pepper

Place the tomatoes, onion, hot pepper(s), parsley, Aleppo pepper, oil, and lemon juice in a nonreactive mixing bowl. Toss to mix, then season the tomato salad with salt and black pepper to taste.

NOTE: Red pepper paste—*biber salçasi*—is a spicy red condiment made with dried Turkish red peppers and salt. For information on Aleppo pepper, see page 334. Look for both at a Turkish or Near Eastern market.

Tomato Salad with Walnuts and Pomegranate Molasses

Here's a slightly more elaborate tomato salad—made with pomegranate molasses for acidity (see page 431) and walnuts for crunch—from the Istanbul restaurant Hamdi (see page 298).

2 luscious, red ripe tomatoes, cut into ¼-inch dice,
    with their juices
½ cup walnuts, coarsely chopped
½ small sweet onion, cut into fine dice (about ¼ cup)
¼ cup finely chopped fresh flat-leaf parsley
2 tablespoons extra-virgin olive oil
1 to 2 tablespoons pomegranate molasses (narsharab)
Coarse salt (kosher or sea) and freshly ground black pepper

Place the tomatoes, walnuts, onion, parsley, olive oil, and pomegranate molasses in a nonreactive mixing bowl. Toss to mix, then season the tomato salad with salt and pepper to taste.

The streets of Istanbul are lined with sidewalk grill parlors.

Ground Lamb Kebabs with Cumin and Mint
{ KOFTA }

THE SCOOP

WHERE: Morocco

WHAT: A sort of skinless lamb sausage, seasoned with North African spices and grilled on a flat metal skewer

HOW: Direct grilling, traditionally on a grateless grill

Kofta refers to a large family of ground lamb and beef kebabs popular across North Africa, the Balkans, the Middle East, and Central Asia. The spicing changes from country to country: onion and summer savory in Bulgaria, for example, or sumac and pomegranate molasses in eastern Turkey. Morocco's *kofta* features the inevitable cumin and paprika; and sometimes fresh parsley, cilantro, or mint. What doesn't change is the way the ground meat is molded on flat metal skewers and grilled suspended over the fire on a grateless grill. This ingenious approach keeps the meat from sticking to the grill grate or from falling off the skewers. The result is a sort of intensely flavorful sausage, and you don't need a sausage stuffer or casings to make it. **SERVES 4**

1½ pounds ground lamb or beef, or a mixture of the two, although it's not strictly traditional

½ cup finely chopped onion

2 tablespoons finely chopped fresh mint

2 tablespoons finely chopped fresh cilantro

2 tablespoons finely chopped fresh flat-leaf parsley, or more mint or cilantro

1½ teaspoons coarse salt (kosher or sea)

1 teaspoon ground cumin

1 teaspoon sweet or hot paprika

½ teaspoon freshly ground black pepper

Moroccan tomato-olive relish (optional, see Just the Facts, this page)

Onion Relish (optional, page 337)

Simple Moroccan Hot Sauce (optional, page 414)

Moroccan bread or pita bread

YOU'LL ALSO NEED

Flat metal skewers

ADVANCE PREPARATION

None

1 Place the ground meat, onion, mint, cilantro, parsley, salt, cumin, paprika, and pepper in a mixing bowl. After lightly wetting your hands with cold water, knead the ground meat mixture together by hand, squeezing out any air bubbles.

2 Mold the meat mixture onto flat skewers to make kebabs that are about 1 inch in diameter and 8 inches long. Place the kebabs on a plate lined with plastic wrap and refrigerate them, covered, until you're ready to grill. The kebabs can be made several hours ahead.

3 Set up the grill for direct grilling and preheat it to high. Or, set up the grill for grateless grilling, following the instructions on page 599.

4 When ready to cook, brush and generously oil the grill grate, if using. Arrange the *kofta* kebabs over the heat and grill them until darkly brown and cooked through, about 4 minutes per side. Slide the *kofta* off the skewers onto a platter or plates and serve them with your choice of the Moroccan Tomato or Onion Relish and/or Moroccan Hot Sauce and bread.

THE SCOOP

JUST THE FACTS: The secret to moist *kofta* is to use meat with a 15 to 20 percent fat content. To grill the *kofta* you'll need flat metal or bamboo skewers. For the tomato-olive relish, use the relish ingredients in the list on page 317 and follow the instructions in Step 2, page 318.

Six Tips for Grilling Perfect Ground Meat Kebabs

Kofta. *Lula. Seekh kebab.* All are ground meat kebabs prized in Turkey, the Middle and Near East, and Central Asia. Here are a half-dozen techniques for grilling these kebabs without leaving half of the meat stuck to the grill grate.

1. Mold the meat onto flat metal skewers. Ground meat will fall off a slender round skewer.

2. When molding the meat on the skewers, lightly wet your hands with cold water first. Pinching the meat between your thumb and middle finger and ring finger will give the kebabs the rippled appearance prized by Near Eastern grill masters.

3. Prior to grilling, refrigerate the kebabs resting on the raised sides of a baking dish so as not to squish the meat.

4. When you are ready to cook, set up the grill for grateless grilling so the ground meat won't stick to the bars of the grill grate. To do this, place metal bars or flat bricks at the front and back of the grill and suspend the skewers of meat between them.

5. So how do you know when the kebabs are cooked? The fat will start to sweat out of the meat.

6. When the kebabs are done, use a piece of lavash as a pot holder to slide the grilled meat off the skewers. Blot off any excess fat with the lavash and cover the kebabs with the lavash to keep them warm. Then, when you're ready to serve, toast the grease-soaked lavash on the grill and serve it as a Turkish "nacho."

Ground Lamb Kebabs with Coriander and Cumin

{ LULA KEBAB }

*L*ula (sometimes spelled *lyulya*) is the kebab of choice for a vast swath of Planet Barbecue that extends from the Caucasus Mountains (the mythological birthplace of fire) to the windswept steppes of Central Asia and to noisy grill parlors in Moscow. Think of it as the kebab version of bratwurst or as a hamburger on a stick. There are probably as many versions of *lula* as there are *mangalchiks* (grill masters) to grill it. The basic version starts with finely chopped mutton or lamb, spiced with onion and cumin and molded and grilled on a flat metal skewer. The crustier and greasier the *lula*—at least from an Uzbek point of view—the better. Here's how it's made and served by Uzbek grill master Stalic Khankishiev (to read more about him, see page 333). **SERVES 4**

1½ pounds lamb shoulder, not too lean, or 1¼ pounds lean lamb and ¼ pound lamb tail fat, cut into 1-inch pieces

1 small onion, finely chopped

¼ cup finely chopped fresh flat-leaf parsley (optional)

2 teaspoons ground coriander

1 teaspoon ground cumin

1½ teaspoons coarse salt (kosher or sea), or more to taste

½ teaspoon freshly ground black pepper, or more to taste

2 branches fresh rosemary

2 branches fresh thyme

8 pieces of lavash cut into 4-inch wedges or squares

About 1 tablespoon sumac powder (optional)

1 small sweet onion or torpedo onion, thinly sliced, for serving

YOU'LL ALSO NEED
Flat metal or bamboo skewers

ADVANCE PREPARATION
None

1 Coarsely chop the lamb with its fat. Traditionally, this would be done on a chopping block using a cleaver (grease the chopping block with lamb fat before you start). Alternatively, you can grind the meat and fat in a meat grinder fitted with a small plate or in a food processor. If you are using a food processor, grind the meat in small batches, running the machine in short bursts. Do not overprocess the meat.

2 Transfer the ground lamb to a mixing bowl. Add the onion, parsley,

HOW TO PREPARE GROUND LAMB KEBABS

1. Mince the lamb with a pair of heavy cleavers.

2. Sprinkle in the coriander, cumin, and other seasonings and knead to blend.

3. Using your hands, form the minced lamb into elongated ovals.

4. Thread the meat ovals onto flat metal skewers.

5. Mold the minced lamb onto the skewers to form elongated skinless sausages.

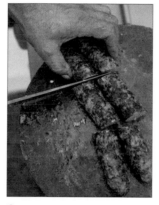

6. Cut the cooked lula into sections approximately 2 inches long for serving.

Uzbek grill master Stalic Khankishiev grills lula on a grateless grill called a mangal.

if using, coriander, cumin, salt, and pepper. After lightly wetting your hands with cold water, knead the lamb mixture together by hand, squeezing out any air bubbles. You can also mix the ingredients with a wooden spoon. To taste for seasoning, grill or fry a small piece of the lamb mixture, adding more salt and/or pepper as necessary.

3 Mold the lamb mixture onto the skewers to make kebabs that are about 1 inch in diameter and 8 inches long. Place the kebabs on a plate lined with plastic wrap and refrigerate them, covered, until you are ready to grill. The kebabs can be made several hours ahead.

4 Set up the grill for direct grilling and preheat it to high. Or, set up the grill for grateless grilling, following the instructions on page 599.

5 When ready to cook, brush and generously oil the grill grate, if using. Arrange the *lula* kebabs over the heat and grill them until darkly browned and cooked through, about 4 minutes per side. After the *lula* kebabs have grilled for 1 minute on the second side, arrange the rosemary and thyme branches on top of the kebabs and continue grilling until done, about 3 minutes longer (see Note).

6 When ready to serve, discard the rosemary and thyme branches. Using a sheet of lavash to protect your hands, slide the *lula* kebabs off the skewers onto a platter or plates. To eat, sprinkle a piece of lavash with sumac, if using. Place a piece of *lula* and some of the thinly sliced onion on top, roll it up, and pop it in your mouth.

NOTE: To help the meat brown more evenly, after cooking it for 1 minute on the second side, use a knife to cut each *lula* crosswise into 2 inch pieces and gently pry them about 1 inch apart.

Lamb Tail Fat

It's the world's most popular grilling ingredient you've probably never heard of. But if you've eaten barbecue anywhere from Marrakech to Mumbai, from Moscow to Mongolia, from Turkey to Turkmenistan to Tashkent, you've surely tasted it. I'm talking about lamb tail fat. This singular ingredient comes from a specially bred sheep called, logically, a fat-tail.

Grill masters have used lamb tail fat for millenia: Fat-tail sheep are portrayed on Babylonian pottery dating from 3000 B.C., and are referenced in the Bible. The fat accumulates at the hind end of the animal under the tail; a sixty-pound sheep carcass can yield as much as ten pounds of tail fat. If you've shopped in a market in the Middle or Near East or Central Asia, you've probably seen it at butcher stalls: clean, large lumps of milk-white fat looking for all the world like melted, hardened candle wax.

OK, I know to most Westerners, the concept of lamb tail fat does not sound terribly inviting. No more inviting than those staples of American barbecue, bacon and lard (the latter essential for biscuits), would sound to the world's billion or so Muslims.

But when it comes to grilling, the hard, snow-white lamb tail fat possesses several genial properties. Thanks to its firm consistency, you can cut it into clean slices. And no matter how finely you chop it, it won't become mushy. This enables you to skewer pieces of lamb tail fat between chunks of meat or vegetables for shish kebabs, much the way Westerners would use pieces of bacon, or add the finely chopped fat to ground lamb to make mincemeat kebabs or burgers. As the kebabs grill, the fat melts, basting the meat and keeping it moist. Thanks to the firm texture of the fat, the ground meat doesn't fall apart on the grill. And despite the fact that it comes from a mature sheep, the flavor of the fat is surprisingly mild.

The virtues of lamb aren't lost on Turkish *kebabi* men, who chop it with shoulder meat to make *kofta* or *lula* kebabs. Azeri grill men slice it into paper-thin sheets to be stuffed, rolled, and grilled. Armenian grill masters insert slices of the milk-white fat in whole eggplants for grilling or between potatoes or onions to make sizzling vegetable kebabs. If you are reading this in what I call Planet Barbecue's "lamb zone," a nearly contiguous grilling region that begins in Morocco and stretches across North Africa, through Asia Minor and Central Asia all the way to India, you can probably find lamb tail fat at your local butcher shop. In the United States, you'd look for it at a halal butcher. The Arabic name is *allyah*. In Russian, lamb tail fat goes by the name of *kurdyuck;* in Uzbekistani, by *dumba*.

If I've failed to make you a believer or haven't piqued your curiosity enough to at least try lamb tail fat, take comfort in the fact that bacon can be a substitute in most of the recipes in this book that call for lamb fat. When the slices of lamb fat are wrapped around or inserted between pieces of meat or grilled vegetables, use slices of bacon, preferably country-style slab bacon. For ground meat kebabs, grind the bacon in a food processor.

FIRE STARTERS

The Man with the Maniacal Cleavers

Host of the Russian cooking show *Not for Women,* **STALIC KHANKISHIEV** is famous for his *lula* (minced lamb kebabs).

UZBEKISTAN

When I first met Stalic Khankishiev, he was brandishing a pair of meat cleavers like some homicidal maniac from a horror film. He flashed them through the air and hammered them on a cutting board, reducing a hefty lamb shoulder into mincemeat so fine, it looked like it had emerged from a meat grinder. Thus armed, he did not look like the sort of guy you would want to meet in a dark alley, and certainly not on the windswept steppes of his Uzbek homeland.

Uzbekistan: The very name evokes images of caravans plying the ancient Silk Road. Of such fabled cities as Samarqand, Tashkent, and Bukhara. Of chopped lamb sizzling on swordlike spits and chicken redolent of Spice Route seasonings roasted over charcoal. Of exotic cooking devices, like the *mangal* and *tandyr*—the former grateless grill; the latter an urn-shaped metal barbecue pit used for roasting chickens or legs of lamb.

A tall, lean, elegant man wearing the embroidered skullcap of a Central Asian Muslim, Khankishiev probably knows more about Uzbek grilling than anyone else in Russia. He comes from the Uzbek city of Ferghana and currently lives in Moscow, where he has made it his life's work to promote the cuisine of his Central Asian homeland.

For Khankishiev, there are three keys to great grilling: the proper fuel, the choice of the meat, and the seasonings. For the fuel, there is only one choice: natural lump charcoal. For the meat, lamb is king in Uzbekistan (as it is throughout Central Asia). When grilling ribs and chops, Khankishiev prefers lambs no older than nine months. For ground meat kebabs, he prefers full-grown mutton, saying the flavor is more intense. He takes pains to use the right ratio of bright red meat to snowy lamb tail fat, about 70 percent meat to 30 percent fat. When it comes to seasonings, he believes in keeping things simple. "We don't use a lot of extravagant sauces or marinades in Uzbek grilling," he says. "Salt. Pepper. Cumin. Ground coriander. Maybe some onion. That's pretty much it."

NAME: Stalic Khankishiev

TERRITORY: Born in Uzbekistan; lives in Moscow

CLAIM TO FAME: Hosts a Russian cooking show called *Not for Women.* Wrote the definitive book on Uzbek cuisine, a stunningly photographed, 75,000-plus copy bestseller called in English, *Kazan, Mangal and Other Manly Pleasures.* Owned an Uzbek restaurant in Moscow.

SPECIALTIES: *Shashlik,* shish kebab; *lula,* cumin- and coriander-spiced mince lamb skewers; and *plov,* lamb, dried fruit, and rice pilaf cooked over a wood fire

KHANKISHIEV SAYS:

► When making *lula,* chop the meat just prior to grilling. And chop it by hand with a knife or cleaver: You'll get a better consistency than with a grinder or food processor.

► Ground meat shouldn't be too lean.

► The wood of fruit trees and grapevines makes the best charcoal. You can't grill properly over gas.

► People tend to make two big mistakes in grilling. The first is overmarinating the meat. A half hour or so will do it. The second is failing to maintain the proper distance between the food and the fire. Hold your hands four inches (about ten centimeters) apart. That's how far the meat should be from the embers.

Stalic Khankishiev with his trademark meat cleavers perfect for mincing lamb.

Ground Lamb Kebabs with Turkish Hot Peppers
{ ADANA KEBAB }

THE SCOOP

WHERE: Adana, Turkey

WHAT: Fiery grilled ground lamb kebabs served on lavash with onion relish

HOW: Direct grilling, preferably on a grateless grill

JUST THE FACTS: In Turkey, the kebabs would be made with finely chopped lamb with a 60 to 40 ratio of meat to fat. (OK, it's not something you or I would eat every day.) The lamb would be freshly chopped for the kebabs, using a giant crescent-shaped knife, called a *zirh*. The incendiary agent of choice is Aleppo pepper, rust-colored hot pepper flakes that are simultaneously milder and more flavorful than North American hot pepper flakes. They have a metallic, almost lemony tartness. If you use American hot red pepper flakes, add a squeeze of lemon juice.

It's war in Turkish barbecue and Adana has fired the first salvo. The grill masters of Turkey's fourth largest city have trademarked their spicy ground lamb kebab that's flavored with the blood-red flakes of a local chile pepper named for a town in nearby Syria, Aleppo. The move outraged grill masters in the rival city of Gaziantep, an ancient Silk Road trading post equally renowned for its grilled ground lamb kebabs—one version flavored with local hot peppers, others made with the surreally green local pistachio nuts or a variety of fragrant seasonal fruits. Of course, these are just two barbecue hot spots in a country where grilling is a national obsession and ancient art, not to mention the birthplace, linguistically speaking at least, of shish kebab, which takes its name from the Turkish words for sword, *shish,* and meat, *kebab.*

The basic recipe for all Turkish ground lamb kebabs starts with chopped meat from the shoulder, leg, or breast, depending on the preference of the grill master, and waxy white tail fat; the flavorings are custom mixed. Each type of kebab goes on its own skewer—a narrow metal strip, a wide metal strip, a square bar, and so on—so the grill master can tell the cooked kebabs apart. If you like your lamb crusty on the outside, spice-blasted and succulent inside, and served sizzling hot off the coals, these kebabs have your name on them. **SERVES 4**

1 to 2 tablespoons Aleppo pepper, or
   1 to 3 teaspoons hot red pepper flakes
   and 2 teaspoons fresh lemon juice
1½ pounds finely chopped ground lamb
¼ cup finely chopped fresh flat-leaf parsley
1 tablespoon sweet or hot paprika, preferably
   Turkish
1½ teaspoons coarse salt (kosher or sea)
½ teaspoon freshly ground black pepper

2 large or 4 small pieces of lavash
Onion Relish (recipe follows)

YOU'LL ALSO NEED
Flat metal skewers

ADVANCE PREPARATION
None

1 Place the Aleppo pepper in a small bowl with 1 tablespoon of hot water. Let stand until pastelike, about 5 minutes.

2 Place the ground lamb in a mixing bowl. Add the pepper paste, parsley, paprika, salt, and black pepper. After lightly wetting your hands with cold water, knead the lamb mixture together by hand, squeezing out any air bubbles.

3 Divide the lamb mixture into 4 equal portions. Mold the lamb mixture onto the skewers to make flat skinless sausages that are about 7 inches long, 1 inch wide, and ½ inch thick, pinching the meat with your thumb, middle finger, and ring finger. Place the kebabs on a baking dish with raised sides, or on a platter lined with plastic wrap. Refrigerate the kebabs, covered, until you are ready to grill.

4 Set up the grill for direct grilling and preheat it to high. Or, set up the grill for grateless grilling, following the instructions on page 599.

5 When ready to cook, brush and generously oil the grill grate, if using. Arrange the kebabs over the heat and grill them until browned outside and cooked to taste, 3 to 4 minutes per side for medium. (Turks prefer their meat well-cooked.)

6 Using the lavash to protect your hands, slide the grilled kebabs off the skewers onto a platter or plates. Blot the lamb fat off the kebabs onto the lavash, then grill it until lightly toasted, 1 to 2 minutes per side, turning with tongs. Watch the lavash; it can burn quickly. Cut the toasted lavash into 4-inch squares for serving with the lamb, and serve at once with the onion relish on the side.

GROUND LAMB KEBABS WITH TURKISH HOT PEPPERS AND VARIATIONS | page 336

VARIATIONS

Once you have mastered the basics of Turkish ground lamb kebabs—the ratio of meat to fat, how to mold the meat on the skewer, grateless grilling, and so on—you can make an almost endless variety of skewers. This is exactly what Mustafa Demircan did for me on a recent visit to Istanbul. Demircan owns what may be the most highfalutin grill restaurant in Turkey—Mabeyin—housed in a nineteenth century sultanic mansion (you can read more about him and the restaurant on page 338). Here are some of the classic kebabs. Serve them with lavash and the Onion Relish.

Ground Lamb Kebabs with Pistachio Nuts
(Fistik Kebab)

These kebabs are a specialty of Demircan's native Gaziantep, renowned throughout the Near East for its sweet, fat, luscious electric-green pistachio nuts. To make the kebabs mix together:

1½ pounds finely chopped ground lamb
¾ cup shelled pistachio nuts, preferably from Gaziantep,
    Turkey (look for them at Near Eastern markets and
    in natural food stores)
1½ teaspoons coarse salt (kosher or sea)
½ teaspoon freshly ground black pepper

Prepare the kebabs and grill as described on page 335.

Vegetable Kebabs
(Sebzeli Kebab)

The primary vegetable here is a hot red bell pepper. In North America you can use a red bell pepper along with a red jalapeño, or use a poblano pepper, which has the right flavor and heat but the wrong color. Sometimes this is called a bride's kebab. To make the kebabs mix together:

1½ pounds finely chopped ground lamb
1 medium-size red bell pepper or poblano pepper, cored,
    seeded, and finely chopped
1 small onion, finely chopped

1 red jalapeño pepper (optional, use if using red bell pepper),
    seeded and chopped (for hotter kebabs, leave the seeds in)
½ cup chopped fresh flat-leaf parsley, chopped finely but not
    too finely
2 cloves garlic, minced
1½ teaspoons freshly ground black pepper
1½ teaspoons coarse salt (kosher or sea)
1 teaspoon ground cumin

Prepare the kebabs and grill as described on page 335.

Onion Kebabs
(Sogar Kebab)

One of the most popular grilled dishes in Turkey, *sogar* kebabs are made with a small onion that looks like a shallot. You can use either pearl onions or shallots. Traditionally the grilled onions are stewed in a covered metal dish with *narsharab* (pomegranate molasses) for a few minutes before serving. To make the kebabs you'll need:

12 small (1-inch) onions or shallots, peeled and
    cut in half through the stem end
1½ pounds finely chopped ground lamb
1½ teaspoons coarse salt (kosher or sea)
½ teaspoon freshly ground black pepper
½ teaspoon ground cumin (optional)
2 tablespoons pomegranate molasses
    (narsharab, see Just the Facts on page 431)

A selection of Turkish minced lamb kebabs. From right to left: sebzeli kebab (vegetable kebabs), adana kebab (hot pepper kebabs), fistik kebab (pistachio kebabs). Note how each kebab goes on a slightly different shaped skewer, so the grill master can tell them apart even when cooked.

Skewer an onion half through the cut side on a metal skewer. Skewer another half onion, cut side facing the first onion half, leaving a 1½-inch gap between them. Skewer a third onion half so that the rounded part touches the rounded part of the second one. Skewer another half onion, through the cut side, leaving a 1½-inch gap between. Skewer 2 more onion halves in the same pattern, for a total of 3 onions (6 halves) on the skewer. Repeat with the remaining onion halves. Mix together the remaining ingredients through the cumin, if using, and mold the mixture onto the skewers in the gaps between the onions. Grill the kebabs as described on page 335.

To serve, unskewer the grilled meat and onions. Keep the meat warm on a plate. Transfer the onions to a metal saucepan with a lid. Drizzle a little pomegranate molasses over the onions. Cover the pan and cook the onions over low heat until soft, 5 to 10 minutes. Serve the onions and lamb with lavash and the remaining pomegranate molasses drizzled on top and Onion Relish on the side.

Ground Lamb and Plum Kebabs
(Can Eriği Kebab)

Another kebab from Gaziantep, Turkey's barbecue heartland, is made with a tart green plum called *can eriği*. It looks like a greengage but is considerably more tart. Half-ripe greengages or any plum will do. A similar kebab is made with crab apples. To make the kebabs you'll need:

1½ pounds finely chopped ground lamb
1½ teaspoons coarse salt (kosher or sea)
½ teaspoon freshly ground black pepper
12 small (1-inch), tart greengage or other plums,
    cut in half lengthwise and pitted

Mix the lamb with the salt and pepper and assemble and grill the kebabs the same way as the Onion Kebabs, 3 plums (6 halves) per skewer.

Onion Relish

Onion relishes are a constant on the world's barbecue trail—some flavored with flat-leaf parsley, others with chopped cilantro, all served with every imaginable grilled meat and seafood. The following version comes from Turkey, but similar relishes are found as far north as Moscow, as far south as India, as far west as Morocco, and as far east as Indonesia. Two things make this version unique: The first is twisting the sliced onions in a cotton dish towel to wring out the juices. This removes the onion's eye- and mouth-stinging pungency, and the resulting onion water makes a great flavoring for marinades. However, you can skip this step and still get a great onion relish, provided you slice the onion just before serving—the longer the sliced onion is exposed to air, the more pungent it will become.

The second twist is the use of sumac powder as a souring agent. The tart powder is ground from the purple sumac berry and used as a grilled-meat seasoning throughout the Middle and Near East. Think of it as powdered lemon. If sumac is unavailable, you can substitute lemon juice. **MAKES ABOUT 1½ CUPS**

1 red onion, cut in half lengthwise and thinly sliced crosswise
1 teaspoon coarse salt (kosher or sea)
1 bunch fresh flat-leaf parsley, coarsely chopped
2 tablespoons sumac powder, or 1 tablespoon fresh lemon juice

1 Place the onion in a mixing bowl lined with a clean cotton dish towel. Add the salt and toss to mix. Let the onion mixture stand for about 5 minutes. Working over the bowl, squeeze the onion as tightly as possible by gathering up and twisting the ends of the dish cloth to wring out the onion juice. Set the onion water aside for another use.

2 Place the onion, parsley, and sumac in a mixing bowl and toss to mix. Serve the relish within 1 hour of mixing.

FIRE STARTERS
The Child Prodigy

GAZIANTEP, TURKEY

Mustafa Demircan has been a grill master for fifty years. He has the scars on his arms to prove it. To meet him today, dressed in a dark suit with a necktie, the owner of a posh restaurant housed in a nineteenth century Ottoman villa, you'd never guess he grew up the son of a poor butcher. Or that he claims to have started in the business when he was five years old, chopping meat with a *zirh,* the scimitarlike knife used by Turkish grill masters to chop meat, that was almost as big as he was.

Demircan comes from the cultural epicenter of Turkish barbecue—Gaziantep. Saying that your grill master comes from "'Antep" is the Turkish equivalent of boasting that your pit man hails from Texas or Kansas City. It was there, in this ancient Silk Road city, that Demircan learned how to mold chopped lamb onto the *cis* (a flat swordlike skewer), applying the decorative rippled finger marks that reveal a true Turkish kebab master. It was in Gaziantep that he learned to add the right dose of red and black pepper to make his fiery *adana kebab,* and to use only the local supernaturally green pistachio nuts to make Maybeyin's signature *fistik kebab.* It was in Gaziantep that he learned to steam the grilled onions with pomegranate molasses to make Turkey's beloved *sogar kebab,* featuring ground lamb and onions.

Here I'm getting a lesson in Turkish kebab-making from Mustafa Demircan, owner of the magisterial restaurant, Mabeyin, in Istanbul.

But like any ambitious young man born in the provinces, Demircan aspired to strut his stuff in the nation's capital. In 1974, at the age of twenty-two, he opened his first restaurant in Istanbul. Today, he presides over a staff of eighty-five, serving as many as four-hundred guests at a seating in a dining room remarkable for its crystal chandeliers and brocade fabrics. But when this reporter showed up, Demircan was not above doffing his suit coat, skewering the meat, fanning the coals, and grilling the kebabs that have made him one of the most respected grill masters in Istanbul.

"It's about art, not just money," Demircan says. He seems to have a messianic sense of mission, and he still personally trains new employees. "I love to teach and my restaurant is my school," he says. To complete the metaphor, he gestures to his "blackboard"—the charcoal-burning *mangal* (Turkish grill) stretching along the back wall of his immaculate white-tiled kitchen. Despite the opulence of the dining room, you have the sense that Demircan wants you to taste the simple, big-flavored Gaziantep barbecue he grew up on.

NAME: Mustafa Demircan

TERRITORY: Turkey (and he's proud to say he has never traveled beyond his homeland's borders)

CLAIM TO FAME: Chef-owner of Mabeyin in Kisikli, Istanbul, Turkey

SPECIALTIES: *Adana kebab,* fiery chopped lamb kebabs; *fistik kebab,* pistachio kebabs; *sogar kebab,* chopped lamb and onion kebabs drizzled with pomegranate molasses; *sebzeli kebab,* chopped lamb and vegetable kebabs

DEMIRCAN SAYS:

▶ For the best flavor, use lambs that are about a year old and weigh about 26 kilos (57 pounds). Here in Turkey, we like lamb that tastes like lamb.

▶ Lightly wet your hands with cold water before molding the chopped meat on the skewer. This keeps the meat from sticking to your fingers.

▶ The best fuel for grilling is natural lump charcoal made from oak.

▶ Don't serve meat hot off the grill. Let it rest for a few minutes on a warm metal tray before serving—this helps "relax" the meat, making it juicy and tender.

Ground Chicken Shashlik with Onion and Dill

The prospect of poultry "meatballs" may not prompt gasps of anticipatory pleasure on the North American grill circuit, but elsewhere on Planet Barbecue they are both prevalent and highly prized. (Consider the Japanese *tsukune* on page 30.) The Uzbek version features flavors common to Central Asia: garlic, onion, and dill. And of course, enough chicken fat to keep the meatballs from drying out over the high dry heat of the grill. This recipe comes from the popular restaurant called Uzbekistan in downtown Moscow. **MAKES 8 KEBABS; SERVES 4**

1½ pounds skinless, boneless chicken thighs
    or breasts
2 ounces chicken fat, or 2 ounces fatty bacon
1 clove garlic, minced
1½ teaspoons coarse salt (kosher or sea),
    or more to taste
½ teaspoon freshly ground black pepper,
    or more to taste
¼ cup coarsely chopped sweet onion
3 tablespoons chopped fresh dill
Lavash or pita bread, for serving

YOU'LL ALSO NEED
Flat metal or bamboo skewers

ADVANCE PREPARATION
For the best results, make the kebabs 2 to 4
    hours ahead to refrigerate until firm.

1 Cut the chicken and chicken fat or bacon into 1 inch pieces and place them in a food processor fitted with a metal blade. Add the garlic, salt, and pepper. Process the chicken to a coarse puree, running the processor in short bursts. Add the onion and dill and run the processor in short bursts just to mix. Transfer the chicken mixture to a bowl and refrigerate it for 1 to 2 hours. This is optional, but it will make the chicken kebabs easier to form.

2 Divide the chicken mixture into 8 equal portions. Lightly oil your hands with vegetable oil, then mold the chicken mixture onto skewers to make kebabs that are about 1 inch in diameter and 5 inches long. Place the kebabs on a plate lined with plastic wrap and refrigerate them, covered, until you're ready to grill. Ideally the kebabs should be refrigerated for 1 to 2 hours, but you can grill them right away.

3 Set up the grill for direct grilling and preheat it to high. Or, set up the grill for grateless grilling, following the instructions on page 599.

THE SCOOP

WHERE: Uzbekistan and Russia

WHAT: Grilled ground chicken kebabs blasted with garlic, onion, and dill

HOW: Direct grilling

JUST THE FACTS: Traditionally, the kebabs would be made with chicken thigh meat with plenty of chicken fat added for richness. Chicken fat has gone out of fashion in health-conscious North America, but elsewhere on Planet Barbecue it is highly prized for its ability to add richness and flavor while maintaining the desirable consistency. You can buy chicken fat from your butcher, or collect it from whole chickens (that's what the waxy yellow-white lumps are just inside the cavity of the whole chicken). Store the chicken fat in a plastic bag in the freezer until you have enough to make these kebabs. If chicken fat isn't your thing, use fatty bacon.

4 When ready to cook, brush and generously oil the grill grate, if using. Arrange the chicken kebabs over the heat and grill them until golden brown and cooked through, 4 to 6 minutes per side. Using a piece of lavash or pita bread to protect your hands, slide the chicken kebabs off the skewers onto a platter or plates. Serve at once.

Romanian "Sliders" (Garlicky Grilled Skinless Sausages)

{ MICI }

THE SCOOP

WHERE: Romania

WHAT: Romania's answer to the American slider—a grilled short, stubby, skinless sausage (it looks like an oversize wine cork) served with mustard and hard rolls

HOW: Direct grilling

JUST THE FACTS: Two things set *mici* apart from the other grilled ground-meat patties or sausages: the blend of meats (traditionally pork, lamb, *and* beef) and the addition of beef stock or water and baking powder. The liquid helps give the *mici* their characteristic spongy texture. The meat should be well marbled; 15 to 20 percent fat is ideal.

What do Dracula and *mici* (pronounced MEE-chee) have in common? In a sense, both are defined by garlic. With regard to Dracula, who may have been inspired by a real-life Romanian ruler with the sinister name of Vlad the Impaler, eating massive doses of garlic was considered one of the best ways to ward off the dreaded vampire. With regard to the sausage, when it comes to making *mici* (or *fleica*—Romanian skirt steak, see page 135), there's no such thing as *too* much garlic. The name of these skinless sausages may mean "small" in Romanian, but their flavor is colossal. And the scent of grilling *mici* is *the* smell of summer in Romania. **MAKES 8; SERVES 4**

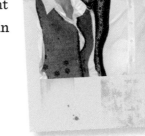

Waiters in traditional garb at the restaurant Terasa Doamnei in downtown Bucharest.

1½ pounds ground meat, ideally 8 ounces ground beef, 8 ounces ground pork, and 8 ounces ground lamb, but any two meats will do

2 to 4 cloves garlic, minced

1 teaspoon coarse salt (kosher or sea)

1 teaspoon freshly ground black pepper

1 teaspoon baking powder

1 teaspoon ground coriander

1 teaspoon dried marjoram or oregano

½ teaspoon ground cumin

½ cup beef stock, preferably homemade, or ½ cup water

Small hard rolls, for serving

Dijon mustard, for serving

ADVANCE PREPARATION

2 hours or as long as overnight for refrigerating the mici mixture

1 Place the meat, garlic, salt, pepper, baking powder, coriander, marjoram, and cumin in a mixing bowl and mix well with a wooden spoon. Beat in the beef stock. Refrigerate the *mici* mixture, covered, for at least 2 hours or as long as overnight; the longer the *mici* mixture is refrigerated, the stronger the flavor will be.

2 Divide the *mici* mixture into 8 even portions. Lightly wet your hands with cold water, then roll each portion into a cork shape about 1 inch in diameter and 3 inches long. Place the *mici* on a plate lined with plastic wrap and refrigerate them, covered, until you're ready to grill.

3 Set up the grill for direct grilling and preheat it to high.

4 When ready to cook, brush and oil the grill grate. Place the *mici* on the hot grate and grill them until browned and cooked through, 1½ to 2 minutes per side, 6 to 8 minutes in all, turning with tongs. Transfer the grilled *mici* to a platter or plates and serve with hard rolls and mustard.

Mici *(literally "small" or "pint-size"): prized by Romanians as much as burgers are in the U.S.A.*

Bratwurst "Hot Tub"

The bratwurst came to Wisconsin with German and Austrian immigrants in the late 1800s. It became synonymous with the state's culture in the 1940s, when an Austrian-born butcher named Ralph Stayer created the Johnsonville bratwurst, named for a village west of Sheboygan. (The village was named after Andrew Johnson, the seventeenth president of the United States.) Stayer's genius lay as much in branding and marketing his brats, as bratwurst are affectionately known in these parts, as in formulating the perfect ratio of lean pork to fat, salt, pepper, and for a sweet note, nutmeg or mace, stuffed into a natural casing. When grilled and served with German-style hot mustard on a crusty roll known locally as a *semmel*, the sausage becomes nothing less than gustatory nirvana.

Several great debates rage locally: Do you parboil the brats before grilling? No, insist purists. Do you prick the sausage to release some of the steam and fat? Again, no, insist the purists. What's the best method for cooking

THE SCOOP

WHERE: The Badger State, U.S.A. (Where else?)

WHAT: Wisconsin's favorite sausage—Wisconsin's sausage fetish—grilled, then served in a tub of grilled onions, butter, and beer

HOW: Direct grilling or indirect grilling

JUST THE FACTS: None, but for authenticity's sake, you should use a Wisconsin-made bratwurst and a Wisconsin beer, like Leinenkugel's.

the brats? Direct grilling over a moderate fire, say the purists. Being a Yankee, now living in Miami, I'm reluctant to wade into the controversy, but I've grilled enough brats over the years to have my own preferred method—one which dodges the risks of setting this highly flammable food on fire while at the same time leaving it astonishingly crusty on the outside, plump and moist inside, and even imbuing it with the soul of American barbecue, a smoke flavor. You guessed it: My preferred method for cooking brats is indirect grilling with wood smoke. As for the bratwurst hot tub, it arose to meet a dire need of Packers fans and other Wisconsin sports fanatics—how to grill the brats before the kickoff or during halftime and keep them warm and moist so you can enjoy them during the game. If you live in the Badger State, you're surely familiar with the procedure, and if you don't, it will quickly become part of your repertory. Without further delay, I give you the bratwurst "hot tub." **SERVES 4 TO 6**

12 uncooked Wisconsin bratwursts (about 3 pounds)

1 large sweet onion, cut crosswise into ½-inch slices

4 tablespoons (½ stick) salted butter, plus more butter for the rolls (optional)

Coarse salt (kosher or sea) and freshly ground black pepper

2 bottles beer (24 ounces), preferably from Wisconsin

12 crusty rolls, such as semmel rolls or kaiser rolls

Hot or sweet German-style mustard

3 cups sauerkraut (optional), at room temperature

YOU'LL ALSO NEED

2 cups hickory, oak, or other wood chips or chunks (optional), soaked in water or beer to cover for 1 hour, then drained; bamboo skewers, preferably flat; a large aluminum foil pan, like a turkey roaster

ADVANCE PREPARATION

The brats can be grilled up to 2 hours ahead—that's the point.

1 To grill: *If you are using the direct method* (the Wisconsin method), set up the grill for direct grilling and preheat it to medium. Leave one-third of the grill bare for a safety zone. When ready to cook, brush and oil the grill grate. Arrange the brats on the hot grate about 1 inch apart. Grill the brats, turning them with tongs, until they are crusty and golden brown and cooked through, 8 to 10 minutes per side. In the event of a flare-up, move the brats to the safety zone.

If you are using the indirect method, set up the grill for indirect grilling, place a drip pan in the center, and preheat the grill to medium. When ready to cook, brush and oil the grill grate. If you are using wood chips or chunks and a charcoal grill, toss the wood on the coals. If you are using a gas grill, add the chips or chunks to the smoker box or place them in a smoker pouch under the grate (see page 603) and continue to preheat the grill until you see smoke. Arrange the brats in the center of the grate over the drip pan and away from the heat. Cover the grill and cook the brats until they are crusty and golden brown and cooked through, 30 to 40 minutes.

Bratwurst on the grill. The flames produce a crackling crisp crust, but take care not to let the sausages burn.

2 Use an instant-read meat thermometer to test for doneness, inserting it through one end to the center of a brat. When done the internal temperature should be about 165°F.

3 As the brats are cooking, skewer the onion slices on bamboo skewers. Place the large aluminum foil pan on the grill grate, add the butter, and let it melt. Lightly brush the onion slices with some melted butter (you'll need about 1 tablespoon) and season them with salt and pepper. Grill the onions until they are golden brown on both sides, 3 to 4 minutes per side. If you are working on a grill set up for indirect grilling, place the onions directly over the heat. Add the onions to the foil pan with the butter, removing and discarding the skewers.

4 Add the beer to the foil pan, let it come to a boil, and boil for 3 minutes. Move the pan to a cooler part of the grill so the beer stops boiling. As the bratwursts are done, add them to the pan with the beer. Position the pan at the rear or side of your grill so that the beer and brats stay warm but don't quite boil; boiling will overcook the brats. (If your grill has a safety zone, position the pan so about half of it is over the safety zone.) Nestled in their "hot tub," the brats will stay warm and moist for up to 2 hours—enough time for you to cook them ahead of time, imbue them with the flavor of smoke and fire, and enjoy them during the game. If you are using a charcoal grill and want to hold the brats longer than 1 hour, you will need to replenish the coals after 1 hour.

5 To serve the brats, slather the rolls with mustard. You can butter and grill the rolls if you like; most Wisconsinites wouldn't bother. Add a brat, some grilled onion, and sauerkraut, if desired.

VARIATIONS

Bagna Cauda—**Italian Sausage "Hot Tub":** Literally "hot bath," *bagna cauda* refers to a warm anchovy dip served with bread sticks and vegetables in Italy's Piedmont region. I've borrowed the name for an Italian sausage hot tub. Prepare the Bratwurst "Hot Tub" recipe, substituting sweet or hot Italian sausage for the bratwurst and white wine for the beer. In addition to the grilled onions, add some grilled bell peppers to the wine. Substitute Italian rolls for the *semmel* rolls and pickled peppers or hot pepper relish for the sauerkraut.

Chicken Sausage "Hot Tub" with Apples and Apple Cider: This variation comes to us from alert reader and "Barbecue Board" user Mike Markowitz of Los Angeles. Prepare the bratwurst recipe, substituting chicken apple sausage for the bratwurst and apple cider for the beer. In addition to the grilled onions, add some grilled apple slices.

How to Grill Sausage Without Flare-Ups

▶ Work over a moderate heat. Over high heat, the sausages are more apt to split and you're more likely to get flare-ups.

▶ Don't crowd the grill. Leave yourself a large safety zone with at least 30 percent of the grill fire-free. That way, if you get flare-ups, you have a safe area where you can move the sausages until the flames die down.

▶ Use tongs, not a barbecue fork, for turning the sausage. Stabbing releases the juices and fat, provoking more flare-ups.

▶ But the best method of all is the least conventional: indirect grilling. The sausages come out with crackling crisp casings and an extraordinarily moist interior. No splitting. No bursting. And if you toss wood chips on the coals, you'll wind up with a bold smoke flavor.

Bratwurst with Curry Sauce
{ CURRYWURST }

In 1993, a charming novella skyrocketed to the top of Germany's best-seller list: *Die Entdeckung der Currywurst* (it means "the invention of curried bratwurst"), by Uwe Timm. The book's subject was one of Germany's most bizarre and beloved street foods: thin slices of a starchy white sausage slathered with a sweet curried tomato sauce and served in a rectangular paper dish with toothpicks. Tradition holds that *currywurst* was born in Berlin in the 1950s, but Timm traces its origins to Hamburg, a city utterly destroyed (like most of Germany) during the Second World War. In the months immediately following the war, the local economy was based on barter. The book traces the adventures of a Mrs. Lena Brücker, who managed to barter a silver equestrian badge for some lumber, the lumber for chloroform, the chloroform for some squirrel skins, the skins for a coat, and so on, until she found herself the surprised owner of a load of skinless veal sausages, a tin of curry powder, and a carton of ketchup bottles.

As Mrs. Brücker hauled these treasures to her fifth floor walk-up apartment, she dropped the box with ketchup. With tears streaming down her cheeks and loathe to waste anything edible in hunger-racked postwar Germany, she fished the glass shards out of the spilled ketchup, now flavored with curry powder. With skepticism she tasted the ketchup . . . and uttered the German equivalent of "Eureka!" The next day, she served veal sausage with curried tomato sauce on a Hamburg street corner. The rest, as they say, is history. Today, *currywurst* turns up throughout Germany (and beyond). There's even a special machine for slicing the sausage into perfect coin-shaped rounds. Most *currywurst* comes cooked in a frying pan or in a grill pan, but occasionally you'll find a vendor who grills the sausage over charcoal. If you do, you're in for a treat. Of course, no one, especially not the late Mrs. Brücker, will tell you exactly how the "secret sauce" is made. Here's my best guess. **SERVES 4**

2 tablespoons vegetable oil

¼ cup very finely minced white onion

1 teaspoon mustard seeds or dry mustard

1 tablespoon curry powder

½ teaspoon freshly ground black pepper

¼ teaspoon freshly grated nutmeg

¼ teaspoon anise seed

1 cup ketchup, preferably Heinz

4 weisswurst or other cooked or uncooked white veal sausages
  (about 1½ pounds total)

YOU'LL ALSO NEED
Toothpicks, for serving

ADVANCE PREPARATION
None, but the curry sauce can be made several days ahead.

1 Heat 1 tablespoon of the oil in a medium-size saucepan over medium heat. Add the onion and mustard seeds and cook until the onion just begins to brown, 3 to 4 minutes. Stir in the curry powder, pepper, nutmeg, and aniseed and cook until fragrant, about 1 minute. Stir in the ketchup and let the sauce simmer gently until thick and richly flavored, 3 to 5 minutes. The curried tomato sauce can be made several days ahead of time but it should be rewarmed before serving.

2 Set up the grill for direct grilling and preheat it to high. If you are using uncooked sausage, leave one-third of the grill bare for a safety zone.

3 When ready to cook, brush and oil the grill grate. Arrange the sausages on the hot grate about 1 inch apart. Grill the sausages until they are crusty and brown on all sides, and cooked through, 2 to 3 minutes per side for cooked sausage; 8 to 10 minutes per side for uncooked sausage. In the event of a flare-up, move the sausage to the safety zone.

4 Transfer the grilled sausages to a cutting board. Cut each sausage crosswise into ¼-inch-thick slices. Mound the sausage slices in shallow bowls, one sausage per person, and spoon the curried tomato sauce on top. Serve with toothpicks.

BRATWURST WITH CURRY SAUCE

Germany: Grilled Meats—for Better or for Wurst

Idar-Oberstein may not top your list of places to visit in Germany. But to come to the land of Goethe and Beethoven and bypass these twin towns nestled between the Rheinpfalz hills and the Nahe River in western Germany would be to miss out on two of the most remarkable dishes on Planet Barbecue. The first bears the curious name of *schwenkbraten*—thick meaty pork steaks perfumed with allspice and nutmeg and grilled on a hanging grate in the fireplace. The second is *spiessbraten,* an onion-stuffed pork neck roast spit roasted over a smoky birch wood fire. Together, they constitute some of the best barbecue you've probably never heard of.

Germany? Grilling? Everyone knows Greek *souvlaki* and Italian *bistecca alla fiorentina.* I venture to say you'd be hard-pressed to name a single German grilled delicacy. *Steckerlfisch?* Huh? *Schweinshaxen?* Never heard of it. *Spanferkel?* Sounds like a hand tool. Germany is the Cinderella of European barbecue—unknown and underappreciated—but come the stroke of midnight (and usually

Sausage vendor near the Museuminsel, Berlin's museum island in the Spree River.

earlier), it's the belle of Europe's barbecue ball.

Like barbecue in the United States, German grilling is highly regional, ranging from *Berliner currywurst,* grilled sausage with curried tomato sauce, to *Nürnberger Würstchen,* bratwurst grilled over pinecones, to Saarbrücken's onion-, garlic-, and paprika-spiced, wood-grilled pork steak. As for *steckerlfisch*

(trout or mackerel stuffed with herbs and roasted on sticks over a camp-fire), and *schweinshaxen* (crusty, juniper- and mugwort-scented rotis-seried ham hocks), both are Bavarian specialties served by the thousands to barbecue buffs at Munich's inimitable Oktoberfest.

In the early seventeenth century a German graphic artist portrayed a first in the world of barbecue—a

Rich with Grilling Surprises

The central food market in old town Munich.

All dressed up and ready to grill. Two girls in traditional Bavarian garb.

Germany has a diverse and sophisticated grill culture. So why hasn't anyone heard of it?

whole ox studded with whole chickens, capons, ducks, and geese—and roasted over an industrial-strength bonfire. In 2005, German grill masters made history again—and the *Guinness Book of World Records*—creating the world's longest shish kebab, more than a kilometer of spit-roasted meat and vegetables, a feat spearheaded by the grill restaurant, Kneshecke, in the town of Dipperz in Hesse, Germany (a record since bested by Denmark and Malaysia).

"Everyone who has more than two square meters of garden has a grill," observes my German grill buddy, Marco Greulich (who won first place in the German barbecue contest and was pronounced *Deutscher Grill König*—German Grill King). "Germany is one place where, even when the electricity goes off, everyone eats well."

THE GRILL: Germans use a variety of grills, the most distinctive being the *schwenker*, a "swaying" or "swinging" grate suspended from a tripod over the fire or in a fireplace. Charcoal- and wood-burning rotisseries are popular for roasting ham hocks and *spanferkel* (suckling pig). Conventional grills, with grill grates positioned over a firebox, are used for grilling sausages. Germans also roast potatoes and other root vegetables in the embers in the fireplace.

The schwenker, Germany's unique "swinging grill." The grate hangs on a chain and swings on a pivot, insuring even grilling no matter how quirky your fire.

THE FUEL: Unlike most of Planet Barbecue, the preferred grilling fuel in Germany is neither gas nor charcoal, but wood, especially *buche* (beech wood) and *eiche* (oak).

THE FLAVORINGS: Germans season with a simple palate—onion, garlic, salt, pepper, and sometimes sweet spices, like allspice and nutmeg. By direct grilling or spit roasting over a smoky wood fire, Germans often achieve the smoke flavor (and smoke ring) associated with traditional American barbecue.

Spiessbraten, onion-stuffed pork roast spit-roasted over a beechwood fire. A specialty of Idar-Oberstein.

MUST TRY DISHES:

Currywurst: A fine-grained white sausage known as bratwurst in Germany (most North Americans would call it *weisswurst*) grilled or griddled and served with a curried tomato sauce. On page 344 you'll find the story of how *currywurst* was invented.

Schweinshaxen: Crackling-crisp, juniper-spiced, spit-roasted pig's "knuckle" (a giant ham hock; you'll find the recipe on page 245)

Schwenkbraten: A spiced pork neck steak cooked on a "swinging" or "swaying" grill—there's a recipe on page 218.

Spanferkel: Spit-roasted suckling pig

Spiessbraten: A cylindrical roast cut from the neck of the hog, stuffed with onions, spiced with salt and pepper, and rotisseried over beech wood (there's a recipe on page 206). In Oberstein, the term also refers to a pork steak grilled on a swinging grill.

Steckerlfisch: Trout or mackerel stuffed with herbs and roasted on a stick over a wood fire.

THE CONDIMENTS: Icicle Radish Salad (page 209) is the traditional accompaniment to *spiessbraten* and *schwenkbraten*. *Schweinshaxen* comes with bread dumplings. Grilled sausages are served with sharp mustard.

IF YOU CAN EAT AT ONLY ONE RESTAURANT: In Munich, you would go to the almost century-old Bauerhaxen for *schweinshaxen*. In Idar-Oberstein, you'd go to the restaurant Im Haag for *spiessbraten* (the pork steak version). For *spiessbraten* (the onion-stuffed roast), you'd get yourself invited to a private home.

WHAT TO DRINK: A crisp white wine from the Nahe or Rhine. Or, of course, beer.

THE MOST SINGULAR DISH IN THE REPERTORY: A slice of grilled bread topped with herbed butter or cottage cheese. It's called an Obersteiner "filet mignon"—a playful insult bestowed by the grillers of Idar on the grill masters of Oberstein. (What better way to insult a griller in this meat-eating part of the world than by designating grilled bread as "filet mignon"?) The recipe is on page 88.

Schweinshaxen, juniper- and mugwort-marinated, spit-roasted ham hocks. A specialty of Munich.

Sausage Kebabs with Pepper Sauce
{ PINCHOS DE CHORIZO }

Here's a whole meal on a single skewer: the meat (two types of sausage), the vegetables (onion and bell pepper), even the starch in the form of *papas criollas*—Colombia's tiny, buttery Creole-style potatoes. It's a thing of beauty, not to mention an object of pride for a Colombian grill mistress named Mariela Alian, who operates a pushcart grill on the edge of Cartagena's open-air food market. You can eat the whole shebang off the skewer or as a sandwich with Lemon-Garlic Mayonnaise (see the facing page). **SERVES 4**

FOR THE KEBABS

8 small (1 inch) new potatoes
Coarse salt (kosher or sea)
1 medium-size onion, peeled
1 red bell pepper, cored and seeded
2 cooked chorizo sausages (about 6 ounces each)
2 cooked garlic sausages (about 6 ounces each), or substitute a 12-ounce piece of kielbasa

FOR THE BASTING MIXTURE/ PEPPER SAUCE

1 Cubanelle pepper, or 1 small green bell pepper, cored, seeded, and coarsely chopped
1 clove garlic, coarsely chopped
¼ cup chopped fresh cilantro
6 tablespoons extra-virgin olive oil or vegetable oil
3 tablespoons distilled white vinegar
¼ teaspoon freshly ground black pepper
Coarse salt (kosher or sea)

YOU'LL ALSO NEED

4 long bamboo skewers; an aluminum foil grill shield (see page 611)

ADVANCE PREPARATION

You can assemble the kebabs up to 4 hours ahead.

1 Prepare the kebabs: Place the potatoes in a saucepan and add salted water to cover by 3 inches. Bring to a boil over high heat and let the potatoes boil until just tender and easy to pierce with a skewer, 6 to 8 minutes. Drain the potatoes in a colander, rinse them under cold water until cool, and drain them again.

2 Cut the onion crosswise in half and cut each half in quarters. Break each quarter into layers. Cut the red bell pepper into 1-inch squares.

3 Cut the sausages into 2-inch pieces. Make a series of parallel slashes, on opposite sides, each ¼ inch deep and ¼ inch apart in each piece of sausage.

4 Assemble the kebabs, alternating pieces of chorizo and garlic sausage (skewered lengthwise), onion, bell pepper, and potato. Refrigerate the kebabs, covered, until you are ready to grill. Set aside any leftover pieces of onion for the basting mixture.

5 Make the Basting Mixture/Pepper Sauce: Place the Cubanelle pepper, garlic, cilantro, and any left-over onion scraps in a food processor and puree until smooth. Work in the olive oil, vinegar, and black pepper, then season the mixture with salt to taste; it should be highly seasoned. Alternatively, you can puree all these ingredients in a blender. Set the sauce aside.

6 Set up the grill for direct grilling and preheat it to medium-high.

7 When ready to cook, brush and oil the grill grate. Arrange the sausage kebabs on the hot grate with the aluminum foil shield under the exposed ends of the skewers to keep them from burning. Grill the kebabs until nicely browned on the out-side and heated through, 3 to 4 minutes per side, 6 to 8 minutes in all. Baste the kebabs with some of the sauce as they grill.

8 Transfer the grilled kebabs to a platter or plate. Spoon a little more sauce on top of them and serve.

VARIATION

Colombian Sausage Sandwiches with Lemon-Garlic Mayonnaise: Here's how to turn the sausage street kebabs into a double-fisted sandwich. First make the lemon-garlic mayonnaise: Place 1 minced clove garlic and ½ teaspoon finely grated lemon zest in a nonreactive mixing bowl and mash to a paste with the back of a spoon. Stir in ¾ cup of mayonnaise and 2 tablespoons of fresh lemon juice. The Lemon-Garlic Mayonnaise can be prepared several hours ahead. Cover and refrigerate it until you are ready to serve.

Grill the Sausage Kebabs with Pepper Sauce. Then, cut 4 long crusty rolls almost in half through the side and slather them with the Lemon-Garlic Mayonnaise. Place the grilled kebabs in the rolls, close the sandwiches, and pull out the skewers.

South African Farmer's Sausage
{ BOEREWORS }

If there is one dish that symbolizes South African *braai* more than all others, surely it's the coarsely ground, richly spiced, supremely succulent beef sausage known as *boerewors* (farmer's sausage). No *braai*—South African barbecue—is complete without it. Many families own hand-cranked meat grinders for making the sausage from scratch, and rare is the butcher shop that does not have a stainless-steel sausage stuffer (it looks like a horizontal metal cylinder) for filling the casings. Naturally, the formula varies from family to family and region to region, but the essential elements—ground beef with plenty of fat, cumin, and coriander (reminiscent of the cooking of the Cape Malays), and cinnamon, and nutmeg (reminiscent of that of Cape Town's founders, the Dutch)—remain constant. The *boerewors* here was inspired by a

THE SCOOP

WHERE: South Africa

WHAT: Juicy grilled beef sausage flavored with coriander, cumin, and other African spices

HOW: Direct grilling or indirect grilling

JUST THE FACTS:
To make truly authentic *boerewors* you'll need a sausage stuffer and casings. A sausage stuffer is a funnel-like device, either hand cranked or motorized, that extrudes the spiced ground meat into the sausage casings, the cleaned small intestines of sheep or hogs. This may sound both gross and complicated, but actually it is neither.

To ready the casings for stuffing, soak them in three changes of water to cover (each soaking should last 5 minutes). Pull one end of the casing over the faucet and turn on the cold water. Flush out the inside of the casing for 2 minutes. Drain the casing well before stuffing.

In Step 2, you'll find instructions for stuffing sausage (it's easier than you think). Alternatively (and not terribly traditionally), you can grill *boerewors* as a skinless sausage on a flat skewer in the manner of a *kofta* kebab or even grill it in patties like burgers.

lively meat market/grill emporium in Soweto called Ray's Butchery. You know, the sort of place, where in true Sowetan fashion, every weekend they set up a grill outdoors next to a sound system with speakers the size of Volkswagens. **SERVES 6 TO 8**

3 pounds coarsely ground beef, not too lean, ideally with a fat content of 25 to 30 percent
1 tablespoon coarse salt (kosher or sea)
2 teaspoons freshly ground black pepper
2 teaspoons ground coriander
2 teaspoons ground cumin
1 teaspoon ground nutmeg or mace
½ teaspoon ground cinnamon
1 small onion, minced (optional)
6 feet sausage casings, soaked and rinsed (see Just the Facts, this page)
Crusty bread, for serving
Dijon or spicy brown mustard (optional), for serving

ADVANCE PREPARATION
You can make and grill the *boerewors* right away, but, for the best results, let it cure in the refrigerator for 12 to 24 hours.

1 Place the beef, salt, pepper, coriander, cumin, nutmeg, cinnamon, and onion, if using, in a mixing bowl and stir with a wooden spoon to mix (you may find it easier to do the mixing in a stand mixer fitted with a dough hook).

2 Knot one end of the casing. Using a sausage stuffer or a piping bag with a ½-inch-round tip, stuff the meat mixture into the casing. Many South Africans coil the *boerewors* into a single large spiral. Others twist the sausage every 6 inches to make individual links. Tie off the other end of the casing. Refrigerate the sausage on a wire rack on a baking sheet until

you are ready to grill. You can grill the sausage right away, however, you'll get a more complex flavor if you let it dry and cure for up to 24 hours, uncovered, in the refrigerator.

3 To grill: You can grill the *boerewors* either using the direct method, as they do in South Africa or, to reduce the chance of it splitting, you can use the indirect method.

If you are using the direct method, set up the grill for direct grilling and preheat it to medium. Leave one-third of the grill fire-free for a safety zone. When ready to cook, brush and oil the grill grate. If the *boerewors* is in links, separate them. Arrange the *boerewors* on the hot grate and grill it, turning with tongs, until browned and crisp and completely cooked through, 8 to 10 minutes per side. If the *boerewors* is in a single large spiral, use a couple of large spatulas to turn it.

If you are using the indirect method, set up the grill for indirect grilling, place a drip pan in the center, and preheat the grill to medium. When ready to cook, brush and oil the grill grate. Arrange the *boerewors* in the center of the grate over the drip pan and away from the heat. Cover the grill and cook the *boerewors* until it is crusty and golden brown and cooked through, 30 to 40 minutes.

4 Use an instant-read meat thermometer to test for doneness, inserting it through one end deep into the center of the *boerewors*. When done, the internal temperature should be about 165°F. Serve the *boerewors* with crusty bread and mustard, if desired. In South Africa, *boerewors* is often eaten with a knife and fork.

Poultry

"**A** chicken in every pot." Such was the aspiration of the early seventeenth century French king Henry IV for his subjects. (The same wish has been attributed to several American presidents, notably Herbert Hoover.) "A chicken on every grill," might be more appropriate. Travel the world's barbecue trail, and you'll find an astonishing array of grilled poultry. From the lemongrass-stuffed *lechón manok* (Filipino rotisserie chicken, so named because the crisp skin resembles that of *lechón,* spit-roasted pig) to Bolivian grilled chicken breasts served with incendiary *llajua* (locoto chile sauce) to Moroccan-style game hens blasted with paprika and cumin.

Such is chicken's popularity on Planet Barbecue that no live-fire cooking technique is too outrageous to cook it. Not beer canning (grilling the bird upright on an open can of beer), a technique pioneered in the United States and represented in this chapter by an Australian grill master who seasons his bird with Asian pesto. Not *al mattone,* grilling under a brick, a popular Tuscan chicken preparation seasoned with rosemary- and sage-scented salt. Not salt crusting, a technique of high drama that seals in flavor and moistness, here demonstrated by South American grill visionary, Francis Mallmann. Of course, there's more than theatrics to these techniques—all are designed to compensate for chicken's notorious tendency to dry out on the grill.

CLOCKWISE FROM THE TOP: *Flames leap up from a grill in Bogota, Colombia; Uzbek chickens being lowered into a* tandyr; *Grilling sugarcane-marinated chicken in the Mauritius Islands; Francis Mallmann's Salt-Roasted Chicken from Garzón, Uruguay.*

But chicken is just the beginning, for the world's grill masters fire up other birds with equal enthusiasm and aplomb. Duck, seasoned with star anise and soy sauce, for example, and spit roasted in the style of Nha Trang, Vietnam. Or goose, brined and smoked as they do at the Auberge Schulamit in Rosh Pina, Israel. Quail, spatchcocked and marinated in orange juice and wine in the style of the Republic of Georgia (a specialty of Kabanchik restaurant in Moscow). And, of course, America's iconic bird, turkey, here brined in orange juice and brown sugar and smoked.

Who needs a chicken in every pot when you've got a grill? If it flies or has wings, chances are that someone on Planet Barbecue has devised a way to grill it.

Previous page: Chickens on a wood-burning rotisserie at Los Caracoles, a restaurant in Barcelona, Spain.

Lemongrass Rotisserie Chicken
{ LECHON MANOK }

The name says it all. *Lechón* is the Spanish word for suckling pig, a crisp-skinned, succulent glory enjoyed in Spain and throughout Spain's former colonies. The cellophane-like crispness of the skin and the buttery richness and moistness of the meat are so prized that the dish has given its name to a spit-roasted chicken that shares these attributes. This is Filipino fast food at its best—you'll find *lechón manok* shops on virtually every street in Manila. You order it through a window cut in the wall next to a charcoal-burning rotisserie. The vendor chops it into bite-size pieces with a cleaver on a well-used butcher block and serves it with the Philippines' ubiquitous garlic-vinegar-soy dipping sauce. Here's an easy lemongrass- and ginger-blasted version you can make at home. If you don't have a rotisserie, you can grill it using the indirect method. Don't be alarmed by the number of ingredients; the preparation time shouldn't take you more than fifteen minutes. **SERVES 2 TO 4**

1 whole chicken (3½ to 4 pounds)

1 cup pineapple juice

½ cup soy sauce

¼ cup patis (fish sauce) or more soy sauce

¼ cup rice wine or dry sherry

3 tablespoons vegetable oil

2 tablespoons calamansi juice
   (see the Calamansi Dipping Sauce
   on page 356) or lime juice

1 medium-size onion, finely chopped

3 cloves garlic, finely chopped

2 star anise, or ½ teaspoon Chinese five-spice
   powder

1 teaspoon freshly ground black pepper

2 stalks lemongrass

1 medium-size leek, trimmed and rinsed,
   or 2 scallions

1 piece (1 inch) fresh ginger, flattened
   with the side of a cleaver

2 tablespoons annatto oil (see Note)
   or more vegetable oil, for basting

Vinegar and Soy Dipping Sauce
   (optional, recipe follows)

Calamansi Dipping Sauce (optional, recipe follows)

YOU'LL ALSO NEED

Butcher's string or a bamboo skewer

ADVANCE PREPARATION

6 to 24 hours for marinating the chicken

1 Remove and discard the fat just inside the body and neck cavities of the chicken. Remove the package of giblets and set it aside for another use. Rinse the chicken, inside and out, under cold running water, then drain and blot it dry, inside and out, with paper towels.

How to Truss a Whole Chicken or Duck

To truss the bird with string, place the chicken on its back on a work surface with the legs toward you. Tuck the wing tips under the back of the bird. Cut a piece of butcher's string about 30 inches long. Bring the string around the drumsticks and rear part of the chicken about 2 inches in from the tail end and loop the ends over to make a simple knot. Then draw the ends of the string over the thighs and around the wings. Turn the chicken over. Loop the ends of the string over again, pinning any neck skin under the string; pull it tight. Tightly tie the ends of the string together—this gives the chicken a compact form, which makes it perfect for roasting.

To truss the bird with a bamboo skewer, place the chicken on its back on a work surface with the legs toward you. Tuck the wing tips under the back of the bird. Starting from the inside of a drumstick, insert the pointed end of a 12-inch bamboo skewer through one of the drumsticks, just under the bone. Push the skewer about halfway through. Now twist the pointed end of the skewer back toward the chicken and insert it through the inside of the other drumstick just under the bone. Twist the skewer back toward the chicken into a vertical position: This will cross the drumsticks over each other and over the cavity, securing them together. Insert the blunt end of the skewer into the cavity and through the back of the chicken. Using poultry shears, cut off the excess skewer. This method gives the chicken a compact form, too.

Place the bird in a deep bowl or large heavy-duty resealable plastic bag (the plastic bag isn't strictly traditional, but it's very effective for marinating).

2 Place the pineapple juice, soy sauce, *patis,* rice wine, vegetable oil, *calamansi* juice, onion, garlic, star anise, and pepper in a large nonreactive bowl and whisk to mix. Add the marinade to the chicken. Let the chicken marinate in the refrigerator, covered, for at least 6 hours or as long as 24, turning the chicken several times so it marinates evenly. The longer the chicken marinates, the richer the flavor will be.

3 Drain the chicken well, discarding the marinade. Using a cleaver, bruise the bulbs of the lemongrass, then fold them in half and place them in the body cavity of the chicken. Stuff the leek and ginger in the body cavity. Truss the bird with butcher's string or a bamboo skewer (see above).

4 To grill: *If you are using a rotisserie,* set up the grill for spit roasting, following the manufacturer's instructions, and preheat the grill to medium-high. When ready to cook, thread the chicken onto the rotisserie spit. Attach the spit to the grill and turn on the motor.

If you are using the indirect method, set up the grill for indirect grilling, place a drip pan in the center, and preheat the grill to medium. When ready to cook, place the chicken in the center of the grate over the drip pan and away from the heat and cover the grill.

5 Grill the bird until the skin is golden brown and crisp and the meat is cooked through, 1 to 1¼ hours. Use an instant-read meat thermometer to test for doneness, inserting it into the thickest part of a thigh but not so that it touches a bone. The internal temperature should be about 170°F. Start basting the bird with annatto oil after 30 minutes, basting it every 10 minutes.

6 Transfer the grilled chicken to a cutting board and remove and discard the trussing string or skewer. Let the chicken rest, loosely tented with aluminum foil, for about 5 minutes. Chop the chicken into bite-size pieces with a cleaver. Serve the chicken with the Vinegar and Soy Dipping Sauce and/or the Calamansi Dipping Sauce, if desired.

NOTE: Annatto oil is made by frying aromatic rust-colored annatto seeds (see page 368) in vegetable oil. Basting the chicken with the oil gives it a distinctive golden color. To make the oil, heat ½ cup of vegetable oil in a small saucepan over medium heat. Add ¼ cup of annatto seeds and cook until fragrant and brown and the oil turns bright orange, 2 to 4 minutes. Immediately strain the oil into a heat-proof bowl and discard the annatto seeds.

Vinegar and Soy Dipping Sauce
{ TOYO AT SUKA }

Almost all Filipino barbecue comes with some version of this bracing, tart, salty sauce. There are surely as many variations as there are Filipinos. The basic model features equal parts soy sauce and vinegar, which you customize by adding black pepper, chopped onion, garlic, and/or chile peppers. Use the sauce for dipping any sort of Filipino grilled meat or seafood. **MAKES ABOUT 1 CUP**

½ cup vinegar, preferably naturally fermented
    Filipino vinegar (see Note)
½ cup soy sauce
2 teaspoons freshly ground black pepper
¼ cup finely chopped sweet onion (optional)
1 tablespoon minced garlic (optional)
1 to 3 small hot chiles, such as Thai bird peppers
    (optional), thinly sliced

Combine the vinegar, soy sauce, and black pepper in a nonreactive mixing bowl. Add the onion, garlic, and/or chile(s) and stir to mix. Divide the dipping sauce among 4 tiny bowls.

NOTE: One good brand of naturally fermented Filipino vinegar is Datu Puti. You could also use distilled white vinegar or rice vinegar.

Calamansi Dipping Sauce

The *calamansi* is a tiny round fruit similar to a lime with intensely sour, fruity, aromatic juice. It's as essential to barbecue in the Philippines as fresh lemon is in Mediterranean grilling or fresh lime is in Mexico. Look for *calamansis* at Asian or Filipino markets, or substitute fresh limes. **SERVES 4**

4 calamansis
4 small hot chiles, such as Thai bird peppers

Cut the top ¼ inch off each *calamansi* and discard it, then place each fruit in a tiny bowl, cut side up, along with a chile. To eat, squeeze the *calamansi* juice into the bowl, then thinly slice the chile to taste and add it to the juice. Use this hot-sour mixture as a dip.

Calamansi: Pinoy (Filipino) barbecue simply doesn't taste authentic without this supernaturally piquant citrus fruit.

FIRE STARTERS

The Barbecue Queen of the Philippines

According to **LYDIA PASION DE ROCA** there are three ingredients for success: imagination, dedication, and the best raw materials money can buy.

MANILA, PHILIPPINES

Her picture smiles from billboards. Motor scooters delivering her wares zip in and out of Manila's notorious traffic. Her name is Lydia Pasion de Roca and I doubt that there's a barbecue buff in the greater Manila region who hasn't sampled—and salivated over—her supernaturally crisp *lechón* (spit-roasted pig). Early each morning at each of her restaurants, an army of cooks stuffs whole hogs with fresh lemongrass, tamarind leaves, and a local green onion that tastes like a cross between a leek and a scallion. The roasting is done on hand-cranked wooden poles in charcoal-fired pits.

The resulting pork is the color of polished teak, with skin so crisp, you can hear it when someone takes a bite. Not the least remarkable thing about Lydia's *lechón* is that she's figured out how to keep the skin crisp for hours—not that her inventory lasts that long. Forty years ago, Lydia concocted a curious condiment to go with the pork, a sauce made with peanuts and pork liver (it tastes better than it sounds). If you're feeling adventurous, try the *sisig;* grilled pigs ears, snouts, cheeks, and the like served in a spicy sauce.

Like many a grilled meat empire on Planet Barbecue, Lydia's Lechon began with an open-air food stall in central Manila in 1968. People tried her pork. People returned and brought friends. "Our first delivery boy was my eldest son, Darly de Roca," Lydia recalls. "He made his deliveries by bicycle." Over time, the food stall became a tiny restaurant, then two, then a half dozen. Today, there are twenty-four Lydia's Lechons around greater Manila, and although Lydia retired and her sons run the business, Lydia remains a household name.

According to Lydia, there are three ingredients for success in the barbecue business: Imagination. Dedication. And the best raw materials money can buy. "But the most important ingredient," says Lydia, "is the one that comes from your heart."

Lydia Pasion de Roca—her lechón (spit-roasted pork here delivered by motor scooter) is a Manila institution.

NAME: Lydia Pasion de Roca

TERRITORY: Manila, Philippines

CLAIM TO FAME: Created the most famous spit-roasted pig in Manila and built the open-air street stall where she started into a twenty-four restaurant chain

SPECIALTIES: *Lechón baboy,* Asian herb-scented, spit-roasted whole hog served with homemade liver sauce. *Lechón paksiw,* leftover roast pork simmered with soy sauce, banana ketchup, and Filipino spices to make a thick gravy eaten over rice.

PASION DE ROCA SAYS:

▶ A grill master's most important tools are her taste buds. It's essential to taste everything you grill.

▶ Don't rush the marinating process (in the Philippines it's not uncommon to marinate meats for forty-eight hours). And above all, don't rush the grilling.

The Philippines:
Asian Grill Secrets Revealed

I often say that there's no such thing as strangers on Planet Barbecue. Just friends who haven't met. Alexander Paman, a Manila-born writer-photographer wrote me a few years ago to fill in what he saw as a gap in my grilling knowledge about *inihaw*—the barbecue of the Philippines. Over the following months, Alex whet my curiosity (and appetite) with tales of *lechón baboy,* herb-stuffed spit-roasted whole hog; *lechón manok,* annatto oil–glazed grilled chicken; and *inihaw na bangus,* herb-grilled milkfish. Long story short, I soon found myself on a Philippine Airlines flight to Manila to experience Alex's beloved Filipino barbecue firsthand.

The grilling of the 7,107 islands that comprise the Philippines is one of the best-kept food secrets in Asia. *Pinoy* (Filipino) grillers use every trick in the book to build complex layers of flavors: marinades that are sharp with vinegar, salty with soy sauce, and fragrant with garlic and lemongrass. Sweeteners that range from the

Filipino grilling: done by women and men alike.

> **"The grilling of the Philippines is one of the best-kept secrets in Asia."**

commonplace cane and date sugars to the unexpected banana ketchup and 7UP. Meats are often marinated for several days, a legacy

of the Spanish, who used *adobo,* a garlic and vinegar or lime marinade found in many of Spain's former colonies, as a flavoring and preservative in the days before refrigeration. There are grilled vegetable salads flavored with the Philippine's notoriously malodorous *bagoong,* fermented shrimp paste. Vinegar-soy-citrus dipping sauces guarantee gustatory pyrotechnics with each bite.

Asian Flavors, Spanish Tradition

In the Philippines barbecue is more than a cooking method—it's a way of life.

Terraced rice paddies in Luzon, Philippines.

Annatto oil: essential glaze and flavoring in Pinoy (Filipino) barbecue.

Fish, fresh out of the water and smoke roasted right on the beach, in the Philippines.

All socioeconomic classes in the Philippines enjoy barbecue: The affluent eat it seated at proper restaurants; the poor stand around sidewalk carts for such uniquely Filipino grilled, er, delicacies as "Adidas" (grilled chicken feet) and "Walkman" (grilled pig ears). (For a full guide to Filipino street food, see page 281.) Come the weekend, family gatherings invariably take place around a blazing barbecue pit or a grill.

THE GRILLS: Filipinos use two basic models: a flat box- or trough-shaped charcoal-burning grill called an *ihawan* and a charcoal-fired rotisserie.

THE FUEL: Lump or coconut-shell charcoal

THE FLAVORINGS: "No other culture uses as much garlic or black pepper as we do," says one Filipino grilling enthusiast. To these flavorings add soy sauce, vinegar, including an intensely flavorful vinegar called Datu Puti, onion, lemongrass, banana ketchup, and the ubiquitous 7UP. Virtually every grilled dish features some combination of these seasonings, but by varying the proportions, grillers give their creations a regional character and personal touch.

MUST TRY DISHES:

Inihaw na bangus: Herb-stuffed grilled milkfish

Inihaw na liempo: Soy-marinated grilled pork belly

Inihaw na panga: Grilled tuna jaw

Inihaw na pusit: Grilled squid, often stuffed with lemongrass and tomatoes

Lechón baboy: Whole hog stuffed with lemongrass, tamarind leaves and other aromatics, spit roasted crackling crisp over charcoal, and served with a spicy, meaty liver sauce

Lechón manok: Spit-roasted chicken (you'll find a recipe on page 353)

THE CONDIMENTS: Virtually all *Pinoy* barbecue comes with one of two dipping sauces: a vinegar-soy dipping sauce called *toyo at suka* and a tiny bowl of fresh *calamansi* juice (from a tiny tart Filipino lime) with sliced chiles. Two other popular condiments include banana ketchup (two popular brands are Jufran and Mafran) and liver sauce (one popular brand is Mang Tomas). The liver sauce tastes better than it sounds—like a rich meat gravy with liver overtones.

Filipino barbecue is often served with turmeric-scented Java rice or *puso* (literally "hanging rice"), a Cebuano dish consisting of rice steamed in a heart-shaped coconut leaf pouch.

HOW TO EAT FILIPINO BARBECUE: Standing at a roadside pushcart or seated in a restaurant. For lunch, for dinner, on the run, with your family, at a village feast, virtually any time of day or night.

IF YOU CAN EAT AT ONLY ONE RESTAURANT: The classic is the Aristocrat, run in Manila by the Reyes family since 1936. In terms of chain restaurants, you could try Lydia's Lechon for astonishingly crisp spit-roasted pig or Bacolod Chicken Inasal for grilled chicken glazed with annatto oil in the style of Bacolod City in the south Philippines. Both restaurants have numerous branches around Manila.

THE MOST SINGULAR DISH IN THE REPERTORY: "Betamax"— small rectangular slabs of coagulated grilled chicken blood

Spit-roasted young pigs lined up at a grill parlor in the La Loma district of Manila.

Uzbek "Tandoori" Chicken

You're probably familiar with India's most famous barbecue dish: tandoori chicken. Similar versions turn up wherever grill masters fire up an urn-shaped clay tandoor, or one of its cousins, the *tanoor* or *tandyr,* for example, in Turkmenistan, Tajikistan, Kyrgyzstan, Azerbaijan, and many other hard-to-pronounce former Soviet Republics and their neighbors. The Uzbek version features a different and simpler seasoning—chicken rubbed with garlic, cumin, coriander, and other spices, but without the yogurt associated with the Indian bird. Tradition calls for the bird to be skinned, which you'll appreciate if you happen to be watching your fat intake. I like chicken skin a lot, so I leave the skin on, although an Uzbek grill master would probably look askance. **SERVES 2 TO 4**

1 whole chicken (3½ to 4 pounds)
3 cloves garlic, coarsely chopped
1 piece (1 inch) fresh ginger, peeled and
    coarsely chopped
2 teaspoons coarse salt (kosher or sea)
2 teaspoons sweet paprika
2 teaspoons ground turmeric
2 teaspoons ground coriander
1 teaspoon ground cumin
1 teaspoon freshly ground black pepper
¼ cup vegetable oil
1 can (12 ounces) club soda or beer (optional)
Lemon wedges, for serving

YOU'LL ALSO NEED

A soda or beer can or a beer-can chicken
    roaster; butcher's string or a bamboo skewer
    for trussing the chicken

ADVANCE PREPARATION

6 hours to overnight for marinating the chicken

1 Remove and discard the fat just inside the neck and body cavities of the chicken. Remove the package of giblets and set it aside for another use. Rinse the chicken, inside and out, under cold running water, then drain and blot it dry, inside and out, with paper towels. Remove the skin from the chicken, if desired. You can pull most of it off with your fingers; use a paring knife to cut the skin away from the wings and ends of the drumsticks. Make 2 deep slashes to the bone in both sides of the chicken breast and in each leg and thigh so that the spices and heat will penetrate the meat more easily.

2 Place the garlic, ginger, salt, paprika, turmeric, coriander, cumin, and pepper in a mortar and pound them to a smooth paste with a pestle, then work in the oil. If you don't have a mortar and pestle, you can make the spice paste in a food processor (a mini processor works better than a full-size processor, but you can use a full-size processor if you scrape down the side of the bowl often with a rubber spatula). Run the processor until the garlic and ginger are finely chopped, then gradually add the oil and puree to a smooth paste.

3 Spoon about 1 tablespoon of the tandoori paste into the neck and body cavities of the bird, spreading it around with the spatula. Place the bird in a baking dish or aluminum foil pan just large enough to hold it. Spread the remaining spice paste over the chicken on all sides. (Alternatively, you can marinate the bird in a large, heavy-duty, resealable plastic bag.) Let the chicken marinate in the refrigerator, covered, for 6 hours or as long as 24; the longer it marinates, the richer the flavor will be.

4 Set up the grill for indirect grilling, place a drip pan in the center, and preheat the grill to medium.

5 If you are cooking the chicken on a can, pop the tab off the can and drink half of the club soda or beer (or pour it out). Using a church key–style can opener, make 2 additional holes in the top. If you are using a beer-can chicken roaster, pour half of the club soda or beer into it. Remove the chicken from the marinade, setting aside any remaining marinade. Hold the chicken upright, with the opening of the body cavity at the bottom, and position the bird on the can or chicken roaster so that it fits snugly into the cavity. If you are using a can, pull the legs forward to form a sort of tripod, so the bird stands upright. The rear "leg" of the tripod is the can. You don't need to do this if you are using a chicken roaster. Tuck the tips of the wings behind the chicken's back. Alternatively, truss the bird with butcher's string or a bamboo skewer (see page 355).

6 When ready to cook, place the chicken, on the can or roaster if using, in the center of the grate over the drip pan and away from the heat. Spoon any remaining marinade over the chicken, then cover the grill. Grill the chicken until it is handsomely browned and cooked through, about 1 hour for a skinless bird, about 1¼ hours if the bird is skin-on. Use an instant-read meat thermometer to test for doneness, inserting it into the thickest part of a thigh but not so that it touches a bone. The internal temperature should be about 170°F. If the top of the bird starts to brown too much, loosely cover it with a small piece of aluminum foil.

7 Transfer the chicken to a cutting board and let it rest for about 5 minutes. Carefully lift the chicken off the can or roaster, if using. Cut the chicken into pieces and serve with lemon wedges.

Beer-Can Chicken with Asian "Pesto"

Despite a reputation for secrecy, grill masters are some of the most open, hospitable people in the world. And nowhere is this truer than in that amazingly welcoming country, Australia. The moment I notified a few Aussie grilling contacts about planning my visit, I was bombarded with invitations. My soon-to-be friend Merilyn Newnham, who works for Australia's largest charcoal manufacturer, Heat Beads, organized an Australian

THE SCOOP

WHERE: Australia

WHAT: Beer-can chicken, Aussie-style, flavored with lemongrass, ginger, and curry

grilling contest, the winners of which would stage a barbecue for me in Melbourne. Which is how, in a single afternoon, I got to taste emu "snags" (sausages), kangaroo shish kebab (see page 188), salt-grilled pineapple (for dessert, no less; see page 577), and even an Aussie riff on beer-can chicken. To make this, Melbourne grill master Julian Wu brings a Southeast Asian twist to the North American favorite—a pestolike marinade made with lemongrass, ginger, and curry. I'm not sure what I prized more: the haunting Southeast Asian spicing or the spirit of bonhomie in which the bird was served. **SERVES 2 TO 4**

FOR THE ASIAN "PESTO"
6 scallions, both white and green parts, trimmed and coarsely chopped
4 cloves garlic, coarsely chopped
3 stalks lemongrass, trimmed and coarsely chopped; save the leaves for stuffing the cavity of the chicken
1 bunch fresh cilantro, rinsed, shaken dry, stemmed, and coarsely chopped
1 piece (2 inches) peeled fresh ginger, coarsely chopped
2 strips (each ½ x 2 inches) lemon zest
2 teaspoons curry powder
½ teaspoon ground cumin
½ cup extra-virgin olive oil
⅓ cup fresh lemon juice
3 tablespoons soy sauce
Freshly ground black pepper

FOR THE BEER-CAN CHICKEN
1 whole chicken (3½ to 4 pounds)
1 can (12 ounces) beer, preferably an Australian brand such as Foster's or Swan Lager, or 1 cup sake, if you are using a beer-can chicken roaster

YOU'LL ALSO NEED
A beer-can chicken roaster, if you are using sake; 2 cups wood chips or chunks (preferably oak or apple), soaked for 1 hour in water or beer to cover, then drained

ADVANCE PREPARATION
3 hours to overnight for marinating the chicken, and allow 1¼ hours for the chicken to grill

1 Make the Asian "pesto": Place the scallions, garlic, lemongrass, cilantro, ginger, lemon zest, curry powder, and cumin in a food processor and finely chop. Work in the olive oil, lemon juice, soy sauce, and pepper to taste and puree to a smooth paste.

2 Remove and discard the fat just inside the neck and body cavities of the chicken. Remove the package of giblets and set it aside for another use. Rinse the chicken, inside and out, under cold running water, then drain and blot it dry, inside and out, with paper towels. Place the chicken in a deep bowl or baking dish just large enough to hold it. Spoon about a quarter of the "pesto" into the neck and body cavities. Pour the remaining pesto over the chicken, turning the bird to coat it on all sides. Let the chicken marinate in the refrigerator, covered, for at least 3 hours or as long as overnight; the longer it marinates, the richer the flavor will be.

3 Pop the tab off the beer can and pour half of the beer over the drained wood chips or chunks. If you are using sake and a beer-can chicken roaster, pour the sake into the roaster.

4 Set up the grill for indirect grilling, place a large drip pan in the center, and preheat the grill to medium.

5 If you are cooking the chicken on a can, using a church key–style can opener, make 2 additional holes in the top. Hold the chicken upright, with the opening of the body cavity at the bottom, and position the bird on the beer can or chicken roaster so that it fits snugly into the cavity. If you are using a can, pull the chicken legs forward to form a sort of tripod, so the bird stands upright. The rear "leg" of the tripod chicken is the can. You don't need to do this if you are using a chicken roaster. Tuck the tips of the wings behind the chicken's back.

6 When ready to cook, if you are using a gas grill, add the wood chips or chunks to the smoker box or place them in a smoker pouch under the grate (see page 603). If you are using a charcoal grill, toss the wood chips on the coals. Stand the chicken up in the center of the grate, over the drip pan, away from the heat. Cover the grill and cook the chicken until the skin is a dark golden brown and very crisp and the meat is cooked through, about 1¼ hours. Use an instant-read meat thermometer to test for doneness, inserting it into the thickest part of a thigh but not so that it touches a bone. The internal temperature should be about 170°F. If you are using a charcoal grill, you'll need to add fresh coals per side after 1 hour. If the chicken skin starts to brown too much, loosely tent the top of the bird with aluminum foil.

7 To serve the chicken, using tongs, carefully transfer the bird on its can or roaster to a platter and present it. Take the chicken to the kitchen, let it rest for about 5 minutes, then carefully lift it off the can or roaster. Halve, quarter, or carve the chicken into pieces and serve at once.

Francis Mallmann's Salt-Roasted Chicken

I arrived in Garzón, Uruguay, after flying all night and driving most of the day. I was looking for Francis Mallmann. The celebrated South American chef–grill master is a tough guy to track down: When he's not at one of his restaurants (located in Mendoza, Argentina, Buenos Aires, and here in Garzón), he's taping a TV show on a glacier in Patagonia, jetting off to some fabulous culinary project in Europe, or chilling in an obscure village without electricity on the Uruguayan coast. But there he was, in his quietly elegant Garzón hotel, in the once moribund ranch town that he's helping resuscitate, his signature salt-crusted chicken about to emerge from a wood-burning oven. Salt crusting is a venerable technique, often used with seafood, but perfect for chicken. The salt adds flavor while sealing in moisture. And the act of cracking open the smoky golden salt crust at tableside with a macho thump of the back of a knife or a cleaver never fails to impress. You can read more about Mallmann on page 576. **SERVES 4 TO 6**

THE SCOOP

WHERE: Garzón, Uruguay

WHAT: One of the coolest dishes on Planet Barbecue—a whole chicken scented with fresh herbs, sealed in a clay-hard salt crust, and roasted between two wood fires

HOW: Indirect grilling

JUST THE FACTS: Mallmann cooks the chicken in what he calls an *infiernillo*, a "little hell," which has a two-tiered fire, or in an *horno de barro*, a wood-burning oven. You'll find a description of these setups on the facing page and in Mallmann's book, *Seven Fires: Grilling the Argentine Way.* I've had excellent results using indirect grilling and tossing wood chunks on the coals for smoke, the method called for here.

1 large whole chicken (5 to 6 pounds)

4 cloves garlic, cut in half crosswise but not peeled

1 lemon, cut in half crosswise

2 sprigs fresh rosemary or thyme

2 fresh bay leaves

Coarsely and freshly ground black pepper

9 pounds—I'm not kidding—kosher salt
    (three 3-pound boxes)

Garlic Parsley Sauce (optional, recipe follows)

YOU'LL ALSO NEED

2 cups wood chips or chunks, or small logs, preferably oak (optional), soaked in water to cover for 1 hour, then drained; butcher's string; 12- to 14-inch cast-iron skillet or roasting pan

ADVANCE PREPARATION
None

1 Set up the grill for indirect grilling, and preheat it to high.

2 Remove and discard the fat just inside the neck and body cavities of the chicken. Rinse the chicken, inside and out, under cold running water, then drain and blot it dry, inside and out, with paper towels. Rub the outside of the chicken with the cut sides of the garlic and one half of the lemon. Place the garlic and the other lemon half in the body cavity of the chicken. Strip the leaves off of 1 sprig of rosemary and set them aside. Place the remaining whole sprig of rosemary and the bay leaves in the body cavity of the chicken. Truss the bird with butcher's string (see the box on page 355). Sprinkle the rosemary leaves over the outside of the bird and season it with pepper.

3 Place the salt in a large bucket or bowl. Stir in enough cold water (about 2 cups) to obtain a slushy mixture with the consistency of wet snow. Scoop enough salt mixture into the aluminum foil drip pan to make a 1-inch deep bed. Arrange the trussed bird on top. Insert the metal probe of an oven thermometer (not an instant-read meat thermometer) in the deepest part of the thigh. Pack the remaining salt around the chicken and thermometer to make a crust that is about 1 inch thick.

4 When ready to cook, if you are using a gas grill, add the wood chips or chunks, if using, to the smoker box or place them in a smoker pouch under the grate (see page 603). If you are using a charcoal grill, toss the wood chips or chunks, if using, on the coals. Place the salt-crusted chicken in the drip pan in the center of the grate away from the heat and cover the grill. Grill the chicken until the salt crust is hard and golden, 1¼ to 1½ hours. When done the thermometer should register an internal temperature of about 170°F.

5 Remove the bird from the drip pan and transfer it in its salt crust to a large baking sheet or roasting pan. Let the chicken rest for about 10 minutes. In front of your guests, crack the salt crust with a mallet, rolling pin, or the back of a heavy cleaver; you may want to spread newspaper over the table where you're working. Break the salt crust off in a couple of pieces. Transfer the bird to a cutting board, and brush any remaining salt off with a pastry brush. Remove and discard the trussing string. Mallmann removes the skin; I like it, so I leave it in place. Cut the bird into quarters or cut the meat off the bone and serve it at once, with the Garlic Parsley Sauce spooned over it.

The Seven Fires of Francis Mallmann

Chef, restaurateur, author, and TV host, Francis Mallmann is the most famous grill man in South America (you can read all about him on page 576). He has spent a lifetime perfecting the ancient art of South American grilling, distilling his knowledge into a must-read book called *Seven Fires: Grilling the Argentine Way*. According to Mallmann, Argentine and other South American grill masters practice seven forms of live fire cooking. Take your pick, but to be strictly authentic, you must grill over wood.

PARRILLA: "The grill." Conventional grilling on a gridiron—a cast-iron grill grate—positioned directly over, and about 4 inches above, the embers of a wood fire. Use a *parrilla* for steaks, chops, fish fillets, and the like.

CHAPA: "The hot plate." A *chapa* is used for pan-grilling on a wood-heated cast-iron plate, known in Spain as a *plancha*. Use a *chapa* for fish, shellfish, fruits, and vegetables.

INFIERNILLO: Mallmann calls this grilling technique "little hell." It's a unique invention based on the premise that if one fire is good, two are better. The fires are built on two tiers and the food cooks in the middle. The bottom fire is lit on a metal or stone base; the top fire on a metal shelf. The *infiernillo* is well suited to cooking roasts, whole salmon, and the salt-crusted chicken on page 363.

HORNO DE BARRO: Wood-burning "clay oven." Found throughout South America, not to mention in Europe, the *horno de barro* is used for baking bread, vegetables, roasts, and salt-crusted chicken using a wood fire.

RESCOLDO: "Ashes." In this method vegetables and other foods are roasted in the gentle heat of wood embers and ashes.

ASADOR: "Bonfire grilling" perfected by the gauchos. The *asador* method is used for roasting whole sheep, small pigs, roasts, and racks of beef ribs on metal stakes in front of a wood fire.

CALDERO: "Cauldron." Cooking stews and soups in a large cast-iron pot in a wood fire is a universal method. The South African equivalent is *potjiekos* (see the "Must Try Dishes" on page 457). Yes, the wood smoke gives a different flavor than a stew cooked in a pot on the stove.

VARIATION

Salt-Roasted Fish: Salt-roasted fish is another Mallmann specialty; it's also enjoyed in Italy and France. Use a whole fish, like a large trout, striped bass, or *branzino*. Clean it well and season and stuff it with the garlic, lemon, herbs, and pepper as described for the salt-roasted chicken. Place the fish in an aluminum foil drip pan on top of a 1-inch bed of salt. Pack the remaining salt around it. A 1½ to 2 pound fish will take about 45 minutes to grill.

Garlic Parsley Sauce
{ SALSA VERDE }

Here's one of the *salsas verdes*—fresh parsley and garlic sauces—that are popular throughout South America. It's simple enough to complement the chicken without overpowering it, but colorful and flavorful enough to bring it alive. Although not traditional, I often add a peeled, seeded, finely diced red ripe tomato. (You'll find a Mexican version on page 130 and an Italian version on page 492.) **MAKES ABOUT 2½ CUPS**

1 cup packed minced fresh flat-leaf parsley

2 cloves garlic, minced

1 cup extra-virgin olive oil, preferably a South American oil, such as TerraMater from Chile

Coarse salt (kosher or sea) and freshly ground black pepper

2 luscious, red ripe tomatoes (optional), peeled, seeded, and finely diced

Place the parsley and garlic in a nonreactive mixing bowl. Whisk in the olive oil in a thin stream. Season the sauce with salt and pepper to taste. Stir in the tomato, if using. The sauce should be made no more than a few hours before serving.

Uruguay: Little Country, Big Barbecue

Guzmán Artagaveytia, co-owner of the popular restaurant La Huella in the chic beach town of José Ignacio, summed it up perfectly: "We come from a little country. The Spanish killed all the Indians, so we have no traditional cuisine. But there's one thing every Uruguayan knows how to do: *asar*—grill meat over a wood fire." And grill they do—over upwardly sloping metal grills at Montevideo's historic Mercado del Puerto (Port Market), on the masonry hearths found in just about all Uruguayan homes, and in the *hornos* (wood-burning ovens) that form the focal point of fashionable resort restaurants, like Garzón, run by celebrity chef Francis Mallmann in an old ranch town turned playground of the rich.

Drive in almost any direction outside Uruguay's capital and you'll see neatly stacked cords of oak logs for sale by the roadside. Pull into any city neighborhood, town, village, or private driveway and you'll smell smoke rising from a *parrilla.* Just exactly what's over the fire

may be perplexing to many North Americans, but if it comes from a four-footed beast, the chances are good someone will grill it. The short list ranges from the usual *bife de chorico,* New York strip, and *ojo de bife,* rib eye—both from Uruguay's fabulous grass-fed cattle—to the somewhat less usual *mollejas,* sweetbreads, and *tira de asado,* thin cross-cut beef short ribs, to the downright unusual, such as *chinchulines,* grilled chitlins.

The typical Uruguayan barbecue, especially at a private home, lasts most of the afternoon. You start with some grilled cheese, slices of *provoleta* cooked directly on the

Holding Its Own at the Grill

Flanked by two barbecue behemoths, Argentina and Brazil, tiny Uruguay can hold its own at the grill.

URUGUAY

COLONIA
MONTEVIDEO
GARZÓN
JOSÉ IGNACIO
PUNTA DEL ESTE
ATLANTIC OCEAN

0   50   100   150
MILES

Gaucho grill session on a ranch in Uruguay's cattle country.

A typical Uruguayan grill: Note the raised metal basket in the center for burning logs down to embers, which are raked under the food.

Distance signs in Punta del Este. In Uruguay, all roads lead to barbecue.

grill grate until it's melted and bubbling, followed by a succession of grilled sausages and organ meats. (With regard to the organ meats, it's best to follow the sage advice of: Don't ask; don't tell.) Next comes a *matambrillo,* a sort of pork skirt steak, cut into bite-size pieces to be eaten on the end of toothpicks, or lamb chops so tiny and tender biting into them feels almost prissy. All this is mere prelude to the serious meats: New York strips, filets mignons, rib steaks, culminating, perhaps, in a *colita de cuadril,* salt-crusted tri-tip.

By this point, you'd have downed several bottles of red wine—a Chilean malbec, for example, or maybe one of Uruguay's little-known, excellent and *rarissime* tannat. Be thankful. You don't need to eat again until tomorrow.

THE GRILLS: Uruguayans do their grilling on two types of grills: a *parrilla,* a grill with a conventional grill grate, and an *horno,* a sort of wood-burning oven. The Uruguayan *parrilla* has two interesting features. First, there's the *canasta para leña,* a U-shaped "basket" in which whole logs are burned to glowing embers, which when small enough, fall through the basket bars to the stone floor of the grill. From there, they're raked under the actual grate, which can be made of V-shaped bars to channel the melting fat to a drip pan, conventional metal bars, or even chain-link fence. The grill grate slopes upward at a 30 to 45 degree angle, which enables the grill master to control the heat and cooking time by moving food closer to or farther away from the fire. You can also grill in an *horno* on a raised gridiron with legs similar to a Tuscan grill.

A Uruguayan street vendor cooks sausage on a portable grill.

THE FUEL: Uruguay is one of the few countries where virtually all the grilling is done over wood, generally oak.

THE FLAVORINGS: Uruguayans don't go in for a lot of fancy rubs or marinades. Salt is the primary seasoning, often applied to steaks by the fistful.

A grill at Uruguay's barbecue central, the Mercado del Puerto (Port Market) in Montevideo. Note how the grate slopes upward to allow for heat control.

MUST TRY DISHES:

Carne de res is beef; *cordero* is lamb; *cerdo* is pork; *pollo* is chicken—and all four might be served at a self-respecting cookout.

Uruguayan steak names are virtually the same as the Argentinean terms listed on page 175. Some other dishes you'll want to know about include:

Bandiola: Pork stuffed with ham, cheese, and peppers, then tightly rolled and thinly sliced crosswise. What results is a sort of meat pinwheel.

Pamplona: A grilled rolled chicken breast or pork fillet stuffed with red bell peppers and cheese. Yes, the whole thing is for you and you're meant to eat it as an appetizer.

THE CONDIMENTS: As in neighboring Argentina, beef comes with a garlic, parsley, and vinegar sauce (more a vinaigrette, really) known as *chimichurri,* but you'll also find mushroom cream sauces served with grilled filet mignon and mustard plum sauces served with pork.

IF YOU CAN EAT AT ONLY ONE RESTAURANT: In Montevideo, dine at La Perdiz (The Partridge) or any of the grill emporiums at the Mercado del Puerto. If you're willing to travel, go to Garzón, the restaurant-hotel of celebrated chef Francis Mallmann.

THE MOST SINGULAR DISH IN THE REPERTORY: *Choto,* coiled grilled lamb intestines; tastes a *lot* better than it sounds.

Uruguayan mixed grill (from left to right): chinchulines (chitlins), morcillas (blood sausages), longanizas (coiled pork sausages), and morones (red bell pepper) roast on the slanting grate of a grill in Montevideo.

Grilled Chicken with Yellow Chiles and Roasted Garlic

As I've said before, when it comes to grilling, Peru is pretty much a two-trick pony. But, oh, what a pair of tricks: sizzling fiery beef heart kebabs called *anticuchos* (you'll find a recipe on page 39) and chicken marinated with hyperactive aromatics and roasted to the color of molten gold on a charcoal-burning rotisserie. Beef hearts remain a tough sell in North America (although many chefs make *anticuchos* with more socially acceptable ingredients like beef steak and shellfish). But Peruvian chicken is one of those crossover dishes that now enjoys wide popularity in Washington, D.C., Los Angeles, and San Francisco—in short, anywhere Peruvian immigrants have spread the gospel of the grilling of their homeland. Here's how they make it in Lima. **SERVES 2 TO 4**

½ cup vegetable oil
¼ cup annatto seeds (achiote), or 2 tablespoons
    ground turmeric
1 small onion, peeled and quartered

Machu Picchu: Where ancient Peru meets the Andean sky.

3 cloves garlic, peeled
2 teaspoons cumin seeds, or 1 teaspoon
    ground cumin
¼ cup chopped fresh cilantro
3 tablespoons ají amarillo paste, or ½ yellow
    bell pepper, diced, plus 1 habañero pepper,
    seeded and diced
1½ teaspoons coarse salt (kosher or sea)
1 teaspoon freshly ground black pepper
3 tablespoons fresh lime juice
1 whole chicken (3½ to 4 pounds)
Lime wedges, for serving

YOU'LL ALSO NEED
Butcher's string or a bamboo skewer

ADVANCE PREPARATION
4 hours to overnight for marinating the chicken

1 Heat the oil in a small saucepan over medium heat. Add the annatto seeds, if using, cook them until fragrant and brown and the oil turns bright orange, 2 to 4 minutes, then strain the oil at once into a heatproof bowl. Discard the annatto seeds. If you are using turmeric, add it to the hot oil and cook it until fragrant and golden, about 30 seconds. Strain the turmeric oil through a fine-mesh strainer or disposable coffee filter. Let the oil cool to room temperature.

2 Heat a dry cast-iron skillet over medium heat (if your grill has a side burner, this is a good time to use it). Add the onion and garlic and cook until browned on all sides, about 2 minutes per side, 4 to 8 minutes in all. (You can also grill the onion and garlic on bamboo skewers.) Transfer the onion and garlic to a plate and let cool.

3 Add the cumin seeds to the hot skillet and toast them over medium heat until very fragrant and lightly browned, about 2 minutes for cumin seeds, 30 seconds to 1 minute for ground cumin. Transfer the toasted cumin to a small bowl and let cool. Grind the cumin seeds to a fine powder in a spice mill or pound them to a fine powder in a mortar using a pestle.

4 Place the browned onion and garlic, toasted cumin, and the cilantro, *aji amarillo,* salt, and black pepper in a food processor and puree to a coarse paste. Add the lime juice and half of the annatto oil; set aside the remaining oil for grilling. Puree the marinade until smooth.

5 Remove and discard the fat just inside the neck and body cavities of the chicken. Remove the package of giblets and set it aside for another use. Rinse the chicken, inside and out, under cold running water, then drain and blot it dry, inside and out, with paper towels. Spoon 1 tablespoon of the marinade into the neck cavity of the chicken and 2 tablespoons into the body cavity. Place the chicken in a large nonreactive bowl or large heavy-duty, resealable, plastic bag and pour the remaining marinade over it. Let the chicken marinate in the refrigerator, covered, for at least 4 hours or as long as overnight, turning the bird several times so that it marinates evenly. The longer the chicken marinates, the richer the flavor will be.

6 Drain the chicken well, discarding the marinade. Truss the bird with butcher's string (see the box on page 355).

7 To grill: *If you are using a rotisserie,* set up the grill for spit roasting, following the manufacturer's instructions, and preheat the grill to medium-high. When ready to cook, thread the chicken onto the rotisserie spit. Attach the spit to the grill and turn on the motor.

If you are using the indirect method, set up the grill for indirect grilling, place a drip pan in the center, and preheat the grill to medium. When ready to cook, place the chicken in the center of the grate over the drip pan and away from the heat and cover the grill.

8 Grill the bird until the skin is golden brown and crisp and the meat is cooked through, 1 to 1¼ hours. Use an instant-read meat thermometer to test for doneness, inserting it into the thickest part of a thigh but not so that it touches a bone. The internal temperature should be about 170°F. Start basting the bird with annatto oil after 30 minutes, basting it every 10 minutes.

9 Transfer the grilled chicken to a cutting board and remove and discard the trussing string. Let the chicken rest, loosely tented with aluminum foil, for about 5 minutes. Chop the chicken into bite-size pieces with a cleaver and serve at once with the lime wedges.

HOW TO SPATCHCOCK A CHICKEN

Y ou can't grill a chicken if you don't know how to spatchcock it. Or to be more accurate, you can't grill a whole chicken using the direct method if you haven't mastered spatchcocking. But why bother? Can't you simply cook the chicken by the indirect method or smoke it? Well, if you happen to live in a part of the world where grills do not come with lids, this is the only way to grill a whole chicken. Since this covers about three quarters of Planet Barbecue, the technique is quite indispensible.

The odd term, spatchcock, which is thought to come from the word *dispatch,* as in the sense of "quick," as in quick to cook, refers to the process whereby you cut out the chicken's backbone and open the bird flat like a book. Here's how you do it.

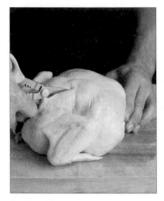

1. *Turn the chicken breast side down. Using poultry shears or a sharp knife and starting at the neck end, make two lengthwise cuts along the backbone, one on each side, from the neck to the tail.*

2. *Cut out and discard the backbone, or save it for stock.*

3. *Open the chicken up like a book. Run the tip of a paring knife along the breastbone and cartilage below the breastbone.*

4. *Run your thumbs along both sides of the breastbone and white cartilage, then pull them out.*

5. *Using a paring knife, cut a 1-inch slit in the skin between each leg and the back end of the breast.*

6. *Insert the end of each drumstick through one of these holes.*

7. *Pull the drumstick through the hole and lay the chicken flat.*

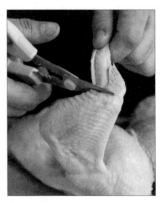

8. *If desired, cut off the wing tips. The spatchcocked chicken is now ready for grilling.*

Cambodian Grilled Chicken
{ MANN OENG K'TEM SOR, MARECH }

The temple complex at Angkor Wat is one of the archeological wonders of the world. It's not, however, the most interesting site in Siem Reap, Cambodia. That honor goes to the less-visited Bayon temple, built at the end of the twelfth century A.D. by the Buddhist king, Jayavarman VII. On its stone walls an amazing series of bas-reliefs tell the story of the victory of the Khmers over the Thais. The obligatory heroic and horrific battle scenes are portrayed, but what caught my eye are the pictures of the army supply trains, encampments, field kitchens, and yes, some of the earliest depictions of Asian barbecue. Specifically, you'll see chicken and other meats skewered on split sticks and grilled over pyramid-shaped fires. Fast forward nine hundred years to the parking lot of Angkor Wat where you'll find chicken grilled on split wooden sticks over an open fire, exactly as it was done during the height of the Khmer empire. This recipe may look complicated, but it's really just a series of simple steps. **SERVES 2 TO 4**

THE SCOOP

WHERE: Siem Reap, Cambodia

WHAT: Grilled chicken with a triple blast of flavor, first from a sweet and salty, garlic-soy marinade, then from an aromatic annatto oil glaze, and finally, from a peppery fresh lime dipping sauce

HOW: In Cambodia, they grill the chicken directly over the fire, which produces a crisp, smoky skin. (It's not like they have a choice; Cambodia's brazier-style charcoal grills are too small for indirect grilling.) If you grill the chicken using the indirect method, you eliminate the risk of flare-ups and keep the meat supernaturally moist. I give instructions for both methods here, but at home I'm more likely to grill the bird using the indirect method.

FOR THE CHICKEN AND MARINADE
1 whole chicken (3½ to 4 pounds)
5 cloves garlic, peeled and cut in half
2 tablespoons sugar
1 teaspoon coarse salt (kosher or sea)
1 tablespoon soy sauce
1 tablespoon Asian fish sauce
    (or more soy sauce)

FOR THE GLAZE
2 tablespoons vegetable oil
1 clove garlic, peeled and gently crushed
    with the side of a cleaver
2 teaspoons annatto seeds (achiote),
    or 2 teaspoons sweet paprika

FOR THE DIPPING SAUCE
1 teaspoon coarse salt (kosher or sea)
1 teaspoon freshly ground black pepper
½ teaspoon sugar (optional)
2 limes

YOU'LL ALSO NEED
A grill basket (optional)

ADVANCE PREPARATION
1 to 4 hours for marinating the chicken

1 Prepare the chicken and marinade: Remove and discard the fat just inside the neck and body cavities of the chicken. Remove the package of giblets

THE SCOOP

JUST THE FACTS:
To grill the chicken you need to spatchcock it, removing the backbone and breastbone so you can grill it flat, like an open book. The technique is explained in full on page 370. Annatto seed, sometimes known by its Spanish name, *achiote*, possesses a vivid orange color, an aromatic, earthy, almost iodiny flavor. If you're in a hurry you can omit the annatto seed glaze and simply baste the chicken with vegetable oil. The dipping sauce is also optional, although it's quick to make.

and set it aside for another use. Rinse the chicken, inside and out, under cold running water, then drain and blot it dry, inside and out, with paper towels. Spatchcock the chicken, following the instructions on page 370. Make 2 deep slashes to the bone in both sides of the chicken breast and in each leg and thigh. Trim or fold the wing tips back behind the wings. Place the bird in a nonreactive baking dish just large enough to hold it.

2 Place the garlic halves, sugar, and salt in a heavy mortar and pound to a paste with a pestle. Work in the soy sauce and fish sauce. If you do not have a mortar and pestle, combine the garlic, sugar, and salt in a small food processor and puree to a paste, then work in the soy sauce and fish sauce. Spoon the marinade over the chicken, forcing it into the slits and turning the bird to coat it well on both sides. Let the chicken marinate in the refrigerator, covered, for 1 hour to 4 hours; the longer it marinates, the richer the flavor will be.

3 Meanwhile, make the glaze: Heat the oil in a small saucepan over medium heat. Add the crushed clove of garlic and cook until just beginning to brown, about 1 minute. Using a slotted spoon, transfer the garlic to a small heatproof bowl. Add the annatto seeds to the saucepan with the oil and cook until fragrant and browned and the oil turns orange, about 2 minutes. If you are using paprika instead of annatto seeds, cook it for only 15 seconds. Strain the oil through a fine-mesh wire strainer into the bowl with the garlic. Set the glaze aside.

4 Prepare the dipping sauce: Place ½ teaspoon each of salt and pepper and ¼ teaspoon of sugar, if using, in 2 small attractive bowls. Have the limes ready; you'll add the lime juice at the last minute. (See Note.)

5 Set up the grill for direct grilling and preheat it to medium. Leave one section of the grill bare for a safety zone.

HOW TO MAKE CAMBODIAN GRILLED CHICKEN

1. Pound the seasoning ingredients to a paste in a mortar with a pestle.

2. Pour the marinade over the chicken.

3. Spread the marinade over the bird and marinate for 1 to 4 hours. The longer it marinates, the richer the flavor.

4. As the chicken grills, baste it with annatto oil, which adds color, luster, and flavor.

6 When ready to cook, brush and oil the grill grate. Drain the chicken and discard the marinade and arrange it on the hot grate or in an oiled grill basket, if using, skin side down. Grill the chicken until it is golden brown and cooked through, 12 to 20 minutes per side. Move the chicken as needed to dodge any flare-ups. Use an instant-read meat thermometer to test for doneness, inserting it into the thickest part of a thigh but not so that it touches a bone. The internal temperature should be about 170°F. Alternatively, you can make a cut in the chicken meat where the thigh connects to the body; there should be no traces of red at the bone. During the last 10 minutes of cooking, start brushing the chicken on both sides with the glaze.

7 To serve, transfer the chicken, skin side up, to a platter. Let it rest for about 2 minutes, then cut it into pieces with a cleaver. Add 2 tablespoons of lime juice to each bowl with the salt, pepper, and sugar for the dipping sauce and stir it with a fork or chopsticks until the salt and sugar dissolves. To eat, dip the pieces of chicken in the salted lime juice.

NOTE: If you are serving 4 people, double the dipping sauce ingredients and divide them among 4 bowls.

VARIATION

Khmer Chicken Grilled Using the Indirect Method: You can also grill the chicken using the indirect method, a process that, although not traditionally Khmer, has the advantage of eliminating all risk of flare-ups. Set up the grill for indirect grilling, place a drip pan in the center, and preheat the grill to medium. Place the marinated chicken skin side up in the center of the grate over the drip pan and away from the heat. Cover the grill and cook the chicken until browned and cooked through, 40 minutes to 1 hour. Start brushing the chicken with the glaze during the last 15 minutes of cooking and baste it again every 5 minutes.

Kelantan Chicken with Malaysian-Thai Marinade
{ AYAM PERCIK }

Kelantan is Malaysia's northeastern-most state, a lush hinterland of rice paddies, coconut plantations, and fishing villages bordering Thailand. Not surprisingly, the local grilling reflects a marked Thai influence in the form of marinades enriched with coconut, fish sauce, and chiles. Here's how a Kelantan-born grill master named Fandi prepares it, and if you've ever found grilled chicken to be dull or unidimensional, this one will light up your mouth like a Chinatown street during the Lunar New Year. **SERVES 2 TO 4**

1 whole chicken (3½ to 4 pounds)
½ cup grated unsweetened coconut
    (fresh or dried)
5 cloves garlic, coarsely chopped
2 shallots, coarsely chopped
2 stalks lemongrass, trimmed and coarsely chopped
1 piece (2 inches) fresh ginger, peeled and
    coarsely chopped
2 to 4 hot red chiles, such as bird peppers or
    serrano peppers, seeded and coarsely chopped
    (for hotter chicken, leave the seeds in) or
    2 tablespoons Malaysian or Thai chile paste
2 teaspoons coarse salt (kosher or sea)
1 teaspoon ground coriander
1 teaspoon ground cumin
½ teaspoon ground turmeric
½ teaspoon freshly ground black pepper
2 tablespoons vegetable oil
    (in Malaysia they'd use coconut oil)
2 tablespoons Asian fish sauce or soy sauce
1 tablespoon toasted sesame seeds
    (optional, see page 68)
Fresh calamansi (an Asian citrus fruit,
    see page 356) or lime wedges, for serving

Creamy Asian Peanut Sauce
    (optional, page 18)

YOU'LL ALSO NEED
A grill basket (optional)

ADVANCE PREPARATION
4 hours to overnight for marinating the chicken

1 Remove and discard the fat just inside the neck and body cavities of the chicken. Remove the package of giblets and set it aside for another use. Rinse the chicken, inside and out, under cold running water, then drain and blot it dry, inside and out, with paper towels. Spatchcock the chicken, following the instructions on page 370. Make 2 deep slashes to the bone in both sides of the chicken breast and in each leg and thigh. Trim or fold the wing tips back behind the wings. Place the bird in a nonreactive baking dish just large enough to hold it.

Skin Side Up or Down?

When grilling spatchcocked chicken or chicken pieces (or butterflied pork shoulder or other meats) using the direct method, do you start skin side up or skin side down? It's a question debated by grilling masters the world over. In general, most start with the skin side down. The reason is simple: You want to melt out the fat and crisp the skin. And the universality of the practice—in the United States, the Caribbean, Europe, and Asia—attests to its success. The risk associated with this practice is that the melting fat will cause flare-ups. There are three easy ways to avoid this problem.

1. Work over a medium-low or medium heat, which is what you should be doing anyway when cooking chicken pieces with the skin on.

2. Avoid crowding the grill grate—leave at least 30 percent of the grate clear so you have a place to move the chicken pieces away from any flare-ups.

3. Grill the chicken using the indirect method. You'll get the same crisp skin and moist meat without the risk of flare-ups.

I've tried starting both with the skin side up and the skin side down, and I prefer skin side down.

2 Place the grated coconut in a dry cast-iron or stainless steel skillet (not a nonstick skillet) over medium heat and cook it until browned and fragrant, stirring with a wooden spoon to prevent scorching, about 3 minutes. Transfer the toasted coconut to a bowl to cool.

3 Place the garlic, shallots, lemongrass, ginger, fresh chiles, if using, salt, coriander, cumin, turmeric, and black pepper in a heavy mortar and pound to a paste with a pestle. Pound in ¼ cup of the toasted coconut, then the vegetable oil, fish sauce, and chile paste, if using instead of the chiles. If the marinade is too thick, thin it with 1 to 2 tablespoons

of water. If you don't have a mortar and pestle, combine these ingredients in a food processor and puree to an aromatic paste. Set the remaining ¼ cup of toasted coconut aside for serving.

4 Spoon the marinade over the chicken, forcing it into the slits and turning the bird to coat it well on both sides. Let the chicken marinate in the refrigerator, covered, for at least 4 hours; the longer it marinates, the richer the flavor will be.

5 Set up the grill for direct grilling and preheat it to medium. Leave one section of the grill bare for a safety zone.

6 When ready to cook, brush and oil the grill grate. Drain the chicken and arrange it on the hot grate or in an oiled grill basket, if using, skin side down. Grill the chicken until it is golden brown and cooked though, 12 to 20 minutes per side. Move the chicken as needed to dodge any flare-ups. Use an instant-read meat thermometer to test for doneness, inserting it into the thickest part of a thigh but not so that it touches a bone. The internal temperature should be about 170°F. Alternatively, you can make a cut in the chicken meat where the thigh connects to the body; there should be no traces of red at the bone.

7 To serve, transfer the chicken to a platter. Sprinkle the top with reserved toasted coconut and the sesame seeds. Serve with *calamansi* or lime wedges and Creamy Asian Peanut Sauce, if desired.

VARIATION

Kelantan Chicken Grilled Using the Indirect Grilling Method: You can also grill the chicken using the indirect method, a process that, although not traditionally Malaysian, has the advantage of eliminating all risk of flare-ups. Set up the grill for indirect grilling and preheat it to medium. Place the marinated chicken skin side up in the center of the grate over the drip pan and away from the heat. Cover the grill and cook the chicken until cooked through, 40 minutes to 1 hour.

TUSCAN-STYLE CHICKEN UNDER A BRICK

Tuscan-Style Chicken Under a Brick

{ POLLO AL MATTONE }

Pollo al mattone is supposed to be one of the glories of Tuscan grilling. So why can't I find it anywhere in Florence? I ask for it at a half dozen restaurants in this medieval city on the Arno. Grill masters proudly gesture at massive hunks of beef, soon to be carved into *bistecca alla fiorentina* (grilled porterhouse steaks, see page 145), but no one seems to care about chicken under a brick. Until I say I must be mistaken—I must have been thinking of a dish from the Piedmont or Rome. You'd think I insulted someone's mother. "Oh, no, we invented it!" insist the Tuscans, "and only we know how to do it correctly." Nothing like wounded civic pride to help you find what you're looking for. Which is how I wound up at Trattoria Omero, a surprisingly bucolic restaurant a short drive from the congestion of downtown, with stunning views of the hills surrounding the city. Sure enough, logs blazed in the fireplace, and spatchcocked chicken sizzled away on a grill with V-shaped bars to channel the fat off the fire. OK, so they used machined-steel weights instead of the traditional bricks. The crisp salty skin, the rosemary-, sage-, and garlic-scented meat were right on the money. **SERVES 4**

3 cloves garlic, coarsely chopped

2 tablespoons stemmed fresh rosemary leaves, plus the remainder of the bunch for serving (optional)

2 tablespoons stemmed fresh sage leaves, plus the remainder of the bunch for serving (optional)

2 teaspoons freshly ground black pepper

½ cup coarse salt (kosher or sea)

4 whole baby chickens, poussins, or game hens (each 1 to 1¼ pounds), or 2 whole chickens (each 3½ to 4 pounds)

About ½ cup of the best quality extra-virgin olive oil, for serving

2 lemons, cut into wedges, for serving

YOU'LL ALSO NEED

2 to 4 bricks wrapped in aluminum foil or metal grill presses

ADVANCE PREPARATION

None

1 Place the garlic, 2 tablespoons each of chopped rosemary and sage, and the pepper in a food processor fitted with a metal chopping blade and run the machine in short bursts to finely chop. Add the salt and process to mix. Transfer the rub to a jar with a tight-fitting lid. This makes about ¾ cup of herbed salt rub, more than you'll need for this recipe. The leftover rub is also excellent for seasoning veal, pork, and pheasant and will keep for several weeks in the refrigerator.

2 Remove and discard the fat just inside the neck and body cavities of the chickens. Remove the packages of giblets and set them aside for another use. Rinse the chickens, inside and out, under cold running water, then drain and blot them dry, inside and out, with paper towels. Spatchcock the chickens, following the instructions on page 370. Generously season the birds on both sides with the herbed salt rub.

3 To grill: The direct grilling method is traditional, but using the indirect method will give you a crisp, moist bird without the risk of flare-ups or burning.

If you are using the direct method, set up the grill for direct grilling and preheat it to medium. Leave one section of the grill bare for a safety zone. When ready to cook, brush and oil the grill grate. Arrange the birds skin side down on the hot grate at a diagonal to the bars. Place the bricks or grill presses on top of the birds.

Grill the chickens until they are crisp and golden brown on the bottom, 8 to 12 minutes, per side for baby chickens; 12 to 20 minutes per side for full-size chickens. Use an instant-read meat thermometer to test for doneness, inserting it into the thickest part of a thigh but not so that it touches a bone. The internal temperature should be about 170°F. Give each bird a quarter turn after 4 minutes on each side to create a handsome cross-hatch of grill marks.

If you are using the indirect method, set up the grill for indirect grilling, place a drip pan in the center, and preheat the grill to medium. Arrange the birds skin side up in the center of the grate over the drip pan and away from the heat and place the weights on top. Cover the grill and cook the birds until golden brown and cooked through, 30 to 40 minutes for baby chickens; 40 minutes to 1 hour for full-size chickens.

4 Line a platter or plates with the remaining rosemary and sage sprigs (this step is optional, but it looks great and it adds a fantastic flavor). Place the grilled birds on top, generously drizzle olive oil over them, and serve with lemon wedges.

Jordanian Grilled Chicken

THE SCOOP

WHERE: Jordan and Israel

Bob Dylan stayed here. So did Lauren Bacall, Marc Chagall, and Sir Winston Churchill. For more than a century, the American Colony Hotel has stood as an oasis of calm and elegance amid the hurly-burly and political upheavals of Jerusalem. In other words, it's about the last place you'd expect to find memorable grilling. But such is the local obsession with *shawarma* and shish kebab, and with *kofta* and *shashlik,* that at least one remarkable grilled dish has found its way onto the menu of the hotel's formal restaurant, Arabesque. Called Jordanian chicken, it reflects the Middle Eastern penchant for juxtaposing sweet and salty flavors—cinnamon, cardamom, and raisins, for example, against the earthy tones of cumin and caramelized onions. **SERVES 2 TO 4**

2 large sweet onions, thinly sliced
6 bay leaves
1 whole chicken (3½ to 4 pounds)
2 teaspoons salt (kosher or sea)
1 teaspoon ground cumin
1 teaspoon ground coriander
1 teaspoon sweet paprika
1 teaspoon freshly ground black pepper
4 tablespoons vegetable oil, or 1 tablespoon
    vegetable oil and 3 tablespoons butter,
    plus oil or melted butter for brushing
    the bread
3 tablespoons pine nuts
3 tablespoons raisins
4 cardamom pods
½ teaspoon ground cinnamon
Taboon (Jordanian bread) or another puffy
    Middle Eastern–style flatbread,
    such as pide (page 107) or pita

ADVANCE PREPARATION
At least 1 hour for marinating the bird

1 Arrange a quarter of the onion slices and 2 bay leaves in the bottom of a baking dish.

2 Remove and discard the fat just inside the neck and body cavities of the chicken. Remove the package of giblets and set it aside for another use. Rinse the chicken, inside and out, under cold running water, then drain and blot it dry, inside and out, with paper towels.

Spatchcock the chicken following the instructions on page 370.

3 Place the salt, cumin, coriander, paprika, and pepper in a small bowl and stir to mix. Season the chicken halves on both sides with this rub. Drizzle 1 tablespoon of oil over the chicken, rubbing it and the spices onto the meat.

4 Arrange the chicken in the baking dish on top of the onion slices and bay leaves. Arrange one-third of the remaining onion slices and 2 bay leaves on top. Let the chicken marinate in the refrigerator, covered, for 1 to 2 hours.

5 Heat the remaining 3 tablespoons of oil or 3 tablespoons of butter in a saucepan over medium heat. Add the remaining sliced onion, the pine nuts, raisins, cardamom, and cinnamon, and the remaining 2 bay leaves and cook until the onion is caramelized (soft and golden brown), stirring with a wooden spoon, 8 to 14 minutes. You may need to lower the heat so that the onion browns without burning. (If you want to do all of the work outside, you can caramelize the onion on the side burner of the grill.) Remove and discard the bay leaves and cardamom pods, and set the caramelized onion mixture aside.

6 Set up the grill for direct grilling and preheat it to medium. To be strictly authentic, you'd grill over charcoal, and if you do use charcoal, build a two-zone fire (see page 611).

7 When ready to cook, brush and oil the grill grate. Remove the chicken from the onion marinade, discarding the onion. Arrange the chicken halves

THE SCOOP

WHAT: Chicken grilled with Middle Eastern spices, topped with caramelized onions, raisins, and pine nuts

HOW: Direct grilling

JUST THE FACTS: Like so much grilled chicken on Planet Barbecue, this one starts with spatchcocking the bird—that is, opening it up like a book. This speeds up the cooking time and gives you a higher ratio of meat to bone.

on the hot grate, skin side down. Grill the chicken until the skin is golden brown and the meat is cooked through, 12 to 20 minutes per side. Move the chicken as needed to dodge any flare-ups. Use an instant-read meat thermometer to test for doneness, inserting it into the thickest part of a thigh but not so that it touches a bone. The internal temperature should be about 170°F. Move the chicken to the side of the grill to keep warm.

8 Brush the bread with oil or melted butter and lightly toast it on the grill, 30 seconds to 1 minute per side. Watch the bread carefully; it can burn quickly.

9 To serve, arrange the bread on a platter or plates. Arrange the grilled chicken on top. Spoon the caramelized onion mixture over the chicken and serve at once.

Thai Grilled Chicken

{ GAI YAANG }

American expat and friend, Alan Drezner, digs into gai yaang som tam, Thai grilled chicken with green papaya slaw.

I came to Bangkok intent on finding the best grilled chicken in Thailand. Good luck—I might as well have been looking for the greatest cheesesteak in Philadelphia or the overall finest cheese in France. You must visit Likit Gai Yaang on Ratchadamnoen Road near the National Boxing Stadium, insisted one informant. No, your best bet is the rotisserie joint next to the Skytrain station on Convent Road, said another. There's that pushcart behind the River City shopping center, mused a third, or that stall at the hawker center just off Silom Road. The truth is, there must be eight thousand "best" grilled chickens in Bangkok, let alone Thailand, so what follows here are what a police artist would call composite mug shots. The first version features the flamboyant lemongrass, ginger, and curry grilled chicken you associate with southern Thailand. The second strikes the more earthy garlic, coriander, and fish sauce

tones you find in the Northeast. The traditional accompaniment to Thai grilled chicken is green papaya salad. **SERVES 2 TO 4**

Thai Grilled Chicken with Lemongrass and Ginger

4 cloves garlic, coarsely chopped

1 piece (3 inches) fresh ginger or galangal, peeled and coarsely chopped

3 stalks lemongrass, trimmed and coarsely chopped

3 tablespoons fresh cilantro root or cilantro leaves, coarsely chopped

1½ tablespoons sugar

1 tablespoon freshly ground black pepper

1 tablespoon curry powder

⅓ cup soy sauce

3 tablespoons vegetable oil, plus 2 tablespoons oil for basting

1 chicken (3½ to 4 pounds), quartered (2 legs and 2 breasts)

About ½ cup sweet Thai chile sauce (see Note)

ADVANCE PREPARATION

4 hours to overnight for marinating the chicken

1 Place the garlic, ginger, lemongrass, cilantro root, sugar, pepper, and curry powder in a heavy mortar and pound to a coarse paste with a pestle. Work in the soy sauce and oil. If you don't have a mortar and pestle, combine these ingredients in a food processor and puree to a coarse paste.

2 Rinse the chicken quarters under cold running water, then blot them dry with paper towels. Make 3 deep slashes in each piece of chicken (this helps the chicken absorb the marinade and speeds up the cooking). Arrange the chicken quarters in a nonreactive baking dish just large enough to hold them in a single layer. Spoon the marinade over the chicken, forcing it into the slits and turning the pieces to coat well on both sides. Let the chicken marinate in the refrigerator, covered, for at least 4 hours or as long as overnight, turning the pieces several times so they marinate evenly. The longer the chicken marinates, the richer the flavor will be.

3 Set up the grill for direct grilling and preheat it to medium.

Sidewalk kitchen—a common sight in Bangkok.

A golden Buddha: Calm amid Thailand's frenzy.

4 When ready to cook, brush and oil the grill grate. Drain the chicken quarters and arrange them on the hot grate skin side down. Grill the chicken until it is darkly browned on the outside and cooked through, 6 to 10 minutes per side. Start basting the chicken with oil after about 5 minutes. Watch for flare-ups; if they occur, move the chicken to a cooler part of the grill.

5 Transfer the grilled chicken to a platter or plates and serve with small bowls of sweet Thai chile sauce for dipping.

NOTE: Sweet Thai chile sauce is a syrupy, garlicky condiment that's more sweet than it is hot (OK, it's a little hot). One good brand available at Asian markets and most supermarkets is Mae Ploy. Or order online at www.importfoods.com.

Thai Grilled Chicken with Fish Sauce and Coriander Root

6 cloves garlic, coarsely chopped
¼ cup coarsely chopped fresh cilantro root or cilantro leaves
3 tablespoons sugar
2 teaspoons cracked black peppercorns
1½ teaspoons coarse salt (kosher or sea), or more to taste
¼ cup Asian fish sauce or soy sauce
3 tablespoons vegetable oil, plus 2 tablespoons oil for basting
1 chicken (3½ to 4 pounds), quartered (2 legs and 2 breasts)
About ½ cup sweet Thai chile sauce (see Note above)

ADVANCE PREPARATION

4 hours to overnight for marinating the chicken

1 Place the garlic, cilantro root, sugar, peppercorns, and salt in a heavy mortar and pound to a coarse paste with a pestle. Work in the fish sauce and the 3 tablespoons vegetable oil. If you don't have a mortar and pestle, combine these ingredients in a food processor and puree to a coarse paste.

2 Rinse the chicken quarters under cold running water, then blot them dry with paper towels. Make 3 deep slashes in each piece of chicken (this helps the chicken absorb the marinade and speeds up the cooking). Arrange the chicken quarters in a nonreactive baking dish just large enough to hold them in a single layer. Spoon the marinade over the chicken, forcing it into the slits and turning the pieces to coat well on both sides. Let the chicken marinate in the refrigerator, covered, for at least 4 hours or as long as overnight, turning the pieces several times so they marinate evenly. The longer the chicken marinates, the richer the flavor will be.

3 Set up the grill for direct grilling and preheat it to medium.

4 When ready to cook, brush and oil the grill grate. Drain the chicken quarters and arrange them on the hot grate skin side down. Grill the chicken until it is darkly browned on the outside and cooked through, 6 to 10 minutes per side. Start basting the chicken with oil after about 5 minutes. Watch for flare-ups; if they occur, move the chicken to a cooler part of the grill.

5 Transfer the grilled chicken to a platter or plates and serve with small bowls of sweet Thai chile sauce for dipping.

VARIATION

Thai Chicken Grilled Using the Indirect Method: You can also grill the chicken using the indirect method, a process that has the advantage of eliminating all risk of flare-ups. Set up the grill for indirect grilling and preheat it to medium. Place the marinated chicken quarters skin side up in the center of the grate over the drip pan and away from the heat. Cover the grill and cook the chicken until browned and cooked through, 30 to 40 minutes. Start basting the chicken with oil during the last 15 minutes of cooking, basting it every 5 minutes.

Cumin-Grilled Chicken Breasts with Fiery Bolivian Salsa
{ POLLO ASADO CON LLAJUA }

I'd been hearing about grilled chicken with *llajua* (pronounced yak-wa), Bolivia's ubiquitous tomato and chile grilling sauce, almost since the day a tall musician of Bolivian descent named Gabriel Berthin started dating my stepdaughter, Betsy. "Hot," Gabriel said. "Real hot." (Hmmm, salsa or stepdaughter?) Well, Gabriel is now my son-in-law, and *llajua* has become a staple of the Raichlen grilling repertoire. And it's hard to imagine any sort of Bolivian grilled chicken, beef, pork, or lamb without this incendiary condiment to reinforce the fire.

Gabriel's family uses bone-in chicken breasts on the theory that the bones add flavor and keep the chicken from drying out, and they grill them directly over charcoal. That's what I've called for here; if you choose to use skinless, boneless breasts, shorten the grilling time. **SERVES 4**

FOR THE LLAJUA

1 to 2 locoto or rocoto chiles, Scotch bonnets or jalapeño peppers

2 luscious, red ripe tomatoes, cored and coarsely chopped (peeling is optional)

1 clove garlic coarsely chopped (optional)

3 tablespoons extra-virgin olive oil

2 tablespoons red wine vinegar or fresh lemon juice, or 1 tablespoon of each, or more to taste

Coarse salt (kosher or sea) and freshly ground black pepper

3 tablespoons chopped fresh cilantro or flat-leaf parsley

FOR THE CHICKEN

4 half chicken breasts, 8 to 10 ounces each if bone-in and with skin-on, about 6 ounces each if skinless and boneless

1½ teaspoons coarse salt (kosher or sea)

1 teaspoon freshly ground black pepper

1 teaspoon ground cumin

2 tablespoons extra-virgin olive oil

ADVANCE PREPARATION

30 minutes to 1 hour for marinating the chicken

1 Make the *llajua:* Stem and cut the chile(s) in half lengthwise, then slice them crosswise into ½-inch pieces. (Gabriel's family is very specific about this way of cutting the chile.) For a milder *llajua,* seed the chiles; for a spicier one, leave the seeds in. Place the tomatoes, garlic, and chile(s) in a food processor and puree to a coarse paste. Work in the olive oil and wine vinegar. Season the *llajua* with salt and black pepper to taste; the salsa should be highly seasoned. Work in the cilantro, running the processor in short bursts. Alternatively, you can puree the ingredients in a blender, adding the cilantro at the very end. You will have about 1½ cups. The *llajua* can be made up to 2 hours ahead.

2 Prepare the chicken: Rinse the chicken breasts under cold running water, then blot them dry with paper towels. Generously season the chicken breasts on both sides with the salt, black pepper, and cumin. Drizzle the olive oil on both sides of the chicken breasts, rubbing the oil and spices onto the meat with your fingertips. Let the chicken breasts marinate in the refrigerator, covered, for 30 minutes to 1 hour.

3 Set up the grill for direct grilling and preheat it to high.

4 When ready to cook, brush and oil the grill grate. Arrange the chicken breasts on the hot grate at a diagonal to the bars. Grill the chicken breasts until golden brown and cooked through, 4 to 6 minutes per side for bone-in breasts, 3 to 5 minutes per side for boneless breasts. Give each breast a quarter turn on each side after 2 minutes to create a handsome crosshatch of grill marks.

5 Transfer the grilled chicken breasts to a platter or plates. Serve the chicken with the *llajua* spooned on top or on the side.

Lemongrass and Curry Grilled Chicken Breasts

WHERE: Luang Prabang in northern Laos

WHAT: Chicken breasts marinated in a fragrant paste of lemongrass, garlic, and curry, grilled until crusty and golden

HOW: Direct grilling

Travel the world's barbecue trail and you'll find lots of grilled chicken. What you won't find outside of North America is a lot of grilled skinless, boneless chicken breasts. The reason is simple: The breast contains less fat and flavor than dark meat. It's also more expensive and more likely to dry out on the grill. So when I found these chicken breasts, fragrant with curry and lemongrass, sizzling hot off the grill, at the night market in the French-Colonial town of Luang Prabang in northern Laos, I knew I had tasted a rarity—a chicken dish that would play equally well to health-conscious, convenience-loving North America and flavor-addicted Southeast Asia. In Laos, the chicken would be grilled on a split stick over a charcoal-filled clay brazier. Here's how to do it on a grill with a conventional grate. The lemongrass, curry, and cilantro speak loudly enough for themselves. **SERVES 4**

2 stalks lemongrass, trimmed and thinly sliced crosswise, or 3 strips lemon zest

2 cloves garlic, coarsely chopped

2 tablespoons chopped fresh cilantro or dill

1½ teaspoons curry powder

1 teaspoon coarse salt (kosher or sea)

1 teaspoon sugar

½ teaspoon freshly ground black pepper

2 tablespoons vegetable oil, plus 1 tablespoon for basting

4 skinless, boneless half chicken breasts (each about 6 ounces, 1½ pounds in all)

Lime wedges, for serving

ADVANCE PREPARATION

1 to 4 hours for marinating the chicken

1 Place the lemongrass, garlic, cilantro, curry powder, salt, sugar, and pepper in a heavy mortar and pound to a paste with a pestle. If you don't have a mortar and pestle, finely chop these ingredients in a food processor. Gradually work in the 2 tablespoons of oil.

2 Rinse the chicken breasts under cold running water, then blot them dry with paper towels. Arrange the chicken breasts in a baking dish just large enough to hold them in a single layer. Spread the lemongrass marinade over the chicken breasts, turning

THE SCOOP

JUST THE FACTS: Pounding the marinade ingredients in a large heavy mortar with a pestle will give you a richer flavor than pureeing them in a food processor; however, you can certainly use a processor.

LEMONGRASS AND CURRY GRILLED CHICKEN BREASTS

to coat both sides. Let the chicken marinate in the refrigerator, covered, for at least 1 hour or as long as 4 hours; the longer it marinates, the richer the flavor will be.

3 Set up the grill for direct grilling and preheat it to high.

4 When ready to cook, brush and oil the grill grate. Drain the chicken breasts and arrange them on the hot grate at a diagonal to the bars.

Grill the chicken breasts until golden brown and cooked through, 3 to 5 minutes per side, giving each breast a quarter turn on each side after 1½ minutes to create a handsome crosshatch of grill marks. After 3 minutes, start basting the chicken breasts with the 1 tablespoon of oil as they grill to keep them moist, taking care not to touch raw chicken with the basting brush.

5 Transfer the grilled chicken breasts to a platter or plates and serve them with the lime wedges.

Chicken Grilled in Lemon Leaves
{ GA NUONG LA CHANH }

THE SCOOP

WHERE: Hanoi, Vietnam

WHAT: Sweet-salty, turmeric-scented chicken pieces grilled in fragrant fresh lemon or basil leaves

HOW: Direct grilling

JUST THE FACTS: Metropole chef Nguyen Thi Kim Hai makes these kebabs with chicken thighs, not breasts. And chicken thighs are what I use; however, breast meat will work if you prefer. I've made the sauce optional. The Metropole serves it, but the chicken is so intensely flavorful, you can do without.

If the walls could talk. Just about everybody who was anybody visiting Hanoi in the last century stayed at the hotel Metropole. From French colonials to the former American defense secretary Robert McNamara and his nemesis, Ho Chi Minh; from Jane Fonda to Joan Baez to, more recently, Sheryl Crow. And all, undoubtedly, at some point during their stay, enjoyed a house specialty: *gà nuóng lá chanh,* chicken grilled in fresh lemon leaves. Like most Vietnamese grilling, this is a simple dish, but the contrast of flavors—salty fish sauce, pungent turmeric, fragrant fresh lemon leaves—will take your breath away. I know, I hear your concern already: Where will you get fresh lemon leaves? If you live in southern California or Florida, you or a neighbor may have a lemon tree in your garden (be sure the leaves come from a tree not sprayed with pesticides). If you don't have lemon leaves, here's a surprising but equally stunning work-around; wrap the chicken and a sliver of lemon zest in fresh basil leaves. Naturally, the flavor will be quite different, but the Vietnamese also have a long tradition of grilling meats in fresh basil. **SERVES 6 AS AN APPETIZER, 4 AS A MAIN COURSE**

1½ pounds skinless, boneless chicken thighs, or 2 pounds
    bone-in chicken thighs
About 30 fresh lemon leaves or large basil leaves
Coarse salt (kosher or sea) and freshly ground black pepper
1 large or 2 medium-size shallots, minced (about ¼ cup)
2 tablespoons palm sugar or light brown sugar
2 teaspoons ground turmeric, or 1 tablespoon finely grated
    peeled fresh turmeric
¼ cup Asian fish sauce
3 tablespoons vegetable oil
About 24 small pieces fresh lemon zest (each piece about
    ¼-inch square; optional)
Lemon Chile Dipping Sauce (optional, recipe follows)

YOU'LL ALSO NEED
Small bamboo skewers; an aluminum foil grill shield
    (see page 611)

ADVANCE PREPARATION
30 minutes to 2 hours for marinating the chicken

1 Rinse the chicken under cold running water, then blot it dry with paper towels. If you are using bone-in chicken thighs, cut out and discard the bones or save them for another use (see the box below for instructions). Cut the chicken into approximately 1½-inch squares. Place the chicken in a large nonreactive mixing bowl.

2 Cut 4 to 6 of the lemon or basil leaves into hair-thin slivers. The easiest way to do this is to roll the leaves into a tight roll, then cut them crosswise.

3 Season the chicken with salt and pepper. Add the slivered leaves and the shallot(s), palm sugar, and turmeric and toss to mix. Stir in the fish sauce and oil. Let the chicken marinate in the refrigerator, covered, for at least 30 minutes or as long as 2 hours; the longer the chicken marinates, the richer the flavor will be.

4 Drain the chicken, discarding the marinade. Wrap each piece of chicken in a whole lemon leaf or basil leaf. If you are using lemon leaves, the leaf will go half or three-quarters of the way around the piece of chicken; that's fine. If you are using basil leaves and lemon zest, place squares of zest on the chicken pieces before wrapping them with the basil. Skewer the wrapped chicken pieces through the thin side so that the skewer pins the leaves to the chicken and the flat side of the chicken will be exposed to the fire. Skewer 2 pieces of chicken on each skewer. The chicken can be prepared several hours ahead to this stage. If you are not grilling the chicken skewers immediately, cover them with plastic wrap and refrigerate them.

5 Set up the grill for direct grilling and preheat it to high.

6 When ready to cook, brush and oil the grill grate. Arrange the chicken skewers on the hot grate with the aluminum foil shield under the exposed ends of the skewers to keep them from burning. Grill the chicken until the lemon leaves and meat are nicely browned and the chicken is cooked through, 2 to 3 minutes per side. Serve the chicken at once with the Lemon Chile Dipping Sauce, if desired.

The Thighs Have It

Travel Planet Barbecue and you'll find that most everywhere grill masters prefer the dark meat of chicken thighs to the white meat of the chicken breast. The reason is simple: The thigh meat is richer and has a higher fat content, so there's more flavor and less chance of the meat drying out over the dry heat of the grill. Chicken thighs also cost less than the breast meat.

To bone a chicken thigh, place the thigh skin side down on a cutting board. Make a cut in the side to and around the bone and open the thigh like a book, then cut out the bone.

Lemon Chile Dipping Sauce

This recipe is loosely modeled on Vietnam's ubiquitous *nuoc cham,* a dipping sauce. Like any self-respecting American barbecue sauce, it is simultaneously sweet, salty, tart, garlicky, and aromatic, but it achieves these flavors without being thick like ketchup. It's simply the most delicate and refined barbecue sauce I know of on Planet Barbecue. **MAKES ABOUT 1 CUP**

3 tablespoons Asian fish sauce

3 tablespoons fresh lemon juice

2 tablespoons sugar

1 lemon leaf or fresh basil leaf (optional), cut into
   hair-thin slivers

2 tiny hot red chiles, cut crosswise into paper-thin slices

Place the fish sauce, lemon juice, and sugar in a nonreactive mixing bowl and whisk until the sugar dissolves. Whisk in enough water to make the sauce mellow and palatable, ½ cup or to taste. Divide the sauce among 4 to 6 tiny bowls. Float a few slivers of lemon or basil leaf and chile slices on top of each serving.

Chicken grilled in lemon leaves, using a Vietnamese grill basket.

Serbian Chicken Bundles
{ PILECI PAKETICI }

WHERE: Belgrade, Serbia

WHAT: Cheese-, ham-, and bacon-stuffed grilled chicken thighs

HOW: Direct grilling

JUST THE FACTS: *Kajmak* is a thick Serbian cream similar to clotted cream, mascarpone, or sometimes sour cream.

Don't look for the restaurant Don in a tourist guidebook to Belgrade. It's a dive, a truck stop, my interpreter explains unapologetically. There's nothing about the location—a garage and warehouse district—or the bare-bones decor to prove him wrong. But one sight of the unexpectedly immaculate kitchen, dominated by a charcoal grill on a masonry base, and one taste of the *pljeskavica,* a giant garlic- and chile-laced veal and beef burger (see page 315), or the *pileći paketići,* ham- and cheese-stuffed chicken bundles, and you know you're in the hands of a master. Presiding over the grill is a tiny woman named Jelena Stuparevic, and she not only grills everything to order, she molds each burger and sausage and stuffs each piece of chicken and pork from scratch. These grilled chicken bundles turn up all over Belgrade. Jelena's, gooey with cheese, smoky with ham, and tangy with mustard, were my hands-down favorite. **SERVES 4**

1 tablespoon vegetable oil

4 ounces thickly sliced, smoky country-style bacon, cut crosswise into ¼-inch slivers

8 bone-in chicken legs (about 5½ pounds total), 8 boneless chicken legs with skin (about 3 pounds total), or 8 half chicken breasts, preferably with skin (about 3 pounds total)

Garlic salt

Freshly ground black pepper

1 to 2 tablespoons Dijon-style mustard

4 ounces thickly sliced smoked ham, cut into ¼-inch dice

4 ounces mildly tangy cheese, such as Edam, Gouda, or Gruyère, cut into ¼-inch dice

¾ cup kajmak, clotted cream, or mascarpone (optional)

YOU'LL ALSO NEED

Large wooden toothpicks or small bamboo skewers

ADVANCE PREPARATION

None, but the chicken bundles can be assembled up to 6 hours ahead.

1 Heat the oil in a small frying pan. Add the bacon and cook until lightly browned, 3 to 4 minutes, stirring with a wooden spoon. Drain the bacon in a strainer over a bowl to catch the fat. Let the bacon and the bacon fat cool to room temperature, then set them aside separately.

2 Rinse the chicken under cold running water, then blot it dry with paper towels. If you are using bone-in chicken legs, bone them (see the box for instructions). If you are using half chicken breasts, butterfly each by cutting it through the thin side almost to, but not through, the other side. Using a meat mallet, scaloppine pounder, or the side of a heavy cleaver, lightly flatten each piece of chicken. Generously season the chicken with garlic salt and pepper.

3 Place the cooked bacon in a small bowl and stir in the ham and cheese. Place a piece of chicken, skin side down, on a work surface and spread some mustard over the top. Place a spoonful of the ham and cheese mixture on top of one half of the piece of chicken. Fold the other side over the ham

MAKING CHICKEN BUNDLES

1. Make lengthwise cuts along the inside of the chicken leg to the bone.

2. Cut around and under the bone to loosen it.

3. Remove the bone, scraping back any meat with the tip of the knife.

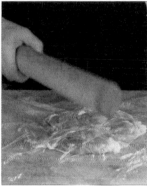

4. Flatten the chicken leg with a rolling pin, pounding it between two sheets of plastic wrap.

5. Spread the top of the flattened chicken leg with mustard, then add the ham and cheese mixture.

6. Using the plastic wrap to help you, fold the chicken leg in half to form a neat bundle.

and cheese mixture to form a neat bundle. Using a toothpick or skewer, pin the chicken bundle shut. Repeat with the remaining pieces of chicken.

4 Set up the grill for direct grilling and preheat it to medium. (To minimize flare-ups, it's better to work over a medium rather than high flame.)

Grill the Serbian Chicken Bundles until browned on both sides.

5 When ready to cook, brush and oil the grill grate. Brush the outside of the chicken bundles with the reserved bacon fat and season them with more garlic salt and pepper. Arrange the chicken bundles on the hot grate, on the diagonal to the bars. Grill the chicken bundles until they are browned on the outside and cooked through, 5 to 8 minutes per side.

6 Transfer the chicken bundles to a platter or plates. Don't forget to remove the toothpicks or skewers. If a sauce is desired—not that you need it—spoon the *kajmak,* clotted cream, or mascarpone on top.

VARIATION

More Chicken Bundles: Some Serbian grill masters wrap strips of bacon around the chicken bundles prior to grilling, rather than adding the diced bacon to the filling. Others add diced onion or hot peppers to the filling. At the Belgrade restaurant, Dacho, partially cooked chicken bundles are dredged in cornmeal, then finished on the grill.

Jerk Chicken Legs in the Style of Yallahs with Hellfire Hot Sauce

Yallahs is the first sizable town you drive through on the way from Kingston to Port Antonio, Jamaica. Capitalizing on the opportunity to feed hungry passersby, the locals have lined the main street with 55-gallon steel drum grills, one after another, each accompanied by an industrial-strength sound system. The town specialty is jerk chicken—or more precisely, jerk chicken legs. These succulent, mahogany-hued chicken legs are considerably less salty and fiery than the jerk one associates with Boston Beach (see page 199 for a jerk pork recipe). Here's how chicken legs

JERK CHICKEN LEGS IN THE STYLE OF YALLAHS WITH HELLFIRE HOT SAUCE

THE SCOOP

JUST THE FACTS: The Jamaican *escallion* is a member of the onion family. It looks like an overgrown scallion and tastes like a cross between an American scallion, a shallot, and garlic. *Escallions* are hard to find in North America, so I've called for this aromatic trio instead. (If you live in an area with a large Caribbean community, you may be able to find *escallions*. If so, use four *escallions* in place of the scallions, shallots, and garlic.)

The grill masters of Yallahs cook their chicken over charcoal, but because no smoke is added, you can achieve fine results on a gas grill.

are "jerked" by a tall, lanky grill jockey named Eric Morgan. If you do want a little more heat, Eric serves an incendiary Scotch bonnet salsa on the side. **SERVES 4**

2 pounds bone-in chicken legs, or 1½ pounds boneless chicken legs or thighs, with skin

1 bunch scallions, both white and green parts, trimmed and cut into 1-inch pieces

2 shallots, coarsely chopped

3 cloves garlic, coarsely chopped

1 to 2 Scotch bonnet chiles or habañero peppers, seeded (for a hotter chicken, leave the seeds in)

1 teaspoon fresh thyme, or ½ teaspoon dried thyme

1½ teaspoons coarse salt (kosher or sea)

1 teaspoon freshly ground black pepper

½ teaspoon ground allspice

¼ cup vegetable oil or water, or more as needed

Hellfire Hot Sauce (recipe follows)

ADVANCE PREPARATION

4 hours to overnight for marinating the chicken

1 Rinse the chicken legs under cold running water, then blot them dry with paper towels. Arrange the chicken legs in a nonreactive baking dish or bowl just large enough to hold them in a single layer.

2 Place the scallions, shallots, garlic, Scotch bonnet(s), thyme, salt, pepper, and allspice in a food processor fitted with a chopping blade and puree to a smooth paste, running the machine in bursts. Add enough oil or water to obtain a pourable consistency.

3 Pour the marinade over the chicken legs, turning them to coat all over. Let the chicken marinate in the refrigerator, covered, for at least 4 hours

or as long as overnight; the longer the chicken legs marinate, the richer the flavor will be. Turn the chicken legs several times so they marinate evenly.

4 Set up the grill for direct grilling and preheat it to medium. Leave one section of the grill bare for a safety zone.

5 When ready to cook, brush and oil the grill grate. Drain the chicken legs well, discarding the marinade. Arrange the chicken legs skin side down on the hot grate and grill them until they are nicely browned and cooked through, 6 to 10 minutes per side, turning with tongs. If the chicken skin or meat starts to burn or you get flare-ups, move the chicken to the safety zone. When cooked, the meat at the bone will have lost all traces of pink; make a tiny slit with the tip of a knife to check it.

6 To serve, place the chicken on a chopping block or substantial cutting board, and, using a cleaver, hack the chicken meat into bite-size pieces. Jamaican jerk is always served in bite-size pieces and is always eaten with your fingers.

Hellfire Hot Sauce

A s a rule, Jamaican jerk is served without sauce, but Eric Morgan provides his customers with this hellish relish should additional heat be desired. If you have sensitive skin, wear rubber gloves when handling Scotch bonnets, and avoid touching your eyes or other sensitive parts of your body. **MAKES ABOUT 1 CUP**

1 cup distilled white vinegar

2 teaspoons coarse salt (kosher or sea), or to taste

1 to 3 Scotch bonnet chiles, seeded and thinly sliced crosswise (for a hotter sauce, leave the seeds in)

½ medium-size sweet onion, thinly sliced crosswise, slices broken into rings

Place the vinegar in a nonreactive bowl. Add the salt and whisk or stir until it dissolves. Stir in the Scotch bonnet(s) and onion. Let the sauce "ripen" for 1 to 2 hours before serving. It will keep for several days. Spoon as much as you desire (or can bear) over the chicken.

Grilled Chicken with Yogurt, Hot Pepper, and Garlic

Every barbecue culture has its version of grilled chicken. Turkey's uses a relatively small number of seasonings—yogurt, tomato paste, garlic, and Turkish red pepper—to create a mouth-blasting range of flavors. As in all good barbecue, there are multiple layers of flavor, first from the yogurt and tomato marinade, then from the crusting of salt and hot pepper flakes. And nobody does it better than Musa Dagdeviren, chef-owner of the restaurant Çiya, on the Asian side of Istanbul. **SERVES 4**

2 tablespoons Aleppo pepper, or 2 teaspoons American-style hot red pepper flakes plus 4 teaspoons sweet paprika

1 cup Turkish- or Greek-style plain yogurt

3 tablespoons extra-virgin olive oil

2 tablespoons red wine vinegar

2 tablespoons tomato paste

Coarse salt (kosher or sea) and freshly ground black pepper

6 cloves garlic, peeled and crushed with the side of a cleaver

2 lemons, 1 thinly sliced crosswise, seeds removed, 1 cut into wedges, for serving

1½ pounds skinless, boneless chicken thighs or breasts, cut into 1 x 1 x ½-inch pieces

YOU'LL ALSO NEED

Flat metal or bamboo skewers

ADVANCE PREPARATION

1 to 4 hours for marinating the chicken

1 Place 1 tablespoon of the Aleppo pepper or 1 teaspoon of hot red pepper flakes and 2 teaspoons of paprika in a small bowl, add 1 tablespoon of warm water, and let stand until a thick paste forms, about 5 minutes.

2 Place the pepper paste in a large nonreactive bowl. Add the yogurt, olive oil, wine vinegar, tomato paste, 1½ teaspoons of salt, and 1 teaspoon of black pepper and whisk to mix. Stir in the garlic and lemon slices.

3 Rinse the chicken under cold running water, then blot it dry with paper towels. Add the chicken to the marinade and stir to coat evenly. Let the chicken marinate in the refrigerator, covered, for at least 1 hour or as long as 4; the longer the chicken marinates, the richer the flavor will be.

4 Thread the chicken through the thin side onto skewers so that the flat side of the chicken will be exposed to the fire.

5 Set up the grill for direct grilling and preheat it to high. Ideally, you'll set up the grill for grateless grilling, following the instructions on page 599.

6 When ready to cook, brush and oil the grill grate. Generously sprinkle each chicken kebab on both sides with salt, black pepper, and the remaining Aleppo pepper or hot red pepper flakes and sweet paprika. Arrange the kebabs on the hot grill and grill them until nicely browned and cooked through, 2 to 4 minutes per side. Serve the kebabs at once with the lemon wedges.

Chicken Brochettes in the Style of Fez

A grill mistress assembles brochettes (Moroccan shish kebabs).

The best chicken *brochettes* in Marrakech are grilled by a . . . woman. I know, I know: The statement smacks of heresy in a machismo grill culture like that of Morocco, but the ladies who own the restaurant Dar al Fassi not only know their way around the kitchen, but around the grill. *Fassi* means women from Fez, and this upscale restaurant, done in white and brass, and located in a shopping complex outside the old city walls is owned, run, cooked for, and served by women. No less remarkable is that you can order Dar al Fassi's haute Moroccan cuisine à la carte, as opposed to the formal, fixed price, multicourse meals normally served at the better restaurants in Marrakech. (Mind-boggling as a full-scale Moroccan banquet is, it's not something you can eat every night.) As for Dar al Fassi's chicken *brochettes,* the bright notes of fresh mint and cilantro, along with the base tones of cumin and turmeric, make these kebabs you could eat every night—and then some. **SERVES 4**

1½ pounds skinless, boneless chicken thighs or breasts,
    cut into 1 x 1 x ½ inch–pieces

3 tablespoons finely chopped fresh mint

3 tablespoons finely chopped fresh cilantro

3 tablespoons finely chopped flat-leaf parsley, or
    more mint or cilantro

1½ teaspoons coarse salt (kosher or sea)

1 teaspoon ground cumin

1 teaspoon ground turmeric

½ teaspoon freshly ground black pepper

2 tablespoons vegetable oil

Moroccan-style rice or couscous, for serving

Onion and Parsley Relish (page 319), for serving (optional)

YOU'LL ALSO NEED

Flat metal or bamboo skewers

ADVANCE PREPARATION

30 minutes to 1 hour for marinating the kebabs

1 Rinse the chicken under cold running water, then blot it dry with paper towels. Place the chicken in a large nonreactive mixing bowl. Add 2 tablespoons each of the mint, cilantro, and parsley and the salt, cumin, turmeric, and pepper, and stir to mix. Stir in the oil. Let the chicken marinate in the refrigerator, covered, for 30 minutes to 1 hour.

2 Thread the chicken through the thin side onto skewers so that the flat side of the chicken will be exposed to the fire.

3 Set up the grill for direct grilling and preheat it to high.

4 When ready to cook, brush and oil the grill grate. Arrange the chicken *brochettes* on the hot grate and grill them until golden brown and cooked through, 4 to 6 minutes per side. Serve the *brochettes* at once, sprinkled with the remaining 1 tablespoon each mint, cilantro, and parsley. Moroccan-style rice or couscous would make a good accompaniment, as would Onion and Parsley Relish.

Pancetta Orange Chicken Kebabs

La Cabrera is the sort of place everyone dreams about stumbling on in Buenos Aires—oozing with atmosphere from its art- and artifact-covered walls to its über-generous meat dishes, but not so touristy that you won't find plenty of *porteños* (as the residents of Buenos Aires are called) dining there too. If hell were on earth, its mouth would be La Cabrera's kitchen, and how the grill men manage to turn out so much meat in such an infernal and confined space remains a mystery. This dish is remarkable for its main ingredient, chicken, an anomaly in a country where people eat beef ten to twelve times a week. And that's not to mention the ingredients that are more characteristic of the Caribbean than of Argentina: fresh orange and rum. **SERVES 4**

THE SCOOP

WHERE: Buenos Aires, Argentina

WHAT: Chicken wrapped in pancetta and skewered with rum-marinated orange slices and grilled kebab style over charcoal

HOW: Direct grilling

JUST THE FACTS:
La Cabrera uses pancetta, a sort of Italian bacon, which is cured but not smoked, to make the kebabs. Smoky North American country-style bacon would give the kebabs even more flavor.

2 large oranges

½ cup dark rum

3 tablespoons salted butter

Coarse salt (kosher or sea) and freshly ground black pepper

1½ pounds skinless, boneless chicken thighs or breasts

6 slices of pancetta, or 6 slices of country-style bacon (about 6 ounces), cut crosswise into 4- to 5-inch pieces

YOU'LL ALSO NEED

Metal or bamboo skewers

ADVANCE PREPARATION

30 minutes to 1 hour for marinating the oranges; the kebabs can be assembled up to 6 hours ahead

1 Cut one of the oranges in half lengthwise. Remove the seeds, if any, with a fork. Place each orange half on a cutting board and cut it crosswise into ¼-inch thick slices, including the skin. Place the orange slices in a nonreactive saucepan and add the rum. Squeeze the juice from the second orange over the orange slices. Gently stir to mix. Let the oranges marinate for 30 minutes to 1 hour.

2 Using a slotted spoon, remove the orange slices from the pan and set them aside. Bring the rum and orange juice mixture to a boil over medium-high heat and let it boil until about ¼ cup of liquid remains. Add the butter and let the mixture return to a boil. Season with salt and pepper to taste.

Set half of the orange and rum mixture aside to use as a sauce. The rest will be used for basting the chicken.

3 Rinse the chicken under cold running water, then blot it dry with paper towels. Cut the chicken into pieces about 2 inches long, 1½ inches wide, and ¾ inch thick. Season the chicken generously with salt and pepper. Wrap each piece of chicken crosswise in a slice of pancetta or bacon. Skewer the chicken pieces so that the long sides are perpendicular to the skewer, placing an orange slice between the pieces of chicken. The kebabs can be made up to 6 hours ahead and refrigerated, covered.

4 Set up the grill for direct grilling and preheat it to medium-high. Leave one section of the grill bare for a safety zone.

5 When ready to cook, brush and oil the grill grate. Arrange the kebabs on the hot grate and grill them until the chicken is golden brown and cooked though, 4 to 6 minutes per side. Should the dripping pancetta fat cause a flare-up, move the kebabs away from the flames. Baste the kebabs with some of the orange and rum mixture on both sides as they grill.

6 Transfer the grilled chicken kebabs to a platter or plates. Remove the hot skewers and pour the reserved orange and rum sauce on top.

Two Chicken Tikkas

Tikka is the Hindi word for pieces, as in bite-size chunks of meat, distinguishing these kebabs, cooked like shish kebab, from the larger chunks of meat cooked on a vertical spit in a tandoor. Here are two *tikkas* from northern India. **SERVES 4**

Cashew Cream Chicken Tikka

If you've held back from Indian grilling in the fear that it's all spicy or fiery, these soulful kebabs are your ticket. I first sampled them at the Ganesh restaurant in the Karol Bagh district of New Delhi. *Restaurant* is a grand word for this corner grill and fry shop, which is packed with customers day and night, but there are a handful of tables and stools under the obligatory blaring television, and they do observe the courtesy (hygiene?) of serving on aluminum foil–wrapped plates. This particular *tikka* reflects what Indians call the "Afghan-style"—flavored with almond or cashew butter, but without the extravagant spicing associated with traditional tandoori. The nut butter and cream give the meat a mild, sweet flavor. Excellent by itself and irresistible when served with Green Herb Chutney.

1½ **pounds skinless, boneless chicken thighs or breasts**
2 **cloves garlic, coarsely chopped**
1 **piece (2 inches) fresh ginger, peeled and coarsely chopped**

1 **jalapeño or serrano pepper, seeded and chopped**
1 **teaspoon coarse salt (kosher or sea)**
½ **teaspoon ground cardamom, or more to taste**
¼ **teaspoon freshly ground white pepper**
¼ **teaspoon ground cumin**
¼ **cup almond or cashew butter**
1 **cup strained yogurt (Greek-style)**
¼ **cup heavy (whipping) cream**
¼ **cup chopped fresh cilantro**
2 **tablespoons unsalted butter, melted for basting (optional)**
Green Herb Chutney (recipe follows)
Indian bread (optional, pages 98 to 101), for serving

YOU'LL ALSO NEED
Flat metal or bamboo skewers

ADVANCE PREPARATION
4 hours to overnight for marinating the chicken

1 Rinse the chicken under cold running water, then blot it dry with paper towels. Cut the chicken into pieces 1 x 1 x ½ inch. Thread the chicken through the thin side onto skewers so the flat side of the chicken will be exposed to the fire. Arrange the chicken kebabs in a nonreactive baking dish just large enough to hold them in a single layer.

2 Place the garlic, ginger, jalapeño pepper, salt, cardamom, white pepper, and cumin in a food processor and pulse to finely chop. Add the almond or cashew butter and yogurt and puree to a smooth paste. Add the cream and cilantro and pulse just to mix. Do not overprocess or the cream may curdle.

3 Pour the marinade over the chicken kebabs, turning to coat all sides. Let the chicken marinate in the refrigerator, covered, for at least 4 hours or as long as overnight, turning the kebabs a few times so they marinate evenly. The longer the chicken marinates, the richer the flavor will be.

4 Set up the grill for direct grilling and preheat it to high.

5 When ready to cook, brush and oil the grill grate. Drain the chicken kebabs, discarding the marinade. Place the chicken kebabs on the hot grate and grill them until golden brown and cooked through, 2 to 4 minutes per side. The last 2 minutes of grilling, baste the kebabs with the melted butter, if using. Serve the chicken *tikka* at once with the Green Herb Chutney and, if desired, one of the Indian breads.

Green Herb Chutney

This piquant green sauce accompanies barbecue throughout northern India, and there are almost as many versions as there are tandoori parlors in New Delhi.

The basic ingredients are fresh mint and/or fresh cilantro, with spinach leaves frequently added for a richer color and flavor. The souring agent can be yogurt, tamarind, lemon juice or a combination of two or three of these. Here's my version. **MAKES ABOUT 1½ CUPS**

1 bunch cilantro, rinsed, shaken dry, stemmed,
    and coarsely chopped
1 bunch fresh mint, rinsed, shaken dry, stemmed,
    and coarsely chopped
1 cup fresh stemmed spinach leaves
1 cup plain whole milk yogurt
1 tablespoon fresh lemon juice, or more to taste
Coarse salt (kosher or sea) and freshly ground black pepper

Finely chop the cilantro, mint, and spinach in a food processor. Add the yogurt and lemon juice, season with salt and pepper to taste, and run the machine in short bursts just to mix. Add enough water—1 to 2 tablespoons—to give you a thick but pourable sauce. Taste for seasoning, adding more salt and/or lemon juice as necessary; the chutney should be highly seasoned.

Saffron Chicken Tikka

{ ZAFRANI MURGH TIKKA }

In the sixteenth and seventeenth centuries, northern India experienced a renaissance. Enlightened rulers from Persia came to rule Rajasthan and Uttar Pradesh. They attracted vast retinues of artists, writers, and architects. The Jami Masjid mosque in Old Delhi and the Taj Mahal in Agra, both built by the Emperor Shah Jahan, bear witness to this extraordinary era of artistry. A Persian influence also survives in modern Indian grilling, as seen in these chicken kebabs, perfumed with saffron, mace, and cardamom—ingredients you'd expect to find in modern-day Iranian cooking. Flavorful but not fiery, flame-charred but moist, these fragrant kebabs represent Mogul cuisine at its best.

1½ pounds skinless, boneless chicken thighs or breasts
2 cloves garlic, peeled and coarsely chopped
1 piece (1 inch) fresh ginger, peeled and coarsely chopped
2 tablespoons fresh lemon juice
1 teaspoon saffron threads
½ cup thick (Greek-style) plain yogurt
½ cup heavy (whipping) cream
1 teaspoon coarse salt (kosher or sea)
½ teaspoon freshly ground white pepper
½ teaspoon ground cardamom
½ teaspoon mace
2 tablespoons unsalted butter, melted for basting (optional)
Indian "Puff Pastry" (optional, page 98)
Green Herb Chutney (optional, recipe on facing page)

YOU'LL ALSO NEED
Flat metal or bamboo skewers

ADVANCE PREPARATION
At least 4 hours or as long as overnight for the
    marinade

1 Rinse the chicken under cold running water, then blot it dry with paper towels. Cut the chicken into pieces 1 x 1 x ½ inch and place it in a nonreactive mixing bowl.

2 Place the garlic, ginger, lemon juice, and 1 to 2 tablespoons water in a blender and puree until smooth, scraping down the sides of the blender with a spatula. Pour this mixture over the chicken and stir to mix. Let the chicken marinate in the refrigerator, covered, for 1 hour.

3 Place the saffron in a small bowl, add 2 teaspoons hot water, and let the saffron soak for 5 minutes.

4 Add the saffron and water mixture, the yogurt, heavy cream, salt, pepper, cardamom, and mace to the chicken and stir to mix. Let the chicken marinate in the refrigerator, covered, for at least 3 hours or as long as overnight, stirring it a few times so that it marinates evenly. The longer the chicken marinates, the richer the flavor will be.

5 Drain the chicken, discarding the marinade. Thread the chicken through the thin side onto skewers so the flat side of the chicken will be exposed to the fire.

6 Set up the grill for direct grilling and preheat it to high.

7 When ready to cook, brush and oil the grill grate. Arrange the chicken kebabs on the hot grate and grill until golden brown and cooked through, 3 to 4 minutes per side. During the last 2 minutes of grilling, baste the kebabs with the melted butter, if using. Serve the saffron chicken *tikka* at once with the Indian "Puff Pastry" and/or Green Herb Chutney, if desired.

Yakitori Like They Make It in Japan

THE SCOOP

WHERE: Tokyo

WHAT: Japanese fast food—chicken kebabs grilled and glazed with a sweet soy master barbecue sauce

HOW: Direct grilling

JUST THE FACTS: Choose your favorite part of the chicken or a mix of parts for this dish. To be strictly authentic, you'd grill the chicken over charcoal on a tiny, slender hibachi. If you use a larger, American-size grill, slide an aluminum foil grill shield (see page 611) under the exposed parts of the skewers to keep them from burning.

There must be a thousand restaurants in Tokyo like the Izakaya-Tamotsu near the train station in the Chiyoda-Ku ward: eight stools lined up at an L-shape counter; two rickety tables with beer crates for chairs outdoors. This rough-and-tumble yakitori parlor serves up every imaginable cut of grilled chicken, from the leg, wing, neck, and skin to the liver, gizzard, heart, and embryonic eggs—and a great deal more, including asparagus and ginkgo nuts, tiny sweet potatoes, and eggplant topped with shaved bonito flakes. All this comes from a closet-size kitchen dominated by a charcoal grill barely the width of a single skewer. But the real treasure here is the pot of *tare* (yakitori sauce) that has been simmering uninterrupted and building flavor for years. For more about yakitori, see the facing page. **SERVES 6 TO 8 AS AN APPETIZER, 4 AS A MAIN COURSE**

Izakaya-Tamotsu— a quintessential neighborhood yakitori parlor.

Yakitori

It's the epitome of Japanese barbecue and some of the best in Asian fast food. At its most authentic, yakitori consists of grilled chicken, plain and simple, without the fireworks of rubs or marinades. The grill it's cooked on measures perhaps two feet long and just a couple of inches across—the ideal size for cooking tiny kebabs without burning the exposed part of the bamboo skewers. When asked about the charcoal fire, the owner of Izakaya-Tamotsu explained in about the only words he knew in English that it burned in excess of 1,000°F.

But what really makes Japanese yakitori authentic is the dipping sauce. For as at a Jewish Passover Seder, you dip not once, but twice in a soy and mirin (sweet rice wine) mixture called *tare* (pronounced TAH-re). The first dip takes place halfway through the grilling, and serves to glaze the mixture onto the meat. The second dip coats the meat like a sauce. The process lacquers the chicken with a glaze that is sweet, salty, silky textured, and absolutely irresistible.

This master sauce, usually ignored in American versions of yakitori, is what distinguishes a great yakitori parlor from an ordinary one. For like the master sauce of China, the *tare* is used over and over, acquiring more flavor with each dipped grilled chicken skewer (the sauce is replenished at the end of each grill session). It's not uncommon in Japan to find sauces that are months or years old, with a concentrated flavor that will bowl you over.

So how do the Japanese address the food safety issue? Well, for one, Japanese chickens are raised in much more hygienic conditions than ours—you can even order chicken sashimi in Japan. And because the yakitori is dipped halfway through the grilling process and again at the end, the sauce is never cross-contaminated with raw chicken. But just to play it safe, when making yakitori in the United States, I recommend keeping the sauce hot on the grill and boiling it well after each use.

FOR THE TARE

1 cup chicken stock, preferably homemade

1 cup soy sauce

½ cup mirin (sweet rice wine), sake, or
  dry white wine

¾ cup sugar, plus 2 tablespoons if using sake
  or white wine

1 scallion, trimmed, white part gently crushed
  with the side of a cleaver (see Notes)

1 clove garlic, gently crushed with the side of a cleaver

1 slice peeled fresh ginger (¼ inch thick),
  gently crushed with the side of a cleaver

1 strip lemon zest (½ x 2 inches)

FOR THE YAKITORI

1½ pounds chicken, any of the following:
  Skinless dark meat
  Dark meat with skin
  White meat
  White meat with pieces of fat
  Chicken wing pieces, wing tips removed
  Chicken skin only
  Chicken livers and/or hearts
  Embryonic chicken eggs (see Notes)
  Toasted sesame seeds (see page 68), for serving

YOU'LL ALSO NEED

Small bamboo skewers or double-pronged
  skewers; an aluminum foil grill shield
  (optional, see page 611)

ADVANCE PREPARATION

None, although you can make the *tare* and assemble the yakitori
  several hours ahead.

1 Make the *tare*: Place the chicken stock, soy sauce, mirin, sugar, scallion white, garlic, ginger, and lemon zest in a nonreactive saucepan and bring to a boil over medium heat. Let the *tare* simmer until thick and syrupy, 6 to 10 minutes, stirring often to prevent scorching. Strain the *tare* into a deep narrow saucepan you can place on the grill;

there must be at least 3½ inches of *tare* in the pot. Discard the solids from the *tare*.

2 Make the yakitori: Cut the chicken into ½-inch cubes and thread it onto skewers. Fill each skewer only halfway; leave the other half bare as a handle. Typically, when skewering the meat, a Japanese grill master will intersperse lean pieces of chicken with pieces of fat or skin. You can grill only one type of chicken meat or you can serve a variety of chicken pieces: dark meat, white meat, chicken skin, and so on, skewering each part of the chicken separately. If you are not grilling the yakitori immediately, refrigerate them covered with plastic wrap. The yakitori can be prepared several hours ahead to this stage.

3 Set up the grill for direct grilling and preheat it to high.

4 When ready to cook, brush and grease the grill grate (a piece of chicken fat or skin held in tongs works great for greasing). Keep the pot of warm *tare* on one corner of the grill. If you are using a hibachi or other slender grill, arrange the chicken skewers on the hot grate so that the bare ends hang over the edge. On a larger grill, arrange the yakitori on the grate with an aluminum foil shield under the exposed ends of the skewers to keep them from burning.

5 Grill the yakitori until the chicken is partially cooked (it will be white on the outside), about 2 minutes per side. Dip each yakitori in the sauce, then return it to the grate. Continue grilling the yakitori until the chicken is well browned and cooked through, 1 to 2 minutes per side longer. The outside should cook to a shiny glaze and the meat should feel firm to the touch when done. Take care that the yakitori don't burn.

6 Dip each grilled yakitori in the *tare* one more time and transfer them to a platter or plate. Sprinkle with sesame seeds and chopped scallion greens, if using, on top and serve at once. Although it's not strictly traditional, I like to serve a little reserved *tare* in a tiny bowl as a dipping sauce.

NOTES: Save the scallion greens for another use or finely chop them for sprinkling over the yakitori. This isn't strictly traditional, but it does add color and flavor.

Embryonic chicken eggs are the unhatched eggs found in hens at the time of processing.

Chicken Liver Yakitori with a Balsamic-Soy Glaze

The word *yakitori* means grilled chicken, but the simple name doesn't begin to describe the variety, complexity, and deep cultural significance of Japan's favorite grilled meat. Yakitori parlors dot Japan's gastronomic landscape, ranging from noisy holes-in-the-wall where commuters grab a quick snack and a few beers before embarking on the long trip home, to neighborhood hangouts, where local bachelors might come for dinner several times a week, to snazzy restaurants, where a seat at the counter around the grill is as hard to come by as a ticket to a U2 concert. Birdland, in the glittering Ginza district in Tokyo, belongs to the last category, and its mercurial chef-owner, Toshihiro Wada, has been known to refuse to serve customers he doesn't believe are sophisticated enough to appreciate his distinctive style of grilling. In a country where grill masters prize simplicity above all else, Wada juxtaposes Eastern and Western flavors, like the soy sauce and balsamic vinegar in the recipe here. What results are sweet-sour-salty chicken livers that will make believers out of people who don't normally like chicken livers. For the sake of accuracy, I should tell you that chef Wada serves his grilled chicken livers on the still bleeding side of rare. They're even batter cooked to what for Westerners, at least, is a more palatable medium-rare or medium. (For more about Wada, see page 404.) **SERVES 6 AS AN APPETIZER, 4 AS A MAIN COURSE**

1½ **pounds chicken livers**
½ **cup good-quality balsamic vinegar**
½ **cup soy sauce**
Very coarse sea salt and freshly ground black pepper

YOU'LL ALSO NEED
Small flat bamboo skewers; a spray bottle; an aluminum foil grill shield (see page 611)

ADVANCE PREPARATION
None

1 Trim any sinews or bloody or green spots off the chicken livers. Skewer the livers on bamboo skewers.

2 Place the balsamic vinegar and soy sauce in the spray bottle and shake to mix.

3 Set up the grill for direct grilling and preheat it to high.

4 When ready to cook, brush and oil the grill grate. Arrange the skewered chicken livers on the hot grate with the aluminum foil shield under the exposed end of the skewers to keep them from burning. Grill the chicken livers until cooked to taste, 2 to 3 minutes per side for medium-rare; 3 to 4 minutes for medium. Spray the chicken livers with the balsamic vinegar mixture as they grill. Season the grilled chicken livers with salt and pepper and serve at once.

VARIATION
Balsamic- and Soy-Glazed Chicken Yakitori: OK, so you don't like chicken livers. This preparation is terrific made with chicken thighs or breast meat. Cut the chicken into pieces that are 1 inch square and ½ inch thick and skewer them through the thin side. Grill the chicken kebabs, until cooked through, 3 to 4 minutes per side, spraying them with the balsamic vinegar mixture.

THE SCOOP

HOW: Direct grilling

JUST THE FACTS: You'll need one unconventional tool for this dish—a spray bottle for applying the glaze. Looks cool as all get out and makes the chicken livers taste even better.

The Japanese yakitori grill is long and slender. Note how the ends of the skewers extend over the sides so they don't burn.

Japan's Mr. Fussy

Toshihiro Wada—the most famous yakitori master in Tokyo.

TOKYO, JAPAN

For years, I'd been hearing about an upscale yakitori parlor called Birdland, but each time I called to make a reservation, I was told it was booked. So I showed up in person, notebook and camera in hand, and had the good fortune to score a seat. Like many yakitori parlors, Birdland is located underground at a train station (more accurately, at the Ginza stop of the Tokyo Metro). But there, all similarity ends. For starters, this is a proper restaurant, with mauve walls and a sleek, blond wood U-shape counter. Secondly, it is owned by a marquee chef, Toshihiro Wada, who caters to an equally marquee clientele that includes the likes of Jamie Oliver and Joël Robuchon.

The patron dining next to us described Mr. Wada as *otaku* ("very fussy"—or less politely, "a pain in the ass"), and you'd need to be fussy (or at least highly demanding about the wholesomeness of your ingredients) to serve the first dish he prepared for us, a tiny kebab of rare chicken breast. Rare chicken would be off-putting to most Americans, but if you can get beyond the initial squeamishness, it tastes a bit like beef carpaccio. According to Mr. Wada, the choicest morsel for this preparation is the muscle on the left side of the breast.

To demonstrate the yakitori master's range, Mr. Wada served in rapid succession crusty kebabs of grilled chicken skin and neck meat with salt and pungent *sansho* pepper;

blood-rare chicken livers sprayed with balsamic vinegar and soy sauce glaze; chicken gizzards seasoned with sake and tarragon vinegar and sprinkled with white pepper and coarse salt; and then amazingly succulent chicken "oysters," the fleshy nugget of meat at the top of the thigh, accompanied with supertart and incredibly aromatic *sudachi* lime.

So what's the Birdland connection? When Mr. Wada was a college student, he had a part-time job in a yakitori parlor behind a jazz bar named for the famous Birdland jazz club in New York. He majored in business management, which may explain two curious practices at the restaurant. The used yakitori skewers are collected, scrubbed, sterilized, and saved for reuse the next day. "They have more flavor than new skewers and are easier to insert in the meat," said Mr. Wada. And at the end of the evening, the costly *binchotan* charcoal is lifted with tongs from the grill, placed in an airtight metal bucket, and saved for use the next day.

Sometimes success breeds its own problems, and I recently heard that Birdland no longer accepts reservations from foreigners. Apparently, the fussy Mr. Wada seems to be unwilling to deal with the language barrier, misunderstandings about reservations, and above all, the general repugnance on the part of most Americans to eat rare chicken. Perhaps you can arrange to be brought here with Japanese business associates or friends.

NAME: Toshihiro Wada

TERRITORY: Born in Hitachi City (the birthplace of the electronics firm). Lives and grills in Tokyo.

CLAIM TO FAME: Chef-owner of one of the most exclusive and hard-to-get-into yakitori restaurants in Tokyo: Birdland

SPECIALTIES: Yakitori made with every imaginable cut of grilled chicken—and just to warn you, Wada likes to serve chicken rare; *negi-ma,* chicken thigh and Japanese leek kebabs sprinkled with *kinome* (*sansho* pepper plant leaves); and *kachokaballo,* a tiny kebab of diced grilled Italian cheese

WADA SAYS:

▶ Listen to your ingredients; Wada literally says "feel the voice of your ingredients."

▶ Educate your palate by eating good food prepared by other grill masters.

▶ Above all, concentrate.

▶ Don't follow the instructions in the barbecue manual too closely.

▶ Fire up your imagination before you fire up your grill.

Israeli Smoked Goose

I wager it's been a while since you've seen goose on a restaurant menu, much less at a barbecue joint. But if this dark, rich, fatty bird has been reduced to the role of a nursery tale character in North America, it still enjoys wide popularity among the Israelis—especially those of Eastern European descent. (Until recently, Israel was a major producer and exporter of foie gras—another reason goose is so popular in that country.) So that's why I'm fighting Friday night traffic from Tel Aviv to Rosh Pina. My destination? The Auberge Shulamit, a restaurant and inn built in the 1920s in this artist town overlooking the Sea of Galilee. It turns out that Auberge Shulamit founders, Gadi Berkuz and her daughter Lea, learned how to smoke goose, beef, and even eggs (see page 13) over cherry and other woods from a pit master from the American South. If you've never tried goose, here's your opportunity, and if you've been disappointed by oven-roasted goose, as I have, this brined, smoked bird will make you a believer. **SERVES 6**

WHERE: Israel

WHAT: A foolproof way to cook an often tough, fatty bird—brined, smoke-roasted goose

HOW: Indirect grilling or smoking

JUST THE FACTS: Your only challenge for this recipe will be procuring a goose. If you live in a town with a large Eastern European or Orthodox Jewish community, you can probably special order it at a butcher shop. One good mail-order source is Schlitz Goose Farms (www.roastgoose.com). As an alternative, you can brine and smoke a turkey the same way.

FOR THE GOOSE AND BRINE

1¼ cups kosher salt

1¼ cups sugar

4 bay leaves

2 sprigs fresh thyme, or 2 teaspoons dried thyme

1 medium-size onion, thinly sliced

1 tablespoon black peppercorns

1 goose (12 to 14 pounds), or 3 whole goose breasts (1½ to 2 pounds each)

FOR THE HORSERADISH SAUCE

1 piece (2 to 4 inches) horseradish root (the more, the better), peeled

¾ cup mayonnaise, preferably Hellmann's

¾ cup sour cream, or more mayonnaise if you keep kosher

1 tablespoon fresh lemon juice

Coarse salt (kosher or sea) and freshly ground black pepper

YOU'LL ALSO NEED

Butcher's string (optional); 5 cups hardwood chips or chunks, preferably cherry, soaked for 1 hour in water to cover, then drained

ADVANCE PREPARATION

24 hours for brining the goose, and allow about 3 hours for grilling using the indirect method or 5 to 6 hours for smoking the goose

1 Make the brine: Place the salt, the sugar, and 1 quart of warm water in a large stockpot or clean bucket and whisk until the salt dissolves. Whisk in 3 more quarts of cool water and the bay leaves, thyme, onion, and peppercorns.

2 Remove and discard the fat just inside the neck and body cavities of the goose. Remove the package of giblets, if any, and set it aside for another use. Rinse the goose, inside and out, under cold running water, then drain and blot it dry, inside and out, with paper towels. Place the goose in the stockpot with the brine. Place a heavy weight, like a saucepan or a large resealable plastic bag filled with ice, on top of the goose to keep it submerged. Brine the goose in the refrigerator for 24 hours.

3 Meanwhile, make the horseradish sauce: Finely grate the horseradish into a nonreactive mixing bowl. Add the mayonnaise, sour cream, if using, and lemon juice and whisk to mix. Season the horseradish sauce with salt and pepper to taste; the sauce should be highly seasoned. Set the horseradish sauce aside.

4 Drain the goose well, discarding the brine, and blot the goose dry with paper towels. For a more professional-looking presentation, truss the bird with butcher's string following the instructions on page 355.

5 To grill: *If you are using the indirect method,* this is best done on a charcoal grill. Set the grill up for indirect grilling, place a large drip pan in the center, and preheat the grill to medium. When ready to cook, if you are using a charcoal grill, toss 2 cups of the wood chips or chunks on the coals. If you are using a gas grill, add the wood chips or chunks to the smoker box or place them in a smoker pouch under the grate (see page 603). Place the goose, breast side up, in the center of the grate over the drip pan and away from the heat and cover the grill. If you are using a charcoal grill, you'll need to add fresh coals to each side of the grill every hour and add 1½ cups of wood chips or chunks to the coals after the first and second hours.

If you are using a smoker, set it up following the manufacturer's instructions and preheat it to 250°F. When ready to cook, place the goose in the smoker, breast side up.

6 Cook the goose until dark golden brown and cooked through, about 3 hours using the indirect method; 5 to 6 hours using a smoker, depending on the temperature outside. Goose breasts will take about 1 hour using the indirect method; 2 to 2½ hours in the smoker. Use an instant-read meat thermometer to test for doneness, inserting it into the thickest part of a thigh or breast but not so that it touches a bone. The internal temperature should be about 180 to 190°F. Another test for doneness is to pierce the side of the thigh or breast with a slender skewer; the juices should run clear.

7 Transfer the goose to a platter or cutting board and remove and discard the trussing string, if any. Let the goose rest for 10 to 15 minutes, loosely tented with aluminum foil. Carve the goose into slices and serve it with the horseradish sauce.

Baste the Israeli Smoked Goose generously and often.

Brown Sugar- and Orange-Brined Smoked Turkey

Here's a bird near and dear to us, for the Aztecs and other native Americans domesticated turkeys long before the arrival of Columbus. Benjamin Franklin regarded turkey so highly, he wanted to name it—not the bald eagle—our national bird. So how did a fowl with such deep American roots come to be called turkey? In the sixteenth century, many luxury consumer products came from or through Turkey. Thus labeling this New World fowl a "Turkie bird" helped lend it cachet and earn it commercial acceptance. Here's a new twist on an American Thanksgiving icon, and brining and smoking virtually guarantee your bird will be moist. I prefer indirect grilling to smoking for turkey as smoking tends to make the skin leathery, while indirect grilling keeps it crisp. But I've given you both options. **SERVES 8**

THE SCOOP

WHERE: North America

WHAT: About the best bird you'll ever serve for Thanksgiving. Thanks to a chemical process known as osmosis, the brine keeps the turkey meat moist—even during prolonged smoking.

HOW: Indirect grilling or smoking

JUST THE FACTS: For the best results, use a free-range, organic turkey.

1 large orange
4 whole cloves
4 bay leaves
4 strips orange zest (each ½ x 2 inches),
    plus the juice of the orange
1¼ cups kosher salt
1¼ cups firmly packed dark brown sugar
1 medium-size onion, thinly sliced
1 stick (3 inches) cinnamon
1 tablespoon black peppercorns
1 turkey (12 to 14 pounds)
4 tablespoons (½ stick) salted butter, melted,
    for basting
Madeira Orange Gravy (recipe follows)

YOU'LL ALSO NEED

Butcher's string; about 5 cups hardwood chips or
    chunks, preferably hickory, soaked for 1 hour
    in water to cover, then drained

ADVANCE PREPARATION

24 hours for brining the turkey, and allow about
    3 hours for grilling the turkey using the
    indirect method or 5 to 6 hours for smoking
    the turkey

1 Make the brine: Using a vegetable peeler, remove 4 strips of orange zest, each ½ x 2 inches, from the orange. Using the cloves, pin the bay leaves to the orange zest strips.

2 Place the salt, the brown sugar, and 1 quart of warm water in a large stockpot or clean bucket and whisk until the salt dissolves. Whisk in 3 quarts of cool water. Add the bay leaves with the orange zest and the onion, cinnamon, and peppercorns to the brine. Juice the orange, discarding any seeds, and add the orange juice to the brine.

3 Remove and discard the fat just inside the body cavities of the turkey. Remove the package of giblets and set it aside for another use. Rinse the turkey, inside and out, under cold running water, then drain and blot it dry, inside and out, with paper towels. Place the turkey in the stockpot with the brine. Place a heavy weight, like a saucepan or a large resealable plastic bag filled with ice, on top of the turkey to keep it submerged. Brine the turkey in the refrigerator for 24 hours.

4 Drain the turkey well, discarding the brine, and blot the turkey dry with paper towels. For a more professional-looking presentation, truss the bird with butcher's string following the instructions on page 355.

5 To grill: *If you are using the indirect method,* this is best done on a charcoal grill. Set up the grill for indirect grilling, place a large drip pan in the center, and preheat the grill to medium. When ready to cook, if you are using a charcoal grill, toss 2 cups of wood chips or chunks on the coals. If you are using a gas grill, add the wood chips or chunks to the smoker box or place them in a smoker pouch under the grate (see page 603). Place the turkey, breast side up, in the center of the grate over the drip pan and away from the heat and cover the grill. Start basting the turkey with butter after it has cooked for 1½ hours and baste it again every 20 or 30 minutes. If you are using a charcoal grill, you'll need to add fresh coals to each side of the grill every hour and add 1½ cups of wood chips or chunks to the coals after the first and second hours.

If you are using a smoker, set it up following the manufacturer's instructions and preheat it to 250°F. When ready to cook, place the turkey in the smoker, breast side up. Start basting the turkey with butter after it has cooked for 2 hours and baste it again every 30 minutes.

6 Cook the turkey until dark golden brown and cooked through, about 3 hours using the indirect method; 5 to 6 hours using a smoker, depending upon the temperature outside. Use an instant-read meat thermometer to test for doneness, inserting it into the thickest part of a thigh but not so that it touches a bone. The internal temperature should be about 170 to 180°F. Another test for doneness is to pierce the side of the thigh with a slender skewer; the juices should run clear.

7 Transfer the turkey to a platter or cutting board and remove and discard the trussing string. Let the turkey rest for 10 to 15 minutes, loosely tented with aluminum foil, before carving. Serve the turkey with the Madeira Orange Gravy.

Madeira Orange Gravy

Another Thanksgiving tradition—this one with roots in Colonial America, for in the eighteenth century, the sweet, brown, fortified Portuguese wine known as Madeira enjoyed the sort of enthusiasm that cabernet sauvignon does today. A fat separator (it looks like a measuring cup with a spout attached on the bottom) is a great help for separating the meat juices from the fat. **MAKES ABOUT 3 CUPS**

Turkey drippings from the drip pan
2 to 2½ cups turkey or chicken stock, preferably homemade
2 tablespoons (¼ stick) salted butter
2 tablespoons flour
1 teaspoon grated orange zest
¼ cup Madeira
¼ cup heavy (whipping) cream
Coarse salt (kosher or sea) and freshly ground black pepper

1 Strain the turkey drippings into a fat separator. Wait a few minutes, pour the drippings into a large measuring cup, stopping when the fat starts to come out. Add enough turkey stock to obtain 2½ cups of liquid.

2 Melt the butter in a large heavy saucepan over medium-high heat. Stir in the flour and orange zest and cook until the mixture is lightly browned, 3 to 5 minutes; do not let it burn.

3 Remove the pan from the heat and gradually whisk in the turkey stock, Madeira, and cream. Return the pan to the heat and let the sauce simmer, whisking often, until thick and the alcohol flavor from the Madeira has cooked off, 4 to 6 minutes. Season the gravy with salt and pepper to taste; it should be highly seasoned.

Turkey Shawarma

S hawarma is the Middle Eastern version of a large shish kebab known as *doner* in Turkey and gyro in Greece. (It's called *tacos al pastor* in Mexico, but that's another story, which I tell on page 212.) It's made by impaling flat strips of meat (lamb, chicken, or turkey) on an oversize spit with a flat base and then roasting it on an upright rotisserie. There are at least three advantages to this singular method of cooking: The dripping fat bastes the meat below it, instead of falling into the drip pan, as on a horizontal rotisserie; the meat can be sliced to order from the outside in, which gives everyone a crusty end cut; and the slices of meat are piled on pita bread with fresh vegetables, pickles, salad, and yogurt or tahini sauce, so you get a whole meal—and a healthy one—in a single sandwich.

THE SCOOP

WHERE: Israel

WHAT: Crisp thin slices of cumin- and turmeric-scented grilled turkey served on pita bread

HOW: Direct grilling

JUST THE FACTS: *Shawarma* is traditionally roasted on a vertical spit. I'm going to assume you don't have a vertical rotisserie, but a similar effect can be achieved by direct grilling.

Shawarma: Roasted on a vertical rotisserie, it's the Middle Eastern answer to Turkish doner and Greek gyro.

Carving shawarma to order. A skinny roast means lots of turnover—hence fresher shawarma.

Traditionally, *shawarma* was made with lamb, but more and more Israeli pit masters use thinly sliced chicken or turkey. The seasonings are what Israelis call "Oriental style," meaning a North African spice mixture of turmeric, cumin, salt, and three kinds of pepper (white, black, and hot). *Shawarma* is Israeli fast food, as ubiquitous as falafel, and to my mind, twice as good. For home grillers I've adapted the *shawarma* so you grill the turkey slices using the direct method. This is actually quicker and easier; you lose the drama of the turning rotisserie spit but you get crustier, more authentic-tasting meat. What follows is a composite of *shawarmas* I enjoyed around Israel. **SERVES 8**

2½ pounds of boneless turkey breast

1 tablespoon ground turmeric

2 teaspoons coarse salt (kosher or sea)

2 teaspoons ground coriander

1 teaspoon ground cumin

1 teaspoon freshly ground black pepper

1 teaspoon freshly ground white pepper or more black pepper

1 teaspoon hot paprika or cayenne pepper

1 onion, cut crosswise into ¼-inch slices

3 to 4 tablespoons extra-virgin olive oil, plus more olive oil (optional), for brushing the pita

8 pita breads

Middle Eastern Sesame Sauce (optional, recipe follows)

Tel Aviv Tomato Relish (recipe follows)

1 cup sour dill pickles or pickled eggplants, thinly sliced

ADVANCE PREPARATION

1 to 4 hours for curing the turkey

1 Rinse the turkey breast under cold running water and blot it dry with paper towels. Cut the turkey sharply on the diagonal across the grain into slices that are ¼ inch thick and 4 to 5 inches wide. If the turkey comes with pieces of fat, count yourself lucky as the melting fat will keep the bird moist. Place the turkey slices in a large baking dish.

2 Place the turmeric, salt, coriander, cumin, black pepper, white pepper, and paprika in a small bowl and stir to mix. Sprinkle the turkey slices on both sides with most of the rub. Sprinkle the onion slices with the remaining rub and layer them with the turkey. Drizzle a few tablespoons of olive oil over the turkey, spreading it onto the meat with your fingertips. Let the turkey cure in the refrigerator, covered, for 1 to 4 hours; the longer it cures, the richer the flavor will be.

3 Set up the grill for direct grilling and preheat it to high.

4 When ready to cook, brush and oil the grill grate. Arrange the turkey and onion slices on the hot grate and grill them until browned and cooked through, about 2 minutes per side. Transfer the grilled turkey slices to a cutting board, piling several slices in a stack, then thinly slice them crosswise. Slice the onions the same way.

5 Brush the pita breads with some of the turkey juices or olive oil. Warm the pitas briefly on the grill, 15 to 30 seconds per side. Place some sliced turkey and onions on each pita and top it with the sesame sauce, if using, the tomato relish, and sliced pickles or pickled eggplant, as desired, and serve at once.

Middle Eastern Sesame Sauce

Tahini is a condiment popular throughout the Middle East. It's especially prized in Israel, where the Kashruth (Jewish dietary laws) prohibit mixing meat and dairy products. Thus, the yogurt and cucumber or yogurt and mint sauce served with grilled lamb in Turkey and Lebanon, would not be consumed by observant Jewish barbecue buffs, but tahini has the creamy mouthfeel and even a bit of the chalky taste one associates with yogurt. Tahini is available in most supermarkets. **MAKES 1½ CUPS**

1 cup tahini
½ cup fresh lemon juice
Coarse salt (kosher or sea)

Place the tahini in a mixing bowl. Whisk in the lemon juice; the tahini will become thinner. Whisk in ¼ to ½ cup of hot water; the tahini sauce will thicken; the sauce should be thick and creamy, with the consistency of heavy cream. Season the sauce with salt to taste.

Tel Aviv Tomato Relish

This is representative of the many tomato relishes served with Mediterranean grilling. There are lots of options for peppers, from a mildly hot horn pepper, popular throughout the Middle East, to jalapeño or serrano peppers. **MAKES ABOUT 3 CUPS**

3 luscious, red ripe tomatoes, cut into ¼-inch dice, with their juices
1 small red onion, cut into ¼-inch dice
1 to 4 hot peppers of your choice, seeded and cut into ¼-inch dice (for a hotter relish, leave the seeds in)
¼ cup chopped fresh flat-leaf parsley (optional)
¼ cup extra-virgin olive oil
3 tablespoons fresh lemon juice, or more to taste
Coarse salt (kosher or sea)

Combine the tomatoes, onion, hot pepper(s), parsley, olive oil, and lemon juice in a nonreactive mixing bowl and stir to mix. Taste for seasoning, adding salt to taste and/or more lemon juice as necessary; the relish should be highly seasoned.

Israeli Grilled Game Hens

Avazi is one of the most famous grill joints in Israel—the sort of place where politicians come, in the words of one customer, "before they become prime ministers." ("The sort of place where prime ministers come before they're indicted," quips another.) But whatever your political views, this noisy restaurant in Tel Aviv's populist Hatikva neighborhood will grab your vote for its massive *meze* (Middle Eastern–style appetizer samplers) and its heaping portions of reasonably priced, intensely flavorful grilled meats. Avazi built its fame on its grilled foie gras (see page 57), but the typical guest is more likely to order another longstanding house specialty, a spice-rubbed, grilled spatchcocked baby chicken that's always crusty on the outside and so moist inside it oozes when you cut into it. Serve the chicken with lemon wedges or with the fiery Tel Aviv Tomato Relish, if desired. **SERVES 4**

THE SCOOP

WHERE: Israel

WHAT: Spatchcocked grilled game hens, pumped up with cumin, turmeric, and pepper

HOW: Direct grilling

JUST THE FACTS: Baby chicken (*poussin* in French) is widely available in Israel and considerably less so in North America, so I call for game hens here. Instructions for spatchcocking (how you do it and why) are found on page 370.

1 tablespoon coarse salt (kosher or sea)

1 tablespoon ground turmeric

2 teaspoons ground cumin

2 teaspoons freshly ground black pepper

1 teaspoon freshly ground white pepper or
    more black pepper

1 teaspoon MSG (optional)

4 game hens (each 1 to 1¼ pounds)

2 to 4 tablespoons extra-virgin olive oil

Lemon wedges, for serving

Pita breads, for serving

Tel Aviv Tomato Relish (optional, page 411),
    for serving

ADVANCE PREPARATION
None

1 Place the salt, turmeric, cumin, black pepper, white pepper, and MSG, if using, in a small bowl and mix well with your fingers or a fork.

2 Remove and discard the fat just inside the neck and body cavities of the game hens. Remove the packages of giblets, if any, and set them aside for another use. Rinse the game hens, inside and out, under cold running water, then drain and blot them dry, inside and out, with paper towels. Spatchcock the game hens following the instructions on page 370. Make 2 deep slashes to the bone in each leg and thigh. Trim or fold the wing tips behind the back. Arrange the game hens on a baking sheet. Set aside 1 to 2 tablespoons of olive oil for basting the game hens. Lightly brush each hen on both sides with the remaining olive oil and season each generously with the rub.

3 Set up the grill for direct grilling and preheat it to medium.

4 When ready to cook, brush and oil the grill grate. Arrange the hens on the hot grate skin side down. Grill the hens until they are darkly browned and cooked though, 8 to 12 minutes per side. Use an instant-read meat thermometer to test for doneness, inserting it into the thickest part of a thigh but not so that it touches a bone. The internal temperature should be about 170°F. During the last 10 minutes of cooking, using a clean basting brush, baste the hens on both sides with the second batch of olive oil. Watch for flare-ups; if they occur, move the hens to a cooler part of the grill.

5 Transfer the grilled game hens, skin side up, to a platter or plates. Serve the hens with lemon wedges for squeezing, pita bread, and tomato relish, if desired.

VARIATIONS

Israeli Game Hens Indirectly Grilled: You can also grill the game hens using the indirect method, a process that, although not traditionally Israeli, has the advantage of eliminating all risk of flare-ups. Set up the grill for indirect grilling, place a drip pan in the center, and preheat the grill to medium. Rub and baste the game hens as described in Step 2, then place them skin side up in the center of the grate over the drip pan and away from the heat. Cover the grill and grill the game hens until they are browned and cooked through, 30 to 40 minutes. Start brushing the hens with olive oil during the last 15 minutes of cooking and baste them again every 5 minutes.

Israeli Grilled Chicken: You can also prepare a 3½ pound spatchcocked chicken in a similar way. You'll need a little less rub. The cooking time will be 12 to 20 minutes per side for chicken grilled using the direct method, 40 minutes to 1 hour for chicken grilled using the indirect method.

"Iceberg" Game Hens with Moroccan Spices

The Iceberg is the sort of place you'd want to live near if you had an apartment in Marrakech—a neighborhood corner restaurant with a charcoal-burning grill out front on which tall piles of spatchcocked baby chickens are roasted the color of burnt orange, then dispersed throughout the neighborhood from morning to midnight. Think your local rotisserie chicken joint with *harissa* (Moroccan hot sauce), and I'm not sure what would be more appealing: the aroma or the convenience. Serve the game hens with a chunk of Moroccan bread dunked in the poultry drippings. **SERVES 4**

4 game hens (each 1 to 1¼ pounds)
1 sweet onion, coarsely chopped
2 tablespoons sweet paprika
1 tablespoon ground cumin
1 tablespoon ground coriander
1 tablespoon coarse salt (kosher or sea)
2 teaspoons freshly ground black pepper
2 tablespoons fresh lemon juice
3 or 4 tablespoons vegetable oil,
    plus oil for basting
Moroccan bread, pita bread, or hard rolls
Simple Moroccan Hot Sauce (recipe follows)

ADVANCE PREPARATION
4 hours to overnight for marinating the game hens

1 Remove and discard the fat just inside the neck and body cavities of the game hens. Remove the packages of giblets, if any, and set them aside for another use. Rinse the game hens, inside and out, under cold running water, then drain and blot them dry, inside and out, with paper towels. Spatchcock the game hens, following the instructions on page 370. Make 2 deep slashes to the bone in each leg and thigh. Trim or fold the wing tips behind the back. Arrange the hens in a nonreactive baking dish just large enough to hold them in a single layer.

2 Place the onion, paprika, cumin, coriander, salt, and pepper in a food processor and puree to a smooth paste. Work in the lemon juice and enough vegetable oil to obtain the consistency of heavy cream. Pour the marinade over the game hens, turning them a couple of times to coat well. Let the birds marinate in the refrigerator, covered, for at least 4 hours, preferably overnight; the longer they marinate, the richer the flavor will be.

3 Set up the grill for direct grilling and preheat it to medium.

4 When ready to cook, brush and oil the grill grate. Drain the game hens, discarding the marinade. Arrange the hens on the hot grate skin side down.

THE SCOOP

WHERE: Marrakech, Morocco

WHAT: Chicken marinated and grilled with onion, paprika, cumin, coriander, and pepper and served with Moroccan hot sauce

HOW: Direct grilling

JUST THE FACTS: The Iceberg restaurant grills baby chickens—what the French would call *poussins* and what I would call the perfect size bird for one person. The closest equivalent in the States would be a game hen. Alternatively, you can substitute one 3½- to 4-pound roasting chicken.

Grill the hens until they are darkly browned and cooked through, 8 to 12 minutes per side. Use an instant-read meat thermometer to test for doneness, inserting it into the thickest part of a thigh but not so that it touches a bone. The internal temperature should be about 170°F. Start basting the game hens with oil after 5 minutes. Watch for flare-ups; if they occur, move the hens to a cooler part of the grill.

5 Transfer the grilled game hens, skin side up, to a platter or plates. Serve the hens with bread and the Simple Moroccan Hot Sauce.

VARIATION

"Iceberg" Game Hens Indirectly Grilled: You can also grill the game hens using the indirect method, a process that, although not traditionally Moroccan, has the advantage of eliminating all risk of flare-ups. Set up the grill for indirect grilling, place a drip pan in the center, and preheat the grill to medium. Place the marinated game hens skin side up in the center of the grate over the drip pan and away from the heat. Cover the grill and grill the game hens until they are browned and cooked through, 30 to 40 minutes. Start basting the hens with oil during the last 15 minutes of cooking and baste them again every 5 minutes.

Simple Moroccan Hot Sauce
{ HARISSA }

Harissa belongs to a broad family of fiery grill condiments that includes Indonesian *sambal* and Provence's *rouille*. **MAKES ABOUT 1 CUP**

¼ cup sweet or hot paprika
1 to 3 teaspoons hot red pepper flakes
⅓ cup boiling water
1 teaspoon coarse salt (kosher or sea)
1 teaspoon ground coriander
½ teaspoon ground cumin
2 cloves garlic, minced
1 medium-size ripe tomato, peeled, seeded, and diced
2 tablespoons extra-virgin olive oil

1 Place the paprika and hot pepper flakes in a heat-proof mixing bowl and add the boiling water. Let stand until a thick paste forms, about 5 minutes.

2 Transfer the pepper paste to a food processor. Add the salt, coriander, cumin, garlic, and tomato and puree to a smooth paste. Add the olive oil and enough water (2 to 4 tablespoons) to obtain a thick but pourable sauce.

With a skewer maker, who turns the sandalwood handles for the skewers on a foot-powered lathe,

Youssef Benjelloun, my guide in Marrakech, next to the grill at Iceberg restaurant on Bani Sadir Street.

Vietnamese Spit-Roasted Duck with Star Anise and Honey

When it comes to roast duck, China grabs the limelight. But excellent duck turns up throughout Asia—typically seasoned with the bold flavors of garlic, ginger, soy sauce, and honey and often roasted on a spit. After all, when it comes to extracting the abundant fat in a duck, nothing beats the rotisserie. The lateral heat and slow gentle rotation melt out the fat and crisp the skin, a virtue not lost on pit masters from Malaysia to Vietnam. This duck comes from a bay front resort called Ana Mandara, in the Vietnamese beach resort town of Nha Trang, and while resorts catering to Westerners don't always dish up authentic cuisine, this one delivers the goods from charcoal-fired pits where local grill masters roast duck on hand-turned rotisseries. **SERVES 2 TO 4**

WHERE: Nha Trang, Vietnam

WHAT: A whole duck glazed with honey, soy sauce, and sesame oil

HOW: Spit roasting or indirect grilling

JUST THE FACTS: This recipe is pretty straightforward, but there's one ingredient you may not know about—star anise, a star-shaped spice with a smoky licorice flavor. Star anise grows in northern Vietnam. Look for it in Asian markets or substitute Chinese five-spice powder, of which star anise is a primary ingredient.

1 duck (about 5 pounds)

6 cloves garlic, peeled and flattened with the side of a cleaver

6 slices (¼ inch thick) peeled fresh ginger, flattened with the side of a cleaver

6 large sprigs fresh cilantro, plus 3 tablespoons finely chopped cilantro, for serving

3 star anise, or 1 teaspoon Chinese five-spice powder

3 tablespoons soy sauce

3 tablespoons honey

3 tablespoons rice wine, sake, or dry sherry

4 tablespoons Asian (dark) sesame oil, for basting

ADVANCE PREPARATION

Allow 12 to 24 hours for marinating the duck and 12 to 24 hours, if possible, for drying it. You'll also need to allow about 1½ hours for spit roasting the duck.

Vietnamese duck spit roasted over charcoal at Ana Mandara resort in Nha Trang.

1 Prick the duck skin all over with the tines of a carving fork to help release the fat. It's important to prick only the skin, not the meat under it; pricking the meat will cause it to dry out. Place 2 cloves of garlic, 2 slices of ginger, 2 sprigs of cilantro, and 1 star anise or ¼ teaspoon of five-spice powder in the cavity of the duck. Place the duck in a large resealable plastic bag (OK, I know this is not traditional in Vietnam, but it's a very effective way to marinate the duck).

2 Place the remaining 4 cloves of garlic, 4 slices of ginger, 5 sprigs of cilantro, and 2 star anise or ¾ teaspoon of five-spice powder in a nonreactive mixing bowl. Add the soy sauce, honey, rice wine, and 2 tablespoons of the sesame oil and stir until well combined. Pour the marinade over the duck. Let the duck marinate in the refrigerator, covered, for 12 to 24 hours, turning the bird a couple times so it marinates evenly. The longer the duck marinates, the richer the flavor will be.

3 Dry the duck (optional, see Note): Drain the duck well, discarding the marinade. Place the duck on a wire rack, such as a cooling rack, over a baking dish or roasting pan in the refrigerator. Let the duck dry, uncovered, for 12 to 24 hours.

4 Set up the grill for spit roasting, following the manufacturer's instructions, and preheat the grill to medium-high. Place a drip pan under where the duck will be positioned.

5 When ready to cook, thread the duck onto the rotisserie spit in such a way that one set of prongs holds the legs apart. Spit roast the duck until it is a deep golden brown and the skin is very crisp, 1¼ to

VIETNAMESE SPIT-ROASTED DUCK WITH STAR ANISE AND HONEY | page 415

1½ hours. Use an instant-read meat thermometer to test for doneness, inserting it into the thickest part of a thigh, but not so that it touches the bone or the spit. The internal temperature should be about 180°F for medium-well done; 190°F for well-done (in Vietnam duck is customarily enjoyed medium-well to well done). Start basting the duck with some of the remaining 2 tablespoons of sesame oil after 30 minutes, basting it again once every 15 minutes.

6 Transfer the grilled duck to a cutting board and let it rest for 5 minutes. Using a cleaver, cut the duck into eight 8 pieces: 2 wing-breast pieces, 2 breast pieces, 2 thighs, and 2 drumsticks. Serve the duck at once, sprinkled with the chopped cilantro.

NOTE: I have made drying the duck optional, but if you have time to do this, the skin will be that much more crisp. My assistant Nancy uses a hair dryer to dry the skin. She puts the duck on a rack, points the hair dryer at it, and turns it on at low heat.

Quail "Kabanchik" Grilled in the Style of the Republic of Georgia

My tickets were bought; my visa paid for. My plan was to fly from Frankfurt to Tbilisi. I'd always wanted to visit Georgia, first because, according to the Ancient Greeks, this tiny republic, sandwiched between the Caucasus Mountains and the Black Sea, was the mythological birthplace of fire (more about that on page xii). And second, because according to every Russian I've ever met, of all the former republics of the Soviet Union, Georgians do the best grilling. But a week before my trip, Russia invaded Georgia (or Georgia provoked Russia) and that was that for my visit. So I settled for a crash course in Caucasus grill culture at a Georgian restaurant in Moscow called Kabanchik. There, in a dining room decorated like a Georgian farmhouse with a magisterial *mangal* in an equally magisterial fireplace, surrounded by garlands of garlic and smoked cheese and Georgian music played on a military-strength sound system, I ate *shashlik* (shish kebabs) and ground turkey kebabs, *tkemali* (Georgian sour plum sauce), and *satsibili* (tomato sauce). I drank rough red wine and ate wood oven–baked Georgian bread, and for an evening at least, I got a glimpse of what barbecue must be like in Tbilisi. Here's grilled quail bursting with Georgian flavors—wine, garlic, oranges, brandy—along with Georgia's national barbecue sauce, the sour plum condiment *tkemali*. **SERVES 4**

12 quail (see Just the Facts, page 417)

⅓ cup Dijon mustard

3 cloves garlic, minced

Coarse salt (kosher or sea), and freshly ground black pepper

⅔ cup dry red wine

4 strips orange zest (each ½ x 2 inches)

½ cup fresh orange juice

4 strips lemon zest (each ½ x 2 inches)

½ cup fresh lemon juice

¼ cup Cognac

½ cup extra-virgin olive oil, plus olive oil for basting

Russian "Ketchup" (optional, page 183), for serving

ADVANCE PREPARATION

2 hours to overnight for marinating the quail

1 Rinse the quail under cold running water and blot them dry with paper towels. Spatchcock the quail, following the instructions on page 370. Arrange the quail in a nonreactive baking dish just large enough to hold them in a single layer.

2 Place the mustard in a nonreactive mixing bowl. Add the garlic, 1 teaspoon of salt, and ½ teaspoon of pepper and whisk to mix. Whisk in the wine, orange zest and juice, lemon zest and juice, and Cognac, followed by the olive oil. Taste for seasoning, adding more salt and/or pepper as necessary.

3 Pour the marinade over the quail, turning them several times to coat well. Let the quail marinate in the refrigerator, covered, for 2 hours or as long as overnight, turning them several times so they marinate evenly. The longer the quail marinate, the richer the flavor will be.

4 Set up the grill for direct grilling and preheat it to medium-high.

5 When ready to cook, brush and oil the grill grate. Drain the quail well and discard the marinade. Arrange the quail skin side down on the hot grate, at a diagonal to the bars. Grill the quail until the bottom is golden brown, 5 to 8 minutes, giving each quail a quarter turn after 3 minutes to create a handsome crosshatch of grill marks. Turn the quail and grill the second side the same way. Total cooking time will be 10 to 16 minutes. Start basting the quail with olive oil after 5 minutes and baste the quail several times.

6 Transfer the quail to a platter or plates. Serve the quail with Russian "ketchup," if desired.

Fish

"**W**hat is barbecue?" It's a question I ask every incoming class at Barbecue University. The answers vary, of course, depending on where you come from. A Texan would respond "brisket"; a North Carolinian, "pulled pork"; and if you are from Kansas City, you'd say "spareribs." In other words, some sort of grilled or smoked meat. So you may be surprised to learn that one of the first recorded barbecue recipes—found in a third century Greek foodie manifesto called the *Deipnosophistae* (Dinner Table Philosophers)—featured fish, or more precisely bonito wrapped in grape leaves and grilled in the embers. As it turns out, on much of Planet Barbecue, the "meat" of choice for grilling comes from the sea.

Nowhere is this truer than in Southeast Asia, where grill masters cook everything from *garoupa* (similar to North American grouper) to snakehead (a long slender fish; you can substitute trout) to skate grilled over coconut shell charcoal. The *garoupa* comes "Portuguese style," marinated in Malaysian spices; the snakehead is stuffed with lemongrass and crusted with salt (it's a popular Bangkok street food); while the skate is one of Singapore's national dishes, electrified with chiles, lemongrass, and other Asian spices and grilled in banana leaves. Further afield, you'll find barramundi grilled in paperbark, a specialty of the Australian outback; tandoori kingfish; and even a Korean *bool kogi*—here a dish traditionally made with beef rib steak is made with puffer fish (blowfish).

CLOCKWISE FROM TOP LEFT: *Fish grilled Greek island style—on fig leaves over charcoal; Meng Kee—a go-to spot for grilled fish in Kuala Lumpur. Laotian grilled fish: fresh from the Mekong River and hot off the grill; Khmer chef Sarun Pich prepares the marinade for Cambodian grilled fish.*

If all this sounds overly exotic, rest assured that Planet Barbecue serves up grilled fish dishes of merciful simplicity that will satisfy even the most diehard steak lover. You'll find grilled hake fillets topped with fried garlic in the style of the Basque region in Spain. Blood-rare tuna steaks stung with wasabi hellfire from Guam. And, of course, there are smoky caper-sauced swordfish steaks done the way we grill them at my home in Martha's Vineyard.

Wherever you live, when it comes to grilling fish, we all face the same challenges: how to keep the fish from drying out or sticking to the grill grate or from falling apart when you turn it. In this chapter, you'll learn how to grill fish on a skewer, in a grill basket, on a cedar plank, and wrapped in banana leaves. The possibilities are endless.

Previous page: Whole fish grilled to perfection at an outdoor stall in Indonesia.

Planked Salmon with Juniper Rub and Berry Glaze

True or false? Planking (grilling on cedar or alder planks) originated in the Pacific Northwest. For extra points, name the decade: the fifties? or the nineties? The answers aren't quite as obvious as you may think. It's true that the Indians of the Pacific Northwest traditionally cooked whole salmon (split open through the belly) on cedar stakes in front of a roaring fire (they did this back when Lewis and Clark visited and they still do). But planking is equally well documented on the East Coast, where coastal Connecticut Indians nailed shad fillets to oak boards to roast in front of a bonfire.

As to the date of its first popularization, you were right if you named the fifties. The *1850s,* that is, when an American food writer named Eliza Leslie included a recipe for planked shad cooked before a fire in her *New Cookery Book,* published in 1857.

Richard Hetzler, executive chef of the Mitsitam Café at the National Museum of the American Indian in Washington, D.C., prefers the traditional live fire approach. His rub has the fresh piney scent of juniper berries; his glaze uses berries Native Americans would have gathered wild and sweetened with another Indian invention, maple syrup. Mitsitam is an upscale cafeteria with cook stations themed broadly by regional Native American cuisine. In the Pacific Northwest station you will find a wood-burning fire pit where planked wild salmon sizzles. The result is America's favorite fish, perfumed with cedar and juniper and glazed with sweet-sour berries. It's crusty on the outside and moist inside, and thanks to the plank, it never sticks to the grill grate. **SERVES 4**

FOR THE BERRY GLAZE

2 cups mixed fresh berries (I like a blend of wild blueberries, marionberries, gooseberries, and raspberries)

¼ cup maple syrup, or more to taste

FOR THE JUNIPER RUB

1 teaspoon juniper berries

1 teaspoon black peppercorns (not native to the Americas, but exceedingly tasty with salmon)

2 teaspoons coarse salt (kosher or sea)

1 piece salmon fillet (1½ to 2 pounds), preferably wild

YOU'LL ALSO NEED

A cedar grilling plank (12 to 14 by 6 to 7 inches), soaked in water to cover for 1 hour, then drained (see Note); squirt gun

ADVANCE PREPARATION

None, but the berry glaze can be prepared several hours ahead.

1 Make the berry glaze: Put the berries and maple syrup in a heavy saucepan and add 2 tablespoons of water. Cover the pan and cook over medium heat until the berries begin to soften, about 2 minutes. Uncover the pan, reduce the heat to medium-low, and cook the mixture down to a thick puree, about 10 minutes, stirring often with a wooden spoon. Add a little more water if needed to keep the glaze liquid; do not let it burn. Taste for sweetness, adding more maple syrup as necessary.

2 Make the juniper rub: Place the juniper berries and peppercorns in a spice mill or coffee grinder and grind to a fine powder. Add the salt, running the motor in short bursts.

3 Run your fingers over the salmon fillets, feeling for bones. Remove any you find with needle-nose pliers or tweezers.

4 Set up the grill for indirect grilling and preheat it to medium-high.

5 Just before cooking, very generously season the salmon on both sides with the juniper rub. Arrange the salmon skin side down on the plank. Spoon half of the berry glaze over the fish. Place the plank in the center of the grate, away from the heat, and cover the grill. Grill the salmon until the top is sizzling and golden brown and the fish is cooked through, 20 to 30 minutes. When done, the salmon will break into firm flakes when pressed with a finger. The plank may become singed at the edges, but it shouldn't catch fire. If it does, extinguish the flames with a squirt gun.

6 Transfer the fish on the plank to a platter and serve it right off the plank, spooning the remaining berry glaze on top.

NOTE: One easy way to soak the cedar plank is on a baking sheet with raised sides; place a weight on the plank to keep it submerged.

Planked Bluefish with Lemon Mustard

Bluefish is a dark, rich, oily fish that is ineffably delicious when caught and eaten the same day and less good when any less fresh than that. If you live in a coastal community in the East (Nantucket, Martha's Vineyard, Cape Cod, or the Jersey Shore, for example), you're in business—make friends with a local fisherman. If not, the same recipe can be prepared with wild salmon. **SERVES 4**

⅔ cup mayonnaise, preferably Hellmann's
⅓ cup grainy Meaux-style mustard
2 teaspoons finely grated lemon zest
1 tablespoon fresh lemon juice
1½ to 2 pounds bluefish fillets
Coarse salt (kosher or sea) and cracked black
    peppercorns

YOU'LL ALSO NEED
A cedar grilling plank (12 to 14 x 6 to 7 inches),
    soaked in water to cover for 1 hour, then
    drained (see Note); squirt gun

ADVANCE PREPARATION
None

1 Place the mayonnaise in a mixing bowl. Whisk in the mustard, lemon zest, and lemon juice.

2 Set up the grill for indirect grilling and preheat it to medium-high.

3 Just before cooking, very generously season the bluefish on both sides with salt and pepper. Arrange the fish skin side down on the plank. Using a rubber spatula, spread the glaze over the top of the fish. Place the plank in the center of the grate, away from the heat, and cover the grill. Grill the fish until the top is sizzling and golden brown and the fish is cooked through, 20 to 30 minutes. When done, the bluefish will break into firm flakes when pressed with a finger. The plank may become singed at the edges, but if you're indirect grilling, it shouldn't catch fire. If it does, extinguish the flames with a squirt gun.

4 Transfer the fish on the plank to a platter and serve it right off the plank.

NOTE: One easy way to soak the cedar plank is on a baking sheet with raised sides; place a weight on the plank to keep it submerged.

Alder-Smoked Salmon

THE SCOOP

WHERE: British Columbia, Canada

WHAT: Salmon cured with brown sugar, dill, and mustard, then smoked over smoldering alder

HOW: Smoking or indirect grilling on a charcoal grill

JUST THE FACTS: You have two options for smoking: the traditional way—low and slow in a smoker, in which case leave yourself 1 to 1½ hours for smoking; or grilling the salmon using the indirect method at a higher temperature (adding wood smoke), in which case it will take about fifteen to twenty minutes. Sorry, folks; this won't work on a gas grill.

In 1985, Canadian fishing enthusiast Ted Bradley got tired of the traditional Vancouver method of smoking salmon. (Add sawdust to the fire, explains Bradley. Drink a rum and Coke, add more sawdust to the fire, drink another rum and Coke, then scrape off the burnt part of the fish before serving.) So he decided to eliminate the guesswork. The device he came up with looks like a miniature refrigerator with a thermostatically controlled burner that uses hockey puck–size cakes of sawdust to provide the smoke: the Bradley Smoker. Ted's alder-smoked salmon builds on a tradition begun by the Indians of British Columbia: preserving Pacific salmon by smoking and drying. The mustard and dill may remind you of another cured (but not smoked) salmon—Swedish gravlax. Once you taste the homemade stuff, it's hard to go back to store-bought. I've adapted the recipe so you can make it on a wide range of smokers. **SERVES 8 AS AN APPETIZER, 4 AS A LIGHT MAIN COURSE**

1½ to 2 pounds wild king or coho salmon fillet with skin, or
    1½ pounds skinless salmon fillet, preferably wild
2 tablespoons vegetable oil
2 tablespoons chopped fresh dill
2 tablespoons cracked or coarsely ground black pepper
1 tablespoon dry mustard
1 firmly packed cup dark brown sugar
½ cup coarse salt (kosher or sea)

YOU'LL ALSO NEED

2 cups alder wood chips or chunks, soaked for 1 hour in water
    to cover, then drained, or alder sawdust disks or pellets

ADVANCE PREPARATION

2 to 4 hours for curing the fish, plus smoking the fish will
    require 1 to 1½ hours.

1 Run your fingers over the salmon fillets, feeling for bones. Remove any you find with needle-nose pliers or tweezers. Brush the salmon on both sides with the vegetable oil.

2 Place the dill, pepper, mustard, brown sugar, and salt in a mixing bowl and mix them with your fingers, breaking up any lumps in the brown sugar. Cut a piece of plastic wrap that is a little more than twice as long as the salmon fillet and place it on a work surface. Spread half of the dill and mustard rub in the center of the plastic wrap in the shape of the fillet. Arrange the salmon on top of the rub, then spread the remaining rub over the salmon. Tightly wrap the salmon in the plastic (the package should be airtight) and let it cure in the refrigerator for 3 to 4 hours.

3 Unwrap the salmon and rinse off the rub. Blot the fish dry with paper towels.

4 To grill: *If you are using a smoker,* set it up following the manufacturer's instructions and preheat it to 200° to 225°F. When ready to cook, oil the grate. Arrange the salmon skin

HOW TO SMOKE SALMON

1. *Remove any pin bones with needle-nose pliers.*

2. *Mix the ingredients for the rub, breaking up any lumps in the brown sugar with your fingers.*

3. *Soak the wood chips in water to cover, so they smolder and smoke, rather than immediately catching fire.*

4. *Place the soaked wood chips directly on the lit coals.*

5. *Smoke the salmon in the center of the grate over the drip pan.*

Serve the alder-smoked salmon with sour cream, capers, and grilled toast points (or pita).

side down, if any, in the smoker and smoke it until cooked through, 1 to 1½ hours, or as needed.

If you are grilling using the indirect method, set up a charcoal grill for indirect grilling, place a drip pan in the center, and preheat the grill to medium. When ready to cook, brush and oil the grill grate. Toss the wood chips or chunks or the disks or pellets on the coals. Arrange the salmon skin side down on the grate over the drip pan and cover the grill. Grill the salmon until cooked through, 15 to 20 minutes.

5 When done, the salmon will break into firm flakes when pressed with a finger. You can serve the salmon hot, but most people will prefer the fish chilled.

Fish on the Grill

When it comes to cooking fish, there's no better method than grilling. That's the good news. The less good news is that grilling fish presents a triple challenge to the aspiring grill master. Unlike steak, grilled fish has a tendency to stick to the grill grate. Unlike chicken, it's prone to falling apart when you go to turn it. And unlike well-marbled meat, if you're not careful, fish is easy to dry out on the grill.

I wish I could tell you there's a one size fits all approach to grilling fish. The fact is that each type of fish—and in many instances each cut—has a grilling method that suits it best. Firm, dense steak fish, like tuna or swordfish, for example, respond to direct high heat grilling, the way you'd cook beefsteak. Delicate fish, such as sardines or snapper, do well grilled wrapped in grape leaves, as they do in Portugal, or banana leaves, as they do in the Yucatán. Oily fish, like bluefish or mullet, seem to taste best hot smoked or cold smoked. And many fish, especially salmon, taste fantastic grilled on a soaked cedar or alder plank in a style possibly inspired by the Indians of the Pacific Northwest.

So what's the best method for grilling a particular fish? Use one of the following three strategies: anatomical, technical, or mechanical.

▶ The anatomical strategy is a fancy way of saying pick a species or cut of fish that's firm and dense enough to hold together when you grill it directly over the fire. The short list of candidates includes tuna, swordfish, marlin, and salmon steaks, and small whole fish, like snappers or trout. For these fish, you want to start with a hot grill grate, well cleaned with a stiff wire brush, and generously oiled with a tightly folded paper towel drawn across the bars of the grate before you put the fish on.

▶ The technical strategy calls for using one or more of the techniques that grillers have developed over the years.

1. Lightly brush pieces of fish on both sides with olive or vegetable oil just prior to putting them on the hot grate.

2. Gently slide the pieces of fish forward a half inch or so as you position them on the grate to prevent sticking and brand in grill marks.

3. Don't try to turn the fish too quickly. Yes, it will stick to the grate after the first minute or so, but if you're patient, it will release after two or three minutes.

▶ The mechanical strategy involves the use of special tools, like a fish grate or a fish basket.

A fish grate is a flat, perforated metal plate or wire grid, sometimes coated with a nonstick finish; you place the fish grate on top of a hot grill grate. The theory is that a flat metal plate is easier to oil and gives more support to fragile fish. It's also easier to slide a spatula under fish that has cooked on a flat metal plate rather than on the bars of a typical grill grate. The holes in the metal or spaces between the wire allow for the fire and smoke to flavor the fish.

A fish basket is a rectangular or oval hinged wire basket. A rectangular basket is designed for grilling fish fillets or steaks; an oval basket is meant for grilling whole fish. The beauty of the fish basket is that you turn it with the fragile fish inside. When buying a fish basket, look for one with a removable handle, so you can close the grill lid. When using a fish basket, remember to oil the wire mesh well with cooking oil spray or a paper towel dipped in oil.

Grilled Salmon with Shallot Cream Sauce

Grilling in France is more the work of passionate individuals than a regional specialty or national pastime. And spicing in France tends to be subdued rather than extravagant; this is *not* the place to come if you're looking for complex spice rubs—except if you travel to Nantes. The largest city in Brittany, Nantes was the port from which French ships sailed to the East and West Indies during the great age of exploration and colonization. Curry powder and other spices—major exports from the French colonies— arrived in Nantes' warehouses for distribution to the rest of France. This curry powder–based rub makes the perfect counterpoint to the rich, oily flesh of the salmon. The dish also features an interesting optional grilling technique: cooking the fish under a metal pie tin. The pie tin holds in the wood smoke and heat, speeding up the cooking time. It's a handy solution for when you cook on a grill that doesn't have a lid. **SERVES 4**

FOR THE SALMON AND RUB

4 teaspoons curry powder

2 teaspoons coarse salt (kosher or sea)

2 teaspoons freshly ground white or black pepper

4 skinless salmon fillets (each 6 to 8 ounces), preferably wild

2 tablespoons extra-virgin olive oil

FOR THE SHALLOT CREAM SAUCE

2 to 3 shallots, minced (about ½ cup)

1 cup dry white wine, such as Muscadet

1 cup crème fraîche or heavy (whipping) cream

6 tablespoons (¾ stick) cold salted butter, cut into ½-inch pieces

Coarse salt (kosher or sea) and freshly ground white or black pepper

1 tablespoon finely chopped fresh chives or scallion greens, for garnish

YOU'LL ALSO NEED

Oak logs for building a fire or about 2 cups oak chips or chunks, soaked in water to cover for 1 hour, then drained; a metal pie tin or aluminum foil pan (optional)

ADVANCE PREPARATION

15 to 30 minutes for marinating the fish

1 Prepare the rub and salmon: Place the curry powder, salt, and pepper in a small bowl and mix with your fingers.

2 Run your fingers over the salmon fillets, feeling for bones. Remove any you find with needle-nose pliers or tweezers. Arrange the salmon fillets in a baking dish just large enough to hold them in a single layer. Season the salmon on both sides with the curry mixture, rubbing the spices onto the fish with your fingertips. Drizzle 1 tablespoon of the olive oil over both sides of the salmon fillets, rubbing it onto the fish with your fingertips. Let the salmon marinate in the refrigerator, covered, for 15 to 30 minutes.

3 Meanwhile, make the sauce: Place the shallots and white wine in a heavy saucepan, bring to a boil over high heat, and let boil until the wine is reduced to about ¼ cup. Whisk in the crème fraîche or heavy cream and let boil until reduced by about half. Reduce the heat to medium-high and gradually whisk in the butter. Do not let the sauce boil once all of the butter is added or it may curdle. Remove the pan from the heat. Season the sauce with salt and pepper to taste; it should be highly seasoned. The shallot cream sauce can be made up to 30 minutes ahead of time; keep it warm at the back of the stove or grill. Do not let it boil.

4 Set up the grill for direct grilling and preheat it to high. Ideally, you'll grill over oak wood embers (see page 603 for instructions on grilling over a wood fire).

5 When ready to cook, if you are using a charcoal grill, toss the wood chips or chunks on the coals. If you are using a gas grill, add the wood chips or chunks to the smoker box or place them in a smoker pouch under the grate (see page 603). Brush and oil the grill grate. Lightly brush the salmon fillets with the remaining 1 tablespoon of olive oil. Arrange the salmon on the hot grate at a diagonal to the bars. Grill the salmon until cooked to taste, 3 to 4 minutes per side for medium. When done, the salmon will break into firm flakes when pressed with a finger. If desired, give each piece a quarter turn on each side after 1½ minutes to create a handsome crosshatch of grill marks. For extra smoke flavor, you can invert a metal pie tin or aluminum foil pan over the fish to trap the smoke.

6 Transfer the fish to a platter or plates and spoon the shallot cream sauce over it or serve the sauce on the side. Sprinkle the chives over the fish and serve at once.

Salmon Glazed with Belgian Cherry Beer

You've probably heard of Belgium's legendary cherry beer, kriek (pronounced creek) lambic, even if you've never tried it. (And if you've never tasted it, run, don't walk, to buy some—its complex flavor can hold its own against wine.) What you may not realize is how food- and grill-friendly this tart, dry ale brewed with sour morello cherries really is. This dish was inspired by my Belgian grill master friend, Peter De Clercq (see page 430), and it will give you a new perspective on teriyaki. **SERVES 4**

1 bottle (12 ounces; about 1½ cups) kriek
    lambic beer
1 cup soy sauce
⅓ cup mirin (sweet rice wine), sake, or
    cream sherry
¾ cup firmly packed brown sugar
    (add 2 more tablespoons if using
    sake instead of mirin)
3 strips orange or tangerine zest
    (each ½ inch wide by 2 inches long;
    remove them with a vegetable peeler)
2 cloves garlic, peeled and crushed with
    the side of a cleaver
1 slice (¼ inch thick) fresh ginger, crushed
    with the side of a cleaver
1 scallion, trimmed, white part crushed
    with the side of a cleaver, green parts
    finely chopped for garnish
4 skinless salmon fillets (each 6 to 8 ounces),
    preferably wild, or 4 salmon steaks
    (each about 1 inch thick and 6 to 8 ounces)

YOU'LL ALSO NEED
A fish basket (optional)

ADVANCE PREPARATION
1 to 2 hours for marinating the salmon

1 Place the kriek lambic, soy sauce, mirin, brown sugar, orange zest, garlic, ginger, and scallion white in a large heavy saucepan over high heat. Bring the marinade to a boil, stirring until the sugar dissolves. Let the marinade boil until syrupy (like maple syrup) and reduced by about one third, 6 to 10 minutes, stirring from time to time. Remove the pan from the heat and let the marinade cool to room temperature (you can speed up the cooling by placing the pan in a bowl of ice).

2 Run your fingers over the salmon fillets, feeling for bones. Remove any you find with needle-nose pliers or tweezers. Arrange the salmon in a non-reactive baking dish just large enough to hold it in a single layer. Pour the cooled marinade over the salmon and let it marinate in the refrigerator, covered, for 1 to 2 hours.

3 Drain the fish from the marinade. Pass the marinade through a strainer into a saucepan and discard the solids. Bring the marinade to a boil over high heat and let it boil until reduced to a glaze (it should be the consistency of barbecue sauce), about 5 minutes, then set it aside.

4 Set up the grill for direct grilling and preheat it to high.

5 When ready to cook, brush and oil the grill grate. Arrange the fish fillets on the hot grate at a diagonal to the bars. Grill the salmon until nicely browned on the outside and cooked through, 3 to 4 minutes per side for medium. When done, the salmon will break into firm flakes when pressed with a finger. If desired, give each piece of salmon a quarter turn on each side after 1½ to 2 minutes to create a handsome crosshatch of grill marks. Start basting the fish with the reduced marinade after 2 minutes, basting both sides.

Alternatively, you can grill the salmon in a well-oiled fish basket, which is a great way to keep the fish from sticking to the grill grate. There's no need to create crosshatch marks if you use a grill basket.

6 Transfer the grilled salmon to a platter or plates. Spoon any remaining marinade on top. Sprinkle the scallion greens over the salmon and serve at once.

JUST THE FACTS: To be strictly authentic, you must use a Belgian cherry-flavored beer called kriek lambic. It's becoming more and more widely available; two good brands include Boon and Lindemans. In recent years, several American breweries, for example, the New Glarus Brewing Company in New Glarus, Wisconsin, and Samuel Adams, in Boston, have begun brewing cherry beer. As for the fish, you know my stated preference for the robust texture and flavor of wild salmon over farmed.

The Bruegel of Belgian Barbecue

MALDEGEM, BELGIUM

You might say Peter De Clercq, owner of the Elckerlijc restaurant in Belgium, came to his grill mastery through marriage. Starting out as a butcher, he worked for his soon to be father-in-law, who saw in the young man a deep respect for Belgium's quality meats and a passion for live-fire cooking. So he made Peter an irresistible offer: "Marry my daughter and I'll give you half my house to open a restaurant."

Never mind that the house was on the outskirts of a nondescript town called Maldegem—in other words, in the middle of nowhere (its chief virtue is its proximity to Brugge). That there was absolutely no reason to go there—unless you wanted to sample the food of a butcher turned grill master whom no one had heard of. And while Belgium may boast of superlative seafood and french fries, it lacks even the most rudimentary tradition of grilling.

Together Peter and his father-in-law designed the massive wood-burning grill that would become the restaurant's spiritual heart and focal point. The wood burns in a raised metal basket at eye level: The embers drop through the metal bars into a fire pan below (the system resembles the grills you find in Uruguay). Five minutes in front of the blast furnace fire is enough to give you sunburn.

> To say that the artist, chef Peter De Clercq, is obsessed with barbecue would be like saying that Steve Jobs has a passing interest in technology.

Far from being a handicap, the lack of a local grilling tradition spurred Peter's creativity. He cooked Belgium's legendary mussels in a foil bag over the fire and grilled North Sea oysters with wild berry jam and ginger (see page 506). He used Belgium's superlative beers to make marinades, glazes, and even a sabayon to serve with grilled vegetables. Not surprisingly, an entire meal is available grilled, from Belgium's superb smoky Breydel bacon as an appetizer, to a honey-marinated grilled apple "steak" with mare's milk ice cream for dessert (see page 569).

Today, the 120-seat restaurant plays to an international clientele, and if you're expecting a rustic barbecue joint, you're in for a surprise. With its exposed brick walls, massive beams, expanses of glass, and gray-clothed tables set with square white plates, Elckerlijc has the cool contemporary feel of a hip bistro in Amsterdam or New York.

"Life revolves around fire," Peter observed recently in an interview in a French magazine. Every day he puts his money where his mouth is. And, yes, his charcoal-crusted paintings are available for purchase.

NAME: Peter De Clercq

TERRITORY: Belgium

CLAIM TO FAME: The short list of De Clercq's accomplishments includes an internationally acclaimed restaurant, Elckerlijc; a series of best-selling cookbooks; and a line of grilling foods and accessories. His *Petermolen* (a play on the Flemish word for peppermill) TV show has made him a media darling and household name. In 2003, De Clercq won a World Barbecue Association championship in Jamaica.

SPECIALTIES: Grilled sea scallops served with burnt chicory. Herb-grilled lobster. Grilled apples with mare's milk ice cream.

DE CLERCQ SAYS:

▶ For me, the only fuels are wood and charcoal, and if you use the latter, the best comes from oak or beech.

▶ To get more flavor from your fire, toss olive pits on the coals. You can also use grilling spices (bay leaves, rosemary, coriander seed, allspice, and juniper berries, and the like) tossed right on the embers.

▶ I like to grill fish whole with the scales on. They protect the flesh from the fire.

▶ There's a lot you can do with live fire, but you can't achieve great results from frozen or poor-quality meats.

Salmon Shashlik

The location is downtown Moscow, a stone's throw from the Kremlin. But with a little imagination and enough *kvass* (a fermented bread drink) or Pivo (Uzbek beer), you could think you're at a country palace in Bukhara. The restaurant Uzbekistan is *the* go-to spot for Uzbek food in Moscow, and the *mangals* and wood-burning oven and rotisserie let you know they mean business when it comes to grilling. One of the many things they grill well here gives you a break from the relentlessly carnivorous parade of meat kebabs consumed around Moscow: *shashlik* made with salmon. The saffron, garlic, and mayonnaise marinade doubles as a glaze, ensuring fish that is always flavorful and never dried out. Salmon steaks could be prepared in a similar manner (with less time spent cutting and skewering the fish). SERVES 4

1½ to 2 pounds skinless salmon fillet, preferably wild
½ teaspoon saffron threads (see Note)
1 cup mayonnaise, preferably Hellmann's
½ teaspoon finely grated lemon zest
1 tablespoon fresh lemon juice
1 clove garlic, minced
1 tablespoon minced fresh flat-leaf parsley
Coarse salt (kosher or sea) and freshly ground black pepper
2 tablespoons vegetable oil, for brushing the salmon
2 to 4 tablespoons pomegranate molasses, for serving

YOU'LL ALSO NEED
Flat metal or bamboo skewers

ADVANCE PREPARATION
30 minutes to 1 hour for marinating the fish

1 Run your fingers over the salmon fillet, feeling for bones. Remove any you find with needle-nose pliers or tweezers. Cut the salmon fillet into roughly 1½-inch cubes. Skewer the pieces of salmon by inserting the skewers through the thin side of each piece so the fillet can be arranged flat on the grill. Arrange the salmon kebabs in a nonreactive baking dish just large enough to hold them in a single layer.

2 Place the saffron and 1 teaspoon of water in a small bowl and stir to mix. Let soak for 3 minutes. Place the mayonnaise, lemon zest, lemon juice, garlic, and parsley in a nonreactive mixing bowl and whisk to mix. Whisk in the saffron mixture and season with salt and pepper to taste; the marinade should be highly seasoned. Pour the marinade over the salmon, turning the kebabs to coat both sides. Let the salmon marinate in the refrigerator,

THE SCOOP

WHERE: Moscow, Russia

WHAT: Salmon kebabs glazed with garlic, saffron, and mayonnaise

HOW: Direct grilling, ideally on a grateless grill

JUST THE FACTS: This recipe uses an ingredient common throughout the former Soviet eastern republics (not to mention throughout the Middle and Near East): *narsharab*—pomegranate molasses. It's made by boiling down pomegranate juice and sugar. This thick, crimson, sweet-sour condiment is drizzled over Russian, Caucasus, and Central Asian barbecue, although with a lighter touch than a sweet, smoky, tomato-based sauce would be applied to barbecued chicken or ribs in North America. Look for pomegranate molasses in Russian, Middle Eastern, or Iranian grocery stores.

covered, for 30 minutes to 1 hour, turning the kebabs once or twice.

3 Set up the grill for direct grilling and preheat it to high. Ideally, you'll set up the grill for grateless grilling so the fish doesn't touch the grill grate (see the instructions on page 599). If you are grilling in the conventional manner, be sure to brush and oil the grill grate very well.

4 Brush one side of each salmon kebab with a little vegetable oil and arrange it oiled side down on the hot grate. Grill the kebabs until the bottoms are nicely browned and the sides turn opaque, 2 to 4 minutes. Brush the tops of the kebabs with oil. If you are grilling the fish on the grate, use a metal spatula to loosen the fish. Turn the kebabs and grill until cooked through, 2 to 4 minutes longer, 4 to 8 minutes in all. When done, the salmon will break into firm flakes when pressed with a finger.

5 Transfer the salmon kebabs to a platter or plates. Drizzle a little pomegranate molasses over each kebab and serve at once.

NOTE: Saffron threads are better than saffron powder, but ½ teaspoon of the powder can be used in a pinch. For that matter, if you don't have saffron, you can make a highly credible version of these kebabs with ½ teaspoon of ground turmeric or paprika instead.

Tandoori Grilled Kingfish

Do not try this at home: Mr. Hari Chand Gangwani owns the popular Ganesh restaurant in the Karol Bagh district of New Delhi. His claim to fame (or at least notoriety) is his ability to pluck fried fish out of a pan of boiling oil with his bare hands. What he's retrieving is one of the house specialties—kingfish marinated in yogurt, chickpea flour, and Indian spices. But the *real* don't-miss dish here is the same fish with the same seasonings seared in India's upright barbecue pit, the tandoor. Think of this as Indian fish and chips on the grill. Kingfish is a dark-fleshed, rather full-flavored fish, and Mr. Gangwani uses a singular technique to remove any fishy flavor: He premarinates it in garlic water. You could certainly substitute another dark-fleshed fish, like mackerel, bluefish, or salmon (salmon is spectacular), or even a milder fish, like halibut. **SERVES 4**

Kingfish grills in a burst of flame at Ganesh restaurant in New Delhi.

1½ to 2 pounds kingfish or other dark-fleshed
   fish steaks or fillets
8 cloves garlic, coarsely chopped
2 pieces (2 inches) fresh ginger, peeled and
   coarsely chopped
1 small onion, coarsely chopped
1½ teaspoons coarse salt (kosher or sea)
1½ teaspoons freshly ground black pepper
1½ teaspoons ground turmeric
1½ teaspoons ground cumin
1 teaspoon ajwain (carom seeds) or
   caraway seeds
1 or 2 cups Greek-style plain yogurt
   (see Step 3)
1 egg (optional), lightly beaten with a fork
1 cup chickpea flour (optional)
3 tablespoons unsalted butter, melted, or
   vegetable oil, for basting
Green Herb Chutney (page 398), for
   serving
Indian bread (optional, pages 98 and 100),
   for serving

YOU'LL ALSO NEED
Bamboo or metal skewers

ADVANCE PREPARATION
3 to 4 hours for marinating the fish

1 Cut the fish fillets into 2-inch pieces. Place the fish in a large nonreactive bowl.

2 Place half of the garlic, half of the ginger, and 2 cups of water in a blender and blend just to mix. Strain the garlic water over the fish. Let the fish marinate in the refrigerator, covered, for 15 minutes. Drain the fish well, discarding the garlic water.

3 Place the remaining garlic and ginger, and the onion, salt, pepper, turmeric, cumin, and *ajwain* or caraway seeds in a food processor and puree to a smooth paste. Add 1 cup of yogurt and the egg and chickpea flour, if using, and puree to a smooth paste, running the machine in short bursts. If you are not using the egg and chickpea flour, add an additional 1 cup of yogurt and run the processor just to mix. The marinade should be thick but pourable; you may need to add a couple of tablespoons of water. Pour the marinade over the fish and stir to mix. Let the fish marinate in the refrigerator, covered, for 3 to 4 hours.

4 Drain the fish, discarding the marinade. Skewer the pieces of fish by inserting the skewers through the thin side of each piece onto skewers so that they can be arranged flat on the grill.

5 Set up the grill for direct grilling and preheat it to high. Ideally, you'll set up the grill for grateless grilling so the fish doesn't touch the grill grate (see the instructions on page 599). If you are grilling in the conventional manner, be sure to brush and oil the grill grate very well.

6 Arrange the fish kebabs on the hot grill and grill them until golden brown on both sides and cooked through, 3 to 5 minutes per side. When done, the fish will break into firm flakes when pressed with a finger. During the last 2 minutes, baste the kebabs with melted butter or oil.

7 Serve the grilled kingfish with the Green Herb Chutney and, if desired, one of the Indian breads.

Tuna Steaks alla Fiorentina

THE SCOOP

WHERE: Tuscany, Italy

WHAT: Bible-thick tuna steaks charred black on the outside, sushi-rare inside, doused with extra-virgin olive oil, and sprinkled with cracked pepper

HOW: Direct grilling

JUST THE FACTS: Use sushi-grade tuna—fish fresh enough to eat raw—and the best olive oil money can buy. You are more likely to find tuna that fresh at a fishmonger than at a supermarket. For the olive oil, I refer you to the Fresh-Pressed Olive Oil Club (www.theoliveoilsecret .com). It has spoiled me for supermarket oils, which can languish on store shelves for months (if not longer). Unlike wine, olive oil does *not* improve with age.
    For the richest, most authentic flavor, grill the fish over wood, preferably olive or oak.

Virtually all of the recipes in this book come from grill masters or grill cultures—part of a cannon, as it were, that includes the greatest grilled dishes in the world. So indulge me if I give you one dish that exists more in my imagination than in the real world of barbecue, but that captures the spirit of Italy's great grilling region, Tuscany. Think of it as a seafood riff on classic *bistecca alla fiorentina* (see page 145 for a recipe). While I've never seen this dish on a menu in Tuscany, theoretically, you could find it in the great Tuscan sea and fishing port Livorno. (The same Livorno where pan-fried fish comes dressed up with capers and olives; I've given you this sauce as a serving option here.) Grill the tuna hot. Eat it rare. And get ready for a fish steak that can give a beef T-bone a run for its money. **SERVES 4**

4 superfresh thick tuna steaks (each about
    1½ inches thick and 6 to 8 ounces)
1 tablespoon best-quality extra-virgin olive oil,
    plus ½ cup oil (optional), for serving
Coarse sea salt and cracked black peppercorns
Livornese Sauce (optional, recipe follows)
Arugula, Endive, and Shaved Parmesan Salad
    (optional, recipe follows)

YOU'LL ALSO NEED
Oak or olive wood for building a fire, or about
    2 cups unsoaked oak or olive wood chips or
    chunks (optional)

ADVANCE PREPARATION
None

1 Set up the grill for direct grilling and preheat it to high. Ideally, you'll grill over wood embers (see page 603 for instructions on grilling over a wood fire).

2 When ready to cook, if you are using a charcoal grill, toss the wood chips or chunks on the coals. If you are using a gas grill, add the wood chips or chunks to the smoker box or place them in a smoker pouch under the grate (see page 603). Brush and oil the grill grate. Lightly brush the tuna steaks on both sides with the 1 tablespoon of olive oil. (Lightly is the operative word here; too much oil and the fish will taste sooty.) Crust the fish with salt and cracked peppercorns, pressing them onto the fish.

3 Arrange the fish steaks on the hot grate and grill them until darkly browned on the outside but still very rare inside, 2 to 3 minutes per side. When done, the tuna should feel quite soft when poked. If desired, give each steak a quarter turn on each side after 1½ minutes to create a handsome crosshatch of grill marks.

TUNA STEAKS ALLA FIORENTINA

4 Transfer the grilled fish steaks to a deep, attractive serving dish. If you are not using the Livornese Sauce, slowly pour the ½ cup of olive oil over them. Cut the tuna steaks crosswise into ¼-inch slices. Spoon all of the liquid that accumulates in the bottom of the dish over the sliced fish several times. Otherwise top it with the Livornese Sauce, if using. Serve the tuna at once, with the arugula salad on the side, if desired.

Livornese Sauce

Livornese (in the style of Livorno) refers to a style of cooking pan-fried fish with sautéed capers, olives, and onions. Pan-fried? Blasphemy. How about some real fire and brimstone—a Livorno sauce for grilled tuna? **MAKES ABOUT 1¼ CUPS**

⅓ cup best-quality extra-virgin olive oil
¼ cup drained capers
¼ cup pitted kalamata olives
¼ cup coarsely chopped fresh flat-leaf parsley
2 cloves garlic, thinly sliced
1 large or 2 medium-size luscious, ripe red tomatoes, peeled, seeded, and cut into ¼-inch dice
A few drops of fresh lemon juice (optional)

Heat the olive oil in a skillet over high heat (the side burner of your grill is a good place to do this). Add the capers, olives, parsley, and garlic to the skillet and cook until the capers are crisp and the garlic is just beginning to brown, about 3 minutes. Add the tomato and lemon juice, if using, and let boil until richly flavored, about 1 minute. Serve the sauce at once.

Selecting the Parmigiano-Reggiano for an Arugula, Endive, and Shaved Parmesan Salad to go with grilled fish or beef.

Arugula, Endive, and Shaved Parmesan Salad

Here's a simple salad you can serve before or alongside the tuna. For the full effect, you must use a genuine imported Parmigiano-Reggiano cheese. Look for these words stamped into the rind to know you've got the real McCoy. **SERVES 4**

1 bunch baby arugula, rinsed, dried, and stemmed
2 Belgian endive, cut crosswise into ¼-inch slices
2 tablespoons extra-virgin olive oil
2 tablespoons fresh lemon juice, or more to taste
Coarse salt (kosher or sea) and freshly ground black pepper
1 chunk (3 ounces) Parmigiano-Reggiano cheese

Place the arugula, endive, olive oil, and lemon juice in a nonreactive bowl but do not toss them until just before serving. Taste for seasoning, adding salt and pepper to taste and more lemon juice as necessary. Using a vegetable peeler, shave the Parmigiano-Reggiano in broad thin strips over the salad and serve at once.

The sun sets over the Arno River in Florence. The covered bridge in the foreground is the historic Ponte Vecchio, built in 1345.

Guam "Volcano" Tuna
{ PEPPER-CRUSTED TUNA WITH GINGER-WASABI DIPPING SAUCE }

Guam has a hyperactive barbecue scene, with an annual festival that gives away tens of thousands of dollars in prize money. No family or social event is complete without the firing up of a grill (often half of a 55-gallon drum). Given Guam's proximity to the Philippines and Japan, it comes as no surprise that soy sauce, ginger, and wasabi should figure prominently in the local grilling. Here's the Pacific Island version of a grilled blackened tuna from my Guamanian barbecue buddy, Steven Cruz. The tuna is crusted with Old Bay seasoning. (OK, it's a long way from Baltimore to Guam, but apparently this Maryland seafood seasoning enjoys great popularity on the island.) Ginger, wasabi, and chiles give the dipping sauce a triple blast of heat. **SERVES 4**

FOR THE DIPPING SAUCE

1 tablespoon wasabi powder, or
    1 tablespoon wasabi paste
1 piece (2 inches) fresh ginger, peeled
    (for 1 tablespoon grated)
1 lemon
¾ cup soy sauce
1 scallion, both white and green parts,
    trimmed and sliced crosswise
    paper-thin
1 hot chile, thinly sliced crosswise
    (see Note)

FOR THE TUNA

4 tuna steaks (each about 1½ inches thick and
    6 to 8 ounces)
6 to 8 tablespoons cracked black
    peppercorns
2 tablespoons Old Bay seasoning
Coarse salt (kosher or sea)
½ cup extra-virgin olive oil
Lemon or lime wedges, for serving

ADVANCE PREPARATION

None; the beauty of this dish is its spontaneity. However, the dipping sauce can be prepared 1 hour ahead.

1 Prepare the dipping sauce: If you are using powdered wasabi, place it in a mixing bowl and add 1 tablespoon of warm water. Stir to form a paste and let stand for about 5 minutes. If you are using wasabi paste, place it in a mixing bowl. Grate the ginger on a fine grater into the bowl; you should have about 1 tablespoon. Cut the lemon in half and cut a thin slice off one half. Cut the slice in quarters, remove any seeds, and set the lemon quarters aside for garnishing the sauce. Squeeze the juice from the remaining lemon into the bowl, squeezing it through your fingers to catch any seeds. Add the soy sauce, scallion, and chile and stir to mix well. Divide the sauce among 4 small bowls. Float a quarter lemon slice in each bowl. The dipping sauce can be prepared up to 1 hour ahead.

2 Prepare the tuna: Place the tuna steaks on a large plate and thickly crust them with cracked peppercorns, pressing the pepper onto the fish on both sides and the edges. Generously season the tuna with Old Bay seasoning and salt. Place the olive oil in a shallow bowl.

Party time in Guam, where grilling is a daily pastime.

3 Set up the grill for direct grilling and preheat it to high.

4 When ready to cook, brush and oil the grill grate. Dip each piece of tuna in the olive oil on both sides, then arrange it on the hot grate. The dripping oil may and should cause flare-ups—it's supposed to. The flames will help sear the crust. Grill the tuna until it is dark and crusty on the outside but still very rare inside, 2 to 3 minutes per side, turning with tongs. When done the tuna should feel quite soft when poked.

5 Transfer the grilled tuna steaks to a cutting board and cut them into ¼-inch slices. Cut down through the steaks, holding the blade perpendicular to the cutting board. Each slice will have a dark crusty exterior and a blood-rare center. Fan out the slices on a platter or plates. Garnish the tuna with lemon or lime wedges and serve the bowls of dipping sauce alongside.

NOTE: Guamanians would use a slender red chile called *donne*. A Thai chile or serrano pepper would work well.

Grilled Swordfish with Garlic Caper Butter

THE SCOOP

WHERE: Martha's Vineyard, Massachusetts, U.S.A.

WHAT: Simply the best way I know to cook swordfish—grilled over wood and topped with butter-fried garlic and capers

Here's a dish close to home and near to my heart, for during swordfish season, Barbara and I make it as often as possible. And whenever I'm traveling Planet Barbecue, the mere thought of it makes me homesick. We're talking quick—thirty minutes max from start to finish—but the flame-charred fish and tart, salty fried caper sauce explode right off the plate. Use the freshest swordfish you can find, and I'd rather see you substitute another, fresher fish than using swordfish that looks tired or old (prepared this way, tuna or salmon steaks would be great). **SERVES 4**

FOR THE FISH

4 swordfish steaks (each at least 1 inch
thick and 6 to 8 ounces)

Coarse salt (kosher or sea) and freshly
ground or cracked black peppercorns

2 tablespoons extra-virgin olive oil

2 lemons, 1 cut in wedges, for serving

FOR THE SAUCE

4 tablespoons (½ stick) unsalted butter

3 cloves garlic, thinly sliced

3 tablespoons drained capers

YOU'LL ALSO NEED

Unsoaked oak or other hardwood logs, or
chips, or chunks

ADVANCE PREPARATION

None

1 Prepare the fish: Rinse the swordfish steaks and blot them dry with paper towels. Place the swordfish in a nonreactive baking dish and very generously season it on both sides with salt and pepper. Drizzle the olive oil over both sides of the fish, rubbing it and the salt and pepper onto the fish with your fingertips. Cut the whole lemon in half and squeeze the juice over the fish, turning to coat both sides. Let the fish marinate in the refrigerator, covered, for 15 minutes.

2 Set up the grill for direct grilling and preheat it to high.

3 When ready to cook, brush and oil the grill grate. Drain the swordfish. Ideally, you'll grill over a wood fire (see page 603 for instructions). Alternatively, you can use wood chips or chunks to add a smoke flavor. If you are using a charcoal grill, toss the wood chips or chunks on the coals. If you are using a gas grill, add the wood chips or chunks, if desired, to the smoker box or place them in a smoker pouch under the grate (see page 603). (You want a light wood flavor—that's why you don't soak the wood.) Arrange the swordfish on the hot grate at a diagonal to the bars. Grill the fish until cooked through, 3 to 4 minutes per side. When done, the swordfish will break into firm flakes when pressed with a finger. If desired, give each swordfish steak a quarter turn after 1½ minutes to create a handsome crosshatch of grill marks. Transfer the steaks to a platter and cover them loosely with aluminum foil to keep warm.

4 Make the sauce (you can start it while the fish is on the grill): Melt the butter in a saucepan. Add the garlic and capers and cook over high heat until the garlic begins to brown and the capers are crisp, about 2 minutes. Immediately pour the sauce over the swordfish steaks and serve at once, with the lemon wedges.

THE SCOOP

HOW: Direct grilling

JUST THE FACTS: For two months a year, we're lucky enough to get harpooned swordfish at our local fish market, Edgartown Seafood Market. So what's the big deal about that? Harpooned fish is landed the same day it's caught, unlike long-line swordfish, which languish in the water or on the hold of the fishing boat for up to a week. It's unbelievably fresh and unbelievably good.

Grilled Turbot with "Holy Water"
{ RODABALLO A LA PARRILLA }

WHERE: The Basque region in northeast Spain

WHAT: A whole grilled baby turbot glazed with sherry vinaigrette

HOW: Direct grilling over charcoal

JUST THE FACTS: Turbot is a delicate white fish in the sole family. It's widely available in Europe but somewhat less so in North America. Part of the pleasure of this dish comes from eating the flame-charred fish skin. Taste and texture wise, halibut comes close to turbot and is easy to find in North America. If you don't like grilling or eating whole fish, you could prepare halibut fillets the same way.

First of all, forget about getting the original recipe for "holy water," the sherry glaze that goes on Elkano's renowned grilled turbot. "Only three people know how to make it," says Luis Mari Manterola, the restaurant's grill master for more than three decades. "We prepare it at night when the restaurant is closed." Elkano is the granddaddy of grilled seafood restaurants in the Basque fishing town of Getaria outside of San Sebastián. Turbot is the house specialty, grilled as simply as possible (with the head and skin intact) in a fish basket over charcoal and glazed with that secret sherry vinaigrette. What results is fish that's white as milk and almost as sweet, with flesh so flaky and moist you'll dream about it long after you've tasted it. Sure, I can tell you the ideal weight for a turbot, and the exact cooking time. But as for that sherry glaze, what follows is my best guess, based on versions prepared around Getaria and along the Basque coast. **SERVES 4 TO 6**

1 shallot, coarsely chopped

1 clove garlic, coarsely chopped

3 tablespoons sherry vinegar (see Notes)

3 tablespoons fresh grapefruit juice plus ½ teaspoon grapefruit zest

3 tablespoons extra-virgin olive oil, preferably Spanish

3 tablespoons vegetable oil

1 tablespoon fresh lemon juice, or to taste

½ teaspoon honey

Coarse salt (kosher or sea)

½ teaspoon freshly ground white pepper

½ cup txakoli wine (see Notes)

1 small whole turbot (about 3 pounds), cleaned, scaled, and fins removed, with head and tail intact or 4 halibut fillets (each 6 to 8 ounces)

Freshly ground black pepper

YOU'LL ALSO NEED

A squirt bottle for the "holy water"; a spray bottle for the wine; a large fish basket (optional)

ADVANCE PREPARATION
None

1 To make the "holy water," place the shallot, garlic, sherry vinegar, grapefruit juice and zest, olive oil, vegetable oil, lemon juice, honey, 1 teaspoon of salt, the white pepper, and ⅓ cup of water in a blender and blend until emulsified. Taste for seasoning, adding lemon juice or salt, if needed. Place the mixture in a squirt bottle. This makes a little more "holy water" than you need. The excess will keep for several days in the refrigerator and goes great with almost any sort of grilled seafood. Shake well before using.

2 Place the wine in a spray bottle and set it aside.

3 Set up the grill for direct grilling and preheat it to medium.

4 When ready to cook, season the turbot generously with salt and black pepper on both sides. Brush and oil the fish basket, if using, or brush and oil the grill grate. Place the fish in the fish basket, if using. Place the basketed or unbasketed fish on the hot grate dark side down if grilling a whole turbot. Grill the turbot until it is crisp and golden brown on both sides (this is easier to tell on the white side) and cooked through, about 10 minutes per side. To check for doneness, make a small cut with the tip of a paring knife in the deepest part of the flesh above the backbone. The flesh will come away cleanly from the bone. Grill halibut fillets over high heat until cooked through, 3 to 4 minutes per side. When done, the fillets will break into firm flakes when pressed with a finger.

5 After the fish has grilled for 2 minutes, spray it with the wine and continue spraying both sides every 2 minutes.

6 Transfer the grilled turbot to a platter. Shake the "holy water" and squirt some over the fish. Bone the fish, if necessary, and serve it squirting more "holy water" on each portion.

NOTES: As the name suggests, sherry vinegar is made from sherry wine. Look for it at specialty food shops and natural food stores. Or you can substitute 2 tablespoons of rice vinegar or distilled white vinegar and 1 tablespoon of dry sherry.

Txakoli is a crisp, tart Basque wine; if it's unavailable, spray the fish with any dry white wine of your choosing.

Grilled Hake with Fried Garlic

Basque chefs like Juan Mari Arzak and Martín Berasategui grab the headlines for their culinary pyrotechnics (think of their food as the culinary equivalent of the Gehry-designed Guggenheim Museum Bilbao). What you may not realize is that the Basque country is also a hotbed of grilling, done for the most part with a simplicity that stands in striking contrast to the foams, jellies, and deconstructions of Spain's culinary avant-garde. A sprinkle of sea salt, a splash of vinegar or olive oil—these are the seasonings favored by the majority of Basque grill masters. This simple grilled hake, topped with olive oil and fried garlic and spiced with a guindilla chile is inspired by Beti Jai ("Always a Holiday"), a popular restaurant tucked away in the warren of narrow streets in the old quarter of San Sebastián. **SERVES 4**

THE SCOOP

WHERE: The Basque Country in northeast Spain

WHAT: Grilled hake fillets topped with sizzling fried garlic and guindilla chiles

HOW: Direct grilling

JUST THE FACTS:
Hake is a white-fleshed, Atlantic fish with a mild flavor and gelatinous texture. Cod, haddock, or halibut would make reasonable substitutes. Guindilla chiles are small, elongated, medium-hot Spanish chiles usually sold dried. Hot red pepper flakes make a reasonable substitute.

4 hake fillets (each about 1 inch thick and 6 to 8 ounces)

Sea salt and freshly ground black pepper

5 tablespoons extra-virgin olive oil

4 cloves garlic, thinly sliced crosswise

1 dried guindilla chile, thinly sliced crosswise, or ½ teaspoon hot red pepper flakes

2 tablespoons chopped fresh flat-leaf parsley

YOU'LL ALSO NEED

A fish basket (optional)

ADVANCE PREPARATION

None

1 Set up the grill for direct grilling and preheat it to high.

2 When ready to cook, generously oil the fish basket, if using, or brush and generously oil the grill grate. Season the hake fillets on both sides with salt and black pepper. Place the fish in the fish basket, if using. Place the basketed or unbasketed fish on the hot grate. Grill the hake until browned on both sides and cooked through, 3 to 4 minutes per side. When done, the hake will break into firm flakes when pressed with a finger. Transfer the grilled fish to a warm heatproof platter or plates and keep warm.

3 Heat the olive oil in a small skillet over high heat (if your grill has a side burner, this is a good occasion to use it). Add the garlic and cook until fragrant and golden brown, 1 to 2 minutes. Add the guindilla chile or hot pepper flakes and cook until aromatic and just beginning to brown, about 10 seconds. Immediately pour the garlic and oil over the hake, sprinkle the parsley on top, and serve at once.

HOW TO GRILL HAKE

1. *Place the hake fillets in an oiled grill basket.*

2. *Grill the hake until browned on both sides. The beauty of the grill basket is that you turn it, not the fragile fish fillets.*

3. *Fry the garlic and guindilla peppers in olive oil in a pan over the coals or on your grill's side burner.*

Once the fish has finished grilling and is out of the basket, top it with a few spicy spoonfuls of fried garlic.

FIRE STARTERS
The Grilled Fish Master General

Simplicity has been **PEDRO ARREGUI'S** mantra ever since he opened Elkano restaurant in 1964.

GETARIA, SPAIN

"When I started the restaurant, no one in Getaria grilled seafood," recalls Pedro Arregui, founder of Elkano. The site was a grocery store run by Arregui's mother in a fishing village near San Sebastián on the Spanish Basque seacoast. Then, as now, Arregui made a virtue of simplicity, grilling whole turbot, skin and all, in a grill basket that looks a bit like a medieval torture device. The public tasted; the public liked; and today, thanks to Arregui, Getaria has become Spain's seafood barbecue central, with one grilled fish restaurant after another lining the port.

Elkano takes its name from a local hero, Juan Sebastián Elkano, the Spanish navigator who completed Ferdinand Magellan's around-the-world journey after Magellan was killed in the Philippines in 1521. Arregui decorated his dining room in the style of a wooden sailing ship, complete with plank walls and brass-rimmed portholes. The seafood comes off the fishing boats daily and is kept alive in vivariums in the basement. The grill, a sort of raised outdoor hearth in front of the restaurant, burns natural lump charcoal as it has from day one.

Today, Elkano is run by Arregui's children. Your meal might start with *nekora*, smokily grilled crab, followed by *kokotxas*, grilled hake throats (tastes like fish, slithers down your throat like oysters).

Next comes a basket of grilled clams served with nothing—not even melted butter—or perhaps a grilled spiny lobster sauced with shallot vinaigrette. All this is a prelude to the house specialty: whole grilled turbot (see page 440).

If you've never eaten turbot before, one of the Arreguis will make sure you appreciate the difference between the meat on the white side (the top) of the fish ("a little drier and meatier" they'll explain), and the meat on the dark side (the bottom, "a little wetter and more gelatinous"). "You know us Basques," they'll say, "We love our fish to have a gelatinous texture." The family obsession with freshness attracts an international clientele. The day my wife, Barbara, and I lunched at Elkano, we heard German, Danish, French, Dutch, and English being spoken. The satisfaction was universal.

Aitor Arregui, son of Pedro Arregui, founder of Elkano restaurant in Getaria in the Basque Country—keeping the fires burning.

NAME: Pedro Arregui

TERRITORY: Basque Country, Spain

CLAIM TO FAME: Introducing grilled fish to Getaria, Spain

SPECIALTIES: Seafood, especially grilled turbot

ARREGUI SAYS:

▶ There's only one way to keep fish from sticking to a grill basket: Use it every day.

▶ Use the freshest possible fish. Grill it as simply as possible. And keep the condiments simple.

Halibut Grilled in Banana Leaves with Lemongrass and Thai Basil

WHERE: Thailand

WHAT: Halibut fillets blasted with lemongrass, basil, and other Thai herbs and wrapped and grilled in banana leaves

HOW: Direct grilling

JUST THE FACTS: Two somewhat uncommon ingredients used in this recipe are coriander root and Thai basil. The coriander roots have a sweeter, earthier flavor than the coriander leaves (usually called cilantro), but you could certainly substitute the leaves. Thai basil has smaller leaves and a more pungent licorice flavor than Italian basil, but again, you could substitute the latter. Both ingredients are available at Asian and Indian markets. Halibut is a delicate white fish found on both coasts of the United States and Canada. Any white fish or mahimahi or bluefish would work well instead.

I t's a problem that bedevils grillers all over Planet Barbecue: How *do* you keep delicate fish fillets from sticking to the grate? Thai grill masters use a technique that has the added advantage of sealing in such vibrant Asian flavors as lemongrass and Thai basil. And the result looks cool as all get-out. (Never underestimate the power of looking cool as all get-out.) The banana leaf wrapping technique turns up throughout Asia (see the *otak-otak* on page 448, for example, or the Singaporean skate wings on page 450), not to mention in Latin America and the Caribbean. The charred banana leaf imparts an herbaceous smoke flavor, but if it's unavailable, you can grill the fish in grape leaves or aluminum foil and still get convincing results. **SERVES 4**

FOR THE HERB PASTE

2 stalks lemongrass, trimmed and cut crosswise into ¼-inch slices

¼ cup lightly packed Thai basil leaves or regular basil leaves

2 cloves garlic, peeled, each clove cut in half

1 tablespoon rinsed, chopped fresh cilantro (coriander) roots, or 2 tablespoons coarsely chopped fresh cilantro leaves

1 to 2 Thai chiles or serrano peppers, seeded (for hotter fish, leave in the seeds)

1 teaspoon coarse salt (kosher or sea)

2 tablespoons Asian (dark) sesame oil or vegetable oil

4 banana leaf squares (each 8 x 8-inches, see Note)

4 halibut fillets (each about ¾ inch thick and 6 to 8 ounces)

Honey Lime Dipping Sauce (recipe follows)

YOU'LL ALSO NEED

Wooden toothpicks or butcher's string

ADVANCE PREPARATION

30 minutes to 2 hours for marinating the fish, and the herb paste can be prepared up to 12 hours ahead.

1 Make the herb paste: Place the lemongrass, basil, garlic, cilantro, chile(s), and salt in a heavy mortar and pound to a paste with a pestle, then work in the sesame oil. If you don't have a mortar and pestle, finely chop the lemongrass, basil, garlic, cilantro, and chile(s) in a food processor, then add the salt and work in the sesame oil. You should wind up with a thick, fragrant flavorful paste. The herb paste can be prepared up to 12 hours ahead.

2 Place a banana leaf square on a work surface, dark side down. Place a spoonful of herb paste in the center and spread it into a rectangle the size of one piece of fish. Arrange a piece of fish on top and top it with another spoonful of herb paste, spreading it over the fish with the back of a spoon. Fold the ends, then the sides of the banana leaf over the fish the way you'd fold up a burrito, blintz, or egg roll. Secure the banana leaf with toothpicks or tie it in place with butcher's string. Repeat with the remaining banana leaf squares, herb paste, and fish. Let the fish marinate in the refrigerator for at least 30 minutes or as long as 2 hours.

3 Set up the grill for direct grilling and preheat it to high.

4 When ready to cook, brush and oil the grill grate. Arrange the fish packets, seam side down to start, on the hot grate and grill until the banana leaf is nicely browned and the fish is cooked through, 3 to 5 minutes per side. To test for doneness,, insert a slender metal skewer through the side of one packet for 15 seconds; when the fish is done the skewer will feel very hot to the touch when removed.

5 Serve the fish in the banana leaf packets at once with the dipping sauce, instructing everyone to pull out the toothpicks or cut any butcher's string to open the packets. (Part of the pleasure of this dish is the blast of herb fragrance you get when you open the banana leaf.)

NOTE: Banana leaves are sold both fresh and frozen at Asian, Indian, and Hispanic markets. If you use a fresh, rather than a thawed frozen banana leaf, be sure it comes from a tree that has not been treated with pesticides. To make a fresh banana leaf pliable, you'll need to soften it by grilling it or heating it over the burner of a stove for 15 to 30 seconds per side. If banana leaves are not available, you can use bottled grape leaves; soak them well in cold water to remove the salt. Or, wrap the halibut, or any fish you may be cooking, in heavy-duty aluminum foil.

Honey Lime Dipping Sauce

Sweet-sour sauces turn up throughout Southeast Asia, where they're used as dips for grilled meats. When you stop to think about it, the flavor profile—sweet-tart-salty—resembles that of many North American barbecue sauces, although the thin, clear, watery texture is similar only to a North Carolina vinegar sauce. Warm the honey in a shallow pan of simmering water to make it easier to pour and measure. **MAKES ABOUT 1 CUP**

¼ cup honey
¼ cup fresh lime juice
¼ cup Thai or Vietnamese fish sauce or soy sauce
¼ teaspoon minced garlic
1 Thai or other hot chile, thinly sliced crosswise

Place the honey, lime juice, fish sauce, garlic, chile, and ¼ cup of water in a nonreactive mixing bowl and whisk until well combined. Divide the sauce among 4 small serving bowls and serve alongside the fish.

Lotus flowers at the Jim Thompson House, a popular museum in Bangkok known for its collections of traditional Thai art and architecture.

PLANET BARBECUE

Malaysia: Home to Multicultural Grilling

If you want to dispel a lot of stereotypes about barbecue, just visit Malaysia. *Grilling is a guy thing, right?* Not at Hotel Equatorial Melaka, where a female chef named Bong Geok Choo makes some of the best *otak-otak* (grilled fish mousse) in Asia. *It's just not barbecue without meat.* Not for Azlinah Kudari (another grill mistress), who's known up and down the Strait of Malacca for her Portuguese grilled fish, turmeric grilled prawns, and cockles roasted over charcoal. *A vegetarian at a barbecue goes hungry.* Not at Tomyam Klasik, for although the meat offerings span several menu pages, this sprawling restaurant in Kuala Lumpur earns wide acclaim for its *tauhu bakar,* grilled tofu served with a spicy sweet-sour fruit sauce called *rojak.*

Malaysia is a land of paradoxes, not the least of which is whether there really is such a thing as Malaysian grilling at all. After all, this long slender nation on Southeast Asia's west coast is comprised of Malays, Indians, Chinese,

Chef Bong Geok Choo about to prepare her legendary otak-otak (grilled fish mousse).

and a dozen other nationalities. Each has its own distinct style of grilling, which is often served side by side at crowded markets and outdoor food courts by grill masters who speak different languages and worship different deities but show a surprising tolerance for the ways of their brothers and sisters in fire.

Indian *kebabi wallahs* dish up tandoori chicken and *roti* and naan that would easily pass muster in New Delhi. Chinese grill masters sizzle *bak kua* (chopped pork jerky) and sweet soy-glazed chicken wings over coconut shell charcoal. Malaysia's Muslims eschew the popular *char siu* (barbecued pork) of their Chinese neighbors, grilling instead lamb, goat, mutton, and an incredible variety of seafood. The one grilled dish you could consider pan-Malaysian—saté (tiny

Grilling at Asia's Crossroads

With Thailand, Cambodia, and Vietnam to the north and Singapore and Indonesia to the south, Malaysia offers some of the world's most vibrant flavors and grilling techniques.

Freshly grilled fish on the 24-Hour Food Street in Kuala Lumpur.

Fiery chiles fuel Malaysian barbecue.

kebabs)—actually comes from Indonesia.

This diversity may pose a challenge for civic governance, but it makes for fantastic eating. Visit one of Malaysia's teeming hawker centers or food streets and you can eat your way around Planet Barbecue-Asia without walking more than a couple of blocks.

Chiles, limes, galangal—some of the seasonings used by Malaysia's flavor-obsessed grillers.

THE GRILL: Depending on their ethnic background, Malaysians grill on a long slender saté grill, a larger charcoal-burning fish grill, in a tandoor, or on a charcoal-fired rotisserie.

Chicken saté served by the bunch at Saté Kajang in Kajang, Malaysia.

THE FUEL: Coconut shell charcoal, and to control the heat, the coals are fanned with a straw fan (the traditional method) or the now more prevalent electric fan.

THE FLAVORINGS: Malaysians season with a bold hand, using big-flavored spice pastes *(rempah)* of garlic, shallot, ginger, galangal, turmeric, lemongrass, pandanus leaves, *belacan* (shrimp paste), and more. Typically, the pastes are fried prior to being spread on the seafood or meat. Chinese grill masters flavor sweet-salty marinades with sugar, rice wine, oyster sauce, and soy sauce. Malaysia's Indians use the yogurt, ginger, garlic, and spice marinades associated with Indian tandoori.

MUST TRY DISHES

Ayam percik: Spicy grilled chicken from the province of Kelantan (see page 374).

Otak-otak (sometimes written otah-otah): Lemongrass- and chile-scented fish mousse enriched with coconut milk and grilled in banana leaf packets. See page 448 for a recipe.

Portuguese grilled fish: Malaysian grilled fish bears homage to the region's first European settlers, the Portuguese, but there's nothing Iberian about the seasonings, a mixture of fried garlic, ginger, chiles, lemongrass, and coconut milk blended into a fiery paste (you'll find a recipe on page 460).

Saté Kajang: Lemongrass- and turmeric-scented saté in the style of Kajang, a city less than an hour's drive from Kuala Lumpur; see page 17 for a recipe.

Tauhu bakar: Grilled tofu with fruity *rojak* sauce; see page 561 for a recipe.

THE CONDIMENTS:

Sambal: One of a dozen or so chile-based sauces or relishes served with grilled meat, fish, and poultry.

Kejap manis: A thick, sweet soy sauce and, through a convoluted path, the etymological ancestor of ketchup.

Cili: A hot red chile sauce reminiscent of Thailand's Sriracha.

Rojak: A thick, sweet-sour sauce made with tamarind or other fruits.

IF YOU CAN EAT AT ONLY ONE RESTAURANT: For a total immersion in Malaysian street barbecue, head for Jalan Alor (appropriately nicknamed the "24-Hour Food Street") in Kuala Lumpur.

Malaysia's most famous saté comes from Saté Kajang, headquartered in the town of Kajang; the restaurant has branches throughout Malaysia.

Azlinah Kudari grills cockles in Malacca, Malaysia.

THE MOST SINGULAR DISH IN THE MALAYSIAN GRILL REPERTORY: Grilled horseshoe crab—a specialty of Panang—available only during a full moon, when the crabs are at their best for harvesting and eating.

Malaysian Grilled Fish Mousse

{ OTAK-OTAK }

WHERE: Malaysia and Singapore

WHAT: Fish mousse electrified with exotic Asian herbs and spices, made buttery rich with coconut milk, and grilled in banana leaves

HOW: Direct grilling

JUST THE FACTS: There are two ways to approach this recipe. The first is to take one look at the ingredient list and dismiss it as hopelesly esoteric. The second is to use the formula as a broad framework, substituting flavorings readily available for some of the less familiar ingredients used in Malaysia. This approach will reward you with one of the truly great dishes on Planet Barbecue.

I f you happen to visit Melaka, Malaysia, Bong Geok Choo is the sort of chef you want to have prepare your dinner. Meticulous. Deeply rooted in the culinary traditions of her native coastal Malaysia. And, most important, while schooled in the ways of an executive hotel chef, she learned to cook from a food-savvy grandmother. Choo is my guide to one of the most popular grilled dishes in Southeast Asia (and one of the least-known dishes in the West): *otak-otak*. Imagine a fish mousse rich and creamy with coconut milk and fragrant with a veritable spice market of Asian seasonings—ginger, galangal, chiles, lemongrass, fresh turmeric, and Kaffir lime leaves, to name just a few. You wrap the whole shebang in a banana leaf and grill it over charcoal. The leaf chars, imparting an herbal smoke flavor. If grilled fish were a controlled substance, this would be the equivalent of a Southeast Asian spliff. One bite and you'll understand why variations on this grilled fish mousse turn up from Singapore to Cambodia, from Indonesia to Laos. **MAKES 12 PIECES; SERVES 4 AS A LIGHT MAIN COURSE, 6 TO 12 AS AN APPETIZER**

HOW TO MAKE OTAK-OTAK

1. Combine the flavorings and pureed fish with a spoon. Don't overstir—the mixture should remain a little lumpy.

2. Spoon the fish mousse onto a square of banana leaf.

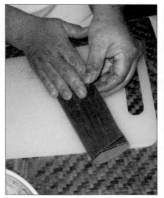

3. Fold in the sides of the banana leaf to enclose the mousse.

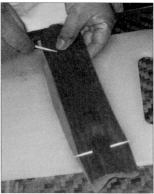

4. Pin the ends of the banana leaf packet shut with toothpicks. The otak-otak is ready for grilling.

4 dried small Asian red chiles, soaked in warm water for
   30 minutes, or 1 teaspoon hot paprika

2 fresh red chiles, such as red jalapeño or red Anaheim
   peppers, seeded and coarsely chopped

2 to 3 shallots, coarsely chopped (½ cup)

3 cloves garlic, coarsely chopped

2 teaspoons turmeric powder, or 1 piece (1 inch)
   fresh turmeric, coarsely chopped

2 stalks lemongrass, trimmed and coarsely chopped

1 piece (1 inch) fresh ginger, peeled and coarsely
   chopped (about 1 tablespoon)

1 piece (1 inch) fresh galangal, peeled and coarsely
   chopped (about 1 tablespoon), or 1 more tablespoon
   coarsely chopped ginger (see Notes)

6 macadamia nuts or candlenuts

½ teaspoon shrimp paste (optional, see below),
   toasted, or 1 teaspoon fish sauce or soy sauce

1½ teaspoons coarse salt (kosher or sea)

¼ cup unsweetened shredded coconut

2 fresh Kaffir lime leaves (see Notes), or ½ teaspoon
   finely grated lime zest (the oil-rich outer rind)

1½ pounds skinless Spanish mackerel fillets, or
   fillets of halibut, bluefish, salmon, or other fish,
   cut into 1-inch pieces

2 tablespoons cornstarch or tapioca powder

1 tablespoon light brown sugar

½ cup unsweetened coconut milk

2 egg whites

12 rectangular pieces of banana leaf, each about
   8 x 12 inches (see Note, page 445)

YOU'LL ALSO NEED
Wooden toothpicks

ADVANCE PREPARATION
The packages of fish mousse can be assembled up to
   4 hours ahead.

1 Tear open the soaked peppers, if using, and discard the seeds. Place the soaked peppers or paprika, fresh chiles, shallots, garlic, turmeric powder, lemongrass, ginger, galangal, if using, macadamia nuts, shrimp paste or fish sauce, and salt in a food processor. Puree to a smooth paste, running the processor in short bursts. Transfer

the spice paste to a large mixing bowl. It's not necessary to wash the processor bowl.

2 Place the coconut in a dry skillet and cook over medium heat, stirring with a wooden spoon, until lightly toasted and just beginning to brown, about 5 minutes. Transfer the coconut to the mixing bowl with the spice paste, discarding any oil from the coconut that's left in the skillet.

3 If you are using Kaffir lime leaves, roll them lengthwise into a tight cylinder and cut them crosswise into hair-thin slivers. Fluff the slices with your fingers and add them to the mixing bowl with the spice paste. If you are using lime zest, add it to the mixing bowl.

4 Puree the fish in the food processor, running the machine in short bursts. Work in the cornstarch and brown sugar. Transfer the pureed fish to the mixing bowl and stir to mix with a wooden spoon.

5 Add the coconut milk to the fish mixture little by little and stir with a wooden spoon to mix. Add the egg whites one by one, stirring just enough

Shrimp Paste

Shrimp paste is one of the secret weapons in the Southeast Asian grill master's arsenal, loaded with meaty, salty, fishy, proteinaceous flavors. The foul-smelling but delectable paste is made from fermented mashed shrimp and salt. In Malaysia it is known as *belacan*. The Indonesian version is called *trasi*. Filipinos have *bagoong*. (You'll find these at Asian markets.)

To bring out the shrimp paste's full complex flavor, you cook it first, either by grilling it on the end of a skewer, roasting it on a piece of aluminum foil in a toaster oven, or panfrying it in oil. Cook the shrimp paste until it is lightly browned and aromatic. The cooking time for about ½ teaspoon will be 2 to 4 minutes. This also helps remove some of the malodorous fermented shellfish smell.

to mix the ingredients. The fish mousse should remain a little lumpy, which is why I have you mix the coconut milk and egg whites in with a wooden spoon, rather than in the food processor (this lumpy consistency is much prized by Malaysians). However, if you're in a hurry, you can do all the mixing in a food processor; run the machine in short bursts.

6 Place a piece of banana leaf on a work surface, dark side down and with a short edge toward you. Spoon about 4 tablespoons of the fish mousse mixture in a free-form oval in the center. Starting with one of the long edges of the leaf, fold it over the mousse, then repeat with the other edge so that the mousse is encased (the process is like folding a business letter). Pin each end about 1 inch in with a toothpick to seal the packet. The packet will be about 12 inches long and 3 inches wide. Repeat with the remaining pieces of banana leaf and fish mousse. The packets of fish mousse can be prepared several hours ahead and refrigerated, covered.

7 Set up the grill for direct grilling and preheat it to high.

8 When ready to cook, brush and oil the grill grate. Arrange the fish mousse packets on the hot grate seam side down and grill the packets until the banana leaf is browned and the fish mousse is cooked through, 3 to 5 minutes per side. To test for doneness, insert a slender metal skewer through the side of one packet for 15 seconds; when the fish mousse is done the skewer will feel very hot to the touch when removed.

9 Serve the *otak-otak* in the banana packets, instructing everyone to pull out the toothpicks to open the packets.

NOTES: Galangal is a rhizome in the ginger family, with ginger's peppery bite, but without its sweetness. Ginger makes a reasonable substitute.

Kaffir lime leaf is a perfumed leaf with a haunting, aromatic lime flavor. There's no equivalent, but finely grated or thinly slivered lime zest is better than nothing.

Singapore-Style Skate Grilled in Banana Leaves

THE SCOOP

WHERE: This particular recipe comes from Singapore, but similar dishes are found in Thailand and Malaysia

Food grilled in banana leaves (and other leaves for that matter) turns up across Planet Barbecue. I've sampled versions in countries as diverse as Mexico, Malaysia (see page 448), and the Philippines. The technique predates the invention of grill grates and even pots and pans—it evolved from a simple desire to keep the ashes off delicate foods roasted directly on or next to the embers. Leaf grilling has several benefits: First, the banana leaf seals in flavor and moisture (the fish steams as well as grills, keeping it from drying out). The leaf itself imparts a smoky herbal flavor as

SINGAPORE-STYLE SKATE GRILLED IN BANANA LEAVES

WHAT: Skate, a fish of growing popularity in North America and wildly popular in Europe and Asia, boldly spiced with fried lemongrass, chiles, and ginger and wrapped and grilled in banana leaves

HOW: Direct grilling

JUST THE FACTS: Skate (aka ray) is a flat, rhomboid-shaped fish whose "wings" possess a bone-white, delicately flavored flesh. You may be able to find it at a good fish market or at an Asian market. Similar in flavor and texture to skate, halibut makes a good substitute, but many fish are suited to this preparation, including striped bass, redfish, catfish, and darker, more robust fish, like kingfish.

To be strictly authentic, you'd need several flavorings that are readily available in Southeast Asia and somewhat esoteric here. If you live in a place with a large Asian community, you should have no trouble finding fresh turmeric and galangal (both are aromatic roots); shrimp paste, a malodorous but tasty condiment made with fermented shellfish; and candlenuts, which look like large macadamia nuts, but taste more aromatic. There are readily available substitutes for each of these, and the recipe tells you how to make this dish with ingredients you can buy on a single trip to a large supermarket.

it chars on the outside (not unlike what Bill Clinton never inhaled). Unwrapping the banana leaf packet is fun (in the way eating anything with your fingers is fun), and in many countries the banana leaf serves as a plate on which to eat your dinner. Here's a Singaporean version, from the Gluttons Bay hawkers center, featuring skate seasoned with an intensely aromatic paste of lemongrass, ginger, and turmeric. You could think of it as turbocharged fish sticks. **SERVES 4**

FOR THE SPICE PASTE

8 macadamia nuts or candlenuts, coarsely chopped

1 piece (5 inches) fresh ginger, peeled and coarsely chopped, or 1 piece (2½ inches) fresh ginger and 1 piece (2½ inches) fresh galangal, each peeled and coarsely chopped

4 shallots, coarsely chopped

4 stalks lemongrass, trimmed and coarsely chopped

4 cloves garlic, coarsely chopped

4 Thai chiles or serrano or jalapeño peppers, seeded and coarsely chopped (for hotter fish, leave the seeds in)

2 teaspoons powdered turmeric, or 1 piece (1 inch) fresh turmeric, peeled and coarsely chopped

Freshly ground black pepper

2 tablespoons Asian fish sauce or soy sauce

5 tablespoons vegetable oil

1 teaspoon shrimp paste (optional)

4 pieces skinless, boneless skate wing or delicate white fish fillets, such as halibut (each 6 to 8 ounces)

Coarse salt (kosher or sea)

4 rectangular pieces of banana leaf, each about 10 x 12 inches (see Note, page 445)

YOU'LL ALSO NEED
Wooden toothpicks

ADVANCE PREPARATION
30 minutes for preparing the spice paste; it can be made several hours ahead.

1 Make the spice paste: Place the macadamia nuts, ginger, galangal, if using, shallots, lemongrass, garlic, chiles, turmeric, and 1 teaspoon of black pepper in a heavy mortar and pound to a paste with a pestle. If you don't have a mortar and pestle, place those ingredients in a food processor and puree to a fine paste, running the machine in short bursts. Work the fish sauce into the spice paste.

2 Heat the oil in a wok over medium-high heat. Add the shrimp paste, if using, and cook until toasted and aromatic, about 1 minute. Increase the heat to high, add the spice paste, and cook it until dark and fragrant, 4 to 6 minutes, stirring with a wooden spoon. Transfer the paste to a plate or bowl and let cool to room temperature. Using a spoon or spatula, thickly spread each piece of fish on both sides with the paste, then lightly season both sides of each piece of fish with salt.

3 Place a piece of banana leaf on a work surface, dark side down and with a short edge toward you. Arrange a piece of fish in the center of the banana leaf. Starting with one of the long edges of the leaf, fold it over the fish, then repeat with the other edge so that the fish is encased (the process is like folding a business letter). Fold over the two ends and pin the banana leaf through the ends with a toothpick to seal the packet. The packet will be about 6 inches by 4 inches. Repeat with the remaining pieces of banana leaf, fish, and spice paste. The fish packets can be prepared several hours ahead and refrigerated.

4 Set up the grill for direct grilling and preheat it to high.

5 When ready to cook, brush and oil the grill grate. Arrange the fish packets, seam side down, on the hot grate and grill until the banana leaf is browned and the fish is cooked through, 3 to 5 minutes per side. To test for doneness, insert a slender metal skewer through the side of one packet for 15 seconds. When the fish is done, the skewer will feel very hot to the touch when removed.

6 Serve the fish in the banana leaf packets, instructing everyone to pull out the toothpicks to open the packets.

Blowfish or Halibut "Bool Kogi"

One of Korea's national dishes, *bool kogi* is thin-sliced, sweet-salty rib eye steak crustily grilled over charcoal. So what am I doing at a restaurant with a picture of a blowfish on the marquee and blowfish on the menu? For that matter, isn't blowfish (aka pufferfish or *bok,* in Korean) another name for Japan's infamous *fugu*—the delicate white fish that, when improperly filleted, contains a deadly toxin that kills dozens of Asians every year? And if blowfish is so dangerous, why have legions of well-dressed Korean businessmen made their way down a maze of sinuous back alleys to eat a fish that's customarily served raw or in soup, not grilled? The answer is simple: because Mrs. Shin Hyo Yeon decided to make this spicy, smoky grilled blowfish the specialty of her tiny restaurant, Cheol Cheol Globefish Restaurant, when she moved from the fish-loving port city of Pusan to Korea's political and commercial Seoul. If you like fish—and not just blowfish—that's pungent with garlic, fiery with chile paste, and served crusty and hot off the grill, run don't walk to your fishmonger and get ready to try this. **SERVES 4**

At the Cheol Cheol Globefish restaurant in the Jung-Gu district of Seoul.

JUST THE FACTS:
Why include a recipe in this book for a fish that's virtually impossible to find outside Korea and Japan? The truth is that by the time the blowfish is marinated in a pungent mixture of garlic and Korean chile paste and grilled over charcoal, it loses all trace of its subtle flavor and texture and any of a half dozen readily available white fishes would make credible substitutes. So you can enjoy a chile- and garlic-blasted version made with more commonplace halibut, grouper, or mahimahi, with a lot less foraging and very nearly equal pleasure in taste. But you will need to track down one ingredient that is less than common, Korean chile paste (made with fermented chiles and soybeans and called *kochujang* or *gochujang*), available at Korean and Asian markets, or on the Web from www.koamart.com. In a pinch, you could substitute Vietnamese or Thai chile paste. The flavor won't be quite the same, but the pyrotechnics on your tongue will be.

FOR THE FISH AND MARINADE

¼ cup Korean chile paste or another Asian chile paste
¼ cup soy sauce
¼ cup Asian (dark) sesame oil or vegetable oil
4 scallions, both white and green parts, trimmed and finely chopped
4 cloves garlic, minced
1 tablespoon sugar
2 teaspoons Korean chile powder or hot paprika
1 teaspoon freshly ground black pepper
1½ pounds skinless blowfish, halibut, grouper, or striped bass fillets

FOR SERVING

Boiled potatoes dotted with toasted sesame seeds and minced scallions
A selection of Korean accompaniments (see page 52)

YOU'LL ALSO NEED

A fish grate or fish basket (optional)

ADVANCE PREPARATION

15 to 30 minutes for marinating the fish

*Shin Hyo Yeon grills her signature blowfish **bool kogi** at Cheol Cheol Globefish Restaurant in Seoul.*

1 Prepare the fish and marinade: Place the chile paste, soy sauce, sesame oil, scallions, garlic, sugar, chile powder, and pepper in a large nonreactive mixing bowl and whisk to mix.

2 Thinly slice the fish sharply on the diagonal to obtain pieces that are about 2-inches square and ¼-inch thick. (Koreans like to grill fish and meats in thin slices so as to maximize the amount of flesh directly exposed to the fire.) Stir the fish into the marinade and let marinate in the refrigerator, covered, for 15 to 30 minutes.

3 Set up the grill for direct grilling and preheat it to high. Koreans grill on grates that look like ½- or ¼-inch screening. The closest equivalent in North America would be a wire fish grate. A wire grill basket makes another attractive option. If you are using a fish grate, oil it well when it is hot and just before putting the fish on. If you are using a fish basket, oil it well before adding the fish.

4 When ready to cook, brush and oil the fish or grill grate. Arrange the fish on the hot grate. Don't worry about draining the fish; any excess marinade will cook into a savory glaze. When done, the fish will break into firm flakes when pressed with a finger. Grill the fish until lightly browned and cooked through, 2 to 3 minutes per side.

5 Transfer the fish to a platter or plates and serve at once, with boiled potatoes and the Korean accompaniments.

Grilled Snook with Apricot Glaze

Grilled snook turns up at *braais* (barbecues) throughout South Africa, but there isn't a better place to try it than at Die Strandloper. This fish camp (the name means "beach walker") lies nestled amid the dunes of Langebaan on the Western Cape. The staff grills over a driftwood fire and the "silverware" at Die Strandloper means a couple of empty mussel shells for cutting and eating your fish. **SERVES 4**

8 tablespoons (1 stick) salted butter
2 cloves garlic, minced
2 tablespoons finely chopped flat-leaf parsley
6 tablespoons apricot jam
¼ cup fresh lemon juice
Coarse salt (kosher or sea) and freshly ground
    black pepper
1½ to 2 pounds snook fillets or other firm,
    rich white fish fillets
1 to 2 tablespoons vegetable oil, for oiling
    the fish

YOU'LL ALSO NEED

Oak logs for building a fire or about 2 cups oak
    chips or chunks, soaked for 1 hour in water to
    cover, then drained; a fish basket (optional)

ADVANCE PREPARATION
None

1 Melt the butter in a nonreactive saucepan over high heat. Add the garlic and parsley and cook until fragrant but not brown, about 3 minutes. Add the apricot jam and lemon juice and simmer, whisking to blend, 3 to 5 minutes. Season with salt and pepper to taste; the apricot glaze should be highly seasoned. The glaze can be prepared several hours ahead; reheat it just before serving.

2 Set up the grill for direct grilling and preheat it to high. Ideally, you'll grill over oak wood embers (see page 603 for instructions on grilling over a wood fire).

3 When ready to cook, lightly brush the fish with oil on both sides and season it generously with salt and pepper. If you are using a charcoal grill, toss the oak chips on the coals. If you are using a gas grill, add the oak chips or chunks to the smoker box or place them in a smoker pouch under the grate (see page 603). Brush and oil the fish basket, if using, or brush and oil the grill grate. Place the basketed or unbasketed fish on the hot grate. Grill the fish until nicely browned on the outside and just cooked through, 3 to 4 minutes per side. When done, the fish will break into firm flakes when pressed with a finger. Start basting the fish with the apricot glaze after 2 minutes of grilling, basting it again several times.

4 Transfer the grilled fish to a platter or plates. Baste it one final time and serve it with any remaining apricot glaze on the side.

THE SCOOP

WHERE: Western Cape, South Africa

WHAT: South Africa's most prized fish, glazed with garlic and apricot jam and grilled in all its simplicity—ideally over wood

HOW: Direct grilling

JUST THE FACTS: Snook is a rich, oily, meaty white fish that tastes like an admittedly unlikely cross between halibut and bluefish. I can't think of a substitute that has quite the same texture or flavor. However, the fruity, garlicky glaze here goes well with any number of grilled fishes, from halibut to striped bass to dark oily fish like Spanish mackerel and bluefish.

South Africa: Where *Braai* Is a Way of Life

There are many places you could start your exploration of South African grilling. At a butcher shop in Soweto, where customers buy steaks and chops by the slice to be seasoned and grilled on the sidewalk on a communal charcoal-filled, 55-gallon steel drum. In a typical Johannesburg backyard, where red-blooded South African males spend the weekend, tongs in one hand and beer in the other, fussing over *boerewors* (farmer's sausage) and *sosaties* (shish kebabs) on the *braai* (barbecue grill). At tables set with fine linens, china, silver, and crystal, sagging under platters of springbok and kudu (antelope) grilled over an open fire and served under the stars on a luxury safari in Kruger National Park.

But the best place to begin might just be a rough-and-tumble seaside grill joint called Die Strandloper on the Western Cape. After all, it was here that the first Europeans, intrepid seafarers from Portugal, navigated South Africa's treacherous southern coast. It was here (more accurately in nearby

A Zulu woman wearing a traditional hat, grinds maize to make mealie pap, in KwaZulu-Natal.

Cape Town) that the Dutch, under Jan van Riebeeck, established South Africa's first permanent European settlement in 1652. It was in Cape Town that French Huguenots, fleeing religious persecution in Europe, planted the first vineyards in Franschhoek. And it was in Cape Town that indentured workers from India and Malaysia, the Cape Malays, came to work the farms and gold and diamond mines.

Each wave of immigrants added its own unique ingredients to the South African barbecue melting pot. The Portuguese brought a tiny fiery red chile from Brazil, the *piri-piri*. Today, it is an indispensible flavoring in two South African national grilled dishes—*piri-piri* chicken and *piri-piri* prawns. The Dutch brought such stolid staples as *boerewors,* South Africa's national grilled beef sausage, and *rooster brood,* bread baked or grilled with wood, then slathered with farmstead gooseberry jam. The Cape Malays spiced up South

Grilling at Africa's Southern Tip

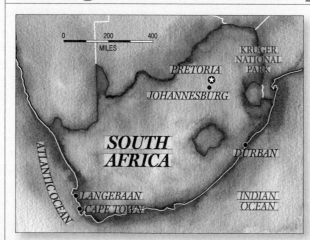

South African barbecue is a melting pot of Portuguese peppers, Dutch cheese and preserves, French wines, East Indian spices, and native game meat.

Fresh produce at a roadside farm stand. Indispensable for South African braai (barbecue).

Giraffes roam free in Kruger National Park.

African barbecue with tamarind, curry powder, coconut milk, and chutney. The French blessed South Africa with a viticultural industry that makes Constantia sauvignon blanc and Stellenbosch cabernet sauvignon some of the world's best wines for *braai*.

Of course, all these are recent refinements to a barbecue tradition that very likely began a half million years ago or more. South African fossil traces of *Australopithecus* (a tool-making, but noncooking human ancestor), *Homo erectus* (the first human predecessor to use fire), and *Homo sapiens* show that they laid the groundwork for a style of barbecue that has become South Africa's preferred pastime and national obsession.

Under African skies: Safari dinner cooked over a campfire.

THE GRILL: At its most rudimentary (and most elemental), a campfire with a grill grate positioned over it. Refinements include conventional charcoal and gas grills, not to mention a grateless, heated flattop grill we North Americans would call a griddle.

THE FUEL: Wood, charcoal, and gas

THE FLAVORINGS: South Africans like their meats highly seasoned, but which seasoning they use depends on their ethnic background. Afrikaners (South Africans of Dutch descent) juxtapose sweet and salty flavors; for example, salty grilled meat with fruit jam. Cape Malays favor East Indian seasonings such as curry powder and coconut. Everyone loves *piri-piri*, the fiery Brazilian-Portuguese chile used in the form of both powder and sauce to spice up grilled meats.

MUST TRY DISHES:

Biltong: Game or beef jerky, traditionally smoke-dried over a wood fire.

Boerewors: South Africa's national sausage—grilled ground beef flavored with coriander, nutmeg, cloves, and other spices (see page 349).

Groenmielies: Butter-basted grilled corn on the cob.

Potjiekos: A savory stew cooked in a three-legged cast-iron pot over a wood fire. Like the burgoo of the American South, *potjiekos* is an indispensable part of a South African *braai*, even though it's cooked in a pot, not directly on the grill.

Rooster brood: Grilled or wood oven–baked bread. Also refers to a grilled (literally) cheese sandwich (see page 105).

Grilling lobsters at Strandloper in Langebaan on the western Cape.

Snook: A buttery, rich-flavored fish grilled over driftwood and served with an apricot-garlic glaze (see page 455).

Sosatie: Red wine–marinated pork and lamb shish kebab (you'll find a recipe on page 251).

THE CONDIMENTS: Monkey Gland Sauce (see page 254) is the thick, sweet-sour, fruit-based sauce that serves as South Africa's barbecue sauce (don't worry; it contains no primate parts). Cape Malay condiments widely enjoyed throughout South Africa include chutney, *achar* (a spicy pickle sauce), and *blatjang* (a spicy, fruit chutneylike condiment traditionally flavored with shrimp paste). And no self-respecting *braai* is complete without *mealie pap*, cornmeal mush.

IF YOU CAN EAT AT ONLY ONE RESTAURANT: For meat—especially game—go to Carnivore, the Johannesburg branch of the famous Nairobi grill restaurant. For grilled seafood, check out Die Strandloper. For *piri-piri* (or as they spell it, *peri-peri*) chicken, visit a fast food joint called Nando's; you'll find outposts everywhere.

WHAT TO DRINK: Castle Lager or another South African beer, or any of South Africa's excellent wines.

THE MOST SINGULAR DISH IN THE SOUTH AFRICAN GRILL REPERTORY: *Moerkoffie*, "grilled coffee," coffee brewed in a pot on a campfire and finished by plunging a burning stick into the pot (this makes the grounds precipitate to the bottom; see page 596).

Mexican Grilled Fish Tacos
{ TACOS DE PESCADO }

WHERE: Mexico

WHAT: Lime-marinated, cilantro- and butter-basted grilled grouper fillets served on tortillas with *pico de gallo* and sour cream

HOW: Direct grilling

JUST THE FACTS: There are many options for the fish: grouper, snapper, mahimahi, kingfish (or even shrimp), if you're trying to use a fish you'd find in Mexico. In the Northeast, you could use striped bass, black bass, swordfish, or tuna. *Naranjas agrias* (sour oranges) can be found at Latino markets and many supermarkets. They taste like a cross between fresh limes and oranges; a mixture of lime and orange juice works great. Cotija is a sharp Mexican cow's milk cheese available in Mexican markets. Central American *queso blanco* or feta make good substitutes, or you can use a mild cheese like Jack.

Fish tacos are not so much a recipe in Mexico, as a way of eating—and a way of life. There's the protein: fresh fish (preferably that came off a boat that morning), minimally seasoned and served hot off the grill. There's the wrapper: a corn tortilla (preferably made by hand a few hours earlier), served hot off the *comal* or warmed on the grill. To invigorate these ingredients, there's a salsa or several salsas at once: a cool, crisp *pico de gallo* (fresh tomato, onion, and jalapeño salsa) from northern Mexico, or perhaps a *xni pec* (fiery habañero and sour orange salsa) from the Yucatán, or a *chiltomate* (flame-roasted tomato salsa) from Campeche, or a more commonplace *salsa verde* (green tomatillo salsa) you'd find pretty much anywhere in Mexico. You'd also find fresh avocado or guacamole, or fresh or pickled onions, or shredded lettuce or cabbage, or a combination of these ingredients. Finally, you might add the cooling touch of sour cream or grated cheese. What matters most is the freshness of the fish and other ingredients—let freshness, not species, be your guide. The recipe may look involved, but actually it's a series of simple steps. **SERVES 4**

FOR THE FISH

1½ pounds grouper, mahimahi, or other fish fillets

Coarse salt (kosher or sea) and freshly ground black pepper

1 large or 2 medium-size fresh naranja agria (sour oranges) or 3 to 4 tablespoons fresh lime juice mixed with 3 to 4 tablespoons fresh orange juice

FOR THE CILANTRO BUTTER

4 tablespoons (½ stick) salted butter, melted

3 tablespoons chopped fresh cilantro, plus sprigs for serving

1 clove garlic (optional), minced

FOR SERVING

12 fresh corn or small flour tortillas

1 cup sour cream and/or grated Cotija or Jack cheese

1 small head or ½ large head iceberg lettuce or green cabbage (optional), shredded or thinly sliced

1 to 2 ripe avocados, peeled and sliced or diced (see Note), or 1 cup Mexican Guacamole (page 131)

Grilled Tomato Habañero Salsa (recipe follows), Pico de Gallo (page 130), and/or Salsa Verde (page 130)

Lime wedges

ADVANCE PREPARATION

15 to 30 minutes for marinating the fish

1 Prepare the fish: Generously season the fish fillets on both sides with salt and pepper. Arrange the fish in a single layer in a nonreactive baking dish and squeeze the sour orange juice over it. Let the fish marinate in the refrigerator, covered, for 15 to 30 minutes.

2 Make the cilantro butter: Melt the butter in a saucepan over medium-high heat. Add the chopped cilantro and garlic, if using, and cook until sizzling but not browned, 2 to 3 minutes. Remove the pan from the heat and set it aside.

3 Set up the grill for direct grilling and preheat it to high.

4 When ready to cook, brush and oil the grill grate. Arrange the pieces of fish on the hot grate at a diagonal to the bars. Grill the fish until nicely browned and cooked though, 3 to 4 minutes per side, turning it with a spatula. When done, the fish will break into firm flakes when pressed with a finger. Start basting the fish with the cilantro butter after about 2 minutes, basting the fish several times on both sides.

5 Transfer the grilled fish to a platter and thinly slice it. If you like, you can warm the tortillas on the grill.

6 To eat the fish tacos, place a slice of fish on a tortilla. Top it with sour cream or cheese, lettuce or cabbage, pickled onions, if desired, some avocado or guacamole, and some Grilled Tomato Habañero Salsa. Squeeze some lime juice on top. Roll everything up and dig in.

NOTE: Sprinkle the sliced or diced avocado with a few drops of lime juice to keep it from discoloring.

Grilled Tomato Habañero Salsa
{ CHILTOMATE }

Chiltomate belongs to a large family of Yucatán salsas based on fire-charred vegetables and fiery habañero peppers. The traditional way to make it is to roast the tomatoes and onions directly on the embers. You could certainly use a grill. **MAKES ABOUT 2 CUPS SALSA**

1 medium-size sweet onion with its skin on
2 large or 4 medium-size ripe red tomatoes (about 1½ pounds)
2 to 8 habañero peppers
½ cup finely chopped fresh cilantro
3 tablespoons naranja agria (sour orange) juice, or
  1½ tablespoons each fresh lime juice and fresh
  orange juice, or more to taste
Coarse salt (kosher or sea)

YOU'LL ALSO NEED
An aluminum foil pan

1 *If you are using a charcoal grill,* light a chimney starter full of coals and rake them out in a single layer. Arrange the onion on the embers and cook it until charred on all sides and easy to pierce with a skewer, 8 to 12 minutes in all, turning

Sigifredo Chale Velázquez grills tikin xik *on Isla Mujeres in the Yucatán.*

The "dining room" at a typical Mexican beach restaurant, where you eat grilled fish overlooking the water, with your feet in the sand.

with tongs. Transfer the onion to an aluminum foil pan. Arrange the tomatoes on the embers and cook them the same way, 6 to 8 minutes in all. Transfer the tomatoes to the pan. Arrange the habañeros on the embers and cook them the same way, 2 to 4 minutes in all. Transfer the habañeros to the pan.

If you are using a gas grill, preheat it to screaming hot. Grill the vegetables on the hot grate until the skins char, 8 to 12 minutes in all for the onion; 6 to 8 minutes in all for the tomatoes; and 2 to 4 minutes for the habañeros. Transfer the grilled vegetables to an aluminum foil pan and let it cool.

2 Using a paring knife, scrape the burnt skins off the vegetables. You don't need to get off every last bit—a few specks of black will add flavor. For a milder (but still ferocious) salsa, seed the habañeros. Cut the vegetables into 1-inch pieces, then finely chop them or coarsely puree them in a food processor. Work in the cilantro and sour orange juice, running the machine in short bursts. Taste for seasoning, adding salt to taste and more sour orange juice as necessary; the salsa should scream with flavor.

Grilled Baby Grouper in the Style of the Portuguese

THE SCOOP

WHERE: Malaysia

WHAT: Fish grilled in banana leaves with one of Southeast Asia's most vibrant fried spice pastes

HOW: Direct grilling

JUST THE FACTS: I first tasted this dish made with *garoupa*—a handsome white-fleshed fish smaller in size but similar in flavor to the North American grouper I call for here. Other good substitutes in North America include whole snapper, redfish, and black bass. Of course, you can always use fish fillets, like grouper or mahimahi. In this case, shorten the cooking time to three to five minutes per side.

What's a Portuguese-style grilled fish doing at a Malaysian fish restaurant run by a woman in a black Muslim headscarf? Indulge me in a bit of history. For thousands of years (literally), Melaka on the west coast of mainland Malaysia has been a center of the spice trade, first with the Chinese, whose junks sailed around Singapore; then with Islamic merchants, whose dhows crossed the Indian Ocean; then with the Portuguese, who turned Melaka into an armed stronghold from which they wrested the lucrative spice trade from Venetian dominance. The Dutch and then the English took charge a century later, but the Portuguese influence survives to this day in the region's extravagant use of spices. As for the *hijab*-wearing grill mistress, her name is Azlinah Kudari and she's the chef-owner of Gerai No. 11 & 12—a seafood restaurant on a renovated pier jutting into the historic waters of the Strait of Malacca. Her Portuguese-style fish is all about flavor— the sonorous tones of fried ginger, garlic, and chile paste, the bright notes of exotic Malaysian fresh herbs. The recipe may look complicated, but you can prepare it in stages. The mouth-filling flavors will leave you speechless. **SERVES 4**

FOR THE SPICE PASTE

5 cloves garlic, coarsely chopped

4 red chiles, such as large Thai chiles, red horn peppers,
    or serrano peppers, seeded and coarsely chopped
    (for hotter fish, leave the seeds in)

1 piece (2 inches) peeled fresh ginger, coarsely chopped

6 macadamia nuts or candlenuts

1 teaspoon coarse salt (kosher or sea)

½ teaspoon MSG (optional)

2 to 4 tablespoons Asian chile paste

1 cup unsweetened coconut milk

3 tablespoons vegetable oil

½ teaspoon shrimp paste (optional)

2 tablespoons palm sugar or light brown sugar

2 tablespoons fresh lime juice or calamansi juice

½ cup loosely packed, thinly slivered mixed fresh herbs,
    including basil, Thai basil, cilantro, mint, daun kesum,
    daum kadok, Kaffir lime leaf, and/or other Asian or
    different herbs (see Notes)

4 rectangular pieces of banana leaf, each about
    10 x 12 inches

4 grouper fillets (each 6 to 8 ounces, see Notes)

YOU'LL ALSO NEED

Wooden toothpicks

ADVANCE PREPARATION

The spice paste can be made through Step 2 up to
    a day in advance.

1 Make the spice paste: Place the garlic, chiles, ginger, macadamia nuts, salt, and MSG, if using, in a food processor and finely chop them. Add the chile paste and a few tablespoons of coconut milk and puree to a thick paste (set the remaining coconut milk aside). You can also make the spice paste in a blender, in which case, you'll need to add the full 1 cup of coconut milk.

2 Heat the oil in a wok or deep saucepan over medium-high heat. Add the shrimp paste, if using, and cook until aromatic and toasted, about 1 minute. Add the spice paste and cook it until browned and fragrant, 3 to 4 minutes, stirring with a wooden

A Taste of Malaysia

For the grilled baby grouper to be strictly authentic, you need some unusual ingredients.

▶ *Belacan,* Malaysian shrimp paste. You can buy it or one of its Asian cousins, at an Asian market. Anchovies or Asian fish sauce will get you in the ballpark, but there is so much flavor in this spice paste, you can omit the shrimp paste entirely and still wind up with fantastic results.

▶ Palm sugar is a little lighter and nuttier than light brown sugar, but the latter makes a great substitute.

▶ *Calamansi* is a supertart Asian lime.

▶ There is no exact substitute for *daun kesum,* "Vietnamese coriander," or *daum kadok,* aromatic "long life" leaves, but a handful of Western herbs, such as basil and tarragon or parsley, are entirely in the spirit of the original.

spoon. Add the remaining coconut milk and the palm sugar and lime juice and cook until thick and concentrated, about 5 minutes. Remove the wok from the heat and stir in the herbs. Let the herb mixture cool to room temperature.

3 Place a piece of banana leaf, with a short edge toward you on a work surface, dark side down. Spoon one eighth of the herb mixture on top of the banana leaf in a rectangle the size of a fillet. Arrange a fish fillet on the herb mixture, then spoon more herb mixture over the fish. Starting with one of the long edges of the banana leaf, fold it over the fish; repeat with the other edge of the banana leaf (the process is like folding a business letter). Fold over the two ends and pin the banana leaf through the ends with a toothpick to seal the packet. The packet will be about 6 inches by 4 inches. Repeat with the remaining pieces of banana leaf, herb mixture, and fish. The fish packets can be prepared several hours ahead to this stage and refrigerated.

4 Set up the grill for direct grilling and preheat it to high.

5 When ready to cook, brush and oil the grill grate. Arrange the fish packets, seam side up, on the hot grate and grill until the banana leaf is browned and the fish is cooked through, 3 to 5 minutes per side. To test for doneness, insert a slender metal skewer through the side of one packet and leave it for 15 seconds; when the fish is done the skewer will feel very hot to the touch. Serve the fish in the banana leaf packets.

NOTES: The exact ratio of the various herbs is less important than their freshness. Just be sure you have a total of ½ cup of herb slivers.

You could also make this dish using small whole fish, each about 1 pound. The spice mix remains the same, but you'll have to use larger banana leaves and increase the grilling time.

Tikin Xik
in the Style of Campeche

THE SCOOP

WHERE: Campeche, on the west coast of the Yucatán, Mexico

WHAT: Whole snappers grilled with achiote marinade, *xcatic* chiles, onions, and lard

HOW: Direct grilling

The polychromatic colonial town of Campeche (a World Heritage site), is home to a remarkable restaurant called La Pigua (named for a local prawn). It's a white tablecloth sort of establishment, not a beach shack, and its dramatic glass-walled dining room with the backlit seventeenth century stone rampart foundations behind it make an architectural statement you'd expect to see in Soho or Roppongi Hills. The chefs in the stainless steel kitchen wear toques—rarely a good sign at a grill joint—and the night I visited, no grill, charcoal or otherwise, was visible. But according to my informants, this was *the* place to experience the Campeche version of *tikin xik*. Sure enough, the moment I arrived, the chef produced an ingenious charcoal-burning grill (it looked like a cross between a wok and a hibachi) that he set on one of the gas burners. He split a fresh snapper the traditional Yucatán way—through the back—and turned out a *tikin xik* that would have done a Mayan potentate proud. The Campechan version uses *naranja agria* (the ubiquitous sour orange) instead of the customary vinegar, and the fish is grilled with vegetables and local chiles. This adds extra layers of flavor and gives the grilling and serving process ceremonial theatrics. **SERVES 4**

FOR THE FISH AND MARINADE

4 fish fillets (each 6 to 8 ounces)

1 cup naranja agria (sour orange) juice, or
    ½ cup each fresh orange juice and lime juice

1 piece (about 2 inches square) achiote paste
    (see Notes)

2 cloves garlic, coarsely chopped

1 teaspoon coarse salt (kosher or sea)

1 teaspoon ground cumin

½ teaspoon freshly ground black pepper

FOR GRILLING THE FISH

1 small red onion, thinly sliced crosswise

1 tomato, thinly sliced crosswise

1 green bell pepper, cored, seeded, and thinly
    sliced crosswise

1 xcatic chile (see Just the Facts, page 464),
    banana pepper, or jalapeño pepper,
    thinly sliced crosswise

1 bunch fresh cilantro, rinsed, shaken dry,
    and stemmed

2 tablespoons lard or salted butter, melted, or
    2 tablespoons olive oil

FOR SERVING

Corn tortillas

Fiery Habañero Salsa (recipe follows) or
    the salsa of your choice

YOU'LL ALSO NEED

A fish basket

ADVANCE PREPARATION

None

1 Prepare the fish and marinade: Place the fish on a large baking sheet.

2 Place the *naranja agria* juice, achiote paste, garlic, salt, cumin, and black pepper in a blender and blend until smooth. Spread the marinade

Campeche-style tikin xik—hot off the grill. The grill basket keeps the fish from sticking.

JUST THE FACTS:
In Campeche they grill whole snappers butterflied open through the back (you can ask your fishmonger to do this), but for the sake of convenience, I suggest you use fillets instead. *Chile xcatic* (pronounced sch-ka-tick) is a yellow, elongated, moderately hot Campechan chile; a banana pepper or even a jalapeño will work in a pinch. As for the lard, well, admittedly, we don't use it much in the United States, but it adds a smoky, meaty flavor you just can't get with the logical substitutes—melted salted butter or olive oil.

over the fish, turning to coat both sides and let the fish marinate for 15 to 30 minutes in the refrigerator, covered.

3 Set up the grill for direct grilling and preheat it to medium-high.

4 When ready to cook, brush and oil the grill grate. Lightly oil the fish basket, then arrange half of the onion, tomato, bell pepper, chile slices, and cilantro in the bottom of the fish basket. Place the fish on top. Arrange the remaining onion, tomato, bell pepper, chile slices, and cilantro on top of the fish and close the fish basket. Just before grilling, drizzle or brush the lard on top.

5 Place the fish basket on the hot grate and grill the fish until browned on both sides and cooked through, 6

to 10 minutes per side depending on the thickness of the fish. Fish fillets, when done, will break into firm flakes when pressed with a finger. To check for doneness on a whole fish (see Just the Facts), insert a paring knife in the deepest part of the flesh above the backbone. When done the flesh will come cleanly away from the bone.

6 Transfer the grilled fish and vegetables to a platter or plates. Serve the *tikin xik* at once with tortillas and salsa.

NOTES: Achiote (annatto seed) is a rust-colored seed that has a tangy, earthy, aromatic flavor with overtones of iodine (iodine in a good way—like the tangy flavor of certain oysters). The seeds are rock hard, and possible to grind in a spice mill, so most Mexicans buy achiote in the form of thick paste,

Tikin Xik

An ancient Mayan dish, *tikin xik,* (pronounced tee-ken-SHEEK) turns up at beach shacks, stylish restaurants, and just about everywhere in between. When it comes to the version that probably most closely resembles the pre-Colombian original, the man to see is Sigifredo Chale Velázquez. A grizzled septuagenarian who grew up on Isla Mujeres off the coast of Cancún and who remembers what life was like here before the arrival of tourism (and electricity), Velázquez runs the grill at La Casa del Tikinxik. For more than four decades, this rustic beach restaurant has been serving *sierra* (king mackerel) fillets so fresh, they're still in rigor mortis. Following a

centuries-old tradition, Velazquez paints the fish with *recado rojo*—the electric orange marinade of the region made with achiote, garlic, and vinegar—then pins it in a fish basket, slaps it over a blazing charcoal fire, and squirts it with a mixture of salt, water, and oil from a plastic squeeze bottle to keep it moist. What results is served under a *palapa* (an open-air thatched hut), with fresh tortillas and an incendiary salsa made of salt, sour orange juice, and Yucatán's infamous habañero pepper. As I eat it (with my fingers), I am reminded again that the ultimate way to eat grilled fish is facing the water it swam in, with your bare feet in the sand.

flavored with other spices and sold in bricks at Mexican markets. One good mail-order source is www.MexGrocer.com. There's no real substitute in terms of flavor, but 1 to 2 tablespoons of sweet paprika will get you the right color.

Tikin xik is traditionally made with whole fish that are butterflied through the back. If you want to try it, have your fishmonger butterfly the fish for you.

Fiery Habañero Salsa

{ X N I   P E C }

The incendiary salsa *xni pec* (pronounced shnee-pek) is the gustatory lifeblood of the Yucatán and there are probably as many versions as there are grill masters to inflict it on their customers. A simple version like this one features fresh habañero peppers, lime juice, and salt. In a more elaborate version, the habañeros might be grilled and/or paired with grilled tomatoes (see the *chiltomate* on page 459). You probably know that the habañero and its close cousin, the Scotch bonnet, are among the world's hottest chiles, so wear gloves when handling them and don't touch your eyes or other sensitive parts. **MAKES ABOUT ½ CUP**

3 to 6 habañero peppers, seeded and coarsely chopped (for hotter salsa, leave the seeds in)
2 teaspoons coarse salt (kosher or sea)
¼ cup naranja agria (sour orange juice), or
 2 tablespoons each fresh orange juice and
 fresh lime juice

Place the habañeros and salt in a food processor and puree or place them in a *molcajete* (a Mexican lava stone mortar) and pound to a paste. Work in the juice. This is strong stuff—use it sparingly.

Greek Fish Grilled in Fig Leaves

This eye-popping fish epitomizes the stunning simplicity and ingenuity of Greek grilling. Simplicity, because when you get down to it, all that's really needed is fish that swam in the Aegean Sea that morning, grilled over locally made natural lump charcoal on fig leaves like those that hang in the arbor of my friends Aglaia Kremezi and Costas Moraitis. Ingenuity, because what better way to solve the perennial problem of keeping fish from sticking to the grill grate than by grilling it on aromatic fresh whole leaves? This dish may be simple, but the fig leaves and oregano (or lavender) impart a haunting smoke flavor that is no less complex for being subtle. **SERVES 4**

THE SCOOP

WHERE: Greece

WHAT: Simply one of the fastest, easiest, tastiest, and most dramatic ways to grill fish, and you can do it either with whole fish or fish fillets

HOW: Direct grilling

JUST THE FACTS:
The first thing you'll need is fresh fig leaves, and if you have a fig tree that has not been treated with pesticides, you're in business. If not, you can substitute fresh or pickled grape leaves, or for a tropical twist, even banana leaves. What's important is the herbaceous flavor imparted as the leaves slowly burn over the coals. For that matter, the variety of the fish matters much less than the freshness. In Greece, they'd use a full-flavored fish called sea bream. In North America, you could substitute a small whole fish, like black bass, snapper, or even trout, or fresh fillets, like cod. Finally, bunches of dried Greek oregano are available at Greek markets. Lavender can be found at specialty food shops, natural foods stores, and farmers' markets.

Coarse sea salt (better sea than kosher
    in this instance)
⅓ cup fresh lemon juice
⅔ cup extra-virgin olive oil, preferably
    Greek, plus olive oil for brushing
    the fish
2 whole fish (2 pounds each), or 4 whole fish
    (1 pound each), such as black bass,
    snapper, or trout, cleaned, scaled, and
    fins removed, with heads and tails intact
1 bunch dried Greek oregano or lavender
8 fresh fig leaves, fresh or pickled grape leaves,
    or pieces of banana leaf cut into rectangles
    2 inches larger on all sides than the fish
    (see Note)

ADVANCE PREPARATION
None

1 Place 1 teaspoon of salt and the lemon juice and olive oil in a jar with a tight-fitting lid. Shake to mix. Set the jar of sauce aside.

2 Set up the grill for direct grilling and preheat it to medium-high.

3 Lightly brush the fish on both sides with olive oil and season them generously with salt. Shake the bunch of oregano or lavender over the fish (you can rub it a little between the palms of your hands to dislodge some of the leaves; the idea is to put a *light* sprinkling of herbs on the fish). Set the bunch of oregano or lavender aside.

4 If you are using fig leaves or grape leaves, arrange them on the hot grate, one overlapping the other if necessary, to cover a rectangle a little larger than one of the fish (if you are using banana leaves, place one piece on the grate). Arrange one of the fish on top of the leaf. Repeat with the remaining leaves and fish. Grill the fish until it is cooked on one side, 10 to 15 minutes; the skin will brown and the flesh will turn white.

5 Using a large spatula, turn the fish over. If the leaves are burned, replace

The Greek chimney starter (choni) goes on top of the wood and charcoal, where it funnels the hot air upward, creating a convection that speeds up ignition.

Ocean fresh tsipoures (sea bream) grill on fresh fig leaves on a portable Greek beach grill.

them with new ones. Toss the bunch of oregano or lavender on the coals. Continue grilling the fish in the herb smoke until the second side is cooked, 10 to 15 minutes longer. To test for doneness make a small cut with the tip of a paring knife in the deepest part of the flesh above the backbone. When done, the flesh will come cleanly away from the bone.

6 Transfer the fish to a platter or plates, discarding the leaves. Bone the fish if you are so inclined. Shake the jar with the sauce vigorously to recombine and spoon a little of the mixture over the hot fish. Serve the rest of the sauce on the side.

NOTE: If you are using fig leaves, you'll need 2 for grilling each side of each 2-pound fish or 1 for grilling each side of each 1-pound fish; in either case, you'll need a total of 8 fig leaves.

If you are using grape leaves, you'll need 4 for grilling each side of each 2-pound fish or 2 for grilling each side of each 1-pound fish; in either case you'll need a total of 16 grape leaves.

You can use either fresh or frozen banana leaves in place of the fig leaves. Banana leaves are sold both fresh and frozen at Asian, Indian, and Hispanic markets. If you use fresh, rather than thawed frozen banana leaves, be sure they come from a tree that has not been treated with pesticides.

"Steam" Fish

I first tasted this fish grilled in aluminum foil, but the poet in me craved the more traditional wrapping of the Caribbean: banana leaves. Foil simply seals in moistness, while a banana leaf imparts a smoky flavor all its own. (Grilling foods wrapped in leaves is a technique of great antiquity and geographic spread; for example, see the *otak-otak*—Malaysian fish mousse grilled in banana leaves—on page 448.) Here's how Jamaican Boston Beach grill master Winston David grills snapper steaks topped with carrots, onion, okra, and other aromatic vegetables. What's remarkable is that when you cook the fish on the embers, even wrapped in foil, the vegetables and fish juices caramelize, giving you a lush, smoky flavor you'd associate with grilling directly over the fire. There are two other advantages to this method: One, you can prepare the packets ahead of time and cook them at the last minute (and, how convenient to combine the main course and vegetables). Two, you can customize the fish by varying the vegetables or seasonings. **SERVES 4**

2 carrots, peeled

8 green beans, trimmed and strings removed

8 small or 4 medium-size okra

1 small sweet onion

4 tablespoons (½ stick) salted butter or margarine

4 snapper steaks or other fish steaks or fillets
(each about 1 inch thick and 6 to 8 ounces; see Notes)

Coarse salt (kosher or sea) and freshly ground black pepper

2 tablespoons Jamaican jerk seasoning (see Notes) or
your favorite commercial brand

About 1 teaspoon seasoned salt or vegetable soup mix
(optional)

YOU'LL ALSO NEED

4 pieces of heavy-duty aluminum foil, each about
12 x 16 inches, or 4 pieces of banana leaf of
the same size (see Note, page 467); butcher's string,
if using banana leaves

ADVANCE PREPARATION

None, however the fish can be wrapped several hours
ahead and refrigerated.

1 Thinly slice the carrots sharply on the diagonal. Cut the green beans into 2-inch pieces. Thinly slice the okra and onion crosswise.

2 Place one of the pieces of aluminum foil on a work surface, shiny side down, with the short side toward you. Or place a piece of banana leaf, dark side down, on the work surface, short side toward you. Cut 2 thin slices of butter and place them in the center of the lower half of the foil or banana leaf. Season the snapper on both sides with salt and pepper and, using the back of a spoon, spread about 1½ teaspoons of the jerk seasoning over the fish. Place the seasoned fish on top of the slices of butter, with the short side of the fish toward you. Mound a quarter of the carrots, green beans, okra, and onion on top. Place 2 more thin slices of butter on top of the vegetables; you should use about 1 tablespoon in all for one snapper steak. If you are using seasoned salt or soup mix, sprinkle it over the vegetables (if you are using soup mix, shake it through a strainer to separate out the noodles).

3 If you are using aluminum foil, fold the top of the foil over the bottom and fold the sides in tightly to encase the fish and vegetables. Twist one of the ends into a long thin tail; this looks good and gives you a tight seal. It also gives you a place to grab the packets without puncturing the foil. If you are using banana leaves, fold the sides in and the top over to wrap the fish tightly. Tie the leaf shut with butcher's string. Prepare the remaining fish steaks the same way.

4 *If you are using a gas grill,* set it up for direct grilling and preheat it to high. Arrange the fish packets, vegetable side up, on the hot grate.

If you are using a charcoal grill, light the charcoal and rake it out over the bottom of the grill. Let the coals burn down until lightly ashed over. Arrange the fish packets, vegetable side up, on the embers.

5 Grill the fish until it is cooked through, 5 to 8 minutes per side. To test for doneness, insert a slender metal skewer through the side of one packet for 15 seconds; when the fish is done the skewer will feel very hot to the touch when removed.

6 Transfer the fish packets to a heatproof platter or plates. Let cool for a minute or two, then open the top of the packets with the tip of a sharp knife, taking care not to burn yourself on the hot steam. You eat the fish right out of the packets.

NOTES: There are several options for fish—the snapper steaks called for here or another Caribbean fish, like kingfish, grouper, or mahi-mahi. Casting your net (as it were) farther afield, you could substitute a steak fish, like salmon or swordfish.

If you're feeling ambitious, you can use the jerk seasoning made from scratch that you'll find on page 200. (Check the ingredients list and Step 1 to make the seasoning.) But because you need only two tablespoons of the seasoning, you could certainly use a good commercial brand, like Walkerswood, which is available in most food markets.

The Grilled Fish Divas

In a back alley of Luang Prabang, **MADAM DJAN AND MISS PANIN** serve up a unique grilling experience that is a must on your barbecue life list.

Grill mistress Panin works on a grateless grill stoked with coconut shell charcoal. The deep slashes in the fish ensure even cooking (and look cool as all get out).

LUANG PRABANG, LAOS

5 P.M. Luang Prabang, Laos. Like clockwork, this former French-Colonial capital and Buddhist center—registered on the UNESCO World Heritage List—turns from a somnolent Laotian hill town into a teeming bazaar. The sidewalks throng with vendors from the nearby hill tribes, the Hmong, Lahu, Akha, and Karen, who display their handicrafts in one of the most vibrant night markets in Southeast Asia. The back alleys come alive with flaming grills and sizzling woks, as town folk and tourists alike set about the serious task of procuring dinner. Enter Madam Djan, a short, affable street vendor recognizable by her red apron (most Laotian grillers are women). Madam Djan's specialty is grilled fish from the nearby Mekong and Nam Khan rivers.

Earlier that afternoon, Madam Djan and her "sous-chef," Miss Panin, slashed the fish to the bone at half-inch intervals on both sides, a process that gives the fish the ornamental look of tribal facial scars. The deep scoring fosters the absorption of the marinade and speeds up the cooking time. The women skewer the fish on long sticks split halfway down the middle. These split sticks combine the virtues of a shish kebab skewer and a grill basket and

Madam Djan (in red apron) displays grilled river fish at the night market in Luang Prabang, Laos.

are found throughout Laos and Cambodia. Madam Djan applies the first layer of flavorings—garlic oil and oyster sauce—and hands the fish to Miss Panin, who does the actual grilling, working over a metal trough filled with hot charcoal.

Miss Panin moves like a perpetual motion machine. She pulls a plastic bag over her hand to grab a fistful of unlit charcoal. She adjusts the coals with what looks like oversize chopsticks and fans them to a fiery glow with a square of cardboard. She turns the fish, first to one side, then the other, then exposes the top and bottom to the embers to make sure it's cooked through.

Her work done, Miss Panin hands the grilled fish back to Madam Djan, who applies one final coat of garlic oil and oyster sauce, then slaps the fish onto a banana leaf-lined plate and serves it lollipop style with lime halves for squeezing. Until you've had grilled fish in a back alley in Luang Prabang, your life list for unique grilling experiences is incomplete.

NAMES: Madam Djan and Miss Panin

TERRITORY: Luang Prabang, Laos

CLAIM TO FAME: The duo run the most popular grilled fish stall at the night market in Luang Prabang

SPECIALTIES: River fish grilled over charcoal and glazed with garlic and oyster sauce

MADAM DJAN AND MISS PANIN SAY:

▶ If your fish didn't swim in the river this morning, it isn't fresh.

▶ Add charcoal one piece at a time to maintain a hot fire. To keep your fingers clean, wear a plastic bag over your hand when you grab the charcoal.

Laotian Grilled Fish

THE SCOOP

WHERE: Laos

WHAT: Whole river fish glazed with fried garlic and oyster sauce

HOW: Direct grilling

JUST THE FACTS: Pretty much all of the fish in landlocked Laos comes from the Mekong river or one of its tributaries. In North America, I've prepared this dish with everything from black bass to snapper to trout. Laotians prefer fish small enough to serve one per person—this maximizes the amount of skin exposed to the fire. If whole fish aren't your thing, you could certainly use fish steaks or fillets. Halibut comes out great glazed this way. To minimize sticking, grill the fish in a grill basket.

Oyster sauce (sometimes called oyster-flavored sauce) is a thick, briny-flavored Chinese condiment that often but not always contains oysters. Look for it at Asian markets and at most supermarkets. Two good brands are Lee Kum Kee, which is widely available, and Wok Mei.

For the sake of authenticity, I've included MSG, which is widely used in Southeast Asia. I myself omit it.

In a landlocked country like Laos, you might be surprised by the prevalence and popularity of grilled fish. The explanation can be found in a river, the Mekong, which runs the length of the country from north to south like a mighty artery. The Mekong influences all aspects of Lao society, from transportation to culture to cuisine. And from it and its tributaries come the fish so prized by Lao grill masters, which is also turned into the pungent fermented fish pastes and sauces served as condiments with all manner of grilled foods. Here's how they grill fish in Luang Prabang, a charming French-Colonial town and UNESCO World Heritage site in northern Laos (you can read more about it on page 469). The seasonings are simple—garlic oil and oyster sauce—but the flavor roars off the skewer. In Laos, the fish would be skewered on a split stick and grilled over a grateless grill. In North America, you can grill the fish in a fish basket or directly on the grate. **SERVES 4**

4 small whole snapper, trout, or other fish
(each 12 ounces to 1 pound), cleaned,
scaled, and fins removed, with heads
and tails intact, or 4 fish steaks or fillets
(each 6 to 8 ounces)
½ cup vegetable oil
4 cloves garlic, minced or thinly sliced
About 2 tablespoons coarse salt
(kosher or sea)
About 1 tablespoon MSG (optional)
About 1 tablespoon freshly ground
black pepper
About ½ cup Chinese oyster sauce
Lime halves, for serving

YOU'LL ALSO NEED
A fish basket (optional); banana leaves
(optional), for serving

ADVANCE PREPARATION
None

1 If you are using whole fish, use a sharp knife to make a series of parallel diagonal cuts about ½ inch apart in both sides of each fish, cutting to the bone; this helps the heat and seasonings penetrate the fish to ensure even cooking.

2 Heat the vegetable oil in a small skillet over high heat. Add the garlic and cook until just beginning to brown, 1 to 2 minutes. Immediately pour the garlic and oil into a heatproof bowl and let cool to room temperature.

3 Place the salt, MSG, if using, pepper, and oyster sauce in separate small bowls.

4 Set up the grill for direct grilling and preheat it to high.

5 When ready to cook, oil the fish basket, if using, or brush and oil the grill grate. Spoon a little of the garlic oil over each fish on both sides, spreading it over the fish with the back of the spoon or a basting brush. Season the fish on both sides with salt, MSG, if using, and pepper. Spoon a little oyster sauce over the fish on each side, again spreading it over the fish with the back of the spoon.

6 Place the fish in the fish basket, if using. Place the basketed or unbasketed fish on the hot grate. Grill the fish until nicely browned on the outside and cooked through, 4 to 6 minutes per side. To check for doneness on a whole fish, insert a paring knife in the deepest part of the flesh above the backbone. When done, the flesh will come cleanly away from the bone. When done, fish fillets will break into firm flakes when pressed with a finger.

7 Transfer the grilled fish to a platter or plates (lined with banana leaves if you want to be strictly authentic). Brush the fish with the remaining garlic oil and oyster sauce and season it again with salt and pepper. Serve at once with lime halves.

Canadian Trout Grilled on a Log

This, Canada's answer to planked salmon, began a long time ago with a very long drive—forty miles on a single lane gravel road. The destination was a lake called Marie-Louise in the Laurentian wilderness north of Montreal. The ritual was always the same, remembers my French-Canadian editor and friend, Pierre Bourdon. "My grandfather would stash a few beers in the lake to chill, wedging the bottles under the water with a log. We'd fish all afternoon, then to warm us up, *Grand-père* would build a fire. He'd drink the beer and lay the fish (fillets for us kids) on the wet log. He'd open a little bag of salt and pepper brought for the purpose of seasoning the fish. From one pocket, he'd produce a lemon; from the other, an onion; and he'd slice these ingredients over the fish, using an old penknife. Thus seasoned, the fish would be placed on its log on the fire, where the smoke and steam from the wood would work their magic. I've since had cedar-planked salmon, not to mention all manner of seafood cooked on a *plancha* in Spain, but I can tell you this: Nothing comes close to my grandfather's trout grilled on a log." Serve with—what else?—Canadian beer. **SERVES 2 AND CAN BE MULTIPLIED AS DESIRED**

THE SCOOP

WHERE: Quebec province, Canada

WHAT: Fresh rainbow trout with lemon and onion, grilled on a flaming log

HOW: Direct grilling

JUST THE FACTS: The best fish for this dish is a two-pound rainbow trout—preferably one you caught earlier that afternoon. You can certainly use trout fillets or, for that matter, another cold-water and freshwater fish, like Arctic char. As for the log, maple or oak would be the logical choice in Canada.

1 whole rainbow trout (about 2 pounds), cleaned, scaled, and fins removed, with head and tail intact, or

    1 pound trout fillets

Coarse sea salt and freshly ground black pepper

1 medium-size onion, thinly sliced crosswise

1 lemon, thinly sliced crosswise (remove any seeds with a fork)

1 to 2 tablespoons extra-virgin olive oil or unsalted butter (optional; not part of his grandfather's repertory, but Pierre uses it today)

YOU'LL ALSO NEED

1 maple, oak, or other hardwood log (3 to 4 inches in diameter and 16 to 20 inches long) soaked in a tub of cold water for 2 hours, then drained well. Try to pick a log that's straight and slightly flat on one side. It's OK to use a split log—put the fish on the split side.

ADVANCE PREPARATION

A couple of hours for soaking the log

1 Set up the grill for direct grilling and preheat it to high. Ideally, you'll build a wood fire and let it burn until you have a good hot bed of embers (see page 603 for instructions on grilling over a wood fire). Or you can set up a charcoal grill for grilling in the embers (see page 601) or set up a gas grill for direct grilling.

2 Generously season the inside and outside of the whole trout with salt and pepper and place a few onion and lemon slices in the cavity. Place the trout on the log and arrange the remaining onion and lemon slices on top, alternating and overlapping them. If you are using trout fillets, season them with salt and pepper on both sides. Place the fillets on the log and arrange the onion and lemon slices on top of the fillets. Season the trout with

more salt and pepper. If you're so inclined, drizzle some olive oil on top or top the fish with thin slices of butter.

3 Place the log with the trout on top in the fire, directly on the embers of a charcoal grill, or on the hot grate of a gas grill. If you are using a gas grill, cover it. Cook the trout until it is sizzling and browned, 30 to 50 minutes for a whole trout, 15 to 20 minutes for trout fillets. If cooking a large fish, you may need to turn it with a long-handled spatula to make sure both sides cook.

To check for doneness on a whole fish, insert a paring knife in the deepest part of the flesh above the backbone. When done, the flesh will come cleanly away from the bone. When done, the fish fillets will break into firm flakes when pressed with a finger.

The perfect set-up: Fishing pre-breakfast in pristine waters practically assures grilled trout with your eggs. At least, that's the hope.

Camping and fishing in a gorgeous Canadian setting; the good life, indeed.

CANADIAN TROUT GRILLED ON A LOG | page 471

Barramundi Grilled in Paperbark with Wild Herbs

THE SCOOP

WHERE: Australia's Northwest Territories

WHAT: Australia's most prized fish stuffed with wild herbs, wrapped in the paperlike bark of an aboriginal tree, and charred on the grill

HOW: Direct grilling

JUST THE FACTS: Australians would use a few ingredients that are challenging to find in North America. Fortunately, you can find readily available substitutes for each. Barramundi is a silver-skinned fish with a melt-in-your-mouth texture and an incredibly rich, buttery flavor. East Coast shad or West Coast *hamachi* (yellowtail) would make convincing substitutes and salmon would be a great stand-in, too. Paperbark, true to its name, is the papery bark of an aboriginal tree that is used for wrapping and grilling foods in the Australian bush much the way banana leaves are used in the Yucatán. The cedar grilling papers sold by www.FireandFlavor.com and other companies work great.

If Vic Cherikoff didn't know so much about Australian bush cookery, I wouldn't be eating "fish fries" for breakfast. Fish fries is a polite way of saying fish liver and other innards chopped up and stuffed inside the fish's air bladder and grilled like some piscine sausage. Anthropologist turned chef, TV host, exporter, and aboriginal food expert, Cherikoff has spent the last twenty-five years promoting wattleseeds to the rest of the world (they taste vaguely chocolatey), lemon myrtle (think citrus-flavored basil), and other foods from the Australian outback. And if I'm eating fish fries in his lush backyard in Sydney this morning, it's because Vic has agreed to show me a grilled fish Australia's Aborigines have enjoyed for thousands of years: barramundi stuffed with herbs and wrapped and grilled in paperbark. The bark burns as the fish grills, imparting an incredible herbal smoke flavor. As for the fish fries, like most of the world's hunter-gatherers, the Aborigines eat a diet rich in lean game and wild plants, but very low in fat (we North Americans should only be so lucky). Thus, fish fries become a valuable source of nutritionally essential fats. I'll spare you the details, as you very likely won't be able to find fish fries in North America. If you're looking for a grilled fish that takes just a few minutes to make, looks spectacularly original on the grill, and explodes with herb, smoke, and fire flavors, this barramundi rocks. **SERVES 4**

2 whole barramundi or other fish, such as trout (each about 2 pounds), cleaned, scaled, and fins removed, with heads and tails intact, or 4 fish fillets, such as salmon (each 6 to 8 ounces)
Coarse salt (kosher or sea, optional)
1 cup mixed fresh herbs, such as lemon myrtle, lemon verbena, basil, dill, or tarragon

YOU'LL ALSO NEED

4 sheets of paperbark (each about 16 by 16 inches), or 12 sheets of cedar grilling papers soaked in cool water for 10 minutes, then drained; butcher's string

ADVANCE PREPARATION

None, although the fish can be stuffed and wrapped several hours before grilling.

HOW TO COOK BARRAMUNDI IN PAPERBARK

1. Spread a layer of lemon myrtle leaves a little larger than the fish on a sheet of damp paperbark. (In North America you could substitute lemon verbena and cedar grilling papers.)

2. Stuff the herbs into the cavity of the barramundi.

3. Bring the ends of the paperbark over the fish to enclose it.

4. The wrapped barramundi is ready for grilling.

5. Grill the barramundi until the paperbark is charred and the fish is cooked through.

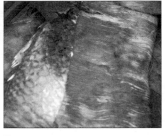

6. Unwrap the fish for serving: Note how the charred paperbark colors and flavors the fish.

Australian bush grilling expert Vic Cherikoff.

Sampling the barramundi bush-style.

1 If you are using fish fillets, cut a deep pocket in one side of each fillet. If you are using salt (the Aborigines don't), generously season the whole fish or fillets inside and out. Stuff the whole fish cavities or the pockets in the fillets with the herbs and place a few around the outside. Wrap each fish or fillet in paperbark or grilling papers, tying it into a neat bundle with string. The fish can be stuffed and wrapped several hours ahead and refrigerated, covered.

2 Set up the grill for direct grilling and preheat it to medium-high. Alternatively, you can grill the fish right on the embers. Rake out lit coals into a single layer.

3 Arrange the fish packets on top of the lit coals or on the hot grate and grill until the paperbark is charred on the outside and the fish is cooked through, 8 to 10 minutes per side for whole fish, 4 to 6 minutes per side for fillets. To test for doneness on a whole fish, insert a slender metal skewer through the side of one packet for 15 seconds; when done, the skewer will feel very hot to the touch when removed.

4 Transfer the grilled fish to a platter or plates and serve it wrapped in the paperbark. Yes, to be strictly authentic, you'd eat the fish with your fingers.

Australia: Grilling in the Land of Oz

The polls are in and the stats say it all: According to *Jetstar* magazine, a whopping 97 percent of Australian families own barbecue grills. And 85 percent say they prefer cooking outdoors, while 50 percent say that the scent of barbecue is their favorite summertime aroma. To state that Oz—as Ozzies (Australians) affectionately call their country—is grill obsessed would be a little like observing that Asians have a passing penchant for rice.

Yet, much as Australians love grilling, there is little consensus on what constitutes Australian barbecue. Beyond the ubiquitous snags (grilled sausages) and shrimp on the barbie, there is no classic canon of grilled dishes; and actually, red meats turn up more than seafood on Ozzie grills. There are no universally embraced flavor combinations or grilling techniques; nothing that would qualify as regional or national grilled specialties; nothing like India's tandoori or Indonesia's satés, although both are popular Down Under.

The barbecue grill, outback style. Where meat meets the open fire.

What there are are superlative raw materials: lamb renowned the world over and beef sold throughout Asia; pristine seafood ranging from Morton Bay bugs (a sort of lobster from the south coast) to barramundi (a silvery fish with a buttery texture and taste); organic vegetables so fresh they would make Alice Waters blush. These ingredients are seasoned the way an Australian's forebears would have done it in the old country: Greek Australians in Melbourne use garlic, oregano, lemon juice, and olive oil; Southeast Asian Australians in Sydney favor lemongrass, chiles, and coconut milk; and so on.

Then there's bush grilling—the simple, primal live-fire cooking you find in the outback, where the Aborigines wrap barramundi in paperbark to be roasted right on the embers (see page 474) and where farmers and railroad workers grill lamb chops on shovels held over

Good Things on the Grill Down Under

Australia: Where superlative raw materials, unrivaled ethnic diversity, and a fanatic national obsession with grilling combine to produce one of the world's most vibrant grill cultures.

The cowboy culture of the outback raises campfire cooking to the level of art.

Uluru—the Red Rock—Australian emblem and backdrop to many an Ozzie grill session.

just have to content themselves with first-rate ingredients, an outdoor grill culture that has virtually every red-blooded male standing over a grill on weekends, and world-class wines and beers to wash down the fruits of their labors. Which eminently works for me.

For many Australians, the "barbie" (grill) is a gas-heated flattop.

a campfire (see page 285) or roast poultry in chicken wire cages positioned directly over an open fire.

"We are just beginning to create a national style," says Melbourne *Herald Sun* food columnist, Bob Hart. "Come back in twenty years and maybe you'll find something called Australian barbecue." Until then, Australians will

Australia's long-burning Heat Beads allow charcoal-grillers to cook up to five hours without replenishing.

THE GRILL: Australians traditionally grill on a flattop gas "barbecue" or "barbie" (as grills are called Down Under). Imagine an American gas grill without a lid. Curiously, many Australian "grills" have gas-heated griddles, not proper grill grates, so much of what passes for Australian "grilling" is actually "griddling."

THE FUEL: For the vast majority of Australians the fuel of choice is propane. Charcoal grillers are in the minority, but their numbers are growing. Australians of Greek descent in Melbourne use a hard lump charcoal made from a wood called mallee root (think of it as Ozzie mesquite). Australia's bestselling charcoal, Heat Beads, may be the world's longest-burning charcoal thanks to the addition of carbonized coal (char). A single chimneyful has been known to burn for five hours.

THE FLAVORINGS: These range from rosemary and garlic to sesame oil and ginger to Australia's excellent olive oil and wine.

MUST TRY DISHES:

Lamb on a shovel (see page 283)

Beer-Can Chicken with Asian "Pesto" (see page 361)

Snags (sausages)

Barramundi in paperbark (see page 474)

Shrimp on the barbie (see page 490)

THE CONDIMENTS: Sweet, but not smoky, red barbecue sauce and such ethnic grilling sauces as Greek *skordalia* (garlic sauce), Japanese teriyaki, and Indonesian *sambal* (fiery chile sauce).

IF YOU CAN EAT AT ONLY ONE RESTAURANT: There are few barbecue or grilling restaurants per se—most Ozzie grilling is done at home. But many contemporary and ethnic Australian restaurants have charcoal- or wood-burning grills. In Melbourne, don't miss Rockpool, opened by Aussie celebrity chef, Neil Perry, who made a mammoth

wood-burning grill the focal point of his restaurant. In a Sydney, check out Wildfire, a collaboration between an Australian restaurant group and American chef Mark Miller. Another distinctly Australian grilling experience: the Coogee Bay Hotel Beer Garden in a Sydney suburb, where you buy your meat and grill it yourself.

WHAT TO DRINK: Beer, like Redoak, Murray's, or Oxford. Or one of Australia's superlative wines, like a reisling or shiraz from the Clare or Barossa Valley.

THE MOST SINGULAR DISH IN THE REPERTOIRE: Kangaroo kebabs

Grilled Eel or Halibut with Sweet Cinnamon and Star Anise Glaze

WHERE: Seoul, South Korea

WHAT: Grilled eel (or other fish) marinated and glazed with a sweet, salty, and profoundly aromatic Korean barbecue sauce

HOW: Direct grilling

JUST THE FACTS: The elaborate glaze and repeated grillings here were conceived for a fish esteemed by most of Planet Barbecue and regarded with skepticism in North America: eel. Unless you're of Asian or Italian extraction, you've probably never cooked eel. If you're willing to try it, look for fresh eel at Asian or Italian fish markets and have the fishmonger fillet it for you. But don't worry if you don't want to experiment with eel. The glaze and grilling process is fabulous for a mild white fish like halibut or grouper.

Eel holds an honored place in the hearts of Asian barbecue fanatics (think Japanese *anago* and *unagi*). Koreans approach the grilling of eel with a zeal that borders on a fetish. This brings me to Ilmijung, a restaurant renowned for its barbecued eel and equally remarkable for its riverside setting and pastoral atmosphere (rare in hyper-urbanized Seoul). You can dine on a dock right on the river or in cozy rooms decorated like peasant cottages. But the star attraction here slithers more than it swims and it comes grilled in several manifestations. The classic features a sweet-salty-spicy lacquer that contains twenty-one ingredients (they're on display in a showcase in the dining room, in case you're curious to know what you're eating). These flavorings range from the predictable (soy sauce and sesame) to the strange (licorice and angelica) to the downright exotic (eel bones and *sansho* peppers).

Of course, it's one thing to know what's in a sauce and quite another to know the exact proportions of each ingredient. What you'll find here will get you to the destination with ingredients readily available in the United States. As for Ilmijung's eel, specially raised for the restaurant in Pusan, it's simply the meatiest, sweetest, richest, fattiest I've ever tasted anywhere. The deep, rich flavor and lacquerlike sheen come from multiple bastings and grillings—I counted eight separate applications. The eel is sandwiched between two wire racks to hold it intact when it's turned—the Korean version of a grill basket. **SERVES 4**

Eel grilled Korean style—on a wire rack that serves as a grill basket. (A second rack is placed on top and holds the eel in place when turning.)

½ cup soy sauce

½ cup sake

¼ cup Asian (dark) sesame oil

¼ cup light corn syrup, such as Karo or Steen's

⅓ cup firmly packed light brown sugar

2 cloves garlic, peeled and lightly crushed with the side of a cleaver

2 slices (¼ inch) fresh ginger, lightly crushed with the side of a cleaver

2 scallions, trimmed, white parts lightly crushed with the side of a cleaver, green parts finely chopped for garnish

1 slice (¼ inch thick) sweet onion, or 1 more scallion

3 tablespoons toasted sesame seeds (see page 68)

2 star anise, or ½ teaspoon Chinese five-spice powder

1 piece (2 inches) cinnamon stick

1 dried Asian hot red pepper, or ¼ teaspoon hot red pepper flakes

1 teaspoon black peppercorns

½ teaspoon ground sansho pepper (see Note), or ½ teaspoon ground Szechuan peppercorns and a pinch of ground coriander (optional)

1½ to 2 pounds eel or halibut fillets

YOU'LL ALSO NEED

A grill basket (optional)

ADVANCE PREPARATION

2 hours for the glaze to stand, plus 1 hour for marinating the eel; the glaze can be prepared up to a day ahead.

1 Place the soy sauce, sake, sesame oil, corn syrup, brown sugar, garlic, ginger, scallion whites, onion slice, 2 tablespoons of toasted sesame seeds, star anise, cinnamon stick, dried hot pepper, peppercorns, and *sansho* pepper, if using, in a large heavy saucepan and bring to a boil over medium heat. Reduce the heat to low and let the glaze simmer gently

Korean eel owes its mahogany sheen and complex flavor to multiple bastings with the sweet soy glaze. The fish is basted six to eight times.

until it is syrupy and richly flavored, 15 to 20 minutes, or as needed, stirring often. Remove the pan from the heat and let the glaze stand at room temperature for 2 hours, then strain it into another saucepan or a clean jar. The glaze can be prepared up to 24 hours ahead and refrigerated, covered.

2 Arrange the eel fillets in a baking dish. Place ⅓ cup of the glaze in a ramekin and very generously brush the eel on both sides with that glaze. Let the eel marinate in the refrigerator, covered, for 1 hour.

3 Set up the grill for direct grilling and preheat it to medium.

4 When ready to cook, oil the fish basket, if using, or brush and oil the grill grate. Place the eel in the fish basket, if using, and arrange it or the unbasketed eel on the hot grate. Grill the eel for 2 minutes per side. Pour a little more glaze into the ramekin and brush both sides of the eel, opening the grill basket so you can coat the eel evenly. (The

reason for adding the glaze to the ramekin is so as not to contaminate the whole batch with fish juices on the brush.)

5 Grill the eel for 2 more minutes per side, then glaze it again. Continue grilling and glazing the eel until it is golden brown on the outside and cooked through, about 8 minutes per side, 16 minutes in all. When done, the eel will break into firm flakes when pressed with a finger.

6 Transfer the grilled eel to a platter or plates. Spoon any leftover glaze on top of the eel and sprinkle the remaining 1 tablespoon of toasted sesame seeds and the scallion greens over it. Serve the eel at once.

NOTE: *Sansho* pepper is an aromatic spice with a minty, lemony flavor. You can buy ground *sansho* pepper at Japanese markets and some specialty food shops. There's no exact substitute, but ground Szechuan peppercorns mixed with a pinch of ground coriander will get you close.

Shellfish

Some of the highest hills in my infamously flat home state of Florida are shell mounds—left by the Calusa Indians centuries prior to the arrival of the Spanish. This serves to remind us that long before cutting-edge chefs took to grilling lobsters and oysters, live fire was firmly established as a superior way to cook shellfish.

Planet Barbecue backs me up on this, as grilled and smoked shellfish turn up on at least six continents: In Mexico, where spiny lobsters are grilled not with salsa, but with a fried garlic sauce called *mojo de ajo.* In Thailand, where cockles are grilled in the shells and dipped in fiery chile lime sauce. In Venice, where scampi come hot off the grill crusted with bread crumbs (you'd think they would burn but they don't). In Australia, where shrimp on the barbie have come to symbolize the Ozzie obsession with grilling.

You want ancient? Grilled shellfish doesn't get much more primal than the *éclade* (mussels grilled on a bed of pine needles, as they do in western France). You want modern? Belgian grill maestro Peter De Clercq grills oysters with ginger, soy sauce, and wild blueberry jam; the combination sounds strange, but it works. And Spain's mad scientist of the grill, Victor Arguinzoniz, reaches for spray bottles of olive oil and wine whenever he grills shrimp.

All are motivated by a simple truth: Nothing brings out the sweetness, the succulence, the briny ocean flavor of shellfish like a bold blast of smoke and fire. So grab your shucking knife and lobster crackers—the feast is about to begin.

Previous page: A Caribbean barbecue smorgasbord.

Piri-Piri Prawns

THE SCOOP

WHERE: Mozambique, Angola, and South Africa

WHAT: Monster prawns glazed with a fiery African red chile sauce

HOW: Direct grilling

When the first Portuguese explorers landed in South America in the sixteenth century, they found a tiny, blazing red chile pepper known locally as *piri-piri* (sometimes called *pili-pili*). Such was its appeal that, within a few decades (an eyeblink in an age when an around-the-world sea voyage lasted several years), the *piri-piri* was being cultivated and cooked in Portuguese colonies that stretched literally around the planet, from Brazil to Mozambique; South Africa to India, Malaysia, and Macao. (If a few decades sounds long, think about how long it took sun-dried tomatoes or balsamic vinegar to make the rounds in our age of jet aviation.) The exact recipe for this dish varies from country to country, but all use some combination of *piri-piri* peppers or sauce, lemon or lime juice, and oil or

PIRI-PIRI PRAWNS

JUST THE FACTS:
Piri-piri describes a small bright red chile and an incendiary vinegary hot sauce made with it. You can find both at African and Brazilian markets, but credible substitutes include hot red Thai chiles, cayenne or serrano peppers, or a hot sauce, like Tabasco or Crystal. As for the prawns, the bigger the better. I like the almost lobster-size prawns that come two to a pound—preferably with the heads on, which gives you extra drama and flavor. If you are substituting shrimp, try grilling them in the shells. That's how they do it in Africa, and this too pumps up the flavor.

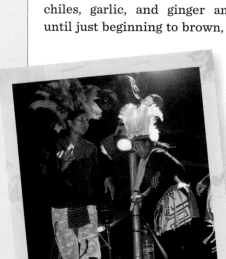

Zulu dancers at Moyo, a restaurant/cultural complex—there's one outside Cape Town and one in Johannesburg.

melted butter. No matter what the mix, this is one of the best ways to grill prawns. **SERVES 4**

6 tablespoons (¾ stick) salted butter

3 piri-piri chiles, or other hot chiles, seeded and minced (for hotter prawns, leave the seeds in)

2 cloves garlic, minced

1 tablespoon minced peeled fresh ginger

⅓ cup fresh lemon juice

3 to 6 tablespoons piri-piri sauce or a hot sauce such as Tabasco

Coarse salt (kosher or sea) and freshly ground black pepper

4 giant prawns in the shells with the heads on (each 8 to 10 ounces), or 1½ to 2 pounds headless shrimp in the shells

ADVANCE PREPARATION

30 minutes to 1 hour for marinating the prawns

1 Melt the butter in a nonreactive saucepan over high heat. Add the chiles, garlic, and ginger and cook until just beginning to brown, about 3 minutes. Immediately, add the lemon juice and *piri-piri* sauce and let simmer until syrupy and richly flavored, about 2 minutes. Season the mixture with salt and pepper to taste; the marinade should be highly seasoned. Let the marinade cool to room temperature.

2 Meanwhile, cut each prawn in half lengthwise and, using the tip of a bamboo skewer or the tine of a fork, remove the vein running the length of the tail. Arrange the prawns, cut side up, in a nonreactive baking dish just large enough to hold them. Spoon half of the *piri-piri* marinade on top and spread it over the prawns. Set the remaining marinade aside to use as a baste and sauce. Let the prawns marinate in the refrigerator, covered, for 30 minutes to 1 hour.

3 Set up the grill for direct grilling and preheat it to high.

4 Bring the reserved marinade to a boil, then remove it from the heat.

5 When ready to cook, brush and oil the grill grate. Drain the prawns, discarding their marinade, and arrange them on the hot grate cut side down so that they all face the same direction. Grill the prawns until they are browned on the cut side, 2 to 3 minutes. (If you are grilling shrimp, they will take about 2 minutes per side.) Turn the prawns, spoon a little of the boiled marinade over them, and continue grilling until the prawns are just cooked through, 3 to 5 minutes longer (they will feel firm to the touch). Do not overcook. Transfer the grilled prawns to a platter or plates. Spoon the remaining marinade on top and serve at once.

How to Peel and Devein Shrimp

Sure, you can buy shrimp that have been peeled and deveined already, but if you're lucky enough to find truly fresh shrimp, chances are you'll need to peel and devein them yourself. Here's how.

To peel a shrimp, grab the legs and pull off the shell; it's a little like peeling a tangerine.

To devein a shrimp there are a number of methods.

▶ Stick one tine of a fork (or use a bamboo skewer) into the back of the shrimp at the midpoint of its curve. Go in deep enough to snag the vein—about ¼ inch. Gently pull the fork away from the shrimp; the vein should come with it. Some shrimp won't have visible veins and in some shrimp that have been previously frozen the vein will break when you go to pull it out. In this case, use one of the other methods that follow.

▶ Insert the slender end of a shrimp deveiner (a long, slender, gently curved plastic device that sometimes has a serrated edge) into the large end of the shrimp. Gently push the deveiner along the shrimp; it will remove the vein.

▶ Using a sharp knife, make two parallel V-shaped cuts in the back of the shrimp running the full length. Remove the vein from the center of the cuts.

▶ You can also butterfly the shrimp: Cut it in half through the belly to but not through the back. Open the shrimp like a book and lightly flatten it with the side of a knife. Scrape out the vein with the tine of a fork or the point of a skewer.

▶ For the best flavor of all, grill the shrimp right in their shells. Make a cut down the back of the shells to remove the vein.

Kuwaiti Chile Shrimp

Most Americans know Kuwait as the country we defended in the first Gulf War and one of our few friends in the volatile Middle East. As for Kuwaiti barbecue—well, I'd venture to say it's a cuisine few of us have experienced. I certainly hadn't until I met Ahmed Jadallah, an engineer and grill fanatic who divides his time between Kuwait City and Salt Lake City (it's a long story involving a woman and a ski slope). It was Ahmed who introduced me to Kuwati-style prawns grilled in their shells, dipped in fiery garlic chile sauce, and eaten the most primal way of all—with your fingers. **SERVES 4**

5 cloves garlic, peeled and coarsely chopped

2 to 4 jalapeño peppers, seeded and coarsely chopped (for a hotter sauce, leave the seeds in)

1 teaspoon ground cumin, or to taste

Coarse salt (kosher or sea) and freshly ground black pepper

⅔ cup freshly squeezed lemon juice (from 3 to 4 lemons), or more to taste

2½ pounds jumbo shrimp or prawns in the shells (the larger the better) with the heads on, or 1½ to 2 pounds peeled and deveined shrimp

2 tablespoons extra-virgin olive oil or vegetable oil

ADVANCE PREPARATION

The dipping sauce can be made up to 4 hours ahead.

THE SCOOP

WHERE: Kuwait

WHAT: Shrimp grilled in the shells and served with a fiery chile garlic sauce for dipping

HOW: Direct grilling

JUST THE FACTS: In Kuwait you'd get huge Arabian Gulf prawns with their heads and shells intact. As the shells char they perfume the shrimp with a rich crustacean flavor. And there's the pleasure anyone from New Orleans will recognize of sucking the juices from the shrimp heads. Choose the largest prawns you can find—two to a pound would be ideal.

1 Place the garlic, jalapeños, cumin, 1½ teaspoons of salt, and 1 teaspoon of black pepper in a food processor and puree to a smooth paste. Work in the lemon juice and enough water (½ to ¾ cup) to obtain a thick but pourable sauce. The sauce can also be made in a blender, in which case, add the lemon juice and ½ cup of water first, then the garlic, jalapeños, cumin, salt, and pepper, adding more water if necessary. Or you can pound the garlic, jalapeños, cumin, salt, and pepper to a paste in a mortar with a pestle, then work in the liquids. Taste for seasoning, adding more cumin, salt, and/or lemon juice as necessary; the sauce should be fiery, tart, and salty. Place the dipping sauce in a serving bowl. The sauce can be made up to 4 hours ahead; taste it for seasoning before serving, adding more as necessary.

2 If you are using whole shrimp with their shells, make a lengthwise cut in the back (kitchen scissors work well for this) and pull or scrape out the vein with the tine of a fork. Lightly brush the shrimp with the olive oil on all sides and season them with salt and black pepper.

3 Set up the grill for direct grilling and preheat it to high.

4 When ready to cook, brush and oil the grill grate. Arrange the shrimp all facing in one direction on the hot grate and grill them until they are sizzling and browned and just cooked through, about 2 minutes per side for regular-size shrimp, 3 to 4 minutes per side for behemoths. When done the shrimp will feel firm to the touch (do not overcook them).

5 Transfer the grilled shrimp to a platter. To eat the shrimp, peel, if necessary, then plunge them in the dipping sauce. Use your fingers and have plenty of napkins on hand.

VARIATION

Kuwaiti Grilled Mackerel or Other Fish: Kuwaitis use the same grilling technique and dipping sauce for all manner of seafood, including oily fish like mackerel. Figure on ¾ pound of fish on the bone or 6 to 8 ounces of fish fillet per person.

Turmeric Grilled Prawns

THE SCOOP

WHERE: Malaysia

WHAT: Prawns marinated electric orange in turmeric, salt, and pepper then grilled over coconut shell charcoal

HOW: Direct grilling

If you want to experience authentic Malaysian grilled seafood, Azlinah Kudari is the woman you want to have prepare it. Recognizable by her black *hijab* (head covering) and a smile that lights up her face, Azlinah runs a waterfront restaurant in the Umbai Baru Floating Grilled Fish Village thirty-two kilometers south of the former spice trading city of Melaka. Umbai Baru is Malaysia's answer to the hawker centers of neighboring Singapore—a clean, modern facility with plumbing, and running water. A decade ago a band of port vendors worked off pushcarts; now they cook in scenic, hygienic surroundings on a pier jutting into the Strait of Malacca. What this means is that, no matter how sensitive your North American digestive system, you get to enjoy astonishingly flavorful Malaysian grilled seafood without subsequent risk of discomfort. Born in Kampong Baru and trained by the best cooks in all of Malaysia—her mother and grandmother—Azlinah is the sort of grill mistress who can work on ten different preparations at once without breaking a sweat. Her prawns feature a marinade that is uncharacteristically simple for a part of the world once defined by its spice trade: turmeric, salt, and black pepper. One flavor-blasted bite lets you know you're in the hands of a master. **SERVES 4**

4 teaspoons ground turmeric, or 1 piece
    (2 inches) fresh turmeric, peeled and
    coarsely chopped
1 piece (2 inches) fresh ginger, if not
    using fresh turmeric, peeled and
    coarsely chopped
2 teaspoons coarse salt (kosher or sea)
2 teaspoons freshly ground black pepper
3 tablespoons vegetable oil, or as needed,
    plus oil for basting
2½ pounds prawns or jumbo shrimp in
    the shells with the heads on, 2 pounds
    headless prawns or shrimp in the shells,
    or 1½ to 2 pounds peeled and deveined
    shrimp
Lime wedges or calamansi, for serving

YOU'LL ALSO NEED
Flat bamboo or metal skewers;
    an aluminum foil grill shield
    (optional, see page 611)

ADVANCE PREPARATION
30 minutes to 1 hour for marinating the prawns

1 Place the turmeric, ginger, if using, salt, and pepper in a food processor and puree to a fine paste. Work in enough oil (about 3 tablespoons) to obtain a thick wet paste. Or you can make the spice paste by pounding these ingredients together in a mortar using a pestle.

2 If you are using prawns with their heads on, make a cut down the back of the body with kitchen shears. Remove the vein using the tip of the tine of a fork or a bamboo skewer. If you are using headless shrimp with the shells on, cut the shells and remove the veins as described on page 485. Place the prawns in a large mixing bowl. Add the spice paste and gently stir to mix. Let the prawns marinate in the refrigerator, covered, for 30 minutes to 1 hour.

3 Set up the grill for direct grilling and preheat it to high.

4 When ready to cook, brush and oil the grill grate. Thread the prawns onto skewers and arrange them on the hot grate. (If you are using bamboo skewers, you may want to slide an aluminum foil shield under the exposed ends to keep them from burning.) Grill the prawns until they are browned on the outside and just cooked through, about 2 minutes per side, turning with tongs. When done, the prawns will feel firm to the touch (do not overcook them). Start basting the prawns with oil after 2 minutes. Serve the grilled prawns at once with lime wedges or *calamansi*.

JUST THE FACTS: In Malaysia, the marinade would be made with fresh turmeric, a bright orange root in the ginger family—the same root that, dried and ground, becomes the turmeric powder familiar to most Americans. (Among much else, it's used as a coloring in ballpark–style mustard.) If you live in an area with a large Southeast Asian community, you may be able to buy fresh turmeric roots at an Asian food market, in which case use a two-inch piece and omit the ginger. My work-around is to mix dried turmeric with fresh ginger—a substitution that not only tastes authentic, but gives you an extra jolt of flavor.

    Calamansi is a tiny round green citrus fruit with a flavor you could describe as a turbocharged lime.

Grilled Shrimp
Sprayed with Olive Oil and Wine

WHERE: The Basque Country in Spain

WHAT: About the simplest way you'll ever grill shrimp and one of the best: You spray it with Spanish olive oil and Basque *txakoli* wine and crust it with crunchy crystals of sea salt—that's it.

HOW: Direct grilling

JUST THE FACTS: Like any dish that contains only three ingredients, this one lives and dies by the quality of its raw materials. For the best results, use fresh (not pre-frozen) and wild (not farmed) shrimp, ideally with the heads intact. The olive oil should be Spanish, extra-virgin, used as soon after it was pressed as possible. (Two good brands are Marques de Valdueza and Castillo de Canena.) (Whatever you do, do *not* use nonstick spray.) *Txakoli* is a crisp dry Basque white wine. If unavailable, you could substitute sauvignon blanc, albariño, or pinot grigio.

Call this less is more food—as in the less you do to it, the more you'll enjoy it. This may surprise you coming from Victor Arguinzoniz, owner of the archly innovative grill restaurant Etxebarri in Spain's Basque Country. (Yes, the same Victor who grills baby eels in a wire mesh pan and smokes milk to make ice cream for dessert; see page 593.) But when it comes to grilling *gambas,* those huge sweet shrimp from Spain's southeast coast, Arguinzoniz insists that less is more. A light mist of olive oil keeps the shrimp moist over the fire, while crunchy crystals of sea salt reinforce the briny flavor—and give you something to crunch with your teeth. The wine is inspired by another Arguinzoniz preparation: oil- and wine-grilled fresh anchovies. Here it rounds out the flavor of the shrimp. **SERVES 4**

2½ pounds jumbo shrimp in the shells with the heads on, or 1½ to 2 pounds peeled and deveined shrimp
¼ cup txakoli or other dry white wine
¼ cup extra-virgin olive oil
Coarse sea salt

YOU'LL ALSO NEED
A spray bottle; an olive oil mister

ADVANCE PREPARATION
None, the spontaneity is the whole point.

1 If you are using shrimp with the heads on, peel and devein the bodies, leaving the tails on (see page 485). Place the wine in a spray bottle. Place the olive oil in an oil mister.

2 Set up the grill for direct grilling and preheat it to high.

3 When ready to cook, brush and oil the grill grate. Mist the shrimp on one side with olive oil. Arrange the shrimp oiled side down on the hot grate so that they all face the same direction. Lightly mist the top of the shrimp with more olive oil and spray with some wine. When the bottom of the shrimp is sizzling and browned, turn the shrimp over. Lightly spray this side with oil and wine. The cooking time is brief, about 2 minutes per side. When done the shrimp will feel firm to the touch (do not overcook them).

4 Transfer the grilled shrimp to a platter or plates, sprinkle them generously with salt, then serve at once.

FIRE STARTERS

Spain's Mad Scientist Griller

Pushing the limits of live-fire cooking, **VICTOR ARGUINZONIZ** reinvents traditional Spanish grilling. No food is safe from fires that blaze in his custom grills.

AXPE, SPAIN

He's been called the mad scientist of barbecue, the Ferran Adrià of the grill. His unassuming restaurant, Etxebarri (pronounced eche-varri), in the Basque town of Axpe, has become a place of pilgrimage for cutting-edge chefs from all over the world. His name is Victor Arguinzoniz and to look at him—white T-shirt and sneaks, hair swept back like some Basque Kevin Costner—you'd never guess he has quietly stood traditional Spanish grilling on its head.

No food is safe from the fires that blaze in his custom-designed grills. Not *kokotxas:* hake throats (a Basque delicacy), which he grills over homemade charcoal. Not *angulas,* Spain's celebrated baby eels, which he grills with garlic and chiles in a metal screen–lined grill pan. Not butter, which Arguinzoniz smokes with oak to spread on, what else? Not grilled bread. Not even milk, which he roasts in a wood-burning oven to make an astonishing smoked ice cream.

A former paper mill executive turned chef, Arguinzoniz taught himself how to cook and run a restaurant. But his passion for grilling he attributes to his grandmother. "As a child, I would watch, mesmerized, as she cooked over the only cooking device she owned—her wood-burning fireplace," Arguinzoniz

That he burns only lump charcoal at the restaurant is a given. That he makes it from scratch from oak and fruitwood logs each morning indicates a passion bordering on obsession.

recalls. "I can still taste the smoke and fire in her cooking every time I fire up the grill."

Despite his Daliesque imagination, Arguinzoniz' cooking remains firmly rooted in traditional Basque flavors. My first meal at Etxebarri featured grilled anchovies sprayed with Spanish olive oil and *txakoli* wine, a cappuccino of *setas* (grilled wild mushrooms), a single, magnificent grilled *gamba* (jumbo prawn) with piquillo pepper sauce, and iconic Basque *chuletón,* grass-fed beef rib steak (see page 164). "I admire the molecular cuisine of guys like Arzak and Ferran," Arguinzoniz says, "but my food is pretty traditional and down to earth."

Like all great chefs, Arguinzoniz has the uncanny ability to make every ingredient taste just like itself, only better. Of course, that was last year. Who knows where Victor's experiments with live-fire cooking have taken him since?

NAME: Victor Arguinzoniz

TERRITORY: Basque Country, Spain

CLAIM TO FAME: Chef-owner of one of the most innovative grill restaurants in the world, Etxebarri

SPECIALTIES: So many and they change often. Grilled bread with smoked butter or smoked *bacalao* (creamed salt cod). *Anchoas a la brasa* (grilled anchovies). *Angulas a la brasa* (grilled baby eels). *Kokotxas a la brasa* (grilled hake throats). Smoked ice cream (see page 593).

ARGUINZONIZ SAYS:

▶ The grill defines the taste, texture, and smell of the food. Use it wisely.

▶ Cook on your grill on a daily basis. Mastery comes through practice.

▶ We make our own charcoal every day. Cheap charcoal or briquettes have an aggressive odor that overwhelms the food.

▶ It's your job to control the fire, not let it control you.

Shrimp on the Barbie (#2)

Australia doesn't have a single national grilled specialty in the way that jerk epitomizes Jamaican barbecue or yakitori says Japan. But one Ozzie (as Australians refer to themselves) dish familiar to grillers the world over is the iconic shrimp on the barbie ("barbie" is an affectionate name for a barbecue grill). Curiously, there's no one traditional way to prepare this: If your forbears emigrated from Asia, you use the sesame, soy, and star-anise flavored marinade found in my first shrimp on the barbie recipe in *The Barbecue! Bible,* hence the name of this one: #2. Here's how you might make it if your ancestors came from southern France or northern Italy. The idea comes from my

SHRIMP ON THE BARBIE (#2)

HOW TO MAKE SHRIMP ON THE BARBIE

1. *Wrap each peeled deveined shrimp in a fresh basil leaf.*

2. *Next, wrap the shrimp and basil in a thin slice of prosciutto.*

3. *Pin the prosciutto and basil in place with toothpicks.*

Flambé the shrimp with Pernod or absinthe just prior to serving.

Ozzie grilling buddy, Bob Hart, who writes for the Melbourne *Herald Sun*. The sweet licorice flavor from the Pernod and basil counterpoints the smoky saltiness of the grilled shrimp and prosciutto. Nice! **SERVES 4**

1½ to 2 pounds jumbo shrimp, peeled and deveined
   (see page 485)
Coarse salt (kosher or sea) and freshly ground black pepper
1 bunch fresh basil leaves
6 ounces very thinly sliced prosciutto, cut lengthwise into
   1½ inch–wide strips
1 to 2 tablespoons extra-virgin olive oil
½ cup Pernod, absinthe, or other anise-flavored aperitif
Lemon wedges, for serving

YOU'LL ALSO NEED
Wooden toothpicks or small bamboo skewers

ADVANCE PREPARATION
None, but the shrimp can be wrapped several hours
   prior to grilling.

1 Season the shrimp on both sides with salt and pepper. Wrap a basil leaf around each shrimp, then wrap it in a strip of prosciutto. Secure the prosciutto in place with toothpicks. Drizzle the olive oil over the shrimp to coat them lightly on both sides or brush on the oil with a pastry brush.

2 Set up the grill for direct grilling and preheat it to high.

3 When ready to cook, brush and oil the grill grate. Arrange the shrimp all facing in the same direction on the hot grate and grill them until the prosciutto is sizzling and crisp and the shrimp are just cooked through, about 2 minutes per side; do not overcook them. Transfer the grilled shrimp to a platter or plates.

4 Pour the Pernod into a small saucepan, place it on the grill, and warm the Pernod until it is just body temperature—do not let it boil. Remove the pan from the heat and, making sure that the area is clear of flammable material and that no one is standing too close, use a long match to ignite the Pernod. Very carefully pour the flaming Pernod over the shrimp and serve them at once, with lemon wedges.

Venetian Shrimp Grilled with Bread Crumbs and Sage

{ GAMBERONI AL FERRI }

WHERE: Venice, Italy

WHAT: Shrimp skewered with fresh sage leaves and grilled with homemade bread crumbs over olive wood charcoal

HOW: Direct grilling

JUST THE FACTS: Venetian shrimp are always fresh and almost always sold and grilled with the heads intact, a practice that adds considerable drama, not to mention the primal pleasure of sucking the flavorful juices out of the heads. If you're lucky enough to live near a fishmonger that sells whole shrimp or prawns, I urge you to try them.

Olive wood chunks are available on my Web site: www.barbecuebible.com/store.

That Venetians serve some of the most pristine seafood on the planet is obvious (thanks to the nutrient-rich waters of the lagoon). It is less obvious that Venetian seafood would be served hot off the grill. After all, this island city possesses no natural source of wood or charcoal, and there are stringent regulations in place forbidding the burning of either, lest a stray spark set fire to a centuries-old palazzo. Where there's a rule in Italy, however, there's always an exception, and the charcoal-burning grill at the Ristorante Da Ivo was installed before the current building code forbade it. So how does Da Ivo grill shrimp? Using a method better suited to panfrying: dredged in dried bread crumbs. You might think the bread crumbs would burn; they don't—at least not if you work over a moderate fire. You might think the shrimp would be dry; they aren't—thanks to a simple sauce of garlic, parsley, and olive oil known as *salsa verde*. Add the scent of flame-singed sage leaves and you wind up with some of the tastiest shrimp you'll experience anywhere. **SERVES 4**

FOR THE SALSA VERDE
¼ cup firmly packed rinsed, stemmed, chopped fresh flat-leaf parsley
1 clove garlic, minced
¼ teaspoon salt, or more to taste
½ cup extra-virgin olive oil

FOR THE SHRIMP
2 pounds jumbo shrimp in the shells with the heads on, or 1½ to 2 pounds peeled and deveined shrimp
1 bunch fresh sage leaves
1 to 2 tablespoons extra-virgin olive oil
1 cup dried bread crumbs, preferably homemade, in a shallow dish

Coarse salt (kosher or sea) and freshly ground black pepper
Lemon wedges, for serving

YOU'LL ALSO NEED
Metal skewers

ADVANCE PREPARATION
The salsa verde can be made up to 2 hours ahead.

1 Make the *salsa verde:* Place the parsley, garlic, and ¼ teaspoon of salt on a cutting board and, using a chef's knife, finely chop them. Alternatively, you can chop them in a food processor. Place the parsley mixture in a small serving bowl and whisk in the ½ cup of olive oil. Taste for seasoning, adding more salt if necessary. Set the *salsa verde* aside.

2 Prepare the shrimp: If you are using shrimp with the heads on, peel and devein the bodies, leaving the tails on (see page 485). Thread the shrimp onto skewers, skewering each shrimp through both the head and tail ends and placing a whole sage leaf between each shrimp and at each end of the skewers.

3 Set up the grill for direct grilling and preheat it to medium-high. Leave one section of the grill unlit or coal-free for a safety zone.

4 When ready to cook, brush and oil the grill grate. Lightly brush each kebab on both sides with olive oil and season them with salt and pepper. Dredge each shrimp kebab in the bread crumbs until lightly coated, shaking off the excess.

5 Arrange the shrimp on the hot grate with the skewers on a diagonal to the bars and grill the kebabs until the bread crumbs are golden brown and the shrimp is just cooked through, 2 to 3 minutes per side. When done, the shrimp will feel firm to the touch (do not overcook them). If the bread crumbs start to burn before the shrimp is cooked through, move the shrimp to the safety zone.

6 Unskewer the grilled shrimp onto a platter or plates. Spoon a little of the *salsa verde* over the shrimp and serve the rest of the *salsa verde* and lemon wedges on the side.

Grilled Shrimp with Fiery Lemongrass Chile Sambal

Reading *Planet Barbecue* you might get the impression that for most of the last three years, I've done nothing but prowl night markets and food stalls. True, a lot of great grilling takes place on Third World street corners, but you can also find some pretty spectacular barbecue at luxury resorts. Consider the ultraposh Amandari in Bali, a hotel built into the top tier of a rice paddy near the artist town of Ubud. At one such barbecue my wife, Barbara, and I dined in an open pavilion next to a lily pond at a table for two strewn with rose petals. Dinner began with a Balinese welcome dance performed by local children in gold-embroidered gowns. The cooking was done on portable charcoal grills by a team of chefs assigned to grill for us and us alone that evening. The succession of dishes—grilled shrimp with fiery

THE SCOOP

WHERE: Indonesia

WHAT: Grilled shrimp with an incendiary Balinese *sambal* (cooked salsa) of lemongrass, chiles, and ginger

HOW: Direct grilling

JUST THE FACTS: First, the bad news: To make this dish truly authentic, you'd need a green market of exotic ingredients—salam leaves, candlenuts, fresh turmeric, greater and lesser galangal—to mention a few. If you live in an area with a large Southeast Asian community or you're an adept shopper on the Internet, you can find these ingredients. The good news is that the vibrant flavor of the spice paste and grilled shrimp can be approximated easily using ingredients readily available at your supermarket. That's the version you'll find here, but if you are so inclined, you can certainly replace the bay leaf with salam leaves, the macadamia nuts with candlenuts, the ground turmeric with fresh, and the ginger with galangal.

lemongrass *sambal,* Balinese grilled chicken, whole grilled fish with Kaffir lime leaves—revealed Balinese cooking in all its polymorphic glory, a profoundly complex cuisine only hinted at at a street corner grill stall.

Sambals are intensely flavorful condiments served with simple grilled foods; the gustatory pyrotechnics of the chiles, lemongrass, and ginger counter the simplicity of the grilled shellfish. **SERVES 4**

FOR THE SAMBAL

4 to 8 bird's eye or Thai chiles, or 2 to 4 jalapeño
    peppers, seeded and coarsely chopped
    (for a hotter sambal, leave the seeds in)
2 stalks lemongrass, trimmed and coarsely
    chopped
4 shallots, coarsely chopped
4 cloves garlic, coarsely chopped
1 piece (1½ inches) fresh ginger, peeled and
    coarsely chopped
6 macadamia nuts
1 bay leaf, crumbled
1 tablespoon light brown sugar
2 teaspoons ground turmeric
1 teaspoon coarse salt (kosher or sea)
½ teaspoon freshly ground black pepper
2 tablespoons vegetable oil

FOR THE SHRIMP AND MARINADE

2 pounds jumbo shrimp in the shells with the
    heads on, or 1½ to 2 pounds peeled and
    deveined shrimp (see Note)
Coarse salt (kosher or sea) and freshly ground
    black pepper
3 tablespoons fresh lime juice
3 tablespoons vegetable oil (optional, use only if
    you are using peeled and deveined shrimp)

ADVANCE PREPARATION

20 minutes for marinating the shrimp

1 Make the *sambal:* Place the chiles, lemongrass, shallots, garlic, ginger, macadamia nuts, bay leaf, brown sugar, turmeric, salt, and black pepper in a food processor and puree to a paste, running the machine in short bursts. Work in the 2 tablespoons of oil and 1 cup of water.

2 Place the *sambal* mixture in a wok or large, deep pot over medium heat. Cook the *sambal* until the water evaporates and the paste turns a golden brown, 20 to 30 minutes. Stir the *sambal* often with a wooden spoon to keep it from burning. Let the *sambal* cool to room temperature, then transfer it to 4 small bowls for serving.

3 Prepare the shrimp and marinade: If you are using shrimp with the heads and shells on, using kitchen shears, make a cut in the shell along the rounded back of each tail. Using the tip of the tine of a fork or a bamboo skewer, scrape out the vein. Place the shrimp in a nonreactive baking dish and season them with salt and black pepper. Drizzle the lime juice and 2 tablespoons of vegetable oil, if using, over the shrimp. Let the shrimp marinate for 20 minutes.

4 Set up the grill for direct grilling and preheat it to high.

5 When ready to cook, brush and oil the grill grate. Drain the shrimp and arrange them all facing in the same direction on the hot grate. Grill the shrimp until browned on the outside and just cooked through, about 2 minutes per side. When done the shrimp will feel firm to the touch (do not overcook them).

6 Transfer the grilled shrimp to a platter or plates and serve the bowls of *sambal* on the side for dipping the shrimp in or spooning on top.

NOTE: As on much of Planet Barbecue, Indonesians grill shrimp in the shells and serve them with the heads on. The shells keep the shrimp from drying out and add a great shellfish flavor when charred. The heads are packed with savory juices for anyone adventurous enough to suck them. You can certainly use peeled, deveined shrimp here. Skewer them on flat bamboo skewers.

Mauritius Shrimp or Squid Kebabs with Ginger Turmeric Glaze

The Republic of Mauritius, an island located in the Indian Ocean off the coast of Africa, has a complicated history. These simple kebabs have everything you'd expect from its melting-pot culture—a wine-based marinade reminiscent of those made by the French, who ruled the island for more than a century; the pungent rhizomes ginger and turmeric, popular with the island's Indian descendants; and the counterpoint of fruity and salty, in this case, fresh pineapple and shellfish, typical of so much of the grilling of the tropics. **SERVES 4**

THE SCOOP

WHERE: The island of Mauritius

WHAT: Kaleidoscopically colorful kebabs of shrimp or squid with pineapple and vegetables

HOW: Direct grilling

JUST THE FACTS: You find these kebabs made with both shrimp and squid at Mauritius island grill shacks. I call for shrimp as the default seafood, but if you live in California or elsewhere where you can get thick calamari steaks or even calamari bodies, this is a great way to grill them. Fresh turmeric is readily available in Mauritius (and at Southeast Asian markets in the United States), so it's included here, but ground turmeric will give you fine results, too.

FOR THE KEBABS

1½ to 2 pounds jumbo shrimp, peeled and deveined, or 1½ pounds calamari steaks, cut into 1-inch squares

4 plum tomatoes

1 large onion, peeled

2 green bell peppers

½ pineapple, peeled, cored, and cut into ½-inch slices

FOR THE MARINADE

½ cup dry white wine

¼ cup vegetable oil

3 tablespoons fresh lemon juice

3 tablespoons soy sauce

3 sprigs fresh thyme, or ½ teaspoon dried thyme

1 tablespoon minced, peeled fresh ginger

1 tablespoon minced, peeled fresh turmeric, or 1 teaspoon ground turmeric

1 teaspoon coarse salt (kosher or sea)

½ teaspoon freshly ground black pepper

YOU'LL ALSO NEED

Flat bamboo or metal skewers; an aluminum foil grill shield (optional, see page 611)

ADVANCE PREPARATION

30 minutes to 1 hour for marinating the kebabs

1 Prepare the kebabs: Cut the firm tomato flesh off the seeds and pulp by making 3 or 4 downward slices to remove the outside of the tomato with the skin intact. The result will be pure tomato flesh, sometimes called the "fillet." Cut each slice of tomato flesh into 1-inch pieces. Finely dice the seeds and pulp and set them aside for the marinade.

2 Cut the onion in half crosswise and cut each half in quarters. Break each quarter into layers. You'll use the larger pieces for making the kebabs. Finely dice the smaller pieces and set them aside for the marinade.

3 Core and seed the bell peppers and cut them into 1-inch squares. Finely dice any scraps of bell pepper and set them aside for the marinade. Cut the pineapple slices into 1-inch pieces.

4 Thread the shrimp and the pieces of tomato, onion layers, bell pepper, and pineapple onto skewers, alternating the ingredients in a regular and colorful pattern. Leave at least 4 inches of the skewer exposed at the end to make a handle. Place the kebabs in a nonreactive baking dish large enough to hold them in a single layer.

5 Make the marinade: Place the white wine, oil, lemon juice, soy sauce, thyme, ginger, turmeric, salt, black pepper and the diced tomato, onion, and bell peppers, in a nonreactive mixing bowl and whisk to mix. Pour the marinade over the kebabs, turning them several times to coat each with marinade. Let the kebabs marinate in the refrigerator, covered, for 30 minutes to 1 hour, turning them once or twice so they marinate evenly.

6 Remove the kebabs from the marinade and strain the marinade into a saucepan, discarding the solids. Bring the marinade to a boil over high heat and let boil until reduced by about half, about 5 minutes. You'll use this mixture for basting the kebabs. The kebabs can be prepared several hours ahead to this stage.

7 Set up the grill for direct grilling and preheat it to high.

8 When ready to cook, brush and oil the grill grate. Arrange the kebabs on the hot grate and grill until nicely browned on the outside and just cooked through, 2 to 4 minutes per side. When done, the shrimp will feel firm to the touch; do not overcook them. (If you are using bamboo skewers, you may want to slide an aluminum foil shield under the exposed ends to keep them from burning.) Start basting the kebabs with some of the reduced marinade after 2 minutes. Transfer the kebabs to a platter or plates and serve at once with the remaining basting mixture spooned over.

Scampi Kebabs with Dalmatian Ham

I'm not sure anyone has ever described barbecue in terms of ballet, but that's exactly what takes place each lunch and dinner behind the glass window that looks into the kitchen of Konoba Varos in Split, Croatia. What else would you call the complex dance of three master grillers working on one charcoal-burning grill, turning out hundreds of orders of grilled seafood and meat—with not a single fish fillet sticking to the grill grate? These grilled shrimp and ham kebabs epitomize Croatian grilling, with its emphasis on pristine ingredients (especially seafood) seasoned and served as simply as possible. The combination of sweet briny shrimp and smoky ham creates a kebab with a flavor that's much greater than the sum of its parts. I've made the onion optional, as not all Croatian grill masters use it. **SERVES 4**

2 pounds jumbo shrimp, in the shells with the heads on, or 1½ to 2 pounds peeled and deveined shrimp (see Note)
1 sweet onion (optional), peeled
6 ounces Dalmatian or other smoked ham, thinly sliced (just shy of ⅛ inch) and cut into 1-inch squares
Coarse salt (kosher or sea) and freshly ground black pepper
Extra-virgin olive oil, for drizzling and basting
Lemon wedges, for serving

YOU'LL ALSO NEED

Flat bamboo or metal skewers; an aluminum foil grill shield (optional, see page 611)

ADVANCE PREPARATION
None

The waterfront of Split, Croatia—a lively city built around the villa of the 3rd century A.D. Roman emperor Diocletian. The villa walls still stand today.

A fish market in Split, Croatia, where the seafood is so fresh, it swam in the Adriatic the night before.

1 If you are using shrimp with the heads on, peel and devein the bodies, leaving the tails on. If you are using onion, cut it in half crosswise, then cut each half in quarters. Break the quarters into layers.

2 Thread the shrimp onto skewers, skewering each shrimp through both the head and tail ends and placing a square of ham and a piece of onion, if using, between each shrimp. Arrange the kebabs in a baking dish and season them on all sides with salt and pepper. Drizzle a little olive oil over the kebabs, turning them to coat on all sides.

3 Set up the grill for direct grilling and preheat it to high.

4 When ready to cook, brush and oil the grill grate. Grill the kebabs until the shrimp are browned on the outside and just cooked through, about 2 minutes per side, basting the kebabs with olive oil after the first minute of grilling. When done, the shrimp will feel firm to the touch; do not overcook them. (If you are using bamboo skewers, you may want to slide an aluminum foil shield under the exposed ends to keep them from burning.)

5 Transfer the grilled kebabs to a platter or plates and serve at once with lemon wedges.

NOTE: For the best results use fresh, not frozen shrimp, ideally with the heads on. For instructions on peeling and deveining shrimp, see page 485.

Lobster the Way We Grill It on Martha's Vineyard

THE SCOOP

WHERE: Massachusetts, U.S.A.

WHAT: Grilled lobster with garlic herb butter—that's it

HOW: Direct grilling

As many of you may know, when I'm not traveling Planet Barbecue, I spend much of the year on Martha's Vineyard. Of course we grill, and naturally, the first thing to hit the embers is the local seafood. For most people lobster means a crustacean boiled in seawater. Boiling helps keep the meat moist, but grilling roasts the shells, and gives the meat a complex flavor you simply can't achieve with a pot of water. Besides, few sights are cooler than a grill full of bright orange lobsters lined up, sizzling over the coals. The only remotely challenging part of this recipe is splitting the lobsters—best done quickly with a large knife. You'll find instructions below, but you may feel more comfortable parboiling the lobsters first. **SERVES 2 AND CAN BE MULTIPLIED AS DESIRED**

My wife, Barbara, and Japanese friends, Shiori and Makoto, enjoy lobster in the rough at Larsen's Fish Market in Menemsha.

6 tablespoons (¾ stick) salted butter

1 clove garlic, peeled and crushed with the
    side of a knife

2 tablespoons chopped fresh flat-leaf parsley, chives,
    tarragon, basil, and/or any other fresh herb

2 Maine lobsters (each about 1½ pounds)

Coarse sea salt and freshly ground black pepper

ADVANCE PREPARATION
None

1 Melt the butter in a saucepan over medium-high heat (you can do this on the stove, on the grill, or on your grill's side burner). Add the garlic and herbs and cook until sizzling and fragrant, about 2 minutes, stirring with a wooden spoon. Do not let the garlic brown. Remove the pan with the herb butter from the heat and set it aside.

2 If you want to parboil the lobsters, pour water to a depth of 3 inches in a very large pot and bring it to a boil over high heat. Add the lobsters and let them boil, covered, for about 3 minutes. Drain the lobsters in a colander, rinse them with cold water until cool, then drain them again.

3 When ready to cook, starting with 1 lobster and using a thick cloth to hold it, place the lobster on a grooved cutting board, or a baking sheet with raised sides, to catch the juices. If you have not parboiled the lobsters, insert a large heavy chef's knife in the back of the head between the eyes; this will dispatch the lobster instantly. Continue cutting the lobster, making a lengthwise cut down the back, pressing the knife to, but not through the soft bottom shell. Pry the lobster open (the process is a little like spatchcocking). Cut off the large claws and set them aside. Remove the papery gray sack from the head and the vein that runs the length of the tail. You can leave or discard the tomale (the green stuff—actually the liver) and/or, if you have a female, the blackish-blue stuff, which is the roe. Of course, I would leave these. Pour any lobster juices into a bowl; you'll baste the lobster meat with these as the lobster grills. Repeat with the remaining lobster. Season the lobsters with salt and pepper to taste.

4 Set up the grill for direct grilling and preheat it to high. Ideally, you'll grill over wood embers (see page 603). Brush and oil the grill grate.

5 Arrange the lobster claws on the hot grate and grill until orange and beginning to brown, 3 to 4 minutes per side if raw, 2 to 3 minutes per side if parboiled. Move the claws to a cooler part of the grill to keep warm. Arrange the lobster bodies on the grate, cut side down, and grill them until the meat starts to brown, about 3 minutes if raw, about 2 minutes if parboiled. Turn the lobsters over and pour any lobster juices over the lobster meat. Continue grilling the lobsters cut side up until the meat is cooked through, 4 to 6 minutes if started raw, 3 to 5 minutes if parboiled first. When the lobsters are cooked the meat will be firm and white; do not overcook them. Baste the lobster meat with the herb butter after it has grilled cut side up for about 2 minutes and baste it again right before serving. Transfer the remaining herb butter to 2 ramekins.

6 Serve the lobster at once, with lobster crackers for the claws and the remaining herb butter for dipping. You eat the lobster with your hands.

JUST THE FACTS: A dish this simple lives and dies by its freshness. For the best results, use live lobsters—preferably from a fish market, not from a tired old lobster tank at the supermarket. One good mail-order source is www.lobsterselect.com. I like female lobsters because of their caviarlike roe; my wife prefers males precisely because they lack the roe. To identify the sex of a lobster, examine the first set of swimmerettes on the underside at the junction of the body and the tail. In a male, these will be hard; in a female they're soft and feathery.

Grilled Maine or Spiny Lobster with Garlic Sauce

{ LANGOSTA CON MOJO DE AJO }

THE SCOOP

WHERE: Mexico

WHAT: Lobster basted with butter and Worcestershire sauce, served with Mexican fried garlic sauce

HOW: Direct grilling

JUST THE FACTS: To most North Americans, lobster means *Homarus americanus* (Maine lobster), recognizable by its large meaty claws. But elsewhere on the world's barbecue trail, the lobster that is most commonly grilled belongs to a family of clawless lobsters (the *Palinuridae*) that includes Florida's spiny lobster, France's *langouste*, and South Africa's rock lobster. And traditionally that's the lobster you would use to prepare this dish. What you lose in claw meat, you gain in tail meat (of which there's more in a spiny lobster). And because the flesh of a spiny lobster is firmer and drier than Maine lobster, it holds up well when exposed to the heat of the fire.

I first tasted this garlic-blasted grilled lobster at a seaside fish shack on Mexico's Isla Mujeres. On receiving my order, the chef walked out on a pier, extracted a spiny lobster from a metal cage in the water, and whacked it in half, using a large chef's knife. The glaze featured an unexpected ingredient: *salsa inglese*—literally "English sauce," as Worcestershire sauce is often called in these parts, which always strikes me as odd because Mexico is one of the few places in North America not at some point colonized by the English. I was also intrigued by the garlic sauce, here called a *mojo,* like the fried garlic sauce popular in Cuba and the Spanish Caribbean, rather than the more common Mexican salsa. Put the lobster, glaze, and garlic sauce together and you get the perfect Mexican grilled seafood dish for people who like bold flavor but not chile hellfire. **SERVES 4**

3 tablespoons salted butter

2 tablespoons Worcestershire sauce

2 tablespoons fresh lime juice, or more to taste

⅓ cup extra-virgin olive oil or vegetable oil

3 cloves garlic, thinly sliced or finely chopped

3 tablespoons minced onion

⅓ cup finely chopped fresh flat-leaf parsley or cilantro, or a mixture of the two

Coarse salt (kosher or sea) and freshly ground black pepper

4 live Maine lobsters (each about 1½ pounds), or 4 live spiny lobsters (each about 1 pound)

ADVANCE PREPARATION

None—unless you decide to parboil the lobsters, but the *mojo de ajo* can be made ahead.

1 Melt the butter in a small nonreactive saucepan over high heat. Add the Worcestershire sauce and 1 tablespoon of lime juice and let boil until syrupy, about 2 minutes. Set the glaze aside.

2 Heat the olive oil in a nonreactive saucepan over medium heat. Add the garlic, onion, and parsley and/or cilantro and cook until lightly browned, 2 to 3 minutes. Add ¼ cup of water and the remaining 1 tablespoon of lime juice and let boil until syrupy and rich flavored, about 2 minutes. Taste for seasoning, adding salt and pepper to taste and more lime juice as necessary. The glaze and the garlic sauce can be made up to 2 hours ahead.

3 If you want to parboil the lobsters, pour water to a depth of 3 inches in a very large pot and bring it to a boil over high heat. Add the lobsters and let them boil, covered, for about 3 minutes. Drain the lobsters in a colander, rinse them with cold water until cool, then drain them again.

4 When ready to cook, starting with 1 lobster and using a thick cloth to hold it, place the lobster on a grooved cutting board, or a baking sheet with raised sides, to catch the juices. If you have not parboiled the lobsters, insert a large heavy chef's knife in the back of the head between the eyes; this will instantly dispatch the lobster. Cut each lobster in half lengthwise. If using Maine lobsters, cut off the large claws and set them

aside. Remove the papery gray sack from the head and the vein that runs the length of the tail of the lobsters. You can leave or discard the tomale (the green stuff—actually the liver) and/or, if you have a female, the blackish-blue stuff, which is the roe. Of course, I would leave these. Pour any lobster juices into a bowl; you'll baste the lobster meat with these as the lobster grills. Repeat with the remaining lobsters.

5 Set up the grill for direct grilling and preheat it to high.

6 When ready to cook, brush and oil the grill grate. Brush the cut side of the lobsters with one

GRILLED LOBSTER WITH GARLIC SAUCE

third of the glaze and season them with salt and pepper. Arrange the lobster claws, if any, on the hot grate and grill until orange and beginning to brown 3 to 4 minutes per side if started raw, 2 to 3 minutes per side if parboiled first. Move the claws to a cooler part of the grill to keep warm. Arrange the lobster halves, cut side down, on the hot grate at a diagonal to the bars. Grill the lobsters until the cut sides are nicely browned, about 4 minutes if raw, about 3 minutes if parboiled, giving each half lobster a quarter turn after 2 minutes to create a handsome crosshatch of grill marks.

7 Turn the lobsters over and pour any lobster juices over the lobster meat. Continue grilling the lobsters cut side up until the meat is cooked through, 3 to 6 minutes longer if raw, 2 to 5 minutes

if parboiled, depending on the size of the lobsters. When the lobsters are cooked the meat will be firm and white; do not overcook them. As they grill, baste the lobsters with the remaining glaze.

8 Transfer the grilled lobsters to a platter or plates. Spoon some of the garlic sauce over each lobster and serve the remainder on the side.

VARIATION

Grilled Shrimp or Fish with Mojo de Ajo: The glaze and garlic sauce work equally well when grilling shrimp or fish. You can thread 1½ pounds of shelled shrimp onto skewers and grill them with the glaze. Or grill 1½ to 2 pounds of fish steaks or fillets with the glaze. Serve the garlic sauce on the side.

Apostles on Horseback

New Zealanders may be as barbecue obsessed as their neighbors in Australia, but besides a traditional method of underground pit roasting called *hangi,* there doesn't seem to be a repertory of uniquely Kiwi grilled dishes. What New Zealanders do boast of is superb raw materials— award-winning olive oils, lamb renowned throughout the world, and seafood that would make even a coastal New Englander's mouth water. The following, from a Kiwi grilling enthusiast named Daniel O'Dea, riffs on British angels on horseback (oysters with bacon): scallops grilled in honey-cured smoked bacon and basted with a honey and lime glaze. Barbecue doesn't get much simpler—or better—than this. SERVES 4

¾ cup crisp dry white wine, such as a New Zealand
   sauvignon blanc

⅓ cup fresh lime juice

⅓ cup honey

1 teaspoon coarse salt (kosher or sea)

Freshly ground black pepper

1½ pounds sea scallops

6 ounces thickly sliced bacon, preferably natural honey cured,
   cut crosswise into 4-inch strips

YOU'LL ALSO NEED

Wooden toothpicks; 2 cups of your favorite wood chips for
   smoking (optional), soaked for 1 hour in water to cover,
   then drained

ADVANCE PREPARATION

30 minutes to 1 hour for marinating the scallops

1 Place the wine, lime juice, honey, salt, and pepper in a large nonreactive bowl and whisk until the salt dissolves.

2 If you're reading this in New Zealand (or Europe), you can buy and grill your scallops with the roe (the coral colored eggs) intact. In North America you'll be buying trimmed scallops. All you need to do is remove and discard the small crescent-shaped muscle on the side of each scallop. This is optional (I call it "circumcising" the scallop), but it will make the scallop more tender. Stir the scallops into the marinade and let marinate in the refrigerator, covered, for 30 minutes to 1 hour.

3 Drain the scallops well, discarding the marinade. Wrap each scallop in a strip of bacon, securing it with a toothpick.

4 Set up the grill for direct grilling and preheat it to medium.

5 When ready to cook, brush and oil the grill grate. If you are using a charcoal grill, toss the wood chips or chunks on the coals. If you are using a gas grill, add the wood chips or chunks to the smoker box or place them in a smoker pouch under the grate (see page 603). Arrange the wrapped scallops on the hot grate and grill them until the bacon is browned and crisp and the scallops are just cooked through, 2 to 3 minutes per side, plus 1 or 2 minutes on the edges to crisp the bacon; 6 to 10 minutes in all. If the bacon fat causes a flare-up, move the scallops to another part of the grill. Transfer the grilled scallops to a platter or plates or simply serve them hot off the grill.

Seafood trailer shack on New Zealand's Kaikoura Coast. Fresh and unpretentious is how Kiwis like their seafood.

Me and my friend Lionel with a fresh haul of scallops.

Oysters Smoked on the Half Shell

THE SCOOP

WHERE: Martha's Vineyard, Massachusetts, U.S.A.

WHAT: Oyster roast New England style— smoke-grilled on the half shell

HOW: Direct grilling

JUST THE FACTS: It helps to grill the oysters in a shellfish rack, which holds the bivalves level so you can grill them without spilling the juices. Two models are the Great Grate (www.greatgrate.com) and my own shellfish rack (www.barbecuebible.com/store).

Permit me a moment of hometown chauvinism. The best smoked oysters in the world are served right here on my island summer home: Martha's Vineyard. More precisely, you find them at the Water Street restaurant in our vintage nineteenth-century whaling village, Edgartown. The Water Street chef has the good sense to start with superlative shellfish from Katama Bay and smoke roast them with nothing more than a pat of sweet butter. The smoky, briny succulent result is barbecue bliss on a half shell. **MAKES 12 OYSTERS; SERVES 2 TO 3 AS AN APPETIZER, 1 TO 2 AS A LIGHT MAIN COURSE**

12 large oysters in the shell
3 tablespoons unsalted butter, cut into 12 pieces
Crusty bread, for serving

YOU'LL ALSO NEED
An oyster knife for shucking the oysters;
  1½ cups hickory, oak, or apple wood chips
  or chunks, soaked for 1 hour in water
  to cover, then drained; a shellfish rack
  (optional; see Just the Facts, this page)

ADVANCE PREPARATION
None; the beauty of this preparation is its
  spontaneity.

1 Set up the grill for indirect grilling, place a drip pan in the center, and preheat the grill to medium-high. For the best results, use a charcoal grill. If you are using a gas grill, add the wood chips or chunks to the smoker box or place them in a smoker pouch under the grate (see page 603).

2 Just before grilling, shuck the oysters, discarding the top shells (see Note). Swipe the knife under the oysters to loosen them from the bottom shells. Take pains not to spill the juices. Arrange the oysters in a shellfish rack, if using, and place a piece of butter on top of each oyster.

3 When ready to cook, if you are using a charcoal grill, toss the wood chips or chunks on the coals. Place the oysters on the shellfish rack, if using, in the center of the grate over the drip pan and away from the heat, and cover the grill. Grill the oysters until the butter is melted and the oysters are just barely cooked, 5 to 10 minutes or to taste (I like them warm but still raw in the center). Serve the oysters with crusty bread, grilled, if desired.

NOTE: To shuck an oyster, insert the tip of a shucking knife into the hinge of the bivalve (the narrow end, where the shells are connected). Gently twist the blade to pry the shells apart. Then, slide the blade under the top shell to cut the muscle. Then, slide the blade under the oyster to loosen it from the shell.

Hanoi-Style Grilled Oysters

Here's another stop in our around-the-world tour of grilled oysters, this one from the Quan An Ngon food court in Hanoi. The recipe is embarrassingly simple, but if you like oysters smoky and hot off the grill (like they do in Tomales Bay, California), you'll be bowled over by the point-counterpoint of scallion oil, salt-pepper-lime dipping sauce, and oysters cooked in their juices on the half shell. **MAKES 12 OYSTERS; SERVES 2 TO 3 AS AN APPETIZER, 1 TO 2 AS A LIGHT MAIN COURSE**

¼ cup vegetable oil

2 scallions, green parts only, thinly sliced crosswise

4 teaspoons coarse salt (preferably sea)

4 teaspoons freshly ground white pepper

12 large oysters in the shell

2 large juicy limes, cut in half

YOU'LL ALSO NEED

An oyster knife for shucking the oysters; a shellfish rack (optional; see Just the Facts, facing page)

ADVANCE PREPARATION

None

1 Combine the oil and scallion greens in a small bowl and stir to mix. The scallion oil can be made up to 2 hours ahead.

2 Divide the salt and white pepper among 4 tiny bowls, mounding each on one side of the bowl in a neat pile.

3 Set up the grill for direct grilling and preheat it to high.

4 Shuck the oysters, discarding the top shells (for instructions on shucking

oysters, see Note, facing page). Take pains not to spill the juices. Arrange the oysters in a shellfish rack, if using. Place about a teaspoon of scallion oil in each oyster.

5 Arrange the oysters on the hot grate, on the shellfish rack, if using, and grill them until the juices bubble and the oysters are just barely cooked, 3 to 6 minutes.

6 Serve the grilled oysters at once, instructing everyone to squeeze about 1 tablespoon of lime juice into a bowl of salt and white pepper. Stir the dipping sauce with chopsticks or a fork to mix. Dip a hot oyster into the salt, pepper, and lime juice mixture and pop it into your mouth. Outrageous!

THE SCOOP

WHERE: Vietnam

WHAT: Oysters grilled on the half shell with scallion oil, lime juice, and pepper

HOW: Direct grilling

JUST THE FACTS: There are numerous possibilities for oysters depending on where you live: Katama Bays from Martha's Vineyard, Wellfleets from Cape Cod, Pemaquid Points from Maine, Blue Points from Long Island, Tomales Bays from California, Kumatos from Washington State, and so on. Choose large oysters with deep shells to hold the juices. In Vietnam, the oysters would be grilled on a sort of wire grid that holds the shells level. In the United States, you can use a shellfish rack (see Just the Facts, facing page).

Oysters Hanoi style, grilled over charcoal and served with salt, pepper, and fresh lime.

Grilled Oysters
with Ginger, Soy, and Jam

THE SCOOP

WHERE: Belgium

WHAT: Oysters grilled on the half shell with a sweet-salty topping of ginger, fruit jam, and soy sauce

HOW: Direct grilling

JUST THE FACTS: The oyster of choice at Peter De Clercq's restaurant Elckerlijc (see page 430) is the *fine de claire*, a large, juicy, deep-shelled oyster cultivated in France. Any fresh oyster will work, but a deep shell is useful for holding the filling. As for jam, I've had excellent results with blueberry, boysenberry, and red currant.

OK, I know it sounds weird: oysters grilled with berry jam and soy sauce. And I wish I could point to a barbecue tradition of great antiquity for the combination; for example, that's how the Belgae grilled oysters when the Romans conquered the Germano-Celtic tribes that would give their name to Belgium. But they didn't and I can't. So you're just going to have to trust me that the yin and yang of sweet berry jam and mirin (sweetened rice wine) contrasted with the briny tang of oysters and soy sauce really does add up to something wondrous on a half shell. The combination was pioneered by Belgian grill master Peter De Clercq (you can read more about him on page 430). **MAKES 12 OYSTERS, SERVES 2 TO 3 AS AN APPETIZER, 1 TO 2 AS A LIGHT MAIN COURSE**

12 large oysters in the shell
About 2 tablespoons of wild blueberry,
    boysenberry, blackberry, black currant, or
    red currant jam
About 2 tablespoons minced peeled fresh ginger
About 2 tablespoons soy sauce
About 2 tablespoons mirin (sweet rice wine),
    sake, or cream sherry
About 2 tablespoons seasoned rice vinegar

YOU'LL ALSO NEED
An oyster knife for shucking the oysters;
    a shellfish rack (optional; see Just the Facts
    on page 504)

ADVANCE PREPARATION
None

1 Set up the grill for direct grilling and preheat it to high.

2 Shuck the oysters, discarding the top shells (for instructions on shucking oysters, see Note, page 504). Take pains not to spill the juices. Arrange the oysters in a shellfish rack, if using.

3 Place a small spoonful (¼ to ½ teaspoon) of berry jam in each oyster. Add a small spoonful of chopped ginger, followed by a few drops of soy sauce, mirin, and rice vinegar.

4 Arrange the oysters on the hot grate on the shellfish rack, if using, and grill them until the juices and sauce bubble and the oysters are just barely cooked, 3 to 6 minutes. Serve the oysters at once on the half shell.

Thailand: The Art of Street Corner Grilling

Midnight. Bangkok: The sun has gone down, and with it, the blast furnace heat of Thailand. In their stead comes the fiery glow of a thousand barbecue grills—on pushcarts, at hawker centers, and at the open air restaurants that sprout like mushrooms on the sidewalks come nightfall. Thailand has always had an outdoor eating culture, and nowhere is this more exuberantly apparent than at the myriad of eateries specializing in *yaang,* grilling.

I'm strolling along a major Bangkok thoroughfare, Sukhumvit Road. In rapid succession I pass grill stalls selling satés and salt-crusted whole snakehead fish, sausages snipped into bite-size balls with scissors, crusty flame-roasted rice

Street vendor with kai ping, Thai grilled eggs.

The Soul of Southeast Asian Grilling

From the highlands of Chiang Mai and Chiang Rai to the palm-lined shores of the Gulf of Thailand and the Andaman Sea, Thailand offers its grill masters an extraordinary selection of meats, seafood, produce, and spices for grilling.

Amanpuri resort in Phuket, Thailand: Water, palm trees, and the graceful lines of a traditional Thai house.

Buddhism amid barbecue—part of the paradox that is Thailand.

cakes with fiery chile dip, and grilled bananas slathered with coconut milk caramel. And that's in a single city block. Travel farther afield (to the next Skytrain stop, for example), and you'll find every imaginable grilled shellfish (grilled cockles, squid, cuttlefish, or head-on prawns, anyone?) and, of course, *gai yaang*—Thailand's iconic and beloved fish sauce- and garlic-marinated rotisserie chicken served with *som tam,* a sort of coleslaw made from green papaya.

Thais distinguish among three distinct styles of grilling. *Yaang* refers to food that is slowly grilled over a medium fire (after being *maak,* marinated in fish sauce and aromatics). *Ping* is the Thai word for "grilled quickly" ("roasted over charcoal"). *Pao* ("burned," literally) refers to quick grilling over a strong flame.

Thai barbecue reflects the grilling styles of its neighbors: the garlic, salt, and cilantro root seasoning pastes of Laos to the northeast and the aromatic lemongrass and coconut milk marinades of Malaysia to the south. As in Cambodia, you find coconut-basted grilled corn and grilled whole river fish (served with a sweet-salty, fish sauce–based, chile-laced dipping sauce). And as in Indonesia, Thais devour

vast quantities of the tiny, bite-size chicken or pork satés—known locally as *gai ping* or *moo ping*—and served with a mild, creamy, garlicky peanut sauce. Thai grill masters rebaptize each dish by coconut shell charcoal fire, electrifying each with a sweet-salty-fiery flavor dynamic that makes Thai grilling some of the most distinctive and satisfying in Asia.

Jumbo prawns from the Gulf of Siam.

THE GRILL: The Thai grill looks like a mini *mangal*—a long, slender rectangular box filled with blazing charcoal. Grill grates are rare. Instead, cooks do their grilling on skewers or in grill baskets stretched across the coals.

Grilling chicken satés in Bangkok.

THE FUEL: Coconut shell charcoal, fanned to the desired temperature with a straw or electric fan

THE FLAVORINGS: Thais like a yin-yang combination of sweet and salty—sweet from palm sugar (It tastes like American light brown sugar or Canadian maple sugar); salty from *nam pla*, a sauce made from fermented fish and sea salt. The fireworks come from garlic, shallots, lemongrass, ginger, galangal (a peppery cousin of ginger), and Thailand's insanely hot *phik khi nu* (literally mouse dropping) chile.

MUST TRY DISHES:
Gai yaang som tam: Spit-roasted or spatchcocked grilled chicken served with crunchy green papaya slaw—sort of like the pork and coleslaw of Memphis, Tennessee.

Yam nua yaang: Fiery grilled beef salad (thinly sliced grilled beef served over lettuce, onions, and other vegetables, with a dusting of crunchy toasted rice powder); this dish comes *yam*-style, which refers to its spicy, lemony dressing.
Goong pao: Marinated, charcoal-grilled king river prawns served in their charred shells, typically accompanied by a spicy chili-lemon-garlic sauce called *nam jim*.

Pla yaang ma-kaam: Whole grilled fish served with sweet and sour tamarind sauce.

Some of the best grilling in Thailand takes place on Bangkok's sidewalks.

Moo ping: Pork satés served with a side of *khao niew* (sticky rice). See below for the most famous *moo ping* vendor in Bangkok.
Sai-krok isaan: Crisp grilled cured pork and cellophane noodle sausages. As with most Isaan (northeastern Thai dishes), *sai-krok* comes with a side of sliced cabbage, fresh string beans, cucumber, basil, and garlic.
Khao tung: Grilled rice cakes served with *nam prik pao* (roasted sweet chili paste).

THE CONDIMENTS: Thailand has three basic barbecue/dipping sauces (generically *nam jim*)—*nam jim saté* (the sweet creamy peanut sauce served with saté); *nam jim jaew* (a thin, sweet-salty dipping sauce made with tamarind, fish sauce, lemon or vinegar, sugar, and sliced chiles and used for dipping slow-grilled chicken, pork, or beef); and *nam jim* seafood (a tart spicy dipping sauce made with garlic, chiles, fish sauce, and sugar—served with grilled fish, prawns, crab, and other shellfish).

IF YOU CAN EAT AT ONLY ONE RESTAURANT: To experience Thai grilling at its most authentic, you have to hit the streets. You'll find excellent grilling at any Bangkok hawker center or outdoor food court. According to locals and expats, Bangkok's most famous *moo ping* stall stands at the corner of Silom and Convent Roads, where the grill master has been grilling bite-size pork satés for more than 20 years. Open from 10 P.M. to 3 A.M. most nights. Other grilling hotspots can be found on Silom Road near the Sala Daeng BTS (a Skytrain stop) and on Sukhumvit Road at the Nana and Asok intersections.

WHAT TO DRINK: Singha beer or sugary Thai iced tea or coffee, enriched with sweetened condensed milk

THE MOST SINGULAR DISH IN THE REPERTORY: *Kai ping*, spiced eggs grilled in the shells

Thai Grilled Cockles or Clams with Chiles and Limes

THE SCOOP

WHERE: Bangkok, Thailand

WHAT: Bivalves grilled in the shells and served with Thai sweet-sour-hot dipping sauce

HOW: Direct grilling

JUST THE FACTS: I first tasted this dish made with cockles, those small briny mollusks of Molly Malone fame, with their deeply ridged, almost spherical shells. Littleneck clams of the sort we dig in Martha's Vineyard work equally well.

River City is a hulking shopping complex on the banks of the Chao Phraya River. But before you dismiss it as a tourist trap, let me tell you that chef-anthropologist Mark Miller comes here to buy Khmer antiques and that yours truly acquired a very handsome seventeenth-century map of Asia at the Old Maps & Prints shop on the fourth floor. Foodwise, the restaurants in the building are about as inviting as airport fast food joints (actually, the food at Bangkok's amazing new Suvarnabhumi Airport is markedly better), but if you wander the streets behind River City, you'll find a cluster of hawker stands where the real Bangkok eats real Thai food. These cockles came from a husband and wife grill team, and the combination of briny shellfish—just hours out of the sand—roasted over coconut shell charcoal, then dipped in a simple sweet, sour, fiery chile lime sauce will give you a new appreciation of bivalves. **SERVES 6 AS AN APPETIZER, 4 AS A MAIN COURSE**

1 clove garlic, minced

3 tablespoons sugar, or more to taste

6 tablespoons fresh lime juice (2 to 3 limes)

3 tablespoons Asian fish sauce, or more to taste

1 small green chile, such as a Thai chile or serrano pepper, thinly sliced crosswise

1 small red chile, such as a Thai chile or serrano pepper, thinly sliced crosswise

1 scallion, green parts only, thinly sliced crosswise

2 pounds fresh cockles or littleneck clams in the shell, well scrubbed with a stiff bristle brush

YOU'LL ALSO NEED

4 bottle caps (the old-fashioned sort you pry off a bottle of soda or beer)

ADVANCE PREPARATION

None

1 Make the sauce: Place the garlic in a nonreactive mixing bowl, add 1 tablespoon of sugar, and mash to a paste with the back of a wooden spoon. Add the remaining 2 tablespoons of sugar and the lime juice and fish sauce and stir or whisk until the sugar dissolves. Stir in the chiles and scallion greens. Add ⅓ cup of cold water. Taste for seasoning, adding more sugar and/or fish sauce as necessary. The sauce should be simultaneously sweet, salty, fiery, and sour. If the fish sauce flavor is too strong, add another tablespoonful or so of water. Divide the dipping sauce among 4 small bowls for serving.

2 Set up the grill for direct grilling and preheat it to high.

3 Arrange the cockles or clams on the hot grate, working in several batches if necessary. Grill the shellfish until the shells just start to open, 3 to 6 minutes for cockles; 4 to 8 minutes for clams. Transfer the grilled shellfish to a platter or plates.

4 To eat, pry the shellfish the rest of the way open with a bottle cap, then dip the shellfish in the dipping sauce and eat with your fingers.

VARIATION

Shellfish in Sauce: Although it's not strictly traditional, here's another way I like to serve these grilled bivalves. Place the sauce in a large heatproof bowl or an aluminum foil pan. Grill the cockles or clams as described. As the shells open, taking care not to spill the juices, transfer the shellfish to the bowl with the sauce. Toss the shellfish with the sauce and serve at once.

Grilled Clams with Korean Cocktail Sauce

These clams come from the Korean port city of Sorae, where a fishmonger turned restaurateur named Lee Myong Chol serves shellfish at his eponymous seafood restaurant/fish market. Sorae is the sort of town any true foodie dreams of discovering, built around a teeming seafood market provisioned by fishing boats that arrive daily and that is chaotic enough to make you feel like you're in preindustrialized Asia, not the ultramodern Korea of the twenty-first century. The bivalves pack a double wallop of flavor, first in the form of a vegetable relish made with peppers, carrot, and scallions, then from a sort of cocktail sauce based on Korea's ubiquitous chile sauce. The master recipe calls for clams, but whole bay scallops in the shell and giant green-shelled mussels would be cooked the same way. All would be served with one utensil not typically found at the tables of most American grill joints—scissors. This enables you to snip even the largest, toughest bivalves into tiny pieces in the shell, rendering them as tender as the most delicate littlenecks. **MAKES 12; SERVES 2 TO 3 AS AN APPETIZER, 1 TO 2 AS A LIGHT MAIN COURSE**

Lee Myong Chol, outside his restaurant, with impeccably fresh shellfish for grilling.

THE SCOOP

WHERE: Sorae, South Korea

WHAT: Clams grilled on the half shell

HOW: The clams are shucked to order and grilled directly in the shells. To shuck a clam, hold the bivalve in the palm of your hand with the hinge facing the base of your thumb. In your other hand, hold the edge of the blade of a shucking knife against the lip of the shells, and squeezing with your fingers, force the blade between the top and bottom shells (be very careful; you don't want the blade to slip). Slide the knife through the lip and under the inside of the top shell to cut the muscle. Slide the blade under the clam to loosen it from the bottom shell.

JUST THE FACTS:
You won't get far in Korean barbecue without getting to know about *kochujang* (sometimes transliterated *gochujang*), an intensely aromatic and flavorful, but not terribly fiery, paste made from Korean dried red chile peppers, fermented soybeans, and rice powder (it tastes a lot better than it sounds). *Kochujang* turns up in a wide range of Korean grilled dishes, from the clams here to the blowfish *"bool kogi"* on page 453. Most often *kochujang* is used as a marinade ingredient, but sometimes it's served as a condiment. Look for it at Asian or Korean markets or order it online at www.koamart.com. You can substitute a Chinese chile paste, like the Lan Chi brand chile paste with garlic.

FOR THE VEGETABLE RELISH

2 tablespoons very finely diced sweet onion, such as Vidalia

2 tablespoons very finely diced peeled carrot

2 tablespoons very finely diced, seeded poblano or serrano pepper

1 scallion, green part only, thinly slivered

FOR THE KOREAN COCKTAIL SAUCE AND CLAMS

⅓ cup Korean chile paste

2 tablespoons fresh lemon juice or rice vinegar, or more to taste

1 teaspoon sugar, or more to taste

½ teaspoon freshly ground black pepper

12 large clams in the shell or 18 cherrystones, well scrubbed with a stiff bristle brush

Lemon wedges, for serving

Feeding green onions into a shredder to make one of the many salads that accompany Korean barbecue.

Korean grill restaurants provide guests with gloves for handling the hot shells of grilled bivalves.

YOU'LL ALSO NEED

An oyster knife for shucking the clams; a shellfish rack (optional; see Just the Facts on page 504)

ADVANCE PREPARATION

None, but the sauce can be prepared up to 6 hours ahead.

1 Make the vegetable relish: Place the onion, carrot, poblano or serrano pepper, and scallion green in a small bowl and stir to mix.

2 Make the Korean cocktail sauce: Place the chile paste, lemon juice, sugar, and black pepper in a small nonreactive bowl and whisk to mix. Taste for seasoning, adding more lemon juice and/or sugar as necessary; the sauce should be a little sweet and sour and very flavorful.

3 Set up the grill for direct grilling and preheat it to high.

4 Shuck the clams, discarding the top shells (see Just the Facts, page 511). Take pains not to spill the juices. Arrange the clams in a shellfish rack, if using. Place a spoonful of vegetable relish in each clamshell and top it with a spoonful of cocktail sauce.

5 Arrange the clams on the hot grate on the shellfish rack, if using, and grill the clams until the juices and sauce bubble and the clams are just barely cooked, 3 to 6 minutes. Serve the clams on the half shell, with lemon wedges.

Mussels Grilled on Pine Needles
{ E C L A D E D E M O U L E S }

Icall it the "pay dirt" moment—the satisfying realization that comes when you walk up to a grill or sit down at a restaurant and know that your hunch was correct, that your journey (in this case, a five-hour drive from Spain to France) was worth it; that you've come upon a remarkable, entirely new form of barbecue. The location was the Ile de Ré in the Charentes region. The dish in question was *éclade,* from the French verb *éclore* (to open, as a rosebud does), and it refers to fresh mussels grilled on a bed of flaming pine needles. The heat causes the mussels to open, while the smoke from the burning pine needles perfumes the shellfish in a way you can't even imagine.

You eat the mussels with your fingers—not a terribly French thing to do—using an empty shell as pinchers to transfer the sweet bivalves from the shells to your mouth. To call the combination of sea saltiness and pine smoke sublime would be an understatement, and to wash the mussels down with anything less than a crisp, dry Muscadet would be criminal. And the best place to try *éclade* is at La Bouvette, a rustic restaurant surrounded by vineyards and with a wood-burning grill (you'll find more about La Bouvette and its remarkable grill master, Laurent Mertz, on page 515).

Use the freshest mussels you can find. Of course, it helps that *éclade* originated in the Charentes region, which has been the epicenter of French mussel cultivation for seven hundred years. **SERVES 4 AS AN APPETIZER, 2 AS A MAIN COURSE**

3 pounds mussels in the shell (45 to 60 mussels)
1 tablespoon raspberry vinegar (optional)
Melted butter (optional), for serving

YOU'LL ALSO NEED
2 quarts dried pine needles and two 9 x 13–inch aluminum foil pans

ADVANCE PREPARATION
None

1 Scrub the mussels well with a brush under cold running water, discarding any with cracked shells or shells that fail to close when tapped. Using needle-nose pliers, pull out and discard any clumps of black strings at the hinges of the mussels. Poke holes in the bottom of one of the foil pans with a screwdriver or knife tip, then twist it to make a ½-inch hole. The holes should be spaced about 2 inches apart.

2 Fill the perforated pan with the pine needles; they should be loosely mounded rather than tightly packed. Arrange the mussels on top.

HOW TO GRILL ON PINE NEEDLES

1. Poke a series of ½-inch holes in the bottom of a foil pan with an old oyster knife or screwdriver.

2. Fill the pan with loosely mounded dry pine needles.

3. Arrange the mussels on top of the pine needles. Do not overcrowd the pan.

4. Place the pan over a hot fire and grill until the pine needles catch fire.

3 Set up the grill for direct grilling and preheat it to high. Ideally, you'll grill over a wood fire. Charcoal is the second best choice, but you can also grill the mussels on a gas grill.

4 When ready to cook, place the pan with the mussels on the hot grate. The pine needles will start to smoke and catch fire after a few minutes. You may need to use a butane match or lighter to help ignite the pine needles. Once the pine needles have caught fire, place the second foil pan upside down over the mussels and pine needles.

5 Check the mussels after a few minutes and once the shells begin to open, sprinkle the mussels with the raspberry vinegar, if desired. Cover the mussels again and grill them until the shells all open and the bivalves are cooked, 5 to 8 minutes total. The vinegar is optional (I don't bother with it), but that's how they do it at La Bouvette.

6 Transfer the smoking, steaming pan with the mussels to a heatproof platter and serve the mussels at once, discarding any that have not opened. You eat the mussels with your fingers right out of the pan. You can dip the mussels in melted butter, but you really don't need it.

Once the pine needles catch fire, cover them with another foil pan.

VARIATIONS

Eclades can also be made with *vanets* (bay scallops)—Nantucketers, are you listening?—or *crépidules* (slipper shells, also known as slipper limpets), a briny shellfish that migrated to France on the hulls of D-Day landing barges

NOTE: If you can't find pine needles, you can grill the mussels on a bed of hay. Can't find hay? For a really interesting, if not wholly authentic variation, arrange the mussels on soaked cedar planks and grill them using the indirect method over the highest possible heat. The cooking time will be 10 to 15 minutes.

FIRE STARTERS
The French Flame Master

Specializing in grilling, **LAURENT MERTZ** makes one of the most spectacular dishes on Planet Barbecue: *Eclade de Moules*.

LE BOIS-PLAGE ON ILE DE RE, FRANCE

Laurent Mertz stands next to his grill—a flame-blackened stone hearth with fire-warped metal bars that could have come from a medieval castle. It is, in fact, of recent construction, built in 1993 in an old grange on the picturesque Ile de Ré off the west coast of France that now houses Mertz' thirty five–seat restaurant, La Bouvette. *Bouvette* in the local patois is a place where you come for a glass of wine and midmorning snack. Today it's an anomaly, a French restaurant that specializes in grilling. It's also one of the few places in France where you can find one of the most spectacular dishes on Planet Barbecue: *éclade de moules* (mussels grilled on a bed of blazing pine needles).

It is remarkable enough that a Burgundy-born chef who trained at top restaurants on the Côte d'Azur and in Paris should wind up on a windswept island once best known for its seventeenth century forti-fications (designed by Louis XIV's military architect, Vauban) and vir-tually deserted eight months a year (the other four months, it has the feel of a French-speaking Martha's Vineyard). That Mertz has chosen to stake his reputation on a cook-ing technique that fell out of favor in France a century ago is nothing short

Top: Laurent Mertz with his signature éclade.
Bottom: Eclade prepared the traditional way: in a chestnut pan filled with pine needles and cooked under an iron skillet.

of amazing. Yet every day, Mertz builds an oak fire in one of his two wood-burning grills (one indoors, one outdoors). Every day, he grills wondrously fresh *seiche blanche* (delicately flavored local squid), enormous *coquilles Saint-Jacques* (sea scallops from the icy Atlantic),

buttery salmon with equally buttery *nantais* sauce (see page 427), and even—heresy of heresies—foie gras. And every day he plays to capacity crowds.

So what's Mertz' secret to becoming a master griller? "Above all, you need to have the *coup d'oeil pour le feu*," Mertz says—the ability to read a fire. "When you cook on a stove, you control the heat. When you grill with wood, it's the fire that decides."

NAME: Laurent Mertz

TERRITORY: Born in Burgundy. Lives and works on the Ile de Ré off France's Atlantic coast

CLAIM TO FAME: Chef-owner of La Bouvette—once featured on the cover of *The New York Times* food section

SPECIALTIES: *Eclade de moules* (mussels grilled on a bed of pine needles). Grilled foie gras. Curry-grilled salmon with *beurre nantais*.

MERTZ SAYS:

▶ Work over a moderate fire. When people complain that grilled fish tastes dry, the reason is simple: They cook it too fast over too hot a fire.

▶ Grilling requires an equal measure of patience and attention. You're constantly moving the food from hot spots to cool spots and back again.

▶ Forget charcoal or gas. You just can't get the right flavor unless you burn wood. (Mertz burns only oak.)

Hanoi-Style Grilled Squid with Chiles and Lime

{ MUC NUONG OT }

THE SCOOP

WHERE: Vietnam

WHAT: Squid or cuttlefish marinated in a sweet-hot paste of chile, sugar, and garlic, served with a salt-pepper-lime dipping sauce

HOW: Direct grilling

JUST THE FACTS: There are two options for grilling the squid. The first is to place the squid bodies in a grill basket. The second is to skewer them lengthwise on bamboo skewers. There are also two options for the dipping sauce: a sweet chile sauce (think of it as turbocharged ketchup) or a salt, pepper, and lime sauce.

Quan An Ngon is the sort of place that should be on every traveler's wish list—a food court in the heart of Hanoi offering the vibrant flavors of Vietnamese street food in a clean, upscale setting. This is where Hanoi's yuppies hang out: a tidy courtyard shaded from the Southeast Asian sun by mammoth umbrellas, with tables and Western-height chairs (the stools at most Vietnamese street stalls require uncomfortable squatting), and most importantly, refrigeration and running water for the culinary concessionaires. In short, it's the sort of place where you can enjoy the explosive flavors of Vietnamese street food while minimizing the risk of gastrointestinal discomfort afterward. Upon arriving, ask for *cac con nuóng* ("barbecue") or simply follow the smoke to the grill stalls, where all manner of seafood and meats are seared on screaming hot charcoal grills. The marinades are mixed to order. The flavors are out of this world. **SERVES 4**

FOR THE SQUID

1½ pounds cleaned squid

¼ cup Vietnamese chile paste, or 1 to 3 teaspoons hot red pepper flakes

2 tablespoons chile oil or vegetable oil

2 tablespoons sugar

1½ teaspoons coarse salt (kosher or sea)

1 teaspoon MSG (optional)

2 cloves garlic, minced

FOR THE DIPPING SAUCE, OPTION #1

½ cup sweet chile sauce, such as Mae Ploy

FOR THE DIPPING SAUCE, OPTION #2

4 teaspoons coarse salt (kosher or sea)

4 teaspoons freshly ground white pepper

2 large juicy limes, cut in half

YOU'LL ALSO NEED

A flat grill basket or bamboo skewers

ADVANCE PREPARATION

15 minutes for marinating the squid

1 Prepare the squid: Place the squid in a large mixing bowl and stir in the chile paste, oil, sugar, salt, the MSG, if using, and the garlic. Let the squid marinate in the refrigerator, covered, for 15 minutes.

2 If you are using the sweet chile sauce for dipping divide it among 4 tiny bowls. If you are using the salt, pepper, and lime dipping sauce, mound

1 teaspoon of salt and 1 teaspoon of white pepper in each of 4 tiny bowls and place a lime half next to each.

3 Set up the grill for direct grilling and preheat it to high.

4 When ready to cook, brush and oil the grill grate. Drain the squid, discarding the marinade. Arrange the squid flat in a grill basket or skewer it lengthwise on bamboo skewers. Place the squid on the hot grate and grill until lightly browned and just cooked through, 1 to 2 minutes per side. Do not overcook the squid or it will become tough.

5 Transfer the grilled squid to a platter or plates. To eat the squid, use chopsticks to dip pieces of squid on the sweet chile dipping sauce. Or if you are using the salt, pepper, and lime dipping sauce, squeeze about 1 tablespoon of lime juice into each one of the bowls with the salt and pepper. Stir the mixture into a paste with the tip of a pair of chopsticks. Dip pieces of squid in this mixture and pop them into your mouth.

Squid grilling in a basket over hot charcoal.

Ordering grilled squid at the Quan An Ngon food court in Hanoi.

Dilled Grilled Squid with Beet Skordalia

In preparation for my research trip to Australia, I spoke with a lot of Ozzie grill masters. Melbourne, I was told, boasts one of the largest Greek communities outside of Athens, and a strong Greek influence is apparent in the local grilling. Consider this dill- and garlic-scented squid served with a crimson beet *skordalia* (a sort of garlic-potato mayonnaise), the creation of Stavros Abougelis, owner of a popular Melbourne restaurant that bears his name. **SERVES 4**

THE SCOOP

WHERE: Australia

WHAT: Grilled squid perfumed with garlic and dill and served with beet "mayonnaise"

HOW: Direct grilling

JUST THE FACTS:
Australian squid comes in meaty white sheets a quarter inch thick—comparable to the Pacific squid steaks available on America's West Coast. If you can buy this, you're in luck, because thick squid will cook into the diamond-patterned rolls so prized by Asians. To achieve this effect, you score the squid in a crosshatch pattern on both sides. This won't work as well with thin East Coast squid, but you'll still wind up with great grilled squid.

1½ pounds cleaned squid, preferably large squid "steaks"

2 large lemons

2 cloves garlic, minced

3 tablespoons chopped fresh dill, plus dill sprigs for garnish

Coarse salt (kosher or sea) and freshly ground black pepper

3 tablespoons extra-virgin olive oil

Beet Skordalia (recipe follows)

YOU'LL ALSO NEED

Bamboo skewers (optional)

ADVANCE PREPARATION

30 minutes for marinating the squid

1 If necessary, make a lengthwise cut through the squid bodies on one side to open them up into a flat sheet. Using a sharp knife, score the squid bodies on both sides in a crosshatch pattern,

Squid "steaks" marinated in a mix of fresh herbs and Australia's fine extra-virgin olive oil need just a couple of minutes on the grill.

making the cuts about ¼ inch apart and as shallow as possible, no deeper than ⅛ inch. The scoring serves a decorative purpose but it also tenderizes the squid and helps it absorb the marinade. It's easier to score a large squid steak than small squid but you can do either—or if you prefer, omit the scoring of small squid.

2 Place the squid in a large nonreactive mixing bowl.

3 Using a Microplane or zester, finely grate 1 teaspoon of lemon zest from one lemon. Cut that lemon in half and seed it. Cut the other lemon into wedges, seed them, and set them aside for serving.

4 Add the lemon zest, garlic, and chopped dill to the squid and toss to mix. Season with salt and pepper to taste. Squeeze the lemon juice from one half lemon (about 2 tablespoons); save the second half for the *skordalia*. Pour the lemon juice and olive oil over the squid and turn to coat. Let the squid marinate in the refrigerator, covered, for 30 minutes.

5 Set up the grill for direct grilling and preheat it to high.

6 When ready to cook, brush and oil the grill grate. Drain the squid, discarding the marinade. If using small squid, skewer the heads and the tentacles separately on bamboo skewers. Skewer the clusters of tentacles side by side. Arrange the squid on the hot grate and grill until it is lightly browned and just cooked through, 1 to 2 minutes per side. The key to tender squid is to grill it quickly—the minute it turns opaque and is cooked through, it's done. Overcooking will give you a mouthful of shoe leather.

7 Arrange the grilled squid on a platter and garnish with dill sprigs. Spoon the Beet Skordalia into a serving bowl and place it in the center of the platter. Serve the grilled squid with lemon wedges and dollops of *skordalia*.

Beet Skordalia

Grilling squid with Stavros Abougelis in Melbourne, Australia.

First created in ancient Greece, *skordalia* was the first "mayonnaise" (in the sense of an emulsified sauce), although in those days, it was thickened with pounded almonds and soaked bread, not potatoes. *Skordalia* is easy to make and the addition of beet gives it a vivid red color and unforgettable flavor. Resist the temptation, however, to use your food processor to make it, or the potatoes in the sauce will become gummy. **MAKES ABOUT 1 CUP**

1 small boiling potato (4 to 6 ounces), peeled and
    cut into ½-inch dice
Coarse salt (kosher or sea)
1 can (8¼ ounces) beets, drained, juices reserved
    (see Note)
2 cloves garlic, minced
1 tablespoon minced fresh dill
2 tablespoons fresh lemon juice, or more to taste
6 to 8 tablespoons extra-virgin olive oil
Freshly ground black pepper

1 Place the potato in a large nonreactive saucepan and add water to cover by 4 inches. Season with salt to taste. Gradually bring the water to a boil over medium heat and let boil until the potato is very soft, about 8 minutes. Drain the potato well in a colander, then return it to the pot. Add the drained beets and puree with a potato masher or through a ricer. Let cool to room temperature.

2 Stir in the garlic, dill, and lemon juice. While beating with a wooden spoon, add enough olive oil in a thin stream to make a thick sauce; the *skordalia* should have the consistency of mayonnaise. For a redder color, add a little of the reserved beet juice. Taste for seasoning, adding salt and pepper to taste and more lemon juice as necessary.

NOTE: You can also use 4 to 6 ounces of fresh beets. Peel and cut into ¼-inch dice. Boil until tender, 20 to 30 minutes, then drain.

Grilled Octopus with Greek Herbs

THE SCOOP

WHERE: Greece

WHAT: Octopus marinated in wine and herbs and smoke grilled over bunches of dried oregano—as commonplace in Greece as shrimp on the barbie is in Australia

HOW: Direct grilling

JUST THE FACTS: You'll need to know about two special ingredients: octopus and Greek oregano. If you live near a neighborhood with a large Greek community, you can get both with one-stop shopping. Otherwise, look for fresh or frozen octopus at your local fish market or even the supermarket (mine always carries it). Octopus is normally sold cleaned and parboiled, so all you need to do is grill it. Greek oregano has a pungent lemony flavor—you need bunches of it to toss on the fire. In a pinch, you could toss a few tablespoons of Mexican or Italian dried oregano or even a bunch of fresh oregano on the fire (dried oregano smokes better than fresh).

It's minus 4 degrees Fahrenheit and snowing as I write this. It was 80 degrees and sunny when I first tasted this handsome, herb-grilled octopus, at a beach barbecue on the island of Kea in the Greek Cyclades. My hosts—Greek culinary expert Aglaia Kremezi, author of *The Foods of Greece* and *The Foods of the Greek Islands: Cooking and Culture at the Crossroads of the Mediterranean,* and Costas Moraitis, her husband, a biblical scholar turned epicurean—had set up a portable charcoal-burning grill called a *shara.* The azure waters of the Aegean shimmered a few meters away, almost close enough to touch. As with most Greek grilling, the octopus emphasized freshness and simplicity over sophistication: the tang of red wine and garlic, the aromatic smoke of Greek oregano placed directly on the embers. When seafood is this fresh, you don't need a lot of fireworks. But don't just take my word for it: You can experience this octopus firsthand at the cooking school/culinary immersion program run by Aglaia and Costas on the island of Kea (www.keartisanal.com). **SERVES 4**

FOR THE OCTOPUS AND MARINADE

1½ to 2 pounds cleaned octopus tentacles
1 small red onion, thinly sliced
3 cloves garlic, peeled and crushed with the side of a knife
1½ teaspoons dried or chopped fresh oregano, preferably Greek
1 teaspoon hot red pepper flakes or Aleppo pepper (see page 393), or more to taste
½ teaspoon freshly ground black pepper
½ cup extra-virgin olive oil, preferably Greek
1 cup dry red wine
¼ cup fresh lemon juice, or ¼ cup red wine vinegar

FOR GRILLING AND SERVING

1 bunch dried oregano, preferably Greek, or 1 bunch fresh oregano, or 3 tablespoons dried oregano
Coarse salt (kosher or sea)
1 lemon, cut into wedges

ADVANCE PREPARATION

2 hours to overnight for marinating the octopus

1 Rinse the octopus, blot it dry, and place it in a large nonreactive bowl. Add the onion, garlic, oregano, the hot pepper flakes, and black pepper and stir to

Aglaia Kremezi and Costas Moraitis stage a beach barbecue near their home on the island of Kea.

mix. Add the olive oil and stir well. Stir in the wine and lemon juice. Let the octopus marinate in the refrigerator, covered, for at least 2 hours or as long as overnight; the longer it marinates, the richer the flavor will be.

2 Set up the grill for direct grilling and preheat it to medium-high. To be strictly authentic, you'd grill over lump charcoal.

3 When ready to cook, brush and oil the grill grate. Drain the octopus well, discarding the marinade. Toss the bunch of oregano on the fire, spreading the sprigs over the coals, if you are grilling with charcoal, or on the Flavorizer bars or heat diffusers of a gas grill. Immediately place the octopus on the hot grate over the oregano and grill it until nicely browned on both sides, 3 to 6 minutes per side, turning with tongs.

4 Transfer the octopus to a platter or plates. Season the octopus with salt and serve it with lemon wedges.

GRILLED OCTOPUS WITH GREEK HERBS

Greece: Firing Up the Grill for 3,000 Years

Greeks do some of the best grilling in Europe. They've certainly had time to practice. When a blind poet named Homer wrote the *Iliad,* he filled the first masterpiece of Western literature with mouthwatering accounts of steers roasted with salt, basted with olive oil and wine (probably retsina), and grilled wrapped in sizzling slices of beef fat. Now, as then, Greek grilling remains a study in splendid simplicity—the primal flavor of flame-roasted meats and seafood speaking loudly for themselves.

Grilled fish at a seaside taverna in Plakias, Crete.

Greece is and has always been defined by the sea. After all, there are more than 1,400 Greek islands (more than 150 are inhabited), and this nation of eleven million has more than 8,500 miles of coastline. Wherever you find people along that coastline—be it a big city like Piraeus or a tiny village like Imerovigli on the island of Santorini, you'll find *tavernas* (casual restaurants) specializing in grilled seafood.

But Greece is also defined by its mountains—remember Mount Olympus? Sheep and goats thrive in landscapes too hilly to support cattle, leading to the predominance on *taverna* menus of lamb dishes, like *païdekia* (crackling crisp baby lamb chops no bigger than lollipops), *souvlaki* (lamb shish kebab), and *gyro* (thin shavings of vertically roasted sliced or ground lamb served on pita). Less well known are Greece's the pork dishes, but I still dream about *kandosouvle* (hot-spiced, spit-roasted pork chunks) and the oregano-scented whole hog I sampled on the island of Kea (you can read about it on page 259).

Modern Greeks do two basic kinds of grilling. *Ste karbonia* means "grilled over charcoal"—often in

Grilling's Ancient Heartland

Surrounded by water and comprised of more than 1,400 islands, Greece and Greek grilling look to the sea for inspiration.

Fast food Greek-style: Gyro roasting on a vertical rotisserie.

Morning delivery by a fishing boat in Crete. Grilled seafood doesn't get fresher than this.

a hinged grill basket or on skewers positioned over a grateless grill called a *psestaria*. *Ste souvla* means "spit roasted," and in Greece this can mean anything from rotisseried lamb or hog to a sort of organ meat mixed grill called *kokoretzi*. The slow turning of the meat on the spit is mesmerizing. The flavors are out of this world.

Sea bream grilled on fig leaves (page 465) and octopus grilled with Greek herbs (page 520)

THE GRILL: Greeks cook on three types of grills: a troughlike grateless grill called a *psestaria,* which resembles the Russian *mangal;* a conventional horizontal rotisserie, popular for spit roasting whole lambs and hogs; and the vertical rotisserie used for cooking lamb to make the popular *gyros* (incidentally, the same "gyro" as in gyroscope). Greek grills rarely have grill grates: The food is grilled in hinged grill baskets.

THE FUEL: Hardwood charcoal. The grill master burns a pile in one corner of the grill and the embers are raked under the food as needed.

THE FLAVORINGS: Greeks work with a simple palate of flavors: sea salt, oregano, olive oil, lemon, and on occasion, fennel, onion, and garlic. As you move north and west, the heat level increases.

MUST TRY DISHES:

Grilled meat dishes

Arni: Lamb. The choicest cut is *païdaekia*—crusty, tender grilled baby lamb chops (page 295).

Bifteki: A sort of hamburger made from ground veal and beef

Brizola: Steak

Gyro: The Greek cousin of Turkish *doner* and Middle Eastern *shawarma*—thinly sliced or ground spiced lamb roasted on a vertical spit and served on pita.

Kandosouvle: Spicy, spit-roasted pork chunks (see page 205)

Souvlaki: Lamb or pork shish kebab

Grilled seafood

Astakos: Spiny lobster

Lavraki: Greek sea bass

Oktopous or *chtapodi:* Octopus

Sardela: Sardines

Tsipoura: Sea bream

THE CONDIMENTS: Greek grilled seafood comes with the simplest of sauces—olive oil mixed with lemon juice and sometimes oregano. Meats are served with lemon wedges for squeezing. *Gyro* and *souvlaki* come with thick Greek yogurt or *tzatziki* (yogurt-cucumber-mint dip) and sliced fresh and pickled vegetables.

A traditional Greek barbecue starts with *mezes*—Greek *tapas.* You'll also get a salad as remarkable for its luscious, sweet, ripe red tomatoes as for its snow-white slab of salty feta cheese. And a loaf of crusty sesame-dotted bread, which may come grilled if the pit master is feeling ambitious.

HOW TO EAT IT: With knife and fork or with your bare hands, as simply as possible, preferably outdoors

IF YOU CAN EAT AT ONLY ONE RESTAURANT: Vlahika (literally the Country Guy), one of the dozens of *hasapotavernas* (butchers' taverns) that line the main route between Athens and Piraeus. Athenians love to flock to these restaurants on the weekend. The fact is, it's hard to find a bad one.

WHAT TO DRINK: Start your meal with a glass of ouzo, an anise-flavored spirit that turns milky white when you add water. As with many European barbecue cultures, Greeks are likely to serve wine with grilled food.

THE MOST SINGULAR DISH IN THE GREEK GRILL REPERTORY: *Kokoretzi*—lamb's brains, heart, liver, spleen, and testicles skewered on a spit, wrapped in small intestine, and spit roasted over charcoal. It's better than it sounds.

Spit roasting lamb in the streets. A community Easter feast near Delphi, Greece.

Nha Trang Mixed Grill

WHERE: Nha Trang, Vietnam

WHAT: Grilled shrimp, squid, fish, and beef marinated with fish sauce and chiles, served in the style of one of the most famous grill houses in Vietnam

HOW: Direct grilling

JUST THE FACTS: To get the full effect, serve a variety of seafoods and meats. The seafood would include shrimp (preferably with the heads and shells intact), spiny lobster or slipper lobster, cuttlefish, squid, and a fish fillet, like halibut or pompano. (When grilling slices of delicate fish fillet, use a hinged grill basket for easier turning.) For meat, you could use thin slices of sirloin or top or bottom round (that's what they use in Vietnam), or even a super tender cut, like tenderloin tips. Or you could grill pork chops or chicken. To simplify the recipe, pick a single ingredient, such as shrimp, squid, or halibut, to marinate and grill.

Nha Trang is Vietnam's ultimate beach town, situated on a huge crescent-shaped bay fringed by a white sand beach. A popular R & R destination during the Vietnam War, it has survived subsequent invasions of Russian and European tourists and more recently, Chinese and Japanese, without for a minute shedding its own unique Vietnamese personality. And whatever their nationality, just about everyone who visits for more than a day or two winds up at Lac Canh, a funky landmark. Lac Canh is the sort of restaurant that draws Saturday night crowds on weeknights and New Year's Eve crowds on Saturday nights. The house specialty is barbecue—pristine seafood fished that morning from Nha Trang Bay, and beef that is famous throughout Vietnam—marinated in a sweet and salty mixture of fish sauce, garlic, and sugar. You grill the seafood and fish ingredients yourself on a charcoal brazier, which is brought to your table loaded with glowing coals. Add a cool, crisp Vietnamese salad plate and a custom-mixed sour-salty-hot dipping sauce and you get barbecue that lights up your mouth like the fireworks in a Tet (Vietnamese New Year's) sky. For an added measure of authenticity, place a hibachi with heatproof tiles or an inverted baking sheet underneath it in the center of an outdoor table and have everyone grill their food to taste. **SERVES 6 TO 8**

FOR THE MARINADE

2 cloves garlic, coarsely chopped

2 stalks lemongrass, trimmed and coarsely chopped

2 tablespoons sugar

2 hot red peppers, such as Thai chiles, or 1 to 2 tablespoons Vietnamese chile paste

1 teaspoon freshly ground black pepper

3 tablespoons fish sauce

3 tablespoons oyster sauce, or more fish sauce

3 tablespoons vegetable oil

FOR THE SEAFOOD AND MEAT

3 pounds shellfish and fish, for example:

12 ounces shrimp in the shells with the heads on, or peeled and deveined shrimp

12 ounces cleaned squid

12 ounces halibut fillets

12 ounces beef sirloin, round, or tenderloin tips

FOR THE SALAD PLATE

1 head Boston lettuce, separated into whole leaves and rinsed

2 red ripe tomatoes, cut In half lengthwise (through the stem end) and thinly sliced

1 large or 2 small cucumbers, peeled and thinly sliced

1 medium-size sweet onion, such as a Vidalia or Walla Walla, cut crosswise into paper-thin slices

FOR THE DIPPING SAUCE

¼ cup coarse salt (kosher or sea)

1 tablespoon Vietnamese chile paste or hot red pepper flakes

8 limes, cut in half

YOU'LL ALSO NEED

A hinged grill basket for grilling the slices of fish (optional)

ADVANCE PREPARATION

1 to 2 hours for marinating the seafood and meats

1 Make the marinade: Place the garlic, lemongrass, sugar, fresh chiles, if using, and black pepper in a heavy mortar and pound to a paste with a pestle. Pound in the 1 to 2 tablespoons of chile paste, if using, and the fish sauce, oyster sauce, and oil. Alternatively, you can puree the garlic, lemongrass, sugar, fresh chiles, if using, and black pepper in a food processor and then work in the chile paste, if using, fish sauce, oyster sauce, and oil.

2 Prepare the seafood and beef: If you are using shrimp with their heads on, make a cut down the back of the body with kitchen shears. Remove the vein using the tine of a fork or the tip of a bamboo skewer. Place the shrimp in an attractive bowl and stir in one fourth of the marinade.

3 Cut the squid into 1-inch pieces and place it in an attractive bowl. Stir in one third of the remaining marinade.

4 Using a sharp knife, cut the halibut sharply on the diagonal into ½-inch-thick slices. Place the halibut in an attractive bowl and stir in one half of the remaining marinade.

5 Thinly slice the beef across the grain and place it in an attractive bowl. Stir in the remaining marinade. Let the halibut, shrimp, squid, and beef marinate in the refrigerator, covered, for 1 to 2 hours.

6 Prepare the salad plate: Arrange the lettuce leaves, tomatoes, cucumbers, and onion slices on a serving platter and set it aside.

7 Make the dipping sauce: Place the salt in a small mixing bowl and stir in the chile paste or hot pepper flakes. Divide the mixture sauce among 8 tiny bowls. Next to each bowl, place 2 lime halves.

The traditional Vietnamese grill is a charcoal-filled clay brazier surmounted by a wire grid.

Lac Canh, where every night is like Saturday night, and Saturday night is like New Year's.

8 Set up the grill for direct grilling and preheat it to high.

9 When ready to cook, brush and oil the grill grate. If you are using a fish basket, oil it as well (an oiled paper towel or cooking oil spray works well for this). Place the slices of halibut in the basket and fasten the basket shut. Place the bowls of marinated shrimp, squid, and beef near the grill.

10 Arrange the shrimp, squid, halibut, and beef on the hot grate. Grill the shrimp until they are browned on the outside and just cooked through, about 2 minutes per side. Grill the squid until it is lightly browned and just cooked through, 1 to 2 minutes per side. Grill the slices of beef until sizzling, browned, and cooked to taste, 1 to 2 minutes per side for medium rare. Grill the halibut until golden brown on both sides, 2 to 3 minutes per side. Transfer the grilled seafood or beef to a plate or platter for serving. (If you are grilling on a hibachi, you can use chopsticks to serve hot off the grill.)

11 To eat the mixed grill, place a piece of grilled seafood or beef on a lettuce leaf. Top it with a slice of tomato, cucumber, and onion and roll it up. Squeeze some lime juice into a dish with the chile paste and salt and stir it with the tip of a chopstick to make a dipping sauce. Dip the lettuce leaf bundle in the dipping sauce and pop it into your mouth.

Vegetables and Vegetarian Dishes

Given the staunchly carnivorous impulses associated with barbecue, you may be surprised to learn that some of the first archaeological evidence of grilling involved vegetables. That nearly 800,000 years ago, a prehistoric grill master (a human ancestor called *Homo erectus*) roasted olives, grapes, and barley in a campfire in what is now near the Israeli-Jordanian border. That more than 10,000 years ago, Cro-Magnon hunter-gatherers with minds and faces virtually indistinguishable from our own enjoyed wood fire–seared peas, acorns, and crab apples alongside the prodigious amounts of wild game that comprised the early human diet.

The fact is that since the dawn of humanity and the birth of live-fire cooking, grilling has always been one of man's preferred ways to cook vegetables. A quick tour of Planet Barbecue turns up Cambodian grilled corn (and a similar grilled corn half a world away in Cartagena, Colombia), Japanese *shishito* peppers grilled with salt and sesame oil (and pickled grilled peppers in Romania), Argentinean fire-roasted squash, and onions spit-roasted on the rotisserie in São Paulo.

CLOCKWISE FROM TOP LEFT: *Fiery chiles for making piri-piri, Azerbaijan; My son-in-law, Gabriel, grills corn on Martha's Vineyard; Pepper and tomatoes grilled Armenian–style; Rice vendor outside Cambodia's Angkor Wat Temple. The rice grills in hollow sections of bamboo.*

When you stop to think about what grilling actually does to a vegetable, it's surprising we don't cook more of our produce over live fire. The high, dry heat caramelizes the plant sugars, accentuating the vegetable's natural sweetness. The outside of the vegetable acquires a crackling skin and crisp crust, not to mention a handsome chiaroscuro dappling for people who like to eat with their eyes as well as their palates.

You'll also find some of the world's greatest grilled vegetarian dishes in this

Even the potato, a relative newcomer to the world's melting pot, turns up on grills across Planet Barbecue, from German ember-roasted, herb and cheese-topped spuds to Uruguayan wood-fired "smashed" potatoes; from Armenian potato and bacon kebabs to "knish on a stick"—Azeri grilled mashed potatoes.

chapter, including Indian tandoori *paneer* (grilled kebabs of cheese, peppers, tomatoes, and onion) and Malaysian sweet-and-sour grilled tofu, not to mention one of the favorite snacks of Laotian school children: grilled rice "pops." You'll even find a vegetarian version of Spain's legendary paella, because yes, the authentic way to cook paella is over an open wood campfire.

Previous page: Barbecuing corn on a grateless grill in the Far East.

Grilled Bananas

This Colombian side dish is so simple I'm almost embarrassed to include the recipe. Almost. It's just that the bananas become so sweet and smoky—and the preparation is so quintessentially Colombian—that I would be remiss to leave them out. These bananas accompany grilled meats at Bogotá's landmark chophouse, Lomos, but they'd also make a terrific dessert, especially if accompanied by the rum-flavored whipped cream on page 572. **SERVES 4**

4 ripe apple or finger bananas, or 4 small
   conventional bananas

ADVANCE PREPARATION
None

1 Set up the grill for direct grilling and preheat it to medium high.

2 Using the tip of a paring knife, make a lengthwise slit in the concave side of each banana. The slit should be about ¼ inch deep and should run the length of the banana to within ½ inch of each end.

3 When ready to cook, brush and oil the grill grate. Arrange the bananas on the hot grate, slit side up, so that they are parallel to the bars of the grate; prop the bananas upright between the bars. Grill the bananas until the skins are darkly brown and the flesh inside, visible through the slits, is bubbling and tender. This will take about 15 minutes: 5 minutes slit side up, 5 minutes with the banana lying on one side, and 5 minutes with the banana lying on the other side. Do not invert the bananas or the juices will leak out. Serve the bananas at once. To eat the bananas, scoop the flesh out of the skins.

THE SCOOP

WHERE: Bogotá, Colombia

WHAT: Bananas grilled in their skins, period

HOW: Direct grilling (traditionally over charcoal)

JUST THE FACTS: The fruit of choice is the short stubby *banana bocadillo*—literally, bite-sizer. The closest equivalents in North America would be an apple banana or a finger banana. You can also use small conventional bananas. The bananas should be ripe (fully yellow and just beginning to form brown sugar spots) but not soft.

Coconut-Grilled Corn
{ POD OENG }

Grilled corn turns up all over Planet Barbecue, and whenever I see it, I screech the car (or Tuk Tuk or pedicab) to a halt. This has lead to some disappointments; for example, in the Balkans, where the corn was so tough and devoid of natural sugar even the cattle must struggle to eat it. On

THE SCOOP

WHERE: Siem Reap, Cambodia

WHAT: Grilled corn basted with spiced coconut milk

HOW: Direct grilling

JUST THE FACTS:
This dish is simple and easy to make, but you will need to shop for a few ingredients. Coconut milk, the heavy cream of the tropics, is available in cans at most supermarkets. Look for unsweetened coconut milk; one good brand is Chaokoh. Pandanus leaf is the slender, sword-shaped leaf of the screw pine; it's used as a wrapper and flavoring in Southeast Asian cooking. You can find it dried in Asian markets, but a couple of bay leaves will give you a similar flavor without requiring you to make a special trip. Palm sugar is the sweetener of choice in much of Asia; light brown sugar is similar in texture and flavor.

the other hand, in Cambodia, I was rewarded by some of the best grilled corn I'd ever tasted. Served outside the Angkor Wat temple complex by Sray Much, a grill mistress with an incandescent smile, it was smoky, with pandanus leaf-scented coconut milk brushed on to accentuate the corn's innate sweetness. Pandanus leaf has a fresh, aromatic flavor that may remind you of pine needles. **SERVES 4**

¾ cup unsweetened coconut milk
2 tablespoons palm sugar or light brown sugar, or more to taste
1 piece (2 inches) pandanus leaf, or 1 or 2 bay leaves
¼ teaspoon salt
4 ears sweet corn, husked or husk stripped back and tied together as shown below

ADVANCE PREPARATION
None, but you can certainly make the coconut basting mixture several hours ahead of time

1 Combine the coconut milk, palm sugar, pandanus leaf or bay leaf, and salt in a small saucepan over medium heat and let simmer gently until the sugar dissolves, 3 to 5 minutes. Taste for sweetness, adding more sugar if necessary. Remove the pan from the heat and let the basting mixture cool to room temperature.

2 Set up the grill for direct grilling and preheat it to high.

3 When ready to cook, brush and oil the grill grate. Place the corn on the hot grate and grill it until nicely browned on all sides, 2 to 3 minutes per side, 8 to 12 minutes in all, turning with tongs. Start basting the corn with some of the coconut milk mixture after a few minutes and baste it again several times as it grills.

4 Baste the corn one final time, transfer it to a platter or plates, and serve.

HOW TO GRILL CORN CAMBODIAN-STYLE

1. Strip the husk back from the ear of corn, leaving it attached at the bottom. (The action is a little like peeling a banana.)

2. Using a strip of corn husk, tie the remaining husks together under the ear to form a handle. Remove the corn silk.

3. As the corn grills, baste it with the pandanus leaf-scented coconut milk.

Cambodian grilled corn sizzling hot off the grill.

Grilled Corn Around the World

Corn may have started as a New World food, but it quickly became a staple across Planet Barbecue. And as many a global grill master knows, there is no better way to cook it than on the grill. The high, dry heat of the fire caramelizes the plant sugars, making ordinary corn taste sweeter, and transporting sweet corn, like the ears from Hokkaido, Japan, to a realm normally reserved for candy. Grilled corn looks great and, like ribs, it gives you the dual pleasures of eating with your hands and sinking your teeth directly into a food hot off the grill—knife and fork be damned.

In North America, a debate rages as to whether it's better to grill corn with the husk on or off. Partisans of grilling it husk-on argue that the husk protects the

Sampling grilled corn from a sidewalk vendor in Cartagena, Colombia.

Corn grilled with coconut milk, a specialty of Siem Reap, Cambodia.

delicate kernels. They'll go to extreme lengths, such as stripping the husk back, removing the silk, buttering the corn, replacing the husk, and tying the ear up like a tamale.

Partisans of the husk-off school believe that when you grill corn in the husk, you're actually steaming it rather than grilling it—that what makes grilled corn so appealing is the browning of the kernels when the corn sugars caramelize. This can occur only when the husk is stripped back. When removing the husk, I like to strip it back the way you'd peel a banana, leaving it attached at the stem and folding it back and under the ear. Then I tie the ends together to form a sort of handle. Using an aluminum foil grill shield will keep the husk from burning.

Here's how corn is grilled in six hot spots around Planet Barbecue. Tellingly, in each of these places they grill the corn without the husk.

CAMBODIA: Cambodians grill corn over a charcoal fire and baste it with a mixture of coconut milk, palm sugar, and pandanus (screw pine) leaf; the recipe starts on page 529.

COLOMBIA: In Cartagena, itinerant street vendors serve corn that is grilled over charcoal and slathered with butter and grated cheese; you'll find the recipe on page 534.

INDIA: After being grilled over charcoal, in India corn is doused with fresh lime juice and dusted with cayenne pepper.

JAPAN: The Japanese grill thin rounds of corn from Hokkaido over odorless *bincho-tan* charcoal (see page 602) and serve it in stark simplicity—the corn is so amazingly sweet, it doesn't need any accompaniments.

MEXICO: Mexican corn is grilled over charcoal, slathered with mayonnaise, crusted with grated Cotija cheese, and seasoned with fresh lime juice and chile powder.

TRINIDAD AND TOBAGO: In Trinidad and Tobago, they grill corn husk off and baste it with garlic-cilantro butter.

Cambodia: SE Asia's Best Barbecue Secret

In the late twelfth century A.D. a fierce battle took place in what is now northern Cambodia between an invading army from Thailand and the local Khmers. The Khmers triumphed in a city known ever since as Siem Reap (literally Siam defeated). That's the same city of Angkor Wat fame, but there's another temple complex that's far more interesting from a grill enthusiast's point of view (and has a lot fewer tour buses parked outside): Bayon. Built by the Khmer king Jayavarman VII, Bayon commemorated not just the victory but the daily life and culture of the victors. To this end, Jayavarman's sculptors carved a series of splendid stone friezes that depict everyday life in twelfth century Cambodia, from transportation to entertainment to cooking.

The exquisite art of traditional Khmer ballet.

Which brings us in a roundabout way to Cambodian barbecue, because depicted on the stone walls of Bayon are the clay braziers filled with blazing lump charcoal and the long, split wooden skewers loaded with lake fish, poultry, and frogs that you still find at Cambodian grill joints today. These are some of the world's earliest depictions of barbecue—an art that, in Cambodia at least, has changed little in eight hundred years.

Cambodian grilling offers some of the most refined, explosive flavors in Southeast Asia: seafood and meats spiced with aromatic marinades, served with equally pungent dipping sauces made with tropical fruits and fermented fish pastes. Chiles came later, brought from their native America to Southeast Asia by sixteenth-century Portuguese seafarers.

In the West, one doesn't normally think of barbecue as health food, but westerners could learn a lot about healthy meat-eating from the way Cambodians grill and serve steak. The steak itself would be subsize by North American standards: A single rib eye would feed

Home of Refined Street Food

Bayon Temple in Siem Reap, where some of the earliest depictions of Asian grilling appear on the stone walls.

Chiles and limes: essentials of Cambodian grilling.

Home of a great Khmer civilization that once ruled Southeast Asia, Cambodians have been grilling the same way for more than 1,000 years.

Grilling in banana leaves at Siem Reap's central food market.

three or four. But accompanying the small portion of red meat would be a lavish assortment of fresh vegetables and spicy condiments. The act of eating becomes an intricate assemblage of flavors, textures, and temperatures, with lettuce leaves serving as both the wrapper and plate.

Besides meat, Cambodians take great pride in grilled seafood and vegetables—unlike many barbecue cultures. Whole grilled river and lake fish and fish mousses are electrified with chiles and lemongrass and wrapped and grilled in banana leaves. And when it comes to vegetables, Cambodia boasts some of the best grilled corn on Planet Barbecue—basted with coconut milk and perfumed with the aromatic pandanus leaf (screw pine). See page 529 for the recipe.

Like most Southeast Asian grilling, Cambodian barbecue is essentially street food, grilled as you watch and dished up from pushcarts and rickety market stalls and roadside stands. The flavors are complex enough to turn up at luxury resorts like Siem Reap's incredible Amansara. Cambodian grilling may not be well known outside of Southeast Asia. I daresay it's worth the journey.

THE GRILL: Cambodians do their grilling in red terra-cotta braziers that look like large clay flower pots. They have no grill grate. Foods are cooked on split bamboo sticks or in grill baskets directly over the embers.

THE FUEL: Natural lump charcoal

THE FLAVORINGS: Like most Southeast Asians, Khmers season their meats with sweet-salty spice pastes of lemongrass, garlic, ginger, galangal, chiles, pepper, sugar, and the malodorous but tasty fish sauce, *toeuk trey*, and fish paste, *pra hok*.

MUST TRY DISHES:

Chaoeng chumny chrouk oeng: Ginger Garlic and Honey Grilled Baby Back Ribs (see page 236).

Mann oeng k'tem sor, marech: Cambodian grilled chicken (see page 371)

Pod oeng: Coconut-grilled corn (see page 529)

THE CONDIMENTS: Cambodian grilled meats are always served with one or more dipping sauces, ranging in simplicity from refreshing salt, pepper, and lime sauces reminiscent of those of Vietnam to the sweet, salty, and garlicky dipping sauces suggestive of Thailand. Oh, then there are dips made from stinky fermented fish paste that you're not likely to enjoy unless Khmer blood runs in your veins.

HOW TO EAT IT: With chopsticks or your fingers—preferably with a crowd

THE MOST SINGULAR DISH IN THE REPERTORY: Grilled eggs, made by seasoning beaten eggs with fish sauce, sugar, and pepper and grilling them, kebab style, on bamboo skewers in the hollowed shells

Have brazier, will travel. An impromptu grill session on a Cambodian beach.

Colombian Grilled Corn with Butter and Cheese

Sometimes the idea of a dish surpasses its execution, for example, the grilled corn served on the cobblestone streets of one of the most perfectly preserved colonial cities in South America: Cartagena (the same Cartagena pictured in the original *Romancing the Stone*). The corn came the way I normally like it—husk off and charred over charcoal on a portable brazier, but the ears were starchy and dry and the "butter" turned out to be margarine of dubious freshness. Here's how Colombian-style corn should be made, and if you're lucky enough to try it with sugar-sweet summer corn and freshly grated Pecorino Romano, you'll never think about corn quite the same way again. **SERVES 4**

4 ears sweet corn
3 tablespoons salted butter, at room temperature
1 cup (about 4 ounces) finely grated Pecorino Romano, Asiago, or other hard grating cheese
Freshly ground black pepper

YOU'LL ALSO NEED
Butcher's string; 4 bamboo skewers, or 4 wooden chopsticks (optional); basting brush

ADVANCE PREPARATION
None

1 Cut the top ½ inch off each ear of corn. Strip a husk back as though you're peeling a banana and tie it together at the base of the corn cob to form a handle; use butcher's string or a piece of the corn husk for tying (see the photos on page 530). Alternatively, you can husk the corn and stick each ear on a thick bamboo skewer. Remove the silk. Repeat with the remaining ears of corn.

2 Set up the grill for direct grilling and preheat it to high.

3 When ready to cook, brush and oil the grill grate. Place the corn on the hot grate and grill it until nicely browned on all sides, 2 to 3 minutes per side, 8 to 12 minutes in all, turning with tongs.

4 To serve, using a basting brush, spread the softened butter over the corn. Working over a plate, thickly sprinkle each ear with cheese and black pepper.

Bacon-Grilled Eggplant

This is one of the most singular vegetable dishes on Planet Barbecue—whole eggplants that have been stuffed with bacon and paprika and charred on the grill. The bacon and paprika imbue the eggplant with incredible smoke and spice flavors. **SERVES 4**

4 small eggplants (3 to 4 ounces each),
    or 2 medium-size eggplants
    (about 1 pound total)
Coarse salt (kosher or sea) and freshly
    ground black pepper
2 teaspoons vegetable oil
4 thick slices of country-style bacon
    (each about 4 inches long, 1 inch wide,
    and ¼ inch thick; 1 to 1½ ounces each)
1½ tablespoons sweet or hot paprika

ADVANCE PREPARATION
None, but the eggplants can be stuffed several
    hours ahead.

1 Using a paring knife, cut a deep lengthwise slit in each eggplant. The slit should run almost but not quite to each end and cut almost completely through the eggplant. Gently pry open the eggplants with your fingers and season them generously inside with salt and pepper.

2 Heat the oil in a medium-size skillet over medium heat. Add the bacon and cook until browned, 2 to 3 minutes per side. Drain the bacon on paper towels, reserving the fat in the skillet.

3 Generously season the bacon on both sides with paprika. Insert 1 slice of bacon in the slits of small eggplants, 2 slices in the slits of medium-size eggplants. Sprinkle any remaining paprika inside the slits. The eggplants can be prepared up to this point several hours ahead. Refrigerate them, covered, until ready to grill.

4 Set up the grill for direct grilling and preheat it to medium-high.

5 When ready to cook, brush and oil the grill grate. Arrange the eggplants on the hot grate slit side up. Grill the eggplants until darkly browned on the bottom, 3 to 4 minutes. Turn each eggplant to grill on one side, then the other, for 3 to 4 minutes per side. Carefully turn each eggplant and grill the slit side until it is browned, 1 to 2 minutes. The eggplants will be done after grilling 10 to 14 minutes in all, somewhat longer for larger eggplants. Baste them with the reserved bacon fat as they grill. When cooked, the eggplants will be very soft to the touch and easily pierced with a skewer. Transfer the eggplants to a platter or plates and serve at once.

THE SCOOP

WHERE: The Caucasus Mountains, Republic of Armenia

WHAT: Eggplant stuffed with bacon

HOW: Direct grilling

JUST THE FACTS: Tradition calls for stuffing the eggplants not with bacon but with thin slices of lamb tail fat (see page 332). I've come to prefer the smoky flavor of bacon to the more neutral flavor of lamb tail fat. Pick a country smokehouse bacon like Nueske's (www.nueskes.com).
    Armenian eggplants are smaller and sweeter than American eggplants. The 3 to 4 ounce slim eggplants sold at Italian produce markets and natural foods stores come the closest in texture and flavor. If you are using conventional eggplants, choose the longest, most slender specimens you can find.

ROTISSERIE ONIONS | facing page
KOSOVAN GRILLED MUSHROOMS | page 540

Rotisserie Onions

Brazilians spit roast everything: Meat. Poultry. Cheese. Even pineapple (see page 578). But onions? Would you really want to tie up your rotisserie for an hour to make them? The answer is yes, for at least three reasons. First, the lateral heat and gentle rotation make the onions supernaturally sweet and tender inside and deliciously caramelized outside. Second, the process looks cool as all get out. And finally, these spit-roasted onions were created by Fuad "Dinho" Zegaib, one of the pioneers of Brazilian barbecue and founder of the São Paulo steak house Dinho's. Enough said. **SERVES 4**

4 large sweet onions (each 12 ounces to 1 pound), with their skins, stem and root ends intact
Best-quality extra-virgin olive oil (optional)
Best-quality aged balsamic vinegar (optional)
Coarse salt (kosher or sea) and freshly ground black pepper (optional)

ADVANCE PREPARATION
None, but allow yourself 45 to 60 minutes cooking time to achieve the requisite tenderness.

1 Set up the grill for spit roasting, following the manufacturer's instructions, and preheat the grill to medium-high.

2 When ready to cook, thread the onions onto the spit through the stem end, using the forked prongs to hold the onions in place. Attach the spit to the grill and turn on the motor. Spit roast the onions until they are dark golden brown and very tender, 1 to 1¼ hours. Use the "Charmin" test (see page 612) to check for doneness; when done, each onion should be squeezably soft and easy to pierce with a skewer.

3 Carefully unskewer the onions onto a platter or plates. Cut the onions open from the top and eat them right out of the skins. Season the onions with olive oil, balsamic vinegar, and salt and pepper, if desired, but the onions are so flavorful, they really need nothing but a fork.

VARIATION
Onions Grilled Using the Indirect Method: If your grill lacks a rotisserie or if the rotisserie is otherwise occupied, you can grill the onions using the indirect method. Set up the grill for indirect grilling and preheat it to medium-high. Arrange the onions on the grill, root side down, on grill rings (you can find these on my website, www.barbecuebible.com/store) or aluminum foil rings. Cover the grill. The cooking time will be 1 to 1¼ hours. For an extra layer of flavor, toss some soaked hardwood chips on the coals or, for a gas grill, place them in the smoker box or in a smoker pouch (see page 603).

THE SCOOP

WHERE: São Paulo, Brazil

WHAT: Whole onions spit roasted until mahogany brown and marshmallow soft—a process that transforms the abundant sugars naturally found in onions into a smoky sweetness suggestive of caramel

HOW: Roasted whole on the rotisserie

JUST THE FACTS: Onions with high sugar content include Walla Wallas, Mauis, and Texas sweets.

PLANET BARBECUE

Brazil: Land of Churrasco, Rodízio, and Fogo de Chão

Mention Rio Grande do Sul to Brazilian barbecue buffs (and they're *all* barbecue buffs in Brazil) and their eyes will blaze like a bonfire. For whether they come from cosmopolitan São Paulo or laidback Rio, they know that Rio Grande do Sul—Brazil's southernmost state—is where it all began: Where the first *vaqueiros* (as Brazilians call their cowboys) built campfires and roasted sides of beef (today reduced to more manageable racks of beef ribs) on upright stakes in front of smoky wood fires. Where Brazil's passion for fire-roasted meats grew into a national obsession.

The cowboys called their barbecue *fogo de chão* (bonfire or campfire), and this became Brazil's first barbecue. From these rustic beginnings, Brazil has developed some of the world's most sophisticated live-fire cooking, served at stylish restaurants like Dinho's and Rubaiyat

The Land of Barbecue Buffs

Brazil, the Americas' most populous country, boasts an incredibly vibrant, varied grill culture.

Iguaçu Falls: A natural wonder shared by two barbecue giants: Brazil and Argentina.

Great grilling and Ipanema beach—what more can a visitor to Rio ask for?

Pineapple Porto Alegre-style: hot off the rotisserie.

in São Paulo and Plataforma in Rio. And barbecue has become one of Brazil's best-known exports, enjoyed at restaurant chains like Fogo de Chão throughout North America and beyond (you can read about it on page 170).

At the heart of Brazilian barbecue lies an industrial-strength rotisserie on which meats, poultry, seafood, and even cheese, bread, and fruit turn on horizontal spits over a charcoal fire. The waiters carry these saberlike spits through the dining room (a process known as *espeto corrido*, which you could loosely translate as "running spits"), carving the food right onto the customers' plates. Meats are served in dazzling variety—eight or ten different cuts at a typical *churrascaria;* two dozen at a really good place. The food is served with such largesse (the salad bar alone typically stretches the length of the dining room) that guests need stop signs (provided by the restaurant) to advise the waiters when they can't eat another bite.

THE GRILLS: Brazilians use three types of grill. The first is a rotisserie with spits turning horizontally over a long rectangular firebox filled with charcoal. Often the spits are driven by motors built right into the wall. The *parrilla* is a conventional grill with a flat grate positioned over the fire. A *fogo de chão* is a campfire around which large cuts of meat, like racks of beef ribs, are roasted on vertical stakes. *Rodízio* means "switching"—a reference to how the waiters offer customers different meat each time they pass through the dining room.

THE FUEL: Natural lump charcoal

THE FLAVORINGS: Brazilians season with a simple palette—very coarse salt, often applied by the fistful, for seasoning red meats, and *tempeiro,* a salt and lime juice–based marinade, for white meats, like chicken and seafood.

MUST TRY DISHES: At most Brazilian *churrascarias* you pay a fixed price that entitles you to sample every item cooked on the rotisserie plus the salad bar and all the side dishes. Each of these are fabulous; the items with asterisks indicate iconic dishes you mustn't miss.

Bife de chorizo: Butterflied rib eye steak

Bife de tira: New York strip butterflied through the short end to create a long steak

*Costela: A rack of sizzling, salty, crusty, meaty beef ribs roasted in front of a campfire

Frango: Chicken

Linguiça: A garlicky Brazilian/Portuguese sausage

*Picanha: Brazil's most important contribution to the world of barbecue— spit-roasted fat cap sirloin (see page 153)

THE CONDIMENTS: *Molho à campanha* (country sauce; see page 155) is a sort of salsa made with onions, peppers, chiles, oil, and vinegar. *Farofa* is a crumbly sauté of cassava flour, bacon, onions, and other vegetables. You sprinkle it over the meat to absorb the juices (you'll find a recipe on page 217). Other typical accompaniments include soupy black beans, white rice, and *couve minera,* sautéed shredded kale.

HOW TO EAT IT: The meats are brought to the table on swordlike spits and carved directly onto your plate. Most restaurants provide you with tongs for grabbing the meat as it comes off the spit and a sign or medallion that's green on one side and red on the other to enable you to regulate the flow of the meal. The waiters continue serving the meat until you instruct them to stop by displaying the red side of the sign.

IF YOU CAN EAT AT ONLY ONE OR TWO RESTAURANTS: Two good chains found in most major Brazilian cities are Fogo de Chão and Porcão.

WHAT TO DRINK: Brazil's national cocktail is the *caipirinha,* a sort of daiquiri made with *cachaça* (a powerful cane spirit), sugar, and mashed chunks of lime.

THE MOST SINGULAR DISH IN THE REPERTORY: There are many: the spit-roasted onions served at Dinho's in São Paulo (see page 537); the rotisserie pineapple served at Galpão Crioulo (see page 578). And you'll find rotisserie chicken hearts at almost any Brazilian *churrascaria*—a dish that may seem singular to North Americans, but that's old hat for Brazilians.

Meats on spits at a Brazilian churrascaria—carnival for carnivores.

Kosovan Grilled Mushrooms

WHERE: Kosovo and throughout the Balkans

WHAT: Grilled mushrooms with garlic and parsley. Simple. Easy. And unbelievably good.

HOW: Direct grilling

JUST THE FACTS: Almost any fresh mushroom can be grilled, from commonplace button mushrooms and creminis to exotic boletus, chanterelles, and hen of the woods.

Like most Europeans, Kosovars are mushroom fanatics. Mushrooming is not only a weekend pastime, it's an important source of income. Indeed, a lot of the truffles, porcini, and other exotic mushrooms sold in Western Europe actually come from Kosovar forests. The following recipe was inspired by Kosovar grill master, Velisic Blagoje, but virtually identical preparations can be found from the Spanish Atlantic to the Black Sea. For a heart-healthier version, mix the garlic and parsley with 3 tablespoons of olive oil instead of butter. For Mexican or Colombian–style mushrooms, substitute cilantro for the parsley and add minced serrano or jalapeño pepper to the butter mixture. **SERVES 4**

4 tablespoons (½ stick) salted butter, at room temperature
2 cloves garlic, minced
3 tablespoons finely chopped fresh flat-leaf parsley, tarragon, or another fresh herb, such as basil or tarragon
Freshly ground black pepper
1 pound mushrooms, such as boletus, chanterelles, cremini, portobellos, or button mushrooms

YOU'LL ALSO NEED
Grill basket or bamboo skewers

ADVANCE PREPARATION
None

1 Place the butter in a mixing bowl. Add the garlic and parsley. Whisk the butter until it is light and creamy, then season it with pepper to taste. Alternatively, you can melt the butter in a saucepan over medium-high heat. Add the garlic and parsley, season with pepper to taste, and cook over high heat until the mixture is sizzling and aromatic, 1 to 2 minutes. Do not let the garlic brown. Set the garlic-herb butter aside.

2 Wipe the mushrooms clean with a damp paper towel or dishcloth. (Do not rinse the mushrooms or they will get soggy.) Trim the ends off the stems. Depending on the size and shape of the mushrooms, it will be easier to grill them in a grill basket or shish kebab-style on skewers.

3 Set up the grill for direct grilling and preheat it to high.

4 When ready to cook, brush and oil the grill grate. Lightly brush the mushrooms with the garlic-herb butter. Place the mushrooms on the hot grate and grill them until niccly browned and tender, 2 to 4 minutes per side, basting them with more garlic-herb butter. Don't apply too much butter or too thickly or it will drip, flare up, and make the mushrooms sooty.

5 Transfer the grilled mushrooms to a platter or plates and serve at once, with any remaining garlic-herb butter spooned on top.

VARIATION

Garlic-Herb Portobello Skewers: The portobello, that oversize cousin of the common button mushroom, makes a great mushroom for grilling. You could think of this variation as vegetarian satés. And to reinforce the Asian theme you could substitute chopped cilantro or shiso leaf—a sort of Japanese mint—for the parsley.

You'll need 4 portobello mushrooms to make these satés. Prepare the garlic-herb butter as described in Step 1 on the facing page. Remove and discard the stems of the portobellos. Wipe the caps clean with a damp paper towel or dishcloth, then cut the caps into finger-wide strips. Skewer each strip lengthwise on a bamboo skewer. Grill the skewered mushrooms with the garlic-herb baste as described in Step 4, placing an aluminum foil shield under the exposed ends of the skewers to keep them from burning (see page 611), if desired. The grilled portobellos are particularly good sprinkled with ¾ cup of grated Parmigiano-Reggiano cheese.

Romanian and Serbian Grilled Pickled Peppers
{ ARDEI COPTI }

I once taught a student who did a Peace Corps stint in Romania. Come autumn, she would awaken to a smell reminiscent of our collective college days—the sweet, smoky reek of dried leafy matter burning on an open fire. No, it wasn't a giant pot party, although it sure smelled that way. It was the scent of peppers being grilled over the fire prior to pickling, an aroma that permeates the air each fall from the Danube to the Black Sea. In this the Balkans and Slavs have it hands down over the Italians, as grilling gives a pickled pepper a smoky dimension that makes mere *peperoncini* pale in comparison. Romanians add dill; Serbs add garlic; and Bulgarians pair the pickled peppers with grilled eggplant. While I've eaten grilled peppers on six continents, Romania is the only country where I've seen the stems wrapped in foil. The foil handles allow you to pick up and eat the peppers with your hands without getting ash or oil on your fingers. **SERVES 4**

JUST THE FACTS:
Romanians use a long, slender, flavorful, but unfiery pepper similar to a North American Cubanelle. Other good choices would include Anaheim and New Mexico peppers, horn peppers, or even miniature bell peppers.

Romanian Grilled Peppers

12 large Cubanelle or Anaheim peppers
    (about 1½ pounds)
1 teaspoon coarse salt (kosher or sea), or to taste
½ cup distilled white vinegar
½ cup vegetable oil
3 tablespoons chopped fresh dill

ADVANCE PREPARATION
The peppers can be grilled and pickled several days or even weeks before serving. Allow at least 2 hours for them to pickle.

1 Set up the grill for direct grilling and preheat it to high.

2 When ready to cook, brush and oil the grill grate. Place the peppers on the hot grate and grill them until the skins are darkly browned and blistered, about 2 minutes per side, 6 to 8 minutes in all.

3 Transfer the peppers to a cutting board and let them cool to room temperature. (No, you don't have to place them in a paper bag or bowl covered with plastic wrap. I've found no appreciable difference in ease of peeling.) Using a paring knife, scrape the charred skins off the peppers. There's no need to remove every last bit; a few black spots will add a charred color and flavor. Place the peppers in a shallow earthenware dish.

4 Combine the salt and vinegar in a nonreactive mixing bowl and whisk until the salt dissolves. Whisk in the oil and dill. Pour the pickling mixture over the peppers, turning them with tongs to coat with marinade. Let the peppers marinate in the refrigerator, covered, for at least 2 hours or as long

as 2 weeks; the longer they marinate, the richer the flavor will be.

5 When ready to serve, cut small (½ x 1 inch) strips of aluminum foil and wrap them around the pepper stems. This step is optional, but it looks cool. Serve the peppers at room temperature with the marinade.

Serbian Grilled Peppers

Serbs use hotter peppers than Romanians and add garlic instead of dill. The peppers are yellow to pale green in color, like a banana pepper; the heat is appreciable and decisive, without the palate-torturing intensity of the Scotch bonnet. The flavor is less grassy and bell peppery than that of a jalapeño and also less hot. Two good choices in North America are horn peppers and banana peppers. This is a good dish to make ahead; refrigerate it until you are ready to serve. **SERVES 4**

1½ pounds small, slender hot peppers, such as
    horn or banana peppers
1 teaspoon coarse salt (kosher or sea)
½ cup distilled white vinegar or red wine vinegar
½ cup vegetable oil
2 to 3 cloves garlic, peeled and crushed with the
    side of a knife

1 Set up the grill for direct grilling and preheat it to high.

2 When ready to cook, brush and oil the grill grate. Place the peppers on the hot grate and grill them until lightly browned, 2 to 3 minutes per side, 4 to 6 minutes in all. You want to brown but not actually char the skin.

3 Transfer the grilled peppers to a nonreactive bowl or crock or, for longer storage, a sterilized jar and stir in the salt, vinegar, oil, and garlic. Let the peppers cool to room temperature, then refrigerate until serving.

Grilled Peppers Around the World

Nothing brings out a pepper's sweetness like the fiery heat of the grill. The sheer diversity of grilled pepper dishes around Planet Barbecue attests to the popularity of both the method and the result. Note that by "pepper," I mean a member of the *capsicum* family (which embraces everything from the mild bell pepper to the incendiary Scotch bonnet). This does not include white, black, or green peppercorns *(piper nigrum)*.

ARDEI COPTI: Pickled peppers Romanian-style—grilled, then marinated with vinegar, oil, and garlic

CHLADA FELFLA MECHWIYA: Moroccan Grilled Pepper Salad (see page 62)

MORONES ASADOS: Argentinean fire-roasted red bell peppers, grilled whole and served plain—or with garlic and anchovies in salads (see page 66)

PEPERONI ARROSTITI: Italian roasted peppers—dressed with olive oil and sea salt

POBLANOS ASADOS: Fire-charred poblano peppers. An indispensable accompaniment to Mexican *carne asado* (grilled beef tacos) and *queso fundido* (melted or grilled cheese)

TANDOORI SIMLA MIRCH: Indian bell peppers stuffed with potatoes and cheese and grilled in a tandoor

SHISHITO YAKI: Japanese Grilled *Shishito* Peppers with Sesame Oil and Salt (see page 544)

SIRKELI SARMISAKLI BIBER IZGARA: Turkish roasted red peppers with garlic and vinegar

XNI PEC: "Dog's nose" salsa, literally, a Yucatán grilled habañero salsa so fiery, it makes your nose run (one explanation for the name)

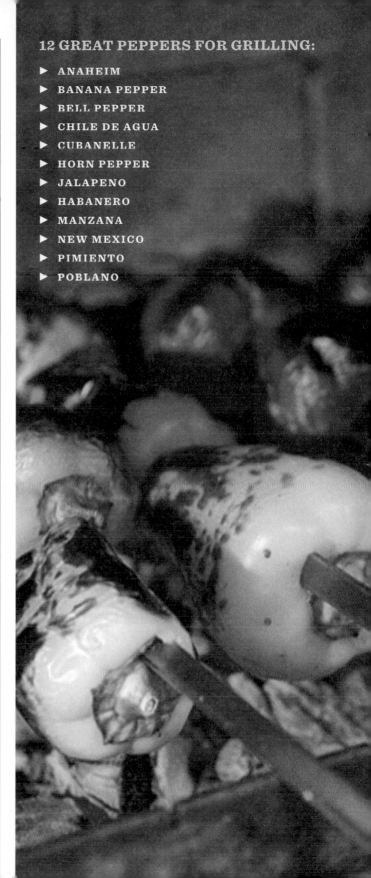

12 GREAT PEPPERS FOR GRILLING:

- ▶ ANAHEIM
- ▶ BANANA PEPPER
- ▶ BELL PEPPER
- ▶ CHILE DE AGUA
- ▶ CUBANELLE
- ▶ HORN PEPPER
- ▶ JALAPENO
- ▶ HABANERO
- ▶ MANZANA
- ▶ NEW MEXICO
- ▶ PIMIENTO
- ▶ POBLANO

Grilled Shishito Peppers with Sesame Oil and Salt

There's no reason you need to ferret out Izakaya-Tamotsu. (But if you want to, the address is 2-3-2 Yuraku-cho, Miyauchi Building 1 F, Chiyoda-ku, Tokyo.) There are thousands of similar establishments in Tokyo: tiny yakitori bars with a handful of stools at an L-shape counter and a handful of tables on the sidewalk in nice weather. Straw baskets line the counter, one piled with shiitakes (stems and caps to be grilled and served separately), others filled with tiny taro roots, grapelike ginkgo nuts, miniature eggplants, or baby finger-size *shishito* peppers—all ready for grilling. The grill measures perhaps two feet long and just a couple of inches across, ideal for grilling a tiny kebab without burning the end of the skewer. When asked about the charcoal fire, Izakaya's owner explained in about the only English words he knew that it burned at more than 1,000°F. Japanese *shishitos* have the sweet grassy flavor of grilled green peppers everywhere, with enough heat to make you sit up and take notice. This is one of the simplest—and best ways—I know to grill any green vegetable: asparagus, scallions, leeks, and so on. **SERVES 4**

1 pound shishito peppers
2 tablespoons Asian (dark) sesame oil
Large flat crystals of coarse sea salt

YOU'LL ALSO NEED
Bamboo skewers; an aluminum foil grill shield
     (see page 611)

ADVANCE PREPARATION
None

1 Skewer the *shishito* peppers crosswise on bamboo skewers, leaving about half of the skewer exposed. Lightly brush the peppers on both sides with the sesame oil and season them with sea salt.

2 Set up the grill for direct grilling and preheat it to high.

3 When ready to grill, brush and oil the grill grate. Arrange the skewered peppers on the hot grate with the aluminum foil shield under the exposed ends of the skewers to keep them from burning. Grill the peppers until sizzling and browned on both sides, 2 to 4 minutes per side. Serve the peppers hot off the grill with extra salt on the side for sprinkling.

Armenian Potato Kebabs

I t's pretty hard to top the combination of potatoes and bacon especially when they're grilled. Which brings me to one of my favorite Armenian restaurants in Moscow, the appropriately named and picturesquely decorated Yerevan (Yerevan is also the capital of Armenia). Of all the grill cultures of the former Soviet republics, Armenians show the most enthusiasm for vegetables. If you've never before grilled potatoes, these smoky, earthy kebabs are a fine place to start. **MAKES 4 KEBABS, SERVES 4 AS AN APPETIZER OR SIDE DISH**

12 new potatoes (each about 1½ inches across; about 1 pound total), scrubbed
Vegetable oil (optional)
Coarse salt (kosher or sea)
Freshly ground black pepper
3 thick slices of smoky bacon, cut into 1 inch squares, or a 3 to 4 ounce chunk of lamb fat, cut into 1 inch squares and ¼ inch thick
1 tablespoon melted bacon fat, lamb fat, butter, or vegetable oil for basting
Sweet paprika

YOU'LL ALSO NEED
Four small bamboo skewers

ADVANCE PREPARATION
You will need to precook the potatoes, either by parboiling them or grilling them using the indirect method. The kebabs can be assembled and refrigerated several hours ahead.

1 Precook the potatoes (this can be done up to 24 hours ahead):

If you are grilling the potatoes, use the indirect method. Set up the grill for indirect grilling, place a drip pan in the center, and preheat the grill to medium-high. When ready to cook,

prick the potatoes with a fork in a few spots, brush them with oil, and season them with salt and pepper. Place the potatoes in the center of the grill over the drip pan and away from the heat and cover the grill. Grill the potatoes until you are just able to pierce them with a slender skewer, 10 to 15 minutes.

If you are parboiling the potatoes, place the potatoes in a pot, add cold salted water to cover by 4 inches, and bring to a boil over high heat. Boil the potatoes until barely tender, 5 to 8 minutes. Use a bamboo skewer or fork to test for doneness; you should be just able to pierce them. Drain the potatoes well in a colander, rinsing them under cold running water until cool.

2 Cut each potato in half. Generously sprinkle the bacon pieces on both sides with paprika.

3 Thread the potatoes and the pieces of bacon onto the skewers starting by skewering 1 half potato through its cut side. Skewer a second potato half through the rounded side, then skewer

THE SCOOP

WHERE: Armenia

WHAT: Bacon and potato shish kebabs

HOW: Direct grilling

JUST THE FACTS: The fat of choice in Armenia—as it is throughout the Caucasus region and Central Asia— is lamb tail fat, available from halal butchers. (The photos on page 546 show how to make the potatoes using the traditional lamb fat.) Using thick sliced smoky country-style bacon produces excellent potato kebabs that are very much in the spirit of the original.

a piece of bacon so that it is flat against the potato. Skewer another potato half through the cut side, followed by a potato half skewered through the rounded side. Skewer another piece of bacon flat against the potato. Finally skewer 2 more potato halves, the first through the cut side and the second through the rounded side. Repeat with the remaining skewers, potatoes, and bacon. The kebabs can be prepared several hours ahead to this stage and refrigerated, covered.

4 Set up the grill for direct grilling and preheat it to high.

5 When ready to cook, brush and oil the grill grate. Brush the potatoes on all sides with the melted bacon fat, and season them generously with salt, pepper, and paprika. Arrange the kebabs on the hot grill grate. Grill the kebabs until the potatoes are golden brown and the bacon is sizzling and cooked through, 2 to 3 minutes per side, 8 to 12 minutes in all. Transfer the kebabs to platters and serve at once on the bamboo skewers.

VARIATION

Armenian Potato Kebabs with Onion: I like the way adding pieces of onion to the kebabs builds on the earthy flavors of the bacon and potatoes. To do this cut a medium-size onion in half crosswise, then cut each half in quarters. Break the quarters into layers and skewer pieces of onion on the kebabs between the bacon and the potatoes.

POTATO KEBABS THE ARMENIAN WAY

1. *Season cubes of lamb fat or bacon with sweet paprika.*

2. *Insert a bamboo skewer through the cut side of a half precooked potato.*

3. *Add a piece of lamb fat or bacon.*

4. *Place another potato half on the skewer. The idea is to place the lamb fat (or bacon) next to the broad side of the potato half to maximize contact with the fat.*

Potato kebabs served Armenian-style—on a sheet of lavash bread.

5. *In Armenia you'd grill the potato kebabs in a grill basket on a grateless grill called a mangal. In North America, you can cook the kebabs directly on the grill grate.*

Grilled Potatoes with Herbed Cheese

I n the staunchly male world of German barbecue, Maritta Stauch stands out, first of all because she's a woman, and a tall, striking redhead at that. But the chef-owner of the Berghotel Kristall, located high on a hill outside Idar, can *schwenken* ("swing" grill, see page 218) with the best of them. She even installed a custom-designed grill in the fireplace of her popular dining room. Like any good *schwenker* (griller), she serves up wood-roasted pork neck steaks and fillets, sirloin, and lamb chops, but what kept me returning for seconds were her *schwenken kartoffeln* (beechwood fire-roasted potatoes). Add a creamy topping of *quark mit kräuter* (a sort of smooth cottage cheese flavored with garlic and fresh herbs) and you get a spud that makes a North American baked potato with sour cream seem, well, boring. **MAKES 8 HALF POTATOES, SERVES 4 TO 8**

FOR THE HERBED COTTAGE CHEESE

1 cup large-curd cottage cheese

¼ cup sour cream

4 tablespoons (½ stick) salted butter, at room temperature

1 small clove garlic, minced

1 tablespoon finely chopped fresh chives

1 tablespoon finely chopped fresh dill

1 tablespoon finely chopped flat-leaf parsley (optional)

Freshly ground white or black pepper

FOR THE POTATOES

4 large baking potatoes (each 12 to 16 ounces; see Note), scrubbed

2 tablespoons (¼ stick) salted butter, melted, or 2 tablespoons extra-virgin olive oil

Coarse salt (kosher or sea) and freshly ground black pepper

YOU'LL ALSO NEED

2 cups wood chips or chunks, preferably beech (optional), soaked in water to cover for 1 hour, then drained

ADVANCE PREPARATION

None, but allow yourself 1 hour for smoke roasting the potatoes. You can make the herbed cheese up to 6 hours ahead

1 Make the herbed cottage cheese: Place the cottage cheese in a food processor and puree until smooth. Add the sour cream and room temperature butter and process to mix. Add the garlic, chives, dill, and parsley, if using, and run the processor in short bursts to mix; do not overprocess or the mixture will turn green. Season with pepper to taste. You can make the herbed cheese up to 6 hours ahead and refrigerate it, covered. Let the herbed cheese warm to room temperature before serving.

2 Grill the potatoes: Set up the grill for indirect grilling, place a drip pan in the center, and preheat the grill to medium-high.

3 Prick the potatoes in a few spots with a fork. Brush the potatoes all over with the melted butter or olive oil and season them generously with salt and pepper.

4 When ready to cook, if you are using a charcoal grill, toss the wood chips or chunks, if using, on the coals. If you are using a gas grill, add the wood chips or chunks, if using, to the smoker box or place them in a smoker pouch under the grate (see page 603). Place the potatoes in the center of the grill over the drip pan and away from the heat and cover the grill. Grill the potatoes until tender, 40 to 60 minutes. Usc a slender skewer to test for doneness; it should pierce the potatoes easily.

5 To serve, cut the potatoes in half and squeeze the sides to loosen the flesh. Top each potato half with generous spoonfuls of the herbed cottage cheese and serve at once.

NOTE: Maritta Stauch uses a thin-skinned white potato grown on her father's farm near the hotel, but baking potatoes or large Yukon Golds will work great.

VARIATIONS
Grilled Potatoes with Herbed Cheese Using the Direct Method: To grill the potatoes using the direct method you will need to parboil them first. Place the potatoes in a large pot, add cold salted water to cover by 4 inches, and bring to a boil over high heat. Boil the potatoes until barely tender, 30 to 40 minutes. Use a slender skewer to test for doneness; you should be just able to pierce them. Drain the potatoes well in a colander, rinsing them under cold running water until cool. The potatoes can be prepared up to 24 hours ahead to this stage and refrigerated, covered.

Set up the grill for direct grilling and preheat it to medium-high. Ideally, you'd grill over a beech wood fire (see page 603 for instructions). Alternatively, you can use beech wood chips or chunks to add a smoke flavor. If you are using a gas grill, add the wood chips or chunks to the smoker box or place them in a smoker pouch under the grate (see page 603).

When ready to cook, brush and oil the grill grate. If you are using a charcoal grill, toss the wood chips or chunks, if using, on the coals. Place the potatoes on the hot grate and grill until browned, smoky, and heated through, 2 to 3 minutes per side, 8 to 12 minutes in all. Alternatively you can cut the potatoes crosswise into ¾ inch-thick slices and grill them until browned, smoky, and heated through, 2 to 3 minutes per side. Serve the potatoes topped with the herbed cottage cheese.

Potatoes in the Embers: In other parts of Germany the potatoes would be roasted in their skins right in the embers—just as portrayed in Vincent van Gogh's painting *The Potato Eaters.* According to my grilling colleague Klaus Marx (see page 221), you wind up with black fingers, a black face, and a smile as wide as Lake Constance.

Ember roasting is generally done in a fireplace. Rake a mound of embers into a rectangle large enough to hold the potatoes. Shovel a ½-inch or so layer of ash on top. Arrange the potatoes on top of the ashes. Shovel another ½-inch layer of ash over the potatoes and top with more hot embers. Roast the potatoes until they are easily pierced with a fork, 1 to 1½ hours. Serve the roasted potatoes with the herbed cottage cheese.

Tandoori Potatoes
{ TANDOORI ALOO }

If you want to master meatless barbecue, India is the place to do it. This nation of more than a billion people has nearly as many vegetarians as there are people in the entire United States. Over the centuries, Indian grill masters have evolved a highly sophisticated style of vegetarian barbecue, creating dishes bursting with flavor (not to mention essential dairy and grain proteins). It's grilling so complex and satisfying, you'll never miss the meat. *Tandoori aloo* (tandoori potato) turns up at grill parlors throughout northern India. The best I've ever tasted was at the landmark restaurant Moti Mahal in Old Delhi. It came packed with cheese, slathered with spice paste, and crusted with sesame seeds. The recipe may look complicated, but actually it's a series of simple steps.   **MAKES 4 POTATOES; SERVES 4 AS A SIDE DISH, 2 AS A MAIN COURSE**

THE SCOOP

WHERE: India

WHAT: Cheese-stuffed potatoes, glazed with yogurt spice paste and grilled in a sesame crust

HOW: Indirect grilling

JUST THE FACTS: In India, these potatoes would be stuffed with *paneer* (sometimes spelled *panir*), a mild, sweet, white cow's milk cheese. You can buy it at an Indian market or online at www.igourmet .com. Many Western cheeses work well as a substitute, from Monterey Jack to white cheddar to Gruyère. Indian grill masters would roast the potatoes on a vertical spit in a tandoor. You can achieve a similar effect by indirect grilling.

FOR THE POTATOES AND STUFFING

4 white or baking potatoes (each about 8 ounces), scrubbed

Vegetable oil (optional)

Coarse salt (kosher or sea) and freshly ground black pepper

2 tablespoons chopped fresh cilantro

1 scallion, both white and green parts, trimmed and finely chopped

1 hot green chile pepper, such as a serrano or small jalapeño, seeded and minced (for hotter potatoes leave the seeds in)

1 tablespoon sesame seeds

4 ounces paneer or other cheese (see Just the Facts), coarsely grated

2 tablespoons (¼ stick) butter (salted or unsalted, whatever you have on hand), melted or at room temperature

FOR THE YOGURT SPICE PASTE

2 cloves garlic, coarsely chopped

2 teaspoons chopped peeled fresh ginger

2 teaspoons sweet or hot paprika

1 teaspoon salt, or more to taste

1 teaspoon ground coriander

½ teaspoon ground cumin

½ cup thick (Greek-style) plain yogurt

4 teaspoons vegetable oil

2 teaspoons fresh lemon juice

¼ teaspoon freshly ground black pepper

½ cup sesame seeds

ADVANCE PREPARATION

Allow yourself time to precook and cool the potatoes. The potatoes can be precooked up to a day in advance.

Moti Mahal— one of the first tandoori restaurants in New Delhi.

1 Precook the potatoes (this can be done up to 24 hours ahead).

If you are grilling the potatoes, use the indirect method: Set up the grill for indirect grilling, place a drip pan in the center, and preheat the grill to medium-high. When ready to cook, prick the potatoes with a fork in a few spots, brush them with oil, and season them with salt and pepper. Place the potatoes in the center of the grill over the drip pan and away from the heat and cover the grill. Grill the potatoes until you are just able to pierce them with a slender skewer, about 40 minutes.

If you are parboiling the potatoes, place the potatoes in a large pot, add cold salted water to cover by 4 inches, and bring to a boil over high heat. Boil the potatoes until barely tender, about 30 minutes. Use a bamboo skewer or fork to test for doneness; you should be just able to pierce them. Drain the potatoes well in a colander, rinsing them under cold running water until cool.

2 Cut each potato in half crosswise. Cut a very thin slice off the bottom of each half potato so you can stand it upright. Using a melon baller or spoon, hollow out each potato half to within ¼ inch of the side, transferring the potato to a mixing bowl. Finely chop or mash the potato. Reserve the potato shells.

3 Add the cilantro, scallion, chile pepper, sesame seeds, *paneer,* and butter to the chopped potato and stir to mix. Season with salt and black pepper to taste; the filling should be highly seasoned. Stuff the filling into the hollowed-out potato halves. The potatoes can be prepared up to 6 hours ahead to this stage and refrigerated.

4 Make the yogurt spice paste: Place the garlic, ginger, paprika, 1 teaspoon of salt, and the coriander and cumin in a food processor and finely chop them. Add the yogurt, oil, and lemon juice and puree to a smooth paste, scraping down the side of the processor bowl with a rubber spatula. Taste for seasoning, adding the black pepper and more salt as necessary. Transfer the spice paste to a shallow bowl. Place ¼ cup of the sesame seeds in a shallow bowl and the remaining ¼ in a measuring cup.

5 Set up the grill for indirect grilling and preheat it to high.

6 When ready to cook, brush and oil the grill grate. Spoon half of the yogurt spice paste over the potato halves, then sprinkle the paste with the sesame seeds in the measuring cup. Dip the bottom of each potato half in the remaining yogurt spice paste, then in the remaining sesame seeds. Arrange the potatoes upright on the grill over the drip pan and away from the heat. Grill the potatoes until they are golden brown on the outside and bubbling in the center, 15 to 25 minutes. Transfer the potatoes to a platter or plates and serve at once.

VARIATION

Tandoori Potatoes in the Style of Baked Stuffed Potatoes: Here's an Indian version of an American-style stuffed baked potato.

Prepare the Tandoori Potatoes recipe, substituting 2 jumbo baking potatoes for the smaller potatoes. Cook them until soft, then cut each in half lengthwise, hollow them out with a spoon, and mash the flesh. Prepare the filling as described and stuff it back into the potato skins. Spread half of the yogurt spice paste on the bottoms of the potato skins and half over the filling. Crust the potatoes with sesame seeds and grill as described.

Potato vendor weighs his wares in Varanasi, India.

Smashed Potatoes
{ PAPAS APLASTADAS }

That grilled potatoes should turn up throughout South America makes sense—after all, Latinos are grill maniacs and the potato originated in the Andes Mountains. That the widespread practice here is to grill potatoes wrapped in aluminum foil (*al plomo*—literally "in lead") seems counterproductive. After all, the foil blocks out the fire and smoke flavors. At least one restaurant, La Huella in José Ignacio, Uruguay, bucks the trend, roasting its potatoes in their skins in an oak-burning oven. Did someone say "oak-burning oven?" The next best thing is smoke roasting on the grill. SERVES 4

4 large baking potatoes (each 12 to 16 ounces), scrubbed

2 tablespoons (¼ stick) salted butter, melted, plus 4 to 6 tablespoons (½ to ¾ stick) butter at room temperature

Coarse salt (kosher or sea) and freshly ground black pepper

YOU'LL ALSO NEED

2 cups wood chips or chunks, preferably oak, soaked in water to cover for 1 hour, then drained; potato masher or pestle

ADVANCE PREPARATION

The potatoes are best grilled and mashed right before serving.

1 Set up the grill for indirect grilling, place a drip pan in the center, and preheat the grill to medium-high.

2 Prick each potato in a few spots with a fork. Brush the potatoes all over with the melted butter and season them generously with salt and pepper.

3 If you are using a charcoal grill, toss the wood chips or chunks on the coals. If you are using a gas grill, add the wood chips or chunks to the smoker box or place them in a smoker pouch under the grate (see page 603). Place the potatoes in the center of the grill over the drip pan and away from the heat and cover the grill. Grill the potatoes until tender, about 1 hour. Use a slender skewer to test for doneness; it should pierce the potatoes easily.

4 Transfer the grilled potatoes to a cast-iron skillet. Coarsely mash each one—skin and all—with a potato masher or pestle. Add the room temperature butter, season the potatoes with salt and pepper to taste, and mash the potatoes a few more times—enough to mix in the butter and break up any large chunks of potatoes but not so much that the potatoes are pureed. The potatoes should look rather like they were run over by a car. Serve the potatoes at once.

THE SCOOP

WHERE: José Ignacio, Uruguay

WHAT: Mashed potatoes like you've never tasted: whole spuds smoke roasted in their skins, then mashed with butter and sea salt

HOW: At the restaurant La Huella, they roast potatoes in a wood-burning oven; indirect grilling with wood smoke produces a similar effect

JUST THE FACTS: For the best flavor, use organic potatoes.

PLANET BARBECUE

Azerbaijan: The Best Barbecue No One Knew About

Azerbaijan may not top your list of the world's barbecue hot spots (many people would be hard-pressed to tell you where Azerbaijan *is*). But this Caucasus Mountain republic, sandwiched between Armenia and the Caspian Sea, has some of the best live-fire cooking of the former Soviet Union.

In fact, it took only one meal at an Azeri restaurant in Moscow to convince me to buy a ticket and make the five-hour overnight flight from Moscow to Baku.

Well, that and a desire to stick my toe in the Caspian Sea. This body of water, the world's largest lake, first appeared on my radar back in my restaurant critic days, when you could still afford (sort of) beluga, osetra, and other caviar from genuine Caspian Sea sturgeon. It also turns out to be a focal point of Near Eastern barbecue, bordered by Russia to the north, Iran to the south, and Turkmenistan and Kazakhstan to the east—in short, one of the primal heartlands of grilling, where lamb perfumed with Spice

Baklava seller. No Azeri barbecue is complete without a sweet dessert.

Route seasonings has sizzled over charcoal for most of human history.

You don't have to travel far in the Azeri capital, Baku, to find barbecue: at outdoor eateries in the waterfront park across from the hotels where international oil execs stay (Azerbaijan is a major petroleum exporter); in the courtyard restaurants of the fabulous medieval quarter, dominated by a mysterious stone tower; in the old Jewish neighborhood, today

home to a splendid new synagogue (Azerbaijan is one of the few Arab nations with warm relations with Israel).

But the best place to experience barbecue is at one of the sprawling country-style restaurants, like Neolit, on the outskirts of Baku. Neolit ("Neolithic") is a veritable city, complete with a music stage, wedding hall, and outdoor village with open-air pavilions, where Azeris can eat under grape arbors,

A Meeting of East and West

The Caucasus Mountains, land of lambs, goats, and wild herbs.

Azerbaijan, where the grilling of the Caucasus Mountains meets the flavors of the Caspian Sea.

A Baku spice market: The go-to source for Azeri rubs and spice pastes.

just like they do in the countryside. Often, each dining area has its own *mangalchik* (grill chef), bread baker, and orchestra.

Neolit chef Mehman Huseynov (read about him on page 592) grills everything, from whole lambs spiced with turmeric and roasted in a *tandir,* to finely minced Caspian sturgeon, and of course, every conceivable incarnation of *lula,* as ground meat kebabs are known in these parts. He even grills ice cream for dessert.

Baku, Azerbaijan, is easy to fly to from London and Moscow. Once there, you'll be rewarded by a culture that is at once exotic and westernized, familiar yet otherworldly. And of course, the barbecue is out of this world.

Azeri grill master, Asif Babayef. Born in Baku; currently grills in Moscow. You can read about him on page 290.

THE GRILLS: Azeri grills come in two basic models. The *mangal,* a troughlike metal box across the top of which are placed skewers of food or grill baskets (see page 605), is used for direct grilling. The *tandir* is the Azeri version of India's tandoor—an upright metal and clay barbecue pit with a fire at the bottom over which chickens and even small lambs are roasted—hung from a rod stretched across the top.

Rolling dough to make lavash (Azeri flatbreads).

THE FUEL: Natural lump charcoal

THE INGREDIENTS: As in most countries in the Near East and Central Asia, lamb is king—followed by chicken, veal, and sturgeon. The spicing is relatively simple: salt, pepper, turmeric, cumin, onion, and garlic. One ingredient widely used in Azeri grilling not familiar in the West is lamb tail fat, a hard, waxy fat that takes the place of butter, olive oil, and bacon. Read about it on page 332.

MUST TRY DISHES:
Bademjan: Grilled eggplant
Gov urmasi: Pit-roasted lamb—often a whole baby lamb
Lula: A minced meat kebab, sort of like Turkish or Middle Eastern *kofta;* while lamb (and very fatty lamb at that) is the most popular meat, you'll also find *lula* made with chicken, sturgeon, and even mashed potatoes.
Shashlik: The backbone of Azeri grilling, if you were to find yourself in the hands of a

good *mangalchik* and you sampled a different *shashlik* every hour, you could spend several full days exploring the Azeri repertory and not eat the same kebab twice.

THE CONDIMENTS: Azeris don't use barbecue sauce, per se, but every grilled dish comes with a tangy relish of sliced red onion and flat-leaf parsley. All restaurants make it fresh daily; at good restaurants, the onions and parsley are chopped to order. You might also get a bowl of a tart purplish sumac powder.

HOW TO EAT IT: Azeri barbecue comes with thin sheets of a flat bread similar to Armenian lavash. Use it to roll up pieces of meat and the onion relish and pop them into your mouth.

IF YOU CAN EAT AT ONLY ONE RESTAURANT: Neolit, just outside Baku

THE MOST SINGULAR DISH IN THE REPERTORY: Grilled ice cream—you can read about it on page 590.

"Knish on a Stick"
{ GRILLED MASHED POTATOES }

THE SCOOP

WHERE: Azerbaijan

WHAT: Onion-scented mashed potatoes grilled shish-kebab style—really

HOW: Direct grilling on a grateless grill

JUST THE FACTS: To be strictly authentic, you'd use an ingredient widely available and beloved in Azerbaijan but ignored in North America—lamb tail fat. This waxy white fat (think of it as the lard of the Near East; see page 332 for more information) keeps things moist, just as butter or cream would in Western mashed potatoes. It has the added advantage of not melting or disintegrating as it grills. I'm going to assume that a trip to a halal market to buy lamb tail fat is not in your future, so I'm going to propose a delectable, if nontraditional (and from a Muslim's point of view, sacreligious), work-around: bacon. The smoke flavor raises these grilled mashed potatoes to a whole new level.

OK, here it is, a Planet Barbecue first: Mashed potatoes like you've never seen—or tasted—before, unless you live in the oil rich Caucasus nation of Azerbaijan. Flavored with caramelized onion (so far so good) and lamb fat (OK, maybe not so good, but bacon makes a great substitute), these potatoes are guaranteed to melt in your mouth, not to mention enhance your reputation for out-of-the-box grilling. So how do you grill mashed potatoes? (Aside from the obvious: carefully?) The secret is to mold and grill them on wide, flat metal skewers. In Azerbaijan, the kebabs would be grilled on a grateless grill called a *mangal* (see page 605), so there's no risk of the soft potato mixture sticking to the grill grate. When grilling on a Western-style grill with a grate, you'll need to oil the grate *really* well, or better yet, set up the grill for grateless grilling. **SERVES 4 TO 6**

1½ pounds Yukon Golds or other yellow potatoes
Coarse salt (kosher or sea)
1½ tablespoons vegetable oil or unsalted butter
1 medium-size onion, finely chopped
½ teaspoon ground cumin
Freshly ground black pepper
2 ounces bacon (about 2 slices), or 2 ounces
    lamb tail fat, cut into ¼-inch slivers
Lavash, for serving

YOU'LL ALSO NEED

A potato masher or ricer; flat metal or bamboo
    skewers

ADVANCE PREPARATION

1 to 2 hours for chilling the mashed potatoes

1 Place the potatoes in a large pot, add cold salted water to cover by 4 inches, and bring the potatoes to a boil over high heat. Boil the potatoes until just tender, about 30 minutes. Use a skewer to test for doneness; it should pierce the potatoes easily. Drain the potatoes in a colander and let cool until warm enough to handle, then remove and discard the skins.

2 Heat the oil in a medium-size skillet. Add the onion and cumin and cook over medium heat until the onion is caramelized, a deep golden brown, 6 to 8 minutes, stirring often and lowering the heat as necessary to keep the onion from burning. Season the onion mixture with salt and pepper to taste.

3 Using a food processor, very finely chop the bacon or lamb fat or put it through a meat grinder.

HOW TO MAKE "KNISH ON A STICK"

1. *Puree the cooked potatoes through a meat grinder or with a potato masher. (Do not use a food processor, or the kebabs will taste gummy.)*

2. *Mix in the onion, cumin, and bacon or lamb tail fat, kneading the ingredients together with your fingers.*

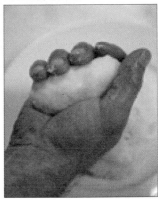

3. *The seasoned potato mixture ready for skewering. Chill the mixture for 1 to 2 hours so it's easier to work with.*

4. *Mold a 2-inch ball of potato mixture into an oblong. Oil your hands to prevent sticking.*

5. *Slide the potato oval onto a flat metal skewer.*

6. *Squeeze the potato mixture onto the skewer with your fingers to create a long slender kebab. Note the rippled pattern—the signature of an Azeri grill master.*

7. *Grill the potato kebab on a grateless grill (if possible) over charcoal.*

8. *Slide the grilled potato kebab off the skewer and cut it into 2-inch lengths.*

4 Mash the potatoes by putting them through a ricer. Or place the potatoes in a deep flat-bottomed mixing bowl and mash them with a potato masher. It's best not to puree the potatoes in a food processor; they will become gummy. If you must do this, run the food processor in short bursts. Stir in the onion mixture and the bacon. Taste for seasoning, adding more salt and/or pepper to taste. Refrigerate the potato mixture, covered, for 1 to 2 hours so that it will be easier to mold.

5 Lightly oil your hands to keep the potato mixture from sticking to them, then take a 2-inch ball of the mashed potatoes and mold it onto a flat skewer to form a cylinder about 1 inch thick and 6 to 8 inches long. Place the kebab on a plate lined with plastic wrap. Repeat with the remaining mashed potatoes. Refrigerate the kebabs, covered, until you are ready to grill.

6 Set up the grill for direct grilling and preheat to high. Ideally, you'll set up your grill for grateless grilling (see page 599).

556 VEGETABLES AND VEGETARIAN DISHES

7 When ready to cook, if you are using a grill grate, brush it well and oil it generously. You may also wish to brush the potato kebabs with oil if you are grilling directly on the grate. Arrange the potato kebabs on the grill and grill them until golden brown on the outside and cooked through, 3 to 6 minutes per side, 6 to 12 minutes in all.

8 To serve, using a piece of lavash to protect your hand, slide the potato kebabs off the skewers onto a platter or plates. Cut the potato kebabs crosswise into 2-inch pieces and serve at once.

VARIATION

Grilled Mashed Potatoes with Cheese: You can also replace the lamb fat with grated cheese to enrich the potatoes. Make the "Knish on a Stick" substituting ½ cup of finely and freshly grated Parmigiano-Reggiano cheese for the bacon.

Grilled Butternut Squash

THE SCOOP

WHERE: Buenos Aires, Argentina

WHAT: Butternut squash grilled to a candy sweetness

HOW: Indirect or direct grilling over a moderate fire, followed by direct grilling over a hot fire

JUST THE FACTS: The squash is grilled twice: the first time to cook the vegetable and the second time to caramelize the slices. In the best of all possible worlds you'd grill over wood embers. You can approximate the effect by indirect grilling with wood chips.

Being the unabashed carnivores that they are, Argentineans don't pay a lot of attention to vegetables. But the few they do grill—peppers, eggplants, onions—come off the fire as smoky and sweet as grilled vegetables anywhere on Planet Barbecue. To this short list, I have a new vegetable to add: whole butternut squash fire roasted in the skin. I first sighted the squash at Campobravo, a grill restaurant in the trendy Palermo district of Buenos Aires. The grilling process gives the squash "steaks" a soft, creamy consistency and seems to intensify their sweetness. **SERVES 4 TO 6**

1 whole butternut squash (2 to 2½ pounds)
2 to 3 tablespoons unsalted butter, melted, or
 vegetable oil
Coarse salt (kosher or sea) and freshly ground
 black pepper
Granulated sugar or cinnamon sugar (optional)

YOU'LL ALSO NEED
1½ to 2 cups oak wood chips or chunks
 (optional), soaked for 1 hour, then drained

ADVANCE PREPARATION
None, but leave yourself time for grilling
 both the whole squash and then the slices
 (about 1½ hours in all). Or grill the whole
 squash up to 48 hours ahead and then grill
 the slices at the last minute

1 To grill: *If you are using the indirect method,* set up the grill for indirect grilling, place a drip pan in the center, and preheat the grill to medium. When ready to cook, if you are using a charcoal grill, toss the wood chips or chunks on the coals. If you are using a gas grill, add the wood chips or chunks to the smoker box or place them in a smoker pouch under the grate (see page 603). Place the squash in the center of the grate over the drip pan and away from the heat and cover the grill. Grill the squash until tender, about 30 to 40 minutes.

If you are using the direct method, set up the grill for direct grilling and preheat it to medium. When ready to cook, brush and oil the grill grate. If you arc using a charcoal grill, toss the wood chips or chunks on the coals. If you are using a gas grill, add the wood chips or chunks to the smoker box or place them in a smoker pouch under the grate (see page 603). Place the squash on the hot grate and grill it until well browned on all sides and very tender, 4 to 6 minutes per side, 16 to 24 minutes in all, turning with tongs. Lower the heat if the squash skin starts to burn.

2 When cooked, the squash will feel soft when the sides are squeezed (the so-called "Charmin test," see page 612) and will be easy to pierce with a skewer. You can slice and grill the squash now or let it cool to room temperature, then refrigerate it, covered, until you are ready to finish grilling it.

3 Just before serving, set up the grill for direct grilling, if you haven't already done so, and preheat it to high.

4 Cut the squash crosswise into 1-inch slices, discarding the seeds. Brush each slice with melted butter or oil and season it generously on both sides with salt and pepper. Lightly sprinkle sugar over the squash slices, if desired.

5 When ready to cook, brush and oil the grill grate. Arrange the squash slices on the hot grate and grill until golden brown, about 2 minutes per side, turning with tongs. Serve the squash at once.

Paella "Primavera" on the Grill

I never ate a vegetarian paella in Spain, but given the sheer diversity of this iconic rice dish, it wouldn't surprise me to learn that such a dish exists. I created this meatless version for a vegetarian episode in my first *Primal Grill* TV show. But what does paella have to do with grilling? Well as it turns out, traditional Spanish paella is cooked over a campfire. And, yes, on account of the variable heat of the fire, not to mention the wood smoke, paella tastes different cooked on a wood fire than it does when you make it on the stove.

For a really dramatic presentation, fire up two kettle grills. Use one for cooking the rice and the second one for grilling the vegetables. Or use a large charcoal grill, like a Weber Ranch, or a large gas grill. If your grill space is limited, grill the vegetables first—this could even be done at a previous grill session—and grill the paella right before serving. **SERVES 4**

FOR THE RICE

½ teaspoon saffron threads

6 tablespoons extra-virgin olive oil, preferably Spanish

1 medium-size onion, finely chopped

1 red bell pepper, cored, seeded, and cut into 2 x ¼–inch strips

2 cloves garlic, thinly sliced

3 tablespoons finely chopped flat-leaf parsley

1 ripe tomato, seeded and cut into ¼-inch dice

2 cups Valencia-style rice, such as bomba or Calasparra
    (see Notes)

1 cup cooked, drained garbanzo beans (chickpeas)

½ cup dry white wine

4 to 5 cups vegetable stock, preferably homemade

Coarse salt (kosher or sea) and freshly ground
    black pepper

FOR THE VEGETABLES

8 baby bell peppers, skewered on bamboo skewers

1 large sweet onion, peeled and cut into 8 wedges,
    each skewered crosswise with a toothpick

1 medium-size zucchini, trimmed and cut sharply on the
    diagonal into ¼-inch-thick slices

1 medium-size yellow squash, trimmed and cut sharply on
    the diagonal into ¼-inch-thick slices

12 cherry tomatoes, skewered on bamboo skewers

2 tablespoons extra-virgin olive oil, preferably Spanish

Coarse salt (kosher or sea) and freshly ground
    black pepper

3 tablespoons chopped fresh herbs, such as rosemary, oregano,
    thyme, and/or basil, or 1½ tablespoons mixed dried herbs

12 cloves garlic in their skins, skewered on bamboo skewers

¼ cup cooked green peas (or if you have an unbelievable
    amount of patience, fresh raw peas skewered on a slender
    bamboo skewer)

YOU'LL ALSO NEED

Bamboo skewers and wooden toothpicks; logs or chunks of
    hardwood for the fire or 2 cups hardwood chips or chunks,
    soaked for 1 hour in water to cover, then drained; a Tuscan
    grill (optional, helpful if working on a wood fire); a paella pan
    (see Notes); a grill hoe or a long-handled wooden spoon

ADVANCE PREPARATION

None. The beauty of this dish is that you make it to
    order with everyone watching.

1 Place the saffron in a small bowl with 2 teaspoons of warm water and let it soak for about 5 minutes.

2 Set up the grill(s) for three-zone grilling (see page 611). Ideally, you'd grill over a campfire (see page 603 for instructions on grilling over wood). Alternatively, you can work on two kettle grills, a large charcoal grill, or a large gas grill and use wood chips or chunks to add a smoke flavor.

3 When ready to cook, if you are using a charcoal grill, toss the wood chips or chunks on the coals. If you are using a gas grill, add the wood chips or chunks to the smoker box or place them in a smoker pouch under the grate (see page 603). Place the paella pan over the hottest zone of the grill. (If you are working with 2 charcoal grills, cook the rice on one grill and the vegetables on the other.) Add the 6 tablespoons of olive oil and a little of the chopped onion and heat it until the onion sizzles in the oil. Add the remaining chopped onion and the red bell pepper strips and cook over high heat, stirring with a long-handled implement, like a grill hoe, until the onion begins to brown, about 4 minutes. Add the sliced garlic, parsley, and diced tomato after the bell pepper and onion have cooked for about 2 minutes. If the mixture starts to burn, slide the pan to a cooler part of the grill.

4 Stir in the rice and cook until the grains look shiny, about 1 minute. Add the garbanzo beans and cook for about 1 minute. Stir in the saffron mixture and white wine and let boil for about 1 minute. Stir in 4 cups of the vegetable stock and season the rice with salt and black pepper to taste. Adjust the heat by moving the paella pan closer to or farther away from the hot zone to obtain a gentle simmer. Let the rice simmer gently until soft, about 20 minutes. Add the remaining 1 cup of stock, if needed, but do not stir the paella.

5 Meanwhile, lightly brush the baby bell peppers, onion wedges, zucchini, yellow squash, and cherry tomatoes with the 2 tablespoons of olive

PAELLA "PRIMAVERA" ON THE GRILL | page 557

Paella the Authentic Way

Paella, that magnificent rice dish from Valencia, Spain, may seem like the last thing you'd expect to cook on the grill. However, the authentic, traditional way to prepare it is simmered over a campfire. First documented during the eighteenth century near the coastal city of Valencia, paella has much in common with American barbecue. It was poor people's food, cooked over an open fire, usually fueled by orangewood or vine clippings and even pine cones. It was cooked by laborers for laborers—for the midday meal—and nearly always by men. As in the world of barbecue, paella masters developed their own jealously guarded "secret" recipes and put them to the test in heated competitions. Even today, a "Paella King" is crowned each year in Galicia, Spain.

Originally, the ingredients for *paella valenciana* were gathered close by—the most important being the unique strains of short-grain rice known as *arroz bomba* or Calasparra that grew (and still grow) in the eastern Spanish region of Murcia. Local produce, like bell peppers and runner beans, added color, while two other traditional Spanish seasonings, saffron and sometimes *pimentón* (smoked Spanish paprika), pumped up the flavor. Protein came in whatever form you could scrounge it: shrimp, clams, chicken or duck, even rabbit or snails.

So what constitutes an authentic paella today? It depends on where you are and the occasion. Even in Valencia, paella has multiple personalities: *Paella de mariscos* comes crammed with shellfish or other seafood. *Paella mixta* includes seafood and meat, such as chicken, pork, chorizo sausage, or all of these. There's even a green paella from Alicante flavored with rabbit, snails, and green herbs.

---

oil. Season the vegetables on both sides with salt and black pepper and sprinkle half of the herbs over them. If you are working over a campfire, position a Tuscan grill over the embers. On the second charcoal grill, if you are using two, or on another section of the grill, after brushing and oiling the grill grate, arrange the peppers, onion, zucchini, yellow squash, cherry tomatoes, and skewered garlic on the hot grate and grill them until golden brown, even darkly browned, on the outside and tender. This will take 3 to 6 minutes per side, depending on the vegetable; the peppers and onion will take longer than the zucchini, squash, and tomatoes. You may have to work over a lower heat (or at the edge of the grill) for the garlic; it should be tender and browned, but not burnt. In the event you have been obsessive enough to skewer the peas, place them on the grate and grill them until lightly browned and cooked through, 1 to 2 minutes per side.

6 During the last 5 minutes that the paella cooks, remove and discard the skewers from the vegetables and slip the burned skins off the garlic. Add the grilled vegetables, the peas, and the remaining herbs to the rice. Taste the paella for seasoning, adding more salt and/or black pepper as needed. If you've done this right and the stars are in alignment, the rice will be tender just as all of the stock is absorbed and the vegetables are cooked and you'll have a crisp rice crust, called *soccarat,* on the bottom. Serve immediately, giving everyone a portion of the rice crust.

NOTES: Paella pans and Spanish ingredients are available from www.latienda.com or www.thespanishtable.com.

The rice of choice is bomba or Calasparra—short-grained Spanish rices similar to Italian arborio. (You can substitute arborio, but you may need to add more liquid to keep it from drying out.)

Grilled Tofu with Chile Peanut Sauce

{ TAUHU BAKAR }

Barbecue is a communal activity on most of Planet Barbecue. The owners of the Tomyam Klasik restaurant on the outskirts of Kuala Lumpur take the concept over the top. Their sprawling open-air dining room is large enough to accommodate eight hundred or so of your extended family members or friends. On a typical Sunday afternoon, they might host a half-dozen parties of forty people or more. To come to Tomyam Klasik solely for the grilled tofu would be to ignore a menu that runs several pages, featuring every imaginable meat and seafood (from venison to squid) from virtually every corner of Malaysia (and neighboring Thailand, too). But to fail to order the tofu would be to miss one of the greatest grilled meatless dishes on the planet. The secret? Charring the tofu over a blistering-hot fire and serving it with cool, crisp pineapple and cucumber and an intensely flavorful chile peanut sauce. Rarely has bean curd met fire with such felicitous results. **SERVES 4**

3 tablespoons vegetable oil

4 cloves garlic, minced

2 medium-size shallots minced
    (about 6 tablespoons)

1 piece (1½ inches) fresh ginger,
    peeled and coarsely chopped

2 tablespoons minced fresh cilantro

1 teaspoon shrimp paste (optional)

¼ cup Malaysian or Chinese chile paste

¼ cup firmly packed palm sugar or
    light brown sugar

½ cup hoisin sauce

¼ cup finely chopped roasted peanuts

1 tablespoon sesame seeds

1 large or 2 small cucumbers, peeled and seeded

½ fresh pineapple, peeled

2 cups fresh mung bean sprouts

About 1½ pounds fried or extra-firm regular tofu

ADVANCE PREPARATION

The sauce can be made several hours ahead. If you are using fresh tofu, allow 30 minutes for pressing it.

1 Heat the oil in a wok or shallow saucepan over medium-high heat. Add the garlic, shallots, ginger, cilantro, and shrimp paste, if using, and cook until fragrant and lightly browned, about 3 minutes. Stir in the chile paste and palm sugar and cook until the sugar dissolves, about 1 minute. Add

THE SCOOP

WHERE: Kuala Lumpur, Malaysia

WHAT: Grilled tofu "steaks," served with a sweet, spicy but not terribly fiery sauce of garlic, chile, and peanuts

HOW: Direct grilling

JUST THE FACTS: Malaysians like to grill fried tofu. Thanks to its firm, elastic consistency, it doesn't fall apart on the grill the way fresh tofu does. You can buy already-fried tofu at Asian markets. However, you can certainly substitute extra-firm regular (not silken) tofu, provided you press the liquid out first.

Shrimp paste (*belacan*) is a malodorous condiment used throughout Southeast Asia. It tastes a lot better than it smells, especially after it has been grilled or fried. I've made it optional. You could substitute one teaspoon of fish sauce or leave it out entirely.

the hoisin sauce, 2 tablespoons of the peanuts, and the sesame seeds and cook until fragrant, about 1 minute. Add ⅔ cup of water, reduce the heat to medium, and let the sauce simmer until it is thick and richly flavored, about 5 minutes, stirring often. If the sauce is too thick, add a little more water. The chile peanut sauce can be made several hours ahead and stored at room temperature.

2 Cut the cucumbers crosswise into 1½ inch-long pieces. Cut each piece lengthwise into approximately ¼-inch x ¼-inch sticks. Cut the pineapple crosswise into ¼ inch-thick slices. Cutting around the core, cut each pineapple slice into sticks that are approximately 1½ inches long and ¼ inch wide. Arrange the cucumber, pineapple, and mung bean sprouts in individual piles on a platter.

3 Starting at a short end, cut each piece of tofu in half through the thickness to obtain 2 broad "steaks." If you are using fresh, not fried tofu, you will need to press it to drain off the liquid and make the tofu firmer. Position a baking sheet or cutting board on a slant in a sink. Arrange the 4 pieces of tofu on top. Then place a second baking sheet or cutting board on top of them. Place a heavy weight, such as a cast-iron skillet, on top of the baking sheet or cutting board and let the tofu drain for 30 minutes.

4 Set up the grill for direct grilling and preheat it to high.

5 Lightly brush each piece of tofu on both sides with a little of the chile peanut sauce. Spoon the remaining sauce into a bowl and sprinkle the remaining 2 tablespoons of peanuts on top.

6 When ready to cook, brush and oil the grill grate. Arrange the tofu pieces on the hot grate and grill them until nicely browned on both sides, 2 to 4 minutes per side. If you like, give each piece a quarter turn after 1 minute to create a handsome crosshatch of grill marks.

7 Transfer the grilled tofu to the platter with the cucumber, pineapple, and bean sprouts and serve at once. Eat the grilled tofu with some of the chile peanut sauce spooned over it, alternating bites of crisp cool cucumber, pineapple, and bean sprouts.

Grilled Cheese Kebabs
{ TANDOORI PANEER }

Grilled and smoked cheeses are a constant on the world's barbecue trail—Argentina's grilled *provoleta,* for example, or Italy's smoked buffalo milk mozzarella. India's version comes on a colorful kebab with tomato, onion, and poblano or bell pepper. Hanging on skewers, it serves as a billboard outside many New Delhi tandoori parlors. Basted with ginger-cilantro butter, *paneer* looks great and tastes even better, and if you serve it at your next barbecue, the vegetarian attendees will be forever in your debt. **SERVES 4**

THE SCOOP

WHERE: New Delhi, India

WHAT: Polychromatic kebabs of grilled cheese, tomatoes, and peppers

THE SCOOP

HOW: Direct grilling; traditionally cooked on a vertical spit in a tandoor

JUST THE FACTS: *Paneer*, or *panir*, is a mild, milk-white Indian cheese made from cow's milk in a manner not unlike Italian mozzarella. In addition to its fine flavor, *paneer* possesses the genial property of being able to stand up to high heat without melting, which makes it a perfect cheese for grilling. If you live near an Indian market, you can buy it ready-made, or buy it online at www.igourmet.com. Alternatively, you could use another firm, mild white cheese, like Greek haloumi, Latino-style *queso blanco*, or Italian mozzarella.

4 poblano peppers or green bell peppers (see Note)

4 red ripe tomatoes

1 large or 2 medium-size red onions

2 pounds paneer cheese, haloumi, queso blanco, or mozzarella

8 tablespoons (1 stick) salted butter

3 tablespoons finely chopped fresh cilantro

2 cloves garlic, minced

1 tablespoon minced peeled fresh ginger

1½ teaspoons ground turmeric

Freshly ground black pepper

½ cup sesame seeds

Lemon wedges, for serving

YOU'LL ALSO NEED

Wide (at least ⅜ inch) metal or bamboo skewers

ADVANCE PREPARATION

None

1 Cut the poblano peppers into 2-inch square pieces, discarding the core and seeds. Cut each tomato into 4 wedges. Cut the seeds and pulp out of each tomato wedge (save them for stock); the remaining wedges of tomato should be about ¼ inch thick. Cut each wedge in half crosswise. Cut the onion(s) in half crosswise and cut each half in quarters. Break the quarters into layers. Cut the cheese into pieces that are 2 inches square and ½ inch thick.

2 Skewer a piece of pepper followed by a piece of tomato, a piece of onion, and a piece of cheese, inserting the skewer through the flat side. Repeat this sequence until all of these ingredients are used up.

3 Melt 3 tablespoons of the butter in a heavy saucepan over medium heat. Add the cilantro, garlic, ginger, and turmeric and cook until fragrant but not brown, 2 to 3 minutes. Add the remaining 5 tablespoons of butter and cook until melted, about 1 minute.

4 Set up the grill for direct grilling and preheat it to high.

5 When ready to cook, brush and oil the grill grate. Brush the kebabs on all sides with some of the cilantro-garlic butter and sprinkle the sesame seeds all over them. Arrange the kebabs on the hot grate and grill them until nicely browned on all sides, 2 to 3 minutes per side, 8 to 12 minutes in all, turning them as the cheese starts to melt and basting them with the remaining cilantro-garlic butter. Serve the kebabs at once with lemon wedges.

NOTE: Indian bell peppers have a bit of heat—poblano peppers are a good substitute.

Laotian Rice "Pops" with Dipping Sauces

Grilled rice cakes are enjoyed throughout Asia—in Japan, for example, where they might be stuffed with miso or bean paste to make a popular snack called *onigiri* (you find this not only at yakitori parlors, but at kiosks in train stations). Or in Thailand, where *khao-tung,* round grilled rice cakes, come with *nam prik pao,* roasted sweet chile jam, dished up by sidewalk grill jockeys. Here's the Laotian version, from a vendor in the French colonial town of Luang Prabang, who set up her pushcart grill in front of the local high school. (I'd sure rather have seen my kids eat grilled rice cakes as an afterschool snack than your average American fast food.) Any Asian short grain sticky rice will work for this recipe; prepare it according to the instructions on the package. Take your choice of the dipping sauces, or if you're feeling ambitious, make all three. **MAKES 8 AND CAN BE MULTIPLIED AS DESIRED**

Vegetable oil
3 cups cooked Asian sticky rice, cooled to room
  temperature

ONE OR MORE OF THE FOLLOWING
SAUCES
Sweet chile sauce
¾ cup Thai sweet chile sauce,
  such as the Mae Ploy brand
3 tablespoons fresh lime juice
2 tablespoons chopped roasted peanuts

Chile fish sauce
⅓ cup Asian fish sauce
¼ cup sugar
¼ cup fresh lime juice
2 to 4 Thai or other hot chiles,
  thinly sliced crosswise

Laotian "spicy" (hot sauce)
1 stalk lemongrass, trimmed, peeled, and minced
1 clove garlic, minced
½ cup Asian chile paste (see Note)
3 tablespoons fresh lime juice, or more to taste

2 large eggs, beaten, in a shallow bowl

YOU'LL ALSO NEED
Wide flat bamboo skewers; an aluminum foil grill
  shield (see page 611)

ADVANCE PREPARATION
The rice will be easier to grill if you cook it and
  form the "pops" several hours or even a day
  ahead

1 Several hours ahead, lightly oil your hands and divide the rice into 8 equal portions. Form each into an oblong about 4 inches long, 2 inches wide, and ½ inch thick. Insert a bamboo skewer through one of the short ends, packing the rice around the skewer. Arrange the rice "pops" on a plate lined with plastic wrap and refrigerate them until you are ready to grill. Actually, it's good to chill them for several hours before grilling; they'll be less likely to fall apart.

2 Make one or more of the dipping sauces.

For the sweet chile sauce, combine the chile sauce, lime juice, and 2 tablespoons water in a bowl and whisk to mix. Transfer the sauce to small shallow bowls for dipping and sprinkle the peanuts on top.

For the chile fish sauce, combine the fish sauce, sugar, and lime juice in a bowl and whisk until the sugar dissolves. Whisk in 3 tablespoons water, or more to taste. Transfer the sauce to small shallow bowls for dipping and sprinkle the sliced chiles on top.

For the Laotian "spicy" (hot sauce), place the lemongrass, garlic, chile paste and lime juice in a bowl and whisk to mix. Taste for seasoning, adding more lime juice, if needed. Transfer the sauce to small shallow bowls for dipping.

3 When ready to grill, set up the grill for direct grilling and preheat it to high.

4 Brush and oil the grill grate really well. Place the bowl with the beaten egg near the grill. Gently dip each rice pop in the beaten egg, letting the excess drip off. Gently arrange the pops on the hot grate, with the aluminum foil shield under the exposed ends of the skewers to keep them from burning. Grill the pops until golden brown on both sides, 2 to 4 minutes per side. Serve the pops hot off the grill with the bowls of dipping sauce.

NOTE: Asian chile pastes are usually available in the ethnic section of larger supermarkets or at Asian groceries. They vary widely in heat from brand to brand, so experiment. Two good ones are Huy Fong (sold as *sambal ulek*) and Lan Chi.

Rice cakes grilled over charcoal in Luang Prabang, Laos.

Afternoon treat for Laotian school kids: Rice "pops" hot off the grill with chile sauces for dipping (or with a banana leaf as a plate).

Desserts

Just when you think you've seen it all in the world of live-fire cooking, a grill master confounds you afresh. Take, for instance, Mehman Huseynov, the hyperkinetic chef and TV star I've nicknamed the "Emeril" of Azerbaijan (you can read about him on page 592). "The strangest thing I've ever grilled? Ice cream," he observed casually during an interview a few years ago at the sprawling Neolit restaurant in Baku. "Ice cream? I don't believe it," I said, and as much to disprove my incredulity as to demonstrate a dish unique in the annals of barbecue, he promptly dipped balls of vanilla ice cream in beaten egg and shredded coconut, skewered them on flat metal skewers, then seared them so quickly over a raging hot fire, that the coconut crust browned while the ice cream in the center stayed frozen. Yes, it was grilled ice cream and yes, you'll find the recipe here.

This just goes to show the great lengths to which creative grillers will go to bring a meal cooked over live fire to a memorable close. And they will go far—to the point of grilling pineapples with sea salt in Australia, wine-marinated apples in Belgium, and "birds nest" (hair-thin shredded wheat pastries) in Turkey. No technique is excluded: not direct grilling, used by Thai grillers to cook coconut caramel bananas; not indirect grilling, used by Arizonans to cook cactus pear crisp; not spit roasting, used by Brazilians to cook whole pineapples; and not even

CLOCKWISE FROM TOP LEFT: *Belgian grill wunderkind Peter De Clercq with his honey grilled apples; Turkish "birds nest" pastries lifted with tongs to drain off the excess syrup; Campfire coffee the way they do in the South African bush; Salt-grilled pineapple—an upscale dessert from Down Under.*

smoking, used by the Spanish grilling iconoclast Victor Arguinzoniz to flavor the milk for home-churned ice cream.

You'll find grilled desserts from all around Planet Barbecue, including a not-so-commonplace s'more (made with a social conscience, no less) and dramatic Catalan creams, caramelized as they do in the southwest of France with a wood fire–heated poker. And to bring your barbecue to a close, have some South African coffee brewed on a campfire and topped off with a burning log.

It's just another day on Planet Barbecue.

Previous page: Thai grill mistress Saisuwan and her legendary coconut-caramel bananas (see page 573).

Grilled Apples with Honey and Apple Wine

Peter De Clercq needs no introduction. Not to upscale grilling enthusiasts in Belgium and beyond who watch his popular TV shows, read his books, buy his innovative grilling accessories, and come from all corners of western Europe to dine at his restaurant, Elckerlijc. Certainly not to anyone who has read about his jaw-dropping oysters grilled with ginger and jam (see page 506) and cherry beer–glazed salmon (see page 428) in this book. Like me, Peter believes that no meal is complete without a grilled dessert—in this case, thick slices of fresh apples, marinated in apple wine, and seared on the grill. If you order this dish at his restaurant, you'll have the unique opportunity to try mare's milk ice cream, which has an interesting sweet musky flavor you'd never mistake for Häagen-Dazs. Boiling the marinade down makes a thick, buttery, caramel-like basting sauce. **SERVES 4 GENEROUSLY OR 6 TO 8 AFTER A BIG MEAL**

6 tablespoons (¾ stick) unsalted butter
½ cup honey
½ cup apple wine, ½ cup hard cider, or
   ¼ cup apple cider plus ¼ cup dry
   white wine
1 piece (3 inches) vanilla bean, split, or
   1 teaspoon pure vanilla extract
1 cinnamon stick (3 inches)
4 firm, sweet-tart apples, such as Pink Lady
   or Fuji
Vanilla ice cream, for serving
Fresh mint leaves, for garnish

ADVANCE PREPARATION
2 to 4 hours for marinating the apples

1 Place the butter, honey, apple wine, vanilla, and cinnamon in a saucepan and bring to a boil over high heat, stirring with a wooden spoon. Reduce the heat and let the marinade simmer until syrupy, about 2 minutes. Remove the pan from the heat and let the marinade cool to room temperature.

2 Core the apples (leave the skin on) and cut them crosswise into ½-inch-thick slices. Arrange the apple slices in a baking dish or container just large enough to hold them in a single layer and pour the honey marinade over them. Turn the apple slices a couple of times to coat well with the marinade. Let the apples marinate in the refrigerator, covered, for 2 to 4 hours.

3 Strain the marinade off the apples into a saucepan and bring it to a boil over high heat. Let the marinade boil until thick and syrupy, 3 to 6 minutes. Remove and discard the vanilla bean, if using, and cinnamon stick.

4 Set up the grill for direct grilling and preheat it to high.

5 When ready to cook, brush and oil the grill grate. Arrange the apple slices on the hot grate and grill until golden brown on both sides, 3 to 5 minutes per side. If desired, give each slice of apple a quarter turn halfway through grilling on each side to create a handsome crosshatch of grill marks. As the apples cook, baste them with the boiled marinade.

6 Scoop the ice cream into bowls or onto dessert plates. Fan out the grilled apple slices on top. Spoon any remaining marinade on top. Garnish with mint and serve at once.

Smoke-Roasted Apples with Japanese Sweet Bean Paste

THE SCOOP

WHERE: Japan and the United States

WHAT: A Japanese twist on a North American favorite—a "baked" apple stuffed with sweet *azuki* bean paste, brown sugar, and cream cheese and smoked with apple wood

HOW: Indirect grilling

JUST THE FACTS: *Azuki* bean paste looks like red axle grease, coats your tongue like Nutella, and has a sweet, musky flavor that's utterly unique. You can find it at Asian markets. Alternatively, you can substitute apricot, raspberry, or another fruit jam.

Sharing a beer with Chef Moreno in my kitchen prior to the challenge.

His name is Kumahachi Moreno and he's one of the most famous television chefs in Japan. He showed up at my door one July 4th weekend bearing a bag of Japanese "mystery" ingredients for me to grill. My efforts would be videotaped and the results shown on Japanese television. Seemed like a good idea, but when Moreno opened his bag, out came *gobo* (burdock root), *natto* (fermented soybeans), uncooked cod roe, and flat painted cans of *azuki* (sweet red bean) paste. Decidedly not what most Americans are accustomed to grilling. I sliced the cod roe over freshly-shucked oysters, which I roasted on a wood-burning grill. The burdock went on bamboo skewers with scallions to be grilled yakitori style on a hibachi. The *natto* went on tortillas with jalapeños and grated cheddar to make grilled quesadillas. I spooned the *azuki* paste into hollowed out apples—Fujis, no less—and topped them with cream cheese, brown sugar, and butter to be smoke-roasted over applewood in a kettle grill. I held my breath and hoped for the best. Mr. Moreno and his Japanese film crew had never seen the likes of the meal that followed. The oysters came out great, served with wasabi-flavored whipped cream. The film crew ate the *natto*-stuffed quesadillas with gusto. A mouthful of the fibrous burdock root taught me why burdock is never grilled in Japan. The red bean paste–stuffed apples—the outside tender and smoky, the filling both piquant and sweet—prompted high-fives all around—definitely a first on both sides of the Pacific. **SERVES 4**

4 firm sweet-tart apples, such as Fujis

2 tablespoons azuki bean paste

2 tablespoons cream cheese (I use whipped cream cheese)

2 tablespoons dark brown sugar

2 tablespoons unsalted butter

YOU'LL ALSO NEED

2 cups applewood chips or chunks, soaked for
 1 hour in water to cover, then drained; grilling rings or
 aluminum foil rings for the apples

ADVANCE PREPARATION

The apples can be stuffed and refrigerated several hours ahead.
 They taste best hot off the grill.

1 Using a small melon baller, core the apples from the top. The idea is to remove the stem end and seeds, creating a cavity in the apple, but leave the bottom intact to hold in the filling. Place 1½ teaspoons of *azuki* bean paste in the cavity of each apple. Top with 1½ teaspoons of cream cheese, 1½ teaspoons of brown sugar, and finally 1½ teaspoons of butter. The apples can be prepared to this stage several hours ahead and refrigerated, covered.

2 Set up the grill for indirect grilling, place a drip pan in the center, and preheat the grill to medium.

3 When ready to cook, if you are using a charcoal grill, toss the wood chips or chunks on the coals. If you are using a gas grill, add the wood chips or chunks to the smoker box or place them in a smoker pouch under the grate (see page 603). Arrange the apples upright in the center of the grate over the drip pan and away from the heat and cover the grill. To help the apples stay upright on the grate, position them on grill rings or rings made from crumpled aluminum foil. Grill the apples until they are tender (the sides will be squeezably soft) and the filling is browned and bubbling. Depending on your grill and the temperature outside, this will take 40 minutes to 1 hour.

Grilled Sweet Plantains or Bananas with Guava and Salty Cheese

Take a coffee break in a Spanish-Caribbean country and you might be served a pastry filled with guava paste and cream cheese. Order a cheese course in Spain or Brazil and you're sure to receive a salty cheese, like Manchego, with a slab of sweet, crimson quince paste. Visit the Bogotá home of my friends Marta and Andres Reyes for a barbecue and dessert will likely be grilled guava paste and cheese-stuffed plantains. (Guava and quince pastes are similar and interchangeable, but guava paste has a more perfumed exotic flavor.) Latin Americans love the juxtaposition of strong, sweet, and salty flavors in a single bite, but to the best of my knowledge, nowhere other than Bogotá does the combination come served hot off the grill. **SERVES 4**

THE SCOOP

WHERE: Bogotá, Colombia

WHAT: A dessert like none you've tasted— guava- and cheese- stuffed plantains charred in the skins on the grill

HOW: Direct or indirect grilling

JUST THE FACTS:
The plantain is a jumbo cousin of the banana, but unlike the banana, it's always cooked before eating. Plantains are sold at varying degrees of ripeness. When green, they're starchy like potatoes, and not at all sweet. As the skin yellows and darkens, plantains become sweeter and sweeter. For this recipe you'll want plantains with yellowish-black skins: Hispanic markets sell them this way. Otherwise, you'll need to buy green plantains and let them ripen at room temperature. Or, you can use regular bananas, in which case, I'd select ripe ones that are fully yellow, but without tiny brown sugar spots.

FOR THE FRUIT

4 very ripe plantains or large ripe bananas
6 ounces mild salty cheese such as queso blanco or cream cheese (see Notes)
6 ounces guava paste (see Notes)

FOR THE SPICED WHIPPED CREAM

1 cup heavy (whipping) cream
3 tablespoons confectioners' sugar
1 teaspoon ground cinnamon
¼ teaspoon ground cloves
1 to 2 tablespoons dark rum (optional)

ADVANCE PREPARATION

The plantains can be stuffed and the spiced whipped cream can be made up to 4 hours ahead.

1 Prepare the plantains or bananas: Using the tip of a sharp paring knife, make a deep lengthwise slit in the concave side of each plantain or banana. The slit should run from one end of the fruit to the other and should be about 1 inch deep and almost to, but not through, the skin on the opposite (rounded) side. Gently press the ends of the plantain toward the center and squeeze the sides to open the slit.

2 Cut the cheese into thin strips about 1 inch long and ¼ inch thick (most *queso blanco* comes in 4-inch blocks, so you'll need a couple of strips to fill each plantain). Cut the guava paste into strips of the same size. Stuff the cheese and guava strips into the slits in the fruit, trimming the pieces as needed to fill the plantains.

3 Make the spiced whipped cream: Freeze the metal bowl and beaters of a mixer for 10 minutes to chill. Place the cream in the chilled bowl and beat it until it forms soft peaks. Add the confectioners' sugar, cinnamon, cloves,

and rum, if using, and continue beating until stiff peaks form. Refrigerate the whipped cream until you are ready to serve. The recipe can be prepared to this stage up to 4 hours ahead.

4 Set up the grill for indirect grilling, place a drip pan in the center, and preheat the grill to medium-high. Arrange the plantains stuffed side up in the center of the grate over the drip pan and away from the heat. The plantains should run in the same direction as the bars of the grate, so they will hold the plantains upright. Grill the plantains until they are browned on the bottom, the flesh is soft, and the cheese and guava paste are bubbling, about 30 minutes.

5 Transfer the plantains to a platter or plates. Spoon the spiced whipped cream on top. To eat, spoon the plantain flesh, cheese, and guava out of the skin.

NOTES: A Colombian would use *queso blanco*, a moist, salty white cheese that sort of squeaks against your teeth when you bite into it. It's available at Hispanic markets and at many supermarkets. You could also use cream cheese; it isn't as salty, but its creamy piquancy makes an equally good counterpoint to the perfumed sweetness of the guava paste and plantains.

Guava paste is an aromatic mauve-colored jelly made from the perfumed tropical fruit. (In its natural state, the guava is impossibly seedy, which is why it's mostly consumed as a juice or jelly.) The best brands of guava paste come in flat metal cans and are available in the Latin food section of most supermarkets. Two good brands are Conchita and Goya.

Grilled Bananas with Coconut-Caramel Sauce

To paraphrase Kevin Costner in *Field of Dreams,* if you grill it, they will come. Such turned out to be the case for a Bangkok grill mistress named Saisuwan. Five years ago, she scraped together enough cash to set up a pushcart on Charoen Krung Road behind the Sheraton Hotel. Her grilling skills became so legendary, guidebooks from all over the world sing her praises. Saisuwan serves just one dish—but what a dish—grilled bananas slathered with coconut caramel sauce. You can eat them for breakfast, as a snack, or for dessert, and the moment you finish, you'll very likely find yourself returning for seconds. If you happen to find yourself near the Sheraton hotel in Bangkok, you'll recognize Saisuwan by her trademark white cap and by the sweet scent of bananas grilling over coconut shell charcoal. I give two versions of the caramel sauce. The first is how it's made in Thailand, with palm sugar and coconut milk simply boiled together. The second is how a Frenchman might make the sauce: The sugar is cooked to a deep golden caramel, then enriched with coconut milk. **SERVES 4**

FOR THE COCONUT-CARAMEL SAUCE

½ cup palm sugar or light brown sugar (see Notes)
1 cup unsweetened coconut milk (see page 503)
8 apple bananas, or 4 conventional bananas

YOU'LL ALSO NEED

Flat bamboo skewers (optional)

ADVANCE PREPARATION

The caramel sauce can be prepared up to a day ahead.

1 Make the coconut-caramel sauce: *Version #1:* Combine the palm sugar and coconut milk in a heavy saucepan. Bring to a boil over medium heat, whisking to dissolve the sugar. Let the coconut mixture simmer briskly until it is thick, golden, and very flavorful, about 5 minutes, whisking often. Remove the pan from the heat and let the coconut-caramel sauce cool to room temperature. Place the sauce in a deep bowl. It can be prepared up to a day ahead and refrigerated, covered. Let the coconut-caramel sauce return to room temperature before using.

Version #2: Place the sugar in a heavy saucepan over medium-high heat and cook the sugar until it melts, turns golden brown, becomes very fragrant, and starts to smoke, 3 to 6 minutes. Swirl the pan so the sugar cooks evenly, but do not stir it. Don't let the sugar burn. As soon as the sugar browns, remove the pan from the heat and add the coconut milk.

THE SCOOP

WHERE: Bangkok, Thailand

WHAT: Smokily grilled bananas topped with coconut-caramel sauce

HOW: Direct grilling

JUST THE FACTS: In Thailand, you'd use a short stubby banana with a firm starchy consistency, which keeps it from falling apart on the grill. The closest equivalent I've seen in North America is the apple banana (sometimes labeled with its Spanish name, *plátano manzano*), which is available at many supermarkets. The Thai banana isn't terribly sweet, but don't forget, it will be dipped in coconut-caramel sauce. If apple bananas aren't available, you can use a conventional banana that's a day or two shy of full ripeness.

HOW TO GRILL BANANAS WITH COCONUT-CARAMEL SAUCE

1. Skewer the bananas.

2. Skewering makes the bananas easier to turn and dip in the coconut-caramel sauce.

3. Dip each partially grilled banana in the coconut-caramel sauce, rotating the skewer to coat the banana on all sides.

4. Alternatively, brush the bananas with the coconut-caramel sauce while they're on the grill.

Stand back—the mixture will hiss and sputter like Mount Vesuvius. Return the mixture to the heat and let simmer, whisking, until the sugar dissolves completely. Let the coconut-caramel sauce cool to room temperature. Place the sauce in a shallow bowl. The caramel sauce can be prepared up to a day ahead and refrigerated, covered.

2 Set up the grill for direct grilling and preheat it to high.

3 When ready to cook, brush and oil the grill grate. Peel the bananas and skewer them through one end, if desired. Grill the bananas until they are lightly browned and partially cooked, 1 to 2 minutes per side. Dip the bananas in the coconut-caramel sauce (that's where the skewer comes in handy) or brush the bananas on all sides, using a basting brush, and return them to the grill. Continue grilling the bananas until they are darkly browned and sizzling, 1 to 3 minutes per side longer. Use a bamboo skewer to test for doneness; it should easily pierce the banana. Transfer the bananas to a platter or bowls. Spoon the remaining coconut-caramel sauce on top and serve at once.

NOTES: Palm sugar is the traditional sweetener of Thailand. Don't worry if you can't find it: In this recipe, it's virtually indistinguishable from light brown sugar.

The bananas used for grilling in Thailand tend to be harder and starchier than their North American counterparts. So grill masters, like Saisuwan, use a two-step grilling process, partially flattening the bananas with a heavy weight halfway through. This helps the bananas grill more evenly. To do this, transfer the bananas to a cutting board after the first 1 to 2 minutes of grilling and lightly flatten them with a scaloppine pounder or the side of a heavy cleaver. Dip each banana in the coconut-caramel sauce, or brush both sides with the sauce, and return the bananas to the grill. Continue grilling the bananas until they are golden brown and cooked through, 1 to 3 minutes longer per side.

Bananas Bangkok-style. Hot off the grill and sweet and smoky, the way Thais like it.

Francis Mallmann's Burnt Oranges with Rosemary

Here's a dessert of such startling simplicity and bold in-your-face flavors, just to hear about it will make you want to try it. It comes from the rock star of South American grilling, Francis Mallmann (see page 576). Mallmann uses a traditional South American wood fire–heated, cast-iron griddle called a *chapa;* think of it as an Argentinean *plancha.* When you do it right, the sugar cooks to a dark, smoky caramel crust—without quite burning. If you smell acrid smoke, you've gone too far. And, yes, you can cook the oranges directly on the grill grate. In his book, *Seven Fires: Grilling the Argentine Way,* Mallmann serves the oranges over thick Greek yogurt, but I like crème brûlée ice cream even more. **SERVES 4**

THE SCOOP

WHERE: Argentina and Uruguay

WHAT: Fresh oranges crusted with rosemary and caramelized on a wood-heated cast-iron plate

HOW: Direct grilling

JUST THE FACTS: Mallmann cooks the oranges on a thick, fire-heated iron plate called a *chapa.* You can achieve a similar effect using a cast-iron skillet.

4 large, juicy navel oranges
2 to 3 sprigs fresh rosemary
    (for 3 tablespoons leaves)
¾ cup sugar
1½ cups crème brûlée ice cream or
    plain Greek-style yogurt

YOU'LL ALSO NEED
A chapa, plancha, or 12-inch cast-iron skillet
    (optional)

ADVANCE PREPARATION
The oranges can be prepared up to 1 hour ahead.

1 Cut off both ends of each orange. Using a sharp paring knife, remove the peel and white pith. Cut each orange in half crosswise and, using a fork, remove the seeds, if any. Arrange the oranges on a plate cut side up.

2 Sprinkle the rosemary leaves over the oranges, pressing them into the flesh. The oranges can be prepared to this stage up to 1 hour ahead.

3 Set up the grill for direct grilling and preheat it to high. Ideally, you'll grill over wood (see page 603).

4 If you have a *chapa, plancha,* or cast-iron skillet, preheat it on the grill until it is very hot. If you are grilling directly on the grate, brush and oil it.

5 Just before you are ready to grill, sprinkle the cut part of each orange with the sugar and pat it in with the back of a spoon. Place the orange halves cut side down on the metal plate or on the grill and cook them until the sugar caramelizes, that is, turns dark brown, 2 to 4 minutes. Do not let the sugar burn.

6 To serve, divide the ice cream among 4 shallow bowls. Using a spatula, arrange the orange halves, cut side up, on the ice cream. If you used a pan, spoon any juices in it over the oranges and serve at once.

Seven Fires and Counting

Chef, TV host, and grilling visionary **FRANCIS MALLMANN** brings South American live-fire cooking to the world.

SOUTH AMERICA

Call him a caveman; Argentina's most celebrated chef can sauce and sauté with the best of them (after all, he trained with Alain Senderens and Raymond Oliver in Paris). But Francis Mallmann staked his reputation on a venture so outlandish, only a fire-obsessed South American could pull it off: He taped a TV show based entirely on campfire cooking outdoors on a Patagonian glacier in winter. Chef, restaurateur, TV personality, author—Francis Mallmann enjoys superstar status in South America, and when it comes to roasting a whole steer in front of a bonfire (hint: you need a hydraulic winch to raise it) or serving the South American Jet Set on damask linens at one of his restaurants, this poet, musician, and carpenter turned chef is your go-to guy.

Born in Bariloche, raised in the Patagonian mountains, and educated at an English language boarding school, Mallmann had his first restaurant by the age of nineteen. Since then, he has opened restaurants in Buenos Aires, Mendoza, and Brazil. His hotel and restaurant, Garzón, located a short drive from the überfashionable Uruguayan beach resort of José Ignacio, has almost single-handedly resuscitated the once moribund ranch town. In 1995 Mallmann became the first chef from Latin America to be invited to cook for the International Academy of Gastronomy, joining the likes of Frédy Girardet, Ferran Adrià, and Alain Ducasse. The menu? Mallmann prepared a nine-course meal based on potatoes.

Mallmann uses a curious word to describe his cooking: *barbaric.* He attempts nothing less than to achieve the pinnacle of flavors through the use of live fire, be it the massive heat of a bonfire or the slow steady warmth of dying embers. "To put it simply, I returned to an Argentine cuisine of wood fire and cast iron," he writes in his book, *Seven Fires.* "I am drawn to fire and the aroma of things cooking over wood."

Francis Mallmann tends one of his seven fires.

NAME: Francis Mallmann

TERRITORY: Born in Uruguay. Mallmann has restaurants in Uruguay and Argentina.

CLAIM TO FAME: Chef-owner of the restaurant and hotel Garzón in Garzón, Uruguay, of Patagonia Sur in Buenos Aires, and of Francis Mallmann 1884 in Mendoza, Argentina; *The Times* of London and *USA Today* named Mallmann's restaurants among the top ten places to eat in the world. For twenty years, Mallmann has hosted some of the most popular cooking shows on South American television.

SPECIALTIES: *Tapa de bife,* a steak consisting of the delectably fatty "top" or "cap" of the rib eye; *entraña a la vara,* skirt steak roasted on a stick over an open wood fire; salt-crusted chicken; burnt tomato halves; burnt oranges; and the biggest beef ribs on Planet Barbecue, a specialty of Mallmann's Mendoza restaurant

MALLMANN SAYS:

▶ I adore dissonance in food—two tastes fighting each other. It wakes up your palate.

▶ Always use hardwood to build your fire. I'm partial to *quebracho, coronilla,* and *lenga* (three South American hardwoods). In North America, oak makes the best coals. You can also use maple, birch, and hickory.

▶ Don't be afraid of burning your food. The right amount of charring or burning adds an extra dimension. The element of danger and excitement appeals to me. Take burning too far, and it destroys the dish. Stay just this side of the line and it's lovely.

▶ Pay attention to the wind direction and always position your dining area upwind of the fire. You should also keep your ingredients out of the path of the smoke, which can give your food a bitter taste.

Muscat-Grilled Pineapple with Sea Salt

Pineapple hails from the New World, where it much impressed Christopher Columbus. This simple dessert comes from the opposite side of the globe, from a Melbourne, Australia, grill man named John Ryan (who learned his way around a grill in Kansas City). You start by marinating the pineapple in a sweet dessert wine. The unexpected touch is the coarse crystals of sea salt sprinkled on the grilled fruit at the end, which seem to heighten the pineapple's sweetness. (Candy makers in France have used this technique for decades, adding salt or salted butter to caramel.) Preheat your grill as hot as it will go so you caramelize the surface of the fruit without overcooking the interior. I've made grilling the pineapple with sugar optional. John doesn't do it, but I find you'll get a better crust. **SERVES 4 TO 6**

1 whole ripe golden pineapple (see Note)

2 to 3 cups sweet muscat wine or other dessert wine

1 cup sugar (optional), in a shallow dish

1 pint vanilla, crème brûlée, or dulce de leche ice cream (optional), for serving

1 tablespoon coarse sea salt (the larger the crystals, the better)

1 bunch fresh mint, for serving

ADVANCE PREPARATION
4 hours to overnight for marinating the pineapple

1 Cut the crown (the leafy part) off the pineapple and set it aside, if desired, for garnish. Cut the rind off the pineapple, then using a sharp knife, make a series of spiral cuts to remove the eyes. Cut the pineapple crosswise into ½-inch-thick slices.

2 Arrange the pineapple slices in a large nonreactive baking dish. Pour enough muscat over the pineapple to cover it. Let the pineapple marinate in the refrigerator, covered, for at least 4 hours or as long as overnight, turning the slices a few times so they marinate evenly. The longer the pineapple marinates, the richer the flavor will be.

3 Strain the marinade into a heavy saucepan and bring it to a boil over high heat. Let the marinade boil until thick and syrupy, 5 to 8 minutes; you should have about ¾ cup. Set the boiled muscat syrup aside to cool.

4 Set up the grill for direct grilling and preheat it to high.

5 When ready to cook, brush and oil the grill grate. If you are using the sugar, dip each slice of pineapple in the sugar, crusting both sides and shaking off the excess. Arrange the pineapple slices on the hot grate at a diagonal to the bars. Grill the pineapple until it is golden brown on both sides, 2 to 4 minutes per side.

6 Divide the ice cream, if using, among serving bowls. Transfer the pineapple slices to the ice cream–filled bowls or a platter. Pour the muscat syrup on top. Lightly sprinkle the pineapple with coarse salt. Garnish it with mint sprigs and serve at once.

NOTE: When choosing pineapple, a yellow or golden rind is a sign of sweetness.

VARIATION

A Slightly Thicker Muscat Sauce: If you would like the sauce for the grilled pineapple to be a bit thicker, after you have strained the marinade and brought it to a boil, make a slurry of ½ teaspoon of cornstarch dissolved in 2 teaspoons of water. Whisk this mixture into the boiling wine and let it boil for about 1 minute; the sauce will thicken.

Spit-Roasted Pineapple

THE SCOOP

WHERE: Porto Alegre, Brazil

WHAT: A whole pineapple crusted with cinnamon sugar and caramelized on the rotisserie—like a pineapple upside-down cake, but without the cake

HOW: Spit roasting

JUST THE FACTS: You'll need a screaming-hot rotisserie to achieve the proper caramelization of the sugar and pineapple. If you have a gas grill with an infrared rotisserie, you're in luck. A three-burner gas grill (with the center burner running directly under the pineapple) or a rotisserie on a charcoal grill will also do the trick. Otherwise, you may need to boost the heat for browning. To do so, use a kitchen blowtorch, which is not only extremely effective, but also extremely cool looking.

By the time I arrived at the sprawling *churrascaria* in southern Brazil, the wedding party was in full swing. So were a half-dozen birthdays, a retirement celebration, numerous extended family dinners, and a bevy of hot Saturday night dates. And to serve them, a forest of spits spun furiously on a charcoal-fired rotisserie several yards long. Welcome to Galpão Crioulo ("Creole Grange")—a country-style grill joint in Brazil's barbecue capital, Porto Alegre, with room enough to feed you and the population of several small cities. This cinnamon-grilled pineapple comes served on a spit, just like Brazilian rotisseried meats, and the waiter carves thin slices onto the plate, just as he would *picanha* (see page 153) or spit-roasted beef tenderloin (see page 119). You can certainly serve the fruit with meat, but it also makes a stunningly original dessert. **SERVES 6 TO 8**

1 whole ripe golden pineapple
1 cup sugar
2 tablespoons ground cinnamon
1 teaspoon ground cloves
3 tablespoons butter, melted
Spiced whipped cream
    (optional, see Note and page 572)

ADVANCE PREPARATION
None

1 Cut the crown (the leafy part) off the pineapple and carefully cut the rind off the fruit. Using a sharp knife, make a series of spiral cuts to remove the eyes.

2 Place the sugar, cinnamon, and cloves in a bowl and stir to mix.

3 Set up the grill for spit roasting, following the manufacturer's instructions and preheat the grill as hot as it will go.

HOW TO SPIT ROAST A PINEAPPLE

1. Cut the leafy crown and bottom off of the pineapple.

2. Stand the pineapple upright and cut off the rind lengthwise.

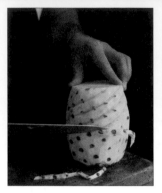

3. Making a series of V-shaped spiral cuts, remove the fibrous "eyes" from the pineapple.

4. Skewer the fruit to the spit. Sprinkle the spit-roasted pineapple with spiced sugar as it grills.

4 Thread the pineapple onto the spit lengthwise so the spit passes through the middle of the fruit (or thread it the traditional way—crosswise). Brush the outside of the pineapple with about 1 tablespoon of butter. Working over a tray or sheet pan, sprinkle one-third of the spice and sugar mixture over the pineapple on all sides and on the ends to crust it as thickly and as evenly as possible.

5 When ready to cook, attach the spit to the grill and turn on the motor. Spit-roast the pineapple until it is darkly browned on the outside, 15 to 30 minutes in all, depending on how hot the fire is (covering the rotisserie will make it even hotter). When the pineapple starts to brown, after 5 to 10 minutes, brush it on all sides with more butter and sprinkle more spiced sugar over it; shake the sugar bowl right over the pineapple as it turns on the rotisserie. Repeat after 5 minutes with the remaining butter and sugar, then continue spit roasting until the pineapple is darkly browned and thickly crusted with sugar.

6 Take the spit to the table and thinly slice the pineapple onto plates. (To be strictly authentic, once the crust of the pineapple is carved off the spit, you'd sprinkle the fruit with more spiced sugar and spit roast it again until darkly browned once more, continuing until all of the sugar mixture has been used up and all the pineapple has been served.) Alternatively, you can remove the pineapple from

Spit-roast the pineapple until the outside is caramelized and crusty.

the spit and cut it crosswise into slices; this is a little more user-friendly in a home setting. Serve the pineapple slices with whipped cream, if desired.

NOTE: In keeping with Brazil, you could flavor the whipped cream with *cachaça* (a Brazilian cane spirit) instead of rum.

VARIATION

"Spit-Roasted Pineapple" without the Rotisserie: If you don't have a rotisserie, you can cut the pineapple crosswise into ½-inch slices, coat each in butter and sugar, and brown the slices on the well-oiled grate of a raging-hot grill.

Cactus Pear Crisp

How do you "bake" a pie or a crisp when your "stove" is a campfire, grill, or fireplace? Our colonial forebears figured it out—they cooked the dessert in a Dutch oven—a large cast-iron kettle nestled in the embers. And they shoveled more embers in the depression in its heavy lid. (Invariably, some smoke from the fire wound up flavoring the dessert.) A few years ago, we were taping my *Primal Grill* TV show in the desert of southern Arizona. A few yards off the set was a cluster of cactuses with flat spiny leaves crowned with egg-shaped cactus pears. The theme of this particular show was "In the Wild," so you won't be surprised to learn that a few minutes later a cactus had been stripped of its fruit and a cactus pear crisp was bubbling away on the grill. **SERVES 6 TO 8**

FOR THE FILLING

1½ pounds cactus pears
¼ to ½ cup sugar
¼ cup unbleached all-purpose white flour
1 teaspoon finely grated lemon zest
2 tablespoons fresh lemon juice, or more to taste
Butter, for greasing the skillet

FOR THE TOPPING

½ cup crumbled gingersnaps
½ cup brown sugar (light or dark, it's your choice)
½ cup all-purpose unbleached white flour
8 tablespoons (½ cup) cold unsalted butter,
    cut into ½ inch slices
Pinch of salt
Vanilla ice cream (optional), for serving

YOU'LL ALSO NEED

One 8-inch cast-iron skillet; 2 cups wood chips
    or chunks, soaked for 1 hour in water to
    cover, then drained

ADVANCE PREPARATION

None, but allow yourself 1 hour for making and
    grilling the crisp.

1 Make the filling: Wearing gloves to protect your hands from the spines, and using a paring knife, cut the top and bottom off each cactus pear. Make a lengthwise slit in the skin and peel it off, leaving a barrel-shaped core of fruit. Cut each peeled pear crosswise into ¼-inch-thick slices.

2 Place the cactus pear slices in a mixing bowl. Sprinkle with ¼ cup of the sugar, the ¼ cup of flour, and the lemon zest and gently stir to mix. Stir in the lemon juice. Taste for seasoning, adding more sugar and/or lemon juice as necessary; the mixture should be sweet, tart, and fruity. Spoon it into the greased skillet.

3 Make the topping: Place the gingersnaps, brown sugar, and flour in a food processor fitted with a metal chopping blade and process to a coarse powder, running the machine in short bursts. Add the butter and salt and process in short bursts until the butter is reduced to pea-size pieces and the mixture feels coarse and crumbly. Do not overprocess or you'll wind up with a gloppy dough. Spoon the topping over the cactus pear mixture.

4 Set up the grill for indirect grilling and preheat it to medium-high.

5 When ready to cook, if you are using a charcoal grill, toss the wood chips or chunks on the coals. If you are using a gas grill, add the wood chips or chunks to the smoker box or place them in a smoker pouch under the grate (see page 603). Place the crisp in the center of the grate away from the heat and cover the grill. Grill the crumble until the top is darkly browned and the filling is bubbling, 30 to 40 minutes. Serve the crisp hot or warm, ideally topped with scoops of vanilla ice cream.

"Birds Nest" on the Grill
{ KUNEFE }

THE SCOOP

WHERE: Istanbul, Turkey

WHAT: The grilled version of a dessert enjoyed throughout the Near and Middle East—crisp, buttery shredded wheat with salty cheese and sweet syrup

HOW: Direct grilling

"**I** know why you're here," said the manager of Köşebaşi. "For *künefe* on the coals." That Turkey is one of the world's top four or five grilling hotspots is common knowledge and that Turks grill everything—from the predictable lamb and eggplant to the more esoteric crab apples, quinces, and pistachio nuts—will likewise come as no surprise. But dessert isn't normally part of the Turkish grill repertory, so when I heard that this upscale grill restaurant, located in Istanbul's fashionable Maçka district, served a grilled dessert, well, who cares if it meant eating lunch for the third time that afternoon. The dessert in question was *künefe,* a sort of shredded wheat, traditionally crisped in butter in the oven, but here grilled over charcoal. This imparts a subtle but discernible smoke flavor you just won't find in oven-baked versions. Then there's the drama of grilling and flipping the pastry—no small feat—and dousing it with syrup. The result makes an astonishing finale for a Turkish or Near Eastern barbecue. **SERVES 4**

Pouring Turkish coffee to go with a grilled dessert.

JUST THE FACTS:
This dessert is super-easy to make, and it will definitely turn heads and make mouths water, but it does require a trip to a Middle Eastern or Greek market to buy a phyllolike dough cut into hair-thin shreds known as *kataifi.* You can also order it online at www .parthenonfoods.com. While you're at it, pick up a salty Turkish or Greek cheese, like Haloumi, and a bottle of rose water. The rose water is optional, but its haunting perfumed flavor will transport you to the Near East. You can grill individual servings in small skillets or make one large *künefe* for four.

1½ cups sugar

1 teaspoon rose water, or to taste (optional)

12 tablespoons (1½ sticks) unsalted butter, at room temperature

1 pound kataifi dough

6 ounces salty Mediterranean cheese, such as Haloumi or a western cheese like Edam or Jack, cut into ¼-inch dice

YOU'LL ALSO NEED

4 small (5-inch) cast-iron skillets, or one 10-inch cast-iron skillet; 2 cups wood chips (optional), soaked for 1 hour in water to cover, then drained

ADVANCE PREPARATION

The dough and cheese can be assembled in the pan several hours ahead and refrigerated, covered.

"Birds nests" cooked the Planet Barbecue way, over a bed of blazing charcoal.

1 Place the sugar in a heavy saucepan with 1 cup of water and bring to a boil over high heat. Let the syrup boil until all of the sugar dissolves, about 2 minutes, shaking the pan so the mixture cooks evenly. Remove the pan from the heat and let the syrup cool to room temperature. Stir in the rose water, if using. Set the sugar syrup aside.

2 Thickly smear the butter in the bottom of the frying pan(s). Fluff the *kataifi* with your fingers and add enough to fill the frying pan(s) halfway. Sprinkle the cheese cubes over the *kataifi* in the pan(s) and place the remaining *kataifi* on top.

3 Set up the grill for direct grilling and preheat it to high. To be strictly authentic, you'd use a charcoal grill. If you are using a gas grill, add the wood chips or chunks to the smoker box or place them in a smoker pouch under the grate (see page 603) and preheat until you see smoke.

4 When ready to cook, if you are using a charcoal grill, toss the wood chips or chunks on the coals. Place the frying pan(s) on the hot grate and grill until the butter is bubbling and the pastry is crisp and browned on the bottom, 3 to 5 minutes. Use a metal spatula to lift one edge to check for doneness. If you're feeling theatrical (or brave), shake the pan(s) with a flick of the wrist to turn over the crisped pastry. Otherwise, use the metal spatula to turn it. Or, slide it onto a plate, place another plate over it, invert the plates, and slide the *künefe* back into the pan. Cook the second side until crisp and browned on the bottom, 3 to 5 minutes longer.

5 Transfer the hot *künefe* to a platter or plates. Douse it with sugar syrup and serve at once.

Fair Trade Chocolate Banana S'mores

Normally, *Planet Barbecue* focuses on the specialties of the world's top grill masters. This dessert has a more socially-conscious goal: to introduce you to an organization—and a way of shopping—that supports farmers and growers in developing countries. As the name suggests, the Fair Trade Federation was founded to guarantee that the people who produce our coffee, chocolate, sugar, bananas, vanilla, and many other staples get paid a fair wage for their labors. (It also encourages sustainable growing techniques that are good for us and for the health of our planet.) So, when you shop for the ingredients to prepare these chocolate banana s'mores, look for the words *"Fair Trade"* on the package. Not only will you grill a great dessert, but you'll also support the farmers and growers who made it possible. For more information, visit www.fairtradefederation.org.

What else is new about this recipe? Chocolate and banana are one of the world's great flavor juxtapositions. Here, they come together in the American classic: s'mores. **MAKES 8 S'MORES**

8 marshmallows

8 squares (2 inches each) Fair Trade bittersweet
    or semisweet chocolate

16 sugar or molasses cookies, gingersnaps,
    oatmeal raisin, or chocolate chip cookies,
    ideally homemade with Fair Trade sugar

1 ripe Fair Trade banana, cut on the diagonal into
    8 thin slices

ADVANCE PREPARATION
None

1 Build a campfire or set up the grill for direct grilling and preheat it to high. Or, if you are using a gas grill that has one, light the side burner.

2 When ready to cook, if using a charcoal grill, rake the lit coals into a mound (don't place the top grate on the grill). Skewer the marshmallows on sticks, skewers, or s'more forks and hold them over the fire. Roast the marshmallows until they are a dark golden brown, 2 to 5 minutes. Some people (yours truly included) believe that a marshmallow is not properly toasted until it catches fire; you blow the fire out before the marshmallow burns completely.

3 Place a square of chocolate on a cookie. Place the hot marshmallow on top and add a banana slice and second cookie to make a sandwich. Squeeze to form a sandwich (if you do it right, the hot marshmallow will melt the chocolate) and pop the whole gooey mess into your mouth.

THE SCOOP

WHERE: The United States

WHAT: A new twist on a campfire classic that assuages your social conscience

HOW: Direct grilling or grilling over a campfire

JUST THE FACTS: For the best results, roast the marshmallows over a log campfire. A grateless charcoal grill works almost as well but will have a little less flavor. Yes, you can use a gas grill—provided you get it screaming-hot.

S'more forks have long extendable handles. You can order them at www.barbecuebible.com /store.

Catalan Cream and Variations
{ CREMA CATALANA }

OK, it's not grilling or barbecue—not technically, at least. But once you've watched Pierre Gironès, owner of the restaurant L'Hostalet de Vivès near Céret in southwestern France, pull an incendiary hot metal poker out of the manorial fireplace where he does his grilling and touch it to the top of his signature *crema catalana* (a crème brûlée–like dessert), once you've seen and smelled the smoke rise with an alchemical hiss and the sugar melt to a vitreous shell, once you've tapped the resulting crust with your spoon to shatter it into a thousand caramel-flavored shards—well, you've witnessed an act of live-fire cooking that's as primal as barbecue itself. **SERVES 6**

FOR THE CUSTARD

1 quart whole milk
1 cinnamon stick (3 inches), or ½ teaspoon
   ground cinnamon
1 piece (1½ inches) vanilla bean, split,
   or ½ teaspoon vanilla extract
3 strips lemon zest (each ½ x 2 inches)
8 large egg yolks
1 cup sugar
3 tablespoons cornstarch
2 tablespoons honey
2 teaspoons anise-flavored liqueur,
   such as anisette
About 1 cup turbinado sugar (see Note) or
   granulated sugar

YOU'LL ALSO NEED

6 crème brûlée dishes (each 3 to 4 inches across
   and ¾ inch deep, traditionally earthenware;
   see Just the Facts); a crème brûlée iron or a
   kitchen blowtorch

ADVANCE PREPARATION

The Catalan creams must be made at least
   3 hours ahead and refrigerated and can be
   made as much as 24 hours in advance.

1 Place the milk, cinnamon, vanilla bean, and lemon zest in a heavy saucepan and bring to a simmer over low heat. Let the milk mixture infuse over the lowest possible heat for 10 minutes.

2 Meanwhile, place the egg yolks, sugar, cornstarch, honey, and anise-flavored liqueur in a large heavy heatproof bowl. Whisk the mixture until smooth and creamy, about 2 minutes. Strain the hot milk into the egg mixture in a thin stream, whisking to mix well. Transfer the egg mixture to the saucepan, place it over medium heat, and let come to a gentle boil, whisking steadily. Cook until the *crema* thickens, 1 to 2 minutes, whisking steadily, then remove the pan from the heat. Do not overcook or the *crema* will curdle.

3 Spoon the *crema* into the crème brûlée dishes, dividing it equally among them and shaking and tapping each to smooth the top. Let the mixture cool to room temperature, then refrigerate it for at least 3 hours, or up to 24 hours ahead. Press a piece of plastic wrap on top of each to keep it from drying out.

4 Just before serving, heat the crème brûlée iron screaming hot, ideally in a wood-burning fireplace, in the embers of a charcoal grill, or laid flat on the grate of a gas grill (you can even heat it on one of the burners of your stove). Evenly sprinkle the top of each Catalan cream with 3 tablespoons of sugar. Press the hot iron onto the surface of a Catalan cream to caramelize the sugar; this will take a few seconds, and a puff of fragrant smoke will rise as the sugar darkens. The sugar should be topaz to a dark golden brown in color, not black (burned sugar tastes, well, like sugar that has been burned). Repeat with the remaining Catalan creams, reheating the iron in between.

To use a kitchen blowtorch to caramelize the sugar, place the Catalan creams on a heatproof surface. Light the flame and adjust it to obtain a pointed red-yellow cone of heat in the center of the lavender-blue flame. Holding the flame about 3 inches above the top of a Catalan cream, move it back and forth until the sugar is evenly browned. The sugar will continue to cook for a few seconds after the flame has been removed; stop torching just when the sugar is topaz colored.

NOTE: Turbinado is sold in the United States under the brand Sugar In The Raw. In England it's known as demerara sugar; the French equivalent is *cassonade*.

VARIATIONS

Crema Catalana with Caramelized Figs:
Another specialty of L'Hostalet, made when fresh figs are in season. The gritty crunch of the fig seeds makes a great counterpoint to the custard. You'll need 9 ripe figs; cut them in half lengthwise.

Prepare the Catalan cream, spooning it into the crème brûlée dishes. Arrange 3 fig halves in each dish, rounded side down, pushing each fig half into the *crema* so that the cut side is flush with the surface. Let the Catalan creams cool as described in Step 3, then sprinkle them with sugar and caramelize them as described in Step 4.

Crema Catalana with Armagnac Prunes:
This version features two delicacies of southwest France—prunes soaked in Armagnac, a brandy from Gascony. Soak 18 prunes in 1 cup of Armagnac in a nonreactive bowl for 2 hours, stirring occasionally. Drain the prunes well—yes, you can drink the Armagnac. It will be fantastic. Prepare the Catalan cream, substituting the whole Armagnac-soaked prunes for the figs.

Pineapple *Crema Catalana:*
Also from L'Hostalet: Substitute 6 rings of fresh pineapple for the figs. Each ring should be about ½-inch thick and cored. Fill the dishes with the *crema* and press the pineapple rings into the top. Sprinkle the sugar on top and caramelize it.

Catalan cream caramelized the traditional way—with a wood fire–heated iron.

France: Méchoui? Mais Oui

When I went to cooking school in Paris (believe it or not, this author has classical French training), we studied all the time-honored cooking techniques: braising, baking, frying, poaching, and sautéing. Grilling was completely ignored. It was as though the most celebrated gastronomic culture in Europe, the birthplace of such culinary luminaries as La Varenne, Carême, Escoffier, Paul Bocuse, and Alain Ducasse (all of whom, incidentally, cooked at some point on wood or charcoal), had chosen to ignore the cooking method that had been practiced in France in neolithic caves, medieval monasteries and castles, Renaissance palaces, and at five-star hotels ever since Frenchmen first put meat to fire.

And that was sure a long time ago. In the Musée National de Préhistoire in Les Eyzies in the Dordogne, you'll find a twenty-thousand-year-old hearth, its stones blackened by fire, on which some prehistoric cook grilled by sandwiching meat between stones and lit embers. At the Pech Merle cavern near

The Eiffel Tower lights up the night sky.

Cahors you'll find another hearth with remnants of some foods our ancestors roasted in the fire, including crabapples, peas, and acorns. And at Préhisto Parc in Tursac near Sarlat, you can visit a community of life-size concrete Neanderthals engaged in the primal arts of hunting, butchering, and roasting meats over a campfire.

The first French cookbook, *Le Viandier (The Victualler),* said to be written by King Charles V's chef,

Taillevent, abounds with recipes for meats that are grilled and spit roasted (the book has remained in print since its debut in the late fourteenth century). Visit a gas station in the French countryside today, and you'll find bundles of grapevine trimmings and bags of lump charcoal ready for a pastime practiced by many but boasted about by few—the backyard barbecue. Not that you'd know it, for most Frenchmen refer to this outdoor feast by the name used

Parlez-Vous Barbecue?

Aged French cheese wheels stacked in the marketplace.

The "Clos de Vougeot" dating back to 1330, is one of the most famous vineyards in France.

Grilling takes place in every corner of France, from the Ile de Ré on the Atlantic coast (home of grilled mussel *éclade*) to Burgundy (renowned for its Charolais beef served with *marchand de vin*—wine merchant's sauce) and the Cote d'Azur. Frenchmen have been grilling in the Dordogne Valley for 40,000 years.

in their former North African colonies: They invite you to a *méchoui*.

Grilling is alive and well in France, although it takes some ferreting out to discover. One good place to start is La Bouvette on the Ile de Ré off the Atlantic Coast, where Burgundy-born chef Laurent Mertz has transformed a local grilled specialty called *éclade* (mussels cooked on a bed of blazing pine needles) into a dish of cult adoration. Or the restaurant L'Hostalet de Vivès (near Céret in Southwest France), where a thirty-year grill veteran named Pierre Gironès grills every imaginable cut of beef, pork, lamb, and rabbit, served with vampire-defying doses of garlicky aioli, and *crema catalana* in a fireplace that looks like it has been burning since the reign of Henri IV.

Parisian restaurants with wood-burning grills include the impossibly snooty, and impossibly difficult to get into, L'Ami Louis and the charmingly old-fashioned Georgette, where steaks and chops—admittedly not always the most tender—are seared in a wood-burning fireplace. Even the celebrated Alain Ducasse has installed a wood-burning grill and rotisserie at his Michelin three-star restaurant at the swank Hôtel Plaza Athénée in Paris, a sure sign that French chefs who are truly obsessed with flavor are not too highfalutin for grilling.

So, why this reticence to include grilling in the classical French culinary canon? "Perhaps it's just too old-fashioned," speculates Laurent Mertz. Yes, but perhaps the future of French cuisine—threatened by changing demographics and economic woes and overshadowed by France's iconoclastic culinary neighbors in Spain—lies in its past.

Le Piqu' Boeuf restaurant in Beaune specializes in grilled Charolais beef.

THE GRILLS: The French do their live-fire cooking on grills and rotisseries. The grills are your basic rectangular firebox or fireplace models with metal grates over the coals. French grills are not covered, so the grilling is direct. Rotisseries range from spits mounted in fireplaces to high-tech models (one designed by Alain Ducasse) with vertical turnspits, variable motor speeds, and thermostatic heat control. The wall rotisseries found at butcher shops and upscale bistros in Paris are unique to France; chickens, saddles of lamb, and even whole fish roast on the horizontal spits of these rotisseries in front of a wall of gas-fired burners.

THE FUEL: Natural lump charcoal or wood for grills; wood or gas for rotisseries

THE FLAVORINGS: As a rule, the French avoid the extravagant spicing of, say, India or Southeast Asia, preferring the more mellow tones of tomatoes, garlic, fresh and dried herbs, wine, and olive oil.

MUST TRY DISHES: The French word for grilled food is *grillade*, but many home cooks use the term of France's former French colonies: *méchoui*.

Bar flambé au fenouil: Whole bass flamed with Pernod over dried fennel branches

Brochette: Shish kebab

Crema catalana: Catalan cream—the southwestern French version of crème brûlée. I know, it's not really grilled, but tradition calls for the sugar to be caramelized by a poker heated red hot in the fireplace (see page 586 for a recipe).

Entrecôte à la bordelaise or marchand de vin: Rib steak with red wine sauce; a *marchand de vin* is a wine merchant

Raclette: A malodorous Alpine cheese melted in front of the fireplace and served spread over country bread

Saucisse: Sausage. Popular sausages for grilling in France include *merguez,* a spicy Moroccan-style sausage, and *andouillette* (chitterling sausage).

HOW TO EAT IT: With a knife and fork: *Après tout,* this is France.

IF YOU CAN EAT AT ONLY ONE RESTAURANT: La Bouvette on the Ile de Ré (see page 515)

WHAT TO DRINK: Wine, of course

THE MOST SINGULAR DISH IN THE REPERTORY: *Eclade de moules*—mussels grilled on a bed of pine needles

Grilled Ice Cream

The strangest thing I've ever grilled? It's a question I'm asked often. So is Azerbaijan's most famous grill master and TV chef, Mehman Huseynov (see page 592), and the hyperkinetic chef has a ready answer: ice cream. Yes, ice cream. Skewered on a slender ribbon of steel, crusted with beaten egg and shredded coconut, and seared over the fire. The secret to grilling ice cream is to dip the frozen balls in egg and coconut several times before grilling. The hot fire cooks these ingredients into a hermetic crust, which seals in the melting ice cream. It's essential to work quickly and over a very hot fire to sear the exterior before the ice cream has a chance to melt.

MAKES 8 TO 12 BALLS; SERVES 4

1½ pints of your favorite ice cream
2 large eggs
1 teaspoon pure vanilla extract
2 cups grated or shredded dried coconut in
    a shallow bowl

YOU'LL ALSO NEED
Flat metal skewers, at least 12 inches long

ADVANCE PREPARATION
4 to 6 hours for refreezing the ice cream

1 Using a large ice cream scoop, scoop the ice cream into 2-inch balls. Place them in a baking dish and return them to the freezer to freeze the balls solid, 1 to 2 hours.

2 Place the eggs and vanilla in a shallow bowl and beat with a fork. Dip each ice cream ball in beaten egg, turning it with forks to coat it all over, then in the coconut, turning it with forks to coat it on all sides. Return each ball to the egg to coat it again, then coat it in the coconut again. Return the balls to the baking dish and freeze them again until solid.

3 When the coconut-covered ice cream balls are frozen solid, skewer them on flat metal skewers and freeze them again.

4 Set up the grill for grateless grilling, following the instructions on page 599 and preheat the grill to as hot as it will go. Arrange 2 bricks on the grate at opposite sides of the grill.

5 Place the kebabs on the grill, resting the ends of the skewers on the bricks. Grill the ice cream balls until the coconut is browned on all sides, 1 to 2 minutes per side, 4 minutes in all. Work quickly; the idea is to sear the coconut without melting the ice cream. Slide the ice cream balls off the skewers into bowls or onto plates and serve at once.

The "Emeril" of Azerbaijan

BAKU, AZERBAIJAN

Last things first. Mehman Huseynov has crossed the final threshold, risen to the ultimate challenge, done the improbable, the impossible, on the grill. He actually grills ice cream. He dips balls of vanilla ice cream in beaten egg, then in shredded coconut, and then threads them onto flat metal skewers and browns them over a blisteringly hot fire (you can read all about it on page 590). As you can imagine, it takes considerable dexterity to brown the crust without melting the ice cream inside it. Then again, this Azeri grill master, chef of the sprawling Neolit restaurant in Baku, has dexterity—and screaming hot fire, well, to burn.

> Huseynov keeps the seasonings simple. "It's really about the meat."

A wiry chef recognizable by his trademark white coat with red piping, Huseynov grew up in Ismayilli in northern Azerbaijan, a region famed for its pit-roasted lamb. (Azerbaijan, you'll remember, is that oil-rich former Soviet Union country sandwiched between the Caucasus Mountains and the Caspian Sea.) He graduated from Baku University Culinary School and has worked as a chef since the age of seventeen. Huseynov currently presides over a staff of 350, running a restaurant that routinely serves two thousand people a day. That's on top of taping a one-hour cooking show five days a week for Lider TV, making him, perhaps, the most famous celebrity TV chef that you've never heard of.

Huseynov's tools of the trade are common currency in the Caspian region—a grateless grill called a *mangal* (you can read about it on page 605) and a pit barbecue called a *tandir* (the Azeri version of an Indian tandoor). He keeps the seasonings simple: salt, pepper, ginger, turmeric, onion, thyme, and parsley. "It's really about the meat," he says. So how do you manage to serve food that's fresh and hot for two thousand customers? He walks me through Neolit's sprawling campus, nodding to a male grill master here, a female bread baker there, a man pushing a cart piled with charcoal—all working in small satellite kitchens. "Neolit may run like a big city," he says, "but we grill like we're in a small village."

NAME: Mehman Huseynov

TERRITORY: Azerbaijan

CLAIM TO FAME: Host of Azerbaijan's premier television cooking show; chef of the sprawling Neolit restaurant in Baku

SPECIALTIES: *Lula*, ground lamb kebab; *govurmasi*, turmeric-rubbed lamb roasted in a *tandir*; *kartof kebab*, mashed potato kebab; *mangal salati*, grilled vegetable salad; *dondurma kebab*, a dessert kebab

HUSEYNOV SAYS:

▶ So what's it take to become a master griller? Imagination. Experience. And, of course, an iron work ethic.

▶ Allah has given you lamb. And you think you can improve on that?

Mehman Huseynov (left) and an assistant show off a chorus line of Azeri *tandir* chickens.

Smoked Ice Cream

All grilled and smoked foods taste great. But some dishes taste so unexpected, so stunningly original, they make you feel like you've rediscovered the art of eating. Consider the smoked ice cream served at Spain's futuristic grill restaurant, Etxebarri (see page 489). The flavor comes from smoking the ingredients with smoldering oak, and if the notion of smoked ice cream sounds weird, the first bite will make you a believer. **SERVES 4**

2 cups heavy (whipping) cream

1 cup whole milk

¾ cup glucose or light corn syrup, such as Karo

½ cup sugar

3 egg yolks

YOU'LL ALSO NEED

An aluminum foil drip pan; 2 cups oak chips or chunks, soaked in water to cover for 1 hour, then drained; an ice cream machine

ADVANCE PREPARATION

Allow yourself 30 minutes to 1 hour for smoking the milk and 1 hour for cooling, churning, and freezing the ice cream.

1 Place the cream, milk, and glucose in a mixing bowl and whisk to blend.

2 To grill: *If you are using a charcoal grill,* set up the grill for indirect grilling and preheat it to medium. When ready to cook, toss the wood chips or chunks on the coals. Place the drip pan with the cream mixture in the center of the grill between the mounds of coals and cover the grill. Grill the cream mixture until richly flavored with smoke, 20 to 30 minutes.

If you are using a smoker, set it up following the manufacturer's instructions and preheat it to 250°F. Place the pan with the ice cream mixture in the smoker and smoke it until richly flavored with smoke, about 1 hour.

3 Place the sugar and egg yolks in a medium-size saucepan and whisk until smooth and creamy. Add the hot cream mixture to the egg mixture, pouring it in a thin stream while whisking vigorously. Place the saucepan over low heat and cook the cream mixture until it thickly coats the back of a wooden spoon, 2 to 3 minutes. Do not allow the mixture to boil or it will curdle.

4 Strain the mixture through a fine-meshed strainer into a bowl and let it cool to room temperature. When cool, transfer it to an ice cream machine and churn until frozen, following the manufacturer's instructions. Serve the ice cream at once.

The Frank Gehry–designed Guggenheim Museum in Bilbao has come to symbolize the innovative spirit of contemporary Spanish cuisine—and grilling.

Spain: The Barbecue in Spain Is Anything but Plain

One sears beef rib steaks over fire with nothing more than fistfuls of sea salt. The other grills *angulas* (baby eels) in a high-tech wire mesh grill pan and smokes butter to spread on grilled bread. Matías Gorrotxategi of the rustic chop house Casa Julián in Tolosa and Victor Arguinzoniz of the exquisitely refined Etxebarri near San Sebastián stand at opposite ends of the barbecue spectrum—one at its most primal, the other at its most thought provokingly inventive. Both represent the glory that is Spanish grilling.

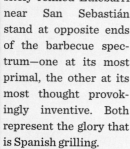

Sardine kebabs at Pedregalejo Beach in Málaga.

Spanish barbecue has one foot in the Stone Age and one foot in the surrealistic, futuristic world of Ferran Adrià. Sixty thousand years ago, a vibrant Neanderthal culture flourished in the mountains and caves of what is now eastern Spain. The cave dwellers left no written records about their grilling, of course (although you can still see traces of their campfires), but at least one grilled dish still popular in Spain may date back to prehistoric times—*calçots*, a sort of leek yanked

from the ground, roasted in the fire, dirt and all, pulled out of its burned skin by hand, and served with *romesco* sauce for dipping.

Fast forward to the twenty-first century, where chefs like Arguinzoniz push the very limits of what we know as live-fire cooking, making charcoal from scratch each morning, grilling and smoking foods

most people wouldn't dream could be cooked with live fire (including milk to make smoked ice cream), even deconstructing and reconstructing the grill. One Arguinzoniz invention is a sort of charcoal burning broiler that grills from above as well as from below.

Between the two extremes stand Moorish *pinchos,* kebabs spiced with

Spanish Grilling Spans 40,000 Years of Human History

Porquets ("Little Piggies"), typical sweets from the Girona Province in Spain.

With water on three sides and mountains to the east, Spain provides its grillers with a prodigious selection of seafood and land foods, with superlative wines, beer, and even hard cider to wash them down.

La Boquería market, Barcelona, Spain.

seasonings brought to Spain from North Africa by the Moors more than a thousand years ago; pristine fish like *rodaballo,* turbot grilled with nothing more than sea salt and served with fried garlic and guindilla chiles; and grass-fed steaks, like the *chuletas* (simple rib steaks) that are the pride of restaurants like Casa Julián. One thing is for sure: Wherever and whenever you see a Spaniard light a grill, get ready for a feast.

The traditional way to cook paella is over an open fire. Here's how they prepare it bigger-than-life at the St. Joan Fiesta on Spain's Costa Blanca.

THE GRILL: Spanish grills can be as simple as open-air campfires or as elaborate as the gleaming, high-performance stainless steel grills at restaurants like Etxebarri. The typical Spanish grill is a metal or stone trough or platform with glowing embers and a cast-iron grate on top. Fish tends to be grilled whole in grill baskets.

THE FUEL: Charcoal or wood

THE FLAVORS: As a rule, Spanish grillers work with a simple range of flavors: salt, generally a very coarse sea salt used for grilling steaks, pepper, garlic, guindilla chiles, olive oil, and lemon juice. As in Italy, less is generally thought to be more.

MUST TRY DISHES:

Calçots: Fire-charred leeklike green onions served with *romesco* sauce; *calçots* are in season in late winter only

Calçots, *Spanish green onions, grilled with their roots, dirt—and all—over a wood fire.*

Chuleta: A bible-thick beef rib steak grilled with a thick crust of coarse sea salt

Me at the famous Casa Julián in Tolosa, Spain, where salt-crusted rib steaks are grilled in an ancient stone hearth.

Escalivada: Mixed grilled vegetables in a light vinaigrette

Merluza a la parrilla: Hake grilled and served with fried garlic sauce

Pa amb tomàquet: Catalan grilled tomato bread

Parrillada: A mixed grill that includes grilled beef, lamb, pork, sweetbreads, and a variety of sausages

Rodaballo: Whole grilled turbot served with a sherry or wine vinaigrette

THE CONDIMENTS: The big three are *alioli,* Spanish garlic sauce; *vinagreta,* vinaigrette; and *romesco,* a thick red sauce made with roasted or grilled vegetables, ground nuts, dried chiles, and toast.

IF YOU CAN EAT AT ONLY ONE RESTAURANT: Etxebarri in the town of Axpe in the Basque region, where you'll experience some of the most cutting-edge grilling on Planet Barbecue

WHAT TO DRINK: Wine—especially Basque *txakoli,* a crisp white wine for seafood, or a hearty red Rioja or Ribera del Duero with beef

THE MOST SINGULAR DISH IN THE REPERTORY: Paella, for although you'd likely never think of this lavish Valencian rice dish as barbecue, the traditional way to cook it is over an open wood fire. The swirling smoke adds a depth of flavor you just can't achieve on the stove.

Grilled turbot with "holy water" (the recipe is on page 440).

South African "Burned" Coffee
{ MOERKOFFIE }

WHERE: The Cape of Good Hope, South Africa

WHAT: Coffee cowboy-style—if the cowboy roamed the range in South Africa

HOW: Direct grilling

JUST THE FACTS: The coffee must be cooked on a wood fire. However, if you have a charcoal grill, you can brew the coffee over the coals and light a single slender log on the coals to finish it.

Here's a fitting conclusion to our tour of Planet Barbecue and a tribute to the primal campfires where barbecue—and humankind—began. In a nutshell, it's coffee, brewed as it has been for hundreds of years by cowboys, herders, fishermen, and other stalwart souls who work, cook, eat, and sleep under the stars: in a pot perched on the embers. Here's how they make it at a seaside fish camp south of Cape Town called Die Strandloper. The secret is to plunge a burning stick into the coffee right before pouring it. This precipitates the grounds to the bottom and adds a decisive smoke flavor—and of course, it looks cool as all get out. **SERVES 4**

½ cup medium-ground coffee
Sugar, for serving
Heavy (whipping) cream (preferably from a farm) or evaporated milk, for serving

YOU'LL ALSO NEED

A wood fire; a pot, preferably an old-fashioned enameled coffee pot such as you would see in an old-time Western movie (see Note)

ADVANCE PREPARATION
None

Coffee South African bush-style: brewed on the fire and finished with a flaming log.

1 Build a wood fire and let most of it burn down to embers. However, keep a few logs mostly whole and on fire.

2 Place the coffee and 1 quart of water in the pot. Set the pot in the embers and let the coffee boil for 10 minutes.

3 Remove the pot from the heat and place it next to the fire. Using long-handled tongs, remove a big, fat, burning stick from the fire—one that is 1 to 2 inches in diameter, about 6 to 8 inches long, and at least partially turned to embers. Plunge it into the coffee. It will hiss like Lucifer. Remove the stick and return it to the fire. Pour the coffee into mugs, preferably tin, leaving the last inch with the grounds in the bottom of the pot. Add sugar and cream to taste.

NOTE: You'll find "frontier"-style percolators and coffee boilers at www.lehmans.com.

The Nuts and Bolts of Live-Fire Cooking

Human beings grill in every corner of Planet Barbecue, yet we do it differently every-where. Our grills are different. Our fuels are different. Our techniques are different. And what we grill is certainly different, depending on—amid much else—where we live, what God we worship, and how much cash we have in our pockets. This chapter tells you everything you need to know about grilling to make the greatest dishes on Planet Barbecue.

The Grill

Travel Planet Barbecue with me and you'll find grills of every size, shape, and design. Despite this incredible diversity, all grills share similar features. Know how they work and you're well on your way to improving your grill skills. What makes a grill?

The firebox: The firebox is where the fire is located. It can be as simple as a stone circle or ember-filled metal box or as sophisticated as the burner manifolds running the width or length of a gas grill. The firebox is where the charcoal or wood burns or the gas glows.

The cook chamber: The part of the grill where the food actually cooks; for most grills the cook chamber is an extension of the firebox.

The grill grate: The grill grate is the proverbial gridiron (yes, this is what gave the football

LID

COOK/SMOKE CHAMBER

GRILL GRATE

TOP VENT

FIREBOX

BOTTOM VENT

ASH CATCHER

Grill grate with raised panels

field its name). Place food on the parallel metal bars or wire screen over the fire and watch it grill to perfection. There's an additional benefit, and that is that the grate gives you a handsome crosshatch of grill marks, contributing to the flavor we associate with the charring that occurs where the meat hits the hot metal. Grill grates are typically made from cast iron (my personal favorite for its branding qualities) or from ¼-inch stainless steel bars, stamped stainless steel, porcelainized enamel, or thick or thin wire. However, a grate is *not* essential. On vast swaths of Planet Barbecue, grills do not have grill grates. The food is suspended over the fire in grill baskets or on metal skewers, producing an equally delicious result (for instructions on grateless grilling, see the facing page).

The airflow: Most charcoal- or wood-burning grills have adjustable vents that let air in at the bottom or on the side and sometimes at the top. These control the airflow, enabling you to control the heat: Increased airflow gives you a hotter fire. The straw or electric fans used by grill jockeys in Southeast Asia and the Near East to oxygenate the embers of a grill serve the same function.

The lid: The lid is a relatively new addition to grill design, but without it there would be no indirect grilling or smoking. Given how common grills with lids are in North America, you may be surprised to learn that most of the world's grills do not have lids.

The Grilling Methods

Given the enormous diversity of grills on Planet Barbecue—not to mention the widely varied techniques and philosophies of the world's grill masters—there actually are only seven basic methods of live-fire cooking. Understanding how they work will make you a better griller, no matter what type of grill you use.

Direct grilling: Direct grilling is what most of the world means when people talk about barbecue or live-fire cooking. As the name suggests, the food is cooked directly over a charcoal, wood, or gas fire. The food is positioned on the grill grate—or on skewers or in a grill basket—3 to 10 inches above the fire. If you are grilling over charcoal or wood, you can rake out the embers to make a two- or three-zone fire (see page 611) and place the food on the grate directly over them. On a gas grill you set the burners to the desired temperature and place the food above the heat source.

In general, direct grilling is done over a high, or medium to medium-high, heat (the smaller the pieces of food, the higher the heat). The cooking time is measured in minutes. Direct grilling

DIRECT GRILLING

1. *Dump the lit coals from the chimney starter into the bottom of the grill. Wear a heavy glove to protect your hand.*

2. *Using a grill hoe, a garden hoe, or other long-handled implement, rake the burning coals to form either a two-zone or three-zone fire (see page 611).*

3. *A three-zone fire: The coals are in a double layer on the top right side (for a strong blast of heat for searing) and in a single layer in the center (for a steady, moderate heat for cooking). The bottom left of the grill is free of coals to give you a safety zone where you can keep food warm or dodge flare-ups.*

is best for small, quick-cooking, and/or tender pieces of food, such as steaks, chops, fish fillets, chicken breasts or pieces, breads, and fruits or vegetables with a high water content.

Grateless grilling: In many parts of the world, from Turkey to Japan to India, grills do not have grates and the food is cooked suspended directly over the fire. The method is particularly good for grilling skewered ground meat kebabs, tofu, and glazed foods that would otherwise stick to the grate. The easiest way to do grateless grilling on an American-style grill, either charcoal or gas, is to place two flat bricks, paving stones, or pieces of metal pipe on the grate, one at the front and one at the back. Position them just far enough apart so that the ends of the skewers will rest comfortably on them as supports. The food will be suspended above the grate and will be fully exposed to the heat.

Grateless grilling: Prop the ends of the skewers on two bricks at opposite sides of the grill so the meat is suspended above the grate.

The setup for indirect grilling on a charcoal grill.

Indirect grilling: As the name suggests, when grilling using the indirect method, the food is cooked next to, not directly over, the fire. This has the advantage of allowing you to cook large cuts of meat thoroughly without burning the exterior and to grill fatty foods without having them singed by flare-ups. Indirect grilling is primarily a North American phenomenon. Elsewhere on Planet Barbecue, grill masters achieve a similar result by grilling large pieces of meat directly over low heat or by using a vessel grill, like a tandoor. Gas or charcoal are the fuels most commonly used for indirect grilling; wood fires get too sooty in a closed environment.

To set up a charcoal grill for indirect grilling, rake the embers into mounds at opposite sides of the grill and place a foil drip pan in the center. Place the food in the center of the grate over the drip pan. On a gas grill, light the front and rear or the outside burners and place the food in the center of the grate to cook. Most gas grills have built-in drip pans. Whether you are using charcoal or gas, once the food is on the grate, cover the grill. As a rule, indirect grilling is done at a moderate temperature (325° to 400°F) for an extended period (1 to 1½ hours for chickens or racks of baby back ribs;

Three Things to Look for When Buying a Grill

STURDY CONSTRUCTION: Your grill will hold a potentially dangerous combustible, not to mention the food you've painstakingly purchased, prepared, and seasoned. Make sure it feels solid and stable.

A RELIABLE WARRANTY: The grill is one of the rare cooking devices you're meant to use and leave outdoors. Metal rusts, moving parts freeze up, and rubber hoses become brittle. Look for a manufacturer that will replace damaged parts willingly and quickly. For more complicated grills, like gas grills, make sure there's a service agent nearby.

RAICHLEN'S RULE FOR BUYING A NEW GRILL: Always buy more grill than you think you need. It will stretch your creativity and you'll grow into it—an investment that will prove well worth the money.

Smoking salmon on a traditional offset barrel smoker. Note the domed water smoker in the background.

up to 4 hours for pork shoulders and whole turkeys). Indirect grilling is best for large, tough, or fatty pieces of meat, like a whole chicken, duck, or turkey, or a leg of lamb or rib roast.

Smoking, aka barbecuing: Smoking is similar to indirect grilling, but you add wood to the fire to generate wood smoke,

Soaking wood chips for smoking. The liquid slows the rate of combustion. Drain before using.

imparting additional flavor to the meat. The practice is most common in North America but is also done in Europe. For low-heat smoking, you build a wood or charcoal fire in the firebox, or use half the normal amount of charcoal in a kettle grill and add 1½ to 2 cups soaked, drained wood chips or chunks. For moderate-heat smoking, you set up the grill for indirect grilling and toss the soaked wood chips or chunks on the coals. Either way, you place the food in the smoke chamber and cover the grill. Note: It is harder to achieve an authentic smoke flavor using a gas grill.

True barbecue, in the style of the American South, Midwest, and West, is done "low and slow" at around 250°F. The process can take up to 6 hours for ribs and 12 to 16 hours for brisket. The best cuts of meat for smoking are tough cuts, like

brisket and spareribs, and large cuts of meat, like mutton and pork shoulders.

There's a hybrid technique called **smoke roasting.** Done with wood chips or chunks at 325° to 400°F, the process is quicker: 1 to 1½ hours for chicken or racks of baby back ribs; 3 to 4 hours for pork shoulders.

Spit roasting: Few sights on Planet Barbecue are more inviting—or hunger inducing—than a duck, rib roast, pork shoulder, or even a whole lamb rotating slowly on a turnspit next to the fire. Nothing compares to the lateral heat and the slow rotation of the spit for crisping and browning meat. It's a self-basting process that maximizes succulence even as it melts out the fat. You can spit roast over charcoal, wood, or gas, setting up the grill as you would for indirect grilling. When grilling with charcoal, rake the embers behind (and sometimes also in front of) the axis where the turnspit will rotate, following the grill manufacturer's directions. Place a drip pan underneath where the food will cook. Many gas grills have dedicated rotisserie burners built into the back of the cook chamber.

As a rule, spit roasting is done at a medium (350°F) to medium-high (400°F) heat. Spit roasting is best for foods that are cylindrical or fatty, like whole chickens, ducks, rib roasts, pork shoulders, legs of lamb, and the like. But you can also spit roast vegetables and fruits, like whole onions (see page 537) or pineapple (see page 577).

Pit roasting: It's a sight as primal as barbecue itself, and it never fails to stir deep emotion. Pit roasting was one of the first methods used to cook food, and it remains one of the most theatrical—and one of the best. At its most primal and elemental, pit roasting involves nothing more than standing large roasts, or even whole animals, on vertical stakes in front of a bonfire. Pit roasting is practiced around Planet Barbecue, especially in North and South America.

Pit roasting can be done above or underground. To pit roast above ground, you build a wood fire and cook the meat or fish by placing it on vertical stakes arranged around the fire. Control the heat by tilting the stakes closer to or farther away from the fire. Despite the raging bonfire, by the time the heat reaches the food it's generally moderate (about 350°F).

Roasting peppers and chiles in the embers.

Roasting salmon on redwood stakes over an open pit fire on the set of Primal Grill.

Cooking times range from 30 minutes for salmon fillets to a half day for a side of beef. Above ground pit roasting is best for whole fish (often butterflied through the belly), whole lambs, goats, and young pigs, and whole racks of beef ribs.

The New England clambake, Polynesian luau, and Mexican *cochinita pibil* are all forms of **underground pit roasting.** Purists may argue that, technically speaking, this is more a form of steaming or baking than live-fire cooking. I say that any culinary activity that requires you to burn large quantities of wood in a hole in the ground to cook dinner deserves attention. To pit roast underground, you dig a hole and line it with stones, then build a raging wood fire on top. When the embers die down, you wrap the food in banana leaves, seaweed, or some other foliage, and place it in the pit. Then you cover everything with dirt and let time and the moist, gentle heat work their

magic. Underground pit roasting requires at least half a day (French-Canadian lumberjacks used to cook beanhole beans for 72 hours). Underground pit roasting is best for whole hogs, sausages, shellfish, and root vegetables.

Roasting in the embers: One of my all-time favorite steaks is a "Caveman T-bone" made by grilling the steak directly on the embers (you'll find the recipe on page 151). This was the original barbecue, and it's still practiced today. Rake out the embers and fan them to blow off any loose ash. Then place the food directly on the glowing coals—the heat will be comparable to that of direct grilling. A related technique, **roasting in hot ashes,** works at a lower temperature. An additional layer of ash and embers is shoveled on top. You need a medium to low temperature for dense foods like potatoes and beets that cook buried in the ashes and embers.

The Fuels

The first "grills" (make that fire pits) burned wood. Actually, the first "barbecue" probably consisted of a bison or an aurochs roasted on the hoof by accident in a forest fire and tasted by one of our curious—no doubt very hungry—human ancestors. Grills have evolved enormously since then, but they still are fired by three basic fuels.

CHARCOAL

Charcoal represents one of man's very first technological achievements; it was in use as early as 200,000 B.C. When wood is burned slowly without oxygen it produces charcoal. The charring removes the water and most of the flavor-producing chemical compounds of the wood, leaving a carbon-rich fuel that burns hot, cleanly, and efficiently. Charcoal also produces a more concentrated fire. No wonder the vast majority of the world's grill masters burn charcoal. But not all charcoals are the same. Here's a scorecard to help you identify the players.

Lump charcoal: Sometimes called **charwood** or **natural lump charcoal,** this is the original charcoal, made by burning trees or logs in a kiln, sealed cave, or even underground. Unlike briquettes, lump charcoal is pure wood—free of binders or petroleum-based accelerants. Lump charcoal burns hot, cleanly, and pure. You can refuel a lump charcoal fire with unlit charcoal without producing the acrid smoke associated with freshly lit briquettes. However, natural lump charcoal burns unevenly, hotter at the beginning, cooler at the end, and it burns out more quickly than charcoal briquettes. When you grill with lump charcoal you'll need to refuel the grill more often than with briquettes, usually after 30 to 40 minutes. Avoid "lump" charcoal that comes in straight-edged rectangular blocks—it's made from lumber scraps, not logs.

Charcoal briquettes: These are designed to burn evenly and maintain a steady "broiling" temperature of at least 600°F for 1 hour. Traditional briquettes contain wood scraps, sawdust, coal dust, borax, and petroleum binders, so it's not surprising that they emit an acrid-tasting smoke when first lit. **Instant-light charcoal** consists of briquettes saturated with lighter fluid. The acrid smoke disappears once the charcoal glows orange and begins to ash over, but you're still grilling over borax, coal dust, and petroleum binders. And, although the petroleum-based accelerants of instant-light charcoal burn off in theory, they can produce an oily taste when less than completely lit. "Natural" briquettes, which contain only wood scraps and starch binders, are meant to eliminate these problems (one good brand is Duraflame). By the way, the contestants at barbecue competitions like those at Memphis in May and Kansas City's American Royal use briquettes and win big.

Binchotan: Japan's superpremium lump charcoal (actually it comes in branchlike cylinders), *binchotan* is used in top yakitori parlors throughout Japan and in the United States. *Binchotan* is traditionally made from *ubamegashi* oak in mud-sealed caves in southwest Japan. It burns very clean and very hot, producing no discernable charcoal flavor. However, it is very expensive; a single piece can cost several dollars. And, *binchotan* takes a long time to light. Use a chimney starter or electric starter or a blowtorch and allow yourself at least 30 minutes for the coals to catch fire. Once the charcoal is lit, however, it burns for a long time.

Coconut shell charcoal: Coconut husks make a fuel that fires tens of thousands of saté grills in Thailand and beyond: coconut shell charcoal. Quick to light, hot burning, and sold in small pieces, it's the perfect charcoal for the small grills used by Asian street vendors.

Coconut shell charcoal

Although coconut shell charcoal is hard to find in the United States, if you do get your hands on some, use it to fire up your hibachi. You'd need an awful lot of coconut shell charcoal to fire a large North American charcoal grill.

WOOD

Wood is the original and, to my mind, still the best fuel for grilling, and grill masters from Montevideo to Munich back me up on this. Charcoal and propane or natural gas produce heat, but only wood gives you both heat and flavor. That flavor is, of course, smoke—made up of carbon compounds like guaiacol, also found in roasted coffee, and syringol, the active ingredient in liquid smoke responsible for the "smoky" flavor.

Wood has two very different uses on Planet Barbecue. As a fuel it imparts delicate flavor of wood smoke. As a smoking agent—whether charcoal, gas, or an electric burner provides the heat—it imparts the heavy smoke flavor associated with traditional North American barbecue. The most common woods used for grilling are oak, used in California, South America, and Europe; beech, used in Germany; grapevine roots and trimmings, used in France and Spain; and mesquite, used in

Split and stacked oak ready for grilling.

Mexico, Texas—and in Hawaii, where it goes by the name of

HOW TO MAKE A SMOKER POUCH

The best way to smoke foods is in a smoker or charcoal grill. If you own a gas grill, you can approximate *some* of the smoke flavor by making a smoker pouch. But, even if you're a diehard gas griller, if you're really serious about achieving a smoke flavor, invest in an inexpensive charcoal grill for smoking.

1. Place an 12 x 18-inch rectangle of heavy-duty aluminum foil on a work surface with the short side facing you. Place 1 cup soaked, drained hardwood chips on the bottom half of the foil.

2. Fold the top half over the bottom and tightly pleat the edges to make a sealed pouch.

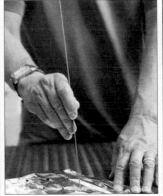

3. Using the end of a metal skewer, poke a dozen holes in the top of the pouch.

4. Preheat your gas grill to high. Lift the grate using heavy-duty tongs or other lifting tool and place the smoker pouch over one of the burners. Return the grate and run the grill until you see smoke. Adjust the grill to the desired temperature and add the food.

kiave. Conventional wisdom holds that you shouldn't use softwoods, like pine and spruce, for grilling, the theory being that their smoke is high in tars and creosote. However, in France, mussels are grilled on pine needles, and in Germany, people grill bratwurst over pinecones—all with fabulous results.

You can use wood four ways for live-fire cooking.

1. Use whole logs for open pit and campfire grilling, as well as in front-loading and South American–style grills.

2. Use split logs and branches in kettle grills and table grills set up for the direct method.

3. Use wood chunks lit in a chimney starter just as you would when grilling with charcoal.

You can also toss wood chips or chunks on a bed of charcoal embers for a smoke flavor.

4. Toss wood chips on the coals for a mild smoke flavor, or soak them in water, then drain and use them in smokers and kettle grills to produce the heavy smoke flavor associated with traditional American barbecue.

You can also get smoke flavor by using pellets or disks made from compressed hardwood sawdust. Pellet "grills" (or more accurately, pellet smokers) like the Traeger, have entered the American barbecue mainstream. The Bradley smoker, popular in Canada, burns hardwood sawdust disks. These fuels give you great flavor, which you can vary by using different hardwoods—just be sure

Add wood chips or chunks to the coals to generate wood smoke. For a light wood smoke flavor, add the wood dry. For the heavy smoke flavor associated with traditional American barbecue, soak and drain the wood before adding it to the fire. Soaking generates clouds of fragrant smoke.

to keep them dry or they lose their combustibility and flavor. And, pellet smokers have turn-of-the-dial heat control, thanks to a built-in electric thermostat, and timers to control the cooking time. However, this fuel is used for smoking, not grilling—and for some purists, the notion of an electronically controlled smoker is just too easy.

GAS

In North America, gas is king. Developed by utility companies, gas grills hit the barbecue scene in the 1950s. Today, almost 70 percent of American families use gas grills. There are two types of gas grill: those that burn natural gas, a fossil fuel based primarily on methane, and those that burn propane, a refined petroleum product comprised of hydrogen and carbon. So why grill with gas? In a word—convenience. The convenience of push-button ignition. The convenience of turn-of-a dial heat control. Gas is less dirty to handle than charcoal and burns cleaner than improperly lit charcoal.

Whether fueled by natural gas or propane, gas grills tend to burn cooler and wetter than charcoal grills, so you don't get quite the same searing and browning as with the heat from charcoal or wood. However, it must be said that the newer, higher powered gas grills come very close to bridging the gap. Still, smoking on a charcoal

Quick, Name the World's Most Popular Grill...
Introducing the *Mangal*

The Weber kettle? (It's sold in more than twenty countries on five continents.) The hibachi? (More than 125 million Japanese must know something about grilling.) The Indonesian saté grill? (You'll find these small, slender grills on roughly two-thirds of the 17,508 islands of the Indonesian archipelago—not to mention in virtually every country in Southeast Asia.) But if I had to guess what is the world's most widely used grill, I'd name the *mangal*. You can find *mangal* grills everywhere from Moldova to Macedonia, from Israel to Uzbekistan. This is *the* grill of Russia, the Balkans, the Middle and Near East, and Central Asia.

The *mangal* is a grill of striking simplicity, a rectangular box filled with blazing charcoal. It has no grate. The food is cooked on flat metal skewers that span the sides of the box, suspended from front to back, or in grill baskets positioned over the grill. Some *mangals* are constructed of stone or brick, built like fireplaces into the wall of a restaurant kitchen. Others are freestanding metal boxes with legs; these can be set up in a backyard or taken on picnics. Typically, burning lump charcoal embers are mounded to one side or in the center on the floor of the grill. The intensity of the heat is controlled by adding or removing embers using a curved metal skewer or a grill hoe, or by moving the skewers of food closer to or farther away from the fire. Ground meat kebabs like the Turkish *kofta* and the Uzbek *lula* (see pages 328 and 330) are grilled on *mangals,* as well as spatchcocked chickens, whole fish and fish fillets, and vegetables.

Shashlik, *Russian shish kebabs, sear on the grateless grill called a mangal.*

grill is easy; on a gas grill it is virtually impossible. Of course, the biggest problem with gas may be image. Grilling over gas just doesn't look as cool as burning wood or messing with charcoal.

Propane cylinders will give you 12 to 18 hours of grilling, depending on the heat, the altitude, and what you're grilling. After that time you need to refill the tank. The first time you fill a propane cylinder, have it "bled" (flushed out) by a professional. To get the propane cylinders home from the hardware store, stand them in plastic milk crates; this keeps them from rolling around in your trunk. Store propane cylinders outdoors, away from the grill, and in an upright position. Always have an extra full propane cylinder on hand; the cylinders have the perverse habit of running out of fuel right in the middle of a grill session. If you have a large underground propane tank to run your furnace or water heater, you might want to ask your gas man to hook up a line from it to your grill.

To grill with natural gas, your grill needs to be specially outfitted, including having larger holes in the burner manifolds. However, natural gas has the advantage of being piped right into your home—no more empty propane cylinders to take to the hardware store.

SOLAR AND ELECTRIC GRILLS

Yes, there are grills that focus the sun's rays to cook food and there are electric heating elements that simulate grilling. Sorry folks, if it doesn't involve live-fire, it isn't in *Planet Barbecue.*

The Six Most Important Types of Grill

There are many ways you could categorize the world's dozens, perhaps hundreds, of different grills. You could group them by fuel, for example: charcoal grills, wood-burning grills, gas grills. You could organize them by region of origin—the grills of South America, for example, or Southeast Asia. But the most useful way, from a griller's point of view, is by the configuration of the fire and where to place the food for cooking. This is what determines at what temperature and how quickly the food will grill. Understanding and controlling these variables goes a long way toward determining your success as a grill master.

	OPEN GRILL	COVERED GRILL	VESSEL GRILL	
DESCRIPTION	The simplest of all grills: a metal or stone box with the burning charcoal, wood, or propane at the bottom and the food positioned directly over the fire. The grill grate is optional.	Add to an open grill a tall lid you can raise and lower and you get a covered grill. This may sound like a simple innovation, and yet the covered grill enables you to add two additional important methods of live-fire cooking to your repertory: indirect grilling and smoking.	A name I coined to describe deep, thick-walled, ceramic grills that rely on the radiant heat of the side walls, as well as the direct heat from the coals, to cook the food. Sometimes the food is cooked directly on the walls (breads) or on a vertical spit positioned inside the firebox instead of on a grill grate.	
INCLUDES	North American and European table grills, South American *parrillas*, the Italian *fogolar*, the Balkan *mangal*, Indonesian saté grill, Asian bucket grills, the Australian flattop grill, and so on.	The kettle grill, gas grill, and 55-gallon steel-drum grill	India's tandoor, Iran's *tanoor*, and closer to home, *kamado*-style cookers, like the Big Green Egg	
WHERE FOUND	In every corner of Planet Barbecue	Primarily found in North America and to a lesser extent in the Caribbean, South Africa, and Australia	Primarily in Central Asia, the Near East, and North America	
FUEL	Charcoal, wood, and gas	Charcoal or gas	Charcoal. (Although in major metropolitan areas in India, some tandoors are heated by gas.)	
TEMPERATURE	In general, the open grill runs at a high temperature (500° to 700°F in North America, as hot as 1,000°F in Asia)	Can be run at a high temperature, but most often operated between 325° and 400°F	Very high (800° to 1,000°F) in the case of the tandoor. Low to high heat in the case of the *kamado* cooker.	
USED FOR	High-heat direct grilling	Direct grilling larger or thicker foods. Indirect grilling and smoking (the latter done primarily on charcoal-burning grills)	High-heat roasting. With the *kamado* cooker, roasting, grilling, and smoking.	
FOODS BEST SUITED	Small, tender, quick-cooking foods like satés, kebabs, steaks, chops, fish fillets, vegetables, and so on	Thick steaks—both beef and tuna—as well as double-thick pork and veal chops. Larger or fattier cuts of meats, like whole chicken and duck, pork shoulder, and baby back ribs.	Flatbreads, like Indian naan, which are cooked right on the walls of the tandoor. Kebabs, chicken, fish steaks, small legs of goat and lamb, peppers, *paneer* cheese—all cooked on a vertical spit.	

Open grill   *Covered grill*   *Vessel grill*   *Smoker*   *Rotisserie grill*   *Campfire*

ROTISSERIE GRILL	SMOKER	OPEN PIT AND CAMPFIRE-STYLE "GRILLS"
The rotisserie adds motion to the static process of grilling. The slow, gentle rotation of a turnspit evens out the cooking process, basting the meat, melting out fat, and browning the exterior. Spit-roasted foods come out crisp on the outside and succulent within.	Smoking is one of the world's oldest methods of cooking and preserving foods, but the smoker as a portable backyard barbecue grill is a North American invention of the 20th century. All the world grills, but not all grill cultures smoke.	In the beginning, grilling (make that cooking) wasn't done on a grill, but over or next to a campfire. This primal method still enjoys wide popularity—especially in the Americas.
The wood-burning rotisseries of Tuscany and Germany, the gas wall rotisseries of France, the charcoal-burning chicken wing rotisseries of Malaysia and Singapore, not to mention the infrared rotisseries built into most high-end American gas grills. In the eastern Mediterranean and Middle East (and elsewhere), grill masters use vertical rotisseries to make Greek *gyro*, Turkish *doner*, and Middle Eastern *shawarma*.	The offset barrel smokers of Texas; the upright water smokers and box smokers of North America, Europe, and China; and the pellet/sawdust smokers (like the Bradley and Traeger), also of North America.	Open pit grilling is epitomized by Argentina's *asado* and Brazil's *fogo de chão*—meats roasted on stakes in front of a fire. Campfire grilling includes the salmon "bakes" of the Pacific Northwest; Connecticut's planked shad; and the roasting of marshmallows on sticks to make that American scout favorite: s'mores
In every corner of Planet Barbecue	North America, Europe, China	Argentina, Brazil, Mexico, Texas and other parts of the U.S.
Wood, charcoal, and gas	Charcoal, wood, or electric or gas with sawdust disks or pellets	Wood
Spit roasting is generally done at a medium to medium-high (325° to 400°F) temperature	True American barbecue is cooked "low and slow" between 225° and 275°F. Smoke roasting is done on a kettle grill at around 350°F. There's also a technique called cold smoking in which the food is smoked without the addition of heat. Cold smoking is beyond the scope of this book.	Moderate
Combines the virtues of direct and indirect grilling. As in direct grilling, the food faces the heat, but as in indirect grilling, the food cooks next to, not directly over the fire.	Smoking; low- to moderate-temperature indirect grilling with wood smoke	Radiant-heat roasting
Cylindrical and/or fatty foods, like whole chickens, chicken wings, ducks, rib roasts, and whole hogs	Traditionally used for tough, flavorful cuts of meat, like brisket and ribs. (The low, gentle heat melts the collagen, making these ornery cuts tender enough to cut with the side of a fork.) Note: When smoking poultry, I prefer to use "smoke roasting"—indirect grilling at a higher temperature to crisp the skin.	Whole lamb, goat, pig, and salmon, rack of beef ribs, and skin-on fish fillets

Lighting the Grill

Now that you've chosen your grilling method, it's time to light your grill. On a gas grill, this is as simple as turning on the gas and pushing the igniter button. Or is it? Here's what you need to know about lighting any grill reliably and safely.

THREE WAYS TO LIGHT A CHARCOAL GRILL

In the United States, you often hear the complaint that a charcoal grill takes too long to light. The truth is that if you have the right tools, charcoal is quick and easy to light, requiring little—if any—more time than it takes to preheat a gas grill. Here are three tried-and-true methods.

A chimney starter: A chimney starter looks like a large coffee can or an upright metal box with a perforated partition inside. The charcoal goes in top; a crumpled newspaper or paraffin fire starter goes in the bottom. You position the chimney starter on the bottom grate of your grill or on a rock or cinderblock—never on a wood deck—and light the newspaper or starter. Thanks to the chimney's upright shape and unique thermodynamics, the charcoal lights quickly and evenly in fifteen to twenty minutes. Briquettes take a bit longer to light than lump charcoal.

Lighting charcoal in a cylindrical chimney starter.

An electric starter: An electric starter is a loop-shaped heating element you place under a mound of charcoal and then plug in (electric starters are especially useful for vessel grills, like the Big Green Egg). Like the chimney starter, the electric starter has the advantage of eliminating the need for petroleum-based lighter fluid. However, it's not quite as fast as a chimney starter and you do need an outlet to plug it into.

Accelerants: Back when I was a kid, we simply doused the coals with lighter fluid. In France and the French West Indies, grill masters often light lump charcoal with wood alcohol. Accelerants have fallen out of fashion in these eco-minded days, and there's always the risk that, if your coals aren't completely lit, your food may acquire a petroleum aftertaste. So make sure the coals are completely lit (glowing orange and beginning to ash over) before grilling.

Forget the great (grate?) charcoal versus gas debate. The most flavorful fuel is wood. And more and more people are discovering the pleasure and taste dividends from grilling with wood. So how do you light the fire?

Chimney starter method: Yes, you can light wood in a chimney starter. Buy hardwood chunks and light them in the chimney starter, just as you would charcoal.

Lighting wood chunks in a square chimney starter.

Teepee method: Build a small teepee of twigs over a ball or twist of loosely crumpled newspaper, leaving enough space in the front to insert a match. Build a larger teepee of sticks over the first teepee, again leaving a space in the front. Finally, build a third teepee of split logs over the first two. Using a long match, light the newspaper.

Box method: Build a small box of twigs, as you would a log cabin, over a ball of loosely crumpled newspaper. Build larger boxes of twigs, sticks, and split logs around it. Light the newspaper with a long match.

Charcoal method: Start with a mound of lit charcoals. Arrange your wood—twigs first, then sticks, then split logs—on top.

Basket method: The basket method is widely used in South America; it requires that the grill have a *cesta*, a U-shaped metal basket. Fill the *cesta* with twigs, then sticks, then split logs, placing crumpled newspaper under the metal bars of the basket. Light the newspaper. As the wood catches fire, keep adding logs, until you have a basket full of burning logs and wood embers. As the embers fall through the bars of the basket, rake them into a pile and do your grilling over them.

Accelerant method: Fireplace shops sell various petroleum- and alcohol-based igniters. Top one of these with twigs, sticks, then split logs, then ignite it. Make sure the accelerant has burned away completely before you start grilling.

SIX THINGS TO KNOW ABOUT LIGHTING A GAS GRILL

What could be easier than lighting a gas grill? Ask someone who burned the hair off his forearm while trying (and usually it's a guy) and you'll understand that, while gas grills are the acme of convenience, a modicum of care should be taken to light them.

1. When you hook up a propane cylinder to your grill for the first time, attach the coupling, *then* open the valve. Make sure you don't smell gas, and if you do, immediately turn off the grill. To check for leaks, make a "detection solution" by mixing equal parts dish soap and water. Brush this mixture on the hoses and couplings; where there's a leak, you'll see bubbles.

2. *Always* have the lid open when you light a gas grill. Failure to do so can result in a potentially fatal gas buildup and explosion.

3. Turn on one of the burners. On many grills the burners must be lit in a precise sequence. Make sure you respect that sequence.

4. If your grill has an igniter button, press it. Some grills have automatic igniters built into the burner knobs. You should hear the click when the igniter sparks. If it doesn't, check the igniter battery, usually an AA, typically located in a plastic tube under or behind the button. Replace the battery as necessary. Try pressing the button a couple of times—the grill should light. If it doesn't, turn off the gas and air out the grill, then try again. Let's assume that you have verified that there's propane in the tank.

5. Once you've lit the grill—or think you have—hold your hand a couple inches above the grate until you feel heat. This lets you know the grill is really lit. Then close the lid for preheating.

6. Leave yourself plenty of time to preheat the grill. This normally takes fifteen to twenty minutes. Sluggish models can take longer. A grill is properly preheated for direct grilling when the thermometer registers 600°F—this is a "2 to 3 Mississippi fire" (see the box on page 610). Even when grilling at a more moderate temperature using the indirect method, preheat a gas grill to high, then reduce the heat.

Three lighting agents: Lighter fluid, fatwood (resin-soaked pine), and paraffin fire starters.

COOKING TEMPERATURES AND HEAT CONTROL

Before you can control the fire, you need to know the target temperatures. There are five. And one good way you check them is by using the "Mississippi test," also known as the "ouch test" (see below).

If you're grilling using the indirect method or you are smoking, your grill probably has a built-in thermometer. If it doesn't, invest in one and insert the probe through one of the vent holes in the lid.

The Mississippi test in action—a good way to judge how hot the grill is.

CONTROLLING THE HEAT ON A GAS GRILL

Controlling the heat on a gas grill is easy. You adjust the burner knobs to obtain the desired temperature, right? Well, that's partially right, but I also recommend double-checking the temperature by using the "Mississippi test." Remember, every grill has hot spots and cool spots.

FOUR WAYS TO CONTROL THE HEAT ON A CHARCOAL GRILL

How do you control the heat on a charcoal grill? Despite the

The Mississippi Test

Travel around Planet Barbecue and you'll see a familiar gesture: The grill master puts his or her hand over the grill to check the heat of the fire. The first goal of every aspiring grill pro is to get to the point where you control the fire, not have it control you. One way to do this is the Mississippi test.

Hold your hand about 3 inches above the fire and start counting: 1 Mississippi, 2 Mississippi, and so on. If the force of the heat makes you say "ouch" by the count of 2 or 3, you have a hot fire. If you get to 4 or 5, you have a medium-hot fire; 6 or 7, a medium fire; and so on. Here's a quick overview.

HEAT	TEMPERATURE	MISSISSIPPI COUNT	USED FOR
High	600° to 800°F (Some infrared grills and electric fan–ventilated yakitori grills attain temperatures of 900° to 1,000°F. This is still considered a hot fire, but you'd use it only for small pieces of food.)	2 to 3	Searing steaks, chops, peppers, and the like
Medium-high	400° to 500°F	4 to 5	Grilling thick steaks and small whole fish, bread, and so forth, using the direct method
Medium	325° to 350°F	6 to 7	Grilling chicken pieces using the direct method; and for most indirect grilling
Medium-low	275° to 300°F	8 to 10	Direct grilling thick or fatty foods, like baby back ribs; slow indirect grilling; smoke roasting
Low	225° to 250°F	12 to 14	Smoking ribs, brisket, and other types of true barbecue

volatile nature of a charcoal (or wood) fire, there are four effective ways to control the heat.

Adjust the airflow: Most charcoal grills have vents on the bottom. Open the vents wide and you get more air and thus a hotter fire. Partially close the vents and you get less air and a cooler fire. Make sure the vents are open when you light your charcoal and set up the grill. If you have trouble starting a charcoal grill, the vents may be clogged with ash.

Build a three-zone or two-zone fire: Another way to control the heat is to rake out the coals in varying thicknesses. To build a three-zone fire, arrange a double-thick layer of coals over one-third of the firebox—the third farthest away from you. This will be the hot zone for searing. Rake out the remaining coals in a single layer in the center of the grill; this will be your moderate zone for cooking. Leave the remaining third of the grill fire-free for a cool or safety zone. By moving the food from the hot to the medium to the cool zone and back, you can effectively control the heat over which the food is grilling.

To set up a two-zone fire, rake the coals into an even layer across two-thirds of the grate. This is your grilling area; the coal-free (fire-free) area is your safety zone.

Monitor the distance: The closer you move the food to the fire, the hotter the heat will be and the quicker the food will cook. Some charcoal grills (like front-loaders) have grates you can raise or lower to bring the food closer to or farther away from the fire. If your grill has a fixed grate, you can mound the coals higher toward the back of the grill and control the heat by moving the food closer to or farther way from the fire.

Make a grill shield: If your food starts to cook (or burn) more quickly than you desire, make a grill shield by folding a piece of heavy-duty aluminum foil in thirds, the way you would fold a letter, and sliding the shield under the food. The shield will block the heat, slowing the cooking process. An aluminum foil shield also works well for keeping the exposed ends of bamboo skewers from burning.

Use an aluminum foil shield to block or reduce the heat of the fire and for keeping the ends of bamboo skewers from burning.

Preparing the Grate

If you've attended one of my classes, read my books, or watched my TV shows, you surely know the Grill Master's Mantra. If not, it goes like this.

Keep it hot. Keep it clean. Keep it lubricated.

What I refer to, of course, is the preparation of the grill grate, because these three simple steps will help give you killer grill marks and go a long way toward eliminating the problem of sticking. The grill should be heated, cleaned, and oiled both before you put the food on *and* after you take it off. This seasons the grate, making it less prone to rust or corrosion. Of course, the best way to keep a grill in top shape is to use it daily.

Keep it hot: Preheat your grill to what I call screaming hot (a "2 Mississippi") fire. It's easier to clean a grill grate when it's hot than when it's cool, and food is less likely to stick.

Keep it clean: A clean grill grate is essential—first, because a dirty grill grate is unappetizing, and second, because the food is more prone to stick. The best way to clean a grill grate is with a few strokes of a stiff wire brush. Argentinean grill masters sometimes plunge the brush

CLEANING A GRILL

The Argentinean way—scrub the grate with a metal brush dipped in salt water.

OILING A GRILL

The Israeli way: rub an oil-soaked half onion—on the tines of a fork—across the bars of the grate.

in a bucket of salt water before brushing to scour the grate. Elsewhere on Planet Barbecue grill masters will clean the grate with a ball of crumpled aluminum foil held at the end of tongs.

Keep it lubricated: Oiling or greasing the hot grate is essential to prevent sticking and produce bold grill marks. Here,

too, grill masters around the world have developed many ingenious strategies. Israelis use half an onion dipped in a bowl of vegetable oil and rubbed across the grate at the end of a barbecue fork. Argentinians rub the grate with a chunk of steak fat. French grillers dip a tightly rolled cotton cylinder (it looks like a cloth egg roll) into a bowl of vegetable oil, then run it across the bars of the grate with tongs. Alternatively, you can substitute a paper towel folded into a tight pad for the cloth. Finally, several companies make spray oils specifically designed for grilling—they won't flare-up when you spray the oil on a hot grill. One good brand is Weber's Grill'N Spray.

The Nine Ways to Check Grilled or Smoked Food for Doneness

"**I**s it done yet?" How many times have you heard this question at a barbecue? How many times have you wondered if what's sizzling away on your grill is cooked to the proper degree of doneness? Fortunately, there are at least nine ways to check the doneness of grilled foods.

1. The visual and olfactory test: First, look at the food and smell it. Properly grilled food will be sizzling and dark golden

brown on the outside. Seared chops and steaks (of the bovine, porcine, and piscine variety) will have a dark visible crust. Food that has been grilled just right has a distinctive smell, too—toasted, caramelized, and smoky.

2. The poke and pinch tests: One of the best ways to judge when meat is done is to poke it with your forefinger (use for steaks) or pinch it between your thumb and forefinger (use for kebabs). To judge whether the meat is cooked to your satisfaction, if it feels:

Soft and squishy, it's rare (or still raw in the center, depending on how squishy).

Gently yielding, it's medium-rare.

Half yielding, half firm, it's medium.

Firm, it's medium-well.

Hard and springy, it's well-done. This well-done test is for steaks and chops grilled directly. However, a well-done brisket will feel soft when you poke it.

The poke test   *The pinch test*

3. The squeeze test: aka the **"Charmin test,"** is used for checking the doneness of such dense, round foods as onions,

Is It Done Yet?

An instant-read meat thermometer is your best guide to knowing when the food is cooked. Here's a general guide to doneness temperatures.

	RARE	MED-RARE	MED	MED-WELL	WELL-DONE
BEEF AND LAMB	125°F	145°F	160°F	180°F	190°F
PORK			160°F	180°F	190°F
CHICKEN, TURKEY, AND QUAIL			170°F	180°F	190°F
DUCK AND SQUAB	125°F	145°F	160°F	180°F	190°F

apples, or potatoes. Squeeze the sides between your thumb and forefinger. If the food feels soft, it's done.

4. The pierce test: Use this test to check the doneness of foods that are hard to see or poke, like ember-roasted sweet potatoes. Insert a slender metal skewer into the center. If it meets no resistance, the food is cooked. You can also use the pierce test to check the doneness of whole or planked fish. Insert a skewer through one of the narrow ends of the fish to the center and leave it there for fifteen seconds. If the skewer feels hot to the touch when you pull it out, the fish is cooked.

The pierce test

5. The cut test: Discouraged in the literature of grilling, the cut test is practiced at some point or other by most people who grill. Using the tip of a paring knife, make a small slit in a steak or chop (ideally on the bottom) and look at the center to check for doneness. This technique should be used sparingly, as it drains the juices from the meat.

6. The flake test: To tell whether grilled fish steaks, fillets, and whole fish are done, press the surface with your forefinger. When the fish is cooked, the flesh will break into clean flakes.

The flake test

7. The shrink test: Use the shrink test to determine the doneness of ribs: The ribs are cooked when the meat has shrunk back enough to leave the last ¼ inch of the bone exposed for baby backs, or ½ inch for spareribs and beef ribs.

8. The tear test: Also for ribs, when the meat is tender enough that you can tear the ribs apart with your fingers, they're done. Or, flex a rack of ribs; if the ribs in the middle of the rack start separating, the rack is done.

9. The instant-read meat thermometer test: This is the most accurate method of all, and yes, even the pros (especially the pros) use it. Insert the slender probe of an instant-read thermometer into the center of the meat; the reading on the thermometer will tell you the internal temperature. Don't let the probe touch any bones or you may get a false reading. If

Instant-read meat thermometer

you are checking a thin piece of meat, like a chicken breast or steak, insert the probe through the side. A digital thermometer will give you the most accurate reading. One good brand is the Thermapen (www.thermo works.com). To verify the accuracy of an analog instant-read meat thermometer, dip the probe in a pot of boiling water. Adjust the locknut on the back of the dial until the needle points to 212°F. (Note: This works only at sea level.)

SAFETY TIPS

Grilling is the world's most popular method of cooking, but I pause here to remind you that it frequently combines fire, alcohol, knives, and testosterone, and it's often done in darkness at night. Here are suggestions to help you grill more safely.

1. Position your grill downwind of your prep and eating areas, out in the open, away from your house and any overhanging trees, and certainly not in a garage, carport, or covered patio.

2. If you grill on a wood deck, invest in a grill pad to catch any stray sparks. One good brand is DiversiTech, available at www .grillpad.com.

3. Yes, it's not only prudent, but manly to have a fire extinguisher on hand. For putting out grease fires, use kosher salt or sand.

4. If a gas grill catches fire, immediately turn off the valve at the top of the propane cylinder. If that doesn't stop the fire, call the fire department. If you smell gas, use a leak detection liquid (see page 609) to find the leak. (Never use a match or lighter.) If a charcoal grill catches fire, simply put the lid on. Close the vents if possible: The absence of air will extinguish the fire.

5. Wear closed shoes. And long pants. That's how most of the world's grill masters dress. It's no fun burning your toes with stray embers.

6. Don't leave meats, mayonnaise, and other perishable foods out in the hot sun. Keep all foods on ice or in an ice-filled cooler until the moment when you're ready to grill them.

7. Avoid cross-contamination. Never put a cooked steak or chicken on the same platter you used to bring out the raw meat. Unless you've boiled the marinade for three minutes first, never put a marinade on a cooked food. Never brush a basting sauce onto raw meat—always wait until the exterior is cooked. You get the idea.

8. Use an instant-read meat thermometer to cook meats to a safe temperature, especially when cooking poultry and ground meats. Cook poultry to at least 170°F; ground meats to at least 160°F.

Four Final Observations

Additional pieces of wisdom gleaned from traveling around Planet Barbecue:

Be prepared: Unlike most cooking, grilling is done outdoors, away from your kitchen. Have all your supplies—tools, oils, seasonings, serving plates, and so forth—on hand *before* you start grilling.

Let there be light: Most grilling is done at night. Have lights that shine on your grill and worktable, so you can see what you're doing and cooking. Invest in a grill light or lighted tool, like my Lumatong (www.barbecuebible .com/store).

Cook the whole meal on the grill: OK, this is a Steven Raichlen thing, not necessarily a Planet Barbecue thing, although the Japanese come pretty close when they grill the chicken, leeks, corn, rice cakes, and gingko nuts for a single meal at a yakitori parlor.

Keep it in perspective: As I always tell my students, there's no such thing as a mistake in the kitchen—just a new dish waiting to be discovered.

Weight Conversions

U.S.	METRIC	U.S.	METRIC
½ oz	. . . . 15 g	7 oz	. . . . .200 g
1 oz	. . . . .30 g	8 oz	. . . . .250 g
1½ oz	. . . . .45 g	9 oz	. . . . .275 g
2 oz	. . . . .60 g	10 oz	. . . . .300 g
2½ oz	. . . . .75 g	11 oz	. . . . .325 g
3 oz	. . . . .90 g	12 oz	. . . . .350 g
3½ oz	. . . . 100 g	13 oz	. . . . .375 g
4 oz	. . . . 125 g	14 oz	. . . . .400 g
5 oz	. . . . 150 g	15 oz	. . . . .450 g
6 oz	. . . . 175 g	1 lb	. . . . .500 g

Approximate Equivalents

1 stick butter = 8 tbs = 4 oz = ½ cup

1 cup all-purpose presifted flour or
   dried bread crumbs = 5 oz

1 cup granulated sugar = 8 oz

1 cup (packed) brown sugar = 6 oz

1 cup confectioners' sugar = 4½ oz

1 cup honey or syrup = 12 oz

1 cup grated cheese = 4 oz

1 cup dried beans = 6 oz

1 large egg = about 2 oz or about 3 tbs

1 egg yolk = about 1 tbs

1 egg white = about 2 tbs

Please note that all conversions are approximate but close enough to be useful when converting from one system to another.

Liquid Conversions

U.S.	IMPERIAL	METRIC
2 tbs	. . . . 1 fl oz	. . . . .30 ml
3 tbs	. . . . 1½ fl oz	. . . . .45 ml
¼ cup	. . . . 2 fl oz	. . . . .60 ml
⅓ cup	. . . . 2½ fl oz	. . . . .75 ml
⅓ cup + 1 tbs	. . . . 3 fl oz	. . . . .90 ml
⅓ cup + 2 tbs	. . . . 3½ fl oz	. . . . 100 ml
½ cup	. . . . 4 fl oz	. . . . 125 ml
⅔ cup	. . . . 5 fl oz	. . . . 150 ml
¾ cup	. . . . 6 fl oz	. . . . 175 ml
¾ cup + 2 tbs	. . . . 7 fl oz	. . . . 200 ml
1 cup	. . . . 8 fl oz	. . . . 250 ml
1 cup + 2 tbs	. . . . 9 fl oz	. . . . 275 ml
1¼ cups	. . . . 10 fl oz	. . . . 300 ml
1⅓ cups	. . . . 11 fl oz	. . . . 325 ml
1½ cups	. . . . 12 fl oz	. . . . 350 ml
1⅔ cups	. . . . 13 fl oz	. . . . 375 ml
1¾ cups	. . . . 14 fl oz	. . . . 400 ml
1¾ cups + 2 tbs	. . . . 15 fl oz	. . . . 450 ml
2 cups (1 pint)	. . . . 16 fl oz	. . . . 500 ml
2½ cups	. . . . 20 fl oz (1 pint)	. . . . . 600 ml
3¾ cups	. . . . 1½ pints	. . . . 900 ml
4 cups	. . . . 1¾ pints	. . . . .1 liter

Oven Temperatures

°F	GAS MARK	°C	°F	GAS MARK	°C
250	½	120	400	6	200
275	1	140	425	7	220
300	2	150	450	8	230
325	3	160	475	9	240
350	4	180	500	10	260
375	5	190			

Note: Reduce the temperature by 68°F (20°C) for fan-assisted ovens.

Photography Credits

FRONT COVER PHOTOS (clockwise from top left): Courtesy of Steven Raichlen; Kevin Foy/Alamy Images; isatori/fotolia; Jeronimo Alba/age footstock; Courtesy of Steven Raichlen; Ben Fink Photography; Photograph of the author by Sylvia Pedras/Courtesy of Steven Raichlen and Primal Grill™; BLOOMimage/Getty Images; dbimages/Alamy Images; Courtesy of Steven Raichlen; Ben Fink Photography; Ben Fink Photography; Jeremy Hoare/age footstock. **BACK COVER PHOTOS:** All Ben Fink Photography. **SPINE PHOTO:** Photography by Sylvia Pedras/Courtesy of Steven Raichlen and Primal Grill™. **HARDCOVER FRONT FLAP PHOTO:** Penny de los Santos. **HARDCOVER BACK FLAP PHOTO:** Ben Fink Photography.

ORIGINAL PHOTOGRAPHY BY BEN FINK PHOTOGRAPHY: pgs. v, vi, 3, 6, 14 (left and middle), 21, 22, 24, 34, 63, 69, 72, 79, 84, 92, 99, 106, 113, 118, 121, 124, 129, 143, 152, 158, 163, 168, 181, 196, 204, 208, 235, 237, 250, 268, 274, 275, 284, 292, 299, 311, 316, 335, 345, 354, 370, 372, 373, 376, 385, 389, 390, 391, 398, 416, 422, 425, 435, 442, 451, 473, 483, 490, 491, 501, 507, 514, 530, 536, 559, 562, 574 (top), 579, 580, 583, 591.

ORIGINAL PHOTOGRAPHY BY PENNY DE LOS SANTOS: pgs. ii, 38, 96, 97, 183, 192 (bottom left), 249, 286 (left), 287, 289, 305, 331, 406, 528 (bottom right), 543, 546, 553 (top), 555, 597, 598, 599, 600 (bottom), 603 (bottom), 604, 605, 607 (covered grill), 608, 609, 611 (top), 612 (bottom left & right), 613 (bottom middle & right).

ORIGINAL MAPS BY SCOTT MACNEILL: pgs. 28, 36, 50, 64, 74, 94, 102, 110, 148, 174, 202, 214, 230, 242, 286, 300, 320, 346, 358, 366, 446, 456, 476, 508, 522, 532, 538, 552, 588, 594.

AGE FOTOSTOCK: Peter Adams p. 446 (bottom right); Aleruaro p. 366 (bottom middle); Giulio Andreini p. 320 (left); ARCO/F. Gierth p. 202 (bottom right); Gonzalo Azumendi p. 286 (bottom right); p. 594 (bottom middle); Tono Balaguer p. 588 (top right); Walter Bibikow p. 366 (right); Randa Bishop p. 215 (left); Christophe Bluntzer p. 110 (top right); Thomas Boehm p. 94 (bottom right); Barbara Boensch p. 595 (top); Jordi Cami p. 174 (top right); Rafael Campillo p. 594 (bottom right); Debra Cohn-Orbach p. 202 (bottom left); Alan Copson p. 232 (top); Jean-Pierre De Mann p. 381 (left); Danilo Donadoni p. 148 (bottom); Greg Elms p. 214 (right); Alain Evrard p. 456 (bottom left); FB-Fischer p. 358 (top right); Giacomo Giannini p. 148 (right); Michel Gotin p. 532 (left); Sylvain Grandadam p. 588 (bottom right); p. 589, Jeff Greenberg p. 233 (bottom); Franck Guiziou p. 94 (left); Amanda Hall p. 36 (right bottom); Dallas & John Heaton p. 286 (top right); J. D. Heaton p. 50 (right top); Christian Heeb p. 539; Gavin Hellier p. 102 (bottom right), p. 231 (middle), p. 447 (top); Jeremy Hoare p. 174 (left); Horizon p. 476 (bottom middle); Richard I'Anson p. 532 (bottom right); Marc Javierre p. 28 (top right); JIRI p. 83; Alan Keohane p. 64 (left); Terrance Klassen p. 538 (middle top); Christian Kober p. 28 (left), p. 191, p. 320 (bottom right); Ton Koene p. 28

(bottom right); Philip Kosche p. 232 (middle); Brian Lawrence p. 149 (top left); Stephan Laude p. 368; Alvaro Leiva p. 594 (left); Yadid Levy p. 112 (right); Jerome Lorieau p. 65 (center), p. 65 (right); Dennis MacDonald p. 231 (bottom); R. Matina p. 523 (bottom); Mattes p. 30 (bottom); McPhoto p. 47, p. 346 (top right); McPhoto/ZAD p. 271, p. 456 (left); Bruno Morandi p. 149 (top right); Bodo Muller p. 156 (right); Michael Owsto p. 522 (bottom middle); Ana Palatnik p. 174 (bottom right); Caroline Pen p. 552 (left); Franco Pizzochero p. 70; Jose Fuste Raga p. 50 (right bottom); Michel Renaudeau p. 65 (left); Rolf Richardson p. 110 (left); Robert Harding Productions p. 508 (bottom center); Martin Rugner p. 588 (left); Sybil Sassoon p. 242 (left); Walter Schiesswohl p. viii-ix; Lorenzo Sechi p. 149 (bottom); Paule Seux p. 102 (top right); Michael Short p. 103 (bottom); Jacques Sierpinski p. 64 (bottom right); p. 394, Johnny Stockshooter p. 74 (top right); Xavier Subias p. 595 (bottom left); SuperStock p. 346 (bottom right); Bjorn Svensson p. 112 (left); Jochen Tack p. 359 (bottom); S. Tauqueur p. 582; Mark Thomas p. 64 (bottom center); Nico Tondini p. 217; Kris Ubach p. 94 (top right); URF p. 533 (bottom); Glenn van der Knijff p. 476 (left); VH p. 36 (right top); Steve Vidler p. 538 (middle bottom); Bildagentur Waldhaeusl p. 367 (top); p. 367 (bottom right); David Wall p. 476 (right); Alexis Wallerstein p. 110 (bottom right); Tony Waltham p. 552 (top right); Florian Werner p. 522 (left); Phil Weymouth p. 477 (top); Konrad Wothe p. 230 (top).

Index

Note: Page references in *italics* refer to recipe photographs.

A

Abougelis, Stavros, 188, 517
Abu-Nassar-Hinnawi (Israel), 91
Achiote paste, about, 213
Adana kebab (ground lamb kebabs with Turkish hot peppers), 334–37, *335*
Aji amarillo (yellow chile peanut sauce), 40–41
Aji (Colombian chile sauce), 185–86
Albania:
    kandosouvle grilled directly over the fire, 206
    pepper-spiced spit-roasted pork, *204*, 205–6
Alder-smoked salmon, 424–26
Allen, Keith, 193, 195
Allen & Son Barbeque (North Carolina), 193, 195, 233
Amanbagh resort (India), 291
Amandari (Indonesia), 493
Amansara resort (Cambodia), 238
Ana Mandara (Vietnam), 415
Anchovies:
    Catalan "bruschetta," 89–90, *90*
    and garlic, roasted bell pepper salad with, 66
Andrés, José, 112
Andrés Carne de Res (Colombia), 111, 123, 136–37
Angkor Wat (Cambodia), 371
Angola:
    piri-piri prawns, 482–84, *483*
Annatto oil. *See* Seeds
Apostles on horseback, 502–3
Appetizers. *See* Starters
Apples:
    and apple cider, chicken sausage "hot tub" with, 343
    grilled, with honey and apple wine, 569–70
    smoke-roasted, with Japanese sweet bean paste, 570–71
Apple wine, grilled apples with honey and, 569–70
Apricot(s):
    Balinese salad, 264
    chutney, 272
    fruit-stuffed leg of kid, lamb, or impala, 270–72
    glaze, grilled snook with, 455
    South African shish kebabs, *250*, 251–53

Arabesque (Jordan), 379
Arcadia (Israel), 71
Arepas con salsa (grilled corn cakes with salsa), 109
Argentina:
    Buenos Aires garlic butter beef roulades, 176–77
    Buenos Aires "heart-stopper" (butterflied New York strip with bacon and eggs), 157–59, *158*
    Francis Mallmann's burnt oranges with rosemary, 575
    grilled butternut squash, 556–57
    grilled peppers in, 543
    grilling, food, and drink, 174–75
    grill masters of, 576
    live-fire cooking methods, 365
    pancetta orange chicken kebabs, 395–96
    the real chimichurri, 159
    roasted bell pepper salad with anchovies and garlic, 66
    unusual grilled foods in, 281
Arguinzoniz, Victor, 488, 489
Armagnac prunes, *crema Catalana* with, 587
Armenia (Republic of):
    Armenian flat bread, 97
    Armenian potato kebabs, 545–46
    Armenian potato kebabs with onion, 546, *546*
    Armenian stick bread, 96–97, *96*, *97*
    bacon-grilled eggplant, 535
    grilling, food, and drink, 286–87
Arregui, Pedro, 443
Arseev, Valery, 182
Arugula, endive, and shaved Parmesan salad, 436
Arzak, Juan Mari, 441
Ashmi, Damir, 5
Asian pears:
    butterflied sesame-grilled beef short ribs, 171–72
    Korean grilled pork belly, 53–54
Auberge Shulamit (Israel), 13, 405
Australia:
    Australian chipotle-glazed lamb "churrasco," 277–78
    Australian lamb on a shovel, 283–85, *284*
    barramundi grilled in paperbark with wild herbs, 474–75, *475*
    beer-can chicken with Asian "pesto," 361–63
    beet skordalia, 519

    dilled grilled squid with beet skordalia, 517–19
    grilling, food, and drink, 476–77
    kangaroo kebabs with grilled olive tzatziki, 188–90, *189*
    muscat-grilled pineapple with sea salt, 577–78
    shrimp on the barbie (#2), *490*, 490–91
Avazi (Israel), 57, 75, 411
Avocados:
    Colombian guacamole, 186
    Mexican grilled beef, 127–32, *129*
    Mexican guacamole, 131–32
Ayo, Juan Jairo Mojica, 184
Azerbaijan:
    grilled ice cream, 590, *591*
    grilled mashed potatoes with cheese, 556
    grilling, food, and drink, 552–53
    grill masters of, 592
    Iranian saffron lemon chicken wings, 26–27
    "knish on a stick" (grilled mashed potatoes), 554–56, *555*
    Persian saffron lemon chicken kebabs, 27
    whole Persian saffron lemon chicken, 27
Azuki (sweet red bean paste), about, 570

B

Babayef, Asif, 290
Baby (and I mean baby) lamb chops with Greek oregano, 295–96
Baby goat or lamb satés with pineapple and sweet soy, 302–3
Baby veal chops with garlic, dill, and Russian "ketchup," 182–83
Bacon:
    apostles on horseback, 502–3
    Armenian potato kebabs, 545–46
    Armenian potato kebabs with onion, 546
    Buenos Aires "heart-stopper" (butterflied New York strip with bacon and eggs), 157–59, *158*
    cheese pork roulade, 255–56, *256*
    cream cheese and chutney open-face poppers, 8
    filets mignons with whisky mushroom sauce, 165–66
    grilled, Hungarian, 46–47
    -grilled eggplant, 535
    -grilled enotake mushrooms, 2–4, *3*
    -grilled prunes, Serbian: village hammers, 5–6, *6*
    "knish on a stick" (grilled mashed potatoes), 554–56, *555*

mint, and chutney, Belgian pork rolls with, 258

pancetta orange chicken kebabs, 395–96

poppers (stuffed grill-roasted jalapeño peppers), 7–8

pork kebabs "Dacho," 247–48

and prunes, pork tenderloin grilled with, with farofa, 216–17

Serbian chicken bundles, 320–21, 388–90, *390*

Serbian stuffed pork loin, 209–11

Bagna cauda–Italian sausage "hot tub," 343

Bali:

Balinese salad, 264

whole hog with Balinese spices, 263

Balkan grilled veal and pork "burgers," 322–23, *323*

Balsamic- and soy-glazed chicken yakitori, 403

Balsamic-soy glaze, chicken liver yakitori with a, 402–3, *403*

Banana leaves:

grilled baby grouper in the style of the Portuguese, 460–62

halibut grilled in, with lemongrass and Thai basil, 444–45

Malaysian grilled fish mousse, 448–50

Singapore-style skate grilled in, 450–53, *451*

Banana(s):

grilled, 529

grilled, with coconut-caramel sauce, 573–74

or sweet plantains, grilled, with guava and salty cheese, 571–72

s'mores, Fair Trade chocolate, 585

Baratov, Nikolai, 248

Barbecue sauce:

bourbon-brown sugar, 229

mustard plum, 223

pineapple, 236

sparkling, 198

Barbecuing. *See* Smoking foods (barbecuing)

Barramundi grilled in paperbark with wild herbs, 474–75

Basil:

Thai, about, 444

Basque Country salt-crusted rib steaks, 164–65

Bazaar burgers, 326–28

Bean paste, sweet, Japanese, smoke-roasted apples with, 570–71

Bean(s):

Balinese salad, 264

Cambodian steak with salads and condiments, 160–62

salad, Tuscan, 146–47

"steam" fish, 467–68

Bean sprouts:

grilled tofu with chile peanut sauce, 561–63, *562*

lemongrass-grilled beef with noodles and salad, 177–79

mung bean sprout salad, 52

Beef:

Basque Country salt-crusted rib steaks, 164–65

Brazilian grilled flank steak, 122

Brazilian matambre, *140*, 140–42

Buenos Aires "heart-stopper" (butterflied New York strip with bacon and eggs), 157–59, *158*

Cambodian steak with salads and condiments, 160–62

caveman T-bones with hellfire hot sauce, 151–53, *152*

Chilean steak with pepper sauce, 133–34

Croatian "cheesesteak," 155–56

filets mignons with whisky mushroom sauce, 165–66

grilled T-bone steak with grape tomato salad, 150–51

hanger steak, about, 144

hanger steak with marchand de vin (wine merchant) sauce, 142–44, *143*

Hill Country brisket, 117–18, *118*

internal cooking temperatures, 613

kangaroo kebabs with grilled olive tzatziki, 188–90, *189*

kebabs, Cartagena, 172–73

kebabs, Peruvian, 39–41

"Kobe," sliders, 310–12, *311*

Kobe-style, about, 312

Korean-style enotakes grilled with, *3*, 4

lemongrass-grilled, with noodles and salad, 177–79

Mexican grilled, 127–32, *129*

Montreal smoked meat, 119

Moroccan "sliders," *317*, 317–18

Nha Trang mixed grill, 524–26

nonya-style flank steak, 138–39

the Paul Newman burger, 307–8

the Paul Newman cheeseburger, 308

poc chuc, 226

really big Bosnian burgers, 315–16, *316*

the real bistecca alla fiorentina, 145–47

ribs, gaucho-style, 167–69, *168*

ribs, over a campfire, grilling, 169

Romanian garlic steak, 135

Romanian "sliders" (garlicky grilled skinless sausages), 340–41, *341*

roulades, garlic butter, Buenos Aires, 176–77

salt-crusted tri-tip, 126–27, *127*

Santa Maria tri-tip, 125–26

Santander cheese steak, 132–33

satés, the best, in Singapore, 32–35, *34*

short ribs, butterflied sesame-grilled, 171–72

South African farmer's sausage, 349–50

spit-roasted rump steak with country salsa, 153–55

spruce-grilled steak, 162–64, *163*

steaks, degrees of doneness, terms for, 147

steaks, grilling myths, 141

stock, about, 340

tenderloin, Brazilian spit-roasted, 119–22, *121*

tenderloin, Italian spit-roasted, 122

tenderloin, salt-crusted, grilled in cloth, 123–25, *124*

tri-tip, about, 127

Turkish "meatball" burgers, 312–13, *313*

Tuscan steaks, two types of, 146

and veal burgers, *318*, 318–19

see also Veal

Beer:

Belgian cherry, salmon glazed with, 428–29

bratwurst "hot tub," 341–43

German whole hog, 261–62

-marinated lamb steaks grilled over herbs and spices, 279–80

Beer-can chicken with Asian "pesto," 361–63

Beet skordalia, 519

Belgium:

beer-marinated lamb steaks grilled over herbs and spices, 279–80

Belgian pork rolls with chutney, mint, and bacon, 258

grilled apples with honey and apple wine, 569–70

grilled oysters with ginger, soy, and jam, 506, *507*

grill masters of, 430

salmon glazed with Belgian cherry beer, 428–29

Bell peppers. *See* Pepper(s)

Benjelloun, Rafih, 272

Berasategui, Martín, 441

Berghotel Kristall (Germany), 547

Berkuz, Gadi and Lea, 13, 405

Berry glaze and juniper rub, planked salmon with, 421–23, *422*

Berthin, Gabriel, 383

Beti Jai (Spain), 441

Bifteki (veal and beef burgers), *318*, 318–19

Binchotan (Japanese lump charcoal), 602

Birdland (Japan), 29, 403, 404

"Bird's nest" on the grill, 582–84, *583*

Bistecca alla fiorentina, the real, 145–47

Blagoje, Velisic, 209, 540

Blowfish or halibut "bool kogi," 453–54

Bluefish, planked, with lemon mustard, 423–24

Bobby's Burger Palace (New York), 324

Bo bun (lemongrass-grilled beef with noodles and salad), 177–79

Bolivian salsa, fiery, cumin-grilled chicken breasts with, 383–84

"Bool kogi," blowfish or halibut, 453–54

Bosnian burgers, really big, 315–16, *316*

Bourbon-brown sugar barbecue sauce, 229

Bourdon, Pierre, 162, 471

Bradley, Ted, 424

Bratwurst:

with curry sauce, 344–45, *345*

"hot tub," 341–43, *342*

Brazil:

Brazilian grilled flank steak, 122

Brazilian matambre, *140*, 140–42

Brazilian spit-roasted beef tenderloin (*filet mignon no espeto*), 119–22, *121*

cheese grilled linguiça, 45–46

country salsa (*molho a campanha*), 155

gaucho-style beef ribs (*costelas de boi*), 167–69, *168*

grilling, food, and drink, 538–39

grill masters of, 170

onions grilled using the indirect method, 537

pork tenderloin grilled with bacon and prunes with farofa, 216–17

rotisserie baby back ribs with garlic and wine, 244–45

rotisserie onions, *536*, 537

salt-crusted tri-tip, 126–27, *127*

spit-roasted pineapple, 578–80, *579*

spit-roasted rump steak with country salsa (*picanha*), 153–55

toasted cassava flour, 217

Bread(s):

Catalan "bruschetta," 89–90, *90*

crumbs and sage, Venetian shrimp grilled with, 492–93

flat, Armenian, 97

grilled Greek, with oregano, 86

grilled, around the world, 87

grilled, Catalan, with country ham, 90

grilled, Vietnamese, 93

grilled, with chocolate, José Andrés', 112–14, *113*

grilled corn cakes with salsa, 109

grilled pita wedges, 10

Indian "puff pastry," 98–100, *99*

in loaves, South African, 105

naan crusted with pumpkin, poppy, and nigella seeds, 100–101, *101*

Obersteiner "filet mignon," 88

pa amb tomàquet, 90

pita, grilled two ways, 91–92, *92*

South African grilled cheese sandwiches, 105–7, *106*

South African grilled rolls, *104*, 104–5

stick, Armenian, 96–97, *96*, *97*

traditional naan, 100

truffled cheese sandwiches with onion, 106–7

Turkish puff, *107*, 107–8

Tuscan grilled toasts (crostini and bruschetta), 83–85, *84*

Vietnamese cinnamon toast, 93

see also Naan; Tortillas

Brik, Hassan Bin, 276

Brochettes d'agneau à la pâte d'arachide (peanut-crusted lamb kebabs in the style of Burkina Faso), 297–98

Brown sugar- and orange-brined smoked turkey, 407–9

Brozin, Robert, 20

Brücker, Lena, 344

Bruschetta:

Catalan "bruschetta," 89–90, *90*

Tuscan grilled toasts (crostini and bruschetta), 83–85, *84*

Buca Lapi (Italy), 145, 180

Buenos Aires garlic butter beef roulades, 176–77

Buenos Aires "heart-stopper" (butterflied New York strip with bacon and eggs), 157–59, *158*

Burgers:

around the world, 314

Bazaar, 326–28

Bobby Flay's Cheyenne, 325–26

"Kobe" beef sliders, 310–12, *311*

Moroccan "sliders," *317*, 317–18

the Paul Newman, 307–8

the Paul Newman cheeseburger, 308

perfecting the, 309

really big Bosnian, 315–16, *316*

Turkish "meatball," 312–13, *313*

veal and beef, *318*, 318–19

"Burgers," Balkan grilled veal and pork, 322–23, *323*

Burke, Mickey, 199

Butter:

garlic, beef roulades, Buenos Aires, 176–77

garlic caper, grilled swordfish with, 438–39

Butterflied sesame-grilled beef short ribs, 171–72

C

Cabbage:

Balinese salad, 264

beef poc chuc, 226

Cambodian steak with salads and condiments, 160–62

Keith Allen's North Carolina pork shoulder, 193–94

Kimchi, 52

Mayan pork chops, 225–26

Mexican grilled beef, 127–32, *129*

Cactus pear crisp, 581–82

Café Atlantico (Washington, DC), 112

Calamansi dipping sauce, 356

California:

Santa Maria tri-tip, 125–26

Cambodia:

Cambodian grilled chicken (*mann oeng k'tem sor, marech*), 371–73, *373*, 533

Cambodian steak with salads and condiments, 160–62

coconut-grilled corn (*pod oeng*), 529–30, 533

ginger, garlic, and honey grilled baby back ribs, 236–38, *237*, 533

grilled corn in, 531

grilling, food, and drink, 532–33

Campfire-style grilling, 604, 607

Campobravo (Argentina), 556

Canada:

alder-smoked salmon, 424–26

Canadian trout grilled on a log, 471–72, *473*

Montreal smoked meat, 119

spruce-grilled steak, 162–64, *163*

Cannon, Steve, 197

Caper(s):

garlic butter, grilled swordfish with, 438–39

Livornese sauce, 436

and pine nuts, bell pepper salad with, 67–69, *69*

Caramel-coconut sauce, grilled bananas with, 573–74

Caribbean pineapple baby back ribs with pineapple barbecue sauce, 234–36, *235*

Carne asada (Mexican grilled beef), 127–32, *129*

Carnivore (Kenya), 54, 56, 267, 457

Carrots:

"steam" fish, 467–68

Vietnamese dipping sauce, 179

Cartagena beef kebabs, 172–73

Casa Julián (Spain), 164

Cassava flour, toasted, 217

Catalan "bruschetta," 89–90, *90*

Catalan grilled bread with country ham, 90

Caveman T-bones with hellfire hot sauce, 151–53, *152*

Charcoal:

binchotan (premium lump), 602

briquettes, 602

coconut shell, 602–3

lump, 602

Charcoal grills:

adjustable vents on, 598, 611

building fires in, 598–600, 611

buying, what to look for, 599

charcoal for, 602–3

cleaning the grill grate, 611–12

common features, 597–98

controlling heat in, 610–11
direct grilling on, 598
grateless grilling on, 599
heat levels and temperatures, 610
indirect grilling on, 599
lighting, 608
oiling the grill grate, 612
preheating, 611
smoking foods on, 600
spit roasting on, 120, 600
starters for, 608
types of, 606–7
Cheese:
arugula, endive, and shaved Parmesan salad, 436
bacon pork roulade, 255–56, *256*
"bird's nest" on the grill, 582–84, *583*
Bobby Flay's Cheyenne burgers, 325–26
Brazilian matambre, *140*, 140–42
and butter, Colombian grilled corn with, 534
cotija, about, 458
cream, and chutney open-face poppers, 8
Croatian "cheesesteak," 155–56
feta, and grilled bell pepper dip, 9–10
goat, and dried tomato poppers, 8
grilled, sandwiches, South African, 105–7, *106*
grilled linguiça, 45–46
grilled mashed potatoes with, 556
herbed, grilled potatoes with, 547–48
herbed, grilled potatoes with, using the direct method, 548
kebabs, grilled, 563–64
Mexican grilled beef, 127–32, *129*
paneer, about, 549, 564
the Paul Newman cheeseburger, 308
pepper Jack, and cilantro, smoked chicken quesadillas with, 15
poppers (stuffed grill-roasted jalapeño peppers), 7–8
potatoes in the embers, 548
salty, and guava, grilled sweet plantains or bananas with, 571–72
sandwiches, truffled, with onion, 106–7
Serbian chicken bundles, 320–21, 388–90, *390*
Serbian stuffed pork loin, 209–11
steak, Santander, 132–33
tandoori potatoes, 549–50
tandoori potatoes in the style of baked stuffed potatoes, 550
village hammers: Serbian bacon-grilled prunes, 5–6, *6*
Cheol Cheol Globefish Restaurant (Korea), 51, 453
Cherikoff, Vic, 474
Chicken:
beer-can, with Asian "pesto," 361–63

breasts, cumin-grilled, with fiery Bolivian salsa, 383–84
breasts, lemongrass and curry grilled, 384–86, *385*
brochettes in the style of Fez, 394–95
bundles, Serbian, 320–21, 388–90, *390*
dumplings, Tokyo-style grilled, 30–31
grilled, Cambodian, 371–73, *373*
grilled, Israeli, 412
grilled, Jordanian, 378–80
grilled, salad with chiles and coconut, *78*, 78–80
grilled, Thai, two ways, 380–82
grilled, with yellow chiles and roasted garlic, 368–69
grilled, with yogurt, hot pepper, and garlic, 393–94
grilled in lemon leaves, 386–88, *388*
grilling, skin side down first, 375
ground, shashlik with onion and dill, 339–40
internal cooking temperatures, 613
kebabs, pancetta orange, 395–96
kebabs, Persian saffron lemon, 27
kebabs piri-piri, 22–23
Kelantan, with Malaysian-Thai marinade, 374–75
Khmer, grilled using the indirect method, 373
legs, jerk, in the style of Yallahs with hellfire hot sauce, 390–93, *391*
lemongrass rotisserie, 353–56, *354*
salt-roasted, Francis Mallmann's, 363–65
satés, Thai, 19–20
satés in the style of Kajang, 17–18
sausage "hot tub" with apples and apple cider, 343
smoked, quesadillas with cilantro and pepper Jack cheese, 15
thighs, deboning, 387
tikkas, two, 397–400, *398*
Tuscan-style, under a brick, *376*, 377–78
Uzbek "tandoori," 360–61
whole, piri-piri, 22
whole, spatchcocking, 370
whole, trussing, 355
whole Persian saffron lemon, 27
wings, honey and soy spit-roasted, 23–25, *24*
wings, Iranian saffron lemon, 26–27
wings, piri-piri, in the style of Nando's, 20–23, *21*
yakitori, balsamic- and soy glazed, 403
yakitori like they make it in Japan, 400–402
Chicken liver:
Tuscan grilled toasts (crostini and bruschetta), 83–85, *84*
yakitori with a balsamic-soy glaze, 402–3, *403*

Chilean steak with pepper sauce, 133–34
Chile (country):
Chilean steak with pepper sauce (*entraña con pebre*), 133–34
Chile paste:
about, 566
blowfish or halibut "bool kogi," 453–54
grilled clams with Korean cocktail sauce, 511–12
grilled tofu with chile peanut sauce, 561–63, *562*
Hanoi-style grilled squid with chiles and lime, 516–17
Kelantan chicken with Malaysian-Thai marinade, 374–75
Laotian rice "pops" with dipping sauces, 565–66, *566*
Chile(s):
Aleppo pepper (Turkish chile flakes), about, 334, 393
Australian chipotle-glazed lamb "churrasco," 277–78
Balinese salad, 264
blowfish or halibut "bool kogi," 453–54
calamansi dipping sauce, 356
caveman T-bones with hellfire hot sauce, 151–53, *152*
chicken kebabs piri-piri, 22–23
Chilean steak with pepper sauce, 133–34
chipotle, salsa de, 131
and coconut, grilled chicken salad with, *78*, 78–80
cumin-grilled chicken breasts with fiery Bolivian salsa, 383–84
fiery habañero salsa, 465
grilled chicken with yogurt, hot pepper, and garlic, 393–94
grilled shishito peppers with sesame oil and salt, 544
grilled tomato-habañero salsa, 459–60
guajillo, about, 213
guindilla, about, 442
hellfire hot sauce, 392–93
jerk chicken legs in the style of Yallahs with hellfire hot sauce, 390–93, *391*
Kuwaiti grilled mackerel or other fish, 486
Laotian rice "pops" with dipping sauces, 565–66, *566*
lemon dipping sauce, 388
lemongrass sambal, fiery, grilled shrimp with, 493–95
and limes, Thai grilled cockles or clams with, 510–11
Mexican guacamole, 131–32
nonya sauce, 139
pepper-spiced spit-roasted pork, 204, 205–6
Peruvian (*locoto*), about, 383
pico de gallo, 130

piri-piri chicken wings in the style of Nando's, 20–23, *21*

piri-piri prawns, 482–84, *483*

the real Jamaican jerk pork, 199–201

Romanian and Serbian grilled pickled peppers, 541–43

salsa verde, 130–31

sauce, Colombian, 185–86

Scotch bonnets, about, 200

shellfish in sauce, 511

"shepherd's tacos," 212–13

shrimp, Kuwaiti, 485–86

spicy tomato relish, 304

spicy Turkish tomato salad, 327

Tel Aviv tomato relish, 411

tikin xik in the style of Campeche, 464–65

tomato-pepper salsa, 32

vegetable kebabs, 336

whole chicken piri-piri, 22

yellow, and roasted garlic, grilled chicken with, 368–69

yellow, peanut sauce, 40–41

see also Chile paste

Chiltomate (grilled tomato habañero salsa), 459–60

Chimichurri, the real, 159

Chocolate:

Fair Trade, banana s'mores, 585

José Andrés' grilled bread with, 112–14, *113*

Chol, Lee Myong, 511

Chong Kee (Thailand), 43

Choo, Bong Geok, 446, 448

Choon, Lim Sin, 48

Chorizo, about, 348

Chubura (Serbia), 255, 257, 321

Chutney:

apricot, 272

and cream cheese open-face poppers, 8

green herb, 398–99

mint, and bacon, Belgian pork rolls with, 258

South African grilled cheese sandwiches, 105–7, *106*

Cilantro:

beer-can chicken with Asian "pesto," 361–63

caveman T-bones with hellfire hot sauce, 151–53, *152*

chicken brochettes in the style of Fez, 394–95

Colombian chile sauce, 185–86

Colombian guacamole, 186

green herb chutney, 398–99

grilled tomato habañero salsa, 459–60

lemongrass-grilled beef with noodles and salad, 177–79

méchoui of lamb or goat with Berber spices, 272–74, *275*

Mexican grilled fish tacos, 458–60

Mexican guacamole, 131–32

pico de gallo, 130

salsa de chile chipotle, 131

salsa verde, 130–31

Cinnamon:

and star anise glaze, sweet, grilled eel or halibut with, 478–80

Jordanian grilled chicken, 378–79

toast, Vietnamese, 93

Cioni, Delfina, Carlo, and Riccardo, 294

Çiya (Turkey), 393

Clams:

grilled, with Korean cocktail sauce, 511–12

or cockles, Thai grilled, with chiles and limes, 510–11

shellfish in sauce, 511

Cockles:

or clams, Thai grilled, with chiles and limes, 510–11

shellfish in sauce, 511

Coconut:

Balinese salad, 264

and chiles, grilled chicken salad with, *78,* 78–80

fresh, how to open, 79

fresh, shredding, 79

grilled ice cream, 590, *591*

Kelantan chicken with Malaysian-Thai marinade, 374–75

Coconut milk:

coconut-grilled corn, 529–30

creamy Asian peanut sauce, 18

fried garlic peanut sauce, *34,* 35

grilled baby grouper in the style of the Portuguese, 460–62

grilled bananas with coconut-caramel sauce, 573–74

Malaysian grilled fish mousse, 448–50

nonya sauce, 139

Coconut shell charcoal, 602–3

Coffee, South African "burned," 457, 596

Collina-Girard, Jacques, xii, xiii

Colombia:

Cartagena beef kebabs (*pinchos de bife Cartagenos),* 172–73

Colombian chile sauce, 185–86

Colombian grilled corn with butter and cheese, 534

Colombian guacamole, 186

Colombian sausage sandwiches with lemon-garlic mayonnaise, 349

eucalyptus-grilled veal roast with Colombian salsas, 184–86

grilled bananas, 529

grilled corn cakes with salsa, 109

grilled corn in, 531

grilled sweet plantains or bananas with guava and salty cheese, 571–72

grilling, food, and drink, 110–11

grill masters of, 136–37

salt-crusted beef tenderloin grilled in cloth (*lomo al trapo),* 123–25, *124*

Santander cheese steak (*lomo Santandereano gratinado),* 132–33

sausage kebabs with pepper sauce (*pinchos de chorizo),* 348–49

Coriander root and fish sauce, Thai grilled chicken with, 382

Corn:

coconut-grilled, 529–30

grilled, around the world, 531

grilled, Colombian, with butter and cheese, 534

Coser, Jair and Arri, 170

Country salsa, 155

Cream cheese and chutney open-face poppers, 8

Creamy Asian peanut sauce, 18

Crema Catalana (Catalan cream and variations), 586–87

Croatia:

Croatian "cheesesteak" (*punjeni ramstek),* 155–56

scampi kebabs with Dalmatian ham, 497–98

Crocodile or pork and shrimp, grilled, with garlic walnut lime sauce, 54–55

Crostini, 83–85, *84*

Cruz, Steven, 78, 437

Cucumber(s):

grilled olive tzatziki, 190

grilled tofu with chile peanut sauce, 561–63, *562*

lemongrass-grilled beef with noodles and salad, 177–79

Mexican grilled beef, 127–32, *129*

Nha Trang mixed grill, 524–26

pork satés in the style of Bangkok's Chinatown, 41–42

relish, Singapore, *34,* 35

salad, 52

sour cream salad, 211

Thai chicken satés, 19–20

Cumin-grilled chicken breasts with fiery Bolivian salsa, 383–84

Curried dishes:

beer-can chicken with Asian "pesto," 361–63

bratwurst with curry sauce, 344–45, *345*

grilled salmon with shallot cream sauce, 427–28

lemongrass and curry grilled chicken breasts, 384–86, *385*

South African shish kebabs, *250,* 251–53

Currywurst (bratwurst with curry sauce), 344–45, *345*

Dacho (Serbia), 5, 247, 321

Da Delfina (Italy), 149, 294

Dagdeviren, Musa, 393

Dar al Fassi (Morocco), 394
David, Winston, 467
De Clercq, Peter, 279, 428, 430, 506, 569
Delmonico's (New York), 314
Demircan, Mustafa, 314, 318, 336, 338
de Roca, Lydia Pasion, 357
Desserts:
    "bird's nest" on the grill, 582–84, *583*
    cactus pear crisp, 581–82
    Catalan cream and variations, 586–87
    Fair Trade chocolate banana s'mores, 585
    Francis Mallmann's burnt oranges with rosemary, 575
    grilled apples with honey and apple wine, 569–70
    grilled bananas, 529
    grilled bananas with coconut-caramel sauce, 573–74
    grilled ice cream, 590, *591*
    grilled sweet plantains or bananas with guava and salty cheese, 571–72
    José Andrés' grilled bread with chocolate, 112–14, *113*
    muscat-grilled pineapple with sea salt, 577–78
    smoked ice cream, 593
    smoke-roasted apples with Japanese sweet bean paste, 570–71
    spit-roasted pineapple, 578–80, *579*
Die Strandloper (South Africa), 104, 455, 457, 596
Dilled grilled squid with beet skordalia, 517–19
Dinho's (Brazil), 537
Dipping sauces:
    Asian pear, 53–54
    calamansi, 356
    ginger-wasabi, 437–38
    honey lime, 445
    lemon chile, 388
    peanut-hoisin, 302–3
    Vietnamese, 179
    vinegar and soy, 356
Dips and spreads:
    creamy Asian peanut sauce, 18
    fried garlic peanut sauce, *34,* 35
    grilled bell pepper and feta cheese dip, 9–10
    Kurdish grilled pumpkin dip, 10–11, *11*
    Mexican guacamole, 131–32
    red pepper dip, 12
    smoked egg pâté, 13–14, *14*
    yellow chile peanut sauce, 40–41
    see also Dipping sauces; Salsas
Djan, Madam, 469
Don (Serbia), 314, 388
Dressing Room (Connecticut), 307, 309
Drinks. *See* Coffee
Duarte, Fernando ("Nando"), 20

Duck:
    internal cooking temperatures, 613
    Vietnamese spit-roasted, with star anise and honey, 415–17, *416*
    whole, trussing, 355
Dumplings, chicken, Tokyo-style grilled, 30–31
Dva Jelena (Serbia), 209

East Coast Grill (Massachusetts), xvii
Eclade de moules (mussels grilled on pine needles), 513–14
Eel or halibut, grilled, with sweet cinnamon and star anise glaze, 478–80
Eggplant:
    bacon-grilled, 535
    Catalan "bruschetta," 89–90, *90*
    grilled, salad, 69–70
    grilled, salad, Filipino, 76–77
    grilled, salad with Jerusalem flavors, 71–73, *72*
    grilled vegetable salad, 60–61
Egg(s):
    Buenos Aires "heart-stopper" (butterflied New York strip with bacon and eggs), 157–59, *158*
    Filipino grilled eggplant salad, 76–77
    smoked, pâté, 13–14, *14*
Eisen Marx (Germany), 218, 221
Elckerlijc (Belgium), 258, 279, 430, 506, 569
El Fogon (Mexico), 212
Elkano (Spain), 440, 443
El Pobre Luis (Argentina), 157, 175
El Príncipe Tutul Xiú (Mexico), 215, 225
Endive, arugula, and shaved Parmesan salad, 436
Entrées (beef):
    Basque Country salt-crusted rib steaks, 164–65
    beef poc chuc, 226
    Brazilian grilled flank steak, 122
    Brazilian matambre, *140,* 140–42
    Brazilian spit-roasted beef tenderloin, 119–22, *121*
    Buenos Aires garlic butter beef roulades, 176–77
    Buenos Aires "heart-stopper" (butterflied New York strip with bacon and eggs), 157–59, *158*
    butterflied sesame-grilled beef short ribs, 171–72
    Cambodian steak with salads and condiments, 160–62
    Cartagena beef kebabs, 172–73
    caveman T-bones with hellfire hot sauce, 151–53, *152*
    Chilean steak with pepper sauce, 133–34
    Croatian "cheesesteak," 155–56

filets mignons with whisky mushroom sauce, 165–66
gaucho-style beef ribs, 167–69, *168*
grilled T-bone steak with grape tomato salad, 150–51
hanger steak with marchand de vin (wine merchant) sauce, 142–44, *143*
Hill Country brisket, 117–18, *118*
Italian spit-roasted beef tenderloin, 122
kangaroo kebabs with grilled olive tzatziki, 188–90, *189*
lemongrass-grilled beef with noodles and salad, 177–79
Mexican grilled beef, 127–32, *129*
Montreal smoked meat, 119
nonya-style flank steak, 138–39
the real bistecca alla fiorentina, 145–47
Romanian garlic steak, 135
salt-crusted beef tenderloin grilled in cloth, 123–25, *124*
salt-crusted tri-tip, 126–27, *127*
Santa Maria tri-tip, 125–26
Santander cheese steak, 132–33
spit-roasted rump steak with country salsa, 153–55
spruce-grilled steak, 162–64, *163*
Entrées (fish):
    alder-smoked salmon, 424–26
    barramundi grilled in paperbark with wild herbs, 474–75, *475*
    blowfish or halibut "bool kogi," 453–54
    Canadian trout grilled on a log, 471–72, *473*
    Greek fish grilled in fig leaves, 465–67
    grilled baby grouper in the style of the Portuguese, 460–62
    grilled eel or halibut with sweet cinnamon and star anise glaze, 478–80
    grilled hake with fried garlic, 441–42
    grilled salmon with shallot cream sauce, 427–28
    grilled shrimp or fish with mojo de ajo, 502
    grilled snook with apricot glaze, 455
    grilled swordfish with garlic caper butter, 438–39
    grilled turbot with "holy water," 440–41
    Guam "volcano" tuna (pepper-crusted tuna with ginger-wasabi dipping sauce), 437–38
    halibut grilled in banana leaves with lemongrass and Thai basil, 444–45
    Kuwaiti grilled mackerel or other fish, 486
    Laotian grilled fish, 470–71
    Malaysian grilled fish mousse, *448,* 448–50
    Mexican grilled fish tacos, 458–60

Nha Trang mixed grill, 524–26
planked bluefish with lemon mustard, 423–24
planked salmon with juniper rub and berry glaze, 421–23, *422*
salmon glazed with Belgian cherry beer, 428–29
salmon shashlik, 431–32
salt-roasted fish, 365
Singapore-style skate grilled in banana leaves, 450–53, *451*
"steam" fish, 467–68
tandoori grilled kingfish, 432–33
tikin xik in the style of Campeche, 462–65, *463*
tuna steaks alla fiorentina, 434–36, *435*
Entrées (ground beef):
    "Kobe" beef sliders, 310–12, *311*
    Moroccan "sliders," *317*, 317–18
    the Paul Newman burger, 307–8
    the Paul Newman cheeseburger, 308
    really big Bosnian burgers, 315–16, *316*
    Romanian "sliders" (garlicky grilled skinless sausages), 340–41, *341*
    South African farmer's sausage, 349–50
    Turkish "meatball" burgers, 312–13, *313*
    veal and beef burgers, *318*, 318–19
Entrées (ground chicken or turkey):
    Bobby Flay's Cheyenne burgers, 325–26
    chicken sausage "hot tub" with apples and apple cider, 343
    ground chicken shashlik with onion and dill, 339–40
Entrées (ground lamb):
    Bazaar burgers, 326–28
    ground lamb and plum kebabs, 337
    ground lamb kebabs with coriander and cumin, 330–32, *331*
    ground lamb kebabs with cumin and mint, 328–29
    ground lamb kebabs with pistachio nuts, 336, *336*
    ground lamb kebabs with Turkish hot peppers, 334–37, *335*
    Moroccan "sliders," *317*, 317–18
    onion kebabs, 336–37
    Romanian "sliders" (garlicky grilled skinless sausages), 340–41, *341*
    vegetable kebabs, 336, *336*
Entrées (ground pork):
    bagna cauda–Italian sausage "hot tub," 343
    Balkan grilled veal and pork "burgers," 322–23, *323*
    bratwurst "hot tub," 341–43, *342*
    Colombian sausage sandwiches with lemon-garlic mayonnaise, 349

Romanian "sliders" (garlicky grilled skinless sausages), 340–41, *341*
sausage kebabs with pepper sauce, 348–49
Entrées (ground veal):
    Balkan grilled veal and pork "burgers," 322–23, *323*
    bratwurst with curry sauce, 344–45, *345*
    really big Bosnian burgers, 315–16, *316*
    veal and beef burgers, *318*, 318–19
Entrées (lamb and goat):
    Australian chipotle-glazed lamb "churrasco," 277–78
    Australian lamb on a shovel, 283–85, *284*
    baby (and I mean baby) lamb chops with Greek oregano, 295–96
    baby goat or lamb satés with pineapple and sweet soy, 302–3
    beer-marinated lamb steaks grilled over herbs and spices, 279–80
    fruit-stuffed leg of kid, lamb, or impala, 270–72
    kangaroo kebabs with grilled olive tzatziki, 188–90, *189*
    Lucknowi lamb chops, 291–92
    Mauritius grilled lamb chops, *292*, 293
    méchoui of lamb or goat with Berber spices, 272–74, *275*
    Moroccan lamb chops with harissa and cumin, 282–83
    onion and coriander brined lamb chops, 288–89, *289*
    peanut-crusted lamb kebabs in the style of Burkina Faso, 297–98
    piri-piri goat kebabs, 303–4
    spit-roasted lamb or goat with garlic and mint, 267–69, *268*
    yogurt-marinated lamb tenderloin kebabs, 298–99, *299*
Entrées (meatless):
    grilled cheese kebabs, 563–64
    grilled tofu with chile peanut sauce, 561–63, *562*
    Laotian rice "pops" with dipping sauces, 565–66, *566*
    paella "primavera" on the grill, 557–60, *559*
    tandoori potatoes, 549–50
    tandoori potatoes in the style of baked stuffed potatoes, 550
Entrées (pork):
    bacon cheese pork roulades, 255–56, *256*
    Belgian pork rolls with chutney, mint, and bacon, 258
    Caribbean pineapple baby back ribs with pineapple barbecue sauce, 234–36, *235*
    German whole hog, 261–62

ginger, garlic, and honey grilled baby back ribs, 236–38, *237*
kandosouvle grilled directly over the fire, 206
Kansas City–style spareribs, 227–29, *228*
Keith Allen's North Carolina pork shoulder, 193–94
Mayan pork chops, 225–26
Nuri's ribs: grilled baby backs with sweet soy glaze, 239–41, *240*
onion-stuffed, spit-roasted pork shoulder, 206–9, *208*
pepper-spiced spit-roasted pork, *204*, 205–6
pork kebabs "Dacho," 247–48
pork satés in the style of Bangkok's Chinatown, 41–42
pork tenderloin grilled with bacon and prunes with farofa, 216–17
Puerto Rican grilled pork chops, 224
Puerto Rican pork shoulder, *196*, 197–98
the real Jamaican jerk pork, 199–201
rotisserie baby back ribs with garlic and wine, 244–45
Russian onion and pork kebabs, 248–51, *249*
Serbian stuffed pork loin, 209–11
"shepherd's tacos," 212–13
South African shish kebabs, *250*, 251–53
South African springbok or pork kebabs with monkey gland sauce, 253–55
spiessbraten grilled on a *schwenker*, 219–20
spit-roasted ham hocks, 245–47
"swinging" pork steaks, 218–20, *220*
Uruguayan pork "skirt steak" with mustard plum barbecue sauce, 222–23
whole hog in the style of a Greek island, 259–61
whole hog with Balinese spices, 263
Entrées (poultry):
    balsamic- and soy-glazed chicken yakitori, 403
    beer-can chicken with Asian "pesto," 361–63
    brown sugar- and orange-brined smoked turkey, 407–9
    Cambodian grilled chicken, 371–73, *373*
    chicken brochettes in the style of Fez, 394–95
    chicken grilled in lemon leaves, 386–88, *388*
    chicken kebabs piri-piri, 22–23
    chicken liver yakitori with a balsamic-soy glaze, 402–3, *403*

cumin-grilled chicken breasts with fiery Bolivian salsa, 383–84

Francis Mallmann's salt-roasted chicken, 363–65

grilled chicken salad with chiles and coconut, *78*, 78–80

grilled chicken with yellow chiles and roasted garlic, 368–69

grilled chicken with yogurt, hot pepper, and garlic, 393–94

"iceberg" game hens with Moroccan spices, 413–14

Israeli grilled chicken, 412

Israeli grilled game hens, 411–12

Israeli smoked goose, 405–6, *406*

jerk chicken legs in the style of Yallahs with hellfire hot sauce, 390–93, *391*

Kelantan chicken with Malaysian-Thai marinade, 374–75

Khmer chicken grilled using the indirect method, 373

lemongrass and curry grilled chicken breasts, 384–86, *385*

lemongrass rotisserie chicken, 353–56, *354*

pancetta orange chicken kebabs, 395–96

Persian saffron lemon chicken kebabs, 27

quail "Kabanchik" grilled in the style of the Republic of Georgia, 417–18

Serbian chicken bundles, 320–21, 388–90, *390*

Thai grilled chicken two ways, 380–82

Tokyo-style grilled chicken dumplings, 30–31

turkey shawarma, *409*, 409–11

Tuscan-style chicken under a brick, *376*, 377–78

two chicken tikkas, 397–400, *398*

Uzbek "tandoori" chicken, 360–61

Vietnamese spit-roasted duck with star anise and honey, 415–17, *416*

whole chicken piri-piri, 22

whole Persian saffron lemon chicken, 27

yakitori like they make it in Japan, 400–402

Entrées (shellfish):
apostles on horseback, 502–3

dilled grilled squid with beet skordalia, 517–19

grilled clams with Korean cocktail sauce, 511–12

grilled Maine or spiny lobster with garlic sauce, 500–502, *501*

grilled octopus with Greek herbs, 520–21, *521*

grilled oysters with ginger, soy, and jam, 506, *507*

grilled shrimp or fish with mojo de ajo, 502

grilled shrimp sprayed with olive oil and wine, 488

grilled shrimp with fiery lemongrass chile sambal, 493–95

Hanoi-style grilled oysters, 505, *505*

Hanoi-style grilled squid with chiles and lime, 516–17

Kuwaiti chile shrimp, 485–86

lobster the way we grill it on Martha's Vineyard, 498–99

Mauritius shrimp or squid kebabs with ginger turmeric glaze, 495–96

mussels grilled on pine needles, 513–14

Nha Trang mixed grill, 524–26

oysters smoked on the half shell, 504

piri-piri prawns, 482–84, *483*

scampi kebabs with Dalmatian ham, 497–98

shellfish in sauce, 511

shrimp on the barbie (#2), *490*, 490–91

Thai grilled cockles or clams with chiles and limes, 510–11

turmeric grilled prawns, 486–87

Venetian shrimp grilled with bread crumbs and sage, 492–93

Entrées (veal and game):
baby veal chops with garlic, dill, and Russian "ketchup," 182–83

eucalyptus-grilled veal roast with Colombian salsas, 184–86

fruit-stuffed leg of kid, lamb, or impala, 270–72

grilled veal chops with sweet-and-sour onions, 180–82, *181*

hunters' kebabs, 187–88

kangaroo kebabs with grilled olive tzatziki, 188–90, *189*

South African springbok or pork kebabs with monkey gland sauce, 253–55

Ermak (Russia), 182

Etxebarri (Spain), 488, 489, 593, 595

Eucalyptus-grilled veal roast with Colombian salsas, 184–86

Fair Trade chocolate banana s'mores, 585

Fair Trade products, 618

Famers' markets, 618

Farofa (toasted cassava flour), 217

Fenugreek powder, about, 291

Fiery habañero salsa, 465

Fig leaves, Greek fish grilled in, 465–67

Figs, caramelized, *crema Catalana* with, 587

Filets mignons with whisky mushroom sauce, 165–66

Filipino grilled eggplant salad, 76–77

Fire pits, lighting, 608–9

Fire spices, 280

Fire starters:
Allen, Keith, 195

Arguinzoniz, Victor, 489

Arregui, Pedro, 443

Babayef, Asif, 290

Brik, Hassan Bin, 276

Cioni, Delfina, Carlo, and Riccardo, 294

Coser, Jair and Arri, 170

De Clercq, Peter, 430

Demircan, Mustafa, 338

de Roca, Lydia Pasion, 357

Djan, Madam, 469

Flay, Bobby, 324

Huseynov, Mehman, 592

Jaramillo, Andrés, 136–37

Khankishiev, Stalic, 333

Kiplagat, Daniel, 56

Lumlerokit, Vichai, 43

Mallmann, Francis, 576

Marx, Klaus, 221

Mertz, Laurent, 515

Panin, Miss, 469

Perunovic, Milica, 257

Samuri, Haji, 16

Wada, Toshihiro, 404

Fish:
alder-smoked salmon, 424–26

barramundi grilled in paperbark with wild herbs, 474–75, *475*

blowfish or halibut "bool kogi," 453–54

Canadian trout grilled on a log, 471–72, *473*

endangered species, note about, 618

Greek, grilled in fig leaves, 465–67

grilled, Laotian, 470–71

grilled baby grouper in the style of the Portuguese, 460–62

grilled eel or halibut with sweet cinnamon and star anise glaze, 478–80

grilled hake with fried garlic, 441–42

grilled salmon with shallot cream sauce, 427–28

grilled snook with apricot glaze, 455

grilled swordfish with garlic caper butter, 438–39

grilled turbot with "holy water," 440–41

grilling, tips for, 426

Guam "volcano" tuna (pepper-crusted tuna with ginger-wasabi dipping sauce), 437–38

halibut grilled in banana leaves with lemongrass and Thai basil, 444–45

Kuwaiti grilled mackerel or other fish, 486

mousse, Malaysian grilled, *448*, 448–50

Nha Trang mixed grill, 524–26

or shrimp, grilled, with mojo de ajo, 502

planked bluefish with lemon mustard,
423–24
planked salmon with juniper rub and
berry glaze, 421–23, *422*
salmon glazed with Belgian cherry
beer, 428–29
salmon shashlik, 431–32
salt-roasted, 365
Singapore-style skate grilled in banana
leaves, 450–53, *451*
"steam," 467–68
tacos, Mexican grilled, 458–60
tandoori grilled kingfish, 432–33
tikin xik in the style of Campeche,
462–65, *463*
tuna steaks alla fiorentina, 434–36, *435*
wild, buying, 618
see also Anchovies
Fish paste (*pra hok*), about, 160
Fish sauce:
Cambodian steak with salads and
condiments, 160–62
Filipino, about, 353
honey lime dipping sauce, 445
Laotian rice "pops" with dipping
sauces, 565
lemon chile dipping sauce, 388
Thai grilled chicken two ways, 380–82
Vietnamese dipping sauce, 179
Fistik kebab (ground lamb kebabs with
pistachio nuts), 336, *336*
Flay, Bobby, 324, 325, 326
Flour, toasted cassava, 217
Fogo de Chão (Brazil), 167, 170, 244, 539
Foie gras:
grilled, with grenadine onions, 58
grilled Israeli spiced, 57–58
France:
Catalan "bruschetta," 89–90, *90*
Catalan cream and variations, 586–87
Catalan grilled bread with country
ham, 90
grilled foie gras with grenadine onions,
58
grilled salmon with shallot cream
sauce, 427–28
grilling, food, and drink, 588–89
grill masters of, 515
hanger steak with marchand de vin
(wine merchant) sauce, 142–44, *143*
mussels grilled on pine needles, 513–14
pa amb tomàquet, 90
Francis Mallmann's burnt oranges with
rosemary, 575
Francis Mallmann's salt-roasted chicken,
363–65
Fried garlic peanut sauce, *34, 35*
Fruit:
-stuffed leg of kid, lamb, or impala,
270–72
see also specific fruits

Galpão Crioulo (Brazil), 578
Game hens:
"iceberg," with Moroccan spices,
413–14
Israeli grilled, 411–12
Game meats:
fruit-stuffed leg of kid, lamb, or impala,
270–72
grilled crocodile or pork and shrimp
with garlic walnut lime sauce, 54–55
grilled ostrich meatballs, 31–32
hunters' kebabs, 187–88
kangaroo kebabs with grilled olive
tzatziki, 188–90, *189*
South African springbok or pork
kebabs with monkey gland sauce,
253–55
Ganesh (India), 397, 432
Gangwani, Hari Chand, 432
Garlic:
and anchovies, roasted bell pepper
salad with, 66
blowfish or halibut "bool kogi," 453–54
butter beef roulades, Buenos Aires,
176–77
caper butter, grilled swordfish with,
438–39
caveman T-bones with hellfire hot
sauce, 151–53, *152*
dill, and Russian "ketchup," baby veal
chops with, 182–83
fried, grilled hake with, 441–42
fried, peanut sauce, *34, 35*
ginger, and honey grilled baby back
ribs, 236–38, *237*
grilled olive tzatziki, 190
grilled shrimp or fish with mojo de
ajo, 502
-herb portobello skewers, 541
Kosovan grilled mushrooms, *536*, 540–41
Laotian grilled fish, 470–71
and mint, spit-roasted lamb or goat
with, 267–69, *268*
Obersteiner "filet mignon," 88
parsley sauce, 365
pita bread grilled two ways, 91–92, *92*
the real chimichurri, 159
roasted, and yellow chiles, grilled
chicken with, 368–69
roasted, preparing, 67
Romanian "sliders" (garlicky grilled
skinless sausages), 340–41, *341*
sauce, grilled Maine or spiny lobster
with, 500–502, *501*
steak, Romanian, 135
Vietnamese dipping sauce, 179
walnut lime sauce, 55
and wine, rotisserie baby back ribs
with, 244–45
yogurt, and hot pepper, grilled chicken
with, 393–94

Garzón (Uruguay), 367, 576
Gas grills:
benefits of, 604
buying, what to look for, 599
cleaning the grill grate, 611–12
common features, 597–98
controlling the heat in, 610
direct grilling on, 598
disadvantages of, 604
grateless grilling on, 599
heat levels and temperatures, 610
indirect grilling on, 599
lighting, 609
natural gas for, 604–5
oiling the grill grate, 612
preheating, 611
propane for, 604–5
smoking foods on, 600, 603
spit roasting on, 120, 600
types of, 606–7
Gaucho-style beef ribs, 167–69, *168*
Georgia (Republic of):
quail "Kabanchik" grilled in the style of
the Republic of Georgia, 417–18
Gerai No. 11 & 12 (Malaysia), 460
Germany:
bratwurst with curry sauce, 344–45, *345*
German whole hog, 261–62
grilled potatoes with herbed cheese,
547–48
grilled potatoes with herbed cheese
using the direct method, 548
grilling, food, and drink, 346–47
grill masters of, 221
Obersteiner "filet mignon," 88
onion-stuffed, spit-roasted pork
shoulder (*spiessbraten*), 206–9, *208*
potatoes in the embers, 548
spiessbraten grilled on a *schwenker*,
219–20
spit-roasted ham hocks
(*schweinshaxen*), 245–47
"swinging" pork steaks
(*schwenkbraten*), 218–20, *220*
Ginelli, Bernard, xiv
Ginger:
beer-can chicken with Asian "pesto,"
361–63
garlic, and honey grilled baby back ribs,
236–38, *237*
German whole hog, 261–62
soy, and jam, grilled oysters with, 506,
507
Thai grilled chicken two ways, 380–82
turmeric glaze, Mauritius shrimp or
squid kebabs with, 495–96
-wasabi dipping sauce, 437–38
Gironès, Pierre, 586
Goat:
baby, or lamb satés with pineapple and
sweet soy, 302–3

fruit-stuffed leg of kid, lamb, or impala, 270–72

kebabs, piri-piri, 303–4

or lamb, méchoui of, with Berber spices, 272–74, *275*

or lamb, spit-roasted, with garlic and mint, 267–69, *268*

Goat cheese and dried tomato poppers, 8

Gómez, Carlos, 132

Goncales, Piedro "Peter," 172–73

Goose, Israeli smoked, 405–6, *406*

Gravy, Madeira, 408–9

Greece:

baby (and I mean baby) lamb chops with Greek oregano (*païdakia*), 295–96

Greek fish grilled in fig leaves, 465–67

grilled bell pepper and feta cheese dip (*htipiti*), 9–10

grilled eggplant salad (*melitzanosalata*), 69–70

grilled Greek bread with oregano, 86

grilled octopus with Greek herbs, 520–21, *521*

grilled pita wedges, 10

grilling, food, and drink, 522–23

kandosouvle grilled directly over the fire, 206

pepper-spiced spit-roasted pork, *204*, 205–6

unusual grilled foods in, 281

veal and beef burgers, *318*, 318–19

whole hog in the style of a Greek island, 259–61

Green beans:

Balinese salad, 264

Cambodian steak with salads and condiments, 160–62

"steam" fish, 467–68

Green herb chutney, 398–99

Greens:

arugula, endive, and shaved Parmesan salad, 436

Cambodian steak with salads and condiments, 160–62

lemongrass-grilled beef with noodles and salad, 177–79

Nha Trang mixed grill, 524–26

Tuscan grilled toasts (crostini and bruschetta), 83–85, *84*

see also Cabbage

Grilling, 597–614

author's final observations, 614

buying ingredients for, 618

with charcoal, 602–3

checking food for doneness, 612–13

direct, 598

first fire-cooked foods, x–xiii

fuel options, 602–5

with gas, 604–5

grateless, 599

heat levels and temperatures, 610

historic timeline, xiv–xvii

indirect, 599–600

Mississippi Test, 610

pit roasting, 601

roasting in the embers, 601

safety tips, 614

smoke roasting, 600

smoking (aka barbecuing), 600

spit roasting, 600–601

underground pit roasting, 601

with wood, 603–4

Grill masters. *See* Fire starters

Grills:

buying, what to look for, 599

campfire-style "grills," 607

cleaning the grill grate, 611–12

common features, 597–98

covered grills, 606

fuel options, 602–5

heat levels and temperatures, 610

mangal grills, 605

oiling the grill grate, 612

open grills, 606

open-pit grills, 607

pellet grills (smokers), 607

preheating, 611

rotisserie grills, 606

smokers, 607

solar and electric grills, 605

types of, 606–7

underground pit barbecue, 607

vessel grills, 606

see also Charcoal grills; Gas grills; Wood-burning grills and fires

Grimpa (Brazil), 119

Ground meats:

bagna cauda–Italian sausage "hot tub," 343

Balkan grilled veal and pork "burgers," 322–23, *323*

Bazaar burgers, 326–28

Bobby Flay's Cheyenne burgers, 325–26

bratwurst "hot tub," 341–43, *342*

bratwurst with curry sauce, 344–45, *345*

chicken sausage "hot tub" with apples and apple cider, 343

Colombian sausage sandwiches with lemon-garlic mayonnaise, 349

ground chicken shashlik with onion and dill, 339–40

ground lamb and plum kebabs, 337

ground lamb kebabs with coriander and cumin, 330–32, *331*

ground lamb kebabs with cumin and mint, 328–29

ground lamb kebabs with pistachio nuts, 336, *336*

ground lamb kebabs with Turkish hot peppers, 334–37, *335*

"Kobe" beef sliders, 310–12, *311*

Moroccan "sliders," *317*, 317–18

onion kebabs, 336–37

the Paul Newman burger, 307–8

the Paul Newman cheeseburger, 308

really big Bosnian burgers, 315–16, *316*

Romanian "sliders" (garlicky grilled skinless sausages), 340–41, *341*

sausage kebabs with pepper sauce, 348–49

South African farmer's sausage, 349–50

Turkish "meatball" burgers, 312–13, *313*

veal and beef burgers, *318*, 318–19

vegetable kebabs, 336, *336*

Grouper:

baby, grilled, in the style of the Portuguese, 460–62

Mexican grilled fish tacos, 458–60

Guacamole:

Colombian, 186

Mexican, 131–32

Guam:

grilled chicken salad with chiles and coconut (*kelaguen*), *78*, 78–80

Guam "volcano" tuna (pepper-crusted tuna with ginger-wasabi dipping sauce), 437–38

Guava and salty cheese, grilled sweet plantains or bananas with, 571–72

Haj Brik (Morocco), 65, 276, 281, 317

Hake, grilled, with fried garlic, 441–42

Halibut:

grilled in banana leaves with lemongrass and Thai basil, 444–45

Nha Trang mixed grill, 524–26

or blowfish "bool kogi," 453–54

or eel, grilled, with sweet cinnamon and star anise glaze, 478–80

Ham:

Brazilian matambre, *140*, 140–42

country, Catalan grilled bread with, 90

Croatian "cheesesteak," 155–56

Dalmatian, scampi kebabs with, 497–98

hocks, spit-roasted, 245–47

poppers (stuffed grill-roasted jalapeño peppers), 7–8

Serbian chicken bundles, 320–21, 388–90, *390*

Serbian stuffed pork loin, 209–11

shrimp on the barbie (#2), *490*, 490–91

Hamdi (Turkey), 298, 301, 328

Hanger steak with marchand de vin (wine merchant) sauce, 142–44, *143*

Hanoi-style grilled oysters, 505, *505*

Hanoi-style grilled squid with chiles and lime, 516–17

Harissa and cumin, Moroccan lamb chops with, 282–83

Harissa (simple Moroccan hot sauce), 414

Hart, Bob, 491

Haxenbauer (Germany), 245

Hellfire hot sauce, 392–93

Hetzler, Richard, 421

Hill Country brisket, 117–18, *118*

Hoisin-peanut dipping sauce, 302–3

Hon, Hang, 93

Honey:

    and apple wine, grilled apples with, 569–70

    German whole hog, 261–62

    lime dipping sauce, 445

    and soy spit-roasted chicken wings, 23–25, *24*

    and star anise, Vietnamese spit-roasted duck with, 415–17, *416*

Hungarian grilled bacon *(solina shutesh)*, 46–47

Hunters' kebabs, 187–88

Huseynov, Mehman, 590, 592

Hwachunok (Korea), 171

Ibiza (Atlanta, Georgia), 272

Ibu Oka (Bali), 243, 263

"Iceberg" game hens with Moroccan spices, 413–14

The Iceberg (Morocco), 413

Ice cream:

    grilled, 590, *591*

    smoked, 593

Icicle radish salad, 209

Ilmijung (South Korea), 478

Impala, lamb, or kid, fruit-stuffed leg of, 270–72

Imperial Fez (Atlanta, Georgia), 272

India:

    green herb chutney, 398–99

    grilled cheese kebabs, 563–64

    grilled corn in, 531

    grilled peppers in, 543

    grilling, food, and drink, 102–3

    Indian "puff pastry," 98–100, *99*

    Lucknowi lamb chops *(lucknowi champ)*, 291–92

    naan *crusted* with pumpkin, poppy, and nigella seeds, 100–101, *101*

    tandoori grilled kingfish, 432–33

    tandoori potatoes, 549–50

    tandoori potatoes in the style of baked stuffed potatoes, 550

    traditional naan, 100

    two chicken tikkas, 397–400, *398*

Indonesia:

    baby goat or lamb satés with pineapple and sweet soy, 302–3

    grilled shrimp with fiery lemongrass chile sambal, 493–95

grilling, food, and drink, 242–43

Nuri's ribs: grilled baby backs with sweet soy glaze, 239–41, *240*

Iran:

    Iranian saffron lemon chicken wings, 26–27

    Persian saffron lemon chicken kebabs, 27

    whole Persian saffron lemon chicken, 27

Israel:

    grilled eggplant salad with Jerusalem flavors, 71–73, *72*

    grilled Israeli spiced foie gras, 57–58

    grilling, food, and drink, 74–75

    Israeli grilled chicken, 412

    Israeli grilled game hens, 411–12

    Israeli smoked goose, 405–6, *406*

    Jordanian grilled chicken, 378–80

    Middle Eastern sesame sauce, 410–11

    smoked egg pâté, 13–14, *14*

    Tel Aviv tomato relish, 411

    turkey shawarma, *409,* 409–11

Italy:

    bagna cauda–Italian sausage "hot tub," 343

    bell pepper salad with capers and pine nuts *(peperoni ai ferri con capperi e pinoli)*, 67–69, *69*

    grilled peppers in, 543

    grilled T-bone steak with grape tomato salad *(tagliata con insalata di pomodoro)*, 150–51

    grilled veal chops with sweet-and-sour onions, 180–82, *181*

    grilling, food, and drink, 148–49

    grill masters of, 294

    Italian spit-roasted beef tenderloin, 122

    Livornese sauce, 436

    the real bistecca alla fiorentina, 145–47

    truffled cheese sandwiches with onion, 106–7

    tuna steaks alla fiorentina, 434–36, *435*

    Tuscan grilled toasts (crostini and bruschetta), 83–85, *84*

    Tuscan-style chicken under a brick, *376,* 377–78

    Venetian shrimp grilled with bread crumbs and sage *(gamberoni al ferri)*, 492–93

Ivanivic, Tomislav, 209

Izakaya-Tamotsu (Japan), 400, 544

Jackfruit:

    Balinese salad, 264

Jadallah, Ahmed, 485

Jam, ginger, and soy, grilled oysters with, 506, *507*

Jamaica:

    grilling, food, and drink, 202–3

    Jamaican seasonings, 200

    jerk chicken legs in the style of Yallahs with hellfire hot sauce, 390–93, *391*

    the real Jamaican jerk pork, 199–201

    "steam" fish, 467–68

Jamaican Boston Beach (Jamaica), 203, 467

Japan:

    authentic yakitori in, 401

    bacon-grilled enotake mushrooms, 2–4, *3*

    balsamic- and soy-glazed chicken yakitori, 403

    chicken liver yakitori with a balsamic-soy glaze, 402–3, *403*

    grilled corn in, 531

    grilled peppers in, 543

    grilled shishito peppers with sesame oil and salt, 544

    grilling, food, and drink, 28–29

    grill masters of, 404

    smoke-roasted apples with Japanese sweet bean paste, 570–71

    Tokyo-style grilled chicken dumplings *(tsukune)*, 29, 30–31

    yakitori like they make it in Japan, 400–402

Jaramillo, Andrés, 136–37

Jerk chicken legs in the style of Yallahs with hellfire hot sauce, 390–93, *391*

Jerk pork, the real Jamaican, 199–201

Jojo (South Africa), 303

Jojo (Soweto butcher), 303

Jordanian grilled chicken, 378–80

Juniper berries:

    planked salmon with juniper rub and berry glaze, 421–23, *422*

    spit-roasted ham hocks, 245–47

Kabanchik (Republic of Georgia), 417

Kalbi (butterflied sesame-grilled beef short ribs), 171–72

Kale *(cavolo nero)*, about, 83

Kallisti (Greece), 314, 318

Kangaroo kebabs with grilled olive tzatziki, 188–90, *189*

Khankishiev, Stalic, 330, 333

Kansas City:

    bourbon-brown sugar barbecue sauce, 229

    Kansas City–style spareribs, 227–29, *228*

Karim (India), 103, 314

Kataifi dough:

    "bird's nest" on the grill, 582–84, *583*

Kauckchan, Onik, 96

Kebabs:

    around the world, 38, 249

    bacon cheese pork roulade, 255–56, *256*

balsamic- and soy-glazed chicken
    yakitori, 403
beef, Cartagena, 172–73
beef, Peruvian, 39–41
Buenos Aires garlic butter beef
    roulades, 176–77
cheese, grilled, 563–64
chicken, pancetta orange, 395–96
chicken, Persian saffron lemon, 27
chicken, piri-piri, 22–23
chicken brochettes in the style of Fez,
    394–95
chicken liver yakitori with a balsamic-
    soy glaze, 402–3, *403*
garlic-herb portobello skewers, 541
goat, piri-piri, 303–4
grilled crocodile or pork and shrimp
    with garlic walnut lime sauce, 54–55
grilled foie gras with grenadine onions,
    58
grilled Israeli spiced foie gras, 57–58
grilled mashed potatoes with cheese,
    556
grilled pork skewers with Filipino
    seasonings, 44–45
ground chicken shashlik with onion
    and dill, 339–40
ground lamb, with coriander and
    cumin, 330–32, *331*
ground lamb, with cumin and mint,
    328–29
ground lamb, with pistachio nuts, 336,
    336
ground lamb, with Turkish hot
    peppers, 334–37, *335*
ground lamb and plum, 337
ground meat, grilling tips, 329
hunters', 187–88
kandosouvle grilled directly over the
    fire, 206
kangaroo, with grilled olive tzatziki,
    188–90, *189*
"knish on a stick" (grilled mashed
    potatoes), 554–56, *555*
lamb, peanut-crusted, in the style of
    Burkina Faso, 297–98
lamb tenderloin, yogurt-marinated,
    298–99, *299*
onion, 336–37
pork, "Dacho," 247–48
pork and onion, Russian, 248–51, *249*
potato, Armenian, 545–46
potato, Armenian, with onion, 546, *546*
salmon shashlik, 431–32
sausage, with pepper sauce, 348–49
scampi, with Dalmatian ham, 497–98
shish, South African, *250*, 251–53
shrimp or squid, Mauritius, with ginger
    turmeric glaze, 495–96
springbok or pork, South African, with
    monkey gland sauce, 253–55

tandoori grilled kingfish, 432–33
Tokyo-style grilled chicken dumplings,
    30–31
two chicken tikkas, 397–400, *398*
vegetable, 336, *336*
yakitori like they make it in Japan,
    400–402
see also Satés
Kelantan chicken with Malaysian-Thai
    marinade, 374–75
Kenya:
    grilled crocodile or pork and shrimp
        with garlic walnut lime sauce, 54–55
    grilled ostrich meatballs, 31–32
    grill masters of, 56
    spit-roasted lamb or goat with garlic
        and mint, 267–69, *268*
    tomato-pepper salsa, 32
Kimchi. *See* Cabbage
Kingfish, tandoori grilled, 432–33
Kiplagat, Daniel, 56, 267
Kish, Ed, 46
Kissoandoyal, Sanjeev, 293
Klein, Jake, 32
"Knish on a stick" (grilled mashed
    potatoes), 554–56, *555*
Kobe beef, about, 312
"Kobe" beef sliders, 310–12, *311*
Kofta (ground lamb kebabs with cumin and
    mint), 328–29
Konoba Varoš (Croatia), 497
Koöftesi (Turkish "meatball" burgers),
    312–13, *313*
Korea. *See* South Korea
Köşebaşi (Turkey), 301, 582
Kosovo:
    garlic-herb portobello skewers, 541
    Kosovan grilled mushrooms, *536*,
        540–41
    Serbian stuffed pork loin, 209–11
    sour cream cucumber salad, 211
Kremezi, Aglaia, 465, 520
Kuang Heng (Thailand), 19
Kudari, Azlinah, 460, 486
Kurdish grilled pumpkin dip, 10–11, *11*
Kuwaiti chile shrimp, 485–86
Kuwaiti grilled mackerel or other fish, 486
Kyong, Kim Su, 171

La Bouvette (France), 513, 515, 589
La Brigada (Argentina), 66
La Cabrera (Argentina), 176, 395
La Casa del Tikinxik (Mexico), 464
Lac Canh (Vietnam), 524
Lachha paratha (Indian "puff pastry"),
    98–100, *99*
La Huella (Uruguay), 551
Lamb:
    Australian, on a shovel, 283–85, *284*
    Bazaar burgers, 326–28

chops, baby (and I mean baby), with
    Greek oregano, 295–96
chops, Greek, about, 296
chops, Lucknowi, 291–92
chops, Mauritius grilled, *292*, 293
chops, Moroccan, with harissa and
    cumin, 281–82
chops, onion and coriander brined,
    288–89, *289*
"churrasco," Australian chipotle-
    glazed, 277–78
ground, and plum kebabs, 337
ground, kebabs with coriander and
    cumin, 330–32, *331*
ground, kebabs with cumin and mint,
    328–29
ground, kebabs with pistachio nuts,
    336, *336*
ground, kebabs with Turkish hot
    peppers, 334–37, *335*
internal cooking temperatures, 613
kangaroo kebabs with grilled olive
    tzatziki, 188–90, *189*
kebabs, peanut-crusted, in the style of
    Burkina Faso, 297–98
leg of, kid, or impala, fruit-stuffed,
    270–72
Moroccan "sliders," 317–18
onion kebabs, 336–37
or baby goat satés with pineapple and
    sweet soy, 302–3
or goat, méchoui of, with Berber spices,
    272–74, *275*
or goat, spit-roasted, with garlic and
    mint, 267–69, *268*
Romanian "sliders" (garlicky grilled
    skinless sausages), 340–41, *341*
steaks, beer-marinated, grilled over
    herbs and spices, 279–80
tail fat, virtues of, 332, 554
tenderloin kebabs, yogurt-marinated,
    298–99, *299*
vegetable kebabs, 336
whole, securing to rotisserie spit, 262
Langosta con mojo de ajo (grilled Maine
    or spiny lobster with garlic sauce),
    500–502, *501*
Laos:
    grill masters of, 469
    Laotian grilled fish, 470–71
    Laotian rice "pops" with dipping
        sauces, 565–66, *566*
    lemongrass and curry grilled chicken
        breasts, 384–86, *385*
La Perdiz (Uruguay), 222, 367
La Pigua (Mexico), 462
Lassen, Louis, 314
Lechon asado (Puerto Rican pork
    shoulder), *196*, 197–98
Léchon manok (lemongrass rotisserie
    chicken), 353–56, *354*

Leipoldt, C. Louis, 251, 252
Lemongrass rotisserie chicken, 353–56, *354*
Lemon leaves, chicken grilled in, 386–88, *388*
Lemon(s):
    chile dipping sauce, 388
    Middle Eastern sesame sauce, 410–11
    mustard, planked bluefish with, 423–24
    preserved, 282–83
    saffron chicken, whole Persian, 27
    saffron chicken kebabs, Persian, 27
    saffron chicken wings, Iranian, 26–27
    Vietnamese dipping sauce, 179
Lettuce:
    Cambodian steak with salads and condiments, 160–62
    Korean barbecue accompaniments, 52
    lemongrass-grilled beef with noodles and salad, 177–79
    Nha Trang mixed grill, 524–26
L'Hostalet de Vivès (France), 89, 586
Lim, Wilfrid, 48
Lime(s):
    Asian *(calamansi),* about, 461
    Balinese salad, 264
    and chiles, Hanoi-style grilled squid with, 516–17
    and chiles, Thai grilled cockles or clams with, 510–11
    honey dipping sauce, 445
    Nha Trang mixed grill, 524–26
    shellfish in sauce, 511
    walnut garlic sauce, 55
Linguiça con queso (cheese grilled linguiça), 45–46
Liver:
    chicken, yakitori with a balsamic-soy glaze, 402–3, *403*
    grilled foie gras with grenadine onions, 58
    grilled Israeli spiced foie gras, 57–58
    Tuscan grilled toasts (crostini and bruschetta), 83–85, *84*
Livornese sauce, 436
Llano y Mamona (Colombia), 184
Lobster:
    about, 500
    Maine or spiny, grilled, with garlic sauce, 500–502, *501*
    the way we grill it on Martha's Vineyard, 498–99
Lomos (Colombia), 132, 529
Loseke, Nancy, 234
Louis' Lunch (Connecticut), 314
Lucknowi lamb chops, 292–93
Lula kebab (ground lamb kebabs with coriander and cumin), 330–32, *331*
Lumlerokit, Vichai, 41, 43
Lydia's Lechons (Philippines), 357, 359

Mabeyin (Turkey), 301, 336, 338
Mackerel or other fish, Kuwaiti grilled, 486
Madeira gravy, 408–9
Malaysia:
    chicken satés in the style of Kajang *(saté Kajang),* 17–18
    creamy Asian peanut sauce, 18
    grilled baby grouper in the style of the Portuguese, 460–62
    grilled tofu with chile peanut sauce *(tauhu bakar),* 446, 561–63, *562*
    grilling, food, and drink, 446–47
    grill masters of, 16
    honey and soy spit-roasted chicken wings, 23–25, *24*
    Kelantan chicken with Malaysian-Thai marinade *(ayam percik),* 374–75
    Malaysian grilled fish mousse *(otak-otak),* 448, 448–50
    nonya-style flank steak, 138–39
    turmeric grilled prawns, 486–87
Mallmann, Francis, 175, 363, 365, 575, 576
Mamoña asado con aji y guacamole (eucalyptus-grilled veal roast with Colombian salsas), 184–86
Mangal grills, 605
Mangoes:
    Filipino grilled eggplant salad, 76–77
    green, about, 77
Manterola, Luis Mari, 440
Mapo Choidaepo (South Korea), 53
Markowitz, Mike, 343
Maroulis, Phillipas, 259
Marx, Klaus, 219, 221
Mauritius grilled lamb chops, *292*, 293
Mauritius shrimp or squid kebabs with ginger turmeric glaze, 495–96
Mayan pork chops, 225–26
Mayonnaise, lemon-garlic, Columbian, sausage sandwiches with, 349
Meat. *See* Beef; Game meats; Goat; Ground meats; Lamb; Pork; Veal
Meatballs:
    ostrich, grilled, 31–32
    Tokyo-style grilled chicken dumplings, 30–31
Mertz, Laurent, 58, 515
Mesa Grill (New York), 324
Metropole (Vietnam), 386
Mexico:
    beef poc chuc, 226
    fiery habañero salsa, 465
    grilled corn in, 531
    grilled Maine or spiny lobster with garlic sauce, 500–502, *501*
    grilled peppers in, 543
    grilled shrimp or fish with mojo de ajo, 502
    grilled tomato-habañero salsa, 459–60
    grilling, food, and drink, 214–15
    Mayan pork chops *(poc chuc),* 225–26

Mexican grilled beef, 127–32, *129*
Mexican grilled fish tacos, 458–60
Mexican guacamole, 131–32
    pico de gallo, 130
    salsa de chile chipotle, 131
    salsa verde, 130–31
    "shepherd's tacos," 212–13
    tikin xik in the style of Campeche, 462–65, *463*
Mickey's Jerk Center (Jamaica), 199
Middle Eastern herb blend, 92
Middle Eastern sesame sauce (tahini), 410–11
Miller, Mark, 277, 510
Mitsitam Café (Washington, DC), 421
Monkey gland sauce, 254–55
Montreal smoked meat, 119
Moon, Youngho, 171
Moraitis, Costas, 465, 520
Moreno, Kumahachi, 570
Morgan, Eric, 392
Morocco:
    chicken brochettes in the style of Fez, 394–95
    grilled peppers in, 543
    grilling, food, and drink, 64–65
    grill masters of, 276
    ground lamb kebabs with cumin and mint, 328–29
    "iceberg" game hens with Moroccan spices, 413–14
    méchoui of lamb or goat with Berber spices, 272–74, *275*
    Moroccan grilled pepper salad, 62, *63*
    Moroccan lamb chops with harissa and cumin, 281–82
    Moroccan "sliders," *317*, 317–18
    simple Moroccan hot sauce, 414
    unusual grilled foods in, 281
Moti Mahal (India), 98, 549
Mousse, Malaysian grilled fish, 448, 448–50
Mozambique:
    piri-piri prawns, 482–84, *483*
Muscat-grilled pineapple with sea salt, 577–78
Musée National de Préhistoire (France), xiii
Mushroom(s):
    Croatian "cheesesteak," 155–56
    enotake, bacon-grilled, 2–4, *3*
    garlic-herb portobello skewers, 541
    grilled, Kosovan, *536*, 540–41
    Korean-style enotakes grilled with beef, *3*, 4
    whisky sauce, filets mignons with, 165–66
Mussels grilled on pine needles, 513–14
Mustard:
    beer-marinated lamb steaks grilled over herbs and spices, 279–80
    lemon, planked bluefish with, 423–24

oil, about, 391
plum barbecue sauce, 223
Serbian chicken bundles, 388–90, *390*

Naan:
  crusted with pumpkin, poppy, and
    nigella seeds, 100–101, *101*
  traditional, 100
Na Brasa (Brazil), 45
Nana (Cambodia), 160
Nando's (South Africa), 20, 457
Naughty Nuri's Warung (Indonesia), 239
Newman, Paul, 307, 309
Newnham, Merilyn, 361
New York grill masters, 324
New Zealand:
  apostles on horseback, 502–3
Nha Trang mixed grill, 524–26
Nigella, pumpkin, and poppy seeds, naan
    crusted with, 100–101, *101*
Nischan, Michel, 307, 309
Nonya sauce, 139
Nonya-style flank steak, 138–39
Noodles and salad, lemongrass-grilled beef
    with, 177–79
Nostromo (Croatia), 155
Nuts:
  cashew cream chicken tikka, 397–99,
    398
  Jordanian grilled chicken, 378–80
  pine, and capers, bell pepper salad
    with, 67–69, *69*
  pistachio, ground lamb kebabs with, 336
  toasting, 68
  see also Peanut butter; Peanut(s);
    Walnut(s)

Obersteiner "filet mignon," 88
Octopus, grilled, with Greek herbs,
    520–21, *521*
O'Dea, Daniel, 502
Olive oil:
  about, 434
  and wine, grilled shrimp sprayed with,
    488
Olive(s):
  grilled, tzatziki, 190
  Livornese sauce, 436
  Moroccan "sliders," *317*, 317–18
Onion(s):
  Armenian potato kebabs with, 546, *546*
  Brazilian spit-roasted beef tenderloin,
    119–22, *121*
  and coriander brined lamb chops,
    288–89, *289*
  grenadine, grilled foie gras with, 58
  grilled mashed potatoes with cheese,
    556
  grilled using the indirect method, 537

Jordanian grilled chicken, 378–80
kebabs, 336–37
"knish on a stick" (grilled mashed
    potatoes), 554–56, *555*
and parsley relish, 319
and pork kebabs, Russian, 248–51, *249*
relish, 337
rings, shoestring, preparing, 326
rotisserie, *536*, 537
-stuffed, spit-roasted pork shoulder,
    206–9, *208*
sweet-and-sour, grilled veal chops
    with, 180–82, *181*
-tomato salsa, 120
truffled cheese sandwiches with, 106–7
Orange(s):
  and brown sugar brined smoked turkey,
    107–9
  burnt, with rosemary, Francis
    Mallmann's, 575
  pancetta chicken kebabs, 395–96
  sour *(naranjas agrias)*, about, 225, 458
Oregano:
  Greek, about, 86, 520
Ostrich meatballs, grilled, 31–32
Ouedraogo, Sala, 297
Oysters:
  about, 505
  grilled, Hanoi-style, *505*, 505
  grilled, with ginger, soy, and jam,
    506, *507*
  shucking, 504
  smoked on the half shell, 504
Oyster sauce:
  about, 25, 470
  Laotian grilled fish, 470–71
  Mauritius grilled lamb chops, *292*, 293

Paella, authentic, notes about, 560
Paella "primavera" on the grill,
    557–60, *559*
Paman, Alex, 44
Pancetta orange chicken kebabs, 395–96
Panin, Miss, 469
Papas aplastadas (smashed potatoes), 551
Parsley:
  garlic sauce, 365
  onion relish, 337
  the real chimichurri, 159
Pâté, smoked egg, 13–14, *14*
Peanut butter:
  creamy Asian peanut sauce, 18
  fried garlic peanut sauce, *34*, 35
  peanut-hoisin dipping sauce, 302–3
  yellow chile peanut sauce, 40–41
Peanut(s):
  Cambodian steak with salads and
    condiments, 160–62
  chile sauce, grilled tofu with,
    561–63, *562*

-crusted lamb kebabs in the style of
    Burkina Faso, 297–98
lemongrass-grilled beef with noodles
    and salad, 177–79
Pepper(s):
  Bazaar burgers, 326–28
  bell, grilled, and feta cheese dip, 9–10
  bell, salad with capers and pine nuts,
    67–69, *69*
  Cartagena beef kebabs, 172–73
  Catalan "bruschetta," 89–90, *90*
  chicken kebabs piri-piri, 22–23
  country salsa, 155
  cream cheese and chutney open-face
    poppers, 8
  Cubanelle, about, 348
  Filipino grilled eggplant salad, 76–77
  goat cheese and dried tomato poppers, 8
  grilled, around the world, 543
  grilled, salad, Moroccan, 62, *63*
  grilled cheese kebabs, 563–64
  grilled corn cakes with salsa, 109
  grilled pickled, Romanian and Serbian,
    541–43
  grilled vegetable salad, 60–61
  hunters' kebabs, 187–88
  kangaroo kebabs with grilled olive
    tzatziki, 188–90, *189*
  Mauritius shrimp or squid kebabs with
    ginger turmeric glaze, 495–96
  paella "primavera" on the grill, 557–60,
    559
  Persian saffron lemon chicken kebabs, 27
  poppers (stuffed grill-roasted jalapeño
    peppers), 7–8
  red, dip, 12
  roasted bell, salad with anchovies and
    garlic, 66
  sauce, sausage kebabs with, 348–49
  -spiced spit-roasted pork, *204*, 205–6
  twelve types, for grilling, 543
  vegetable kebabs, 336, *336*
Peppers, hot. *See* Chile(s)
Pernod, about, 490
Persian saffron lemon chicken kebabs, 27
Peru:
  grilled chicken with yellow chiles and
    roasted garlic, 368–69
  Peruvian beef kebabs *(anticuchos)*,
    39–41
  yellow chile peanut sauce, 40–41
Perunovic, Milica, 255, 257
"Pesto," Asian, beer-can chicken with,
    361–63
Philippines:
  calamansi dipping sauce, 356
  Filipino grilled eggplant salad, 76–77
  grilled pork skewers with Filipino
    seasonings, 44–45
  grilling, food, and drink, 358–59
  grill masters of, 357

lemongrass rotisserie chicken, 353–56, *354*

unusual grilled foods in, 281

vinegar and soy dipping sauce (*toyo at suka*), 356

Phillipas Taverna (Greece), 259

Phothisoontorni, Jutarat, 41

Pich, Sarun, 238

Pickled peppers, Romanian and Serbian grilled, 541–43

Pico de gallo, 130

Pineapple:

baby back ribs, Caribbean, with pineapple barbecue sauce, 234–36, *235*

barbecue sauce, 236

crema Catalana, 587

grilled tofu with chile peanut sauce, 561–63, *562*

Mauritius shrimp or squid kebabs with ginger turmeric glaze, 495–96

muscat-grilled, with sea salt, 577–78

"shepherd's tacos," 212–13

spit-roasted, 578–80, *579*

and sweet soy, baby goat or lamb satés with, 302–3

Pine needles, mussels grilled on, 513–14

Pine nuts:

and capers, bell pepper salad with, 67–69, *69*

Jordanian grilled chicken, 378–80

Piri-piri chicken wings in the style of Nando's, 20–23, *21*

Piri-piri goat kebabs, 303–4

Piri-piri prawns, 482–84, *483*

Pistachio nuts, ground lamb kebabs with, 336

Pita bread grilled two ways, 91–92, *92*

Pit roasting, description of, 601

Planked bluefish with lemon mustard, 423–24

Planked salmon with juniper rub and berry glaze, 421–23, *422*

Plantains, sweet, or bananas, grilled, with guava and salty cheese, 571–72

Plum:

and ground lamb kebabs, 337

mustard barbecue sauce, 223

Pollo al mattone (Tuscan-style chicken under a brick), *376*, 377–78

Pollo asado con llajua (cumin-grilled chicken breasts with fiery Bolivian salsa), 383–84

Pomegranate molasses:

about, 26, 431

and walnuts, tomato salad with, 328

Poppers:

cream cheese and chutney open-face, 8

goat cheese and dried tomato, 8

(stuffed grill-roasted jalapeño peppers), 7–8

Poppy, pumpkin, and nigella seeds, naan crusted with, 100–101, *101*

Pork:

belly, grilled, Korean, 53–54

Caribbean pineapple baby back ribs with pineapple barbecue sauce, 234–36, *235*

chops, grilled, Puerto Rican, 224

chops, Mayan, 225–26

German whole hog, 261–62

ginger, garlic, and honey grilled baby back ribs, 236–38, *237*

internal cooking temperatures, 613

Jamaican jerk, the real, 199–201

jerky, grilled, *48*, 48–49

kandosouvle grilled directly over the fire, 206

Kansas City-style spareribs, 227–29, *228*

kebabs "Dacho," 247–48

loin, Serbian stuffed, 209–11

Nuri's ribs: grilled baby backs with sweet soy glaze, 239–41, *240*

and onion kebabs, Russian, 248–51, *249*

or springbok kebabs, South African, with monkey gland sauce, 253–55

pepper-spiced spit-roasted, *204*, 205–6

rolls, Belgian, with chutney, mint, and bacon, 258

Romanian "sliders" (garlicky grilled skinless sausages), 340–41, *341*

rotisserie baby back ribs with garlic and wine, 244–45

roulade, bacon cheese, 255–56, *256*

satés in the style of Banghok's Chinatown, 41–42

"shepherd's tacos," 212–13

shoulder, Keith Allen's North Carolina, 193–94

shoulder, onion-stuffed, spit-roasted, 206–9, *208*

shoulder, Puerto Rican, *196*, 197–98

and shrimp or crocodile, grilled, with garlic walnut lime sauce, 54–55

skewers, grilled, with Filipino seasonings, 44–45

"skirt steak", Uruguayan, with mustard plum barbecue sauce, 222–23

South African shish kebabs, *250*, 251–53

spiessbraten grilled on a *schwenker*, 219–20

steaks, "swinging," 218–20, *220*

tenderloin grilled with bacon and prunes with farofa, 216–17

and veal "burgers," Balkan grilled, 322–23, *323*

whole hog, carving, 263

whole hog, securing to rotisserie spit, 262

whole hog in the style of a Greek island, 259–61

whole hog with Balinese spices, 263

see also Bacon; Ham; Pork sausages

Pork sausages:

bagna cauda–Italian sausage "hot tub," 343

bratwurst "hot tub," 341–43, *342*

cheese grilled linguiça, 45–46

Colombian sausage sandwiches with lemon-garlic mayonnaise, 349

Romanian "sliders" (garlicky grilled skinless sausages), 340–41, *341*

sausage kebabs with pepper sauce, 348–49

Potato(es):

beet skordalia, 519

Cartagena beef kebabs, 172–73

in the embers, 548

grilled, with herbed cheese, 547–48

grilled, with herbed cheese using the direct method, 548

grilled mashed, with cheese, 556

kebabs, Armenian, 545–46

kebabs, Armenian, with onion, 546, *546*

"knish on a stick" (grilled mashed potatoes), 554–56, *555*

sausage kebabs with pepper sauce, 348–49

smashed, 551

tandoori, 549–50

tandoori, in the style of baked stuffed potatoes, 550

Poultry:

"iceberg" game hens with Moroccan spices, 413–14

internal cooking temperatures, 613

Israeli grilled game hens, 411–12

Israeli smoked goose, 405–6, *406*

quail "Kabanchik" grilled in the style of the Republic of Georgia, 417–18

trussing, 355

Vietnamese spit-roasted duck with star anise and honey, 415–17, *416*

see also Chicken; Turkey

Prawns:

piri-piri, 482–84, *483*

turmeric grilled, 486–87

Préhisto Parc (theme park), x, xii

Preserved lemon, 282–83

Profeta, Mike, 76

Prosciutto:

shrimp on the barbie (#2), *490*, 490–91

Prunes:

Armagnac, *crema Catalana* with, 587

and bacon, pork tenderloin grilled with, with farofa, 216–17

mustard plum barbecue sauce, 223

Serbian bacon-grilled: village hammers, 5–6, *6*

Puerto Rican grilled pork chops, 224

Puerto Rican pork shoulder, *196*, 197–98
Pumpkin, grilled, dip, Kurdish, 10–11, *11*
Pumpkin, poppy, and nigella seeds, naan crusted with, 100–101, *101*

Quail:
    internal cooking temperatures, 613
    "Kabanchik" grilled in the style of the Republic of Georgia, 417–18
Quesadillas, smoked chicken, with cilantro and pepper Jack cheese, 15

Radish, icicle, salad, 209
Ray's Butchery (South Africa), 350
Red pepper dip, 12
Relish:
    cucumber, Singapore, *34*, 35
    onion, 337
    onion and parsley, 319
    tomato, spicy, 304
    tomato, Tel Aviv, 411
Rend, Szabadtüzi, 46
Restaurants and resorts:
    Abu-Nassar-Hinnawi (Israel), 91
    Allen & Son Barbeque (North Carolina), 193, 195, 233
    Amanbagh resort (India), 291
    Amandari (Indonesia), 493
    Amansara resort (Cambodia), 238
    Ana Mandara (Vietnam), 415
    Andrés Carne de Res (Colombia), 111, 123, 136–37
    Angkor Wat (Cambodia), 371
    Arabesque (Jordan), 379
    Arcadia (Israel), 71
    Auberge Shulamit (Israel), 13, 405
    Avazi (Israel), 57, 75, 411
    Berghotel Kristall (Germany), 547
    Beti Jai (Spain), 441
    Birdland (Japan), 29, 403, 404
    Bobby's Burger Palace (New York), 324
    Buca Lapi (Italy), 145, 180
    Café Atlantico (Washington, DC), 112
    Campobravo (Argentina), 556
    Carnivore (Kenya), 54, 56, 267, 457
    Casa Julián (Spain), 164
    Cheol Cheol Globefish Restaurant (Korea), 51, 453
    Chong Kee (Thailand), 43
    Chubura (Serbia), 255, 257, 321
    Çiya (Turkey), 393
    Dacho (Serbia), 5, 247, 321
    Da Delfina (Italy), 149, 294
    Dar al Fassi (Morocco), 394
    Delmonico's (New York), 314
    Die Strandloper (South Africa), 104, 455, 457, 596
    Dinho's (Brazil), 537
    Don (Serbia), 314, 388
    Dressing Room (Connecticut), 307, 309
    Dva Jelena (Serbia), 209
    East Coast Grill (Massachusetts), xvii
    Eisen Marx (Germany), 218, 221
    Elckerlijc (Belgium), 258, 279, 430, 506, 569
    El Fogon (Mexico), 212
    Elkano (Spain), 440, 443
    El Pobre Luis (Argentina), 157, 175
    El Príncipe Tutul Xiú (Mexico), 215, 225
    Ermak (Russia), 182
    Etxebarri (Spain), 488, 489, 593
    Fogo de Chão (Brazil), 167, 170, 244, 539
    Galpão Crioulo (Brazil), 578
    Ganesh (India), 397, 432
    Garzón (Uruguay), 367, 576
    Gerai No. 11 & 12 (Malaysia), 460
    Grimpa (Brazil), 119
    Haj Brik (Morocco), 65, 276, 281, 317
    Hamdi (Turkey), 298, 301, 328
    Haxenbauer (Germany), 245
    Hwachunok (Korea), 171
    Ibiza (Atlanta, Georgia), 272
    Ibu Oka, 243, 263
    The Iceberg (Morocco), 413
    Ilmijung (South Korea), 478
    Imperial Fez (Atlanta, Georgia), 272
    Izakaya-Tamotsu (Japan), 400, 544
    Jamaican Boston Beach (Jamaica), 203, 467
    Jojo (South Africa), 303
    Kabanchik (Republic of Georgia), 417
    Kallisti (Greece), 314, 318
    Karim (India), 103, 314
    Konoba Varoš (Croatia), 497
    Köşebaşi (Turkey), 301, 582
    Kuang Heng (Thailand), 19
    La Bouvette (France), 513, 515, 589
    La Brigada (Argentina), 66
    La Cabrera (Argentina), 176, 395
    La Casa del Tikinxik (Mexico), 464
    Lac Canh (Vietnam), 524
    La Huella (Uruguay), 551
    La Perdiz (Uruguay), 222, 367
    La Pigua (Mexico), 462
    L'Hostalet de Vivès (France), 89, 586
    Llano y Mamona (Colombia), 184
    Lomos (Colombia), 132, 529
    Louis' Lunch (Connecticut), 314
    Lydia's Lechons (Philippines), 357, 359
    Mabeyin (Turkey), 301, 336, 338
    Mapo Choidaepo (South Korea), 53
    Mesa Grill (New York), 324
    Metropole (Vietnam), 386
    Mickey's Jerk Center (Jamaica), 199
    Mitsitam Café (Washington, DC), 421
    Moti Mahal (India), 98, 549
    Na Brasa (Brazil), 45
    Nana (Cambodia), 160
    Nando's (South Africa), 20, 457
    Naughty Nuri's Warung (Indonesia), 239
    Nostromo (Croatia), 155
    Phillipas Taverna (Greece), 259
    Ray's Butchery (South Africa), 350
    Ristorante Da Ivo (Italy), 150, 492
    Saté Kajang (Malaysia), 16, 447
    Schneider (Brazil), 140
    Seyhmuz (Turkey), 326
    Stavros Tavern (Australia), 188, 517
    Tarihi Sultanahmet Köftecisi (Turkey), 313
    Terasa Doamnei (Romania), 187, 340
    Tomyam Klasik (Malaysia), 446, 561
    Uzbekistan (Russia), 288, 339, 431
    Water Street (Massachusetts), 504
    W.A.W. Restaurant (Malaysia), 23
    Wildfire (Australia), 277, 477
    Wood (Singapore), 32
    Yerevan (Russia), 96, 545
    Yhznaya Notch (Russia), 290
    Zübeyir (Turkey), 10, 301
Reyes, Marta and Andres, 571
Rice:
    paella "primavera" on the grill, 557–60, *559*
    "pops," Laotian, with dipping sauces, 565–66, *566*
Ristorante Da Ivo (Italy), 150, 492
Roasted bell pepper salad with anchovies and garlic, 66
Romania:
    hunters' kebabs (*frigărui vânătoreşti*), 187–88
    Romanian and Serbian grilled pickled peppers (*ardei copti*), 541–43
    Romanian garlic steak (*fleica*), 135
    Romanian "sliders" (garlicky grilled skinless sausages) (*mici*), 340–41, *341*
Rooster brood #2 (South African grilled cheese sandwiches), 105–7, *106*
Rooster brood #1 (South African grilled rolls), *104*, 104–5
Rosemary, burnt oranges with, Francis Mallmann's, 575
Rotisseries:
    description of, 606
    outfitting charcoal kettle grill with, 120
    see also Spit roasting
Russia:
    baby veal chops with garlic, dill, and Russian "ketchup" (*telyachya korejkana grile*), 182–83
    grilled vegetable salad (*mangal salati*), 60–61
    grilling, food, and drink, 286–87
    grill masters of, 290
    ground chicken shashlik with onion and dill, 339–40

onion and coriander brined lamb chops, 288–89, *289*

Russian onion and pork kebabs, 248–51, *249*

salmon shashlik, 431–32

Ryan, John, 577

Saffron:

chicken tikka (*zafrani murgh tikka*), *398*, 399–400

lemon chicken, whole Persian, 27

lemon chicken kebabs, Persian, 27

lemon chicken wings, Iranian, 26–27

Saisuwan (Bangkok grill mistress), 573

Salads:

arugula, endive, and shaved Parmesan, 436

Balinese, 264

bean, Tuscan, 146–47

bell pepper, with capers and pine nuts, 67–69, *69*

grape tomato, grilled T-bone steak with, 150–51

grilled chicken, with chiles and coconut, *78*, 78–80

grilled eggplant, 69–70

grilled eggplant, Filipino, 76–77

grilled eggplant, with Jerusalem flavors, 71–73, *72*

grilled pepper, Moroccan, 62, *63*

grilled vegetable, 60–61

icicle radish, 209

roasted bell pepper, with anchovies and garlic, 66

sour cream cucumber, 211

tomato, spicy Turkish, 327

tomato, with walnuts and pomegranate molasses, 328

Salmon:

alder-smoked, 424–26

glazed with Belgian cherry beer, 428–29

grilled, with shallot cream sauce, 427–28

planked, with juniper rub and berry glaze, 421–23, *422*

shashlik, 431–32

Salsa de avocate (Colombian guacamole), 186

Salsas:

country, 155

de chile chipotle, 131

grilled tomato-habañero, 459–60

habañero, fiery, 465

Mexican guacamole, 131–32

pico de gallo, 130

salsa verde, 130–31

tomato-onion, 120

tomato-pepper, 32

Salsa verde (garlic parsley sauce), 365

Salt:

-crusted beef tenderloin grilled in cloth, 123–25, *124*

-crusted rib steaks, Basque Country, 164–65

-crusted tri-tip, 126–27, *127*

-roasted chicken, Francis Mallmann's, 363–65

-roasted fish, 365

Tuscan-style chicken under a brick, 377–78

Samuri, Haji, 16

Sandwiches:

grilled cheese, South African, 105–7, *106*

Keith Allen's North Carolina pork shoulder, 193–94

sausage, Colombian, with lemon-garlic mayonnaise, 349

truffled cheese, with onion, 106–7

see also Burgers

Santa Maria tri-tip, 125–26

Saté Kajang (Malaysia), 16, 447

Satés:

baby goat or lamb, with pineapple and sweet soy, 302–3

beef, the best, in Singapore, 32–35, *34*

chicken, in the style of Kajang, 17–18

chicken, Thai, 19–20

pork, in the style of Banghok's Chinatown, 41–42

Sauces:

barbecue, bourbon-brown sugar, 229

barbecue, mustard plum, 223

barbecue, pineapple, 236

barbecue, sparkling, 198

beet skordalia, 519

chile, Colombian, 185–86

Colombian guacamole, 186

garlic parsley, 365

garlic walnut lime, 55

grilled clams with Korean cocktail sauce, 512

grilled olive tzatziki, 190

hellfire hot, 392–93

Livornese, 436

Madeira gravy, 408–9

mint, sweet-sour, 269

monkey gland, 254–55

Moroccan hot, simple, 414

nonya, 139

peanut, creamy Asian, 18

peanut, fried garlic, *34*, 35

peanut, yelllow chile, 40–41

the real chimichurri, 159

sesame, Middle Eastern, 410–11

vinegar, 193–94

see also Dipping sauces; Salsas

Sausage(s):

bratwurst "hot tub," 341–43, *342*

bratwurst with curry sauce, 344–45, *345*

cheese grilled linguiça, 45–46

chicken, "hot tub" with apples and apple cider, 343

grilling, without tears or flare-ups, 343

Italian, "hot tub"–*bagna cauda*, 343

kebabs with pepper sauce, 348–49

Romanian "sliders" (garlicky grilled skinless sausages), 340–41, *341*

sandwiches, Colombian, with lemon-garlic mayonnaise, 349

South African farmer's, 349–50

Scallions (*escallions*), about, 392

Scallops:

apostles on horseback, 502–3

Scampi kebabs with Dalmatian ham, 497–98

Schlesinger, Chris, xvii

Schneider (Brazil), 140

Schutz, Bob, 125

Seafood. *See* Fish; Shellfish

Seckback, Diego, 126

Seeds:

annatto, about, 197, 224, 356, 368

carom (*ajwain*), about, 433

nigella, about, 108

pumpkin, poppy, and nigella, naan crusted with, 100–101, *101*

toasting, 68

Serbia:

bacon cheese pork roulade (*rolovani punjeni raznjići*), 255–56, *256*

Balkan grilled veal and pork "burgers" (*ćevapčići*), 322–23, *323*

grilling, food, and drink, 320–21

grill masters of, 257

pork kebabs "Dacho," 247–48

Serbian and Romanian grilled pickled peppers (*ardei copti*), 541–43

Serbian chicken bundles (*pileći paketići*), 320–21, 388–90, *390*

Serbian stuffed pork loin (*punjena vesalica*), 209–11

sour cream cucumber salad (*tarator*), 211

village hammers: Serbian bacon-grilled prunes (*seoski cekić*), 5–6, *6*

Sesame oil:

butterflied sesame-grilled beef short ribs, 171–72

and salt, grilled shishito peppers with, 544

Sesame seed paste (tahini), 410–11

Seyhmuz (Turkey), 326

Shallot(s):

cream sauce, grilled salmon with, 427–28

hanger steak with marchand de vin (wine merchant) sauce, 142–44, *143*

"Kobe" beef sliders, 310–12, *311*

Shashlik (Russian onion and pork kebabs), 248–51, *249*

Shellfish
    apostles on horseback, 502–3
    dilled grilled squid with beet skordalia, 517–19
    grilled clams with Korean cocktail sauce, 511–12
    grilled Maine or spiny lobster with garlic sauce, 500–502, *501*
    grilled octopus with Greek herbs, 520–21, *521*
    grilled oysters with ginger, soy, and jam, 506, *507*
    Hanoi-style grilled oysters, 505, *505*
    Hanoi-style grilled squid with chiles and lime, 516–17
    lobster the way we grill it on Martha's Vineyard, 498–99
    Mauritius shrimp or squid kebabs with ginger turmeric glaze, 495–96
    mussels grilled on pine needles, 513–14
    Nha Trang mixed grill, 524–26
    oysters smoked on the half shell, 504
    piri-piri prawns, 482–84, *483*
    in sauce, 511
    Thai grilled cockles or clams with chiles and limes, 510–11
    turmeric grilled prawns, 486–87
    see also Shrimp
"Shepherd's tacos," 212–13
Shrimp:
    on the barbie (#2), 490, 490–91
    grilled, sprayed with olive oil and wine, 488
    grilled, with fiery lemongrass chile sambal, 493–95
    Kuwaiti chile shrimp, 485–86
    Nha Trang mixed grill, 524–26
    or fish, grilled, with mojo de ajo, 502
    or squid kebabs, Mauritius, with ginger turmeric glaze, 495–96
    peeling and deveining, 485
    and pork or crocodile, grilled, with garlic walnut lime sauce, 54–55
    scampi kebabs with Dalmatian ham, 497–98
    Venetian, grilled with bread crumbs and sage, 492–93
Shrimp paste, about, 77, 449, 461, 561
Side dishes:
    Armenian potato kebabs, 545–46
    Armenian potato kebabs with onion, 546, *546*
    bacon-grilled eggplant, 535
    coconut-grilled corn, 529–30
    Colombian grilled corn with butter and cheese, 534
    garlic-herb portobello skewers, 541
    grilled bananas, 529
    grilled butternut squash, 556–57
    grilled mashed potatoes with cheese, 556

    grilled potatoes with herbed cheese, 547–48
    grilled potatoes with herbed cheese using the direct method, 548
    grilled shishito peppers with sesame oil and salt, 544
    "knish on a stick" (grilled mashed potatoes), 554–56, *555*
    Kosovan grilled mushrooms, *536*, 540–41
    Laotian rice "pops" with dipping sauces, 565, *566*
    onions grilled using the indirect method, 537
    potatoes in the embers, 548
    Romanian and Serbian grilled pickled peppers, 541–43
    rotisserie onions, *536*, 537
    smashed potatoes, 551
    tandoori potatoes, 549–50
    tandoori potatoes in the style of baked stuffed potatoes, 550
    see also Salads
Simple Moroccan hot sauce, 414
Singapore:
    the best beef satés in Singapore, 32–35, *34*
    grilled pork jerky *(bak kua)*, 48, 48–49
    grilling, food, and drink, 36–37
    Malaysian grilled fish mousse, *448*, 448–50
    Singapore cucumber relish, *34*, 35
    Singapore-style skate grilled in banana leaves, 450–53, *451*
Skate, Singapore-style, grilled in banana leaves, 450–53, *451*
Sliders, "Kobe" beef, 310–12, *311*
"Sliders," Moroccan, *317*, 317–18
Smashed potatoes, 551
Smoked chicken quesadillas with cilantro and pepper Jack cheese, 15
Smoked egg pâté, 13–14, *14*
Smoke roasting, 600
Smoking foods (barbecuing):
    best foods for, 600
    best meat cuts for, 600
    on charcoal grills, 600
    description of, 600
    on gas grills, note about, 600
    making a smoker pouch, 603
    with wood chips or chunks, 600
S'mores, Fair Trade chocolate banana, 585
Snook, grilled, with apricot glaze, 455
Sogar kebab (onion kebabs), 336
Sour cream:
    cucumber salad, 211
    kajmak, about, 248, 256
South Africa:
    apricot chutney, 272
    chicken kebabs piri-piri, 22–23
    fruit-stuffed leg of kid, lamb, or impala, 270–72

    grilled crocodile or pork and shrimp with garlic walnut lime sauce, 54–55
    grilled snook with apricot glaze, 455
    grilling, food, and drink, 456–57
    monkey gland sauce, 254–55
    piri-piri chicken wings in the style of Nando's, 20–23, *21*
    piri-piri goat kebabs, 303–4
    piri-piri prawns, 482–84, *483*
    South African bread in loaves, 105
    South African "burned" coffee *(moerkoffie)*, 457, 596
    South African farmer's sausage *(boerewors)*, 349–50
    South African grilled cheese sandwiches, 105–7, *106*
    South African grilled rolls, *104*, 104–5
    South African shish kebabs *(sosaties)*, *250*, 251–53
    South African springbok or pork kebabs with monkey gland sauce, 253–55
    spicy tomato relish *(chacalaka)*, 304
    whole chicken piri-piri, 22
South Korea:
    barbecue accompaniments, 52
    blowfish or halibut "bool kogi," 453–54
    butterflied sesame-grilled beef short ribs, 171–72
    grilled clams with Korean cocktail sauce, 511–12
    grilled eel or halibut with sweet cinnamon and star anise glaze, 478–80
    grilling, food, and drink, 50–51
    Korean grilled pork belly *(sam gyeop sal)*, 53–54
    Korean-style enotakes grilled with beef, *3*, 4
Soy (sauce):
    -balsamic glaze, chicken liver yakitori with a, 402–3, *403*
    and balsamic-glazed chicken yakitori, 403
    Indonesian *(kejap manis)*, about, 230, 302
    Nuri's ribs: grilled baby back ribs with sweet soy glaze, 239–41, *240*
    and vinegar dipping sauce, 356
    yakitori like they make it in Japan, 400–402
Spain:
    Basque Country salt-crusted rib steaks, 164–65
    Catalan "bruschetta," 89–90, *90*
    Catalan cream and variations, 586–87
    Catalan grilled bread with country ham, 90
    grilled hake with fried garlic, 441–42
    grilled shrimp sprayed with olive oil and wine, 488

grilled turbot with "holy water" (*rodaballo a la parrilla*), 440–41

grilling, food, and drink, 594–95

grill masters of, 443, 489

José Andrés' grilled bread with chocolate, 112–14, *113*

pa amb tomàquet, 90

paella "primavera" on the grill, 557–60, *559*

smoked ice cream, 593

Sparkling barbecue sauce, 198

Spices, fire, 280

Spicy Turkish tomato salad, 327

Spiessbraten grilled on a *schwenker,* 219–20

Spit roasting:
best foods for, 600–601
on charcoal grills, 120, 600
description of, 600–601
on gas grills, 120, 600

Springbok or pork kebabs, South African, with monkey gland sauce, 253–55

Spruce-grilled steak, 162–64, *163*

Squash:
butternut, grilled, 556–57
Kurdish grilled pumpkin dip, 10–11, *11*
paella "primavera" on the grill, 557–60, *559*

Squid:
dilled grilled, with beet skordalia, 517–19
grilled, Hanoi-style, with chiles and lime, 516–17
Nha Trang mixed grill, 524–26
or shrimp kebabs, Mauritius, with ginger turmeric glaze, 495–96

Starters:
alder-smoked salmon, 424–26
Armenian potato kebabs, 545–46
Armenian potato kebabs with onion, 546, *546*
bacon-grilled enotake mushrooms, 2–4, *3*
the best beef satés in Singapore, 32–35, *34*
Brazilian matambre, *140,* 140–42
Catalan "bruschetta," 89–90, *90*
Catalan grilled bread with country ham, 90
cheese grilled linguiça, 45–46
chicken grilled in lemon leaves, 386–88, *388*
chicken liver yakitori with a balsamic-soy glaze, 402–3, *403*
chicken satés in the style of Kajang, 17–18
cream cheese and chutney open-face poppers, 8
goat cheese and dried tomato poppers, 8
grilled bell pepper and feta cheese dip, 9–10

grilled clams with Korean cocktail sauce, 511–12

grilled crocodile or pork and shrimp with garlic walnut lime sauce, 54–55

grilled foie gras with grenadine onions, 58

grilled Israeli spiced foie gras, 57–58

grilled ostrich meatballs, 31–32

grilled oysters with ginger, soy, and jam, 506, *507*

grilled pita wedges, 10

grilled pork jerky, *48,* 48–49

grilled pork skewers with Filipino seasonings, 44–45

Hanoi-style grilled oysters, 505, *505*

honey and soy spit-roasted chicken wings, 23–25, *24*

Hungarian grilled bacon, 46–47

Iranian saffron lemon chicken wings, 26–27

Korean grilled pork belly, 53–54

Korean-style enotakes grilled with beef, *3,* 4

Laotian rice "pops" with dipping sauces, 565–66, *566*

Malaysian grilled fish mousse, *448,* 448–50

mussels grilled on pine needles, 513–14

oysters smoked on the half shell, 504

pa amb tomàquet, 90

peanut-crusted lamb kebabs in the style of Burkina Faso, 297–98

Peruvian beef kebabs, 39–41

piri-piri chicken wings in the style of Nando's, 20–23, *21*

poppers (stuffed grill-roasted jalapeño peppers), 7–8

pork satés in the style of Bangkok's Chinatown, 41–42

red pepper dip, 12

shellfish in sauce, 511

smoked chicken quesadillas with cilantro and pepper Jack cheese, 15

smoked egg pâté, 13–14, *14*

Thai chicken satés, 19–20

Thai grilled cockles or clams with chiles and limes, 510–11

Tokyo-style grilled chicken dumplings, 30–31

Tuscan grilled toasts (crostini and bruschetta), 83–85, *84*

village hammers: Serbian bacon-grilled prunes, 5–6, *6*

yakitori like they make it in Japan, 400–402

Stauch, Maritta, 547

Stavros Tavern (Australia), 188, 517

Stayer, Ralph, 341

"Steam" fish, 467–68

Stuparevic, Jelena, 306, 314, 388

Sugarcane juice, about, 293

Surgeon's lock knot, tying, 260

Suryatmi, Isnuri, 239

Sweet bean paste, Japanese, smoke-roasted apples with, 570–71

Sweet-sour mint sauce, 269

"Swinging" pork steaks, 218–20, *220*

Swordfish, grilled, with garlic caper butter, 438–39

Tacos:
Mexican grilled fish, 458–60
"shepherd's tacos," 212–13

Tacos al pastor ("shepherd's tacos"), 212–13

Tacos de pescado (Mexican grilled fish tacos), 458–60

Tandoori aloo (tandoori potatoes), 549–50

"Tandoori" chicken, Uzbek, 360–61

Tandoori grilled kingfish, 432–33

Tandoori paneer (grilled cheese kebabs), 563–64

Tandoori potatoes, 549–50

Tandoori potatoes in the style of baked stuffed potatoes, 550

Tarihi Sultanahmet Köftecisi (Turkey), 313

Terasa Doamnei (Romania), 187, 340

Tezçakin, Mehmet, 312

Thailand:
grilled bananas with coconut-caramel sauce, 573–74
grilling, food, and drink, 508–9
grill masters of, 43
halibut grilled in banana leaves with lemongrass and Thai basil, 444–45
honey lime dipping sauce, 445
pork satés in the style of Bangkok's Chinatown, 41–42
shellfish in sauce, 511
Thai chicken satés, 19–20
Thai grilled chicken two ways, 380–82
Thai grilled cockles or clams with chiles and limes, 510–11

Thyme:
about, 200
the real Jamaican jerk pork, 199–201

Thow, Wendy Lokechan, 23

Tikin xik in the style of Campeche, 462–65, *463*

Timm, Uwe, 344

Toasted cassava flour, 217

Tobago:
Caribbean pineapple baby back ribs with pineapple barbecue sauce, 234–36, *235*
grilled corn in, 531

Tofu, grilled, with chile peanut sauce, 561–63, *562*

Tokyo-style grilled chicken dumplings, 30–31

Tomatillos:
salsa verde, 130–31

Tomato(es):
    Brazilian spit-roasted beef tenderloin, 119–22, *121*
    Chilean steak with pepper sauce, 133–34
    cumin-grilled chicken breasts with fiery Bolivian salsa, 383–84
    dried, and goat cheese poppers, 8
    grape, salad, grilled T-bone steak with, 150–51
    grilled, -habañero salsa, 459–60
    grilled cheese kebabs, 563–64
    grilled eggplant salad with Jerusalem flavors, 71–73, *72*
    grilled vegetable salad, 60–61
    Livornese sauce, 436
    Mauritius shrimp or squid kebabs with ginger turmeric glaze, 495–96
    Moroccan grilled pepper salad, 62, *63*
    Moroccan lamb chops with harissa and cumin, 282–83
    Moroccan "sliders," *317*, 317–18
    Nha Trang mixed grill, 524–26
    -onion salsa, 120
    pa amb tomàquet, 90
    paella "primavera" on the grill, 557–60, *559*
    -pepper salsa, 32
    pico de gallo, 130
    relish, spicy, 304
    relish, Tel Aviv, 411
    salad, spicy Turkish, 327
    salad with walnuts and pomegranate molasses, 328
    salsa de chile chipotle, 131
    Santander cheese steak, 132–33
Tomyam Klasik (Malaysia), 446, 561
Tortillas:
    Mexican grilled beef, 127–32, *129*
    Mexican grilled fish tacos, 458–60
    "shepherd's tacos," 212–13
    smoked chicken quesadillas with cilantro and pepper Jack cheese, 15
Trinidad and Tobago:
    Caribbean pineapple baby back ribs with pineapple barbecue sauce, 234–36, *235*
    grilled corn in, 531
Trout, Canadian, grilled on a log, 471–72, *473*
Truffled cheese sandwiches with onion, 106–7
Tuna:
    Guam "volcano" (pepper-crusted tuna with ginger-wasabi dipping sauce), 437–38
    steaks alla fiorentina, 434–36, *435*
Turbot, grilled, with "holy water," 440–41
Turkey:
    Bobby Flay's Cheyenne burgers, 325–26

internal cooking temperatures, 613
shawarma, *409,* 409–11
smoked, brown sugar- and orange-brined, 407–9
Turkey (country):
    Bazaar burgers (*seyhmuz kebab*), 326–28
    "bird's nest" on the grill (*künefe*), 582–84, *583*
    grilled chicken with yogurt, hot pepper, and garlic, 393–94
    grilled peppers in, 543
    grilling, food, and drink, 300–301
    grill masters of, 338
    ground lamb and plum kebabs (*can çriği kebab*), 337
    ground lamb kebabs with pistachio nuts (*fistik kebab*), 336, *336*
    ground lamb kebabs with Turkish hot peppers, 334–37, *335*
    Kurdish grilled pumpkin dip, 10–11, *11*
    onion kebabs (*sogar kebab*), 336–37
    onion relish, 337
    red pepper dip, 12
    spicy Turkish tomato salad, 327
    Turkish "meatball" burgers, 312–13, *313*
    Turkish puff bread (*pide*), 107, 107–8
    vegetable kebabs (*sobzoli kobab*), 336, *336*
    yogurt-marinated lamb tenderloin kebabs, 298–99, *299*
Turmeric:
    fresh, about, 487, 495
    grilled prawns, 486–87
Tuscan bean salad, 146–47
Tuscan grilled toasts (crostini and bruschetta), 83–85, *84*
Tuscan-style chicken under a brick, *376,* 377–78
Tzatziki, grilled olive, 190

United States:
    Bobby Flay's Cheyenne burgers, 325–26
    bourbon-brown sugar barbecue sauce, 229
    bratwurst "hot tub," 341–43
    brown sugar- and orange-brined smoked turkey, 407–9
    cactus pear crisp, 581–82
    chicken sausage "hot tub" with apples and apple cider, 343
    Fair Trade chocolate banana s'mores, 585
    grilled swordfish with garlic caper butter, 438–39
    grilling, food, and drink, 230–33

Hill Country brisket, 117–18, *118*
Kansas City–style spareribs, 227–29, *228*
Keith Allen's North Carolina pork shoulder, 193–94
"Kobe" beef sliders, 310–12, *311*
lobster the way we grill it on Martha's Vineyard, 498–99
oysters smoked on the half shell, 504
the Paul Newman burger, 307–8
planked bluefish with lemon mustard, 423–24
planked salmon with juniper rub and berry glaze, 421–23, *422*
poppers (stuffed grill-roasted jalapeño peppers), 7–8
Santa Maria tri-tip, 125–26
smoked chicken quesadillas with cilantro and pepper Jack cheese, 15
smoke-roasted apples with Japanese sweet bean paste, 570–71
Uruguay:
    filets mignons with whisky mushroom sauce, 165–66
    Francis Mallmann's burnt oranges with rosemary, 575
    Francis Mallmann's salt-roasted chicken, 363–65
    grilling, food, and drink, 366–67
    grill master of, 570
    salt-crusted tri-tip, 126–27, *127*
    smashed potatoes, 551
    unusual grilled foods in, 281
    Uruguayan pork "skirt steak" with mustard plum barbecue sauce, 222–23
Usta, Ibrahim, 326
Uzbekistan:
    grilling, food, and drink, 286–87
    grill masters of, 333
    ground chicken shashlik with onion and dill, 339–40
    ground lamb kebabs with coriander and cumin, 330–32, *331*
    onion and coriander brined lamb chops, 288–89, *289*
    Uzbek "tandoori" chicken, 360–61
Uzbekistan (Russia), 287, 288, 339, 431

Veal:
    and beef burgers, *318,* 318–19
    bratwurst with curry sauce, 344–45, *345*
    chops, baby, with garlic, dill, and Russian "ketchup," 182–83
    chops, grilled, with sweet-and-sour onions, 180–82, *181*
    kangaroo kebabs with grilled olive tzatziki, 188–90, *189*

and pork "burgers," Balkan grilled, 322–23, *323*
really big Bosnian burgers, 315–16, *316*
roast, eucalyptus-grilled, with Colombian salsas, 184–86
Vegetable(s):
grilled, salad, 60–61
kebabs, 336, *336*
paella "primavera" on the grill, 557–60, *559*
see also specific vegetables
Velázquez, Sigifredo Chale, 459, 464
Venetian shrimp grilled with bread crumbs and sage, 492–93
Venison:
hunters' kebabs, 187–88
Vietnam:
chicken grilled in lemon leaves (*gà nuóng lá chanh*), 94, 95, 386–88, *388*
grilling, food, and drink, 94–95
Hanoi-style grilled oysters, 505, *505*
Hanoi-style grilled squid with chiles and lime (*muc nuóng ot*), 516–17
lemon chile dipping sauce, 388
lemongrass-grilled beef with noodles and salad, 177–79
Nha Trang mixed grill, 524–26
Vietnamese cinnamon toast, 93
Vietnamese dipping sauce (*nuoc cham*), 179
Vietnamese grilled bread, 93
Vietnamese spit-roasted duck with star anise and honey, 415–17, *416*
Village hammers: Serbian bacon-grilled prunes, 5–6, *6*
Vinegar:
hellfire hot sauce, 392–93
the real chimichurri, 159
sauce, 193–94
sherry, about, 441
and soy dipping sauce, 356
Vietnamese dipping sauce, 179

Wada, Toshihiro, 403, 404
Walnut(s):
garlic lime sauce, 55
grilled eggplant salad with Jerusalem flavors, 71–73, *72*
Kurdish grilled pumpkin dip, 10–11, *11*
and pomegranate molasses, tomato salad with, 328
Wasabi-ginger dipping sauce, 437–38
Watercress salad, 53
Water Street (Massachusetts), 504
W.A.W. Restaurant (Malaysia), 23
Wheaton, Cary, xvii
Whole chicken piri-piri, 22
Whole hog in the style of a Greek island, 259–61
Whole hog with Balinese spices, 263
Whole Persian saffron lemon chicken, 27
Whyte, Mark, 199
Wildfire (Australia), 277, 477
Willoughby, John, xvii
Wine:
apple, and honey, grilled apples with, 569–70
bagna cauda–Italian sausage "hot tub," 343
hanger steak with marchand de vin (wine merchant) sauce, 142–44, *143*
Madeira gravy, 408–9
muscat-grilled pineapple with sea salt, 577–78
and olive oil, grilled shrimp sprayed with, 488
Wood:
four ways to grill with, 603–4
as fuel, 603
making a smoker pouch, 603
as a smoking agent, 603
Wood-burning grills and fires:
adjustable vents in, 598
campfire grilling with, 604, 607
lighting, 608–9
open pits, 607
pit roasting, 601

smoking foods in, 600
spit roasting, 600–601
types of, 606–7
underground pit roasting, 601, 607
Wood (Singapore), 32
Wrangham, Richard, xi
Wu, Julian, 362

Yakitori:
authentic, in Japan, 401
chicken, balsamic- and soy-glazed, 403
chicken liver, with a balsamic-soy glaze, 402–3, *403*
like they make it in Japan, 400–402
Yellow chile peanut sauce, 40–41
Yeon, Mrs. Shin Hyo, 453
Yerevan (Russia), 96, 545
Yhznaya Notch (Russia), 290
Yogurt:
green herb chutney, 398–99
grilled eggplant salad with Jerusalem flavors, 71–73, *72*
grilled olive tzatziki, 190
hot pepper, and garlic, grilled chicken with, 393–94
Indian "puff pastry," 98–100, *99*
Iranian saffron lemon chicken wings, 26–27
Kurdish grilled pumpkin dip, 10–11, *11*
-marinated lamb tenderloin kebabs, 298–99, *299*
Persian saffron lemon chicken kebabs, 27
tandoori potatoes, 549–50
tandoori potatoes in the style of baked stuffed potatoes, 550
whole Persian saffron lemon chicken, 27

Za'atar (Middle Eastern herb blend), 92
Zegaib, Fuad "Dinho," 537
Zübeyir (Turkey), 10, 301